READING JOSS WHEDON

Television and Popular Culture

Robert J. Thompson, *Series Editor*

READING

JOSS WHEDON

Edited by
RHONDA V. WILCOX
TANYA R. COCHRAN
CYNTHEA MASSON
DAVID LAVERY

SYRACUSE UNIVERSITY PRESS

∞ The paper used in this publication meets the minimum requirements
of the American National Standard for Information Sciences—Permanence
of Paper for Printed Library Materials, ANSI Z39.48-1992.

For a listing of books published and distributed by Syracuse University Press,
visit www.SyracuseUniversityPress.syr.edu.

ISBN: 978-0-8156-3364-8 (cloth)
         978-0-8156-1038-0 (paper)
         978-0-8156-5283-0 (e-Book)

Library of Congress Cataloging-in-Publication Data

Reading Joss Whedon / edited by Rhonda V. Wilcox, Tanya R. Cochran,
Cynthea Masson, and David Lavery. — First edition.
    pages cm. — (Television and popular culture)
  Includes bibliographical references and index.
  ISBN 978-0-8156-3364-8 (cloth : alk. paper) — ISBN 978-0-8156-1038-0
(pbk. : alk. paper) — ISBN 978-0-8156-5283-0 (ebook) 1. Whedon, Joss—
Criticism and interpretation.   I. Wilcox, Rhonda, editor of compilation.
II. Cochran, Tanya R., editor of compilation.   III. Masson, Cynthea, 1962–
editor of compilation. IV. Lavery, David, 1949– editor of compilation.
  PN1992.4.W49R43 2014
  791.45092—dc23   2014003751

Manufactured in the United States of America

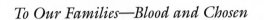

To Our Families—Blood and Chosen

Contents

Contents by Topic

Acknowledgments

The editors wish to acknowledge the work of the stellar contributors to this volume. They are a patient lot: we began work early in 2009, and most of the scholars published herein have been involved with the project from the start. On the other hand, we owe special thanks to Kristopher Woofter and Ensley Guffey, who agreed to work in much less time than a scholar likes, in order to turn in essays on the recently released *The Cabin in the Woods* (2012) and *Marvel's The Avengers* (2012), respectively. We thank as well those who have helped us in the editing process, including Jen Hale and Richard Gess. Outside the bounds of the book, we wish to thank all those who pursue Whedon Studies for the work they have done and are doing—particularly the members of the Whedon Studies Association, *most* particularly those who attend the biennial *Slayage* conference, publish in the journals *Slayage* and *Watcher Junior*, and work on the editorial boards or as external reviewers. Finally, always, we thank Joss Whedon and his creative collaborators for giving us something worth writing about.

READING JOSS WHEDON

Introduction

Much Ado about Whedon

RHONDA V. WILCOX

In May 2012, *Marvel's The Avengers*, a film written and directed by Joss Whedon, broke box-office records for a US opening weekend, having already succeeded wildly in international markets—and the film's audience, as of this writing, continues to grow. In 2011, between production and postproduction work on this superhero summer blockbuster, Whedon and his wife, Kai Cole, had planned to take a vacation. But instead, they chose to spend their recreation time to make a film of Shakespeare's romantic comedy *Much Ado about Nothing*. For those unfamiliar with Whedon, the step from Marvel Comics movie to Shakespeare may seem incongruous, but to many it seems a natural move, part of a unified body of work.

Scholarly writing on Whedon has been produced at a faster rate than on any other figure in television studies. Whedon is important not only because of his television series, but also because he works in more than one medium—as a film writer-director, a composer, a producer, a comic book writer, and an Internet miniseries creator. But it is his television work that has driven the academic engine. His texts are of both social and aesthetic significance; he creates canonical television. Furthermore, he has managed this artistic success on broadcast networks, not HBO. He has to date helmed four noteworthy television series: *Buffy the Vampire Slayer* (1997–2003); *Angel* (1999–2004); *Firefly* (2002), with its accompanying film, *Serenity* (2005); and *Dollhouse* (2009–10), as well as the Internet musical miniseries *Dr. Horrible's Sing-Along Blog* (2008). Then in 2012 came the release of *The Cabin in the Woods* (which Whedon cowrote with director Drew Goddard), followed by *The Avengers* and (in 2013) *Much Ado*.[1]

---

1. *Much Ado* was shown during the 2012 Toronto International Film Festival and distributed in wide release through Lionsgate in 2013.

Since the beginning of *Buffy the Vampire Slayer*, dozens of academic books have been published, including Marcus Recht's 2011 German monograph and Barbara Maio's 2007 Italian edited collection—evidence of Whedon's reputation among international scholars. Many hundreds of serious articles have been published, including (as of January 2013) twelve years of the peer-reviewed journal devoted to Whedon's work, *Slayage*. There have been more than ten international conferences on Whedon, in locales from Tennessee to Turkey. And in 2008 the Whedon Studies Association was established as a legal nonprofit organization. This continuing phenomenon of scholarly response to Whedon supports the claim that he is a major artist. His recent film work is a continuation of, not a departure from, that artistic career. For this volume, which explores the fullness of Whedon's career (rather than a single element), it seems appropriate to start with his most recent choice. Explaining how *Much Ado* and Whedon are a good match (though, like Beatrice and Benedick, on the surface at odds) should serve to introduce some of the methods and themes that anchor the analyses in this collection.

Admirers of Whedon have long known of his interest in Shakespeare. During the run of his first and most famous television series, *Buffy the Vampire Slayer*, Whedon invited cast members to his home for weekend dramatic readings of Shakespeare. Although he has asserted that he watched relatively little television growing up, Whedon told James Longworth that he did enjoy the BBC versions of Shakespeare's plays (Lavery and Burkhead 2011, 51). That intersection of people constituted of Shakespeare lovers who are also Whedon aficionados might take pleasure in thinking of *As You Like It*'s forest upon learning that Whedon has a child named Arden (Shakespeare's mother was born Mary Arden). Connections flow back and forth between life and art. For their part, many fans of Whedon are willing to make comparisons between the two authors, both (we would do well to remember) popular culture figures of their own day. The director of Atlanta's Shakespeare Tavern, for one, declares that "if William Shakespeare were alive today, he'd be Joss Whedon" (Watkins 2012). Not all admirers may be willing to endorse such an equation; after all, Shakespeare is Shakespeare, and Joss Whedon is himself alone. But it is certainly true that Whedon's interest in Shakespeare helps clarify the fact that he is part of a long stream of dramatic literature and a writer aware of his inheritance (see Wilcox 2005, 2–5). His choice of *Much Ado* as his first filmed Shakespeare project is particularly appropriate, particularly revealing of some of the elements of his work that make Whedon an artist who will endure. So, why would Whedon choose to direct and produce *Much Ado about Nothing*?

Before considering the play itself, we might first note an important part of the production of *Much Ado*: Whedon's acting company. The part of Benedick is played by Alexis Denisof, who starred in *Buffy the Vampire Slayer* and its spin-off, *Angel*; Beatrice is done by Amy Acker, who played a main character on both *Angel* and *Dollhouse*; Dogberry is performed by Nathan Fillion, who appeared in a recurring guest role on *Buffy*, as the lead character on *Firefly*, and as a main character in *Dr. Horrible's Sing-Along Blog*; Fran Kranz, of *Dollhouse* and the Whedon cowritten movie *The Cabin in the Woods*, is Claudio; Don John is played by Sean Maher of *Firefly*; and we could go on.[2] Shakespeare worked, as a matter of course, with a repertory company of actors, a group who were so successful that they were named the King's Men. Like many good filmmakers (think of Ingmar Bergman, Woody Allen, Christopher Guest), Whedon has chosen to gather a group of go-to actors with whom he has creative compatibility. In the press release for the film, Whedon calls the production "a love letter—to the text, to the cast" ("*Much Ado about Nothing* Press Release" 2011). Furthermore, Jay Hunter, who worked on *Dollhouse*, is the director of photography, and Kai Cole is coproducer for the film (see Lavery 2012 on the "School of Whedon"). One of the recurring themes in Whedon's work is the importance of human community, of chosen family; and it has become clear, over the years, that this theme in his art is reflected in his everyday, lived experience.

As for the choice of the play itself, it is one of the wittiest of Shakespeare's brilliant texts; the darting humor of Beatrice and Benedick is known by reputation even to those who have not seen or read the play. Among the first of Whedon's qualities to draw attention was his witty language. He was, after all, a Hollywood script doctor (uncredited, he wrote much of the dialogue of *Speed* [1994], for instance). Scholars often note that Whedon is a (and perhaps the first) third-generation television writer, since both his father and grandfather wrote for television: his father wrote for *Benson* (1979–86) and *The Golden Girls* (1985–92), and his grandfather wrote for *The Donna Reed Show* (1958–66) and *The Dick Van Dyke Show* (1961–66) (Wilcox and Lavery 2002, xxi). It is also worth noting that all these shows are *sitcoms*; Whedon grew up with comedy. He himself wrote for the sitcom *Roseanne* (1988–97)

2. Others include Reed Diamond (the security adviser in *Dollhouse*) as Don Pedro, Clark Gregg (Agent Phil Coulson of *Marvel's The Avengers*) as Leonato, and Tom Lenk (Andrew in *Buffy the Vampire Slayer*, with brief appearances also in *Angel* and *The Cabin in the Woods*) as Verges.

at the beginning of his career. Even his darkest work is laced with humor. The humor rests in the web of the story; it grows from character; the full flavor cannot be completely excerpted. But one can imagine that the man who wrote lines for a high school character such as "The dead rose. We should've at least had an assembly" would take serious pleasure in the joy of Beatrice and Benedick's banter ("The Harvest," *Buffy* 1.2). "I love words. I love the sound of words. I love syllables," Whedon says (Lavery and Burkhead 2011, 47), and Whedon's *Much Ado* press release refers to the play's dialogue as being "as fresh and intoxicating as any being written" ("*Much Ado about Nothing* Press Release" 2011). The first scholarly responses to Whedon included commentaries on his language (M. Adams 1999a, 1999b; Wilcox 1999). Joy in the wit of language inhabits both Shakespeare and Whedon, and no script shines with more of that joy than *Much Ado*.

But while many think first of the light and playful verbal fencing of *Much Ado*, the story also harbors darkness. When Beatrice's cousin is falsely accused of deception and unchastity, rejected at the altar by her fiancé, Claudio, she faints—and then her religious counselor advises her that her family and friends should collude in the pretense of her death. Yet the harshest darkness comes in Beatrice's response to Claudio's actions. In her indignation on behalf of her cousin, she moves past the "merry war" of words with Benedick (1.1.57) toward true violence. After all the dance of language, Beatrice makes of Benedick one request, stark in its brevity: "Kill Claudio" (4.1.288). The depth of her anger is startling. Though he resists at first, Benedick becomes convinced, and in grim seriousness presents his challenge to Claudio. No wonder Whedon chose to shoot *Much Ado* in black-and-white. This is no lightweight Hollywood rom-com. It is, in fact, much more like the mixture of light and dark that pervades Whedon's work, where Buffy makes quips about her fashion choices but is also forced to kill her beloved to save the world; where Angel sings ludicrously off-key but must also watch the mother of his child die; where Malcolm Reynolds ends up ruefully naked after a heist but must ferry home the dead body of a war comrade whose life he first saved, then ended. As Whedon says, "No one's going to go see the story of Othello going to get a peaceful divorce. People . . . need things to go wrong, they need the tension. In my characters, there's a core of trust and love that I'm very committed to. . . . But at the same time, you can't keep that safety" (Lavery and Burkhead 2011, 31). He does say "need," not "want": dealing with the darkness is part of what he does. "Ultimately, to access these bare emotions, to go to these strange places, to deal with sexuality, to deal with horror and death, is what people need and it's the reason that we tell these stories" (Lavery and Burkhead 2011, 57). Surely, Whedon understands why Beatrice says, "Kill Claudio."

Beatrice's voice is in the imperative, both grammatically and emotionally. But it also implies a restriction that shows yet another of *Much Ado's* connections to Whedon's key themes: the question of gender. "O that I were a man!" says Beatrice, furious for her cousin's sake. She adds, "What! bear her in hand until they come to take hands, and then with public accusation, uncovered slander, unmitigated rancor—O God, that I were a man! I would eat his heart in the market place" (4.1.302–5). I will gloss over, here, a whole history of gender studies—for example, in not delving into the question of Beatrice's claiming to wish to be male rather than to be a woman freed of gender restrictions.[3] I will simply note that Shakespeare has his character raise the issue of those restrictions. The intelligent, passionate Beatrice is clearly unhappy not to be able to deal out justice herself, as she surely could not have in her time and place. As Stephen Greenblatt says in *Will in the World: How Shakespeare Became Shakespeare*, "Elizabethan society was intensely, pervasively, visibly hierarchical: men above women, adults above children, the old above the young, the rich above the poor, the wellborn above the vulgar" (2004, 76). Whedon is an avowed feminist; he has worked on-screen and off- (for example, through the organization Equality Now) for women's rights. His character of Buffy has given birth to a host of strong females on-screen, such as Sydney Bristow of *Alias* and Rob Thomas's Veronica Mars of the eponymous series and planned 2014 film. It would seem likely that Beatrice's anger at her societally constructed limitations would be something Whedon would want to film.

There is another, less overt, connection that this particular Shakespeare comedy has with some of Whedon's work. Like a Hollywood movie, Shakespeare's play is self-contained; it does not have the long accumulation of character created in one of the serialized novels in weekly parts by Whedon's favorite novelist, Dickens, or quality weekly serialized television such as Whedon has produced. But Shakespeare has managed to give his heroic couple a history. As early as the first scene of the second act, Don Pedro notes that Beatrice has "lost the heart of Signor Benedick," and she responds, "Indeed, my lord, he lent it me awhile, and I gave him use for it. . . . Marry, once before he won it of me with false dice; therefore your grace may well say I have lost it" (2.1.261–66). Beatrice and Benedick have a backstory. Their relationship,

3. On gender issues in the play, see, for example, Wynne-Davies 2001.

in imagination, reaches into the past before the play begins. Technically, they live within a single play—they do not even have the sequels afforded Prince Hal and Falstaff—yet Shakespeare has managed to extend their lives outside their single story. Whedon consistently does the same with his characters. As I have argued before, there is life between the episodes (Wilcox 2005, 178). For Beatrice and Benedick, there is life before the episode of *Much Ado*; we are invited, by Beatrice's comments in the second act, to wonder what has led to their relationship as it stands as the play opens—to wonder what has led to the intense badinage that illuminates their focus on one another. Beatrice's first line in the play, as Don Pedro and his men return from battle, is to ask (however sarcastically) after Benedick; and he, despite his stinging humor, reveals to Claudio that for Benedick, Beatrice is far more beautiful than her cousin (and he says it with the casual assumption that this view could not be questioned [1.1.182–18]). Sometimes audience members question the relationship of Beatrice and Benedick, seemingly invoked by a trick of their friends, who convince Beatrice and Benedick that each loves the other. But do they not? That moment of Beatrice's reference to their past opens up the relationship in a way that correlates (even if briefly) to Whedon's use of the temporal tools at his disposal in his prime medium of television. And Whedon chose to highlight Shakespeare's glance at a backstory by opening the film with a visual representation of a moment in Beatrice and Benedick's conflicted history.[4]

In Whedon's opening, we see a couple apparently the morning after a one-night stand. Their eyes never meet, and he silently leaves. A solitary note of music suggests their isolation. Whedon, almost entirely faithful to Shakespeare's language, added this scene using no words. Thus, with the wordlessness of the famously loquacious Beatrice and Benedick, he shows the difficulty of achieving intimacy. Benedick is also beardless; when next they meet, Benedick is wearing a full beard, like defensive armor (or one of the play's many masks). And their war of words has begun—but Beatrice and Benedick cannot stop talking about each other. Their friends plot to unite the couple by staging conversations in which each separately overhears that the other is in love. At this point, their witty words (which suggest tightly controlled feelings) shift into wildly uncontrolled body language—Acker's and Denisof's pratfalls

4. Compare Kenneth Branagh's use of Ophelia's memories (or is it imaginings?) of her relationship with the prince in *Hamlet* (1996). Interestingly, Branagh did not choose to include a comparable scene for Beatrice and Benedick's backstory in his own film of *Much Ado* (1993).

revealing formerly hidden emotions. (And Benedick shaves his beard again, risking closeness.) At the play's end, Beatrice is silenced when she is to be wed. But Whedon transforms the effect by having another wordless scene at the film's end, reflecting the scene at the beginning. While in the beginning they avoided each other's eyes, now they look deeply, their silence true communication: "Silence is the perfectest herald of joy" (2.1.289). The picture cuts to black with a single, joyful musical note, the metamorphosis of the opening's note of loneliness.

Much Ado's Beatrice and Benedick are the progenitors of a thousand Hollywood rom-com couples whose apparent distaste for each other leads to eventual union. But, like Whedon's characters (and unlike many a Hollywood pair), they are complex, not a simple sunshine duo. Whedon says, in fact, "the text is to me a deconstruction of the idea of love," though, as noted, he has also said that "the entire production is a love letter to the text" ("*Much Ado about Nothing* Press Release" 2011). In sum: the wit of the language; the note of human darkness and violence in the narrative; the acknowledgment, however brief, of gender issues; and the complex characters' expansion beyond the temporal bounds of a single episode all make *Much Ado* a play that would seem likely to appeal to Whedon, the Shakespeare fan. Some critics might see his choice to base a movie on the play as an attempt to gain cultural capital; scholars such as Petra Kuppers mock the "Shakespeare complex" of certain science fiction–fantasy series (2004, 50). But I would argue instead that what we know about Whedon shows that his production of *Much Ado* is an organic part of his growing body of work.

Studying the full range of that body of work is the ambitious project of this volume—and these themes of *Much Ado* are to be seen again and again in Whedon's work. Although we do not cover every single Whedon production (for example, we do not have essays on all of his comics), we do discuss all of what we consider his most important productions, and a sampling of all the major types. For the convenience of readers, we have arranged the essays in this collection in groups based on Whedon's works, beginning with *Buffy* (the series) and moving forward through the years to a section titled "Beyond the Box," covering nontelevised works such as *The Avengers*. Inserted at the relevant points, for the aid of readers who may not be familiar with all of Whedon's works, are brief general introductions to each of the four television series, covering premise, key staff and actors, critical reception, and plot summary. The book also has a concluding section, called "Overarching Topics," which explores multiple Whedon works. However, we (the editors and contributors) see many other connections in Whedon beyond the basic subject of the television series, film, or other text, so we offer readers another way to organize the material in thought. There are essays on narrative and writing; visuals and directing; character; music; myth; symbolism; a set of themes: gender, human identity, community and collaboration, and heroism; and, finally, essays on the extratextual worlds of the business side of television art and the academic study of Whedon.

Whedon has spoken of believing in a "religion in narrative" (Lavery and Burkhead 2011, 28), and he is preeminently a writer. A Wesleyan University film studies graduate taught by scholars such as Jeanine Basinger and Richard Slotkin, he had his first professional experience in cinema with the 1992 filming of his *Buffy the Vampire Slayer* script. He learned then how little creative control writers have in Hollywood; years later, he found that control in television. Horace Newcomb and Robert Alley, in distinguishing television from film, the director's medium, called television *the producer's medium*; we might call it *the writer's medium* as well. Indeed, that was an important part of Newcomb and Alley's point (1983). The term *producer* is given to major writers for a series. Many today would acknowledge that television, with its opportunities of long-term narrative, provides a finer forum for writing than the high-stakes gamble of the single Hollywood film; hence, we see famous film actors such as Glenn Close and Dustin Hoffman turning to television for well-written roles. Whedon's writing is at the core of all he does.

Many of the essays in this volume examine his writing techniques. David Kociemba discusses *Buffy*'s first season and its narrative interconnections with the full seven seasons of story in "From Beneath You, It Foreshadows: Why *Buffy*'s First Season Matters." The first season, half as long as a standard television season of its day, was completely finished before it was broadcast, so Whedon had the opportunity to use foreshadowing within it. However, as Kociemba explains, the foreshadowing goes further: many of Whedon's ideas, developed more fully in later years, were first broached in this season. Janet K. Halfyard addresses the idea of the hero's journey, most famously charted by Joseph Campbell as the monomyth; as she notes, other scholars have explained Whedon's use of the monomyth before, but she illustrates a particular application of that significant narrative structure in "Hero's Journey, Heroine's Return? Buffy, Eurydice, and the Orpheus Myth." Ananya Mukherjea shows how the moral growth of certain characters guides several narrative arcs in "'It's Like Some Primal, Animal Force . . . That Used to Be Us': Animality, Humanity, and Moral Careers in the Buffyverse." My essay "'Can I Spend the Night / Alone?': Segments and Connections in 'Conversations with Dead People'" illustrates Whedon's command of structure as he combines four different script segments written by not only himself but also several other members of the *Buffy* writing staff and creates a beautifully unified whole within a framing device. Richard S. Albright tackles Whedon's use of the story within a story, the narrative within a narrative. Through different characters who tell tales within the series, he examines questions of the untrustworthy narrator in "'Hey, Respect the Narrative Flow Much?': Problematic Storytelling in *Buffy the Vampire Slayer*."

The skill of Whedon's writing technique extends beyond *Buffy*, of course. In "What the Hell? *Angel*'s 'The Girl in Question,'" Cynthea Masson focuses on an episode of *Angel* disliked by many viewers, and parallels its narrative dead-ends (undead-ends?) to existential drama's illuminating blankness. Alyson R. Buckman, in "'Wheel Never Stops Turning': Space and Time in *Firefly* and *Serenity*," applies Bakhtin's idea of the chronotope to clarify the connections between place and story. Victoria Willis discusses the differences in experiencing *Dr. Horrible* through a computer screen, in separated episodes, versus the continuous through-flow of the narrative when seen on DVD, in "Joining the Evil League of Evil: The Rhetoric of Posthuman Negotiation in *Dr. Horrible's Sing-Along Blog*." Marni Stanley covers the comics in "*Buffy*'s Season 8, Image and Text: Superhero Self-Fashioning." She examines the change in medium from television—yet we can see that, once again, there is a season-long arc, and thus a focused story, no mere picaresque hodgepodge. In "Watchers in the Woods: Meta-Horror, Genre Hybridity, and Reality TV Critique in *The Cabin in the Woods*," Kristopher Karl Woofter situates the film within the tradition of the horror genre while suggesting that it serves in addition as a critique of the reality television genre. Ensley F. Guffey also uses genre, specifically the World War II combat movie (and, more specifically, Whedon's professor Jeanine Basinger's interpretation of such movies) to analyze Whedon's megahit film *The Avengers*. Lorna Jowett covers flashback, alternate universes, and the centuries-long lives of vampires (among other things) as devices to extend narrative through time, to enrich backstory, in "Stuffing a Rabbit in It: Character, Narrative, and Time in the Whedonverses." She thus approaches Whedon's creation of character through the advantage of long-term television narrative, referencing all of his television series to do so. J. Douglas Rabb and J. Michael Richardson, in "Adventures in the Moral Imagination: Memory and Identity in Whedon's Narrative Ethics," argue that one of the true uses of Whedon's stories is to create a narrative ethics.

Writing, for Whedon, is born with images, with visuals: "I have a very specific vision when I write, directorially speaking, about everything, about camera angles," he tells us (Lavery and Burkhead 2011, 45). Halfyard discusses the visuals of both setting and costume in "Hero's Journey, Heroine's Return?" I cover the use of on-screen title cards, elements of mise-en-scène, and visual symbolism of mouths, appropriately enough in an episode whose title refers to "Conversations." In "'Enough of the Action, Let's Get Back to Dancing': Joss Whedon Directs *Angel*," Stacey Abbott gives a carefully contextualized analysis of Whedon's work as a director in *Angel*, where he was able to serve as "sidebar guy," directing more experimental episodes that were not narrative linchpins. Willis explores not only the viewer's visual relation to the computer screen for *Dr. Horrible* but also the significant visuals of costuming. Finally, Stanley gives a detailed discussion of the visual impact of the *Buffy* Season 8 comic, with panels that bleed, horizontal visual parallels, Whedon's playing with the surprise of the page turn, and more. The overlap of these discussions of visuals with narrative is, of course, inevitable: the visuals carry narrative (as they do every day in our lives).

Surely, too, the narrative carries character. One of the preeminent advantages of television, comparable (as many scholars have noted) to nine-teenth-century serialized novels, is the ability to develop character through time, and Whedon makes vivid use of this power. "I need people to grow, I need them to change, I need them to learn and explore, you know, and die and do all of the things that people do in life," he told David Bianculli in 2000 (Lavery and Burkhead 2011, 4). Many of the essays in this volume discuss character, but two focus on it in particular. One is Mukherjea's dis-cussion of the "moral careers" of Angel, Willow, Oz, and Buffy. The other is Jowett's examination of the creation of character through careful continuity of intertwined times, sometimes paradoxically contradictory (as in the case of the inserted character Dawn) and sometimes simply complicated. Character is never simple for Whedon.

Like Shakespeare, Whedon is perfectly comfortable using music to enhance a character, deepen a theme, or even advance a plot. (Shakespeare planted a song about men as deceivers in the middle of *Much Ado*.) Probably the most famous instance of Whedon's musical work is the musical episode of *Buffy* for which he wrote both lyrics and melodies. He also wrote melody and lyrics for *Firefly*'s theme song and melody for Shakespeare's *Much Ado* lyrics. Two full volumes of essays have already been devoted to Whedon's music, including one coedited by Janet K. Halfyard. In this volume, Halfyard applies the 1607 Claudio Monteverdi opera *Orfeo* (and other versions of the story of Orpheus, the great musician) to *Buffy*. Moving from four-hundred-year-old opera to twentieth-century rock, I analyze "Conversations with Dead People" through the song Whedon cowrote with singer Angie Hart (who appears in the show) in order to frame the episode. The music of the song's language is evocatively beautiful and structurally suggestive. For *Dr. Horrible*, too, Willis shows that music intertwines with story.

Besides music, another way to make a text more resonant is myth. In fact, we might consider myth to be a subdivision of narrative—yet it seems larger as well. "[*Buffy*] was designed to be the kind of show that people would build myths on," Whedon tells us, and his texts are built with myths, too (Lavery and Burkhead 2011, 16). As noted, Halfyard explores the Orpheus myth and connects it to the hero's—in this case, Buffy's and Angel's—descent to the underworld. Mukherjea applies to *Buffy* the myth of the Hindu goddess Shakti, incarnate as Durga, the commanding woman who rides a lion (compare Buffy with her desert puma). In "Reflections in the Pool: Echo, Narcissus, and the Male Gaze in *Dollhouse*," K. Dale Koontz discusses the Greek myth of Echo and Narcissus and its surprisingly multitudinous applications to *Dollhouse* and its protagonist Echo. Like Halfyard, Cynthea Masson takes us to hell, this time in the *Angel* series, specifically in terms of its similarities to Samuel Beckett's *Waiting for Godot* and Jean-Paul Sartre's *No Exit*. Finally, Guffey discusses the modern myth of America as it inhabits *The Avengers*.

Myth in effect creates a symbolic level of meaning for a text. But there are many uses of symbols that are meaningful without being mythic. One of the primary ways Whedon has functioned as an artist is to engage his audiences' minds by the use of symbolism (see Wilcox 2005, chap. 1). Buffy's high school sits on a mouth of hell, and the straightforward idea of high school as hell is perhaps its most famous symbol. From the earliest episodes, with a controlling mother as a witch, an Internet predator as a demon, and a high school clique as a band of hyenas, Whedon has played with specific symbols. Fairly horrific symbolism of mouths, as noted above, runs through "Conversations with Dead People" (7.7). Mukherjea covers the symbolic use of animals in her essay. Elizabeth L. Rambo discusses the way that Jayne's knitted hat becomes a symbol of family and community in *Firefly* in "Metaphoric Unity and Ending: Sending and Receiving *Firefly*'s Last 'Message.'" Along with the Echo and Narcissus myth, Koontz develops the symbolism of the pool and reflections in *Dollhouse*.

Some might argue that all of this work is done in the service of theme. Often a small, sharp moment can mean more than the largest of themes, and the flavor of a moment makes a story art (or not). But theme gives power to the art, and as Whedon repeatedly has his characters say, "It's about power" ("Lessons," *Buffy* 7.1). Arguably, Whedon's primary theme is gender equality—primary at the very least in the sense that it was chronologically his first great theme. As Whedon has often said, Buffy was born when he envisioned the stereotypical victimized blonde from the horror movies turning in triumph against her attacker (Lavery and Burkhead 2011, 53, 140). She is not the virginal Final Girl (Clover 1992); she is sexually aware, she is fun, and still she does not die. Much academic work has examined the various forms in which Whedon uses gender thematically, perhaps most notably Lorna Jowett's *Sex and the Slayer: A Gender Studies Primer for the "Buffy" Fan* (2005). In this volume, Halfyard looks at the shifting gender positions of Buffy (and other characters) as either Orpheus or Eurydice. Mukherjea discusses the implications of animal imagery for gender in *Buffy*. Koontz reminds us of the significance of the very present male gaze in *Dollhouse*. Sharon Sutherland and Sarah Swan investigate the idea of human trafficking, prostitution, and slavery, especially in terms of the question of choice, in "'There Is No Me; I'm Just a Container': Law and the Loss of Personhood in *Dollhouse*." *Dollhouse* above all has made fans and scholars ask whether what Whedon is putting on-screen can truly be called feminist—but questions have been raised since *Buffy* first went on the air. Examining all the series, Lauren Schultz takes on these questions in "'Hot Chicks with Superpowers': The Contested Feminism of Joss Whedon."

The nature of human identity, of humanity, is another paramount theme in Whedon's work—and it appears in various incarnations, many of which are explored here. A fictional world of monsters and superheroes gives us the chance to ask: what makes us human? Mukherjea examines the line between human and animal—and who are treated as which, and why. Koontz reminds us of the robots in human flesh that Karel Čapek used in *R.U.R.* (Rossum's Universal Robots) and shows us how *Dollhouse*, with its Rossum Corporation, fits into a literary history that also includes the contested humanity of *Blade Runner* (1982) and *A.I.* (2001): stories built around "dolls" who want to be acknowledged as human. Sutherland and Swan focus on the legal status of such "dolls": can one sign away the right to personhood? Rabb and Richardson argue that our own choices of memory create our human identities and that Whedon demonstrates that we each thus make ourselves. His stories suggest that our personal stories—the ways we envision our own lives—constitute existential choices. In "Technology and Magic: Joss Whedon's Explorations of the Mind," Jeffrey Bussolini examines two seemingly very different yet, in the Whedonverses, often equivalent elements—and the ways they impact the human mind, the human self. Finally, Gregory Erickson takes on the vexed question of the soul—and the body—in the many creations of the atheist

Whedon in "From Old Heresies to Future Paradigms: Joss Whedon on Body and Soul."

One of the most compelling themes, to which Whedon returns again and again, is the importance of community, of the chosen family, of human collaboration. As noted above, he seems to enact it with his artistic cocreators as well as to present it through his characters. "Conversations with Dead People" is the epitome of collaboration by the *Buffy* writers—while the episode is also a poignant meditation on isolation. Linda J. Jencson discusses an often-visited trope of the Buffyverse—the apocalypse—in terms of the very real social science of disaster studies, and the resultant operation of human communities, in "All Those Apocalypses: Disaster Studies and Community in *Buffy the Vampire Slayer* and *Angel*." Rambo analyzes the breaking and making of community—both in the episode and behind the scenes—for the final episode of *Firefly* to be filmed. And Guffey details the creation of a team from a set of highly individualistic characters in *The Avengers*: The "Mighty Shield" of Guffey's title literally belongs to Captain America, the Avenger who used to be the little guy but who now directs the heroes—not unlike Whedon himself, as the title's metaphor indicates.

Perhaps pulling all these themes together is the concept of heroism, in all its battered glory. Halfyard's examination of the hero's journey also considers the hero's complicity in the wrong that haunts the Orphic tale. Masson focuses on the desperate, heroic effort we may be called on to make in order to choose any kind of change in this world. Change as movement comes up in Buckman's essay as well; she describes *Firefly*'s Captain Mal Reynolds as not only picaresque rogue hero, but also as Western, science fiction, and road-trip hero, using movement and chronotope to define the heroism of Mal and his passenger (later copilot) River. Willis covers the lack of heroism, the loss of heroism, in the posthumanism of another Nathan Fillion character: Captain Hammer of *Dr. Horrible's Sing-Along Blog*—and, for that matter, in the protagonist who chooses posthumanism as well. In contrast, *Buffy*'s Season 8, as Stanley explains it, shows case after case of existential heroism (among familiar characters and ones we have never before met), in spite of the fact that the heroes are as flawed as we have ever seen in a Whedonverse. Last, Guffey shows why the making of a hero from a flawed human is exactly the story to draw millions of viewers to theaters around the world, if the story has some truth in the telling as well as myth (or in its myth).

These many topics are just a sampling of the ways that Whedon's work calls for analysis. For the most part, these essays are analyses of the texts themselves. (Indeed, we include several essays that are close textual analyses of a single episode or film; see Wilcox, Masson, Rambo, Woofter, and Guffey.) We also, however, provide two essays that place their fulcrums outside the text. Matthew Pateman investigates the business world of television and in particular the Fox network and *Firefly*, a subject of interest to many followers of Whedon's work, since the actions of the network had a serious impact on an artistic creation that has subsequently proved itself to have long-term appeal—and the cancellation of which Whedon publicly mourned. The second of these essays we offer as a kind of conclusion or afterword for the whole volume. Tanya R. Cochran's "Whedon Studies: A Living History, 1999–2013" is a contribution to firmly rooting television studies in general, and Whedon Studies in particular, within the academy. But it also attempts to convey a sense (shared by the editors and contributors) of the significance of Whedon's work in the world beyond the ivory tower as well.

Many of the essays in this collection could be placed in more than one category. There are also more categories that might have been identified; for instance, most of the essays engage the question of genre—something important to the genre-mixing, genre-loving Whedon. We have tried to give some sense of the breadth and significance of Whedon's work, but in no sense is this volume a last word. There is more yet to say; there always will be more to say on Whedon, and that is one of the things that prove him to be an artist. Best of all, *he* has more to say: his revels are not ended.

Part One

Buffy the Vampire Slayer

Buffy the Vampire Slayer

An Introduction

RHONDA V. WILCOX

Buffy the Vampire Slayer, a television series that ran from 1997 until 2003, is the creation that established Joss Whedon's reputation as an artist. It was preceded by a 1992 film for which Whedon wrote the script—a lesser work over which he did not have creative control. For *Buffy*, which was made by his production company, Mutant Enemy, Whedon was the showrunner (joined in that capacity by *Buffy* writer Marti Noxon for the last two years of the series, when *Buffy* moved from the WB network to the UPN). Other key writers included Jane Espenson, Douglas Petrie, David Fury, Rebecca Rand Kirshner, Drew Z. Greenberg, Stephen S. DeKnight, and Drew Goddard. Key staffers also included composer Christophe Beck, editor Lisa Lassek, production designer Carey Meyer, director of photography Michael Gershman, and costume designer Cynthia Bergstrom. In addition to writing and directing many of the episodes himself, Whedon had final review of the overall narrative arc for each season and the specific script of each of the 144 episodes.

The premise of *Buffy* is that a blonde, sexy teenage girl is not the victim of creatures of horror, but instead a superhero capable of defending not just herself but all the world. As the opening voice-over says, "In every generation there is a Chosen One. She alone will stand against the vampires, the demons, and the forces of darkness. She is the Slayer." Her natural desire to lead a normal life conflicts with the duty and self-sacrifice demanded by her vocation. This conflict forms the basis of many of the plots—along with, memorably, the idea of high school as hell, with various high school problems symbolically represented as various monsters (an abusive boyfriend is a Doctor Jekyll/Mr. Hyde, a controlling mother is a witch, and so on). Buffy (Sarah Michelle Gellar), by appearance a typical Southern California teen, the daughter of a divorced mother, is the Slayer of these monsters. Her mentor is Rupert Giles

(Anthony Stewart Head), a member of the mainly British, mainly male Watchers, a group that has through the centuries advised and controlled the single Slayer in all the world (when one Slayer dies, another is activated). At around the time of high school graduation (at the end of the third season), she repudiates their control, though she continues her relationship with Giles. She is aided in her battle against evil by the brave but geeky Xander Harris (Nicholas Brendon) and the brilliant but shy Willow Rosenberg (Alyson Hannigan), who accidentally discover Buffy's secret identity. The teens become closest friends despite warnings from the beautiful, popular, acerbic Cordelia Chase (Charisma Carpenter), who at first believes Buffy may be socially acceptable. However, Buffy's social life and studies are hampered by secret monster fighting—not to mention her loyalty to her courageous but unpopular friends, called the Scooby Gang or Scoobies (in reference to the cartoon *Scooby-Doo*, which features teen mystery sleuths [1969–present]). Also occasionally coming to Buffy's aid is the handsome, mysterious Angel (David Boreanaz), who is revealed to be a vampire—but with a soul; he too fights evil, and he and Buffy become romantically involved.

Each of the seven seasons of *Buffy* has a season-long arc; the series as a whole also has a narrative arc that reflects the hero's journey, Joseph Campbell's monomyth. Whedon planned each season to be able to conclude the series, in case of cancellation. Each season focuses on a major villain or "Big Bad." In the first season (technically a half-season of twelve episodes), Buffy faces the Master, a powerful vampire who briefly (for a couple of minutes) kills her. Xander, with help from Angel, revives her. Because of her brief death, another Slayer, Kendra, is activated, unbeknownst to Buffy and the Scoobies. In the second season, it seems that two vampire lovers, Spike (James Marsters) and Drusilla (Juliet Landau) will be the Big Bad, but when Buffy and Angel make love for the first time, he loses his soul under the terms of a curse: his soul was returned to him to torment him, and if he knows a moment of pure happiness (which happens only on that occasion when he and Buffy make love), his soul departs. The evil vampire Angelus looms over the rest of the season. He arranges the death of Kendra in its final episode. He has earlier in the season killed Giles's beloved, Willow's mentor, the technopagan computer teacher (and secret Gypsy) Jenny Calendar, in a signature Whedon move making clear that even major characters can (and should) die. Jenny has, before her death, rediscovered the magical means to return Angel's soul. To save the world, Buffy must kill him—even though, at the last minute, Willow has managed to return his soul. Thus, at the end of Season One Buffy sacrifices herself; for Season Two, she sacrifices her love. She sees Angel sucked into a hell dimension.

Buffy runs away and is gone over the summer hiatus; in Season Three she returns to some resentment from her mother (Kristine Sutherland) and friends. They are joined by Faith, a Slayer who was activated when Kendra died—a tough Boston girl with serious authority issues. Their Big Bad for the season is the Mayor of Sunnydale (Harry Groener), a seemingly mild-mannered, squeaky-clean politician who has made a demonic pact to be elected again and again through the centuries, and who fully believes he is doing good by bringing order. In the second half of the season, they are joined by Wesley Wyndam-Pryce (Alexis Denisof), a younger, prissier Watcher who makes tightly laced Giles look loose; Wesley, exactly the wrong person, serves as Faith's Watcher. After various conflicts (including her accidental killing of a human), Faith ends up secretly giving her allegiance to the Mayor, who treats her like a daughter. This season also sees the development of the romance begun in Season Two between Willow and Oz, who has become a werewolf (Seth Green), and Xander first with Cordelia and then with Anya (Emma Caulfield), a thousand-year-old female vengeance demon who becomes trapped in the form of a high school girl. For his part, Angel mysteriously reappears from hell, once Buffy in effect renounces him. In the season finale, he departs, saying they cannot be together because of his curse and his desire for her to lead a relatively normal life. The season ends with all the students of Sunnydale High joining to fight and kill the Mayor, who has transformed into a giant demon snake happily representative of all self-satisfied government tyrants.

In Season Four Buffy goes to college; the Big Bad is the Initiative, a secret military-scientific group experimenting with demons—among them Spike, whom they render unable to harm humans by implanting a chip in his brain. Other demons, however, they weaponize, including the Frankensteinian human-demon-cyborg Adam (George Hertzberg). Buffy becomes romantically involved with Riley Finn (Marc Blucas), a graduate student and secretly a lead soldier of the Initiative. Oz departs to keep Willow safe from his inner wolf; she then begins a romantic relationship with Tara (Amber Benson), a fellow witch. The Initiative turns on Buffy (whom it cannot control); Riley must break with them. In the season's penultimate episode, Giles, Willow, Xander, and Buffy mystically join in the final battle (after a season in which their disunity, through the changes of life, has been apparent); in the season's final episode, "Restless," a sequence of four dreams (one for each major character) displays both the psychic consequences of that joining and Buffy's connection to the historically First Slayer.

In Season Five the Big Bad is Glory—a female god who searches for the mystical Key to open the gates to another dimension, so that she can return home—disregarding the fact that everyone in Buffy's dimension will die. The Key has been transformed, for safekeeping, into human form: a young teenage sister Buffy never had, Dawn. The monks who made her have even transformed everyone's memories to believe she was always there. (As early as Season Three, hints of the character's coming had been planted.) In this season Spike realizes, to his dismay, that he loves Buffy. It is also the season marked by the death, by natural causes, of Buffy's mother. At the season's end, when Dawn is about to be killed to open the dimensions, Buffy sacrifices her life to take Dawn's place and save the world—and this time Buffy truly dies and is buried.

In Season Six, Willow, in concert with Xander, Tara, and Anya, returns Buffy to life; Willow is able to use magic to do so because Buffy's was a mystical, not a natural, death. Willow believes they are saving Buffy from a hell dimension, but Buffy tells Spike she believes she was in heaven, and she suffers miserably in her return. Giles departs for England, believing he must leave Buffy to enable her to grow. She and Spike begin a secret affair. Willow struggles with magic as an addiction. The Big Bads of the season are actually human but still deadly—three geeks with scientific and magical skills: Warren (Adam Busch), Andrew (Tom Lenk), and Jonathan (Danny Strong), who has appeared since Season One. In attempting to kill Buffy with a gun, Warren accidentally kills Tara. The resultant grief transforms Willow into Dark Willow, who very nearly ends the world to stop its (and her) pain, and finally is herself stopped by Xander's unconditional, self-sacrificing love.

In Season Seven, the Big Bad is the First Evil, the evil underlying and preceding all evil, which can take the form of anyone who has died (including Buffy). It sets out to attempt to assassinate all potential Slayers, whom Buffy gathers to her to protect. After many conflicts—during which Xander loses an eye in battle, many young Potentials die, and Buffy is temporarily excommunicated from the group—the characters come together to save the world once more. Giles, Faith, and Angel return to Sunnydale (though Buffy sends Angel away to prepare another battle front); Willow becomes imbued with extraordinary power, sharing, by Buffy's choice, the Slayer's power with the Potentials; the regular characters risk their lives together in the battle to defend humanity: Anya and Spike die. The survivors depart the now cratered town of the high school as hell, in a school bus.

Buffy the Vampire Slayer was an immediate popular success. Though some critics complained about the idea of a young woman in short skirts as a hero, many in the popular press acclaimed the series from the start for its witty language, psychologically sound characterization, clever symbolism, engaging narratives, and thoughtful themes. As the series continued, critics also praised the characters' long-term development within impressive continuity of story line, as well as the series' formal experimentation (despite the confines of broadcast, non-HBO television)—for example, the largely silent episode "Hush," the dream episode "Restless," and the musical episode "Once More, with Feeling" (with lyrics and melodies by Whedon). Whedon's careful responsibility for the overall quality of the series, and his ability to attract and work creatively with gifted collaborators, has been generally acknowledged. Academic publications on *Buffy* first appeared in 1999. The series has had scholarship published on it at a faster rate than any other single television series. Sixteen years after the start of the series, academic work continues to flourish, and new viewers continue to discover *Buffy the Vampire Slayer*.

From Beneath You, It Foreshadows

Why Buffy's *First Season Matters*

DAVID KOCIEMBA

The first season of *Buffy the Vampire Slayer* barely exists in the scholarship on the Buffyverse. It has been buried beneath scholarly attention to musicals and dream episodes, theories of love and redemption, and analyses of the series' politics, philosophy, and metaphysics. Character studies begin with the first season but quickly move on to the juicier deaths, damnations, and transformations found in later seasons. The first-season wordplay that *Entertainment Weekly* dubbed "Slayer-speak" gets the most attention (Howard 1997, 84). Many writers discuss this linguistic free-for-all (see M. Adams 2003, 2006; Overbey and Preston-Matto 2002; Wilcox 2005; S. Wilson 2001). They argue the series' use of language builds a community on-screen and off-, disarms foes, expresses character psychology, and teaches the pleasures of speaking truth to power through wit, playful teasing, and sophisticated wordplay. A sense of humor and strong command of language are essential parts of Joss Whedon's progressive politics.

But that is not all that can be found if one digs through Whedon's first season on television. First, the initial season stands on its own as an object worthy of study for the way it prompts active viewers to perform close readings. Also, the foundational themes of the series reveal themselves in these early episodes: the just use of power, reimagining gender, and empathy for enemies as part of heroism. Second, Whedon anticipates and counters many of the criticisms his series would face. Third, Whedon's belief that the series would not last past its first season means that these episodes provide a window into what he initially regarded as essential to *Buffy the Vampire Slayer*. An analysis of the first season reveals the first expressions of ideas that would be given greater depth with the Initiative, Spike and Angelus, and the dream episode "Restless" (4.22). Finally, the unaired "Production Pilot" (1.0) and "Prophecy Girl" (1.12) provide the first glimpses of Joss Whedon's development as a director as well as a unique view of Whedon before his signature traits of artistic collaboration and close relationship with his fan audience fully develop.

The kind of close attention to narrative construction that the first season encouraged was becoming a more common mainstream viewing posture as the television industry began producing more complex narratives. This model of storytelling is neither entirely episodic nor serial, but it is also not a complete merger of both forms. Jason Mittell argues that this new approach rejects "the need for plot closure within every episode," while "individual episodes have a distinctive identity as more than just one step in a long narrative journey." It "foregrounds ongoing stories across a range of genres" (2006, 32), but may downplay or reject the melodrama style and relationship-centered structure. Ultimately, this approach "invites us to care about the storyworld while simultaneously appreciating its construction" (35). Such series make narrative evolution, convolution, and involution central. Mittell traces the approach from its roots in the late 1970s and early 1980s (with *Dallas* [1978–91], *Hill Street Blues* [1981–87], and *Cheers* [1982–93], among others) through the late-1980s programs (for example, *Moonlighting* [1985–89], *thirtysomething* [1987–91], and *Star Trek: The Next Generation* [1987–94]). It flowers during the early 1990s with *Twin Peaks* (1990–91), *Seinfeld* (1990–98), and *The X-Files* (1993–2002) (32–33), culminating in a rich crop of complex series on cable and in broadcast, with *Buffy*, *The Sopranos* (1999–2007), *The Wire* (2002–8), *Arrested Development* (2003–6), and *Lost* (2004–10) as just a few of the shows cited (33–36).

Many new factors helped narrative complexity (and the resulting closer viewing posture) flourish. An influx of talent fueled a rise in quality, as creators sought more control as producers in television than they could reliably retain in film. Long-form series present an artistic challenge impossible in film's constrained time span, especially as the industry increasingly relied on blockbusters in the 1980s. Shrinking audiences after cable television's rise reshaped networks' expectations and forced them to consider the viability of cult shows with boutique audiences; *Hill Street Blues* is an early example. Narrative complexity provided brand separation from inexpensive reality television, serving as a type of counterprogramming. New revenue streams pushed the industry away from least objectionable programming toward most repeatable programming. Due to new revenue streams—including DVD rentals and sales, digital downloads and streaming video, and expanded merchandising opportunities—*Battlestar Galactica* (2004–9) was a smash hit for the Sci-Fi cable network despite a peak audience of 3.8 million viewers. Finally, technological shifts connected audiences and allowed for greater scrutiny of television narratives (Mittell 2006, 30–32). These technologies fostered a greater collective intelligence among viewers who could catalog motifs, archetypes, and thematic connections between episodes, then debate their meaning on fan sites and Listservs or post them to Wikis such as Lostpedia, TV Tropes, or Memory Alpha.

Over the past three decades, mainstream and cult viewers alike learned the kind of close-reading approach assumed in this chapter. As Philip Mikosz and Dana C. Och observe, "To write about *Buffy* is to write about a relationship, a certain investment across a serialized duration, as well as the cognitive relations that are elaborated at all levels of the series, from the season right down to a single shot" (2002, para. 2). The first season of *Buffy* is both a coherent work on its own and one that anticipates the series' later narrative developments.

"It's about Power": The Pilot

The foundational story of the series' first two episodes is about men, women, and sexual violence. The first scene features an aggressive teenage boy and an attractive blonde schoolgirl breaking into school after hours. He comments upon their isolation, clearly savoring her fear. The girl turns into a vampire and drains him. When another blonde schoolgirl walks to the Bronze alone at night, she is followed down an alley. She has lured her follower there to ambush him, kicking him to the ground in a gymnastic attack. These women, Darla and Buffy, are used by Whedon to turn the tables on horror movie clichés; these women embody Whedon's "very first mission statement . . . the joy of female power: having it, using it, sharing it" (Miller 2003, 35).

"Welcome to the Hellmouth" (1.1) and "The Harvest" (1.2) acknowledge and highlight the historical connection between the vampire mythology and the rape myth. While vampires have meant many different things as well— the intimacy of friendship, growing up, oral eroticism, possession, addiction, middle-class fears of the decadent aristocracy, the exotic, AIDS—they have also been about sexualized violence. The iconic vampire myth of the twentieth century is of a man who has no weapon but his body, who often attacks someone of the opposite sex at night when she is alone, especially in her bed. The narrative lingers on these moments when he creeps in, punctures her body, and drains her of her vital bodily fluids. If he does it often enough, well enough, she comes to like it, comes to actively participate in it. "No" eventually means "yes."

The pilot shows vampires to be sexual predators—seductive, stalking, and violent. When a vampire dressed like El DeBarge flirts with Willow at the Bronze, he cups her chin lightly, an older man with an inexperienced, too young lover, a Humbert Humbert to her Lolita. Cordelia refers to Jesse by saying, "Oh yay, it's my stalker." Having been driven off by her verbal mace, Jesse comically states, "Oh right, I'm on the prowl. This is me prowling." Later, as a vampire, Jesse straddles Cordelia's prone body, pins her arms to the ground above her head, and shouts, "Stop struggling! You're not making this easy!"

Yet Jesse, like Willow, is a sexual innocent, easily manipulated by the experienced Darla. Xander emphasizes that Jesse is a victim even as he is a monster, pleading with him in "The Harvest": "I know there's still a part of you in there!" Xander here recognizes the humanity within the human-demon hybrid that is the vampire in *Buffy*. Although Giles harshly rebukes Xander's empathy in the pilot, Buffy says exactly the same words to Angelus as he holds Willow hostage in "Innocence" (2.14). Through Jesse, the series starts its examination of the endless cycle of violence in which victims become victimizers. When we look on the vampire's visage, we see the abuser's face layered over the human face of the abused. That recognition begins with Xander looking at Jesse's vampire face with empathy and dismay.

The series insists on monsters whose humanity cannot be easily erased. Mary Alice Money observes that essential to the series' understanding of heroism is "the ability to perceive, to *know* the inner nature of a person." Beginning with Cordelia in the first season, the series rehabilitates obnoxious, different, and even monstrous characters. The series forces the protagonists and the viewers to see these marginalized figures anew: as "worthy of inclusion, nonhumans who are people after all, strangers who become us" (2002, 98). This undemonization is the subject of "Angel" (*Buffy* 1.7), wherein Buffy discovers Angel's true nature as a vampire with a soul. Spike, Harmony, and Vamp Willow also force the characters and their viewers to see "some part of you" in the familiar face of the monstrous Other. The just use of power requires the ability to see Others with empathy.

Whedon is wise enough to know that not all abuse is physical and not all scars are visible. After Buffy and Willow solidify their budding friendship by discussing boys at the counter in the Bronze, Buffy tells her that she has to meet Giles briefly in the club's balcony. Willow responds, "No, that's okay. You don't have to come back." Alyson Hannigan's stutter-step delivery and her hesitancy and eagerness to please economically present a whole history of social trauma at the hands of popular kids like Harmony, who bullied her for ten years ("Graduation Day, Part One" 3.21). We witness some of the bullying in the pilot when Cordelia scorns Willow's homespun dress and white tights as being from "the softer side of Sears." This moment is so devastating that audiences would easily remember Willow's ensemble when it shows up in her nightmare three years later in "Restless."

Buffy's reaction to Willow's low self-esteem is telling. Sarah Michelle Gellar's pause, her holding of Hannigan's eye, and her slowly dawning smile give Buffy's response a humanity inflected with recognition and compassionate humor. Buffy likely recognizes the source of Willow's insecurity, having perhaps inflicted it on others. Buffy admits she was like Cordelia before her calling, complete with a group of sycophants ("Helpless" 3.12; "Becoming, Part One" 2.21). While the primary cause for Willow's mad, murderous grief in the sixth season is Tara's traumatic death, another factor is the insecurity and self-hate resulting from the emotional trauma of bullying during her formative years. This first-season moment in the Bronze suggests why Buffy takes Willow under her wing, before Willow develops any powers at all. Willow is a part of Buffy's redemption.

Countering Anticipated Criticism with "The Witch" and "Teacher's Pet"

Several critics championed *Buffy* during its first season: Kristen Baldwin and Bruce Frets of *Entertainment Weekly*, Tom Gliatto of *People*, and the editorial board at *Slate* and *Salon* (1997, 68; 1997, 17; Foer 1997; Millman 1997). Joe Queenan (1997) at *TV Guide* wrote, "Far from being the stuff of fantasy or mere over-the-top satire, [*Buffy*] is the most realistic portrayal of contemporary teenage life on television today" (quoted in Stafford 2007, 7–8). But an influential few panned it. *Variety* reviewer Todd Everett damned the pilot with faint praise, saying it would have "potential for early-teen viewing" (1997, 1). John J. O'Connor's dismissive *New York Times* review of the first five episodes observed that the series should appeal to "Humbert Humberts all over America" because the main character wears "hot pants and boots" and "changes from one skimpy outfit to another" (1997, 11). His review scoffs at the idea that such a girl could be a hero.

O'Connor's review demonstrates the series' need to deal with Buffy being considered too femme to be feminist, let alone a hero. Whedon uses two early episodes to shift the traditional depiction of female heroism and how viewers understand it; Xander and Willow guide viewers through that process. (During the first season, teenage girls made up the largest segment of the audience, whereas it was a college-age audience by the second year [Dempsey

1997, 25; Longworth 2002, 215].) As the season had completed filming before its midseason airing, "The Witch" (1.3) and "Teacher's Pet" (1.4) suggest that Whedon anticipated criticisms like O'Connor's and devoted airtime to countering them.

The series tackles the issue of gender codes and predatory gazes head-on immediately after the pilot. "The Witch" explores the romantic triangle among the teens while Buffy becomes a cheerleader, only for them to fight a witch who wants a position on the squad. Xander tells Willow he is so close to her that she's "like a guy," only to have Buffy call him "one of the girls." Buffy even sings about how she wants to be a "macho, macho man." This episode represents hyperfemininity as chosen and performed rather than natural. The script mentions cheerleading's long training sessions, professional coaching, and job prospects. Gender is a performance that requires work and skill. In the pilot, Buffy complains that she used to be "so good" at the masquerade of femininity as she compares a long, dowdy flower-printed dress with a scandalously brief outfit as she prepares to go to the Bronze. This moment implies that appearances are crafted, requiring skill to navigate, and that gender binaries are perilous and present. And these skills aid her work. Buffy uses fashion to identify as a vampire the man luring Willow away by noting that his style is "carbon-dated" ("Welcome to the Hellmouth"). In "Teacher's Pet," Buffy correctly identifies a predatory quality to Natalie French's shoulder pads. But these skills are not always benign. Catherine Madison's witchcraft uses Barbie dolls as instruments of vengeance in service of sexual jealousy ("The Witch"). Catherine's final spell states, "I will look upon my enemy and the dark one will have her soul." That enemy turns out to be Catherine's own image, reflected back at the cosmetologist.

All performances of femininity are presented as paths to power: witchcraft, cheerleading, cosmetology school, and even normalcy. Cordelia wants to lead cheers as a means to increased social power. Buffy wants to use it as a camouflage of normalcy. But it matters how that power is used. The head cheerleader curls her lip in a slight smile as she dismisses the spontaneous combustion of one of the girls during the first day of auditions. A life of feminine ornamentation is not represented as desirable or natural to any impressionable viewers.

Yet, in showing several shots of cheerleaders' panties, the series seemingly panders to immature boys and envious girls. Admittedly, casting attractive actresses such as Gellar, Hannigan, and former National Football League (NFL) cheerleader Charisma Carpenter will draw the kind of objectifying gaze this episode simultaneously solicits and counters. But does "The Witch" demand this kind of reading position? The series would need to use male point of view sequences, close-up framing of bodies, and subjective effects to suture an audience to a (male heterosexual) objectifying perspective rather than promote the appreciation of skillful labor of femininity's performance. It is difficult to say that such editing techniques are utilized,[1] except for the scene in which Xander leers at the cheerleader tryouts. Laura Mulvey's classic description of the gaze's effect manifests through Xander, as "the beauty of the woman as object and the screen space coalesce; she is no longer the bearer of guilt but a perfect product, whose body, stylized and fragmented by close-ups, is the content of the film and the direct recipient of the spectator's look" ([1975] 2000, 490). Xander later jokes about "taking Polaroids outside [Buffy's] window" as part of his admission that he has "got to be a man and ask her out." Yet Buffy and Willow's reaction shots frame Xander's leering gaze at the tryouts with raised eyebrows, tilted heads, and small smiles that suggest his immaturity. Xander needs to see the world through new eyes, to become a new man in place of the sexually immature boy he is.

Xander's daydream in the teaser of "Teacher's Pet" picks up on his comic lechery during "The Witch." "Teacher's Pet" begins with an embarrassingly immature sexualized daydream of rescuing Buffy from a vampire, then rocking out with a guitar solo as she watches adoringly from the audience. For him to feel empowered and potent, she must be weak and solicitous, with eyes wide and lips parted. Xander's daydream of potency and fame prefigures Jonathan's episode-long fantasy in "Superstar" (4.17), suggesting these daydreams are common. It is no wonder Whedon went on to make *Dollhouse*, a series that critiques the fantasies and defense mechanisms that support pornography, prostitution, and emotional disconnection.

Fortunately, the real Buffy has the smarts, ingenuity, and toughness to save Xander from sexual predation. Natalie French, a praying-mantis demon who can assume the form of a very shapely substitute teacher, takes an interest in Xander. Just as Darla toyed with Jesse, Ms. French's flirting takes advantage of Xander's sexual innocence. Luring him to her home, she drugs Xander and cages him in her basement. Just as she is about to rape and murder Xander while in praying-mantis form, he is rescued by Buffy. The B-movie monster costume and Nicholas Brendon's comic acting deflect some of the grotesque

---

1. One may certainly argue that the series creators use Angel's infrequent appearances from the shadows as their way of suturing the audience into a male objectifying point of view. For more on male spectatorship in the series, see Middleton 2007.

horror of such a scenario.² The fact that Xander is male defuses the moment as well. In the parallel inappropriate lover episode focused on Willow, "I Robot . . . You, Jane" (1.8), there is no rape cliffhanger to Willow's online flirtation with a demonic predator. These two early episodes anticipate O'Connor's *Lolita* objection and confront it head-on as a subject of comedy and horror.

The Essential Story of *Buffy the Vampire Slayer*

If the first four episodes are primarily concerned with establishing the series' core themes and relationships, the remaining episodes reiterate previous themes while presenting the first expressions of ideas that later receive fuller expression. These preliminary explorations are more significant than simply setting up later narrative effects. As a midseason replacement on a two-year-old network, Whedon thought the series would "last only a few episodes and no one will see it," according to mentor Jeanine Basinger (2008). The first season therefore hints at what Whedon initially regarded as essential to *Buffy*.

Buffy's writers engaged in retroactive continuity, in which certain tropes, characters, and situations initially intended to stand on their own are invested with new meanings in later episodes. These moments are not simply about the momentum a narrative develops as it is created. Rhonda V. Wilcox writes, "It is possible that the early versions of a pattern are purposeful foreshadowing; it is also possible that they are preliminary explorations or first inklings of an idea which the writers will choose to develop more fully later. Retroactive continuity allows for the effect of foreshadowing" (2005, 115). Whedon and his fellow writers knew the overall arc of a season prior to its start. They planned some events much further out. Whedon told Kristine Sutherland two years in advance that her character, Joyce, was going to die (Havens 2003, 46). Buffy's death is foreshadowed two years in advance in "Graduation Day, Part Two" (3.22). Such narrative connections are basic to Whedon's story construction, argues Jes Battis: "*Buffy* 'double-codes' many of its scenes, using a combination of foreshadowing and subtextual references that the more discerning reader can access" (2003, para. 17). But not all developments are planned far in advance. Whedon left room to react to unexpected developments on set;

---

2. Even the first two episodes skirted the line of decency for some, as Howard Rosenberg (1997), the *Los Angeles Times* television reviewer, blasted the WB for airing the pilot so early in prime time, despite an aired disclaimer that emphasized its TV-PG rating.

Jenny Calendar, Darla, and Spike got additional episodes due to the performances of their actors (Stafford 2007, 140; Havens 2003, 43). Writer Jane Espenson recalls, "In 'Doppelgangland,' [Willow] notices that her vampire self is 'kinda gay.' When we started plotting the Tara arc in Season Four, Joss said, 'Were we planning this back then?' And even he didn't know for sure. . . . Some of it is conscious and some of it is not conscious, but it is clearly there anyway" (Kaveney 2004c, 107–8). Such retroactive continuity is an inherent feature of creating complex narratives in a serial format. Authors such as Charles Dickens knew the overall arc of the plot, but "follow[ed] where the characters led," Wilcox observes. For her, these processes are one way that complex narratives develop "the wonderful quality of much great literature, of seeming both surprising and inevitable" (2005, 115). Retroactive continuity describes narrative elements whose intention, meaning, and reception shift over time. The precarious status of this midseason replacement not only makes the first season of *Buffy* an excellent case study of retroactive continuity but also reveals the foundational elements of the story before retroactive continuity builds on them.

"The Pack" establishes the second season's key elements of betrayal and the unexpected (1.6). In this episode, hyena spirits possess Xander and four bullies during a field trip to the zoo. After the hyena possession takes hold, Xander dumps Willow as a friend, saying, "My feelings for you have been changing. And, well, we've been friends for such a long time that I feel like I need to tell you something. I've, um . . . I've decided to drop geometry. So I won't be needing your math help anymore. Which means I won't have to look at your pasty face again." And then he bursts into delighted laughter at Willow's devastation.[3] In its prankish cruelty and its insight into the young woman's insecurities, this speech is reminiscent of Angelus's devastating talk with Buffy in "Innocence." (Similarly, Xander's attempted sexual assault of Buffy later in the episode prefigures the emotional trauma inflicted by Spike's attempted rape in "Seeing Red" [6.19].) This episode also establishes Xander as an adept liar—he convinces Buffy and Willow that he remembers nothing of his cruelty—which would prove crucial to setting up his role in the grand tragedy of the Season 2 finale. Villainy based in emotional betrayal seems essential to this series. Anthony Stewart Head thought that the pack killing and then eating Principal Flutie had a profound impact, saying, "I thought it was wonderful . . . when he bumped off the principal. At that moment, you

---

3. Willow grimaces at the memory three years later in "Who Are You?" (4.16).

knew there weren't any lines he wouldn't cross and anything goes" (Stafford 2007, 7). Killing off essential characters would be a feature of Whedon's work in *Buffy*, *Angel*, *Serenity*, and beyond.

Just as Whedon uses Principal Flutie to set the pattern for unexpectedly killing off a character, he uses Cordelia to set the pattern for later redemption arcs. The revelation of Cordelia's humanity in "Out of Mind, Out of Sight" (*Buffy* 1.11) sparks her character's evolution in both *Buffy* and *Angel*. When she is the "Queen of Mean," her biting sarcasm not only provides pleasure but also indicates an intelligence and social awareness that belie her public persona as vapid princess. She is the first one to put together that Buffy is not what she seems. Cordelia reveals the costs of holding the social power she wields: "You think I'm never lonely because I'm so cute and popular? I can be surrounded by people and be completely alone. It's not like any of them really know me. I don't even know if they like me half the time." This moment changes a viewer's relationship to Cordelia, revealing the social tyrant as a slave to popularity. Whedon urges viewers to recognize Cordelia's humanity, just as he did with Jesse. Of course, *Buffy* is not an after-school special, so Cordelia returns to her old habits once she is observed hanging with losers by her boyfriend and Harmony.[4] Yet when people are in danger in the season finale, this epically self-involved girl joins the good fight in spectacular fashion. In the second season, she slowly starts to pitch in during nonapocalyptic situations. Like Spike, Cordelia opts for a life well lived without the formal second chance offered to Angel or Buffy by special power or prophecy. In the first season, it is Cordelia who shows what Whedon regarded as vital to his story's theory of redemption, not Angel. Change is hard, it takes work, and there is always the temptation to fall back into old habits. But anyone can do it if Cordelia can. In a way, she is the first Spike, even as Xander is the first Angelus.[5]

The first season also foreshadows another antagonist, the Initiative. In "Out of Mind, Out of Sight," Marcie's social invisibility becomes physical. Once Buffy foils Marcie's plan to maim Cordelia and make her unforgettable, Federal Bureau of Investigation (FBI) agents place Marcie in their custody. Remembering the agents' earlier presence lurking on campus, Buffy intuits, "This isn't the first time this has happened. It's happened at other schools."

---

4. She does the same thing in "Bewitched, Bothered, Bewildered" (2.16) once she realizes that dating Xander has bumped her off the top of the social pyramid.

5. To complete this analysis of Buffy's major boyfriends, Elizabeth Rambo (2009) makes an excellent case that Owen in "Never Kill a Boy on a First Date" (1.5) prefigures Riley.

The agents take Marcie to a classroom with others like her to be taught assassination and infiltration techniques. The facility has glass-enclosed rooms like the Initiative's cells. The idea that the government would be interested in the monstrous is foundational to *Buffy* and many other works by Whedon, who script-doctored the first *X-Men* film, later wrote the third volume of the *Astonishing X-Men* comic series, and once referred to *Buffy the Vampire Slayer* as "*My So-Called Life* meets *The X-Files*" (Tracy 1998, 22).

"Out of Mind, Out of Sight" is a classic example of retroactive continuity. It both stands alone as an episode with an ominous twist ending and represents part of a broader project to keep the mix of the fantastic and the contemporary viable. The series adjusts its narrative logic to compensate as it evolves. In "The Harvest," Giles explains the pandemic of denial in Sunnydale in this way: "People have a tendency to rationalize what they can and forget what they can't." Principal Snyder's crackdown on missing persons and spontaneous cheerleader combustion signals that others in Sunnydale know and respond to these events. The FBI agents in the episode complete the move from local to national. In the third season, the writers add a historical element to this foundational explanation of how the world responds to incursions of the supernatural. Mayor Wilkins has been behind the scenes in Sunnydale for decades, even providing the demon-friendly extensive sewer system. In the fifth season, everybody in Sunnydale knows enough that a rampaging troll is dangerous but hardly worth holding a town meeting. By the sixth season, government black-ops teams fight a covert war against monsters across the globe. As Scott Westerfield puts it, "The fantastic leaves its mark on the world." *Buffy* presents not simply a trespassed world that snaps back to middle-class normality and implies its inevitability, "but it is a world that, like ours, can be and is changed, for better or worse, by the actions of the people who live in it" (2003, 40). For viewers to accept the implicit progressive politics of Buffy's decision to share her power in the series' finale or seek assistance from her community in "Graduation Day," the narrative must consistently teach viewers to take pleasure in a narrative that embraces change rather than remain comfortingly familiar.

The first season explores psyches along with the possibility of moral or social change. "Nightmares" (1.10) is the first season's version of both "Fear, Itself" (4.4) and "Restless." As the characters' darkest fears come to life in response to the distress of an abused, comatose kid, "Nightmares" is like "Fear, Itself" (where a haunted house manifests the protagonists' fears) with some of the formal adventurousness of "Restless." All three episodes feature shared nightmares that reflect the terrors of each individual protagonist (for example, Xander sees Willow suffocating in "Restless"; Buffy's terror of becoming a vampire is visible to all in "Nightmares"). Because Buffy's dreams predict the future, each character's nightmares plausibly anticipate narrative developments as well. As the first glimpse inside the unconscious of these characters, "Nightmares" also encourages viewers to perform close readings based in character psychology. Once the writers revisit that episode twice in the fourth season, retroactive continuity requires viewers to reflect on both the series' narrative construction and the characters' more complex psychology. No early episode fits the new storytelling mode of narrative complexity more.

Willow's dream is the first in "Restless," so it highlights that episode's connection to "Nightmares" to encourage reading the episodes in light of each other. In "Nightmares," the first season's dream episode, Willow gets dragged backstage, costumed in a kimono, told by the director that there is an ugly crowd with a lot of reviewers, and then thrust onstage next to her irked male lead, where Willow can squeak but a single note of the aria.[6] Her actor's nightmare in "Restless" has her cast in her drama class's surreal *Death of a Salesman* (1949) despite having never attended a single class. As soon as she is backstage, Willow asks whether the play is *Madame Butterfly* (1904), as she has "a whole problem with opera." Buffy's role as a 1920s vamp, rather than a Slayer turned into a vampire, reminds viewers of "Nightmares" as well (Pateman 2006, 131–32). In "Restless," Buffy acts like a peppy version of Willow's "Nightmares" director cheerfully telling her, "The place is packed. Everybody's here! Your whole family's in the front row, and they look really angry." In both episodes, Willow fears being noticed and judged. Finally, just before Willow's opera debut in Season 1, Xander finds himself seminude in front of the classroom. In the library afterward, Willow remarks, "Everyone staring? I'd hate to have everyone paying attention to me like that." This fear of being judged by hostile viewers seems grounded in her decade of being bullied by Harmony and Cordelia. The final moments of her dream in "Restless" find her back in the plaid dress and white tights Cordelia mocked in the pilot, giving a book report before a bored and hostile class.

Yet Willow is ambivalent about being noticed. In "Gingerbread" (3.11), her mother has not noticed Willow's new haircut or boyfriend. Willow complains that her mother listens to her colleagues more than her daughter, claiming

---

6. In "Puppet Show" (1.9), Willow flees the stage during her reading of a dramatic scene from *Oedipus Rex* (429 BC) with Buffy and Xander.

that their last in-depth conversation was about the patriarchal bias on *Mister Rogers' Neighborhood* (1968–2001). Willow shouts, "I'm not your sidekick!" at Buffy during "Fear, Itself." In "Two to Go" (6.21), Willow references that moment, saying that after "six years as a side man, now I get to be the Slayer," meaning the most powerful one, and perhaps suggesting the one that gets the attention. One of the most famous lines from *Death of a Salesman* is Linda's plea on behalf of her humble husband that "attention must be paid" to his sacrifices and difficulties as he slowly cracks under the pressure of failure. One part of Willow demands the attention, while another part of her fears that the pressure will cause her to fail, freeze, or snap.

Cordelia, Xander, and Giles have simpler fears. In "Nightmares," Cordelia fears having bad hair, worse attire, and being dragged off to join the chess club against her will. She experiences a similar downward mobility once she starts dating Xander in the second season. Xander faces off against the clown of his sixth birthday party. Punching Bozo out, he slams the clown's act, saying, "You are a lousy clown! Your balloon animals are pathetic! Everyone can make a giraffe!" This scene sets up a wonderful joke two years later when Xander loses the coveted Sunnydale High Class Clown award to a prop comic wearing a balloon hat. More seriously, Xander spends much of the fourth and fifth seasons worrying that he is a buffoon, not a grown man. After the nightmares end, Xander confesses to Willow that he found the vampire version of Buffy attractive, joking, "I'm sick. I need help." Xander's experience with desiring a vampire makes his hostility and revulsion to Buffy's relationships with Angel and Spike more complicated. Meanwhile, Giles fears being lost in the stacks and unable to read. Jane Espenson references this moment in her episode "Something Blue" (4.9) when Willow causes Giles to go blind; Espenson loves to make these kinds of callbacks (Kociemba 2009). Giles's dream in "Restless" features his concern that his work as a Watcher means he has lost out on a fuller life, symbolized through Olivia and her baby carriage. Last, Giles fears that he will fail in his duty to protect Buffy as he kneels by her grave. Buffy would die twice: in "Prophecy Girl" and "The Gift" (5.22). The writers found fertile ground for future narrative and psychological developments in "Nightmares."

Finally, Buffy's nightmare features many elements that are incorporated into the series. Her fear in "Nightmares" of failing to perform in combat comes to pass when the Master hypnotizes her in "Prophecy Girl." Buffy takes a history test unprepared, only to have time speed up as well. Espenson revisits this moment from "Nightmares" in her episode "Life Serial" (6.5), when the Trio makes Buffy experience time as moving faster and looping. Early in

"Nightmares," Buffy's father blames her for his divorce from Joyce, wants to drop his visitation rights, and wishes she had turned out differently. We never see Hank Summers again outside of flashbacks or alternate realities, as he misses Buffy's eighteenth birthday and ends up in Spain with his secretary, "living the cliché" ("Family" 5.5). Buffy transforms into a vampire in "Nightmares." While both Angel and Dracula drink her blood, "the manifestation of Buffy as a vampire . . . is evidently meant to demonstrate the fear that Buffy has of being turned into that which she is supposed to kill, but the fact of that vampire being a demon lodged in a human body is a teasing (if unintentional) presentiment of what we discover about her as a Slayer" (Pateman 2006, 187). Here is a classic case of retroactive continuity: what first revealed only understandable fear later suggests the possibility that Slayers might be partly demonic after "Restless" revisits this moment: "We're not demons," Buffy declares, leading Adam to respond skeptically, "Is that a fact?" "Get It Done" (7.15) confirms the hybrid origins of the Slayer line. In addition, Buffy's fear of becoming monstrous connects to her Season 5 fears about the predatory nature of the Slayer, questioning whether she is patrolling or hunting. (In the first season, Buffy often blithely uses the term *hunting*.) In "Nightmares," Buffy fears that the Master will be released, which occurs during "Prophecy Girl." The Master serves as her spirit guide in this nightmare, confirming the mystical and psychological sources of the nightmares. Buffy's dream in "Restless" features only characters who were once antagonists or threatened a key relationship: Anya, Joyce, Tara, Riley, and Adam. Yet each provides crucial guidance. Finally, the Master buries Buffy alive in "Nightmares," which foreshadows Buffy clawing her way out of her grave after Willow's interrupted resurrection spell in "Bargaining, Parts One and Two" (6.1 and 6.2). Viewers who paid close attention to Buffy's nightmares were richly rewarded through this foreshadowing.

More broadly, Roz Kaveney observes that the first season lays the foundation for Whedon's narrative structure in later seasons and other series (2004b, 19). The antagonist is established early, only to have a radical revision of the rules of the conflict halfway through the season. The second half of the season establishes the emotional obstacles the characters must overcome. Kaveney says these seasons "share a structural pattern as coherent as the statement, development, second statement, recapitulations and coda of the sonata form" (14). The first seasons of *Firefly*, *Dollhouse*, and *Angel* similarly use the mostly anthology format of the first season of *Buffy*.

Whedon's first season on television sets the pattern for his long-form narrative structure, his understanding of villainy and redemption, and his encouragement of viewers to perform close readings of both narrative construction and character psychology.

Whedon in Control: The Production Pilot and "Prophecy Girl"

Finally, the first season shows the beginning of Joss Whedon's artistic development. "I want to speak visually," said Whedon to the *Onion A.V. Club* in 2001. "Writing is just a way of communicating visually. That's what it's all about. But nobody would even consider me to direct. So I said, 'I'll create a television show, and I'll use it as a film school, and I'll teach myself to direct on TV'" (Robinson 2001). His directorial debut was a production pilot designed to show network executives what *Buffy* was going to be. The use of such demos gained prominence in the mid-1990s as a way to cut costs from green-lighting full-blown pilot episodes. Demos are never intended to be broadcast. Whedon steadfastly refused to include it as a DVD extra, despite the demand for it and the archival value, declaring to *IGN FilmForce* in 2003, "Not while there is strength in these bones."

There is a reason for his reaction. The production pilot is rife with mistakes. The sound design lacks score, foleying, and mixing. Whedon does not use music to fill in the fight scene. One dialogue scene features wind in shots from one take but no wind in the other shots. When Cordelia delivers her devastating put-down of Willow's dress, it is a loosely framed full shot with Willow walking out of the frame before the punch line is even delivered. Willow and Buffy have a long talk when they first meet, but it is a long shot in which the camera keeps them in the background with an empty foreground. That is no way to build chemistry between two actresses vital to one's show. Even in closer framings, Riff Regan's Willow grinds many dialogue scenes to a halt. Regan drops cues, pauses lengthily between sentences, uses slow-developing frowns, and generally makes Willow sound slow and deliberate rather than intelligent. The production pilot shows Whedon to be a novice *television* director. Placing actors relatively far away from the camera in dialogue scenes can work on film's bigger screens because viewers can still see facial expressions. Directors have to get in close for television.

The production pilot did not go well for a few reasons. The low budget, brief production schedules, and expectations such productions operate under are clearly factors. The vampires are dusted via extremely clunky stop-motion sequence. More important, Whedon's inexperience impeded things on set, which frustrated him: "I was a first-time guy who didn't know what he was doing, surrounded by old veterans who didn't know what they were doing."

Whedon had gone back to television because, as he explained, "I liked the idea that I would be in charge of every aspect of the show, and the only person I could blame if it failed was me" (Havens 2003, 32). He must have realized after the production pilot that filmmaking was not that simple. Creators need to have a certain amount of on-set experience to even be able to communicate their vision accurately.[7] Television is a collaborative art form.

Whedon's new team working on the Season 1 finale, "Prophecy Girl," his directorial debut, features many who became his frequent collaborators: cinematographer Michael Gershman, Emmy-winning makeup artists Todd McIntosh and John Vulich, set designer Carey Meyer, and *Angel* cocreator David Greenwalt. Many of the problems on display in the production pilot vanish. Whedon uses tighter framing, such as the extreme close-ups on Buffy's face as the Master bites her. Instead of the daytime exteriors that dominated the production pilot, Gershman uses high-contrast lighting in the many night scenes in "Prophecy Girl." The makeup artists have fixed the early problems with the vampire teeth that led *People* reviewer Tom Gliatto to observe that the Master "slurps his lines" (1997, 17). Instead of being stuck with the demo's reliance on preexisting sets and locations, Meyer created the iconic library and an effectively atmospheric low-budget Hellmouth. Whedon uses parallel montage smoothly, tracking action in several different locales. Composer Walter Murphy allows for the use of score to fill in scenes, although Rob Haskins describes his scoring for the series as "competent but rarely inspired" (2010, 45). Murphy's single interesting musical decision is the jarring quotation of the Nerf Herder title theme as Buffy, Angel, and Xander march off to fight the Master. Janet K. Halfyard praises the theme's insertion for reestablishing Buffy's narrative agency and cites its lyrical and reflective reuse in the final scene of the season (2010, 25). Whedon's decision to hire Christophe Beck for the next season paid off with an intricate, motif-laden score that won an Emmy.[8] Quality series tend to be multivocal in ways that do not diminish the concept of auteurism but rather richly expand it. Although that feedback loop among creators would be least on display during the first season, the contrast between the production pilot and the season finale shows its importance even here.

7. Whedon would go on to encourage a number of his writers to direct, including Marti Noxon, Doug Petrie, and David Fury; Jane Espenson took steps in that direction while working with Whedon. See Kociemba 2009.

8. He also hired new directors. Five of Whedon's eleven first-season directors never worked on *Buffy* again, and two more shot just one more episode.

In "Prophecy Girl," Whedon creates the space for melodrama in a series devoted more toward comedy, action, and horror until that point. When Buffy overhears Giles discussing the prophecy of her death, Whedon creates the classic melodrama clash between abstract principles and relationships. Giles cannot see past prophecy and duty, while Buffy reminds Giles of their emotional connection. In tears, Buffy hammers on the personal betrayal of Giles's silence. She accuses Giles of forgetting her precious particularity in his focus on her role as a Slayer when she says, "Giles, I'm sixteen. I don't want to die." For her, these birthrights are imposed, not chosen. Whedon visualizes her emotion through the creation of dead space in the compositions of those medium one-shots, while the intensity of the moment is captured in the gradually tightening framing of the close-ups. It is a classic technique done well. As in the pilot, Buffy rejoins the fight not because of a sense of duty for a role she never chose, but out of a sense of responsibility and caring for Willow. Buffy's tearful rebuke moves Giles (and viewers) from the realm of action and plot resolution to experiencing the more interpersonal values of melodrama.

Whedon reinforces the role of melodrama in "Prophecy Girl" through a touching scene between Joyce and Buffy. Joyce unknowingly references the essence of Buffy's plight by asking, "Is it written somewhere? You should do what you want." Buffy's sadness continues, but she begins to smile and relate to her mother. This early moment of ambivalent bonding counterbalances Giles's and Angel's allegiance to duty. At least one adult gets Buffy's point. Joyce's statement is wrong on many levels, but it is emotionally authentic. Buffy should do what she wants. Eventually, what she wants will match what is expected of her. This moment begins an emotional connection that had not happened yet, making the stakes even higher for Buffy and Joyce's fight in "Becoming, Part Two" (2.22).

Conclusion

The first season was Joss Whedon's one chance to tell the essential story of *Buffy the Vampire Slayer*. As a novice TV creator, he could not assume that his midseason replacement series with the cult title would get some of the top ratings the two-year-old network had achieved to that point. Whedon's essential *Buffy* includes multiple genres, sexual predation, villains whose humor inflicts emotional damage, government conspiracies, a dream episode, and redemption being sought by the least likely characters. The bedrock themes of the series reveal themselves in these early episodes: reimagining gender and generational roles, understanding predators as simultaneously victims, and showing heroes as empathic and playful. The first season's use of intricate foreshadowing "indicated a real commitment to, and respect for, the intelligence of its viewers," Kaveney writes (2004b, 2). Whedon anticipated many of the criticisms his series would face and devotes "The Witch" and "Teacher's Pet" to countering them. Finally, "Prophecy Girl" and the production pilot provide the first glimpses of Joss Whedon as a director, though one with less influence from many of his later collaborators. It is often remarked that the series is a bildungsroman for Buffy, but the first season is one for Joss Whedon as well.

Hero's Journey, Heroine's Return?

Buffy, Eurydice, and the Orpheus Myth

JANET K. HALFYARD

In *Why "Buffy" Matters*, Rhonda Wilcox boldly asserts that "*Buffy* is art, and art of the highest order" and that "in the world of television, there has probably never been a greater work of language than *Buffy the Vampire Slayer*" (2005, 1, 30). Although these claims for a comic horror TV series apparently aimed at a teenage audience might at first seem excessive, the wealth of academic essays and books examining the series are both an acknowledgment of and a testament to the richness of a text that challenges many of the accepted conventions and assumptions of television narratives and of culture itself.[1]

Among the mechanisms it uses to do this are the exploration and reinvention of our mythologies. Myths are, as Nick Lowe defines, stories that are never fixed in a definitive version but are, by their very nature, retellable ("The Greek Myths" 2008). In the same radio program, Mary Beard describes myth as a process that questions, interrogates, and prompts us to think about "how we know what we know and why we do things, a framework for thinking about who we are." Her description of myth as a "thought experiment" seems apt in relation to *Buffy*: certainly, these questions are never far from the surface, and Wilcox in particular has discussed Buffy herself and her narratives

1. In the summer of 2007, I received an unexpected request from Dominic Gray, the projects director of one of the UK's principal opera companies, Opera North. They were holding a conference to celebrate the four hundredth anniversary of the composition of Claudio Monteverdi's opera *Orfeo*, examining the continuing presence of the Orpheus myth in modern culture, and they wondered if there was a connection between Buffy and the Orpheus myth, in particular between Buffy and Eurydice. The result of the subsequent e-mail exchange was an invitation to speak on *Buffy* and the Orpheus myth at their conference, and this essay is based on that paper.

in relation to Joseph Campbell's monomyth (Wilcox 2005, 30–45). In the monomyth, the hero is called to adventure, must pass the threshold that separates worlds, undergoes trials in order to complete the quest, and then returns to the world, hopefully successful in the mission, bestowing a boon upon us that makes the world a better place for all. Laurel Bowman is so struck by the close parallels between Campbell's monomyth and *Buffy* that she suggests "a well-thumbed copy of *The Hero with a Thousand Faces* is probably on Joss Whedon's bedside table" (2002, para. 18).[2]

Wilcox and Bowman both, therefore, identify Campbell's mythic model as an important structuring factor in *Buffy*'s narrative. However, the myth of Orpheus and Eurydice seems to have a particular significance, entering the narrative on several occasions as a reference, a structure, or simply a gesture toward the myth that resonates with *Buffy*'s narrative even when the gesture is a fairly oblique one. Like most myths, the story of Orpheus and Eurydice exists in several different versions, but the essence of the myth is that Orpheus was a great musician, the son of a human king and the muse Calliope. The beauty of his music and his voice was so great that he could charm wild beasts, and even the rocks and trees would move from their places to follow the sound of his music. He married Eurydice, but she died after being bitten by a snake (in some versions of the myth it happened because she was being pursued by Aristeus, who wanted to force himself upon her). Orpheus pursued her into the underworld where Hades and his wife, Persephone, were so enchanted by the sound of his lament that Hades agreed to release Eurydice from death. He made one condition, that Orpheus not look back at Eurydice until he had led her out of the underworld, but on the journey back to the land of the living, Orpheus looked back and so Eurydice was lost to him forever.

Throughout the seven seasons of *Buffy*, the various elements of the Orpheus myth are played out and replayed several times, with different characters taking on different roles and with Buffy herself playing a multifaceted role in relation to the myth. On the one hand, she is the hero of the piece: she is Orpheus, repeatedly venturing into the underworld and returning with the boon of safety from evil and apocalypse. At the same time, as an attractive young woman, she also embodies Eurydice, the object of desire, the damsel in distress. It must also be noted that Orpheus is a very unsuccessful hero: he fails in his mission to save Eurydice. In *Buffy*, Eurydice often seems to

---

2. Richard Slotkin confirms that Whedon studied Campbell at Wesleyan (see Wilcox 2005, 99).

be invoked in the moments that Buffy succeeds where Orpheus failed. That moment of failure offers up the possibility of revisiting the myth with various twists, specifically various reversals and juxtapositions of ideas of success and failure such that the myth itself proves to be a useful mechanism for reading some of the more perplexing moments in *Buffy* and for illuminating the potentially paradoxical aspects of Buffy's nature.

Right from her inception, Buffy has embodied both the hero and the girl the hero is expected to save: this point is inherent in Whedon's original intention of turning on its head the horror movie trope of the little blonde girl who ventures into the dark and is killed by the monster.[3] In Whedon's concept, she is still the seemingly vulnerable little blonde girl, but now she is also the hero who can slay the monster. The result is that she sometimes seems to be playing out the roles of Orpheus and Eurydice simultaneously, their identities superimposed and intersecting, coexisting in the same space, perhaps like the optical effect of Rubin's vase, where the images of a vase and two faces in profile visually compete to operate as either background or foreground figure. Orpheus, in this construction, is Buffy as hero, while Eurydice is Buffy as "normal girl." Eurydice comes into play as an aspect of Buffy primarily at the moments that she most actively resists the role of hero that has been thrust upon her, and where she finds herself making a decision about whether she is prepared to continue. The Orpheus/Eurydice gesture in the narrative articulates the particular tension between the hero and the girl as figure and ground.

The first time that juxtaposition is overtly articulated is in the finale of *Buffy*'s first season ("Prophecy Girl" 1.12). Buffy discovers a prophecy that she will die in her confrontation with the Master, and in the moment that she believes the prophecy to be true, she becomes the heroine, the damsel in need of rescue. This transformation is underlined by the way she dresses for the final battle: she is wearing her prom dress, a semiclassical confection of white floating layers that she wears somewhat incongruously with a modern and less obviously feminine leather jacket, an overt visual juxtaposition of hero and heroine. There is something genuinely Orphic and quite reminiscent of baroque opera (with its long-standing obsession with Orpheus) in the construction of the sequence in which she goes into the Master's lair: she

---

3. Whedon has spoken about this intention on numerous occasions in interviews; he also refers to it in the audio commentary for the first episode of Season 1, "Welcome to the Hellmouth" (1.1).

descends into a candlelit underworld, with the bowed and pointed shape of her crossbow echoing both the bowed and pointed shape of Orpheus's lyre and indeed its physical construction as a strung wooden instrument. Here, we see real competition between Eurydice and Orpheus as figure and ground: like Orpheus with his lute, she descends into the underworld, and like Eurydice, she is first pursued and then bitten and killed. Eurydice is bitten and then descends; Buffy does it the other way around, but the end result is the same. Buffy dies, falling facedown in a pool of water.

She is quickly rescued and resuscitated by Xander performing CPR. In the moment that she comes back to life, the tension between figure and ground resolves—but in the usual manner of Joss Whedon, it is not a simple resolution; instead, it is one of those moments when he adds his own twist to the myth. Whereas before the Orpheus/Eurydice aspects were intersecting, now they are polarized. Buffy lost the leather jacket at the moment of her death, so is now, visually, entirely the heroine, but, psychologically, the hero aspect reasserts itself as she realizes that her death has turned out to be temporary—she looks entirely like the heroine but is now acting as the hero. This transformation is further reinforced by the use of the series theme tune in the underscore at this point as she leads Xander and Angel back to the school for a final confrontation with the Master: and this is the only occasion that the theme tune, exactly as it appears in the title sequence, appears within the body of the show.[4] I examined ideas of gender in the theme tunes of *Buffy* and *Angel* in an earlier essay on these series (Halfyard 2010). Using data from Philip Tagg's analysis of Verbal Visual Associations in relation to music, I demonstrated that Buffy's theme music is overtly masculine in terms of its tempo, timbres, rhythms, dynamics, and phrasing. On this one occasion in 144 episodes of *Buffy*, the title music, the music that encodes the tough, masculine, active elements of her heroic identity, is played as underscore while, dressed like a recently dead Greek heroine, Buffy marches into her final battle with the Master.[5]

The second major articulation of the Orpheus myth bridges the end of Season 2 and start of Season 3, and here the idea of looking becomes

---

4. The theme appears in varied form in the underscore in a number of different episodes, but never in the original version as played by Nerf Herder for the title sequence.

5. It must be noted that this is actually a very problematic sequence. Although one can understand the logic of putting the music here, the combination of the awkwardly low camera angle, the strident music, and the on-screen movement, which looks as if it may have been speeded up a little, conspires to make the sequence more contrived than heroic, but the intent is nonetheless clear.

important. Much has been written on Orpheus and the moment when he looks back at Eurydice: it is one of the most retold parts of the myth, different versions offering different reasons Orpheus looks back. In one version, Orpheus's error is a simple mistake, a loophole in how Hades constructed his condition that Orpheus not look back at her until she was out of the underworld. As he is leading, Orpheus reaches the sunlight first and looks back to see if she is behind him, but she has not yet crossed the threshold, and so is lost on a technicality (Graves 1992, 112). In other versions, most notably in the operas by Monteverdi (1607) and Gluck (1762), Eurydice does not know the nature of the bargain and endlessly pleads with Orpheus to look at her: eventually, he gives in to her nagging, and her doom therefore is her own fault. In *The Gaze of Orpheus* ([1955] 1981), Maurice Blanchot's reading of the myth has Orpheus so overwhelmed with desire for Eurydice that he cannot prevent himself from looking back, and Blanchot makes an explicit connection between Eurydice's disappearance into the underworld and artistic creativity. The overwhelming desire to see her destroys the real Eurydice but leaves Orpheus his creative inspiration: "Eurydice's disappearance symbolizes a loss that is recuperated by the compensatory gift of Orpheus's song" (Huffer 1998, 37).

Eurydice is effectively the sacrifice Orpheus makes that ensures his own greatness: a necessary and justified sacrifice, Blanchot appears to think, apparently unperturbed at reducing Eurydice to the means to Orpheus's artistic ends.[6] Various twentieth-century poets (for example, Rilke, H. D., and Carol Anne Duffy) seem to agree in their reading of the myth that Orpheus was really very selfish, and it seems he looks at Eurydice only when it suits him.[7] She dies, arguably, because he is not paying attention, too occupied with singing to notice that she is being pursued, bitten, and killed; conversely, he fails to bring her back to the world because he cannot resist the temptation to look around at her. All of these ideas associated with the gaze are therefore destructive, specifically of Eurydice, and the idea of the gaze that can either save or destroy whoever is currently cast in the Eurydice role is a persistent

6. There are certain unpleasant resonances of Angelus here, who seems to regard evil as an art form to be perfected and who, Orphically enough, connects this to song when he tells Buffy, "For a hundred years I offered ugly death to everyone I met, and I did it with a song in my heart" ("Angel," *Buffy* 1.7).

7. The poems referred to here are Rilke's *Orpheus. Eurydike. Hermes* (1907); H. D.'s *Eurydice* (1917); and Carol Ann Duffy's "Eurydice" from *The World's Wife* (1999).

one throughout the *Buffy* narrative.[8] Ultimately, Whedon takes the gesture of Orpheus's errant gaze and its role in his failure to save his lover and reverses it in *Buffy*, effectively staking a claim for higher moral authority on the part of his female hero and, in perhaps his most emotive twisting of the myth, allowing her to succeed where Orpheus fails.

But before that success can come, there is a great deal of descending into the underworld—a chain of three descents, in fact; and it is only after the third of these results in a successful rescue and return that we can come back up along the chain and rescue everyone else. The first descent is Angel's: at the end of Season 2, his soul having been restored about thirty seconds too late, Buffy is forced to send him through a gateway into a hell dimension ("Becoming, Part Two" 2.22). Far from not paying attention, Buffy looks deep into his eyes and tells him that she loves him and then stabs him through the chest with a mystical sword and pushes him through the gateway into hell, thus sealing it. In some ways, this is one of her most genuinely Orphic moments: she has just failed to rescue her lover; looking at him and declaring her love serve to compound her own sense of her terrible betrayal of him as she becomes the agent of his doom, consigning him to hell. Here, Angel is Eurydice, and Buffy fulfills the Orphic role of the one who both looks upon and destroys the object of her love, in the very moment that she (or Willow, acting on her behalf) appears to have saved him by restoring his soul.

The next descent is her own: she is so devastated by what she has done that she comprehensively rejects her role as hero and, in her Eurydice persona, metaphorically dies, abandoning her life and removing herself from view, refusing to be seen, descending into the urban underworld of Los Angeles. This is the place we find her in "Anne" (3.1), the opening episode of Season 3, willingly if not happily resident in her own version of hell. The third descent occurs in the same episode. Lily (formerly Chanterelle, latterly Anne)[9] is abducted by demons preying on the dispossessed of Los Angeles, transporting them to another demon underworld dimension to use them as slave labor. Buffy follows Lily into hell, slays the demons, rescues Lily, and leads everyone back into the world. In saving Lily, she reclaims her hero aspect, and so in this

8. The idea of the destructive gaze is perhaps further echoed in Dark Willow's blackened eyes in Season 6. See also Koontz, this volume.

9. Lily adopts Buffy's pseudonym (Buffy's middle name) at the end of this episode, and we meet her again, still calling herself Anne, in Season 2 of *Angel*.

episode we see another major reversal of the classic elements of the myth: Buffy as Eurydice goes into the underworld not just to rescue Lily but to find Orpheus, to reclaim her own heroic aspect, a sequence that culminates in one of the most iconic shots of the series, used as the final shot of the title sequence throughout Seasons 3, 4, and 5, as she pauses and gathers herself for the fight ahead, battle ax raised, a frown upon her face as she surveys the foe before her.

No other shot of Buffy stays in the title sequence as long, and it is superficially quite an unlikely shot to have such status: she does not look obviously powerful. Instead, she appears battered and vulnerable, but grimly determined, a reluctant hero if ever there was one. I would argue that this is Whedon's shot of Eurydice as hero, a vulnerable Buffy in the process of reclaiming her heroic mission, and another intersection of her Orpheus and Eurydice aspects: resistant, reluctant, but still fighting to save the world.

After three descents, therefore, we have the first reemergence, and this precipitates the others. Having rescued Lily, Buffy is able to rescue herself—Eurydice rescuing Orpheus—to return to Sunnydale and become the Slayer again, however reluctantly. This leaves only Angel, Buffy's great love, the one whose apparent death left her in her metaphorical hell and him in his literal one in the first place. Orpheus failed to bring Eurydice back because he looked, because he wanted to look at her, and that desire overrode his ability to obey one simple instruction. The command not to look back equates here to the idea of renunciation: if he could have renounced his own interests in wanting Eurydice back, if he had wanted to reclaim her for her own sake and for the world rather than simply for himself, perhaps he would have succeeded.

A direct inversion of this part of the Orpheus myth functions as the means by which Angel is returned from hell. There is no logical explanation ever offered for how or why Angel is brought back from the underworld, but he is undoubtedly brought back by Buffy at the precise moment that she lets go of him. In the opening episodes of Season 3, Buffy is still in denial about his loss, and at the end of "Faith, Hope, and Trick" (3.3) Giles uses a ruse to persuade her to talk about what happened when she sent him to hell. As she recounts to him for the first time the fact that Willow's soul restoration worked, but too late, the famous "Buffy-Angel love theme," composed by Christophe Beck, is heard in full for the first time in the season, reinforcing the extent to which this theme has always signified Buffy's sense of loss with regard to Angel, as much as or even more than her love for him. Telling the truth about his loss is an important stage in her being able to let go of him and move on, as Giles clearly realizes. Immediately after this scene, she returns to Angel's mansion, places the ring he gave her on the spot where she killed him, and walks away—significantly, without looking back. Again, the use of the love theme at this point further underlines the idea of love and loss and her acceptance that Angel is gone, and it is at this point that we have another of the reversals of the mythic narrative. Buffy plays Orpheus to Angel's Eurydice, and her not looking back—her lack of selfishness, her ability to let go of him—seems to be the direct cause of his return, which occurs immediately after she leaves the mansion. Where the act of looking is associated with losing loved ones, it would seem that not looking can save them. Although the gesture is far from overt, bringing the Orpheus myth into a reading of this scene can provide some explanation for the otherwise mysterious reasons for Angel's return from hell at this point in the narrative. Buffy is at her most heroic in this moment as she renounces her claims upon Angel, renounces her claims to love, and gives him up in order to be able to continue as hero: unexpectedly, such sacrifice is, for once, rewarded.

As the series progresses, we find characters other than Buffy and Angel entering into these mythic gestures. Willow, especially, takes on the role of Orpheus to a variety of Eurydices. As an increasingly powerful witch, it falls to her to bring people back when they are lost to the darkness: in the *Angel* episode "Orpheus" (4.15), Willow retrieves Angel's soul and restores him to the world; when Tara loses her mind in *Buffy*, Season 5, it is Willow who finds and restores her; when Buffy is so horrified by her failure to stop a massacre that she sinks into a catatonic state in the penultimate episode of the same season ("The Weight of the World" 5.21), Willow is the one who uses magic to follow Buffy into the underworld of her mind and brings her out again. Orpheus was a singer so talented that he could control all of nature with the sound of his voice—the animals would stop and listen. Willow rather famously in the series does not sing, but she nonetheless controls magic through the sound of her voice, through speech acts that give her power over the world. We even have a famously unpleasant moment at the start of Season 6 when, Orpheus-like, the power of her voice brings a tiny fawn to her, which she kills as part of her resurrection spell for Buffy ("Bargaining, Part One" 6.1).

The Orpheus myth has a particular resonance in Season 6. Following Buffy's second death at the end of Season 5, Willow takes on the role of Orpheus to Buffy's Eurydice and weaves a spell to bring Buffy back from the dead. There is, therefore, a very clear repetition of Willow and Buffy's Orphic relationship: at the end of Season 5, Willow's intervention to bring Buffy back from her catatonic state leads directly to her death; Willow therefore attempts to reiterate the previous rescue, now with a literal rather than simply a psychic retrieval. She justifies it to herself on the grounds that Buffy may be trapped in a hell dimension, but she is perhaps motivated as much by the fact that she feels responsible, and all of the Scoobies feel lost and helpless without Buffy. They want her back, and the idea that she may be suffering is ultimately merely an excuse for their actions. When she is brought back, Buffy is bewildered and lost. Here we find strong resonances of Rilke's Eurydice, who does not recognize or remember Orpheus when he comes to claim her. Instead, death "filled her abundantly . . . / Like a fruit of sweetness and darkness" and leaves her empty of everything else, no longer interested in or able to understand the world of the living from which she has been severed (Rilke 1996, 502; my translation).

Death, it seems, fulfills and transforms Rilke's Eurydice: there is a richness in the experience for her to which Orpheus is oblivious. Buffy, likewise, is so far gone from the world that initially she no longer recognizes her friends; later, when she admits for the first time that she was not in hell, we find the same idea that her death fulfilled and transformed her, in her confession to Spike: "Time . . . didn't mean anything. Nothing had form. But I was still me, you know? And I was warm . . . and I was loved . . . and I was finished. Complete" ("Afterlife" 6.3). Buffy, then, is a modern rather than an operatic Eurydice, one who wants only to be left alone, completed by death rather than needing to be rescued from it.

The problems she has returning to life reach a climax in "Once More, with Feeling" (6.7). A demon has been summoned to Sunnydale, apparently by Dawn (in fact, by Xander), and the demon asserts his right to take the summoner back to the underworld as his bride. This brings in a new but strongly connected myth: as Bowman notes, Buffy plays Demeter to Dawn's Persephone, bargaining with Hades (2002, para. 14). The scene where Buffy confronts the demon is another moment where the mythological strands intersect and accrete to the narrative. Buffy sings and dances her willingness to take Dawn's place, so casting herself also as Orpheus singing to Hades to release Dawn/Eurydice; Buffy reveals to the rest of her friends for the first time that they tore her out of heaven, so putting Willow back into the role of the selfish Orpheus to Buffy's own reluctantly returned Eurydice; and finally, as Buffy is about to dance herself to death, Spike steps in to save her and pulls her back from the brink. Again, we find an Orphic reversal, where his sudden capturing of her gaze pulls her out of hell rather than sending her into it, giving us another suggestion of and variant on an Orpheus/Eurydice pairing. If Willow is the bad Orpheus in Buffy's resurrection scenario, Spike is the remedy, the anti-Orpheus who truly brings Buffy's Eurydice back to life. His is a constructive gaze that restores her to herself: he saves her by seeing her.[10]

"Once More, with Feeling" does not resolve things—in fact, Buffy does not unequivocally embrace life until the end of the season—and in the later Season 6 episode "Normal Again" (6.17), her Orpheus and Eurydice roles are again polarized. Buffy appears to start hallucinating, and reality splits in two: in the Sunnydale world, she continues as Orpheus-hero, but in the second world, she has been in a psychiatric clinic for the past six years in an undifferentiated schizophrenic state in which the entire Sunnydale world of heroes and monsters is of her own construction. Her death there was a brief period of lucidity in this second reality. Here, she is not a hero but a normal girl: in this world, she is only Buffy as Eurydice. Encouraged by her psychiatrist to remain permanently in this version of reality by killing all her hallucinated friends in Sunnydale, Buffy agrees, saying she wants to be normal again: ultimately, though, she realizes that she has to return, that however much she wants to remain in the safe and normal world, she must go back, must recross the threshold and be the hero again—and so she reembraces her dual roles. Again, because this decision is made in the "normal" world of the clinic, we have a moment when Eurydice apparently makes the decision to take herself back to life: Eurydice becomes the hero.

This situation is, if you like, Buffy as Schrödinger's cat, the explanation of how physics works at the quantum level. There is a cat in a box. Opening the box to see whether the cat is dead or alive will kill the cat, but until you do that, the cat is in fact both dead and alive at the same time: it exists in a state of probability. Opening the box collapses those probabilities into a single state—the cat is dead—but at least the fundamental instability of the previous state has collapsed back into certainty. The final shot of Buffy in this episode is not of her in Sunnydale but of her catatonic (the pun is apt if unintentional) in the clinic. One might interpret this as meaning that the entire Buffyverse is a schizophrenic delusion, not real even in its own universe, but the episode seems to position it more as two possibilities, each equally probable, which Buffy collapses into a single state—the Buffyverse as we know it—at the moment that she makes her decision and, as it were, opens the box and

10. At the end of the season, Spike further subverts the myth by crossing the threshold and undergoing the trials of the underworld not to rescue the girl but to rescue himself, to retrieve his own soul.

kills the cat. However, once Buffy has made her decision, the box is effectively shut again, and we can no longer tell which state is real: they have become two equally likely probabilities.

Perhaps the most remarkable aspect of Whedon's mythmaking is the sheer number of times he revisits and reinvents the hero's journey, twisting and reversing the Orpheus myth not just in *Buffy* but in other narratives. Here, I have primarily looked at how this particular mythic gesture operates in relation to Buffy herself, but the most specific and overt reference to the myth occurs not in *Buffy* but in the *Angel* episode "Orpheus." This episode performs a complex interweaving of multiple levels of mythic gesture. At the start of the episode, Angelus bites Faith, intending either to kill her or to turn her, casting Faith as Eurydice, both bitten by the snake and murdered by Aristeus. Immediately, we have the first reversal, as it is the biter not the bitten who is poisoned, Faith having injected herself with the drug named Orpheus that ostensibly gives the episode its title. The drug itself is a reversal of the mythic role played by Orpheus: Wesley says that it "leads you to hell and leaves you there," whereas in the myth, Orpheus follows Eurydice to hell and at least attempts to bring her out. Angelus and Faith both find themselves in the Orpheus-induced underworld, but rather than playing Orpheus and Eurydice, they switch to a different pair of underworld figures, Faith's Virgil to Angelus's Dante, as they move through the various circles of Angelus's own hell, forced to witness and experience all Angel's good deeds after he was reensouled by the gypsies, such as rescuing a puppy. But the ancient myth reasserts itself in several ways even here: Willow appears in Los Angeles to play Orpheus to Angel's Eurydice, successfully retrieving his soul and leading him back to life; meanwhile, Angel himself reminds us of his love of Barry Manilow's "Mandy" by playing it on the jukebox, and in doing so in this particular episode not only parodies the whole idea of Orpheus's beautiful music but also reminds us that Angel himself is no musician.[11]

Despite this, Angel nonetheless gets to play Orpheus on other occasions. In "The Trial" (*Angel* 2.9), the retelling of the myth is perhaps at its most classical, as Angel descends into an underworld to undergo terrible trials with the specific aim of saving Darla. The twist here, of course, is that Darla is not yet dead but instead newly resurrected, human again, and dying from the

---

11. As if this amount of mythic gesturing were not enough, Whedon throws in a little Oedipus, as Connor attempts to kill his father, itself a reversal of the false prophecy that the father would kill the son.

syphilitic heart condition that would have killed her in the 1600s had she not been turned into a vampire. Yet he is attempting to save both the soul and the life she has not yet lost, caught between the choices of human death and returning to her vampire state. As in the original Orpheus myth, Angel fails at the last moment, just as he believes success is certain. He goes through a not dissimilar process in "That Vision Thing" (*Angel* 3.2) where, again in order to save the girl—Cordelia this time—he descends into hell and undergoes a trial; as ever, though, there is a twist, as this time to save Cordelia he must in fact pull a different soul out of the pit: Billy, the woman-hating, psychic psychopath whom Lilah eventually kills three episodes later.

Elsewhere in the Whedonverses, the entire premise of *Dollhouse* inverts the fundamental Orphic gesture. Instead of heroes who cross the threshold into the underworld to pursue their heroic mission, Echo and other Dolls inhabit the underworld, like souls who have drunk the waters of Lethe, their memories gone. They form a tribe of placid, memoryless Eurydices, content in their state of "death," who are then restored to life and cross the threshold in the opposite direction, venturing out into the world of the living to undergo their trials before sinking back into their Doll state, reclaimed by Hades.

As a series, *Buffy the Vampire Slayer* is underpinned by a rich web of intertextual references from both popular and classical culture, and it is this richness of the text that makes it not just good television but, as Wilcox asserts, art. The series is exceptionally culturally knowing: Whedon is conscious, it seems, that his work is both situated in and commenting on popular culture, and all kinds of writing on *Buffy*, both academic and popular, engage in the process of drawing out the pop-culture references. These tend to exist close to, if not on the surface of, the text: they are normally overt and explicit, and there is a distinct pleasure to be found in recognizing and understanding the idea of being "Keyser Soze–ed," for example (Xander in "The Puppet Show," *Buffy* 1.9). These cultural references function as intertextual shorthand that not only communicates specific ideas but also makes the viewer feel included: recognizing the references has the effect of giving us ownership of the text and its meanings.

The high-cultural references to myth are both less overt and also less completely specific: anything said here about the Orpheus myth is just one way of looking at things—but this is also the nature of myth. As stated at the outset, classics scholars will tell us that myths do not exist in fixed forms but are constantly retold. The availability of mythic readings of *Buffy*, and the narrative's specific mythic gestures of journeys to and returns from the underworld, is important. As a university educator, I am very aware that my students do not know their Greek myths: every year in music history courses, they need to be told the "plot" of Monteverdi's *Orfeo*, and teachers all over the world no doubt bemoan a similar lack of cultural knowledge. Yet in shows such as *Buffy* and *Angel*, we find modern narratives actively engaging in the telling and retelling of old myths, remaking them for a new generation. Our myths have been shaped by our culture, and we have in turn been shaped by them: it is a two-way process. As Wilcox and Cochran say in an essay entitled "Good Myth," "The stories we tell ourselves about our lives, the ways we mentally shape our experiences—these stories construct our worlds for us" (2008a, 1). One of the elements that make Joss Whedon's work great and make it art is the way it continues the age-old process of telling and retelling our myths.

"It's Like Some Primal, Some Animal Force . . . That Used to Be Us"

Animality, Humanity, and Moral Careers in the Buffyverse

ANANYA MUKHERJEA

Joss Whedon has always distinguished his work through his ability to inject fundamental questions of human existence into the fantasy, science fiction, and horror he creates.[1] Such attention to existential questions is, in general, a strength of science fiction and fantasy, but Whedon is producing, in collaboration with others, a particularly rich and extensive body of work that merges genres and straddles formats. The Whedonverses regularly address questions of existence at the turn of the twenty-first century and the delimitation of both the human and the humane (the two do not always overlap). These texts allow readers to ask and answer thorny questions about the nature of being and divisions between orders of being through metaphor, complex characters, and strong story lines.

The work of Joss Whedon is laudable, too, for his consistent attention to matters of social inequity, power and its misuses, and the strife caused by intolerance and exploitation. His work has moral implications—moral in the common ethical sense and also moral in the sense that sociologist Erving Goffman might have understood it. This sense of "morality" (see, for example, Goffman 1963) refers to evaluating one's relationship with society, understanding the goals and limits of that society, and determining what one's own goals and affiliations should be. It is a matter of finding one's place in the

---

1. I presented sections of earlier drafts of this paper at the Popular Culture Association in the South meeting in Louisville, Kentucky (2008), and at SCW4: The *Slayage* Conference on the Whedonverses, Flagler College, St. Augustine, Florida (June 3–6, 2010).

world or, as Buffy phrases it at the end of the television series, the business of letting one's own cookie dough bake ("Chosen" 7.22).

In the Buffyverse, questions of gender, sexuality, and human identity are sometimes posed and prodded through images of and associations with nonhuman animals to interrogate what being human means. For example, the show generally deals with questions of race and racism more effectively through metaphor and the use of monster and animal imagery than through the straightforward human narrative. Critics such as Chinua Achebe (1989) have clearly shown how assertions of animality and savagery can host racist or racialized ideas in the work of an author like Joseph Conrad, whose canonical *Heart of Darkness* is referenced in Season 4's "Restless" (4.22). Similarly, gender, sexuality, and politics of all kinds are implicated in using animals, animality, or associations with animals metaphorically or in problematizing the line distinguishing the human from the animal/monster.

Through the depictions of monsters and monstrous or possessed human characters who display animal characteristics, and through occasional dreams or visions, *Buffy* is filled with animal imagery, allusions, and associations. The joke, in fact, is often in the dissonance between the monstrous blending of species and the "personalities" these characters present, such as the genial but hideously slimy-antlered Chaos demon for whom Drusilla leaves Spike in "Fool for Love" (5.7). A handful of episodes will serve to closely consider the animality, social identities, and "moral careers"[2] (to borrow Goffman's term) of Angel, Oz, and Willow—three characters who exist somewhere between the human and the not-human. I also consider the complicated more-than-human being and purpose of the vampire Slayers, especially as Buffy's contemporary experience of being a Slayer is examined against the precivilized figure of the First Slayer, who is meant to act on instinct, quasi-animalistically, rather than to analyze and question.

Particularly at issue here, two themes are often conveyed in Whedon's works through the metaphoric use of animal representations. The first concerns a series of juxtaposed dualisms: the wild and the civilized (the animalistic

---

2. In his book *Stigma* (1963), Erving Goffman explores how severely stigmatized persons negotiate finding their place in their social worlds and developing a social identity that feels stable and whole to them. Here, the moral career refers to one's path through life—partly determined through external circumstances and others' decisions and partly through one's own choices and work—and the affiliations, priorities, exclusions, and more that make up that identity and map of the social world.

and the human), masculinity and femininity (or, relatedly but distinctly, the male and the female), and individual instinct or urge as opposed to the rational, cultured, and social. In the context of this discussion, these dualisms are considered together. Whedon's feminist perspective means that gender, sexuality, and intimacy are given a narrative focus, neither taken for granted nor subordinate to the rest of the "action" in the story, so that his characters deeply explore what is required of them as women, men, friends, and lovers as they search out their own humanity and moral careers.

The second theme concerns the common but controversial notion that we all have essential selves or basic natures, which we can then attempt to enhance, suppress, or otherwise alter toward an ethically, intellectually established ideal. Sociologically speaking, the existence of an "essential self" is fundamentally unknowable and, therefore, largely irrelevant (see, for a classic and controversial example, Berger and Luckmann 1966). By contrast, the profound influences of history, biography, social environment, and conscious choice on an individual's character are plain to be seen and accessible for analysis. This disregard for the existence of the essential self is not, generally speaking, a popular notion, and many or most conversations about adolescence and moral development now concern discovering "who one really is." Whedon's work stands out because his characters develop both through searching for the already existing essential self *and* through constantly crafting and recrafting a viable self from the changing circumstances of their lives (or undeaths). This integrated understanding of moral selfhood—made explicit in the plot of *Dollhouse*, for example, as Echo must eventually integrate her many imprinted selves with what is left of the girl she used to be—is what I argue Whedon uses animal imagery, references, and associations to articulate in *Buffy*. Representations of animals and animality in *Buffy*[3] serve as indicators of, or ways to explore, the development of selfhood with respect to gender, sexuality, individual agency, and humanity.

---

3. The full text of the series offers many more crucial examples of animal representations than I can adequately address here. There is the fawn that Willow sacrifices to bring Buffy back from the dead ("Bargaining, Part One" 6.1) and the literal kitten-kitty for which the demons gamble ("Life Serial" 6.4). There are also frequent references to the vampires being animal-like, whether it is Spike exulting in his animal viciousness or Willow's evil doppelgänger calling the captive Angel "the puppy" ("The Wish" 3.9). I hope that I or other scholars can consider more of these examples in future work.

Animality and Gender in a Gothic Context

Many commentators have argued that *Buffy* presents a Gothic text (Callander 2001; Bacon-Smith 2003; Harbin 2005; Mukherjea 2008). It is a good example of American Gothic work in that it presents the horrors of both physically misshapen monsters and monsters of evil intent but often locates the latter among human, highly attractive (Glory), or seemingly mild (Mayor Wilkins) characters. *Buffy*'s Gothic aspects provide one lens through which the series allows for rich and layered gendered critique. In *Goth's Dark Empire* (2005), for example, Carol Siegel suggests that Goth subculture's use of Gothic style allows complexified consideration of gendered and sexual identities through the acceptance of androgyny and bisexuality and the exploration of sexual limits. And Cyndy Hendershot, in *The Animal Within: Masculinity and the Gothic*, argues that the "confusion of the two-sex model" in Gothic literature produces horror and fascinates readers (1998, 24). She writes, "Gothic bodies disrupt stable notions of what it means to be human. They break down the demarcations between animal and human, death and life, and male and female. . . . Readings of the body are crucial to gender identity because through them the body serves as the visible image of the subject's ego. . . . Stable gender identity is predicated on the stability of the body itself" (9). In Whedon's works, identities are seldom fixed or simply given but need to be chosen, crafted, and re-created as characters develop.

Near the beginning of Season 2's "Reptile Boy" (2.5) is a scene recognizably Gothic in structure. The camera follows Buffy through a cemetery at night, and the viewer watches as the much taller Angel first startles her (with the ominous phrase, "There's blood on it . . ."), then proceeds to argue with her, and then roughly grabs her by both arms. If, at this point, the viewer were not already confident of Buffy's superhero strength and Angel's genuine affection for her, this would be an uncomfortable scene to watch. Angel goes on to try to convince Buffy of the dangers of a romantic relationship between them, urging her to distinguish between real life and a "fairy tale," in which he kisses her and she wakes up to live happily ever after. Buffy, angry at being scolded and rebuffed, retorts, "No, when you kiss me, I want to die."

This scene is meant to be both upsetting and passionate, and it provides a good example of the short distance between pleasure and pain that Siegel cites as typical of Gothic style and that *Buffy* makes more explicit in the later episode "Passion" (2.17). It is also an example of a certain kind of doubling. Angel is the mature, experienced, timelessly suave man who tries to protect Buffy. At the same time, he seems to be a different prototypical man, perhaps more adolescent, present-day, and familiar as a masculine type, one who is simply shy of intimate involvement and commitment. As Willow chides him later in "Reptile Boy" for his reluctance to go "on a date" with Buffy, "You're going to live forever! You don't have time for a cup of coffee?" Still later in the episode, he transforms into his animalistic vamp face, growling menacingly and inhumanly in preparation for the fight, an effective wingman for Buffy the superhuman warrior. And, at the end of the episode, he approaches her romantically, less abruptly and with a more inviting human face than before, to share a cup of coffee at the decidedly teenage hangout the Bronze.[4] Angel is simultaneously ancient, beyond human, potentially dangerous, and also a bit adolescent, awkward with dating, and extremely human. He goes through a range of masculine expressions in "Reptile Boy." Accordingly, his body changes physically as well, from his vamp face, which Darla calls his "true face" in Season 1's "Angel" (1.7) and which Buffy fully accepts as a seamless part of him in Season 2 ("What's My Line? Part One" 2.9), to one variant or another of his human one.

This episode is particularly concerned with different ways of being masculine or feminine. Cordelia consults a women's magazine for advice on how to appeal to college guys (laugh at everything they say) and gives Buffy minute instructions on how to dress and act before they head to a college fraternity party together. Xander's insistence on following them into the party, perhaps equally motivated by jealousy and a chivalrous urge to protect his friend, leads to a conspicuously chauvinist humiliation wherein he is dressed in women's clothes and hazed by the overtly macho fraternity brothers. In the meantime, Angel must learn to walk a line between monster and human, between man-in-charge and boy-with-a-crush, and between being the protective boyfriend (of sorts) and the supportive ally to Buffy, who is the real powerhouse, if also one of the damsels in distress, in this story. The plot of this episode criticizes and pokes fun at the entitled machismo of corporate old-boy networks and spoiled big men on campus, but it also highlights how sensitive and potent a matter gender always is. Buffy thoroughly cuts down the "reptile boy," the giant, quite intentionally phallic serpent-demon of undomesticated masculinity to which the fraternity brothers feed attractive young women as sacrifices for their own continued success. Angel, however, has to tame both his

4. It is worth remembering that when adults do enter the Bronze, as in Season 3's "Band Candy" (3.6), it is clearly uncomfortable for the young people there and a clear sign to them that something is not right in Sunnydale.

monstrous growl and his masculine defensiveness to become the gentle hero with the cup of coffee who is worthy of Buffy's affection at the end of the episode. To locate the humanity within himself, he has to wrestle with the sort of man he needs to be.

Throughout the series, we see many monsters of the week, several Big Bad's (Angelus, the Mayor, Adam, the First Evil), and some central characters (Angel, Spike, Oz, Giles, Xander, Anya, Willow) shift form radically as they shift sensibilities as well. This sort of Gothic doubling blurs the lines between one category of being and another and, as Hendershot describes it, destabilizes the body, allowing it to house more than one gender, one set of motivations or instincts, one species, and so on. The study of animal imagery and references in *Buffy*, then, provides one access point for considering all the Whedonverses have to offer toward comprehending humanity, society, and identity in all its glorious mess, for understanding why establishing one's own moral career is both so important and so fraught.

Animality and "True Nature"

The practice of using animal imagery and metaphor to convey messages about what is human and what is beyond human, what is civilized and what is wild, is a very old one. For one ancient example, let me offer a common version of the highly syncretic Hindu-Bengali story of the goddess Durga and the demon Mahishasur. In the story of how Durga saved the universe we know, Mahishasur is a half-man, half-demon monstrosity, and therefore doubly dangerous, who then assumes a third, bovine, form to elude Durga as he threatens the goodness in the world. After Durga slays Mahishasur as he shifts out of his buffalo guise, the life and being of the demon spill out through the animal's severed neck. In Bakhtin's sense of transgressing and confounding categories of being, bringing the insides of the body disturbingly to its outside,[5] Mahishasur presents the Gothic grotesque. Mahishasur does embody evil in this story, but, as a hybrid man, it is the evil that is potentially present in all men. "Men" here refers to the outdated, generic "men," as in people, but also to men, specifically, as a gender. With the various male representations of god ultimately unable to defeat Mahishasur, it becomes evident that only a woman can fight him.

---

5. See, for example, Hurley's (2007) discussion of Bakhtin's work as his theory relates to contemporary culture and see also Bakhtin ([1941] 1993).

In much Hindu philosophy, power is embodied in the feminine through the concept of *shakti*. To defeat Mahishasur, the goddess Shakti (who shares a name with the concept) incarnates as Durga, commanding in presence and riding a lion or tiger in most images. Shakti also appears elsewhere, as Kali, as a primal, blood-smeared, matted-haired, wild woman, in appearance not unlike the First Slayer, who also appears dressed in skins, with dreadlocked hair. When Buffy meets her spirit guide who takes the form of the First Slayer, it is a puma, like Durga's cat, that leads Buffy to that meeting. These are examples of the persistent affiliation of the female or feminine with the feline, as I will further discuss regarding Willow and in contrast to references to Angel as "bad dog" or "puppy" ("What's My Line? Part Two" 2.10 and "The Wish" 3.9). This affiliation of both Durga and the First Slayer with wild cats (presumably only tame for the women in question) also suggests that the feminine is *naturally* strong and that exceptionally strong women, like vampire Slayers and goddesses, can tame and relate to wildness.

By attacking Mahishasur at the precise moment of his transformation from beast to man, his one moment of being his "true self," both of and between human and demon, Durga kills him with a mere touch. Threshold, transformative moments can be particularly vulnerable ones, revealing an individual stripped to essentials: adolescence and childbirth are both examples. Durga, representing pure, feminine power, proves much stronger than Mahishasur's naked moment of existential transition. Her purity of form conquers his grotesqueness. However, Durga's defeat of Mahishasur allows the world to be created such that humans can live in it even *with* all their internal conflicts, contradictions, and ambivalence.

I take the time to tell this story[6] because of the resonances with the history of the vampire Slayers. Although it is unlikely that Whedon recalled this story in devising Buffy's, it is part of the broad cultural repertoire within which we viewer-readers watch and interpret *Buffy*. The First Slayer, adorned, like Kali, in the stuff of death—skins and bones—first appears in order to punish Buffy and the Scoobies for compromising their discrete identities in merging to fight Adam ("Restless"). She rebukes Buffy for seeking other purposes to her life beyond that of the Slayer. The Slayer is created to "*be* the kill,"

---

6. Joseph Campbell (2004) offers another, related, interpretation of this story in his book *Pathways to Bliss*. See also Jonah Blank's *Arrow of the Blue-Skinned God* (2000). My mother, Swapna Mukherjea, though, is the one who first related the colloquial history of Durga's battle to me.

to be one and the same with her mission and her lethal ability. Because Buffy refuses this stark purity of purpose and isolation, she ultimately gains the power to move beyond being an unwilling recipient of demon-hybrid powers and instead becomes a bestower of power, along with Willow as embodiment of Wicca-*shakti* (if you will), on all the potential Slayers. Joss Whedon, repeatedly, embraces what is complex and conflicted and pieced together over purity for its own sake.

In more recent nineteenth- and twentieth-century European and American theories about the masculine and the feminine and their interrelationship, their separateness has often been a given; one has been posed as the more evolved and the other as more primal and wild, one as the more adult and formed and the other as more juvenile and still natural. Women were the underintellectual, natural beings of the Victorian era, in need of rational men to culture them; and men were the raw brutes of the American frontier, requiring a woman's civilizing influence to hold the line against savagery, easily understood as an extension of European modernity and the "White Man's Burden" of colonizing and "civilizing" the world. To speak in terms of genders potentially available within any one individual rather than polarized sexes, there are many ways to interpret and cast these convergences of the beast, the civilized, masculinity, and femininity, so as to understand all contemporary people as struggling to find a balance among them.

Season 3's "Beauty and the Beasts" (3.4) links narrated excerpts from Jack London's *Call of the Wild* (which book-ends the episode) with the regular characters Angel and Oz. Angel and Oz (a werewolf) are both coded as morally good and beloved people (not just monsters), striving to be righteous men as opposed to the temporary character Pete, who is not portrayed favorably. These connections are drawn through dialogue and with repeated shots from the perspective of someone or something running through the woods at night. This is the episode that witnesses Angel's first days back from hell and gives us a glimpse into the darkness of normally steady Oz's volatile werewolf nature.

The episode comments on the insecurities of teen masculinity and the intensity of teen love and observes the duality of human or partially human nature. Its focus is on the three male hybrid humans, each more dangerous than a mere man: Angel, just returned from hell and, though still with perfect hair and physique, inarticulate and animal-like; Oz, contending with his changes during the full moon; and the Mr. Hyde–like Pete. It also highlights the ambivalence felt by Buffy, who wants to like the eminently likable Scott

Hope but is drawn back into her passion for Angel; by Willow, who shows a new strength and steel in the lengths to which she goes to prove Oz's innocence; and by Debbie, who is both emotionally and physically "broken," as Buffy puts it, by her relationship with Pete.

The show eventually reveals that it was Pete who mauled a student in the woods and not Oz or Angel, who are both suspected of the attack. Pete is distinguished from the other men because he is the one of the three who makes no attempt to control his baser urges or to interrupt his trajectory toward perfectly possessive and violent machismo with any sort of feminine tenderness. We do see women morph into wild animals in other episodes. Veruca, the werewolf in Season 4, and the praying mantis teacher[7] in Season 1 straightforwardly glorify their animal natures, and both present their animal characteristics as seductive hyperfemininity in their human forms ("Wild at Heart" 4.6 and "Teacher's Pet" 1.4). Both ultimately die. In this sense, there is a similarity to Pete, and one could interpret his violent death as just deserts for his uncritical, domineering masculine exaggeration. Angel and Oz stand out in their beastiness because their wildness is ennobled in being tempered by the attachments these men have with their friends and human lovers and because they resist that wildness. Again, Whedon embraces complexity within individuals and communities. Elsewhere in the series, Angel and Oz do commit violence, as Angelus or when wolf-Oz kills Veruca to save Willow, and they both face punishment for those acts through Angel's tenure in hell and Oz's self-imposed exile.

In her subtle taxonomy of men in the Buffyverse, Lorna Jowett classifies Oz as a "new man," Angel as a "dead boy," and Pete as a "tough guy," the latter typically being the least sympathetic category of man on *Buffy*. Jowett calls Angel "one of the primary examples of masculinity's split personality in *Buffy* [being either very good or very bad]" (2005, 152) and also argues that masculine self-control is at the heart of this episode, as the men seek to conquer and rise above their primal natures. I suggest that this is one of two interpretations and that both are intended to be present and parallel.

The other interpretation is that the impulse-driven beast is not so much true nature as a strong urge, part of the individual's character along with a civilized sociality. The two aspects of the individual—the primal, beastly instinct

7. In speaking of the science teacher whom the praying mantis kills at the beginning of the episode, Giles comments that he liked him, that the man was "*civilized*."

and the mitigated self who must learn to abide by some social rules—are not so much in competition with each other as they are in need of a balanced cooperation. As the individual strives toward this balance, she/he produces her/his identity, which is not fixed or a priori but made and remade through a lifetime of choices, challenges, alliances, and commitments. This is certainly akin to how Goffman understood identity, and I argue it is Joss Whedon's understanding too.

It is a progressive notion, emphasizing both the natural and the civilized, both the individual and the social simultaneously. As Buffy and Willow read to us from Jack London ([1903] 2003), the lead dog answers "the parts of his nature that were deeper than he," implying that he, his identity, exists somewhere between that primal urge and the external interactions with the men and dogs around him. The growling and claws, then, might well refer to these ancient urges and to the bare essence of who a man is, driven primarily by hunger and aggression, but it might also bear witness to the ongoing struggle to make one's self, one's role, one's place in one's chosen society. Goffman calls the initial confrontation of the "normal" person (or, here, the human self) with the stigma (or, here, the animal urge) a "primal scene of sociology" because it is a moment in which the profound way individuals necessarily are defined by their social roles, alliances, and needs becomes perfectly clear (1963, 13). It is a glimpse of the emergence and formation of the social individual. Oz and Angel both give in to their wild instincts in this episode as each attacks Pete, but these attacks are not indiscriminate. Oz attacks only in self-defense, and Angel kills Pete to protect Buffy, at whose feet he then collapses for solace.

Pete, while he turns monstrous, is never exactly animal-like; he remains upright and talkative, while we see wolf-Oz and wild Angel, like London's lead dog, run low to the ground, growling, and inarticulate (reminiscent of wolf-Oz and Angelus growling over the unconscious body of student Theresa in Season 2's "Phases" [2.15])—more fully engaged in the struggle to define themselves intentionally, to locate themselves between the primal and the social, both of the beast and of the human. Pete's monstrosity, by contrast, is intentionally and externally induced and actually a product of his overcivilization of himself through a science experiment gone hideously wrong. I have suggested elsewhere that, for all of us, the monster is always there; it is each individual's fight to be redeemed and to tame, not eradicate, that monster that raises us above our demons and makes us worthy of the society of those we love and admire (Mukherjea 2008).

Facing the Self in "Restless"

Willow

In her book *Why "Buffy" Matters*, Rhonda Wilcox quotes Joss Whedon's commentary on writing the final fourth season episode "Restless," likening the process to the writing of poetry, dealing heavily in the symbolic and the surreal. She further notes, "The seemingly external threat battled in 'Restless' is actually something within (paralleling the idea that the whole dream-set represents aspects within a person, not just separate personalities)" (2005, 165). Willow's section of this collective dream is focused on her attempts to hide herself and her past from the view of others. As Wilcox explains, "Willow does not want to enter [that bright, unknown desert outside Tara's window], but she will be forced to explore herself nevertheless" (167).

In the first segment of "Restless," Willow and Tara are discussing "real names," the real name for the cat, whom they call Miss Kitty in this scene, and Tara's real name, which Tara says that Willow already knows. The question of Willow's real name, however, is not explicitly raised, although it seems to be the central issue for her dream and this scene. Jes Battis (2003) points out that the phrase, "She's not all grown yet," which Willow speaks to explain why the cat has not revealed her true name, applies equally well to Willow, who undergoes an enormous transformation throughout Seasons 4, 5, and 6. Although Willow assures Tara that she need not worry about the cat's name just yet, Tara should maybe worry about what she does not know of Willow's future potential. Willow, however, seems more worried about the past that she would like to hide from Tara. The two worries are connected, and while Dark Willow is devastated by Tara's tragic death at the end of Season 6, her fury is also fueled by resentment of earlier years of unpopularity and social impotence. Willow tells Buffy in "Two to Go" (6.21), "Willow [was] a loser . . . and, now, Willow's a junkie," explaining that, without those moments when Tara would look at her and make her feel wonderful, Willow is no one worthwhile. Later in the episode, fighting Buffy at the Magic Box, Willow exults, "I get it now. The Slayer thing really isn't about violence. It's about power." At this point, Willow's growing thirst to be potent and significant disrupts her heartbroken quest for vengeance, and, ultimately, when Dark Willow seeks to end all the pain in the world by killing all of its people, her desire for power and her all-consuming grief merge as motivation.

That Willow is on her way to drama class in "Restless" is significant, as both Wilcox (2005, 167) and Matthew Pateman (2006, 131–32) have pointed out. Throughout Season 4, she has explored and revealed a series of truths about herself, the two most prominent being that she is an increasingly powerful witch and that she is a lesbian in love with Tara. Both of these facts are referenced in this scene, along with her insecurities and the suggestion that there is still much more for her to learn about herself and either hide or reveal. The muted quality of the interaction between Willow and Tara is contrasted with Miss Kitty's play-menacing. We see this as she first viciously attacks a ball of yarn, throwing her entire body into the assault even as she is simply playing and experimenting with her strength and skills, and as she later stalks threateningly toward the viewer at the end of the scene, mirroring the unknown threat that Willow fears in the desert outside the window.

Miss Kitty is a girl cat (that fact of her sex emphasized by her name), and a mostly black one, and, as mentioned earlier, the feline in general is often strongly associated with the female and feminine: crudely, with female sex; with lesbianism; and with witches, in history and on *Buffy* itself (see "The Witch" 1.3). The fact that Miss Kitty is just a kitten is also important, as she is in the process of learning and developing and has yet, as Tara puts it, to reveal her true name. Pateman writes about Miss Kitty's presence in this scene that her threatening play presents an "emotional prolepsis" to "the most important plot development" for Willow in relation to Tara, "which is her turning into the Big Bad of season 6" (2006, 127). At this moment in Season 4, Willow is also in development, like Miss Kitty, not yet sure of and reticent about her own real name but practicing her power—her attacks and her stalking. Miss Kitty's play-viciousness, on her way to becoming an adult cat with adult claws and fangs, offers a metaphor for Willow's amateur witchcraft, which will soon lead to her grown-up and awesome powers. Her attacks on Glory in Season 5 are a precursor to her morphing into Dark Willow in Season 6, both acts prompted by grievous assaults on Tara's well-being.

Willow's struggles are especially poignant because she is an extraordinary person but also an ordinary one, and therefore easy to empathize with. Viewers who identify with being brainy or socially ill-at-ease or who have suffered unrequited love (which is to say most viewers) understand Willow's pain. Like working-class Xander, Willow offers representation for marginalized groups, first because she is Jewish (as she reminds Buffy repeatedly in Season 3's Christmas-set "Amends," "Still Jewish here!" [3.10]) and, later, as a lesbian. And despite her extraordinary magical abilities, Willow seldom loses her nervousness about them. She becomes Dark Willow, perhaps, because she matures as a witch more quickly than she does emotionally.

Miss Kitty, however, is too young and maybe also too feline to know how to perform intentionally. Although she is playing at viciousness, she certainly seems to play with her whole body and self. She is learning to be a killer, a true cat. In so doing, she represents within Willow both the desire to be unrestrained and the fact that, for everyone and everything that lives socially and intentionally, selves are a process, are learned, and are made. Miss Kitty symbolizes Willow's own search for and production of her real name, but Willow, watching Miss Kitty's process of becoming, also serves as metaphor for herself, both as Willow and as a performer of Willowness, on her way to drama class and making a presentation to her friends and former and current lovers. Willow's task, we learn throughout the following seasons, is to control and use her power without letting it control and use her, to eventually attain balance between the power within her and the responsibilities about her, to find herself between what she has the ability to be and who she needs to be.

Buffy

Pateman, later in his analysis of "Restless," writes about Buffy:

> Buffy asserts to Riley and not-Adam that "we are not demons." This is said as the First Slayer is in frame with, and behind, her, and the clear identification with the First Slayer is unambiguous; that Buffy has . . . mistaken her nature as nondemonic will become apparent as the remaining seasons unfold. *It is, it would appear, Buffy's humanity that is the major point of contrast between the two.* . . . The image of the First Slayer . . . proposes two seemingly antithetical ideas: that Buffy is alone and her job is destruction; and that Buffy is full of love. *In other words, Buffy is both potentially monstrous and full of humanity.* (2006, 187–9; emphasis added)

Wilcox argues that in the Buffyverse "simple dualism is not allowed—virgin/whore, devil/angel, hero/villain" (2002b, 16). When polar opposites are set up in the Buffyverse, it is usually so their polarity can be undermined. Each season's Big Bad, therefore, is difficult to dismiss as completely, undifferentiably evil. Season 2's Angelus shares a body with Angel. Season 3's mayor tends caringly to the lost and wayward Faith. Season 4's Adam seems amoral and inquisitive more than immoral and sadistic. Even the First Evil at the end of the series repeatedly takes the form of people once loved by central characters:

Jenny Calendar, Drusilla, Robin Wood's mother. So, too, as each Slayer on the television series—Kendra, Faith, and the First Slayer—is set in opposition to Buffy, she is also brought into alignment with Buffy, with common purpose and powers and, in some way, an overlap in sensibility. Although these other Slayers all have their own lives and personalities, they also function as foils for Buffy, helping her redraw the limits of who she is and better understand her own identity as it intersects with and diverges from, rather than merging with, the role of vampire Slayer.

The animalistic/primitive First Slayer, like wild Angel and wolf-Oz, runs close to the ground, growls and snarls, and for much of "Restless" is inarticulate. To return to the category-transgressing of the Gothic grotesque, she is difficult to identify or locate, although the threat she poses is clear. Trying to understand the amorphous threat in his own dream in this episode, Giles theorizes, "It's like some primal, some animal force . . . that used to be us." Because the Scoobies recently merged their selves with Buffy's, Giles's theory is at least partly true. However, the First Slayer is both more than and something other than what Giles surmises she is. She does embody the primal drive to kill within all Slayers and provides an example of their primeval forebears, but she is also a girl, however much that girl-self has been suppressed, someone with a history, a destiny, a duty and, one imagines, thwarted dreams and desires.

The First Slayer is differentiated from Buffy and the postmodern Scoobies by her hair (which, as Buffy comments, is not making a good impression in the workplace), her minimalistic clothing, and her manner. Of course, and crucially, she is Black and, thus, marked as racially different, a difference bluntly emphasized by her generically "tribal" attire and dreadlocks. This makes sense with respect to the dominant theory that human life stems from the African continent and that the first recognizable humans resembled the precolonial inhabitants of southern Africa more than they did any other contemporary people. However, it inevitably also relates to modern, late eighteenth- and early nineteenth-century European and North American depictions of Africans as wild, barely human, and constituting a single homogeneous people, with the continued conflation of the primitive, the savage, the subhuman, and the racial Other.

Hendershot (1998) discusses the preoccupation with animality, humanity, and gender in post-Darwinian fiction, as the discrete categories "human" and "animal" began to bleed at the edges through the turn of the twentieth century and inhabitants of the colonizing powers increasingly came in contact with the colonized "savages" and their differences (see chap. 5). The First Slayer seems something like Robert Louis Stevenson's Mr. Hyde, more purely instinct driven, less caught up in matters of emotion or ethics than Buffy, but, importantly, she also single-mindedly and selflessly pursues her duty as a vampire Slayer, disciplining those instincts with that calling (see R. L. Stevenson [1886] 1991). She may appear wild, but she is all business. Unlike Dr. Jekyll to Mr. Hyde, Buffy does not prove weaker than the First Slayer, nor, ultimately, is Buffy without sympathy or understanding for the First Slayer. While the two are presented in a dualistic, mirror-image manner, their relationship is (typical of the Whedonverses) more synthesized than dichotomized. Buffy must face the inhuman and, occasionally, the inhumane within herself and, before the end of the series, witness the human vulnerability that the First Slayer is forced, because of her gender and situation, to relinquish. Before Buffy's dream in "Restless" ends, the First Slayer pauses and cocks her head at Buffy, as if in a more mutual conversation with her than has seemed to be the case up to this point.

Near the end of "Restless," Buffy makes the spirit of the First Slayer retreat by telling her, "You are not the source of me." However, she spends the following seasons closely studying what her legacy, nature, source, and potential end as a Slayer might be. Through Seasons 5 and 6, Buffy takes on, learns, and sometimes discards new roles—as a lover to Riley and to Spike, as a supportive daughter to her sick mother, and then a mother figure to her new sister. Through Seasons 7 and (in the comics) 8, she increasingly becomes an instrument of "just war," a commander more in line with the First Slayer's insistence that her life must be all about the hunt, the precivilized drive to survive and kill or be killed but structured through military hierarchy.[8]

It is appropriate that the spirit guide appears as the First Slayer in Season 5's "Intervention" (5.18) to show Buffy the middle path, that although death is her gift (her enhanced ability to kill as well as her own death to save the world, which also ends her difficult existence on earth), her strength is her capacity to love. Buffy presents, therefore, a Gothic heroine initially trapped within and chafing against a closely defined and monitored role as a vampire Slayer and battling to reconcile her dualistic (death/love) and dangerous nature, to effectively straddle the space between multiple ways of being. The First Slayer initially seems to be Buffy's polar opposite—more "natural," dressed in animal skins, lunging and glaring as opposed to Buffy's pretty cherry-printed dress and swift repartee—when she appears to punish the Scoobies for not following a pure and solitary path, but the First Slayer's function in the series

8. For another perspective on Buffy as just warrior, see Early 2003.

is overall more holistic and far-reaching. The vision Buffy has in "Restless" sparks her voyage of self-discovery through the following seasons. Near the end of the television series, this voyage leads to her refusal of the narrow purpose forced on the line of vampire Slayers through the original violation of the First Slayer's will and body by authoritarian men wielding a demon spirit.

Therefore, the First Slayer's challenge to Buffy begins the journey through which *Buffy* enacts a sort of self-determination for all potential Slayers that is fundamentally feminist. Anya struggles throughout her thousand-year life to fulfill a stable, predefined role as a bride or a "working gal," to be somebody, to step into an acknowledged self, but Buffy leads her sister Slayers toward the goal of choosing or making the multiple roles they want to live, to producing their own moral careers. Whedon's characters invest a great deal of energy and anguish in understanding what makes them human, in possession of what Goffman might term a moral identity, even when those characters are vampires, demons, or cyborgs. Demonic spirits and two deaths aside, Buffy's humanity is proven by her choice to make her own life path, balancing her animal urges and her social ambitions, integrating her many facets, needs, and talents, including the ancient duty and ability to kill demons to protect humanity. As she tells Willow in "Two to Go," being a vampire Slayer is much more than just being a killer.

Conclusion

Joss Whedon's texts routinely present hope in hopeless worlds. His characters find love on the Hellmouth, humor in the face of the apocalypse, and beauty in the terrifying vacuum of outer space. He builds stories about ordinary and extraordinary people collaborating to create worlds both bizarre and recognizable, profoundly feminist, and full of sexual and existential diversity. Although his too frequent use of racial stereotypes and the propensity his Black characters have to die early remain extremely frustrating, a central message of his 'verses—that, whatever our legacies, we still have the right and responsibility to choose our futures—might help to balance that frustration.[9]

9. Whereas Season 1 of *Buffy* featured no recurring Black characters, the Black Jamaican Slayer Kendra is killed by Drusilla in the first part of the conclusion to Season 2 ("Becoming, Part One" 2.21). Kendra is the first of three Slayers of color who are killed on screen. In flashbacks in "Fool for Love" (5.7), Spike kills an unnamed Chinese Slayer during the Boxer Rebellion and the African American Slayer Nikki Wood in 1977 New York. The African American vampire Mr. Trick notably observes that Sunnydale is strictly for "the Caucasian

The struggle for self-determination that Angel, Oz, Willow, and Buffy engage offers an optimistic view of the work of developing social selves, of wrangling with the immensely difficult task of fulfilling one's inner needs while learning to live with others. The Gothic setting of the *Buffy* story, with its monsters and ever-present death and horror, offers the texture needed to explore such weighty questions, and animal images, motifs, and animal-like characteristics provide the vehicle to track the characters' responses to these questions. It is through facing her own mortality and then Angel's, early in the series, that Buffy comes to terms with what it means to live as a vampire Slayer instead of racing away from that destiny. In waiting to bake the raw dough of her human/Slayer potential into the delicious cookie of her more fully realized, socialized Buffy self, she seeks to establish her moral career. The search for a moral identity, a self between the wordless urges within the person and the rules of the society around her, between simple animal existence and purely ethical purpose, is, for Buffy, as for the other major characters in the series, a search for humanity and a place in the world, to survive and to live intentionally and authentically.

---

persuasion" in his introductory episode ("Faith, Hope, and Trick" 3.3), and he is dusted by Faith later that season ("Consequences" 3.15). In Season 4, Riley Finn's Initiative comrade, the African American Forrest Gates, develops an antagonistic relationship to Buffy and, through a disturbing series of events near the end of the season, is killed and reanimated by Adam, then mutilated in a fight with Spike, and later killed a second and final time by Riley himself ("The Yoko Factor" 4.20; "Primeval" 4.21). Kendra, Mr. Trick, and Forrest are the only recurring characters of color on *Buffy* until Robin Wood (Nikki Wood's son) and several potential Slayers, including the African American Rona, join the cast in Season 7. Therefore, it is significant that (unlike lesser but recurring white characters such as Amy and Drusilla) Kendra, Mr. Trick, and Forrest do not make it through an entire season. Seasons 7 and 8 of *Buffy* incorporated more characters of color with longer story lines, changing the racial dynamics in the Buffyverse. For a more thorough discussion of race in *Buffy*, see Ewan Kirkland's "The Caucasian Persuasion in *Buffy the Vampire Slayer*" and Mary Ellen Iatropoulos and Lowery A. Woodall III's forthcoming collection, "Beyond Light and Dark: Race, Ethnicity, Power, and Privilege in Joss Whedon's Works."

"Can I Spend the Night / Alone?"

Segments and Connections
in "Conversations with Dead People"

RHONDA V. WILCOX

Structure helps me get through the day," says Joss Whedon (Lavery and Burkhead 2011, 113).[1] The *Buffy* episode "Conversations with Dead People" (7.7) won the 2003 Hugo Award for Best Dramatic Presentation, Short Form, and one of the reasons was surely its sophisticated use of structure to help convey its meaning. Among other methods, "Conversations with Dead People" effectively uses framing, notably a song that opens and closes the episode, with words written by Joss Whedon for the purpose. Framing has been used throughout narrative history. From *One Thousand and One Nights* (ca. 800–900) and *The Canterbury Tales* (ca. 1380–1400) and *The Taming of the Shrew* (ca. 1592) and *Don Quixote* (1604+) to *The Rime of the Ancient Mariner* (1798) and *Wuthering Heights* (1847) and *Heart of Darkness* (1902) to *Annie Hall* (1977) and *The French Lieutenant's Woman* (1969 novel/1981 film) and *Moonlighting*'s "Atomic Shakespeare" (1986), poems and plays and novels and movies and television and more have used framing to help convey their creators' ideas and feelings. The frame of the tale-telling Canterbury pilgrims links seemingly unconnected tales; the Ancient Mariner "stoppeth one of three" wedding guests to tell a story in which he himself is the protagonist; in the movie *Annie Hall*, Woody Allen provides a preface of jokes that thematically cue us to the film to follow; and there are many variations of technique. Nita Schechet properly distinguishes between "prefatory framing and . . . narrative framing" within the story (2005, 45), and her discussion of

---

1. An early version of this essay was presented at SCW3, The *Slayage* Conference on the Whedonverses, at Henderson State College, Arkadelphia, Arkansas (June 5–8, 2008).

Mary Shelley's *Frankenstein* exemplifies the two.[2] Viewers of early *Buffy* episodes experience prefatory framing with the opening voice-over that explains the Slayer's vocation, and in the last episode of the series, the frame closes when the character of the First Evil reiterates the words of the early voice-over. The First Evil adds commentary on the theme of isolation versus communion, a theme important to the series as a whole—and brightly illuminated in the episode under discussion here: "Into every generation a Slayer is born. One girl in all the world. She alone will have the strength and skill to—There's that word again. What you are. How you'll die. Alone" ("Chosen" 7.22). Symbolism can be used as a framing device as well; for example, Terry Thompson notes the use in *Moby-Dick* of the "framing image [of] Golgotha, the three-crossed hill" of Jesus's crucifixion (2001, 131). Body images, particularly the image of the bloody mouth, perform this symbolic function in "Conversations with Dead People." Indeed, multiple types of framing articulate the structure of this hour of television. The predominant framing, however, is the song that opens and closes the episode, a song that shows us both loneliness and connection.

The writers credited with "Conversations with Dead People" are Jane Espenson, author or coauthor of more than twenty episodes of *Buffy*, and newer staff writer Drew Goddard (later Whedon's partner for *The Cabin in the Woods* [2012]). The episode was written in an even more hurried fashion than usual, over the course of one weekend, so the co–executive producers Joss Whedon and Marti Noxon shared in the writing task, uncredited. In the fourth season episode "Restless" (4.22), each break, or act, was divided into a segment focusing on the dream of a different character. "Conversations with Dead People" also overtly focuses on four character segments, for the characters who speak with dead people: Buffy, Dawn, Willow, and the remaining members of the Nerd Trio, Jonathan and Andrew (specifically, it is Andrew who talks with the dead here). However, instead of separating the characters out by act, à la "Restless," "Conversations with Dead People" interweaves scenes of the various conversations, offering easier opportunity for parallels. Lee Haring, in "Framing in Oral Narrative," notes that when they use frames, "performers often tell trickster tales in clusters or chains . . . so neatly

2. Percy Shelley's preface and Mary Shelley's introduction illustrate the former, while the story's epistolary opening leads us into the latter: we first encounter the letters of Arctic explorer Robert Walton, who then encounters scientist Victor Frankenstein and his story, and then the story of the monster himself.

that when collectors reproduce the clusters in the translations they publish, a reader can deduce principles of sequencing" (2004, 230). "Conversations with Dead People" is structured not with chains but with clusters relating back to the frame, the song (titled "Blue," unnamed in the episode). It should also be noted that interwoven among these four major "conversations" is a completely *wordless* series of scenes featuring the vampire Spike, which constitutes a key element of the resolution of the episode and the forecasting of theme throughout the season. On the DVD commentary, Jane Espenson states that "Joss wrote the segment with Buffy in the cemetery and Marti wrote the segment with Willow and Azura Skye," a.k.a. Cassie, while she herself wrote the Dawn segment, and Drew Goddard wrote the Jonathan and Andrew segment (Marck et al. 2004). Espenson and Goddard credit director Nick Marck (Goddard and Marck are also commentators) with helping to unify the episode; Marck himself focuses on the prefatory/closing song as unifier. He calls their treatment of it a "rock video," saying that "Joss and [singer] Angie Hart wrote this song" and that for the episode as a whole, "the song became the glue" (Marck et al. 2004).

"Conversations with Dead People" takes place about a third of the way through the final season of *Buffy*. It was broadcast immediately after the humorous episode "Him" (7.6); more significant in terms of seasonal and series arc is the preceding episode, "Selfless" (7.5, written by Goddard), in which Anya, in a crisis of identity, returns to killing as a vengeance demon and, despite Anya's being Xander's ex-fiancée, Buffy sets out to kill her. "Conversations with Dead People" comes before the radical breakdown of unity suffered by Buffy and her friends and allies later in the season, when she is expelled from the group, but it occurs at a point of tenuous group unity (demonstrated in "Him" and "Selfless"), and the episode is suffused with melancholy. In the seventh season, the Scoobies battle the First Evil, the incorporeal, seemingly timeless force that precedes evil in beings throughout our world. The First can appear in the form of anyone who has died, and, in conversation with Dawn, it takes the form of Joyce, the mother of Dawn and Buffy; in conversation with Andrew, it takes the form of his fellow Trio member, the murderous Warren (murdered in turn by Willow); in conversation with Willow, though purportedly she receives a message from her dead lover Tara, the messenger takes the form of a teenager the Scoobies tried and failed to save in the season's fourth episode, Cassie—who, like classical mythology's Cassandra, predicted the future but was doomed to be heard with disbelief. Cassie predicted her own death, and the Scoobies should have believed her; here, ironically, Willow should *not* believe what the shape of Cassie tells her.

Like so many frame stories, "Conversations with Dead People" engages in the question of appearance versus reality, reliable and unreliable narrators, and epistemological uncertainty in general. As for the Buffy segment, she encounters the vampire form of Holden Webster, her former classmate at Sunnydale High; her dead person seems, in the end, to be not the First Evil but genuinely what he claims to be—a vampire. However, his death is nonetheless the responsibility of the First, who controlled the one who sired him; thus, Holden Webster too is in effect an agent of the First, and all the segments are in that sense unified. Furthermore, every segment focuses on the longing and loneliness of the living character communing with the dead. As director Nick Marck says, "The characters actually never interact—they're alone in their stories" (Marck et al. 2004). Thus, the structure reiterates the theme.

But it is the preface itself that most strongly unifies the episode. First of all, the episode calls attention to itself as a constructed text in a way that only one other *Buffy* episode does: like the musical "Once More, with Feeling" (6.7), "Conversations with Dead People" flashes a title card on the screen. Life does not have a title. But whereas the title reminds us that we view created fiction, the words that flash on the screen immediately afterward work to the opposite effect: the date November 12, 2002, appears, and then the time, 8:01 p.m. I remember the pleasurable chill I felt when first viewing these words *on* November 12, 2002, at 8:01 p.m. Instead of (or perhaps while) reminding us of the textual construct, these words invite us to be in the moment with the story—an example of what Gérard Genette calls "temporal 'isotopy'" (in *Narrative Discourse*, quoted in Haring 2004, 235). In a few sentences on this use of title and time cards, Matthew Pateman provides perhaps the most in-depth critical commentary to date on "Conversations with Dead People." As he says of the displayed date and time, this "clear sign of the show's constructedness is attempting to force a direct equivalence between its world and the world of the viewer. This tense struggle between the desire to assert a specific realism via an overtly aesthetic gesture is compounded by the episode also having its title displayed. The giving of a title is an emphatic index of its fictionality . . . and one that clearly mitigates against the claims for the particular realism it strives to achieve" (2006, 203).

Furthermore, the prefatory opening gestures toward realism because the filming does not start with the beginning of the song; instead, we begin with a close-up of the instruments and amps as the musicians prepare, as if we were overhearing the tuning up of an orchestra; we are backstage, or onstage, with them. Only then does the singer's performance start, though of course the *episode*'s performance has already begun before she opens her mouth. As

Pateman comments, "That 'Conversations with Dead People' is so profoundly concerned with questions of the authentic versus the counterfeit, simulacra versus the real, means that this aesthetic antagonism provides a supreme and subtle metatextual commentary on its own action" (2006, 203). While Angie Hart sings, we are given glimpses of Buffy, Spike, Dawn, and Willow. Like the characters in the story as they face their dead, we are here pulled between emotional immersion and distancing, between connection and separateness.

Whedon's lyrics themselves are not simply beautiful and emotionally resonant; like the series as a whole, they repay specific attention. In fact, these lyrics adumbrate the events to come in the episode. The words are presented, of course, with accompanying television images: the visual of Angie Hart singing is intercut with shots of certain major characters. I will not attempt to do a thorough exegesis of the lyrics, but I will focus on those words that play a noteworthy part in helping to unify the structure of the episode—the parts that help to connect the segments.

Let me begin with perhaps the most memorable line in the song, a line that is sung at both the beginning and the ending of the episode and that forms part of my title: "Can I spend the night / alone?" This line directly expresses in miniature the division expressed in the overall structure of the episode: the struggle between loneliness and connection. As the episode's cowriter Drew Goddard says, the song "ending with the 'alone' . . . the song [i]s key. The whole theme of this episode is about loneliness and being alone—and how we're alone even when we're surrounded by our friends, and . . . when Joss wrote that song [it was] . . . very clear in his mind about the tone he wanted to set for this episode" (Marck et al. 2004). In the first iteration within the song, the line is simply "Can I spend the night?" In other words, the words first suggest connection with another person. In the second and third iterations, at the end of the preface and at the end of the episode, the word *alone* is added, completely changing the meaning. In prosody, the term for this technique is *enjambment*.

At its most basic level, *enjambment* simply refers to a line of poetry for which the meaning carries through from one line to the next, rather than stopping at the end of the line. An example of an end-stop line would be John Donne's "Goe and catch a falling star, / Get with child a mandrake root . . ." ([1633] 1941a, 3). Enjambment, on the other hand, is illustrated in his poem "The Sunne Rising" with the lines, "Sawcy pedantic wretch, goe chide / Late school boyes, and sowre prentices" ([1633] 1941b, 6). The object of the verb *chide* is found in the following line, so the sense of the sentence is carried through—hence, enjambment. But there are some particularly enjoyable uses of enjambment that combine with wordplay (paronomasia). The effect is similar to antanaclasis, as discussed by Cynthea Masson in reference to *Firefly*; the meaning of the word changes when Saffron says "You would lie with me?" and Inara replies, "I guess we've lied enough" (2008a, 26). In the slightly different instances I refer to, the meaning of the first line must be mentally revised with the addition of the second line in the enjambment. Thus, for example, in songwriter Jackson Browne's "The Pretender" (from the 1976 LP of the same title), we get one sense of the wording when we hear him singing that the Pretender will "believe in whatever may lie," and then another sense when, after the singer's pause, we hear the next words: "In those things that money can buy." Having absorbed the lines separately alerts us to the dual meaning in a way that would not have happened were all the elements connected. Similarly, when we hear Whedon's "Can I spend the night," the meaning is essentially the direct opposite of what happens when we proceed through the enjambment: "Can I spend the night alone"—Can I make it through the night by myself? Indeed, the very last line of the song (the last line of the preface and the episode) is that single word *alone*, itself alone in perfect joining of form and content. This enjambment is a microcosm of the episode, a synecdoche: depending on how you look at it, we are connected or separate.

Other lines of the song are also highly evocative. The very first words are "Night falls; / I fall." The *I* in the song has a shifting reference (as indeed do all the pronouns). It can be the singer Angie Hart; it can also refer to any of the other characters whose images are shown while she is singing, beginning with Buffy. In the words "Night falls; / I fall," the parallel, the structural equivalence (in grammatical terms) of *Night* and *I* seems particularly appropriate for Buffy: "The sun sets, and she appears," as Spike says in "Once More, with Feeling." The word *fall* can itself be read in myriad ways: Buffy sees herself as fallen in a moral sense, excoriating herself later in the episode; she could be seen as, in the old-fashioned term, a "fallen woman"; the Fall in the biblical sense refers to Original Sin, which can be connected to the First Evil, her opponent in this season (see Wilcox 2005, 95–107). But, with her rebirth, Buffy has also fallen out of heaven back into the darkness of her life, fighting creatures of the night. And one might even, on the contrary, connect the phrase with the idea of falling in love ("Can I spend the night?"). At least, and in all of these variations, the words seem to suggest a lack of control. By the end of the episode, Buffy, Willow, Dawn, Andrew, and certainly Spike have, in different ways, fallen into a kind of darkness.

The next words of the song are "And where were you? / And where were you?" Most of the characters in the episode, of course, are trying to connect with someone lost to them: Willow believes she is conveying a message to her beloved Tara; Dawn struggles to speak with what she thinks is her mother; Andrew listens to what he believes to be Warren—with whom Andrew has been infatuated. The words "where were you?" express that longing for communion with another. In terms of the specific context of the song, we hear these words while we see Buffy in a cemetery patrolling alone, and after a shot of the band, the next character we see is Spike, visually suggesting that for Buffy, the *you* in the phrase may refer to him and that for Spike, "where were you?" refers to Buffy. Furthermore, responses to and variations on the phrase occur later in the episode, making more specific connections than just the general theme. "You keep leaving me," says Andrew to the shape of Warren; "I hate it when you leave me." Willow says of Tara, "You're gone." More ominously, the First Evil in the shape of Joyce tells Dawn that "when it's bad," Buffy "won't be there for you"—a lie that does contribute to the later separation of Buffy and Dawn.

Perhaps the most poignant of these echoes comes for someone who *is* there for us—for the Scoobies and all those in the audience who identify with them. That someone is Jonathan. Jonathan is a character who has been with the series since the first season, and in this episode he dies, murdered by his friend Andrew, who succumbs to the conniving of the First. (The French title for this episode is "Connivences.") Jonathan has often (as in the Espenson episode "Superstar" [4.17]) wished to become more popular and appreciated through some grand deed or great gesture. In the first part of "Conversations with Dead People," he and Andrew are still talking about the possibility that they may be taken into Buffy's group and allowed to "hang out at her house." But Jonathan comes to a greater and less selfish understanding of the way to connect—something that may have been building in him for some time, but comes to reality here. In the opening song, Angie Hart sings, "Can I make it right?" And when Jonathan and Andrew are driving back to town in a scene right after the credits, Jonathan mutters to himself, "Gonna make it right." He is acting ethically, acting for the sake of justice, not just to be liked. Like Angel in the *Angel* series episode "Epiphany" (2.16), Jonathan comes to realize that the smallest acts of good will, the humblest good wishes, can be the most important and the most real. With symbolic appropriateness, he expresses this realization after he remembers his high school locker combination: he has unlocked the secret, and he understands the nature of our combination, our connection. When Andrew sarcastically doubts that Jonathan could miss high school, Jonathan replies, "No, I'm serious. I really miss it. Time goes by, and everything drops away. All the cruelty, all the pain, all that humiliation. It all washes away." These words might suggest to us that Jonathan is about to shuffle off the mortal coil. Still, the tone is positive: "I miss my friends. I miss my enemies. I miss the people I talked to every day. I miss the people who never knew I existed. I miss 'em all. I want to talk to them, you know? I want to find out how they're doing." Andrew, preparing himself to kill, says that none of them want to talk to Jonathan; none of them care. But Jonathan responds, "Well, I still care about them. That's why I'm here." Jonathan knows why he is here, which is more than many of us can say. He knows the answer to the song's question "where were you?"—he was at the place where he was "gonna make it right." And despite his exclusion and his wrongdoing, he still feels connected—he *is* connected—because he has empathy; he cares about others, whether or not they reach out to him.

For her part, Willow still wishes she could reach Tara. As noted before, Pateman points out that this episode's title "provides an involutional link back to 'Once More, with Feeling' (self-conscious, artificial, aestheticized television at its most pronounced and glorious)" (2006, 203). The episode makes another direct connection to "Once More, with Feeling" in the Willow segment. To convince Willow that she is truly connecting to Tara, the First in the shape of Cassie mentions certain events that it would seem only Willow and Tara could know. In particular, she mentions the song on the wooden bridge from the musical episode, and "Cassie" tells Willow, "she still sings to you." Tara's song is "I'm under Your Spell." In what Pateman would term involutional response, some of us recall that this song of Tara's love asserts that Tara is metaphorically under Willow's spell, but that later in the musical she learns she is literally under Willow's magic spell. In other words, this is a song about deception, Willow's deception. In "Conversations with Dead People," with miserable irony, mention of this song is offered as a guarantor of truth; however, by the end of the episode, Willow realizes that she has been deceived. During the prefatory song, a visual of the University of California–Sunnydale library appears, and then we see a shot of Willow, alone, as the singer voices "High tide / inside." One might think first simply of the idea of a rising tide of emotion; however, one might also recall Tara's song from "Once More, with Feeling," with the words "The moon to the tide, / I can feel you inside." The pull between them is still there, and the First Evil attempts to abuse that feeling: if the First can get Willow to completely stop using magic, Willow may, as Giles says, "go off the deep end." But if Willow were to disconnect from magic, she would never be able to make that ultimate altruistic connection of Buffy's power shared among all those who could be Slayers ("Chosen" 7.22). Willow earlier went off the deep end after trying to totally reject magic, then suddenly, vengefully, immersing herself in it; the song's words "I died / And where were you?" could recollect the catalyst for that vengeance, Willow's reaction to Tara's death. (Again, the *I* could have multiple referents here: Tara, Buffy, Spike, and Warren are possibilities.) But Willow here recognizes the First's deception when it tries to sway her toward suicide, a message Tara would never convey to Willow. It is her lasting connection with the real Tara that allows her to recognize the deception. In more than one way, the prefatory song has hinted at the struggles in Willow's segment.

But to return to Buffy: One of the important emotional and ethical passages of Season 7 is the change in Buffy and Spike's relationship, which is part of the overall maturation that eventuates in the power sharing of "Chosen." In "Conversations with Dead People," the vampire Holden Webster, Buffy's former schoolmate, is the dead person with whom she converses. He has been a Dartmouth psychology major and has held an internship at the Sunnydale Mental Hospital. When she expresses regret that he has become a vampire, he cheerfully asserts, "No, no, feels great. Strong. Like I'm connected to a powerful all-consuming evil that's going to suck the world into a fiery oblivion. How about you?" "Not so much connected," she replies. When he learns she is "pretty much" the only Slayer, he notes, "So, when you said not connected, that was kind of a telling statement, wasn't it?" While this conversation is going on, Buffy's cell phone is ringing, lying unheard in the grass, as Dawn frantically tries to reach her. Buffy is here literally not connected to her remaining family member, and in true psychoanalytic fashion, "Webs" the vampire therapist pursues the connection between family encoding and Buffy's adult relationships. He leads her to see that her father's cheating on her mother may have left her unwilling to fully engage with a man emotionally. It is during this episode that Buffy finally does admit aloud that Spike loved her, though she was "a monster" to him. And some of the problems in her relationship with him have the same root as her problems in relationships with others: "They haven't been through what I've been through. They're not the Slayer." Thus, as Holden Webster says, "It all adds up to you feeling alone. But Buffy, everybody feels alone. Everybody is, until you die."

This sounds beautiful and sad and Byronically impressive—and, indeed, in many ways it *is* true. But it is also the voice of the evil dead, and it is not the whole truth. However, it is a melancholy part of the truth that much of the episode confronts, including the song. After we first see Buffy and hear the words "where were you?" we see Spike alone at the bar in the Bronze, and we hear the words "Warm skin / Wolf grin." On first hearing the words "Wolf grin," I immediately thought of the usual expression of Spike's face during the years when we were getting to know the character, and I was troubled by the phrase "Warm skin," which did not seem to fit. But in fact, it is a foreshadowing of the dreadful revelation at the end of the episode: Spike, the vampire with a chip in his head that pains him if he hurts humans, the vampire who struggled mightily to regain his soul, has, under control of the First, been drinking from humans again. And human blood is what "makes you warm" ("The Gift" 5.22). "Can I make it right? Can I spend the night?" These words can refer to Spike as well as anyone, considering that he did regain his soul in an attempt to make it right and does of course want to spend the night with Buffy—and, in fact, memorably does in "Touched" (7.20). Two later lines in the song, "I crawled out of the world / And you said I shouldn't stay," could equally well refer to Buffy and Spike, as each of them had to climb out of their own grave.

And the end of the teaser recalls that moment. Just as the first and last episodes of Season 6 display Buffy's hand emerging from the ground, so too this episode displays another's hand emerging from the ground: Holden Webster's, or, rather, the vampire form of Holden Webster. "Here we go," says Buffy; once more we have to deal with what has come up from below—emotionally, spiritually. And we know that if we do not deal with it, then, as the First says, "From beneath you, it devours." (Or as Andrew translates from the "Mexicoan," "It eats you starting with your bottom.") When Buffy first grapples with Holden Webster, she sees him as just another vampire. It takes him a half hour to get her to remember that they did know each other in school. But by the end of the episode, when she thanks him for listening and he says, "Some things you can only tell a stranger," she replies, "You're not a stranger." It is at this moment, when she acknowledges what is left of the real Holden Webster, that she is relaxed enough to mention Spike's name, and therefore comes to discover what is really going on with Spike: Holden Webster has been sired by Spike, which means—in the very same episode in which she acknowledged his love and her own distrust of men—she learns that Spike is killing again. Given the number of times Spike has drawn Buffy into conversations and counseled her, and given the fact that Holden Webster was made a vampire by Spike, it is easy to see "Webs" as Spike's representative in this episode. Holden is indeed not a stranger to her. (As I have said elsewhere, Holden Webster can also be seen as Spike's child, with Buffy almost parentally responsible for his existence too, since she has let Spike roam [Wilcox 2009b, 107–8].) In the last images of the episode, as the song returns, we see Spike with a mouth full of the blood of a young woman and Buffy dusting Holden; the violence of the two images is parallel. Spike kills, and Buffy kills his creature—who, however, is also a *person* with whom she and we, the audience, have connected. Is she thinking, as she dusts him, that she may need to be killing Spike soon? "Can I make it right?" the song asks. "Can I spend the night alone?" Willow, Dawn, Andrew, Jonathan, Spike, and Buffy all are alone at the end of the episode. In hearing the words of the song repeated after what has happened, the doubt and the loneliness are only sharper.

The closing image of Spike is part of a set of images that help to unify the episode and to structure its meaning. In more than one place, body images are used to make connections in "Conversations with Dead People." As Dawn is attacked by the First, it inhabits various items in the house, and she destroys them. At one point, we see an image of her feet lightly, quickly stepping backward through broken glass. Jane Espenson explains that in a part cut from the episode, she had intended Dawn to use the blood from her feet for a spell to enable communication with her mother (Marck et al. 2004). In any case, immediately after we see the shot of Dawn's feet, we hear Holden trying to remind Buffy of their acquaintance by describing the time he dropped a lighting board on her foot during preparations for a school drama production—a nice little segue. One might compare Whedon's use of River's feet in *Firefly* (or, more recently, Pepper Potts's bare feet in *Marvel's The Avengers* [2012]). We have here a reminder of the reality of the body.

Much more significant and more visually arresting, however, are the images of bloody and fearful mouths that occur, clustered near the end of the episode. In the Dawn segment, one of the most frightening moments comes toward the middle of the episode, when lights flash on and off and Espenson's wonderful words "Mother's milk is red today" appear, seemingly in blood, on the wall. It is all too appropriate, then, that late in the episode we see Dawn bloody-mouthed: she has been battered around the room by the force of the First, but she has also been drinking Mother's milk: she takes in the words given to her by the First in the form of Joyce. The visual presentation of the supposed Joyce is pure, glowing white, but we must not forget that Mother's milk is red today.

A few moments later, we see Spike's mouth red from feeding on a victim. The visual parallel of Dawn's mouth with Spike's is a grotesque one. It is the episode's penultimate scene that shows us Spike's face in perhaps the bloodiest form it ever takes.[3] Throughout the episode, we have never heard the character say a word, but the bloody mouth—a mouth he licks with pleasure—seems

3. In "Intervention" (5.18), Spike is himself more battered, but in "Conversations" his mouth is filled with another's blood.

to speak all too clearly of horror, of evil, of betrayal. This implication, however, is just another deception of the First; in the next episode, "Sleeper" (7.8), we learn that the First is controlling him. Because Spike is then willing to ask for help and Buffy is willing to really listen, he can be saved to, in his turn, help save the world when he gives his life in the series' last episode. But for now, we know only the reality of the blood itself and the solemnity of Buffy's face in the next scene as she realizes he is feeding on humans.

The third gruesome image of the mouth appears at the close of Willow's segment. As she comes to understand that some other creature has used Cassie's face, Willow must suffer through vicious verbal cruelty from the First, who mockingly imagines Willow's suicide: "The world would be a better place if you took a razorblade to your wrist. . . . I can see it now. Candlelight, the Indigo Girls playing, picture of your dead girlfriend on your bloody lap." Perhaps because Willow directly recognizes the First, it announces itself to her: Willow recites the warning phrase that the Scoobies and we have heard since the beginning of the season: "From beneath you, it devours." And the supposed Cassie replies, "Oh, not it. Me." Then, grinning more and more widely, she spreads into a horrid mouth, a giant maw that eats itself in the air, suspended. And like all the images of bloody mouths, it is grotesquely appropriate for an episode about conversations with dead people.

The three mouth images are all physically revolting in one way or another. But some viewers may realize that there is another image of the mouth: the Hellmouth, of course. Since the series' first episode, we have known that Buffy's high school sits on the mouth of hell. In "Conversations with Dead People," the scene just before we see Spike's bloody mouth shows us Jonathan, stabbed atop the shield that covers the mouth of hell beneath the school, and his blood covers the shield: blood on another mouth. "I fall," the opening song has said, and now it is the fall into death. Everything seems to be falling as Jonathan dies and Spike is shown, fallen into evil again. The utter silence of all of Spike's brief segments is just as important an element of the episode as any of the conversations. It is a mystery that must be broached. The silence is nondiegetic; he converses with the woman who is to be his victim, but we do not hear. And it is curious to note that, of all the characters, only Spike is in place to hear the song, along with the audience. He is in the Bronze as the singer begins, though there is no indication he is attending to the music. In fact, he leaves it behind, diegetically, when he leaves the Bronze with his blonde Buffy substitute. Nonetheless, Spike, silent, is the only one who is in the same place as the music that hints at the mysteries of the episode. Both his silence and the music give meaning.

"Conversations with Dead People" is beautifully crafted. Ironically, this meditation on solitude is brought to us as a result of perhaps the most successful writing collaboration in *Buffy*. We know that Whedon worked with Espenson, Goddard, and Noxon to make the parts cohere, including at the level of imagery and symbolism. For example, when Espenson suggested having Dawn run out of the Summers house and see Joyce's face in every window, Whedon said, "No, I never intended her to leave the house" (Marck et al. 2004). Is it partly that Dawn is trying to deal with the home, or relationships within a family? Is it part of the overall claustrophobic loneliness of the child alone in the house? Whatever the reason, Whedon was, of course, fine-tuning the metaphoric music of the episode. It is also true, however, that as Drew Goddard says, after they wrote their separate segments, "We had our pages and we were passing them back and forth to each other reading what we had done—it was amazing how it's just the fate of this episode where everything just sort of lined up" (Marck et al. 2004).

I hope I have helped to highlight some of the ways the framing elements help things "sort of line up." The displayed title referring to conversations connects to the images of mouths near the closing, providing a symbolic unification—one kind of structuring, with the first word linking to the later images. And the segments of the episode are even more clearly unified by the "glue" of the framing song that envelopes the whole. Both horror and beauty come from the mouths in this episode. From the tone of the singer's beautiful voice to the lighting to the verbal images, the themes of the show are conveyed. The characters' loneliness shows in structural segmentation, too, as Dawn, Willow, and the rest try to commune with their dead. The representation of the theme pervades the episode even to the level of the single sentence, with the enjambment of "Can I spend the night / alone" hovering over the closing. Or, rather, it lives at the level of the single word; with the dust and ashes of dissolution falling around her, Buffy's solemn, solitary face meets the world, and the word, "alone."

If this were an episode alone, it would be a beautiful thing. It is a beautiful thing, but it is not an episode alone. As Espenson says, the psychological issues explored here (such as Buffy's inferiority complex about her superiority complex) foreshadow much that is to come as the series plays out. Goddard notes that it eventually leads to Buffy and Willow's power sharing—or, as Espenson puts it, this episode "sets up her. smile at the end" of the series (Marck et al. 2004). And the episode is tightly hinged to the next one, not simply in terms of the ongoing narrative: in "Sleeper," we see Spike triggered by another song that is psychologically and symbolically significant. Past argument and struggle, Buffy and Spike and Willow—indeed, all the decent characters—will finally find a way to communicate and to work together in the series' close. But at the seventh episode of the seventh season, we dwell in a moment of loneliness. In one way or another, we all commune with our dead; we all need to learn from our past. Later in *Buffy*, later in life, there may be togetherness. But in some ways, "everybody feels alone; everybody is, until you die." The segments of "Conversations with Dead People" connect to show us our loneliness. And in the end, we hear the song alone.

"Hey, Respect the Narrative Flow Much?"

Problematic Storytelling in Buffy the Vampire Slayer

RICHARD S. ALBRIGHT

Buffy the Vampire Slayer is replete with scenes that depict characters telling stories to each other, stories embedded within the narrative arc of the series itself.[1] Series creator Joss Whedon has said that "stories are sacred" and that he believes in a "religion in narrative" (Lavery and Burkhead 2011, 57, 28). He has also said that "stories are made of other stories," so it is fitting that he would embed stories within stories, in the tradition of Boccaccio's *Decameron*, Chaucer's *Canterbury Tales*, and the *Thousand and One Nights* (Whedon 2005b, 30).[2] Yet despite their frequency in *Buffy*, a surprising number of these narrative situations are problematic, with their stories narrated reluctantly or not at all, marred by interruption, openly disparaged, or resulting in adverse consequences.[3] The series seems to exhibit a noticeable *lack* of respect for narrative flow, to borrow Willow's words when she protests Anya's interruption of her story in the teaser to "Doublemeat Palace" (6.12); or perhaps Whedon's respect for narrative is more akin to that of Laurence Sterne, who famously mocked narrative conventions in *Tristram Shandy*.

Narrative in *Buffy* has previously been analyzed at the level of the episode, multiepisode story arc, season, and series, most notably by David Lavery. Applying Frank Kermode's theories of narrative, in which we use fiction as one means of satisfying our desire for "the sense of an ending" that is missing

1. An early version of this essay was presented at SCW2: The *Slayage* Conference on the Whedonverses, Gordon College, Barnesville, Georgia (May 26–28, 2006).

2. See Wilcox, this volume.

3. Of course, interruptions and disparagements are common in some of the classic narratives I mentioned, as for example, the conflict between the Miller and the Reeve in *The Canterbury Tales*.

from our lives, Lavery has analyzed the different levels of closure attained by the endings of various *Buffy* episodes, using categories such as "Cliffhangery," "Partial Closurey," "Foreshadowy," and "Set-Uppy" (2003, para. 4). As Lavery argues, the series as a whole provides an ending that satisfies our expectations. But below this macro level, the stories that the characters tell each other are often fragmented and lacking coherence, just as beneath the apparent order of the material universe lies the subatomic world of quantum uncertainty. The embedded stories in *Buffy* provide a realistic texture; they resemble the kind of narrative incoherence that often characterizes our own lives, contributing to our desire to impose order upon chaos; and they remind us that any sense of closure we might enjoy at the level of the episode or series is a construct. I want to explore the way *Buffy the Vampire Slayer* employs acts of storytelling within episodes in order to contest the narrative coherence that is achieved at the episode or season level, as well as to advance plot elements and develop characters, and to examine some of the features of the language that the characters use in their storytelling. I am not concerned with simple flashbacks, such as the depiction of Angel's backstory in Parts 1 and 2 of "Becoming" (2.21–2.22) or Anya's backstory in "Selfless" (7.5), because those past events are not narrated by the characters themselves, or with the voice-overs that occur in a limited number of episodes.[4] As a means of gaining insight into the nature of Whedon's narrative religion, I will focus on four episodes that emphasize, and raise important questions about, storytelling: "Faith, Hope, and Trick" (3.3), written by David Greenwalt; "The Zeppo" (3.13), written by Dan Vebber; "Fool for Love" (5.7), written by Douglas Petrie; and "Normal Again" (6.17), written by Diego Gutierrez. Although these episodes were written by different authors, we must remember that Joss Whedon is very much the auteur of the series, remarking that "once the writers are done, I rewrite every script" (quoted in Lavery 2002b, para. 10).

"Faith, Hope, and Trick": Good Storytelling

"Faith, Hope, and Trick" is best remembered for introducing Faith. Yet this episode is also remarkable for its emphasis on storytelling. Not only are the narrative instances numerous, but the Scoobies frequently comment on the

---

4. Obvious examples are the "In every generation" voice-overs used at the beginning of Season 1 and some Season 2 episodes, Angelus's narration of "Passion" (2.17), and Whistler's comments at the end of "Becoming, Part One" (2.21).

stories and the art of storytelling, beginning with the teaser, as Willow, Oz, Cordelia, and Xander prepare to meet Buffy for lunch. Willow suggests, "Maybe we shouldn't be too couple-y around Buffy," to which Cordelia replies, "Oh, you mean 'cause of how the only guy that ever liked her turned into a vicious killer and had to be put down like a dog?" Xander marvels at Cordelia's ability to "cram complex issues into a nutshell." Indeed, she has summarized the dominant story arc of the entire second season in a single sentence, though obviously from Cordy's biased perspective.

Later, when we meet Faith, the presence of two Slayers instantly provokes comparisons, represented by their ability to tell stories. Faith is repeatedly seen to be smooth, confident, and in command (of her stories as well as her audience), whereas Buffy is uncertain, hesitant, and frequently interrupted. As they retire to the Bronze after Faith has slain a vampire, Faith's stories of her exploits have the Scoobies, especially Xander, enthralled, as she describes her nude rescue of a busload of Baptists from three vampires. (It was in the middle of a summer heat wave, and Faith had been sleeping "without a stitch on.") When she comes to the punch line, in which the preacher hugs her gratefully and the police arrive and arrest them, Xander can only respond inanely, "Wow. They should film that story and show it every Christmas."

Faith's claim that slaying makes her "hungry and horny" prompts the others to look meaningfully at Buffy, who sheepishly admits that she sometimes "crave[s] a nonfat yogurt afterwards." Cordelia interrupts with her explanation of why there are two Slayers. Although Buffy has not yet embarked on a full-fledged narration, Faith's swagger, and the degree to which her friends are responding to this new Slayer, clearly have her off-stride, and this encounter sets a pattern in which Buffy will be interrupted and her verbal abilities critiqued. Ironically, Buffy's uncertainty here occurs only two episodes after the season opener, "Anne" (3.1), in which Willow had spoken stammeringly of Buffy's verbal skill in the face of danger ("the Slayer always says a pun or—or a witty play on words, and I think it throws the vampires off"), a skill that, despite Willow's superior academic abilities, she obviously lacks.

But confronted by the blustering Faith, it is Buffy's turn to stammer, as Faith invites her to tell the story of her use of a rocket launcher (seen in "Innocence" [2.14]). Buffy barely begins her tale, leaning forward to say, "Uh, yeah, actually, it's a funny story. There was—" when Xander interrupts to ask Faith to tell a story about her wrestling an alligator. This leads to Faith's asking Buffy to describe her "toughest kill." Buffy cannot bring herself to tell the story of how she had to kill Angel, so she decides to try another: "Oh! Oh, do you guys remember the Three?" When they look puzzled, she realizes,

"That's right, you never met the Three. Well, there was three—," but now Oz interrupts to ask Faith about her "position on werewolves." Willow explains that "Oz is a werewolf," and Buffy adds, "It's a long story." But when Oz succinctly states, "I got bit," Buffy replies wryly, "Apparently not that long."

Despite several attempts, Buffy cannot hold the gang's attention the way Faith can. (There is a similar situation in the *Firefly* episode "Out of Gas" [1.5], written by Tim Minear, in which Shepherd Book is able to captivate the crew with stories, while Simon's stories from his medical career fall flat.) And Oz's characteristic skill at "minimal narrative"—the ability to express complex ideas with an economy of words—echoes Cordelia's conciseness at the beginning of the episode and has again provoked comment from a member of the group.[5] We see two different narrative skills in these scenes: Cordelia and Oz excel at succinctness, while Faith excels at telling stories that enthrall their audience. By contrast, Buffy's own stories are neither succinct nor able to capture and hold her audience's attention, and her lack of narrative competence reinforces the impression that Buffy is no longer the dominant figure in the group. She has lost the quick-wittedness and wordplay that were associated with her dominance over vampires.

A veritable epidemic of storytelling soon ensues. Xander and Willow give Faith a tour of Sunnydale High School, pointing out the places where Angel nearly killed Willow and "where Spike and his gang nearly massacred us all on Parent-Teacher night." Faith dazzles Buffy's nascent boyfriend, Scott Hope, by "telling [him] tall tales." And at several points in this episode, Giles asks Buffy for the specific details of Angel's demise, ostensibly to fashion a binding spell for the demon Acathla. Giles is asking Buffy to shape the raw materials of the events into narrative discourse. But Buffy is evasive until the end of the episode, by which time we have begun to see Faith's stories for what they really are—"tall tales" that cover the fact that Faith has been running away from her fears (and from the vampire that killed her Watcher). Buffy's story is revealed falteringly: "When I killed him, Angel was cured. Your spell worked at the last minute, Will. I was about to take him out, and, um . . . something went through him . . . and he was Angel again. He–he didn't remember anything

---

5. We have seen streamlined narratives before, of course. For example, in "Reptile Boy" (2.5), Willow summarizes the crisis situation quite succinctly: "Guys! Buffy! Snake! Basement! Now!" (see Wilcox 2005, 114–18). Cordelia accomplishes a similar function in "Halloween" (2.6) when she tells Angel, "They don't know who they are, everyone's turned into a monster, it's a whole big thing." However, in these examples, the conciseness is due to time pressure. Furthermore, no one comments on the brevity of Willow's or Cordelia's exclamations.

that he'd done. He just held me. Um, but i–it was . . . it was too late, and I, I had to. So I, I told him that I loved him . . . and I kissed him . . . and I killed him. I don't know if that helps with your spell or not, Giles." Although Giles answers that it will, he later admits to Willow, "There is no spell." Although it is not stated explicitly, Giles clearly believes that Buffy's narration of the events surrounding Angel's death would have therapeutic value. His "binding spell" is a fiction, but unlike Faith's, his fiction is not self-aggrandizing or concealing an unpleasant truth.

The theme of narration as therapy extends into the subsequent episode, "Beauty and the Beasts" (3.4), which opens and closes with Buffy reading to werewolf Oz from Jack London's *Call of the Wild*. Buffy is asked by Mr. Platt, the school psychologist, to explain why she had run away (at the end of the previous season). Once again, Buffy initially resists telling her story, but she is won over by Mr. Platt's sensitivity and insight. Though he does not grasp the supernatural dimensions of Buffy's story, his ability to understand and summarize her situation with Angel (Angel's having "changed" and "got[ten] mean" after they made love is quite accurate) causes her to realize that she can trust the psychologist. He has successfully shaped the raw emotional materials of her life into a coherent narrative, a framework that she can use to articulate her pain. In a poignantly ironic scene later in the episode, she comes to him to tell him that the "Bad Ending Guy" (Angel) has returned, a fact that she cannot reveal to anyone else, only to discover that Platt is dead, mauled by the Mr. Hyde–like Pete. Buffy is finally willing to open her heart to an adult, and he has become a victim of life on the Hellmouth.

Is Buffy, despite her punning skills, narratively challenged? Is narrative the wrong verbal medium for her? After all, in "Gingerbread" (3.11), she refers to "that kid in the story, the boy that stuck his finger in the duck," and wryly observes that the story "makes a lot more sense" after Angel points out that it is a dike, not a duck. Still, despite her spotty academic record, she makes a series of literary allusions that are quite sophisticated. These include "I'm sure we love the idea of going all Willy Loman" ("Band Candy" 3.6), "The girl makes Godot look punctual" ("Enemies" 3.17), and "Stay back . . . or I'll pull a William Burroughs on your leader here" ("New Moon Rising" 4.19). Moreover, some of Buffy's malapropisms are too witty to be based on ignorance, especially where demon names are concerned. For example, in "Faith, Hope, and Trick," "Kakistos" is rendered variously as "kissing toast," "taquitos," and "khaki trousers." Indeed, Buffy scores 1,430 on her college boards, which feat prompts no less an authority than Willow to exclaim that she "kicked ass" ("Lovers Walk" 3.8). More important, she is able to convey tactical plans to the other members of the gang without difficulty or ambiguity. By this point, early in Season 3, she has demonstrated the ability to take charge of a situation and give clear orders to the others, including Giles, all of whom usually agree with her plans. She is more adept at planning a future course of action and anticipating consequences than at narrating past events, particularly where her own emotional life is involved.

Just as Buffy is hesitant to admit to Giles that Angel had been "cured" when she killed him, she is reluctant to tell Faith about her relationship with Angel. In "Revelations" (3.7), Faith has just recounted some of her unfortunate romantic history to Buffy as the two patrol ("Ronnie, deadbeat. Steve, klepto. Kenny . . . *drummer*"). Expecting a reciprocal soul-baring from Buffy, who tries to avoid the subject with "Not much to tell these days," Faith presses her with characteristic directness: "Yeah, but you gotta have stories. I mean, I've had my share of losers, but you . . . you boinked the undead. What was that like?" Buffy can only say, "Life with Angel's . . . *was* complicated. It's still a little hard for me to talk about."

The rhetorical term for Buffy's hesitation is the Greek word *aporia*, which literally means "without passage," denoting a paradox or contradiction that resists articulation.[6] An aporia is a symbol of incoherence. Buffy has hesitated first in her choice of verb tense—*is* or *was*—because no one else knows that Angel has come back. Second, she is unable to articulate the complexities of their paradoxical relationship. Buffy's life is aporetic in several ways: she is a Slayer in love with a vampire, she has had to kill the person she loves to save the world, she wants to have a normal life as a high school student, but in "Helpless" (3.12), she faces the prospect of normalcy with anxiety, and is aware that prior to becoming the Slayer, she was shallow. No wonder she rhetorically hesitates! As she confesses to Jonathan near the end of "Earshot," "My life happens to, on occasion, suck beyond the telling of it" (3.18). Yet for Buffy to suppress the narration of her emotional life inevitably leads to adverse consequences. She conceals news of Angel's return until Xander's discovery in "Revelations" (3.7), and Giles and the other Scoobies feel betrayed; she does

---

6. Referring to Aristotle's demonstration that time can be said both to exist and not to exist, Derrida states, "The word 'aporia' appears in person in Aristotle's famous text, *Physics* IV (217b), which reconstitutes the aporia of time. . . . (*Diaporeo* is Aristotle's term here; it means 'I'm stuck . . . I cannot get out, I'm helpless.')" (1993, 13).

not reveal what she knows about Dawn's identity as the Key until "Blood Ties" (5.13), which hurts and angers her friends and devastates Dawn;[7] and she withholds (except from Spike) her true feelings about her return from the grave until they are revealed in "Once More, with Feeling" (6.7). So story-telling, at least where it involves the sharing of truth and does not stem from motives of self-promotion (both tests that Faith fails), is usually good, and suppression is usually bad.

"The Zeppo": Liking the Quiet

Coming later in the same season, "The Zeppo" is an interesting companion piece to "Faith, Hope, and Trick," because it approaches narrative from the opposite direction, extrapolating the concept of minimal narration to its ulti-mate conclusion. In this popular episode, Xander finds his usefulness to the Scooby gang, and even his masculine identity, threatened. Alluding to the Marx Brothers, Cordelia has ridiculed Xander as the "Zeppo," the group's use-less member. Xander characteristically talks too much and looks foolish in ver-bal confrontations with Jack O'Toole and Cordelia, so he embarks on a quest to discover "the essence of cool." He asks Oz, "Is it about the talking? You know, the way you tend to express yourself in short, noncommittal phrases?"; in response, Oz answers in short, noncommittal phrases such as "Not sure" and "Could be" and warns that Xander is "over-thinking it." Only in the course of his night's adventures with Jack and his magically reanimated fellows does Xander achieve the object of his quest, while the "main" story has the rest of the Scoobies engaged in "a standard *Buffy* apocalypse-stopping episode, delicately heightened to the point of parody," as Rhonda Wilcox elegantly describes it (2005, 141). In effect, Xander's adventures constitute an embedded story, as they represent a digression from the primary narrative, a case of the subtext becoming text (to appropriate a line from "Ted" [2.11]). Staring down Jack in the basement as the final seconds tick away on the bomb the dead boys have planted, Xander asserts with determined calm, "I like the quiet."

Afterward, in the most minimal narrative of all, he does not tell the other Scoobies about his evening, and in a reprise of his verbal contest with Cordelia,

---

7. The story of Dawn's origin in Season 5 is a highly mediated narrative. The dying monk tells the story to Buffy in "No Place Like Home" (5.5); Buffy then tells Giles, who in turn writes it in his Watcher's Diary, which is found by Dawn and the relevant portions read to her by Spike in "Blood Ties" (5.13). Buffy tells the other Scoobies at the beginning of the epi-sode, beginning with the line, "There's something that you need to know . . . about Dawn."

he smiles wordlessly at her and walks away, utterly defeating her. This is not an aporetic hesitation, but a conscious choice not to speak, to "like the quiet." Here the void in narration has become productive, as in "Hush" (4.10), of which Whedon has said, "When you stop talking, you start communicating" ("Hush [featurette]" 2003). Instead of the stammering, babbling Xander, he is the silent Xander, and silent Xander is the cool one (though he does talk to himself throughout the night's adventures). As if to underscore the value of Xander's narrative lacuna, two episodes later, in "Consequences" (3.15), he cannot resist alluding cryptically to a "connection" he has with Faith—the fact that the two have had sex. Although he still keeps the other details of his adventures a secret, this revelation leads to Willow's crying in the bathroom. Later, when Xander speaks to Faith of their "connection," she mocks him and nearly strangles him in her motel room. Thus, the "main" story of "The Zeppo" has been parodied and glimpsed only in fragments, the "true" story is not narrated, and when parts of it are (notably from a motive of self-aggrandizement), adverse consequences ensue.

"Fool for Love": Transgressing Boundaries

One of the most innovative applications of embedded narratives occurs in "Fool for Love" when Buffy reluctantly seeks Spike's assistance after a routine encounter with a vampire has left her impaled on her own stake. Buffy worries that she has "slipped up" and seeks answers in the Watchers' diaries, but they lack information about the deaths of previous Slayers—a narrative gap that is unproductive. Giles hesitatingly reminds her that "the problem is after a final battle, it's difficult to get any . . . well, the Slayer's not . . . she's rather—." Buffy answers, "It's okay to use the D-word, Giles." He does: "Dead. And hence not very forthcoming." But Buffy is still unsatisfied, wondering why the Watchers have not kept fuller accounts. Again, Giles falters: "Well, I suppose if they're anything like me, they just find the whole subject too—" and Buffy interrupts: "Unseemly? Damn. Love ya, but you Watchers are such prigs sometimes." Giles finally completes his thought. "Painful, I was going to say." Giles's hesitation is classic aporia; clearly identifying with the pain and grief of the Watchers who have lost their Slayers, magnified by his own love for Buffy (which, according to the Watchers' Council, is excessive), he is unable to articulate his feelings. It is at this point that Buffy suddenly realizes that Spike possesses the knowledge she seeks.

　　Spike's revelation of how he killed two Slayers is accomplished via four flashback scenes that move steadily from pure mimesis ("showing") to a combination of mimesis and diegesis ("telling"). Television or film is usually better suited to showing than telling, so even when events are narrated—as in a courtroom drama in which a witness is recounting events—we often begin with the narrator's words and then move directly to the action at a lower narrative level, with the narrator's voice-over fading out. And such embedded or "framed" stories often signal a return to the outer frame by resuming the voice-over.

In "Fool for Love," the first flashback begins immediately after Spike swaggeringly asserts to Buffy that "I've always been *bad*" and depicts, in contrast, Spike's humiliation as a failed poet as well as suitor to Cecily, leaving him vulnerable to the vampire Drusilla, who alone recognizes the power of William's imagination. This flashback is entirely mimetic—the events are shown without narration. Presumably, he gives Buffy *some* version of the events because after the flashback they are in the Bronze shooting pool and she comments on his having "traded up on the food chain." But, at this stage in their relationship, it is doubtful that Spike would admit to Buffy such humiliating details as the origins of his nicknames "William the Bloody" and "Spike," both of which refer to his "bloody awful" verses.

The second, much shorter, flashback is introduced by Spike's comment about "get[ting] myself a gang" and shows Spike, Drusilla, Angel, and Darla hiding in a mine shaft, where Spike first learns of the existence of a Slayer. When this flashback ends, Buffy asks him how he killed his first Slayer. Suddenly grabbing Buffy, who reaches for the pool cue to defend herself, Spike states, "Lesson the first: A Slayer must always reach for her weapon. I've already got mine," and he reveals his vampire face. The scene immediately shifts to his battle with the Chinese Slayer during the Boxer Rebellion, in which he defeats his opponent and seduces Drusilla. "The best night of my life," Spike calls it.

Shortly after, in the alley outside the Bronze, Spike imparts his second "lesson" by arguing, "The question isn't 'How'd I win?' The question is 'Why'd they lose?'" The two fight, and as Buffy crouches over Spike with a stake to his chest, he flips Buffy, and we immediately see the same movement depicted in flashback as Spike flips another Slayer (Nikki Wood) aboard a New York subway train in 1977. This scene is much more diegetic, frequently shifting back to Spike and Buffy's fight in the alley, the two choreographing the same moves as we see in the flashback, with Spike providing a running commentary. It is a fascinating merging of the two realities. As 1977-Spike breaks off the handrail on the subway train and twirls it, 2000-Spike twirls the pool cue. In the final moments of the flashback, as Spike is on his knees over the slain Slayer (and in the "present" he is in the alley kneeling before the standing

Buffy), he looks up at Buffy (and also at us) and speaks to her directly from the train, without the mediation of having been brought back to the present. This transgression of time and narrative represents Spike transcending his own flashback, as if his 1977 self is aware of, and speaking to, Buffy, who has not even been born yet. Even in a series where monsters, magic, and fairy tales are real, the effect is disconcerting and uncanny. We perceive a violation of the norms of narrative. In his discussion of the storyteller-listener interaction, Peter Brooks notes that "in the framed-tale structure, the outer frame comes to represent 'the real,' and movement from inner to outer tales suggests the movement of reference, making real" (1992, 220). Thus, the effect of Spike's past persona, the 1977-Spike, penetrating (and given his nickname and the Season 6 story arc, the pun is apt) the outer frame is analogous to breaking down the boundaries between fiction and reality. Sigmund Freud notes that "an uncanny effect is often and easily produced by effacing the distinction between imagination and reality" (1959, 398).

Gérard Genette would call this a "transgression" of the levels of Spike's narrative, giving it the formal term *narrative metalepsis* (1980, 234–35). Note that this metalepsis prefigures the transgressive nature of Spike's relationship with Buffy over the next two seasons. It is unusual enough for a vampire to be in love with a Slayer, but the relationship between the two, particularly in Season 6, transgresses many social norms. It is not just the sex; the sadomasochistic nature of the affair violates Buffy's own standards of behavior and actually made Sarah Michelle Gellar—in the real world that frames *Buffy* the television series—uncomfortable (Miles, Pearson, and Dickson 2003, 243). It is also interesting that Spike's dissolving of the boundaries between narrative levels occurs during the season whose Big Bad wishes to dissolve the boundaries between dimensions.

"Normal Again": Alternate Realities

The sixth season episode "Normal Again" also threatens to efface the boundary between fantasy and reality, and, indeed, storytelling in this episode is problematic on multiple levels. "Normal Again" contains embedded narratives, but we must also consider the larger implications of the episode and its relationship to the narrative arc of the series as a whole. When Buffy is stung by a Kashma'nik demon, its venom induces psychotic hallucinations in which Buffy is a patient in a mental institution in a reality resembling our own. Buffy relates this aporetically to Willow: "It stung me or something, and . . . then I was like . . . no. It, it wasn't *like*. I *was* in an institution. There were, um . . .

doctors and . . . nurses and, and other patients. They, they told me that I was sick. I guess crazy. And that, um, Sunnydale and, and all of this . . . none of it . . . was real." Willow assures her, "You are not in an institution. You have never been in an institution." But Buffy reveals to her that when she saw her first vampires, she told her parents, who "completely freaked out" and sent her to a clinic for a few weeks until she stopped talking about vampires. She wonders now if she never left the institution. The fact that the hallucination has its roots in Buffy's past produces an uncanny effect for her, by effacing the boundary between fantasy and reality.

"Normal Again" dramatizes Buffy's confusion via flash cuts between the events in Sunnydale and Buffy as a mental patient, sometimes midsentence. The embedded asylum story provides an alternative story line that challenges the entire premise of *Buffy the Vampire Slayer*. Like Buffy, the viewer is forced to choose between alternate realities. That is, do we accept the premise that the Buffyverse is an hallucination of a psychotic Buffy Summers, or do we accept the "truth" of Buffy's Slayer identity? Although Erickson and Lemberg point out that this episode "invites troubling interpretations: unless the [mental] institution is somehow real, it makes no linear or literal sense," there is no suggestion in the remaining twenty-seven episodes of the series that the asylum is real (2009, 118).[8] Buffy's attempt to kill her friends is mentioned twice in "Entropy" (6.18), but that episode makes no reference to the asylum.

One asylum scene in particular does remind us that the Buffyverse is a created world and critiques that world's narrative consistency. The doctor explains to Joyce and Hank that Buffy has "created an intricate latticework to support her primary delusion," in which "she's the central figure in a fantastic world beyond imagination." "Intricate lattice work" suggests a complex but unstable structure (perhaps reminiscent of the tower from which Buffy plunges in "The Gift" [5.22]). The psychiatrist identifies two flaws in Buffy's "delusion": According to him, the rewriting of previous history necessitated by the advent of Dawn in Season 5 "created inconsistencies" and is a sign that Buffy's created world is "coming apart." Moreover, in contrast to the "grand overblown conflicts against an assortment of monsters both imaginary and rooted in actual myth," the Trio's ordinariness, their lack of grandiosity, is seen as a narrative failure. And back in the "real" world of Sunnydale, Spike

8. The episode's narrative placement makes it unlike *St. Elsewhere* (1982–88), which raised a similarly disturbing possibility in its series finale.

tells Buffy to "stop with the bloody hero trip for a sec," reminding her that even here she is living a story, a trip.

Ironically, while the (in)famous last scene of the episode, in which the psychiatrist says "I'm afraid we lost her," raises the question of which reality is the "true" one, the world depicted in the mental institution is in some ways more idealized, and therefore more suspect, than Sunnydale. Despite its horrors, in the world of the institution Buffy's mother is alive and still married to her father. Given the trauma of Joyce's death and the psychological damage inflicted by Hank Summers's abandonment of his family, having the nuclear family reunited without Dawn to compete with for her parents' affections might be a desirable fantasy, because in some ways, the nightmare of Buffy's father's abandonment depicted in "Nightmares" (1.10) has come true. The asylum reality represents a fantasy of childlike wholeness where Buffy does not have to worry about leaking pipes, missing the trash collection, or earning money to pay bills—all responsibilities of her adulthood. I submit that the "tidiness" of the world of the mental institution is an indicator of its falsehood. In any case, "Normal Again" challenges the narrative coherence of the overall series. Erickson and Lemberg note that "'Normal Again' forces viewers to acknowledge fictionality, to see the cracks in the narrative—to be aware of an imperfect text" (2009, 118).

No Place Like Narrative: Exposing the Cracks

In fact, Whedon seems to enjoy revealing the cracks in the narrative, exposing its constructedness. In "Superstar," it is Buffy who first perceives that Jonathan, who has used a reality-altering spell to make himself a superstar athlete, musician, chess player, and demon hunter, "just seems too perfect," a perception shared with viewers, who have seen the alteration in the teaser and the opening credits (4.17). And in "Storyteller," the altered reality is Andrew's film version of *Buffy, Slayer of the Vampyrs*, an embedded story that parodies *Buffy* and the conventions of cinematic narrative via its faux *Masterpiece Theatre* introduction. Although most of the characters are annoyed by Andrew's "document for the ages," Anya's reaction is the most pointed: "Why can't you just masturbate like the rest of us?" (7.16). Suggesting that storytelling is akin to masturbation seems a curious strategy for Whedon, who has said that he believes in a "religion in narrative" (Lavery and Burkhead 2011, 28). But then, he also has Buffy say, "Note to self: religion freaky" ("What's My Line? Part One" 2.9).

Whedon's willingness, despite being an atheist, to freely use Judeo-Christian symbols and themes is consistent with his willingness to use problematic narratives to mock, parody, question, contest, and subvert this "religion in narrative," in much the same way that Laurence Sterne's *Tristram Shandy*, a masterpiece of narrative, often parodies narrative styles and conventions. Whedon has characterized *Buffy* as "an action, comedy, romance, horror, musical. It is a hodgepodge"; however, he goes on to say, "Structurally it is a drama. . . . Everything is about the momentum of the storytelling, whether the story is somewhat farcical, or straight-ahead action, or horror" (Lavery and Burkhead 2011, 53–54). We perceive the horror in Caleb's chilling voice-over in "Dirty Girls," after Caleb has put out Xander's eye: "I have found and truly believe that there's nothing so bad it cannot be made better with a story" (7.18). We recognize the farcical in Andrew's parody of Alistair Cooke: "It's wonderful to get lost in a story, isn't it?" ("Storyteller" 7.16). And we sometimes see the two juxtaposed. For example, Season 7's "Lies My Parents Told Me" is a dark and disturbing episode, but an early scene parodies the complexities of the series, plot over the previous three seasons (7.17). Giles and Buffy are in Principal Wood's office, arguing about Spike, and Wood, a latecomer to Sunnydale, is trying to follow the conversation, but he is unable to keep straight the sequence of events. Wood frequently interrupts them for clarification but receives only what Giles calls "abridged version[s]," ultimately concluding, "So he [Spike] has a trigger, a soul, and a chip?" Clearly, this embedded narrative is highly streamlined, because both Buffy and Giles already know all the details. Like Cordelia's synopsis of Season 2 that we saw earlier in our discussion of "Faith, Hope, and Trick," Buffy's rapid-fire summary of Spike's history "cram[s] complex issues into a nutshell." But as a narrative, it is comically unsuccessful where Principal Wood is concerned, and attentive viewers who know Spike's history can enjoy Wood's puzzlement.

Another way that Whedon occasionally mocks his narrative religion is by associating it with questionable characters. Hayden White has noted that historians use the process of narrative emplotment "to make a plausible story out of a congeries of 'facts' which, in their unprocessed form, make no sense at all" (1985, 83), but Principal Snyder's speech in "I Only Have Eyes for You" reflects emplotment run amuck: "I'm no stranger to conspiracy. I saw *JFK*. I'm a truth seeker. I've got a missing gun and two confused kids on my hands. Pieces of the puzzle. And I'm gonna look at all the pieces carefully and rationally, and I'm gonna keep looking until I know exactly how this is all your fault" (2.19). McNeilly, Sylka, and Fisher point out that "Snyder's quest for truth through 'looking' is exactly the narrative trajectory of the episode: to resolve fractured channels into a coherent, truthful view" (2001, para. 16), yet Snyder's "quest" is obviously a parody of the narrative art.

According to Whedon, "Stories are made of other stories" (2005b, 30). Using embedded stories allows Whedon and his apostles to explore (often playfully) narrative possibilities to a greater extent than the demands of the larger-scale story arcs permit. Yet a recurring theme (emphasized in episodes such as "Superstar," "Storyteller," and "Once More, with Feeling") is that the story has to be real, and more than just fun. After all, as Kermode has argued in *The Sense of an Ending*, we use fiction as one means of satisfying the desire for meaning and coherence that are often missing in our lives. Because we cannot gain a perspective of the whole of our lives, we do this fictively, so as to "see the structure whole" (1967, 7–8). As stated earlier, David Lavery has applied Kermode's theories to his analysis of *Buffy* episode endings, as well as his examination of the series as a whole. I would add that Whedon's use of embedded narratives exposes the degree to which we use storytelling to shape and order our lives, and both their frequency in *Buffy* and the problematic nature of so many of them help make the Buffyverse believable. We do not always "respect the narrative flow much." We interrupt each other and criticize each other's storytelling competence, as the Scoobies do in "Faith, Hope, and Trick." We sometimes find that it is better to say nothing at all than to seem foolish, as Xander learns in "The Zeppo." We sometimes conceal or distort the truth or violate narrative conventions, as Spike does in "Fool for Love." And we often have to decide between competing versions of events, as Buffy must in "Normal Again."

At the end of "Storyteller," Buffy tells Andrew to "Stop telling stories. Life isn't a story" (7.16). David Lavery points out that Andrew "abruptly turns off his video camera, pointing his remote at the camera and at us" (2003, para. 40). Does "Storyteller" devalue stories and reject storytelling? Perhaps. But matters are never quite so clearly defined for Joss Whedon, who loves to subvert the obvious. Consider that *Buffy the Vampire Slayer* began with a simple premise: vampires bad, Slayer good. Whedon immediately complicates this binary opposition by suggesting that a vampire could be good (the reensouled Angel). In later seasons, he complicates it further as Spike gradually evolves from foe to friend to lover. And in Season 3, we see a Slayer turn bad (Faith), at least for a time. More germane to the "life isn't a story" argument, "Once More, with Feeling" gave us the line "Life's not a song" (6.7). Ironically, that message was delivered *in a song,* and one thing that wonderful musical proved was that life really *was* a song. Whedon has said, "I think that stories are sacred. I think that creating narrative is a basic human function. It's why we remember some things and not everything. It's why everybody's version of the same event is different. Everybody creates narrative all the time" (Lavery and Burkhead 2011, 56).

It would seem that life is a story after all.

All Those Apocalypses

Disaster Studies and Community
in Buffy the Vampire Slayer *and* Angel

LINDA J. JENCSON

The interdisciplinary field of disaster studies is one aspect of the social sciences that takes the power of mass media very seriously. You will not hear "it's only entertainment" from disaster researchers. When viewers watch real people on the news or fictional characters in films and on television, they are unconsciously absorbing role models for their own future behavior. Popular media help people to think the unthinkable, giving them a repertoire of potential responses available to them should the unthinkable come to pass. Scholars in the field of disaster research are quite clear on the power of mass media to promote the resilience of communities and individuals, or, conversely, to promote dysfunctional behaviors that can literally befuddle people's response to disaster, befuddle those people to death.

In this chapter, I take a look through the lens of disaster studies at Joss Whedon's apocalypse-filled creation *Buffy the Vampire Slayer* and to a lesser extent *Angel*, the spin-off series about Buffy's vampire lover. What kind of messages are Whedon and the other screenwriters who work with him putting out for the potential victim/survivor of natural and human-made disaster? As is well known, Whedon hopes to empower girls, women, and nonsexist men through his texts. Can Whedon manage to empower the potential victim of disaster as well? Can the way that his characters respond to monster attacks, the collapse of a city into a giant crater, or the imminent end of the world give us any clues about how to respond in real-world mass crises? Or do his words and images succumb to the lethal myths of disaster so often portrayed in American visual media? I will approach the question by examining how media portrayals of disaster can influence disaster response in the real world.

Disaster depictions come to consumers through both fiction and non-fiction, primarily the news industry. A study done by disaster researchers affiliated with the University of Colorado, published in *The Annals of the American Academy of Political and Social Science*, sums up mainstream disaster reporting through an examination of coverage in the aftermath of 2005's Hurricane Katrina. Bluntly, they found the media reports to be "highly over-simplified and distorting" (Tierney et al. 2006, 73). For example, incidents of violence among evacuees in the Superdome and the city at large were grossly exaggerated, and a widely repeated quotation from Governor Blanco gave law enforcement the false impression that the city of New Orleans was under martial law, when in fact the Constitution of Louisiana has no martial-law provision. False reports and interpretations were so influential that Tierney's group concludes, "Media stories influenced officials to adopt unproductive and outright harmful response strategies during the emergency" (63). Harmful responses included pulling National Guard and law enforcement off search and rescue after the second day and the use of troops to entrap flood victims in New Orleans while preventing outside aid volunteers and agencies from entering. These acts ensured that no one except Fish and Wildlife officers and the Coast Guard could legally rescue survivors still trapped in attics and on rooftops, essentially leaving an unknown number who could have been saved—perhaps hundreds—to die. Supplies were withheld outside the city, while even the Red Cross and Salvation Army were barred from New Orleans for days, causing even more unnecessary deaths (Tierney et al. 2006; Brinkley 2006; Solnit 2009, 247–66). There are even documented instances of law enforcement fatally shooting innocent flood victims (Solnit 2009, 258–64; Kunzelman 2011). Disaster coverage compounded preexisting ineptitude by falsely confirming leadership's paranoid fears, promoting the mistaken belief that the more than ten thousand survivors trapped in New Orleans (trapped not only by water but also by government troops and law enforcement) were a danger to anyone entering the city as well as to residents of outlying areas above the water line. With few members of the news media having learned from Katrina, a similar case can be made for media distortions contributing to aid delays after the earthquake that devastated Port-au-Prince, Haiti, in 2010 (Jencson 2010a, 2010b).

Tierney's analysts point out common media misconceptions that lead reporters to overlook what really happens in disaster situations. The analysts state further that reliance on certain myths commonly leads news teams to fall for rumor and scant evidence, often reporting events that are not real. The first myth of disaster is that in the absence of authoritative institutions such as police and military, human beings revert to antisocial animals that inevitably panic and turn on one another. The second myth assumes that disasters sort human beings into two categories: victims within the zone of disaster and heroic rescuers from the outside. Individuals who have experienced the disaster firsthand are expected to act like helpless victims, capable only of stunned lethargy or mob violence. Only the outsider who has not been directly impacted is capable of providing aid. These myths combine to create the third myth, the belief that outsiders can bring aid only by first restoring order by force.

Some readers might wonder: helpless victims, mass panic, selfish survival instinct, social breakdown—isn't that what actually happens when disaster strikes? In fact, no. Disaster studies going back to the start of the twentieth century have demonstrated repeatedly that the myths are not representative of reality. Investigative journalist Rebecca Solnit (2009) has compiled a century of scholarly disaster research into a volume accessible to the general reader titled *A Paradise Built in Hell: The Extraordinary Communities That Arise in Disaster.* Not only does she discuss findings that crime often goes down during an event, but she also discusses findings that disaster victims are rarely passive. When they take action, it is seldom in the form of panic. Nor do they often victimize one another. Quite the contrary, the most common human response to disaster is an outburst of hypersocial altruism (see Jencson 2001; Oliver-Smith 1999; Quarantelli 1985; Solnit 2009; Tierney et al. 2006). Rather than dividing people into victims and heroes, disaster usually makes heroes of the victims themselves, who will expend great energy and scarce resources saving, provisioning, and sheltering fellow survivors. The altruistic response among disaster victims is so essentially a part of human nature that even on the eve of World War II, when a massive flood hit Kobe, Japan, in 1938, many Japanese risked drowning to rescue American, Korean, and Chinese nationals among them (Yun Hui Tsu 2008).

When I first encountered the altruistic community built in disaster settings in my own research on the Red River flooding of 1997, I likened it to an emotionally empowering rite of passage, describing the phenomenon with a term from religious studies: *communitas,* a state experienced in intensive tribal initiation rituals that creates a deep sense of bonding among initiates who share the experience. The flood lasted nearly a month. I myself joined fellow citizens sandbagging the homes of total strangers, being fed cookies, sandwiches, and even hot meals by still other strangers. I joined the Red Cross. I responded spontaneously to emergency calls over local television and radio, and went to volunteer headquarters for deployment to sites in Fargo, North

Dakota, and her twin across the river, Moorhead, Minnesota. When the cities north of us (Grand Forks, North Dakota, and East Grand Forks, Minnesota) flooded completely and then caught fire, I joined in taking food and supplies to the fifty-five thousand evacuees. Even though water filled the cities as fast and as deep as Katrina's New Orleans, no one died in the evacuations of the Forks. Fargo and Moorhead cared for the evacuees while we huddled behind our own defensive dikes, some of which were more than fourteen feet high. Once the water receded, I began my first anthropological disaster study, interviewing a sample of the tens of thousands of volunteers who succeeded in saving Fargo and Moorhead. I heard stories of great heroism and generosity. There was, for example, an elderly man who stepped out of line and let a young couple with a new baby have the last pump from a truck of donations delivered to their neighborhood, knowing that his own home would be lost as a result of his generosity. Others told me about water racing up the street and a man who did not have time to retrieve his car keys; neighbors carried the car to dry ground (Jencson 2001).

While I was noting heroism among victims of floods along the Red River, psychologists all over the world were beginning to delineate a common, long-term outcome of disaster *communitas* that they labeled post-traumatic growth (PTG). This type of growth refers to both immediate actions and positive, lifelong changes such as new coping skills, strengthened social ties, courage, faith in one's abilities, an expanded respect for human life, and a hopeful outlook on life that can result from the experience of disaster *communitas* (Weiss and Berger 2010). Great truth infuses the saying, "What doesn't kill you can make you stronger."

Whedon does well depicting PTG. The story arcs for each of the Scoobies (Buffy's gang of demon-fighting friends) and their primary allies clearly show how post-traumatic growth arises from coping with recurring apocalypse. Contrast the strengths of those standing around the crater at the end of the final episode—Buffy, Xander, Willow, Giles—with their many flaws and weaknesses at the beginning of the series ("Chosen" 7.22). The reluctant, sarcastic, difficult teen Buffy has grown to lead an army and defeat the ultimate evil. Xander, the clumsy, unpopular boy everyone picked on, has become an inspiration to others and the emotional glue of the organization. Shy, self-deprecating Willow has attained the power of a world-altering goddess. Even the immature, bungling murderer Andrew (who stands in the background of the primary characters at the edge of Sunnydale's crater) has gained maturity through self-forgiveness, self-sacrifice, and bravery, growing to fight alongside the Scoobies, at one point even having closed the Hellmouth with his repentant tears.

Mary Alice Money (2002) points out the recurring theme of the unde-monization of demons in *Buffy the Vampire Slayer*. This recovery of human-ity constitutes a form of post-traumatic growth experienced by the demons admitted into the Scoobies' circle of *communitas* and solidarity. Angel, Spike, Anya, and even Clem become stronger, more capable, and caring, common outcomes for persons who experience disaster. Thus, Angel becomes even more determined to atone for his centuries of killing after fighting beside Buffy and her friends. Spike, a serial killer and rapist (like his grandsire Angel/ Angelus), finds his soul, heals his Oedipal weakness, and saves the world. Anya, who had spent a millennium as a vengeance demon, torturing and kill-ing, grows to discover an altruistic love of humankind underneath her scars of rejection and rage. Clinical diagnostics for post-traumatic growth include this enhanced humanity, a compassion and appreciation for others that result from the trauma and solidarity of disaster (Tedeschi and Calhoun 1996).

Some viewers might assume that the scarred lives of Whedon's characters are too extreme, too far beyond redemption, that the recovery of Spike's and Anya's humanity (or even Andrew's) constitutes an excessive leap for the will-ing suspension of disbelief. Yet disaster researchers who specifically study the effects of chronic war and captive torture find that, in certain circumstances, torments inflicted by one's fellow humans can enhance compassion and even create a sense of understanding toward one's torturers. Such has been the case for many Palestinian partisans, captured and tortured by Israeli guards, while outside the prison walls their homes had been bulldozed and family members killed. It is not at all uncommon for them to forgive their captors. They leave the prison to return to chronic warfare all around yet become advocates for peace in its midst (Punamaki 2010). It is for this sort of remarkable human growth that fans so appreciate characters such as Buffy, Spike, and Willow, who come to know hell intimately but still seek a better world.

Whedon's main characters obviously make good role models for respond-ing actively in times of crisis, but what about the average citizens of Buffy's Sunnydale or Angel's Los Angeles? At first glance, the premise of *Buffy the Vampire Slayer* does not look promising. Buffy, the "Chosen One," leads a secret group of demon fighters who repeatedly save the unaware citizens of the small suburban city of Sunnydale from vampires, giant snakes ("Gradu-ation Day, Part Two" 3.22), resurrected harbingers of Armageddon, and an alternate-dimension god bent on ripping a hole in reality and letting hell slip through ("The Gift" 5.22). Finally, they save the unknowing townsfolk from the origin of all evil, as the Hellmouth and the entire town (once abandoned) collapse into a giant Sodom and Gomorrah–like crater ("Chosen"). Through one disaster after another, the power imbalance between the knowing Scoobies and the oblivious citizens does stand out, as noted in scholarship on *Buffy.*

This phenomenon of citizen blindness has been termed the "Sunnydale Syndrome." Interestingly, the *Buffy*-derived term has entered the English language in spoken and written form in a variety of locations beyond Whedon Studies, including media studies in general (Arnzen 2008) and organizational systems analysis (Armson 2011, 25–26). *Buffy* scholars, on the other hand, often write about the phenomenon without using the term. One outstanding example is Jeffrey Bussolini's (2005) comparison of Sunnydale with Los Alamos, a town of similar size and demographics. In Los Alamos, the obliteration of life through means of atomic weapons is investigated; ironically, the town is assessed as a positive environment in which to raise kids, despite its abnormal rates of cancer, its mysterious illnesses, and its potential to end all life on earth. Whereas Bussolini writes from a sociological perspective, the concept (but not the term) of Sunnydale Syndrome also appears in Kromer's psychological discussion of self-repression by characters within the Buffyverse (2006). Though the series itself never uses the term, the viewer is made aware of the syndrome's operation in many episodes, including one in which demons are first explained to Oz, who had been suffering from Sunnydale's shared denial and who appreciatively notes that the news "explains a lot" ("Surprise" 2.13). Although citizens in the series did indeed suffer mass denial, they also quite appropriately snapped out of it and opened their eyes whenever demonic threats ceased to pick them off one at a time—whenever demonic annihilation manifested instead as a threat to large groups or to the town as a whole.

One critic, Neal King, refers to the basic premise of *Buffy the Vampire Slayer* as an "idiot plot," one in which many characters must be stupid for the story to progress (2003, 201). This sounds ominously similar to disaster films such as *Earthquake* (1974) and *Dante's Peak* (1997), cited by disaster scholars who accuse them of contributing to the real-world news media's deceptive myths. Building on work begun by E. L. Quarantelli (1985), Solnit states, "You need close-ups . . . individuals to follow, a star to attract audiences." As she further explains, "Heroes are necessary because the rest of us are [portrayed as] awful—selfish or malicious or boiling over with emotion and utterly unclear on what to do or too frightened to do it. Our awfulness requires and produces their wonderfulness" (2009, 124). A real-world result of these common tropes in fiction is that news broadcasts imitate the fiction. Take, for example, news coverage of the 2010 Port-au-Prince earthquake. In the first few days after the event, commentators emphasized the helplessness and passivity of victims, as cameras panned streets where bodies were laid out respectfully and covered in cloth, and nearly all the wounded victims displayed on the screen had homemade bandages. If the victims were so helpless, who was doing all that laying out and bandaging? Who had pulled the living and the dead from the rubble? Of course, the answer is the quake victims themselves, but the audience is not supposed to consider the question or note the discrepancy (Jencson 2010b).

Overall, I was pleasantly surprised when I began reviewing scenes in *Buffy the Vampire Slayer*. For instance, average Sunnydale citizens display very little panic. Even in "Hush" (4.10), when the entire town loses the ability to speak, outsiders quarantine the town, preventing anyone from escaping (similar to New Orleans), and bodies are discovered each morning with their hearts cut out, there are few panic problems. A fistfight is shown, people look depressed, someone has lit a trash receptacle on fire, but there is little panic overall. Consider the *Buffy* episode "Innocence" (2.14), in which a demon (The Judge) attacks a shopping mall. Yes, people are shown running for cover. But no, the normal Hollywood hysterical, screaming females running in the wrong direction are absent. Voices are raised, but they are shouting questions and instructions. These reactions are appropriate behavior, documented to arise spontaneously among intelligent survivors of real-world crises such as the Virginia Tech sniper incident, during which teachers who led others to the best hiding spots and secretaries who e-mailed updates on the sniper's whereabouts to authorities from beneath their desks saved many lives (Powley 2009). Instead of having them in blind, irrational panic, Whedon depicts the people at the mall effectively taking cover and assisting one another in locating exits. Similar scenes of appropriate duck-and-cover moves or evacuation are shown often. One prominent example occurs in "Empty Places" (7.19), when the populace of Sunnydale self-evaluates the signs of impending apocalypse, and, wisely, they evacuate unaided by government. Despite the ensuing traffic jam, Sunnydale appears successfully emptied well in advance of the town's obliteration.

Furthermore, Whedon's Scoobies are not above training their fellow students at Sunnydale High to fight demons as effectively as they do when threatened by the mayor's transformation into a giant snake demon ("Graduation Day, Part Two"). Similarly, unlike news outlets that seem to think the topic of disaster coordination and organization might bore viewers (no matter how much they might benefit should they someday find themselves in a disaster),

Whedon does not skimp on democracy-in-action scenes in the Buffyverse. These scenes are an essential part of interaction and development for main characters. The library, the Summers' living room, and the magic shop are home to scenes of planning and debate that are a regular feature of nearly every episode. And by the final season, they become one of the series' greatest practical education assets, as the Scoobies and the assembled Potentials debate strengths and weaknesses, share knowledge and voice opinions, rein in Buffy's leadership excesses, and make collective plans to which everyone contributes and of which each can claim ownership. *Buffy* evolves far beyond Hollywood's crippling "idiot plot" of helpless masses and active heroes from outside stricken communities.

Angel's message is less centered on empowerment, more focused on explorations of the nature of heroes. Hence, messages that might empower people confronted with crises are mixed confusingly with portrayals of passive crowds awaiting the heroic main characters who, as advertising states, "help the helpless." Nowhere is this mixed message more apparent than in the episode "Hero" (*Angel* 1.9). The victims in crisis are family groups of half-human demons hunted by demon purists in Nazi-like blue uniforms. At the start of the action, we hear the half-human Doyle expressing self-doubt, to which Angel replies, "You never know your strength until you've been tested." Doyle grows to find the strength and courage to save the intended victims, but the victims themselves apparently fail the test, remaining extremely passive throughout—never erecting a barricade or lifting a weapon in their own defense. If we take Doyle's post-traumatic growth as the only role model on display, everything is fine, but what of the other half-blood demons who here represent the general victims of disaster? The misguided moral of the story may be interpreted to be that exceptional people from outside the afflicted group become heroes (and die), while the victims who take no action on their own behalf may go on to live (unexceptional lives). This is far too much like King's idiot plot, and a far cry from the lessons about self-motivated, heroic disaster victims that disaster researchers want policy makers and the general public to absorb.

We have dealt with the myth of passive disaster victims, but what of the notion that they become violent criminals? The news media continue to send correspondents into the field seeking close-ups of big-eyed children staring pathetically into space, offset by mobs of young adults violently looting (Solnit 2009; Tierney et al. 2006). When such scenes are difficult to find in the coverage of any particular event, American and British news outlets sometimes resort to the practice of looping—running the same scene time and again, with a voice-over telling viewers how to interpret what they are shown. The loop may show people shouting and waving their arms, actions the audience is told to understand as violence. The loop may show children picking peacefully through rubble while the commentator insists that looting has broken out. The stories can be enhanced with disconnected scenes of people running and sounds of distant screaming, if the correspondents and their crews can find any (Jencson 2010b).

Mob violence among *Buffy*'s Sunnydale population does happen, but only in situations where people are under some sort of spell. Mob violence is not assumed in the Buffyverse to be human nature. Take, for instance, the attempted looting of the candy factory in "Band Candy" (3.6). It results from consumption of curse-tainted candy, which turns the adult population of Sunnydale into a worst-case stereotype of wild teenagers. Giles even robs a store and knocks a police officer unconscious. Similarly, the mob violence of "Gingerbread" (3.11), in which parents attempt to burn Buffy, Willow, and Amy at the stake, also results from a spell. The episode, in fact, attributes centuries of historic incidents to the magic of this particular demon.

Crowds in *Angel* are less consistent. In Seasons 4 and 5 of *Angel*, ominous signs of the tired disaster-movie stereotypes that foster the news media's disaster myths begin to creep in, showing crowds in crisis at their mob worst. For example, in "Peace Out" (4.21), when the mind-control magic of Jasmine wears off, the Los Angeles population goes on a classic-movie mob spree, setting fires, wrecking cars, and running in random directions. Dialogue for several episodes leading up to these scenes makes it clear that people had lost their free will to Jasmine's magic; their violent panic results when their free will is returned. Are we to believe that mob violence is, after all, "human nature," or are we to understand that the response is an aftereffect of magic and manipulation? I believe Whedon and his cocreators are uncharacteristically unclear in these scenes.

One possible explanation is that the series creators are trying to make a statement about hegemony, although Whedon does so much more clearly elsewhere. Bussolini (2005) points out that the general lack of awareness on the part of the masses in the Buffyverse (an issue that disaster researchers would label low risk perception) is an intentional expression of Whedon's views on hegemony—the ideological perceptions and explanations that the power elites promote to the masses to actively obscure elite power and culpability. A population with blind spots when it comes to certain strategic knowledge is kept malleable and generally submissive to those persons in power. In an astute comparison, Bussolini (as noted above) likens Sunnydale to the real-world town of

Los Alamos, where nuclear experimentation has the genuine power to endanger the real world on a scale comparable to *Buffy*'s many apocalypses. It is also a place where "minor" radiation leaks and environmental damage regularly inflict death and illness upon individuals and families who have been ideologically trained never to seek a cause for their suffering. Bussolini demonstrates that this gradual rate of mortality in Los Alamos (higher than the norm for other parts of the country without nuclear waste under their playgrounds) parallels the gradual mortality rate owing to the "everyday" supernatural threats on Whedon's Hellmouth. Bussolini makes the case that people are not blind by nature, but they can be blinded by the intentional cover-ups of individuals in power. Whedon provides us with a variety of power elites making a constant effort to reduce risk perception among Sunnydale's populace: the control-obsessed Sunnydale High principal, Sunnydale's evil mayor, demonic leaders such as the Master and the First, and human power structures reliant upon secrecy for their continued functioning, such as the Initiative.

Whedon makes stronger statements about the power of hegemony with his portrayal of power elites in *Angel*'s Los Angeles: zombie-raising police officers, jet-setters who are well aware of the demon world and view it as entertainment, and the nearly omnipotent demon-backed law firm Wolfram & Hart. The field of disaster studies recognizes that power elites can endanger the health and safety of citizens. In "The Negation of Disaster," Gregory Button describes Great Britain's consistent history of obscuring the damage and threat to health and environment caused by oil spills. He traces the ability to obscure risk perception to the elites' behind-the-scenes control of the news media through personal ties, sponsorship, and media ownership. These connections create, as he puts it, "a bargaining about the meaning of reality" (1999, 130).

The violent mob that attacks Angel in the 1950s flashback episode "Are You Now or Have You Ever Been?" (*Angel* 2.2) is used metaphorically to make a political statement about hegemony. The crowd's fear and anger emerge after a murder threatens people's sense of safety yet are ultimately the product not only of dark magic but also of dark politics. The episode's title (as well as a replay of a 1952 television broadcast watched attentively by that same crowd in the establishing shots) references the loyalty oath created during the 1950s panic over fears of communism. Senator Joseph McCarthy and other politicians eager to gain unprecedented power used that oath in well-publicized "witch hunt" trials. The characters who make up Angel's lynch mob include homosexuals, a black woman trying to pass as white, and blacklisted Hollywood writers, the persecuted pariahs of their era who threaten one another

with labels of "pansy," "commie," and "red," before turning their manufactured fears on Angel.

We could generalize by saying that Whedon's crowds panic and become violent when manipulated by some type of external leadership. Disaster researchers have fairly consistently found external hierarchies to be a source of much of what goes wrong in times of disaster. The phenomenon is termed "elite panic" (Solnit 2009; Tierney et al. 2006). Elite panic was demonstrated in response to Katrina when law enforcement was dedicated to protecting damaged property from disaster victims rather than protecting disaster vic-tims from the flood (Solnit 2009; Tierney et al. 2006). Elite panic involves an unreasonable fear of disaster victims on the part of the government and economic elites with the power to aid those victims. It stems from a worldview that says the police and military are the only entities standing between civili-zation and mass mayhem. That worldview displays ignorance of the anthropo-logical fact that the most peaceful cultures on earth (M'buti and Aka pygmies, the Pauite, the !Kung, to name only a few) are those cultures without power hierarchies such as organized government and police forces (Harris 1989). The panic of the powerful results from a lack of faith in human nature, a fear of losing top-down social control, and complete failure to comprehend disas-ter *communitas*.

Although the news industry normally tries to find panic among disaster victims, elite panic was exposed for what it is in Haitian earthquake coverage unique to one network, CNN, when unreasonable fear of survivors caused an entire team of doctors to abandon their tent hospital, leaving CNN corre-spondent Dr. Sanjay Gupta, with only the help of his camera crew, to treat the critical crush wounds of patients throughout the night (CNN 2010). The net-work exposed elite panic at its rawest the next day when CNN correspondents came upon two men shot by police; bystanders explained to the news crew that their only crime was carrying bags of rice that had fallen off a truck. As discussed above, the myths of disaster are the normative frame for most news coverage of earthquakes, but CNN was confronted with elite panic so blatant that they threw away the frame and presented what they actually saw, raw, to the viewing public. As an example of how far outside the norms of "regular, by-the-book-and-stereotype" CNN had gone, the decision was made to air the footage of one of the men as he died of his wounds on camera (CNN 2010). It should be noted that in times of disaster, "elite" is a relative notion. People with the means to eat become elite in contrast with people who have lost everything; whatever gives a person greater power in relation to others makes him or her elite.

It is no secret that Whedon is antiauthoritarian (Bussolini 2005; Graeber 1998); consequently, he does a thorough job of depicting elite panic throughout *Buffy the Vampire Slayer*. Principal Snyder expresses contempt for students, treating them with utter mistrust. In "Gingerbread," he calls in police to search lockers and arrest students—and he enjoys it. He even orders police to confiscate Giles's collection of occult books, the very books needed to defeat the actual threat to the school. In the same episode, the demon-manipulated vigilante group Mothers Opposed to the Occult (MOO) might also be interpreted as a case of elite panic, as parents are the traditional holders of power in the American family, and these parents so fear their own children that they are prepared to execute them. Elite panic appears many times during *Buffy*'s seven seasons on television—culminating in the final season as police become a source of dysfunctional violence. Instead of assisting in the evacuation of Sunnydale ("Empty Places"), they "restore order" by arresting citizens. Among their targets is Faith, one of the Slayers essential to averting apocalypse. Throughout Season 4 of *Buffy*, Maggie Walsh, the head of the federal government's military program on demons, exhibits elite panic as she perceives the Slayer's civilian demon fighters as disorderly rivals, incapable of effectively fighting or understanding the demons she studies, fights, and utilizes. Fearing the challenge to her monopoly in demon response, she orders Buffy killed ("The I in Team" 4.13). After Walsh's death at the hand of her own part-demon creation, Adam, the Initiative's new commander, Colonel McNamara, also fears loss of control. He subsequently threatens Riley Finn: "Tomorrow I'm going to institute a court martial to investigate the extent of your involvement with the Slayer and her band of freaks. They're anarchists, Finn. Too backwards for the real world. You help us take them down, you might just save your military career" ("New Moon Rising" 4.19). The colonel wants to restore order, even though it means crushing potential allies against the demons. Similar efforts to restore order by restoring submissiveness and inequity can be traced back to events such as the San Francisco earthquake of 1906 when unofficial soup kitchens were closed by government order, despite dire need (Solnit 2009) and government expended great effort to separate victims deemed worthy of aid from the ones that the government would abandon and persecute (Brown-Jeffy and Kroll-Smith 2009).

Colonel McNamara's fears anticipate actual news statements and formal statements made by government officials in the aftermath of Hurricane Katrina. For instance, the *New York Times* described New Orleans as "a snake pit of anarchy, death, looting, raping, marauding thugs" (Dowd 2005). President George W. Bush was quoted in the *New Orleans Times-Picayune* as saying, "We are going to restore order in the city of New Orleans. The people of this country expect there to be order, and we're going to work hard to get it. In order to make sure there's less violence, we've got to get food to people" ("Bush Stunned" 2005). In this line of thinking, the primary reason to feed starving Americans is that they need to be controlled, not that they have a basic right to survive. Sadly, most Americans still believe the myth of extensive individual and mob violence in post-Katrina New Orleans. In reality, provable prosecutions have centered on actions committed by police and white supremacist elites (Solnit 2009; Kunzelman 2011).

Disaster researchers connect media distortions and misdirected government policies to fears of looting (Quarantelli 1987; Solnit 2009; Tierney et al. 2006). They ask, is it wrong to get life-saving supplies for oneself, one's family, or injured strangers if stores are collapsed or under water and one's money and credit cards have been destroyed along with one's home, workplace, and bank? What about damaged supplies such as medicines expiring in wet, hot, or cold conditions or food without refrigeration, all of which could save a life today but will not be any good in a week or two when the owners can return to claim them? Disaster scholars generally support some type of amnesty that distinguishes supply requisition (a highly social act) from the violent looting of luxury goods (an antisocial act). They advocate that disaster survivors have legal access to perishable necessities gleaned from damaged structures (Solnit 2009).

Where might Whedon stand on the supply-requisition issue during times of disaster? He seems to be against the taking of nonnecessities, as evidenced when Faith leads Buffy to robbery in "Bad Girls" (*Buffy* 3.14). The consequences are clear: Buffy falls under extreme suspicion from her friends, while Faith goes into a complete sociopathic tailspin. On the other hand, consider the series' penultimate episode, "End of Days" (*Buffy* 7.21). The final apocalypse is in progress, citizens evacuated. The Scoobies and Potentials are hungry; stores are deserted, food free for the taking. As part of his personal growth, Andrew becomes a competent provider, bringing supplies back to the Summers' home to feed the hungry. In warm scenes revelatory of character depth, Andrew brings individuals their personal favorite treats.

By the time of "End of Days," several of the Potentials have been injured in battles against the minions of the First. Andrew recruits Anya, the ex-demon, to search Sunnydale's deserted hospital for medical supplies. In my opinion, it is one of the best scenes in the entire series, comparable in depth, humor, and pathos to Buffy's notorious "cookie dough" speech of the next episode ("Chosen"). While searching the shelves of a large supply closet, Andrew cajoles Anya into a colloquy on the nature of human beings and her reasons for staying: "I guess I was kind of new to being around humans before. Now I've seen a lot more, gotten to know people, seen what they're capable of. . . . Here's the thing. When it's something that really matters, they fight. They're lame morons for fighting, but they do. They never quit. So I guess I will keep fighting, too," she tells him. "You loo-oove humans," Andrew fondly taunts her in return ("End of Days"). The scene reveals her post-traumatic growth as a result of her years on the Hellmouth. It is all the more poignant in retrospect; Anya will die in the final battle.

Leading anthropological disaster scholar Anthony Oliver-Smith has said, "Solidarity that is born of crisis is not based on a purely rational calculus but is profoundly embedded in our social nature, in that realm of emotion and thought in which we as individuals are created and recreated through time. . . . Disaster assisters who recognize this potential can foster rather than obstruct an empowerment process that can have implications for the development of community long after the disaster has passed" (1999, 170). Building upon Oliver-Smith, Tierney and her crew of disaster researchers summarize major disaster-response recommendations as follows: strengthen community resilience and reduce reliance on outside aid, build public-private partnerships, reach out and incorporate marginalized groups in response plans, and develop consensus-based response strategies capable of coordinating multiple levels of social structures (2006, 76). Whedon employs a broad range of artistry to engage the emotions as well as the intellect of his fans. So when *Buffy* and *Angel* fans are faced with real-world disaster, what kind of disaster responders is Whedon fostering? How well do the lessons in *Buffy* and *Angel* stand up when compared to the recommendations of experts? Not perfectly, but not badly, either. Many *Buffy* and *Angel* episodes advocate empowering individuals and local communities and developing a consensus regarding appropriate response. Whedon's marginalized groups are his response leaders. He acknowledges and honors the potential for post-traumatic growth and altruism. He finds his heroes realistically among the survivors.

Whedon is not a disaster specialist, after all; he is a screenwriter. He comes from an industry indicted by disaster scholars for contributing to unnecessary deaths by filling the heads of viewers with falsehoods that misdirect policy, waste resources, and squander lives. Whedon falls into some troubling disaster stereotypes, but for the most part, his depictions of crises carry many useful lessons. In fact, his apocalyptic disaster coverage is often more accurate and truthful than most of what passes for "nonfiction" on the evening news.

Part Two

Angel

Angel

An Introduction

CYNTHEA MASSON

*A*ngel, a television series spin-off of *Buffy the Vampire Slayer*, ran on the WB Network from 1999 to 2004. Created by Joss Whedon and David Greenwalt, the series comprises 110 episodes over five seasons. As with *Buffy*, *Angel* was written and produced collaboratively through Whedon's production company, Mutant Enemy. Key show runners included Greenwalt and Jeffrey Bell; key writers included Whedon, Greenwalt, Bell, Steven S. DeKnight, David Fury, Tim Minear, and Mere Smith. Considered darker and grittier than *Buffy*, and set in opposition to *Buffy*'s relatively youthful world of Sunnydale, *Angel* is centered in the urban, often sordid, primarily adult world of Los Angeles. Like *Buffy*, *Angel* blends horror and comedy genres, but elements of noir, melodrama, and detective fiction contribute to the show's hybridity.

The premise of *Angel* is that a vampire (sired by Darla in 1753 and cursed with a soul by "gypsies" in 1898) works toward his potential redemption by fighting evil. Prior to being ensouled, Angel (David Boreanaz)—or Angelus, as he is known in his soulless incarnation—wreaked havoc and bloodshed along-side Darla (Julie Benz), Drusilla (Juliet Landau), and Spike (James Marsters). Newly relocated in Los Angeles, Angel, along with Cordelia from *Buffy* (Charisma Carpenter) and Doyle (Glenn Quinn), establishes Angel Investigations, a makeshift detective agency with the motto "We help the helpless." Season 1 progresses through a succession of standalone episodes in which Team Angel, as they have been dubbed by fans, fights a variety of bad guys. Angel is initially assisted in his efforts through visions provided by Doyle, who has a mystical connection to the Higher Powers (known as the Powers That Be). He also relies on the assistance of Detective Kate Lockley (Elisabeth Röhm), despite the complications caused by Kate's hesitance to work with a vampire. The early episodes of Season 1 work well to establish the characters as a unified team. Consequently, viewers were saddened when, only nine episodes into Season 1, Doyle suddenly died, passing his visionary gift to Cordelia through a kiss ("Hero" 1.9). In the next episode, Wesley (Alexis Denisof)—"rogue demon hunter" and former Watcher on *Buffy*—arrives on the scene, gradually works his way onto the team, and remains an integral character through the rest of the series. Two major plot points from the season's final episode are of particular importance: first, the discovery of the Shanshu Prophecy, which indicates that Angel may eventually become human; second, the resurrection of Darla by the evil law firm Wolfram & Hart.

Season 2 consists of both standalone episodes and a plot arc focused on Darla, who, with the help of Wolfram & Hart lawyer Lindsey McDonald (Christian Kane), aims to lure Angel back to the dark side. Darla has been resurrected as human but desperately wants to become a vampire again. When she fails to convince Angel to sire her, Wolfram & Hart enlists Drusilla to do the job; thereafter, Darla and Drusilla blaze a destructive trail through Los Angeles. Angel, in a state of despair over these events, fires his team and, one desperate night, has sex with Darla. In remorse, Angel has an epiphany; he prevents Kate's death and eventually reunites with his team. Season 2 also establishes three new Team Angel members: first, Charles Gunn (J. August Richards), a vampire hunter who initially views Angel as an enemy but gradually understands that Angel is fighting the good fight; second, Lorne (Andy Hallett), the green-skinned, anagogic host of a demon karaoke bar, who (in the season's final episodes) accompanies Team Angel through a portal into his home dimension, Pylea; and third, scientist Winifred (Fred) Burkle (Amy Acker), who is rescued from slavery in Pylea and returns to Los Angeles with the gang.

Season 3 initially revolves around the visibly pregnant Darla and the eventual birth of her and Angel's son, Connor. As a vampire, Darla is unable to give birth; consequently, she stakes herself, leaving the baby in the wake of her dust. Meanwhile, Daniel Holtz (Keith Szarabajka), an eighteenth-century vampire hunter seeking revenge on Angelus and Darla, has been resurrected in Los Angeles. Initially, Holtz wants only to kill his vampire enemies, but the birth of Connor provides him with an opportunity to take even sweeter revenge. Complicating matters, Wesley has discovered a prophecy claiming "the Father will kill the Son." Out of fear for his safety, Wesley kidnaps Connor, only to have him kidnapped again by Holtz's accomplice, Justine (Laurel Holloman), who nearly kills Wesley in the process. As events unfold, Holtz transports Connor to Quor'Toth, an alternate dimension on a different time line; upon their return only a few weeks later, Connor (Vincent Kartheiser) is a teenager who, having been raised by Holtz, despises Angel. Still wanting vengeance, Holtz commits suicide by having Justine kill him; she uses a weapon to imitate a vampire bite, physical evidence that leads Connor to blame Angel for Holtz's murder. In revenge, Connor locks Angel into a strongbox and sinks it to the bottom of the ocean. Meanwhile, Cordelia, having finally admitted her love for Angel, is intercepted (apparently by the Higher Powers) en route to a rendezvous with him. Thus, the season ends with Angel descending in the dark water of the ocean and Cordelia ascending in a beam of light toward the sky.

Season 4 begins with Wesley, having been excised from the team thanks to the kidnapping, in search of Angel. Meanwhile, Fred and Gunn continue to reside with Connor, not knowing what has happened to either Angel or Cordelia. Shortly after Angel has been found and revived (and Connor has been banished), a Beast appears on the scene and, among other crimes, blots out the sun. Meanwhile, Cordelia reappears, initially with no memories of her former life; she is befriended by Connor, with whom, on the eve of an apparent apocalypse, she has sex and becomes pregnant. After numerous futile attempts to vanquish the Beast, the Team decides to remove Angel's soul in hopes of attaining information about the Beast from Angelus. Angelus escapes and, though he later regrets it, kills the Beast; eventually, with help from *Buffy* characters Willow (Alyson Hannigan) and Faith (Eliza Dushku), Angel's soul is reinstated. The team comes to learn that Cordelia, controlled by someone or something else, was in league with the Beast. Her pregnancy results in the birth of Jasmine, a being who proffers world peace at the price of free will. Though initially under her spell, the team eventually destroys Jasmine. Connor is thus distraught, since his happiness is destroyed along with Jasmine. In exchange for the offer of a stable life for Connor (which involves a complex memory spell), Angel makes a deal with the Senior Partners to take over the Los Angeles branch of Wolfram & Hart.

Season 5 finds the team (minus Cordelia, who remains in a coma since Jasmine's birth) reunited and newly established in the offices of Wolfram & Hart. Gunn is given a brain enhancement that provides him with detailed knowledge of human and demon law, making him the team's primary lawyer. Spike, having died at the end of *Buffy*, is resurrected through unknown mystical means and appears at Wolfram & Hart as a noncorporeal entity who eventually regains his corporeality and reluctantly (at first) helps the team to vanquish evil from inside the notoriously evil establishment. A standout episode of this season is fan-favorite "Smile Time" (5.14), in which Angel is transformed into a puppet. In the subsequent episode, "A Hole in the World"

(5.15), the laughter of "Smile Time" is replaced with tears as Fred dies, having been taken over by an ancient being known as Illyria (Amy Acker). With great difficulty, but with the help of Wesley, Illyria gradually adjusts to her new existence and becomes an integral member of the team. As the series draws to a close, Team Angel makes the potentially suicidal decision to take down the Circle of the Black Thorn, a group of extraordinarily powerful demons. In the process, Angel signs away his future as foretold in the Shanshu Prophecy and, with it, his potential to become human. Though Wesley is killed in the final fight, the remaining weary and wounded team members continue onward, rallied by Angel's battle cry, "Let's go to work" ("Not Fade Away" 5.22).

Like its predecessor, *Buffy*, *Angel* attracted a loyal audience of viewers. Though doing well in the ratings on the WB Network, the series was unexpectedly canceled after five seasons, prompting fans to lobby, unsuccessfully, for its continuation. As they have with *Buffy*, scholars have found fertile ground with *Angel*. The first book-length academic study of the series (*Reading Angel: The TV Spin-off with a Soul*, edited by Stacey Abbott) was published in 2005 by I. B. Tauris. More than a hundred academic articles, many of which appear in *Slayage: The Journal of the Whedon Studies Association*, have likewise contributed to ongoing scholarly interest in the series. Despite its origin as a spin-off series, *Angel* has made a name for itself as a unique entity within the grand realm of the Whedonverses.

"Enough of the Action, Let's Get Back to Dancing"

Joss Whedon Directs Angel

STACEY ABBOTT

In the extensive academic and critical writing on *Buffy the Vampire Slayer*, a great deal of attention has been paid to Joss Whedon's creative vision for the series, with particular focus upon his critically acclaimed episodes "Hush" (4.10), "Restless" (4.22), "The Body" (5.16), and "Once More, with Feeling" (6.7). His auteurial stamp upon the visual and narrative style of *Buffy*, for many, goes without saying. Rhonda V. Wilcox compares Whedon to a "master builder," overseeing and shaping the creative contributions of the team of artists and craftspeople in the production of this show (2005, 5). In describing Whedon as "creator and catalyst and air traffic controller," Wilcox acknowledges both the collaborative framework of television production and Whedon's auteurial skill at pulling all of this talent together into one coherent whole (2005, 8). Furthermore, of the seven episodes that Wilcox analyzes in depth, five were written and directed by Whedon, recognizing his individual creative contribution to the show not only as executive producer and show runner but also as writer and director. David Lavery similarly argues that Whedon is the "mad genius" behind *Buffy* because of his significant contributions to the show as producer, writer, and director (2002a, 252).

The context of Whedon's involvement in *Angel*, however, was quite different. As I have argued elsewhere, while Whedon's role as executive producer enabled him to ensure that *Angel* suited his overall vision for the show, *Angel* was collaboratively conceived by Whedon and *Buffy* producer David Greenwalt (Abbott 2009a, 9–16). Furthermore, show-running responsibilities were given to Greenwalt and later Jeffrey Bell, making Whedon's involvement somewhat more distant than in *Buffy*, *Firefly*, and *Dollhouse*. Whedon

119

acknowledges this difference when he explains, "It's not about having to do the 'big' one, that's the thing I love about *Angel*. With *Buffy* I was beholden to the major episodes, it was my show, my responsibility, and it was very seldom I could do one that was just a sidebar. On *Angel* I really am sidebar guy" (quoted in D. Richardson 2004, 35). Although this distance enabled *Angel* writers like Tim Minear, Stephen DeKnight, and Jeffrey Bell to play a substantial role in shaping the series, this chapter will demonstrate that it also enabled Whedon to take a playful approach to his writing and direction for *Angel*—to be "the sidebar guy" on the show. Without having to bear the weight of the series, Whedon was free to interweave his interests in genre, performance, and cinematic allusion into his televisual storytelling and in so doing experiment with form, narrative structure, and genre conventions.[1]

As the creator of *Buffy*, Whedon took responsibility for establishing and maintaining the major narrative arc for each season as well as thematic developments by writing and/or directing season openers and finales as well as key narrative and thematic episodes that served to underpin the arcs for each season. He wrote five season openers, directing three of them, and wrote *and* directed six of the season finales. In contrast on *Angel*, Whedon wrote and directed only two season openers, "City Of" (1.1) and "Conviction" (5.1); is cocredited for the story of "Judgment" (2.1); and cowrote the series finale, "Not Fade Away" (5.22). As cowriter and director of "City Of," Whedon was responsible for establishing the series' narrative links to its parent show, *Buffy*, setting the film noir–superhero aesthetic and atmosphere for the series, and introducing the show's theme of redemption. Similarly, by writing and directing "Conviction," Whedon took responsibility for rebooting the series visually, narratively, and thematically when the characters of Angel Investigations (AI) took over the Los Angeles branch of their arch nemesis, Wolfram & Hart, for the final season. In these episodes, Whedon's contribution was in keeping with his work on *Buffy*, where he had to take responsibility for the big episodes. The other episodes for which he is credited as cowriter, writer, or director (or a combination) each contribute plot points to the seasonal narrative arcs but are not episodes upon which the seasons pivot. They have

---

1. As executive producer, Joss Whedon had substantial and invisible influence on the series through the planning of the seasonal arcs and providing notes on scripts, uncredited contributions to scripts, and redrafts; however, for the purposes of this chapter, I am focusing upon those episodes where he has a clearly identified screen credit.

elements that are necessary to the overall narrative and possess key character moments, but their raisons d'être are far more idiosyncratic.

Through close analysis of "Waiting in the Wings" (3.13), I will examine Whedon's approach to *Angel* as a writer and director, for it is in this dual role that he maintains creative control over the episode and infuses the series with his artistic and cultural preoccupations. Furthermore, much discussion of his work focuses upon his talent as a scriptwriter, emphasizing his strengths in dialogue and story construction with less consideration for his skills as a director despite the fact that Whedon himself admitted that although he loves writing, he always aspired to being a director, telling *TV Zone*, "One of my first motivations for doing the show [*Buffy*] was that no one was interested in me as a director . . . I thought, 'I'll start a TV show and hire myself. I'll learn to direct'" (quoted in Ferrante 2001, 50).

Whedon describes working in television as his training ground as a director, learning to create high-quality drama under economically and temporally restrictive conditions (Holder with Mariotte and Hart 2000, 323). Over the course of his career on *Buffy*, his skills and confidence as a director developed. David Kociemba (2010) clearly demonstrates that even between the production pilot, Whedon's first attempt at directing, and "Prophecy Girl" (1.12), his "official directorial debut," Whedon developed greater confidence and sophistication in his direction, gained from his experience on the previous eleven episodes as creator, writer, and executive producer.[2] According to Kociemba, "Many of the problems on display in the production pilot vanish," and Whedon begins to use "tight framing," "high contrast lighting," and "parallel montage," all "classical technique[s] done well." Most important, as Kociemba convincingly argues, "Whedon's facility with actors shines."

Whedon's development as a director continued as *Buffy* progressed and he gained greater experience with each season. For instance, in the commentary to the second season episode "Innocence" (2.14), Whedon discusses his preference for the cinematic "long sustained take" that allows for more visually dynamic composition and camera movement while also enhancing the chemistry between the actors on-screen. Whedon (2002) stresses, however, that you are not supposed to notice the shot, explaining that "they are not the Brian-DePalma-see-how-far-I-can-take-my-steadicam-before-I-run-out-of-film kind of shots." In the third season episode "Anne" (3.1), however, he

2. A revised version of Kociemba's 2010 conference paper appears in this volume.

captures the excitement and chaos of the first day of school by using precisely this type of shot. In a Robert Altman–style three-minute-take sequence shot,[3] Whedon follows Giles, Willow, Cordelia, Oz, and Xander, as well as other teachers and students, in and out of disparate conversations as they circulate around the library, corridors, and school lounge. Like its cinematic predecessors in *Touch of Evil* (1958) and *The Player* (1992), this shot calls attention to itself stylistically and sets up the high school space that will be pivotal to the season, particularly the finale, "Graduation Day, Part Two" (3.22), when Buffy lures the Mayor-demon back through the lounge, corridor, and library before blowing up him and the school.

By Season 4's "Restless" (4.22), Whedon, according to David Lavery, uses a similar steadicam sequence shot to capture the surrealism of dreams as Xander walks from "Giles' apartment, through a hallway, and out into Buffy's dorm, into Buffy and Willow's room, and through a closet into his own dank basement apartment." As Lavery explains, this sequence "makes perfect dream sense—for in dreams, after all, are not all places and times contiguous? But the dream contiguity of the diegesis of 'Restless' is in reality the equally surreal contiguity of the extradiegetic actual television shooting set" (2002a, 253). Whedon's use of the long take demonstrates the increasing sophistication of his filmmaking style and his desire to stretch the aesthetic boundaries of mainstream television. This notion is further supported by the fact that Whedon gradually moved beyond episodes that largely serve the narrative arc to directing episodes such as "Hush" and "Restless" that both feed into the series' narrative and experiment with televisual form, in these cases through the creative use of sound or a nonlinear dream structure, respectively. By the premiere of *Angel*, Whedon had directed eleven episodes of *Buffy* and was increasingly prepared to experiment aesthetically and narratively. His work on *Angel* continues this creative trajectory without the pressure to focus on the big episodes.

As evidence of Whedon's whimsical approach to *Angel*, we need look only at the origin stories for "Waiting in the Wings," "Spin the Bottle" (4.6), and "A Hole in the World" (5.15). The inspiration for these episodes originated not out of narrative or thematic necessity but rather through Whedon's extradiegetic interests. "Waiting in the Wings" began when Amy Acker (Fred) told Whedon that she studied ballet for fifteen years and he decided to write

---

3. A long take is a shot that continues for an unusually long time before cutting to the next shot, whereas a sequence shot is a long take that runs for an entire scene without cutting.

an episode that would enable Acker to dance. Whedon (2003c) further points out that much of the action within the script grew out of a desire to see Wesley (Alexis Denisof) "do lots of different things . . . the sword fighting . . . the ballet . . . and of course the heartbreak." Similarly, Season 4's "Spin the Bottle" stemmed from Whedon's desire to "see Alexis fall down again," referring to Alexis Denisof's supreme skill of physical comedy, absent from the show once Wesley became a dark and brooding demon hunter (Whedon 2004b). Finally, the nascent idea for "A Hole in the World" grew out of Whedon's now renowned Shakespeare readings where he had opportunity to see Acker perform a range of stately and villainous characters and decided that he wanted to give her the opportunity to play "regal and scary and different than anything she's gotten to do" . . . so he killed Fred and the demon-god Illyria was born (Whedon 2005a). Although there were undoubtedly other contributing factors to Whedon's choices, these declarations demonstrate that one key factor was his personal affinity with certain actors—all three episodes feature Acker and Denisof—and a desire to indulge their performance.[4] But what began as an indulgence of performance evolved into a creative indulgence in stylistic and generic excess.

Even before looking at how these episodes offer a new spin on the show's generic and aesthetic style, Whedon's "Waiting in the Wings," "Spin the Bottle," and "A Hole in the World" stand out within the series as breaks from the main seasonal narratives. Located halfway through Season 3, "Waiting in the Wings" falls after the birth of Angel's son, Connor, which drives the first half of the season, but before the story takes a darker turn with Wesley's uncovering the prophecy that the Father will kill the Son, his resulting abduction of Connor and subsequent betrayal by his friends, and Connor's eventual return from a hell dimension to wreak revenge upon his father. The episode gives the characters, and the audience, a night off as the team of Angel Investigations gets dressed up and goes to the ballet. The amnesia narrative of "Spin the Bottle," in which a spell goes wrong and the team members of AI lose their recent memories and think they are seventeen again, offers a comedic respite from the almost operatic apocalypse narrative that dominates Season 4. During Season 5's "A Hole in the World," all other cases and narratives are put on hold as the entirety of Wolfram & Hart becomes focused on finding a cure for the mystery illness attacking Fred's

---

4. Whedon has since cast the two as Beatrice and Benedick in his *Much Ado about Nothing* (2012).

system, a fact that is emphatically driven home to the one lawyer who dares suggest that "the whole company can't be working Ms. Burkle's case" and is subsequently shot in the leg by Wesley.

These episodes also provide an opportunity for Whedon to experiment with stylistic, generic, and narrative conventions, briefly disrupting the series' diegesis with his televisual experimentation. In the case of "Waiting in the Wings" and "A Hole in the World," Whedon foregrounds the show's allegiance to melodrama by engaging playfully with the aesthetic and narrative conventions of the genre, while "Spin the Bottle" offers a creative interplay among melodrama, cabaret, and slapstick. It is this experimentation that distinguishes his work on *Angel*. While the *Buffy* episode "Restless" is, with its surrealist and decidedly oneiric, nonlinear structure, the most avant-garde episode of television that Whedon has written and directed to date, it is also primarily in the service of character, narrative, and theme on *Buffy*. As Matthew Pateman has convincingly argued in his detailed analysis of the episode, you can read, or unravel, the entirety of the series through "the conduit of 'Restless'" (2006, 109). This fourth-season episode is a pivotal moment for the seven-season show, as Whedon uses highly innovative means to reflect both backward and forward in terms of the characters', and the show's, development. In contrast, the sidebar quality of "Waiting in the Wings" enables Whedon to reflect upon the televisual medium itself. Whereas "Spin the Bottle" is more ostentatiously experimental in format, "Waiting in the Wings" is equally—if subtly—innovative in style and narrative. As such, it is a highly instructive case study of Whedon's approach to directing on *Angel*.

"Waiting in the Wings": Echoes of the Past

"Waiting in the Wings" is a "special episode." It does not fall into the tradition of after-school specials, "which aim for redeeming social value by focusing on unmediated presentations of social topics," repudiated by Whedon with regards to *Buffy* (Wilcox 2005, 17). Rather, it is special in terms of its story, narrative, and aesthetic construction. Its specialness is first conveyed narratively by the characters as they are each caught up in the magic of the evening, whether it is Cordelia and Fred's pleasure of dressing up or Gunn's rapture in the dance itself. This "specialness" spilled out onto the production, as Whedon describes the shooting of this episode as a magical experience because it was a break from the norm on *Angel*—the script did not require the usual night shooting, the cast and crew got to shoot for two days at the Orpheum Theatre in Los Angeles, and the filming of the ballet was of course very different from the action choreography that they were used to staging. In so doing, Whedon (2003c) offers a break from the show's traditional visual and generic style; as he explains, "enough of the action, let's get back to dancing."

Whereas the focus on dance suggests a relationship with the musical, the aesthetics of the episode more directly allude to the conventions of melodrama, a fact supported by Whedon's references to the work of Vincent Minnelli and Douglas Sirk in his DVD commentary. Furthermore, the title "Waiting in the Wings" echoes one of Douglas Sirk's most famous melodramas, *Written on the Wind* (1956). Whedon's engagement with the conventions of melodrama is highlighted by his emphasis upon the artificiality of the episode's mise-en-scène and its aesthetic construction, a defining characteristic of the genre. The episode is replete with shots that seem out of place in *Angel* and draw attention to their aesthetic beauty. Act 1 begins on a brightly lit and colorful display of women's shoes in an expensive dress shop. As Cordelia and Fred enter the frame, browsing for dresses, Fred draws attention to the anomalous location by asking, "Are you certain this is the place for us?" Later, the image of the lonely ballerina (Summer Glau) standing in the wings of the stage evokes the imagery of the French impressionist Edgar Degas's renowned paintings of ballet dancers. The empty background as the ballerina silently waits, poised to return to the stage, captures Degas's preoccupation with the beautiful but unglamorous world of dancers off the stage. Furthermore, the stillness of the dancer and Ross Berryman's exquisite lighting lends the image a painterly quality, calling attention to the artificiality of its construction.

This stillness, however, is not unique to this image, for it characterizes the imagery throughout the episode, a stylistic choice that is unusual for *Angel*, a show more often defined by fast-paced action. The episode's imagery suggests both painterly traditions and the nineteenth-century tableau vivant, which serves to visually anchor the episode in the Victorian traditions of theater and art where the ballerina's story of love and betrayal begins. This stillness also reinforces the artificiality of the mise-en-scène. For instance, Whedon composes a number of shots with characters overtly posing and being admired by others. Cordelia, dressed for the evening, poses in Angel's doorway with her head tilted coquettishly, while Fred is similarly framed in long shot as she admires her gown and is openly admired by both Gunn and Wesley. Fred waits patiently for Gunn to emerge and pose awkwardly in his tuxedo and squeals with glee when she sees how "pretty" he looks, while Wesley describes Fred as a "vision." Later, Whedon captures the team's wondrous glances around their surroundings as they enter the Orpheum Theatre, filmed in a low-angle panning shot that mirrors Fred's movements as she looks up and turns around, admiring the beautiful location. This emphasis upon posing and looking calls attention to the episode's theatricality. Furthermore, through their color and composition, these images establish that we are entering unusual generic territory, far from the sewers, back alleys, and rooftops that are more commonly associated with *Angel*. These images suggest glamour and sensuousness, and evoke the realms of musicals and melodramas.

The emphasis upon a heightened form of aestheticism is crucial to the emotional impact of melodrama, for, as Geoffrey Nowell-Smith argues, "music and mise en scène do not just heighten the emotionality of an element of the action: to some extent they substitute for it" (1987, 73). This understanding of melodrama was recognized by the master of melodrama Douglas Sirk when he explained that his expressionistic use of color in *Written on the Wind* was designed to "bring out the inner violence, the energy of the characters which is all inside them and can't break through" (quoted in Elsaesser 1987, 43). In "Waiting in the Wings," the opening of the curtain and the beginning of the ballet signal the point at which the heightened emotions of the dance—a form of theater that, like melodrama, is about expressing extreme emotions through music and performance—spill out into the world of *Angel* through the mise-en-scène. From this point, Whedon allows the characters from *Angel* to become immersed in the ballet when actions on and off the stage become increasingly intertwined and the aesthetics of the episode are used to convey the emotions of the scenes playing out. The soft lighting and lushness of the color scheme in the dressing room embody the passion of the love scene enacted by Angel and Cordelia possessed by spirits of the past, while the loneliness of the image of the ballerina in the wings captures the beautiful pain and isolation of missed opportunity, a theme that permeates the episode.

Furthermore, Whedon takes the artificiality of the mise-en-scène beyond visual imagery by emphasizing the artificiality of performance itself. As they prepare to go to the ballet, Cordelia informs Angel that for one night, they can pretend to live different lives when she explains, "Tonight I've decided that we don't have to be our incredibly dreary selves. Tonight we are just a couple of young sophisticates enjoying an evening of classical dance." The choice of ballet, *Giselle*, emphasizes this theme, for it is about a prince who pretends to be a peasant in order to romance the young Giselle, and within the diegesis of "Waiting in the Wings" this ballet reflects and distorts the ballerina's own tragic story of betrayal. Once Angel and Cordelia go into the ballerina's dressing room and become possessed by echoes of the past, they "perform" a passionate love scene as a means of uncovering the truth about the ballet company: Cordelia tells Angel, "All we have to do is play the scene," echoing her earlier pronouncement that for one night, they will get to be different people.

Finally, once Gunn, Fred, and Wesley go backstage, they also begin to "perform" their love triangle, playing all of the emotions in an exaggerated and excessive manner. When Gunn is stabbed, Fred uncharacteristically responds with tears. Her response seems overstated, for it is not the first time that one of them has been hurt or in danger. Furthermore, as they begin to express their feelings for each other, they do so in a manner that is highly performative. Unlike Angel and Cordelia, the feelings they express are their own—they are not possessed by echoes of the past—but the language with which they express them is excessive and literary as compared to their more contemporary speech patterns. Compare Gunn's affectionate description of Fred earlier in the episode as possessing "a little stick figure body" and backhanded compliment when he tells her "Come on, you know you're gorgeous" to his response to her crying: "If you care that much then the wound is definitely deep," which leads to their first kiss. His earlier statements are cagey compliments that do not reveal too much, whereas the latter statement employs more sophisticated rhetoric, using the word *wound* to refer both to his physical injury and, more important, to the figurative wound of love. Furthermore, the melodramatic performance of their love scene enables the characters to openly express what they feel.

Whedon presents Wesley's response to seeing Gunn and Fred together in an even more excessive and stylized fashion, beginning with highly expressive composition as the camera pulls out from a two-shot of Fred and Gunn kissing into a three-shot including Wesley, whose back is to the camera while his reaction is captured in a reflection (Whedon 2003c). The expressiveness of the sequence is enhanced by Denisof's melodramatic performance as he walks away, slumps to the ground, and then looks up toward the camera as he is consumed by echoes of the nineteenth-century Count's rage, conveyed by the flash dissolve to the Count watching the ballet and the increasingly dramatic music.[5] Here the passion and heartache of the ballet begin to intertwine with the melodrama backstage as the music bleeds across the two sequences.

---

5. The Count is a wizard who owns the ballet and is obsessed with the ballerina. When he learned that she loved another man, he pulled her out of time and cursed her to repeat the same performance of *Giselle* every night.

Like Angel and Cordelia's love scene, the possession by emotions from the past allows Wesley's repressed emotions to briefly burst forth before being contained once again. Later Whedon ensures that only the audience is aware of Wesley's anger, disappointment, and heartbreak through the occasional cutaway to Wesley's silent, pained reaction to Gunn and Fred. It is in the representation of this particular love triangle, replete with passion and sexual jealousy, that Whedon most overtly alludes to Sirk's *Written on the Wind*, a film that chronicles the painful and often violent repercussions of two sets of love triangles (Rock Hudson/Lauren Bacall/Robert Stack and Lauren Bacall/Rock Hudson/Dorothy Malone).

Like Sirk, Whedon uses heavily stylized lighting, composition, and performance to project the characters' secret inner turmoil outward—Angel and Cordelia's love for one another, which remains unspoken until the end of the season, and Wesley and Angel's disappointment and heartbreak when both Fred and Cordelia choose someone else. The intertwining of the *Angel* characters' love stories with the performance of the tragic romance of *Giselle* allows Whedon to contrast what is revealed to be a shadow of the ballerina's past performances with the all-consuming emotions felt by Angel and his team. It is revealed toward the end of the episode that the ballerina has been cursed to repeat the same performance of *Giselle* every night, telling Angel, "I don't dance, I echo." In contrast, Whedon has the team members at AI express their real emotions through performance, enabling him as director to "play the emotion the way you feel the emotion here at the ballet," turning the episode into balletic choreography of music, aesthetics, dance, and performance (Whedon 2003c).

"Waiting in the Wings" is a sidebar episode. It has a monster-of-the-week narrative, and its excursion into the ballet was an opportunity for Whedon to indulge his own passion for dance and the cinematic aesthetics of melodrama. This choice ironically came at the expense of his original reason for writing and directing the episode, since the scene with Acker and Denisof dancing, conceived as a comic dream sequence, no longer suited the melodramatic resonance of the rest of the script and had to be cut. It might be easy to dismiss the aesthetic extravagance of this episode as a result of the high-art association with the ballet, but when looked at alongside Whedon's other directorial contributions to the series, particularly "Spin the Bottle" and "A Hole in the World," we see a shared preoccupation with melodrama and a melancholic sensibility that emerge not only from the story but through Whedon's directorial approach to *Angel*.

Melodrama and Melancholy: The Aesthetics of Relationships

This mix of melodrama and melancholy that characterizes much of Whedon's work on *Angel* is best conveyed aesthetically through Whedon's use of the sustained long take. As discussed above, Whedon has openly declared his preference for staging scenes in this manner, and, as a result, it has become one of Whedon's most distinctive stylistic tropes as a director. Whereas his creative use of this technique on *Buffy* served a multitude of purposes, on *Angel*, as I will demonstrate, Whedon returned to it in "Waiting in the Wings," "Spin the Bottle," and "A Hole in the World" in order to represent the evolution of relationships and convey their inherent beauty and anguish.

Whedon's commitment to the long take is an aesthetic choice that is generally uncharacteristic of television production, which tends to rely upon editing. The rationale for this tendency is twofold: first, the director must provide sufficient amount of coverage of a scene for the editor to cut and keep the episode to time. A long take does not provide editing possibilities (Whedon 2002). Second, as Karen Lury has argued, television traditionally favors the close-up, as it emphasizes dialogue, intimacy, and familiarity, whereas the long take generally oscillates between long and medium shots (2005, 28–29). On occasion, Whedon's long takes do move into close-up for dramatic effect, as in the posttitle sequence that (re)introduces the audiences to the cast and primary location of *Serenity* but ends on an extreme close-up of the character River (2005). More often, however, his sequence shots include more than one character, precluding any extensive use of the close-up. In this manner, Whedon evokes familiarity and intimacy through character interaction rather than camera proximity. Even when not staging extensive long takes, he opts for the two- or three-shot rather than the more conventional close-ups of individual characters. These types of shots tend to be longer than a more traditional shot-countershot structure, and, like the long take, they favor character interaction in their composition, generating heightened emotions (Whedon 2004b).

Nowhere are these stylistic choices more evident than in his representation of the love triangle, a theme he first introduced on *Buffy* before exploring it in greater depth on *Angel*. For instance, in the *Buffy* episode "Innocence," Whedon uses the long take as a significant stylistic tool to capture the macabre dynamic that emerges when Angelus rejoins Spike and Drusilla after Angel loses his soul. When Angelus arrives at the factory, Whedon films the three vampires in a long take as they celebrate his return to the fold. The sustained shot emphasizes their unity but also draws attention to their changing relationship dynamics. When Spike and Drusilla were first introduced in "School Hard" (*Buffy* 2.3), informing the head vampire (the Anointed One) that they "are moving in," they are framed in a tight medium close-up as they stand, holding each other while facing the camera. This composition emphasizes their strength in unity. This point is reiterated in "Innocence," as they continue to be framed in a medium two-shot, with Drusilla lying on a table so that she is still on an equal level to Spike, now confined to a wheelchair. Once Angelus is reintroduced, however, Whedon disrupts this unity by placing Angelus at the center of the composition and emphasizing that Drusilla and Spike are no longer on equal levels. Drusilla, walking along a table, towers over both men, while Spike's slightly weakened position in the wheelchair is emphasized when both Drusilla and Angelus have to lean down to speak to him in close-up. The long take also visually expresses Drusilla's kinky delight in now having both men to amuse her. Exclaiming in rather perverse fashion that "we're family again," Drusilla walks to the end of the table, past Angelus, while the camera tilts down and reframes into a medium two-shot as she playfully tells him, "We'll feed." The camera then pans to a medium close-up of Spike as Drusilla leans over to him, seductively completing the sentiment with "and we'll play." This fluid camera movement captures the macabre ménage à trois dynamic that will characterize their relationship but also will lead to their undoing. Later in the episode, Angelus once again disrupts Spike and Drusilla's intimate composition as she sits on Spike's lap. Angelus takes her hand and leads her out of a two-shot and into a three-shot as they both walk away, leaving Spike alone in the background, stuck in his wheelchair. This composition, reinforced by the fact that in "Becoming, Part One" (*Buffy* 2.21) the three vampires are repeatedly framed with Angelus between Spike and Drusilla, foreshadows Spike's increasing isolation that will lead him to betray Angelus in order to get Drusilla back at the end of the season.

On *Angel*, Whedon continues to develop this visual language to capture the changing relationship dynamics within a love triangle by focusing upon the sidebar relationship of Wesley, Fred, and Gunn. In "Waiting in the Wings," Whedon establishes this triangular relationship in three key scenes. As they prepare to go to the ballet, Whedon has Fred and Gunn each admiring the other in a shot-countershot sequence, largely filmed in medium close-up. The tightness of the framing and the shallow focus of the image emphasize that they see only each other. This composition is disrupted when Wesley unexpectedly enters the frame of a medium close-up of Fred to put her wrap over her shoulders. Subsequently, Wesley enters the foreground of the reverse medium shot of Gunn, standing between Gunn and Fred, as he turns back to look at Fred. The composition of these images establishes the potentially romantic dynamic between Fred and Gunn and Wesley's unwitting position between them. Unlike Angelus, Wesley is unaware of his disruption to the moment, and instead of suggesting a possible ménage à trois, this sequence, consistent with the episode's emphasis upon melodrama, establishes the potential for heartache. This possibility comes to fruition when Wesley becomes aware of his missed opportunity with Fred in the sequence described earlier when Whedon films Wesley's discovery of the two lovers in a sustained long take of the couple kissing that pulls out to reveal Wesley's pained reaction. Wesley's heartache is reinforced at the end of episode as he tends to Gunn's stab wound. Wesley is again framed between the couple, this time in the background as Fred and Gunn stare lovingly at each other, painfully blind to Wesley's presence. Whedon uses intimate composition to capture the heartache that will characterize this triangular relationship throughout the series.

Whereas "Waiting in the Wings" employs subtle compositional choices to suggest the burgeoning emotional dynamics that involve these three characters, "Spin the Bottle," with its more self-conscious aesthetic, uses the sustained take to overtly acknowledge the changing dynamics as relationships turn sour. Here Lorne, narrating the episode, tries to explain the reasons for the growing tension and hostility among Fred, Wesley, and Gunn. In a reverse of the three-shot from "Waiting in the Wings," it is now Fred and Wesley who stare at each other, unaware that Gunn, in the background of the image, is watching them. Fred and Wesley in this case stare at each other not with love but rather with knowing complicity in the attempted murder of Fred's evil professor, a murder that Gunn undertook himself to protect Fred. Whedon then reinforces the growing isolation of the members of the group by using a fast-paced tracking shot to track into an individual close-up of each of the characters as Lorne explains the level of secrecy and duplicity among them. This isolation is reiterated at the end of the episode through Whedon's high-angle long shot of Fred, Wesley, and Gunn silently walking away from each other. This episode does not merely mark the beginning of the end of Fred and Gunn's romantic relationship but also signifies the continued deterioration of Gunn and Wesley's friendship.

Finally, in "A Hole in the World," Whedon has moved beyond visually depicting this triangular relationship, although it is still a key factor to the plot. Gunn alludes to his past relationship with Fred when he teasingly tells Wesley that he (Gunn) and Fred are getting back together before giving Wesley his blessing. Rather than focus on the love triangle, Whedon uses the long-take two-shot to contrast two budding relationships—Spike and Angel as well as Wesley and Fred—the first on a trajectory from antagonism to friendship and the second going from romance to tragedy. Whedon opts to film each couple in intimate two-shots throughout the episode. Initially, this aesthetic choice captures an almost claustrophobic antagonism between Spike and Angel as they argue over who would win in a fight, "caveman or astronauts," staged in one long take. Eventually, however, it captures their bond as heroes and unites them against the evil that is destroying Fred, best exemplified in the low-angle long shot of the two vampires as they leave Wesley's office, preparing to fight for Fred's cure, or as they hold hands in the field outside the Deeper Well, waiting for its guardians to be unleashed.

With respect to Fred and Wesley, the first half of the episode, couched in the excesses of romance—Lorne tells them to "go get a balcony"—usually frames them in quite conventional shot-countershots, culminating in a climactic two-shot as they kiss. However, once Wesley takes Fred back to her apartment, not for their desired sexual liaison but so she can die within the comforts of her own home, Whedon frames them in increasingly tight two-shots lying on her bed as they fight to stay together. The two relationships tragically interact in the climax of the episode, as Angel and Spike's painful decision not to save Fred because it would result in the deaths of thousands of innocents is juxtaposed with her death scene in Wesley's arms, filmed in one long take.

Whedon's preference for the sustained take over a shot-countershot enabled him to create an intimacy that enhanced the beautiful pain of the Wesley, Fred, and Gunn love triangle across these three episodes. I have described this relationship, clearly beloved to Whedon for he returned to it frequently, as a sidebar relationship because it does not include the show's lead character, Angel. That description is not to deny its significance to the series' narrative or its emotional resonance for audiences. In fact, it is, arguably, more affecting than the Angel, Cordelia, and Connor love triangle, which is more central to the series' narrative arc. I would argue that this significance is owing in part to its status as a sidebar relationship. It is not expected to cater to and facilitate the show's main plot developments or themes. As such, it is able to develop slowly and haunt the periphery of the series, fostering an atmosphere of melancholy distinct from *Buffy*, aided in no small part by these three sidebar episodes that demonstrate Whedon's passion for melodrama and his growing confidence and sophistication as a writer and director.

Conclusion: The Benefits of Being "Sidebar Guy"

Not being "beholden to the major episodes" of *Angel* enabled Joss Whedon to develop his style as a writer and director by not having to cater to the main narrative arcs of the series. Instead, in the episodes he directed, he was able to explore personal interests in dance and melodrama, as well as creative collaborations with certain actors by allowing them to explore new aspects of their characters (or, in the case of Wesley, return to a previous persona). He was also able to develop his visual style and experiment with storytelling techniques, weaving into his episodes a range of aesthetic and narrational references that enhance how we understand his stories. As "sidebar guy," he was able to be stylistically provocative without risking undermining the seasonal arcs, yet he also demonstrated how far a writer and director could stretch the show's generic parameters without alienating the audience. This sophistication in storytelling and experimentation with form and style, therefore, was not limited to Whedon's contributions to the show (see "Are You Now or Have You Ever Been?" [2.2], "Orpheus" [4.15], and "Soul Purpose" [5.10]).[6] Instead, his work on *Angel* pushed the boundaries and techniques of storytelling within TV and raised the bar on a series that consistently challenged and undermined our expectations and understanding of television.

6. For further discussion of *Angel*'s experimentations with form, narrative, and style, see Abbott 2009a.

What the Hell?

Angel's "The Girl in Question"

CYNTHEA MASSON

I would like to formally nominate this episode as [the] Worst Epi[sode] of *Angel* Ever," posts Doug on May 6, 2004, to the online forum *All Things Philosophical on "Buffy the Vampire Slayer" and "Angel": The Series*.[1] On *Television without Pity*, [O]stentatious writes, "Wow. Of all the shows I've ever considered myself a fan . . . this episode was the worst single episode of any of them. The worst. Hands down" (2004). On *Whedonesque*, ZachsMind laments, "It was fluff. It was filler. It was pab[u]lum. . . . I would have preferred Il[l]yria just killed them all and then burst into flames" (2004). You get the idea, but here is a brief sampling of the most passionately vehement responses to "The Girl in Question" (*Angel* 5.20) posted in the immediate aftermath of its debut on May 5, 2004:

- Catanzey: "The identical [Wolfram & Hart] office was predictable, and sad, because I know they can't afford another set. . . . This whole season has been [Mutant Enemy] slowly tearing a Band Aid off my eyeball—this time, they just yanked that sucker off."
- [S]teffie: "Was this the 'madcap adventures in Italy' episode of the popular sitcom *Cordy*?"[2]

---

1. This paper was first presented at SCW3: The *Slayage* Conference on the Whedonverses, Arkadelphia, Arkansas (June 5–8, 2008). I thank Kathryn Barnwell and Marni Stanley for early editorial feedback and Stacey Abbott for providing me with her SCW2 paper.

2. "Birthday" (*Angel* 3.1) features Cordelia in an alternate dimension as the star of the television sitcom *Cordy*.

- SNeaker: "With the cookie dough, and the jacket and the . . . I'm just so embarrassed for everyone involved with that show. I'm embarrassed for the gaffer. I'm embarrassed for the donut guy."
- [L]uxgladius: "Lamest. Episode. Ever. . . . What's the point of an episode where the subject character isn't even there?"
- The Pez: "Seriously how pathetic could you get to have a storyline centered on someone who isn't there?"
- [S]ervo: "This is the 3rd last episode, and nothing happened. Nothing."
- Kalbear: "It was scattered and weird. And oddly lit. . . . And nothing happened."

"Nothing happens, nobody comes, nobody goes, it's awful": Samuel Beckett, *Waiting for Godot* (1954, 43). I am not suggesting that "The Girl in Question" reworks *Waiting for Godot*. I am, however, convinced that centering the story line on a subject character who is not there is key to understanding this episode as an existential drama.

This antepenultimate episode of the series is set primarily in Italy, where Angel and Spike attempt to rescue Buffy from an old nemesis, The Immortal. Angel's most recent encounter with Buffy (which had occurred during the final episode of *Buffy the Vampire Slayer*) included a conversation in which she described herself as "cookie dough"; figuratively, she claimed not to be fully baked and thus, by implication, not ready to settle down with anyone, including Angel ("Chosen" 7.22). In "The Girl in Question," neither Angel nor Spike has seen or spoken with Buffy for almost a year, yet each still harbors hope of reconnecting with her in Italy. Despite their best efforts in Rome to locate her, including repeated trips to her apartment (which they find occupied by her colleague Andrew) and to a dance club she is rumored to frequent, Angel and Spike do not succeed. Indeed, other than a brief shot of a woman in the club who *could* be Buffy, neither she nor The Immortal appears in the episode.[3] An absent Immortal is also featured in flashbacks to 1894, when Angel (Angelus), Spike (William), Darla, and Drusilla temporarily resided in Italy. Meanwhile, in current-day Rome, with help from the Italian branch of Wolfram & Hart, Angel and Spike work to retrieve the literal head of the "Capo di Famiglia" of the Goran demon clan. Their official mission involves

3. The first issue of *Buffy* Season 8 (Dark Horse Comics, 2007) confirms that the woman glimpsed in Italy is not Buffy. For my paper, the critical point is not Buffy's presence but the repeated attempts by Spike and Angel to reach her.

returning the head to Los Angeles in time to avert violent dissent among rival demon clans.

When contextualized as existential drama, "The Girl in Question" is more than "a weak comedic episode" (Kaveney 2005, 64). Like the absence of Godot in *Waiting for Godot*, the absence of both Buffy and The Immortal works to highlight the relationship between the male leads as they enact the possibility of unending despair. Similarly, the use of an identical set for the Italian branch of Wolfram & Hart evokes the inescapable hell of Jean-Paul Sartre's existential play *No Exit*.[4] "The Girl in Question" may be scattered. It may be weird and oddly lit. And one can certainly argue that nothing happens (in terms of the season's plot development). But to paraphrase Angel himself from "Epiphany" (2.16), *if nothing that happens matters, then all that matters is what happens.*[5] The so-called pabulum of this episode arguably comprises thematic elements of absurd and existential theater evident in *Waiting for Godot* and *No Exit*. Viewed from these sites, "The Girl in Question" becomes a powerful, well-placed reassertion of the dilemma of immortality—that is, the potential for stasis—and the necessity to choose, eternally, to change.

This episode depicts Angel and Spike in a state of inertia—one most obviously illustrated in the final scene. As they lean against Angel's desk together, Angel says, "Movin' on." Spike says, "Oh, yeah." Angel says, "Right now." Spike says, "Movin'." Yet as the final image fades to black, they do not move. This ending is similar to the one in both *Waiting for Godot* and *No Exit*. At the conclusion of *Waiting for Godot*, Vladimir says, "Well? Shall we go?" Estragon replies, "Yes, let's go." The stage directions state, "They do not move" (Beckett 1954, 109). At the end of *No Exit*, recognizing that he will remain in hell with Estelle and Inez "for ever, and ever, and ever" (as he says), Garcin looks at the women and proposes, "Well, well, let's get on with it. . . ." (Sartre [1947] 1989, 46; Sartre's ellipsis). The curtain closes. The lead characters are trapped in a room together for eternity. As Lois Gordon explains, "Their immortality will be spent in the dual role of the tortured

---

4. In "Lovers Walk," Angel is seen reading the French version of Sartre's novel *Nausea* (*Buffy* 3.8). Whedon's visual reference to Sartre is through fiction rather than, for example, *Being and Nothingness*. Using *No Exit*, another fictional work of Sartrean existentialism, thus seems appropriate for discussing the existential elements of an *Angel* episode. For more on Whedon and existentialism, see Abbott 2003, 2005b; Richardson and Rabb 2007. For a discussion of *Nausea* in relation to *Angel*, including a section on the Wesley-Illyria plot of "The Girl in Question," see Masson 2010b.

5. "If nothing we do matters, then all that matters is what we do."

and torturer" (2003, 166). *Waiting for Godot*, according to Gordon, is an "example of human imprisonment" in that "one hears repeatedly . . . 'Let's go,' . . . followed by . . . '(They do not move.)'" (2003, 170). In *Angel*'s "To Shanshu in L.A." (1.22), Wesley relates life to the necessity of moving forward: "We live. We grow. We change," he says. Cordelia, realizing that Angel cannot do these things, responds, "What are you saying, Wesley? That Angel has nothing to look forward to? That he's going to go on forever the same in the world . . . ?" Immortality without forward movement or change is the hell represented in "The Girl in Question."[6]

The opening scene of "The Girl in Question" likewise establishes a focus on inertia. Thus, when Gunn speaks the episode's first line, "We have to act on this now," Angel responds, "Not without a full risk analysis." In other words, he prefers to wait. Similarly, at first Spike wants nothing to do with the mission; he sits in a chair playing a handheld video game and says to Angel, "Do it yourself." Thus, Spike, like Angel, initially refrains from action. We know from the series' final two episodes—"Power Play" (5.21) and "Not Fade Away" (5.22)—that Angel and Spike do choose to make a dramatic move toward change. "The Girl in Question," placed as it is immediately before the big power play, emphasizes the *other* possibility: failure to change or to effect a change. Angel and Spike fail at their mission in this episode, being unable to attain the head of the "Capo di Famiglia" in Italy. More important, they find themselves trapped in repetitive situations or patterns: in their quest for Buffy, in their desire for revenge on The Immortal, in the language spoken by the Italians, and in the offices of Wolfram & Hart. Such repetition reflects a typical strategy of absurd theater as outlined by Martin Esslin: "What passes in these plays are not *events* with a definite beginning and a definite end, but types of *situation* that will forever repeat themselves" ([1961] 2004, 76). In repeating the same situations, Angel and Spike risk remaining who they *were* rather than initiating a move toward who they could become. In *The Existential Joss Whedon*, J. Michael Richardson and J. Douglas Rabb describe "existential freedom" as "the freedom to become better than we were, to transform ourselves completely by adopting new life-defining goals, as both Spike and Angel ultimately do" (2007, 115). Yes, ultimately, they *do*. But "The Girl in Question" illustrates what would happen if they did *not*.

---

6. Mary Alice Money argues that vampires can "become undemonized" through love, change, and choice (2002, 102).

Their perpetual focus on Buffy throughout the episode ensures that Angel and Spike remain trapped in the hell of an unresolved relationship rather than initiating the existential freedom of new goals. In their chapter "Angel in Hell: Love and Moral Choice," Richardson and Rabb discuss hell (via Dostoyevsky) in relation to the inability to love (2007, 122). With regard to Angel's return from hell at the beginning of *Buffy* Season 3, they connect Angel's recovery from hell with the necessity to "exercise existential choice" and "to respond to both reason and love." Thus, they conclude that "in one sense [Angel] never really escapes from Hell at all. He dares not consummate his love with [Buffy] again now that he knows the consequences of the gypsy curse" (130). Though I agree with this, I would also contend that, paradoxically, Angel's perpetual love for Buffy keeps him from escaping another sort of hell—the potential of loving Buffy eternally without essential change or movement away from her. As he says to Spike about his relationship with Buffy, "Ours is a forever love" ("The Girl in Question").

Gunn articulates Angel's problem back in "Heartthrob" when he tells Cordelia, "The 'B' word was the love of his life. And he's what, 250? That ain't no short life" (*Angel* 3.1). Spike suffers a similar immortal-love dilemma. In "Touched," he tells Buffy, "I've been alive a bit longer than you. And dead a lot longer than that. . . . A hundred-plus years. And there's only one thing I've ever been sure of. You" (*Buffy* 7.20). In "The Girl in Question," their continual attempts to reach Buffy illustrate that both Angel and Spike (despite pretenses of moving on) are, in some sense, still waiting for her. As Angel laments, "[Buffy's] not finished baking yet. I gotta wait 'til she's done baking, you know, 'til she finds herself, 'cause that's the drill. Fine. I'm waiting patiently, and meanwhile, The Immortal's eating cookie dough!" Esslin in his discussion of the absurd says, "The subject of [*Waiting for Godot*] is not Godot but waiting, the act of waiting as an essential and characteristic aspect of the human condition. Throughout our lives we always wait for something, and Godot simply represents the objective of our waiting—an event, a thing, a person, death" ([1961] 2004, 50). In the human condition, death will eventually put an end to waiting. In the *vampiric* condition, waiting may be eternal. Thus, the problem for Angel and Spike is not Buffy herself (who, as Andrew tells them, is "moving on"), nor is it their inability emotionally, physically, or sexually to reach her; the problem is their inability to stop attempting to reach her.

This continual pursuit of Buffy in "The Girl in Question" has been discussed by both Stacey Abbott and Lewis Call. Abbott argues that the pursuit "becomes a means for Spike and Angel to preoccupy themselves with their long-standing obsession with each other and to resolve the erotic triangle before the end of the series" (2006, 14).[7] Call argues, moreover, that Buffy's absence permits "the homoerotic relationship between the two male vampires to eclipse their mutual obsession with Buffy" (2007, para. 2). Certainly, I would agree that the episode is about Angel and Spike's relationship, despite Angel's remark to Spike on their way to Rome: "This isn't about us." Spike's request for Angel to get on the motor scooter ("Hop on, little mama") and Angel's response ("I'm not riding on the back") play into the homoeroticism discussed by Call. Likewise, Angelus's reprimand to Darla regarding "concurrent" sex ("You never let us do that") arguably implies a desire for group sex, perhaps a foursome. Nonetheless, I do not think the "erotic triangle" or "obsession" with Buffy is necessarily "resolve[d]" or even "eclipse[d]" within this episode. For one thing, in the final scene, Angel and Spike are still discussing Buffy. With regard to her choice of The Immortal, Spike asks, "What's Buffy thinking? Honestly?" Angel and Spike then proceed to hypothesize on how to attain Buffy for themselves. Spike asks, "Can't we just lock her away in a box where no one can ever touch her?" When Angel rejects that idea, Spike suggests, "We could do a spell. Some sort of mind control." His resignation—"So, what? We just have to live with it? Get on with our lives?"—is worded as a series of questions rather than statements, which results in the *lack* of moving on that I discuss above.

Thus, I would argue that their obsession for Buffy is not eclipsed so much as it is exploited to illustrate the dilemma. Their mutual obsession (including the repeated trips to the apartment and dance club in search of Buffy) provides continual impetus for Angel and Spike not only to cooperate but also to enact their ineffective pattern of pursuit. In the jet on the way to Rome, Angel warns Spike, "This is a dangerous mission that's only gonna get worse if we don't put aside our differences. Look, we have to work together on this to stop The Immortal and save Buffy. Oh, and pick up that demon body thingy." The actual mission is last on the list. In response to Angel's proposition, Spike suggests, "Partners, then?" Angel responds, "Just like old times." Herein lies an aspect of the problem—*just like old times*. The episode's flashbacks make it clear that obsession by Angel and Spike (in the past for Darla and Drusilla, rather than for Buffy, in relation to The Immortal) can last indefinitely.

7. This quotation is from the conference version of Abbott's paper rather than the revised version published later as chapter 4 of her book *Angel* (2009a). For the chapter, Abbott removed the section on "The Girl in Question."

This obsession is evident much earlier in the series. For example, back in Season 2, in regard to Angel's questionable decisions, Cordelia says to Gunn and Wesley, "It's all about Darla. One thing you can say about Angel— at least he's consistent. It's always some little blonde driving him over the edge" ("Redefinition" 2.11). In the same episode, Wesley confirms, "Angel is obsessed with Darla." Similarly, during flashbacks in another episode, Spike avows that Drusilla is part of his destiny, confidently asserting, "We're forever, Drusilla and me" ("Destiny" 5.8). In "The Girl in Question," though the love interest shifts between Darla and Buffy for Angel (and between Drusilla and Buffy for Spike), The Immortal's involvement in both the past and the present situations ensures that the potentially eternal, obsessive pattern is highlighted. Back in the scene on the jet, having consumed several miniature bottles of alcohol, Angel complains, "Really can't get drunk off these things." Spike responds, "Not us, anyway. Vampire constitution. Not always a plus." Thus, before they even reach Rome, their bond as vampires and their mutual understanding of problems associated with the "vampire constitution" have been established. Amid the ongoing futile and repeatedly failed quests to reach Buffy, Angel and Spike support one another *because* each understands what the other is facing *eternally*. As Gordon contends regarding Vladimir and Estragon in *Waiting for Godot*, "The overarching imperative in their relationship is that each distract the other from despair over the human condition" (2003, 179)—or, in this case, over the vampiric condition that makes possible eternal despair.

Of course, Angel and Spike are both pursuing Buffy and simultaneously and continually blaming The Immortal for their inability to reunite with her. In one of the club scenes, having learned that Buffy and The Immortal have already left, Angel says, "He's got her, Spike. He's got Buffy. Why is this always happening to us?" Spike answers, "It's him. The Immortal. This is what he does every time he shows up—I either lose my girl, get beaten by an angry mob, or get thrown in prison for tax evasion." In response to Spike's outburst, Angel responds, "It's different now. We're different." But this very scene shows that they are no different now in relation to Buffy and The Immortal than they were years ago in relation to Darla, Drusilla, and The Immortal. Near the beginning of the episode, Spike defines The Immortal as "the foulest evil hell ever vomited forth." Later in the episode, Angelus (when speaking with Darla) calls The Immortal "my arch-nemesis." In the episode's final scene, when Angel learns that The Immortal has helped them by returning the head to Los Angeles, he announces to Spike, "I really hate that guy." In other words, within the course of the episode, both in the present and in the past, nothing changes in terms of their attitude. The perpetual focus on The Immortal as the cause of their problems arguably represents a form of Sartrean "bad faith." As Peter Ashworth explains, bad faith occurs "in refusing responsibility for a choice by denying having made it. To deny responsibility for the meanings inevitably imposed on the situation is bad faith" (2000, 113). In "The Girl in Question," Angel and Spike repeatedly exercise bad faith by casting blame outward toward an Other and denying responsibility for both their choices and their current circumstances.

The 1894 prison scene, in which Angelus and William are chained to the ceiling in The Immortal's "room of pain," provides a graphic illustration of their static predicament. Rather than take responsibility for the choices that led to being imprisoned, they continue to place blame on a notably absent Other. William says, "That right bastard." Angelus complains, "The Immortal thinks he can do this to us?" William then threatens immortality itself, swearing, "We'll see just how immortal he is when we're done with him." Literally and figuratively, they do not free *themselves* from this prison; instead, The Immortal sends someone to release them. At this point, Angelus assumes that The Immortal's servant is about to kill them and states, "Ferry us to hell, then." Yet they are not killed or sent to hell. Instead, they are provided an exit (so to speak) when The Immortal's servant advises them to "leave this city tonight"; however, rather than leave, Angelus and William choose to continue their pursuit of The Immortal, thereby perpetuating their struggle with him. Thus, like the characters in *No Exit*, when the "door flies open," they shut it (Sartre [1947] 1989, 41). Estelle, Inez, and Garcin, explains M. John Carol Blitgen, "find themselves in a fictional hell with their essences crystallized" (1967, 61). Angel and Spike are in danger of having their essences crystallized if they cannot exit their ineffective pattern of perpetual blame; as Vladimir posits in *Waiting for Godot*, "Habit is a great deadener" (Beckett 1954, 105).

Equally ineffective is their pattern of threatened but unsuccessful vengeance on The Immortal. At the end of the prison scene, Angelus vows, "There's gonna be a reckoning"; he then immediately adds a condition: "after a good meal and a long rest." Angelus, like Angel in the opening scene of "The Girl in Question," *waits* rather than acts. The scene immediately shifts to the bedroom, where Angelus and William discover that The Immortal has had sex with Darla and Drusilla. In regard to her new lover, Darla asks the men, "Have you seen him? With the eyes and the chest and the—immortality." William immediately insists, "We're immortal," to which Darla responds, "Not like him. I mean, he's not some common vampire. He's—I don't know what he is. A giant. A titan straddling good and evil, serving no master but his own considerable desires." The Immortal chooses freely and acts effectively. This quality is a primary difference (in this episode) between Angelus and William (who are imprisoned and ineffectual) and The Immortal (who is free and effectual): in cookie-dough terminology, they're waiting and he's eating.

After Darla and Drusilla leave the room, Angelus says to William, "This is a slight that will not go unmet. . . . I think it's time for blood vengeance." The scene then immediately cuts to Angelus and William attempting to enter a party hosted by The Immortal—we see Angelus asking, to no avail, whether "blood vengeance" is on The Immortal's guest list. Unsuccessful at gaining entrance to the party, Angelus declares, "He mocks us at every turn," and yells toward his absent nemesis, "This isn't over yet, Immortal! This'll never be over!" Once again, the issue here is "never"—the problem is not The Immortal; it is immortality. If Angelus and William had chosen to move on back in the day, Angel and Spike would not be in their current predicament of repeating the same task eternally. "Hell," according to Blitgen's analysis of *No Exit*, "is the failure to recognize the value of free personal choice and to live those choices out" (1967, 63). Angel and Spike fail to recognize that they have a choice to repeat (eternally) or to end (finally) the attempts at vengeance on The Immortal.

Notably, Angel and Spike fail not only to recognize their own free choice but also to respect the choices being made freely by others. Initially, in the 1894 bedroom scene, Angelus and William assume that The Immortal had forced himself upon Darla; however, Darla quickly makes her role in their relationship clear. Thus, when Angelus asks whether The Immortal hurt her, she responds, "Not until I asked him to." Darla thereby recognizes and, indeed, revels in her personal choice. Angelus and William, however, are unwilling to accept that their women *chose* to have sex—or "really great fornication," as Darla describes it. Indeed, even after hearing about the pleasure enjoyed by both Darla and Drusilla, Angelus and William repeatedly use the word *violate* to describe The Immortal's actions toward the women. Laura Diehl calls the men "sexually spiteful" in this scene, noting that William initially "taunts Angelus for being cuckolded by Darla, but he stops dead in his tracks when he sees Drusilla walk out" (2004, para. 44). The word *cuckold* in this scene is a blow to their reputations as virile vampires, capable of satisfying their women. Their reaction to Buffy's relationship with The Immortal is similar. Though Andrew informs them that Buffy and The Immortal "snuggle"—certainly a word free from association with "violate"—Angel and Spike insist that Buffy did not have a choice in the matter. Spike says, "She's under some kind of spell," and Angel replies, "I was just thinking that."

Moreover, though cuckolding is no longer at issue, their reputation is nonetheless insulted during the head-in-exchange-for-money scene, when the Demon Butler taunts, "You must be so lonely. Your girlfriend has become lovers with The Immortal. How unfortunate for you. And how fortunate for her." Perhaps Angel and Spike are unable to respect the choices freely made by the women and, simultaneously, are unwilling to choose to let go of the quest for vengeance because their immortal reputations are at stake. They care what others think of them, regardless of the significance of the relationship; thus, they care about the reactions not only of Buffy, Darla, and Drusilla, but also of Andrew, the Demon Butler, and even the unmet Immortal. In her discussion of *No Exit*, Gordon accuses the lead characters of "the most venal sin in the Sartrean universe"—that is, "the compulsion to define themselves and seek validation through the eyes of Others" (2003, 167). As Garcin famously utters near the end of *No Exit*, "Hell is—other people!" (Sartre [1947] 1989, 45). And as Sartre himself explains in regard to Garcin's words, "There are a vast number of people in the world who are in hell because they are too dependent on the judgment of other people" (1976, 199).

Specific elements of the dialogue in "The Girl in Question" also accentuate the repetitive hell faced by Angel and Spike. As an initial excuse to refuse the Italian mission, Spike says, "I don't even speak the language," to which Angel replies, "We'll get you a book." Shortly thereafter, when Spike shows enthusiasm for the trip (thanks to Buffy), Angel reminds him, "You don't speak the language," to which Spike replies, "I'll get a book." The repetition of these phrases works both as a rhetorical reflection of the repetitive patterns in the episode and as a gesture toward the general *lack* of effective communication with the Italians. Playing with language and, in particular, with the "disintegration of language" is typical of absurd theater (Esslin [1961] 2004, 86). Esslin, in his discussion of Beckett, explains, "In a purposeless world that has lost its ultimate objectives, dialogue, like all action, becomes a mere game to pass the time" (87). Esslin cites "repetition" as one of the "modes of disintegration of language observable in *Waiting for Godot*" (87). In "The Girl in Question," ongoing repetition is particularly notable in the language of the Italians.

Take, for example, Ilona (the chief executive officer of "Wolfram & Hart"), who regularly repeats the same words: "You take my breath away. Ah, I have no breath"; "If you want the world, we give you the world. We give you two worlds, in fact, because this is our way"; "Your problems, they are no more. You have no more problems. What are your problems?" Her declaration regarding gypsies—"We shall speak of them no more"—is spoken again in her next scene. Similarly, the Demon Butler repeats his words: "You give us the money, we give you the head. You give us the money, we give you the head. The money, the head. The money—." "Yeah. We get it," says Angel. But, in fact, they do not get it. The words, though repeated, have no value in terms of results: that is, Ilona does not give them the world or solve their problems, and the Demon Butler does not give them the head. As Spike says, rather than accomplishing the mission, they "end up" (literally and figuratively) "standin' in the strada holdin' the bag." "Strada," of course, along with "Ciao," appears to constitute the extent of Spike's Italian vocabulary. His first use of "strada" occurs in an argument with Angel regarding the lost head: Spike asks, "You gonna stand here in the strada yelling at me all night?" Angel replies, "Did you just say *strada*?" Spike informs him, "It means *street*." And Angel says, "Yeah. I know what it means." They may know what the Italian *word* means, but they do not understand the significance of their Italian journey, even when it is reflected in the language of the Italians. Not until Ilona literally closes the doors of the Italian branch of Wolfram & Hart against them does Angel announce, "We make our own fate."

In "Angel: The Final Season" (2005), a Season 5 DVD featurette, Alexis Denisof equates working at Wolfram & Hart with "working in hell." Certainly, Wolfram & Hart has been depicted as impossible to escape—as with the "in perpetuity" clause of Lilah's contract (which ties her to Wolfram & Hart even after death) or Spike's initial inability (existing as an intangible specter in early Season 5) to venture far from the offices without being mystically retrieved.[8] In "Just Rewards," when Wesley hypothesizes that Spike is the property of Wolfram & Hart, Spike asks, "So what, I'm just stuck here forever?" and then says to Angel, "I bet you're loving this, aren't you?" (5.2). Angel sarcastically replies, "Knowing you'll be haunting me till the end of time. Mmm. It's a dream come true." Though Spike's later recovery of a corporeal state gives him the option to leave physically, he (like Angel) remains on the job. Thus, Angel and Spike may indeed be "stuck here forever" together unless one or both of them chooses to leave—not just geographically, but in a way that will break all connections with Wolfram & Hart.

The mirror-image set for the Rome offices in "The Girl in Question" graphically depicts this problem—a geographical move is not a viable option for escape. No matter where they go physically, their connection with Wolfram & Hart remains the same. Sartre, speaking about *No Exit*, says, "I wanted to

8. Regarding Lilah, see "Home" (4.22); regarding Spike, see "Just Rewards" (5.2).

show by way of the absurd the importance freedom has for us, that is, the importance of changing our actions by acting differently. No matter what circle of Hell we're living in, I think we're free to break out of it. And if people don't break out of it . . . they condemn themselves freely to hell" (Contat and Rybalka 1974, 99, sec. 65/48). Escape from the hell of Wolfram & Hart is indeed what Angel and Spike choose in the series finale, despite the seemingly insurmountable obstacles facing them. "You cannot beat me," claims Hamilton, during his final battle with Angel. "I am part of them. The Wolf, Ram and Hart. . . . My blood is filled with their ancient power" ("Not Fade Away"). Here language does hold value: Angel replies, "Can you pick out the one word there you probably shouldn't have said?" He then acts immediately to drink the power from Hamilton's veins. "You don't stand a chance," retorts Hamilton. "We are legion. We are forever." Angel kills him, saying, "I guess forever just got a hell of a lot shorter." Angel has chosen to change and to effect a change. Immortality is no longer his dilemma.

The radical change enacted in "Power Play" and "Not Fade Away" provides a solution to the stasis represented in "The Girl in Question." Near the beginning of "Power Play," we see Nina and Angel in bed having an obviously postcoital conversation. Nina asks Angel whether he is thinking about his "little Roman friend" (that is, Buffy), and Angel confirms he is not. Thus, this scene, like others in the final two episodes, suggests that Angel has moved on from "the girl in question." The contrast in Angel's attitude is emphasized through effective episode placement—the seemingly pointless antepenultimate episode is readily juxtaposed with the purposeful final two. As Stacey Abbott has said in regard to *Angel*, "It is through the series' expression of the motifs of the non-heroic hero, choice, meaninglessness, purposelessness and the absurd . . . that the series explores more fully the complexity of the vampire with a soul and places Angel on the path to an existential realization" (2003, para. 9). "The Girl in Question," with its nonheroic heroes, its meaningless plot, and its absurdity, emphasizes the importance of choice as a means of transforming the self, of escaping one's personal, oft-repeated hell. As Angel asserts near the end of "Power Play," "The powerful control everything except our will to choose."

Hollis Cate, in "The Final Line of Sartre's *No Exit*," contends that the words "Well, well, let's get on with it" "become a weighty final projection . . . for the theater audience. . . . [T]hey, too, are to 'get on with it' in the midst of existential confrontations from which there is no exit" (1972, 9). Thomas Whitaker, in a chapter titled "Playing Hell: Sartre, Beckett, Genet, and Pinter" makes a similar comment, saying that we as audience must "admit that precisely when Garcin says, 'Well, well, let's get on with it,' the curtains must close upon this hell" (1999, 116). Similarly, "The Girl in Question" draws its audience of devoted fans toward the closing of the curtain on this television series. As Spike says, "We just have to live with it. . . . Get on with our lives." On May 6, 2004, MindPieces posts to *Whedonesque*, "This just may be one of my favorite Angel episodes of all time"; Rob calls it "a comedic masterpiece"; and [P]iranesi says, "It's like a Marvel Comic written by Beckett." But perhaps [C]actusflower says it best in this post to *Television without Pity*: "Dude. I don't get the hate. I thought the ep was a gay romp. . . . And hail to thee oh shirtless Spike. I will miss you." Not to worry, [C]actusflower, shirtless Spike, along with shirtless Angel, has reappeared in a "simple modulation of [the] form" available at your local comic store ("The Girl in Question").[9] Of course, in *Angel: After the Fall*, the entire gang is literally stuck in hell—but that is a topic for another time. For now, let's move on, let's get on with it, or, to take Angel's advice, "Let's go to work" ("Not Fade Away").

9. Illyria speaks the quoted words in "The Girl in Question." Shirtless Spike is featured in the comic *Angel: After the Fall* (published by IDW).

Part Three

Firefly
and
Serenity

Firefly and Serenity

An Introduction

TANYA R. COCHRAN

The television series *Firefly* ran in the United States on the Fox Network from September 20 to December 20, 2002. Executive produced by Joss Whedon and Tim Minear, the series comprises one season of fourteen episodes, three of which were not aired during the series' original broadcast on television and all of which were aired out of intended order. For this and other reasons, *Firefly* was canceled by Fox in December 2002. As with *Buffy* (1997–2003) and *Angel* (1999–2004), *Firefly* was produced by Whedon's company Mutant Enemy. Writers included Cheryl Cain, Ben Edlund, Jane Espenson, Drew Z. Greenberg, Brett Matthews, and José Molina—some of whom were alums from Whedon's other series. Other notable staffers were editor Lisa Lassek, cinematographer David Boyd, production designer Carey Meyer, composer Greg Edmonson, and costume designer Shawna Trpcic. A year after its cancellation, on December 9, 2003, the complete series was released on Region 1 DVD. Based on a considerable number of DVD sales and much fan activism, Universal Pictures chose to back the feature film *Serenity*, which was released on September 30, 2005, as a reiteration and extension of the series. Both the television show and the movie swiftly achieved and maintain today a cult status among devotees, or Browncoats.

On the surface, *Firefly* appears to be a departure from Whedon's previous work on *Buffy* and *Angel*. Most notably, there are no supernatural monsters— no vampires, no demons, no hell gods—in this narrative universe, one set in 2517 on the frontier of space. "Earth-that-was" became overpopulated and, understandably, depleted of the resources needed to sustain all of its inhabitants. As a result, many people migrated to a new star system where planets with many moons could be terraformed, or manipulated to accommodate human life. In this new star system, the government, called the Alliance, represents the amalgamation of the last dominant powers on Earth: the United States and China. However, it has not maintained its power peaceably. When the story begins, the audience learns that the Alliance has recently been engaged in a civil war, one central to the plot of the series and the characters who populate it.

If watched in intended order, "Serenity" (1.1–2) introduces Sergeant Malcolm "Mal" Reynolds (Nathan Fillion) amid a heavy gunfight in Serenity Valley, a position he and his comrades, the Independents, are attempting to hold against Alliance troops. Reynolds is flanked by Corporal Zoe Alleyne (Gina Torres) and a group of soldiers, one of them a visibly traumatized, obviously inexperienced young man. Key to the narrative arc of the series and motion picture is Mal's faith—and his loss of it. Though Mal kisses the cross hanging from a chain around his neck and looks confidently to the sky, reinforcements do not come. Soldiers continue to fall, including the fledgling soldier under Mal's charge. The Independents (or Browncoats—so named for their long russet military jackets) surrender. These moments profoundly mark Mal.

The next scene, according to the title at the bottom of the screen, occurs six years later. Mal floats into view from the top of the screen—upside down. The symbolism is obvious: Mal's world has been altered, 180 degrees altered. Still flanked by Zoe, who is now married to spaceship *Serenity*'s pilot, Hoban "Wash" Washburne (Alan Tudyk), the two scavenge a derelict ship with the help of additional crew member and "muscle" Jayne Cobb (Adam Baldwin). Before long, viewers also meet Kaywinnet Lee "Kaylee" Frye (Jewel Staite), the ship's mechanic, and Inara Serra (Morena Baccarin), a Guild-trained and Alliance-licensed Companion, or elite courtesan, who rents a small shuttle attached to the ship that she uses for business affairs.

Serenity is an outmoded transport vessel, and like *Serenity*, her crew members are ragtag vagabonds; they create a chosen family in her womb-like belly. To subsist, they plunder not unlike pirates yet live by a code not unlike Robin Hood. In addition to their black-market ways, they also hire themselves out as stellar taxi drivers, taking on and letting off passengers as needed. This transportation service allows the other central characters a way onto *Serenity* and into the story line. On the planet Persephone, the audience first meets Shepherd Derrial Book (Ron Glass) and Dr. Simon Tam (Sean Maher), passengers assumed to need only a one-way ride to their next destination ("Serenity" 1.1–2). As it turns out, though, both have quite a few secrets. One of those secrets, the contents of a large box Dr. Tam brings aboard the ship, is soon discovered: his sister, River Tam, who initially appears on-screen naked, coiled in fetal position, and sleeping (apparently a chemically induced sleep) inside the shipping container.

Much of what drives the entire series and the film arc involves this brother and sister. Mal and his crew must hurriedly decide if they will harbor the fugitives. Will they aid and abet Simon in his efforts to protect his sister from what he describes as medical experiments turned abuse conducted by the Alliance on the gifted and now disturbed River? Or will they put out the siblings and the trouble they represent—abandon them? Because Mal's code will not allow him to leave the two behind, the motley crew must now stay on the run for more reasons than ever before, some of them deadly. While watching the crew stay just ahead of—most of the time—their many foes, the audience gets to revel in spaceship chases, attempted witch burnings, drug smuggling, sword fights, and plenty of sexual tension, especially between Mal and Inara.

Though *Firefly* has villains—Badger (Mark Sheppard), Adelei Niska (Michael Fairman), "Saffron" (Christina Hendricks), "The Hands of Blue" (Dennis Cockrum and Jeff Ricketts), and, most disturbing of all, Jubal Early (Richard Brooks)—as well as a meddlesome government, the ultimate "baddies" of the television series are the Reavers. Though the Alliance denies their existence, settlers on the outer planets know they exist and believe them to be humans who have simply been radically changed for the worse by the vast blackness of space. In fact, the Reavers are not understood to be people anymore, as they murder, rape, cannibalize, and use their victims' skins for clothing—and not necessarily in that order, as Zoe insinuates ("Bushwhacked" 1.3). The motion picture *Serenity* gradually explains why Jubal Early pursued River in "Objects in Space" (1.14) and why the Operative (Chiwetel Ejiofor) now pursues her in the film: River's brain—though no one knows it at first, not even River—possesses the answer to the question of the Reavers' origin. In the end, it comes to light that Reavers are, like River, the product of Alliance experimentation, experiments born of "good" intentions gone bad—very bad. Once Mal and crew discover the truth, they vow to share it with as many people as will listen—which they do with the help of the super-tech-savvy anarchist Mr. Universe (David Krumholz)—even if it means dying for their cause.

As mentioned above, on the surface *Firefly* and *Serenity* appear to be a departure from Whedon's work on *Buffy* and *Angel*. But that assumption could not be more mistaken. Whedon has always been interested in heroism, responsibility, consequences, teamwork, emotional resonance, and generic hybridity. The core themes and creative goals that infuse his Sunnydale and Los Angeles occupy his outer space. It is not surprising, then, that *Firefly* had from the outset an active and ardent fan following that was already familiar with Whedon's storytelling. However, in addition to the lack of fantasy elements, what distinguishes *Firefly* and *Serenity* is their message, one read by many audience members as overtly libertarian. As a result, the series and film also found a new fan base, a politically active one at that. For these and other reasons, both visual texts have also attracted the attention of cultural critics and scholars. For example, I. B. Tauris has published the anthology *Investigating "Firefly" and "Serenity": Science Fiction on the Frontier* (Wilcox and Cochran 2008b). Also, a special issue of the journal *Slayage* devoted to the two works was released just prior to the collection's printing. Conference presentations and essays in both journals and collections continue to appear.

Firefly represents for Whedon his third television-crafting venture. It died all too soon only to be resurrected in film as well as (like *Buffy* and *Angel*) comic book form. Though it had a short run on television and has had a limited narrative afterlife, it remains a "shiny" series with a fiercely loyal fandom.

Firefly

Of Formats, Franchises, and Fox

MATTHEW PATEMAN

In 2003, Joss Whedon was interviewed by Michael Patrick Sullivan. In response to a question about networks, Whedon's plaintive reply was, "My only hope is that one day, I'll understand what it is the networks want" (Whedon 2003a). This desire to "understand" came a few months after the cancellation by Fox of *Firefly*, his science fiction western. It may seem curious that an executive producer of the stature and reputation of Whedon would be unable to understand the requirements of a network, and one would have to take the customary pinch of salt with Whedon's quotation, but there is a sense in which his unknowingness is perfectly understandable. In many ways, networks do *not* know what they want themselves, or, rather, they know exactly what they want but are not able to say how to achieve it. They want a format that will gain high ratings, develop into a franchise, and make a lot of money. A pilot is the first expression of that format and as such has to set up the series in a way that the network believes will entice viewers not only to watch this episode, but to return to watch the next episode as well. The job of the executive producer is to create this format, this franchise through the vehicle of the pilot: a conceptually easy schematization that is viciously difficult to produce.

The purpose of this chapter, then, is threefold. First, it seeks to provide a history that makes sense of what Fox may have desired from Whedon regarding *Firefly*. This chronicle includes a short diversion into the aspects of Fox's history, as they pertain to the eventual decision to air *Firefly*, as well as a brief summary of Whedon's contribution to this network history owing to his involvement with both the WB and UPN. In this discussion, I assert the centrality of *Buffy* to any later discussion of *Firefly* in the context of the next two parts of the chapter. *Firefly* needed to be a successful franchise. Fox understandably desired to replicate the success of *The X-Files* (1993–2002) by building on Whedon's success with the *Buffy* franchise. Whedon's job, then, was to produce a show that would have the same impact and franchise possibilities as *Buffy*. For this success to happen, the show had to have a successful format. The final part of the chapter will be a discussion of the idea of format, especially in its manifestation as a pilot of a show. The term *format* is perhaps best understood in television criticism in terms of adaptation study, where the ability to make a version in one country of a show from another country relies upon the ability to "translate" the format from one set of supposed national characteristics to another.[1] It is also a word that is understood in industry terms and allows for a more specific examination of a show than, for example, "genre" might. Graeme Turner's conception of format having a much greater valence in the industry itself than does genre will be helpful in identifying how *Firefly* sought to situate itself not just as a show, but as a franchise: "Formats can be original and thus copyright [*sic*], franchised under license, and traded as a commercial property. Genres, by definition, are not original. Format is a production category with relatively rigid boundaries that are difficult to transgress without coming up with a new format" (2005, 6–7). Given the relatively new use of the term in critical analysis, it may be helpful to provide a brief definition of how I am using it here, which will be elaborated upon as the chapter progresses. Format is determined by the fusion and interaction among a number of intersecting components—which include, but cannot be reduced to, place(s), time(s), genre(s), mise-en-scène, character(s), and plot(s).

The importance of the pilot in establishing the format is clear, and the dissatisfaction of the Fox executives with the pilot offered by Whedon and the subsequent writing of a new pilot by Whedon and Tim Minear (co–executive producer on *Firefly*) illustrate this importance well. A discussion of the opening sections of each of the pilots will, therefore, be the final part of the chapter.

Whedon and the Networks: A Very Brief History

Long before the premiere of the rewritten pilot for *Firefly*, Whedon had been working with Fox, but whereas the production arm of Fox had been collaborators with Whedon since *Buffy* (with Fox owning *Buffy*), the network itself

---

1. See, for example, Beeden and de Bruin 2010 regarding *The Office*. Other examples might include the ABC version of *Life on Mars* (2008–9), a format translation of the BBC show of the same name (2006–7), or the Fox-produced and AMC-aired version of *The Killing* (2011), a format translation of the Danish *Fobrydelsen* (2007–11).

had been less enthusiastic to promote Whedon's work. There had been an opportunity for Fox to schedule *Buffy* after the WB declined its option on the show at the end of its fifth year, and in itself the disputes surrounding this moment in Whedon's pre-*Firefly* career are instructive in terms of the tensions that exist between networks and producers.

In the spring of 2001, Fox productions said it was increasing the licensing fee for *Buffy*. The effect of this increase is that the WB (which was broadcasting *Buffy*) would have to pay significantly more to Fox for each episode it aired. Fox's decision was not surprising. As Lynette Rice (2001) reported at the time: "It's not like the studio expected to make money before now. Producers routinely lose millions in a show's first five years—and that's assuming there is a first five. Up until then, the network pays a nominal licensing fee—anywhere between $900,000 and $1.1 million for a drama—and the studio swallows the deficit. (The WB currently pays $1 million to air an episode of [*Buffy*], less than half of what it costs to make.)" However, Jamie Kellner, the WB founder and then soon-to-be chief executive officer of Turner Broadcasting, felt a different kind of financial model should be offered to new and emerging networks. Kellner was prepared to offer $1.6 million per episode, but the Fox studio was insisting on more than $2 million. Not only, though, did Kellner feel that different business models should be available for the WB, but he was also critical of the value of *Buffy* itself. He made the point that "it's not our No. 1 show. . . . It's not a show like *ER* that stands above the pack." He continued his defense of refusing to pay the renewal fee by saying that *Buffy* was failing to bring in the WB's desired demographic (quoted in Rice 2001). Not surprisingly, Whedon was unimpressed by his own network's lack of enthusiasm for the show that "put the WB on the map critically." He said, "For [the WB] to be scrambling to explain why it's not cost efficient—it's their second highest rated show. . . . They need to step up and acknowledge that financially" (quoted in Rice 2001).

The major concern for analysts was not simply that licenses become more expensive after a fifth season, but that in this instance, there was a sense of "self-dealing." Given *Buffy*'s Nielsen ratings, there was little chance that ABC, CBS, or NBC would seriously consider buying the show (even though rumors did suggest some interest, especially from ABC). *Buffy*'s very best Nielsen rating was 5.2 for the episode "Innocence" (2.14), which was the very heavily promoted lead-in to the WB's new Tuesday. It was more usually in the high 3.0 or low 4.0 category. For the sake of comparison, *The West Wing* routinely scored more than 11.0. *Buffy*'s relatively low score meant that the only networks likely to bid would be UPN or Fox itself. The idea that the company that owned the production could then pull the show and put it on its own network provoked consternation in some quarters, and the battle lines for an industry-shaking argument were being drawn.

In any event, concerns regarding self-dealing proved unfounded in terms of Fox Television buying the show, as UPN, to the surprise of many, bid substantially more than the WB was willing to and acquired the show. With *Buffy* and *Angel* still being aired on UPN and the WB, respectively, it would be *Firefly* that would be Whedon's first foray into the world of the major networks. And Friday night on Fox was to be his challenge.

Friday Night on Fox: A Difficult Fit

Television companies need to make a profit; indeed, it is fair to say that the primary aim of such a company is to make a profit, and the output is simply the mechanism that enables that outcome. This desire for profit does not preclude high-quality television, and there is no inevitable conflict between profit and aesthetic interest. Indeed, Peter S. Grant and Chris Wood very clearly state, "Lavishly financed series like *West Wing*, *CSI* and *The Agency* have sharply raised the standard of production values by which audiences judge television drama. Broadcasters everywhere have reacted by scheduling fewer, albeit more expensive such shows, and filling the air with cheap but popular 'reality TV' fare" (2004, 235). Networks realize the marketing value of a high-quality format and its associated franchise, but to afford it, less expensive forms of television are required to take up the slack. The decision as to what will and what will not be produced will be every bit as much driven by the market analysts as by any sort of aesthetic criteria. Indeed, the analysts' role is to determine the best match between aesthetics, markets, scheduling slots, and franchise potential in order for them then to "have a voice in determining the kinds of programmes made by identifying demographics in particular scheduling slots at which the company overall is aiming" (Nelson 2007, 63).

Fox, in many ways, had been at the forefront of the growth of quality TV and its "reality" financing as well as the targeted notion of market segmentation. Whereas the high-performing and relatively cheap-to-produce reality show *America's Most Wanted* (1988–2011) managed to be Fox's longest-running show in any format, the critically acclaimed Golden Globe–winning *Party of Five* (1994–2000) struggled to be renewed each year and rarely achieved high viewing figures. It could be argued that there is a mutual cross-subsidization at play here: *America's Most Wanted* supports the financial cost of *Party of Five*, while the latter affords the network the cultural capital of award-winning drama. There is much to be said on this subject, but for the purposes of *Firefly*, the important questions relate to Fox's desire to reproduce *The X-Files* phenomenon, the slot into which the show was destined, and the nature of Fox's sports franchises.

Fox had seen enough of Whedon's work and his dedicated fan base to believe that Whedon was the man to re-create the Friday-night 9:00 p.m. hit that had eluded them since *The X-Files*. *The X-Files* itself had suffered at the hands of Fox in its very early days. Peter Roth, who worked with Chris Carter to develop Carter's initial idea into a viable series, explains, "It almost didn't get greenlit as a pilot. It almost didn't get greenlit as a series. It was perceived to be too myopic and singular and not commercial" (quoted in Kimmel 2004, 214). The eventual success of the show, and Fox's desire to recapture the audience that it had seen disappear with its demise, laid the foundation for a number of attempts to mine the same televisual gold. It was not only the ratings that Fox sought, but also the *franchise*. *The X-Files* had been its first franchise, and the ancillary markets had provided huge revenue boosts. *Buffy* and *Angel* were successful franchises, and it was hoped that Whedon would produce another. Chris Carter himself had had two failed attempts: *Millennium* first aired in October 1996, in the midst of *The X-Files'* success. It achieved three seasons but never pulled in the ratings that *The X-Files* had. *Millennium* (1996–99) was replaced by another Carter program, *Harsh Realm* (1999–2000). Only nine episodes were filmed, and not all of them were shown. The pattern had been set that would lead directly to *Firefly*'s demise.

Another effort to fill the vacated *X-Files* slot was *Brimstone* (1998). An ex-cop sent to hell for killing his wife's rapists is given a deal by Satan: if he tracks down and returns 113 evil souls who have escaped from hell, he will be released. Beset by problems from the beginning, executive producer Michael Chernuchin walked off the project before it had even aired. In addition to these internal difficulties, Fox now had to contend with ABC, NBC, and CBS as well as with the new WB and UPN channels, which had learned Fox's lessons well (the WB being set up and run by ex-Fox executives Jamie Kellner and Garth Ancier). *Brimstone* fared badly against a new WB hit, J. J. Abrams's *Felicity* (1998–2002). Again, *Firefly* was destined to have a hard time.

The difficulty faced by *Firefly* was caused to a certain extent by a decision made nearly a decade earlier, in the same year that *The X-Files* came to the television screen. In that year (1993), Fox became a genuine player in the US networks by bidding $1.6 billion for the rights to broadcast NFL football. Having ousted CBS from its position as the football network (and in the process demolishing CBS's Sunday prime-time strategy), Fox had shown it was capable of being a serious sports and outside broadcaster. Three years later, it acquired rights to Major League Baseball, including the important postseason and its divisional playoffs and the World Series. The postseason takes place in September and October and brings in enormous numbers of new viewers. A difficulty, however, is that the regular schedule has to be moved around to accommodate the games. *Firefly* began its doomed brief season in the heart of postseason. Keith R. A. DeCandido makes this point and observes that "a big chunk of the advertising for the show was also shown during those games" (2004, 56). However, the demographic for baseball is not necessarily the same demographic to which *Firefly* would be appealing, and a quotation from an unnamed executive discussing the initial deal in 1996 is pertinent here: "You can promote *The Simpsons* all day long, but if you're promoting it to a sixty-year-old male, he's not gonna watch" (quoted in Kimmel 2004, 214).

Whedon's creation, then, was already in a difficult position. Fox had specific objectives for any show in that time slot, which included re-creating the audience figures and the franchise potential of *The X-Files*. Also, this mission had already been attempted by a number of programs that had fared with various degrees of difficulty. In addition, the launch coincided with one of Fox's greatest assets, but an asset that played havoc with regular scheduling and something a new show could barely afford.

A Difficult Format

As if the time-slot history was not fraught with enough problems, the concept of a space western had always struggled on network television. Ginjer Buchanan (2004) in "Who Killed *Firefly*?" offers a history of both science fiction and westerns on US network television and indicates that there had been no successful westerns except *Deadwood* (2004–6) (which, of course, was HBO, not network) in more than twenty years. Although science fiction had fared better in the same period, it was a niche genre with little chance of pulling in the kinds of viewing figures that Fox would have required. As a result, Whedon had a task on his hands. The viewing figures he had achieved with *Buffy* and *Angel* on the WB and UPN were not going to be anywhere near sufficient to suit Fox, and he was choosing a show whose two main generic modes had not had significant televisual success for more than a decade. In some ways, though, the specific generic makeup of the show is unimportant (not entirely unimportant, but not as determining a factor in its future as Buchanan may suggest).

Of more import is the show's format. As mentioned above, format is determined by the fusion and interaction between a number of intersecting components—which include, and cannot be reduced to, place(s), time(s), genre(s), mise-en-scène, character(s), and plot(s). It is clear that in *Buffy*, Whedon had created a format that had extraordinary cultural purchase and a range of ancillary merchandising possibilities to, importantly, a surprisingly broad demographic. Although *Angel* had been less successful in embedding itself in the general discourses of popular culture, it still offered a range of merchandising possibilities (games, comic books, novels, mouse pads, and postcards, to name only a tiny fraction). Whedon, then, needed to duplicate the format success without repeating too closely the format itself.

The most significant change of artistic direction (and, therefore, format creation) is precisely that *Firefly* has no relationship with the mythos of *Buffy*. Although *Angel* had asserted its independence from *Buffy* and had become a show in its own right, it was still clearly located within the ever-expanding narrative world initially produced by *Buffy* (that is, the Buffyverse). *Firefly* was a completely new entity. The strongest difference was that *Firefly* is an entirely human world: there are no vampires, witches, werewolves, vengeance demons, supernatural law firms, or anything that is not human. Indeed, the absence of nonhumans was a cause for worry for some, not necessarily because of the shift away from the imagined landscapes of *Buffy* and *Angel* but because, according Jane Espenson, "a space show without aliens felt like *Buffy* without vampires" (2004b, 1).

Espenson's comment indicates another change in Whedon's creative vision. Rather than fashion a fictional world set in the present in recognizable locations and infuse them with Gothic, noir, and other aspects, in *Firefly* he created a fictional world set in a distant future and infused it with western and other aspects. This movement from present to future, from supernatural and noir to western, was not a complete break with his aesthetic vision, however. In some ways, the use of science fiction and Western was, if not obvious, not surprising as a progression. His work on *Toy Story* (1995) placed him directly in a sci-fi and western milieu (however attenuated and parodied through the characters of spaceman Buzz Lightyear and Woody the cowboy), *Alien Resurrection* (1997) is a very clear expression of his desire for and skill at science fiction writing, and the *Buffy* episode "Listening to Fear" (5.9) trades on science fiction motifs and ideas. In addition, the figure of Adam in Season 4, with his obvious indebtedness to Shelley's science fiction–horror *Frankenstein*; the *Angel* episode "Happy Anniversary" (2.13); and the character of Fred, also in

Angel, all illustrate how much Whedon enjoys engaging with science fiction. Western aspects inhabit the Buffyverse, not only in very obvious ways such as the episode "Pangs" (4.8) or the horse-and-motor-home chase in "Spiral" (5.20), but more generally as part of a range of shared themes such as the outsider, the protection of home, and so on. I do not wish to overstate the extent to which science fiction and the western are already part of Whedon's aesthetic palette, but it is clear that thematically and formally his work until *Firefly* had engaged to some measure with these areas. Also, the generic and stylistic blurring that is an important aspect of *Firefly* is a continuation of one of the most significant artistic attributes of his oeuvre to date.

The Pilot Problem

Whedon's first attempt at producing a pilot that would create the "rigid boundaries" of *Firefly* was not met with enthusiasm by the network, and he and executive producer Tim Minear very quickly wrote and shot a new pilot. It would be an exaggeration to suggest that the new pilot created a new format, but its emphasis certainly drew attention to aspects of the format that were not necessarily as prevalent in the original pilot.

The job of a pilot is to introduce the format to an audience. All of the elements that make up a format are, of course, present in any episode of any series, and they are all subject to revision and change (characters come and go, locations are added or withdrawn, and so on), but the role of the pilot in establishing the audience's first response to the format makes it especially important. However, it should be obvious that a methodological difficulty exists here. Assessing (or even describing) the establishment of a format in a show that has been and gone and whose format is so well known (at least in all likelihood for many of the readers of this book) means that there is a danger of overdetermining a reading of the two pilots based on what came after. As far as possible, I will keep my comments to a "sum-total" version of the pilots.

The place is space. This space is divided between the ships, *Serenity* in particular, and planets. In turn, these distinct spaces can be divided into areas of *Serenity* (engine room, shuttle, for example), and the different planets, which are distinguished by virtue of being inner planets or outer planets. These planets are then further divided by settlement or city and buildings, streets, and such. The time is the distant future after the seeming destruction of Earth and a devastating civil war. Genres are science fiction and western, and within this very bald delineation there are many styles, such as comedy, action, romance, and more. Mise-en-scène is the area of most difference between the two pilots, and I shall discuss an example of each pilot in relation to that point shortly. All the main characters are introduced in both pilots, but the method of their presentation is necessarily different, and this difference in some ways is related to the mise-en-scène. However, the overall effect of the character introductions, especially as they relate to the twin-genre aspect of western and science fiction, can be described schematically.

Captain Malcolm Reynolds is a science fiction structure (spaceship captain) with a western sensibility, one somewhat compromised, according to John C. Wright (2004), by Mal's failure to live up to a certain kind of chivalry by throwing a villainous henchman into the ship's engine in "The Train Job" (1.2). Zoe Washburne operates structurally as both western and sci-fi—the lieutenant figure, second in command. Her husband is Hoban "Wash" Washburne, structurally basically science fiction, being the ship's pilot, though, as Fred Erisman (2006) points out, he can also be seen as stagecoach driver. Kaylee Frye is sci-fi in her role as ship's mechanic. Simon Tam becomes the doctor and functions as both western and sci-fi in this position. Shepherd Book as the spiritual focus also traverses both traditions. Inara Serra as courtesan or whore is more difficult. Her position both as a character and in terms of the ship's spaces is slightly extraneous: her part of the ship is another ship (the shuttle); she is outside the outsiders, socially of a higher rank and generically perhaps the most "western" (as we discover much later in the unaired "Heart of Gold" [1.13]); and she is the most "Eastern" in terms of the show's co-opting of "oriental" cultures. Nikki Stafford (2011) has also suggested that Inara operates in the context of science fiction because she complicates the western "whore" by also being a confidante-type figure much more in keeping with, for example, Deanna Troi from the *Star Trek: The Next Generation* franchise (1987–94). Jayne Cobb as the thug figure could be from almost any action genre. Finally, River Tam, Simon's sister, is a figure of extreme peculiarity, someone who exceeds easy assimilation into a structure because she seems to sit so far outside of it. Part hidden object (of desire?), part frail waif, part lunatic mystic, she exists in excess of the generic codes into which the others fit (however interestingly new, askance, or revised these generic structures may be). These rather static narratological descriptions do not reveal the developing relationships between the characters; in various forms, that topic will be addressed by other authors. For the purposes of this discussion, I want to indicate how the pilot introduced the characters as aspects of genre and to imply how this introduction contributed to the format.

These characters and their generic and plot-related aspects were introduced differently in each of the two pilots. Using slightly different terminology than has been used here, Keith DeCandido is emphatic in his belief that the "world building" work done by a pilot is simply not done well enough by "The Train Job." Indeed, it was done so badly that he says, "The thing that really killed *Firefly* was 'The Train Job'" (2004, 56). He laments the fact that the civil war was not shown to the viewer but was instead "told in a standard bar-fight scene." The presence of Simon and River Tam was, equally, told to us rather than shown, using dialogue described by DeCandido as "awful expository language" (57). Of particular concern for DeCandido, though, is the character Niska, who is the episode's bad guy. The problem is that, as pilot and "world maker" (or format creator), the bad guy in this episode could reasonably be assumed to be representative of bad guys in later episodes. Niska is very much *not* like most of the series' other villains. Whereas future villains would enact a series theme of the separation within normal civil society between the haves and the have-nots, their villainy an expression of greed and exploitation within this context, Niska is "just a brutal sadistic gangster" (58). DeCandido's observations offer a useful entry point into my discussion of the pilots and their relation to the construction of *Firefly*'s format.

The Format of "Serenity"

It is true that the other pilot, "Serenity" (1.1), opens in the middle of the battle that will become a defining feature of Mal's history, and we witness him and Zoe as soldiers and losing. However, because of the decision to open in medias res, we as an audience have little sense of who is fighting or why. The explosions, gunshots, breathless action, and future-looking equipment give us a sense of the format as action and sci-fi, and this notion is reinforced as we move from the battle to (as a title says) "six years later" and a spaceship, where the captain, Zoe, and Jayne are breaking into a stranded vessel and stealing its cargo, while being pursued by a gleaming silver and gray angular (and beautifully unusual-looking) Alliance spaceship. Many of the key format issues surrounding science fiction, action, the Alliance, and the crew's marginal existence are shown to us.

In addition, we are introduced to other important elements of the series, including the color scheme that will dominate, especially the costumes. The soldiers have all been wearing browns, deep reds, russets, and rusts. The space suits we see after the six-year time gap are largely within this color scheme, as are the clothes of the rest of the crew as we discover them, even Kaylee, who is allowed a degree more color in the T-shirt she wears under her neutral-brown overalls. Wash is dressed in browns and oranges, and his warning to Mal after seven minutes (we have not yet had the opening credits) elicits from Mal an expression in Chinese. Kaylee's first line is also in Chinese, yet there is no other context (verbal or visual) to offer a reason for this choice. The color scheme is essential for any format and is clearly introduced here, but there is an odd sense that any costume decision is only ever a supplement to the primary and originary moment of color, which is military. The overinsistence on the military aspect of Zoe's and Mal's previous lives in the color scheme presents an unevenness to the mise-en-scène of "Serenity" that "The Train Job" does not have, as the colors, though linked to their military past, are not completely determined by the past (we first see their outfits within the context of a western, though we come to know these clothes are from their military past). That said, the relative poverty of Mal and the crew, and the more general sense of poverty in the outer planets, provides an obvious reason for the color scheme, as does the fact of the association with earthiness, soil, and the mixture of dust-bowl western (the only hint of the western as a genre in the opening of "Serenity") and a painfully ironic awareness of the lack of mellow fruitfulness that the autumnal palette suggests but does not deliver. In "Serenity," the "gold bars" that it looks as though Mal has stolen from the stricken ship hint at the theme of money and wealth, and the fact that we discover they are food bars is a neat wrapping up of nutrition in money. The dull, tarnished nature of the gold is a further aspect of the overall contribution of color to format. Barbara Maio (2008) has discussed in great depth the potential contribution of the color scheme to assumed ideological positions held by characters and groups in the show and has traced an initial lineage of the colors in *Firefly* from earlier forms of science fiction and western.

An additional aspect of the format—the camera usage in developing the mise-en-scène—is demonstrated in this "Serenity" opening sequence. The combination of blurred shots, refocusing, and jump cuts when showing the battle and *Serenity*'s crew, while choosing much more stable shots for the Alliance, offers a visual cue to distinguish between the "ordered" world of the Alliance and the authority it has and the much more improvised world of Mal and his crew.

Although this analysis focuses specifically on the teaser, two important postteaser elements warrant brief exploration. The opening credits provide visual information about the characters and the actors who will play them and end with the disarmingly gorgeous shot of the spacecraft above a herd of cattle. If we accept that the costumes thus far have offered an attenuated gesture to the western, then this image may itself also suggest the importance of the western in the format. However, it is an aspect that, for the first ten minutes of the first episode, has been largely absent. The key western component of the format has not been present in "Serenity" (and is not really present until the image of bowler-hatted Badger and the more explicit setting of the shoot-out at White Falls). The credits' theme song, by contrast, does serve to insist on the western. As Christopher Neal writes, the "folksy" theme song "evokes a time in American history when governmental control of the individual was diffuse, at best," and the performance history of the folk song as such (no conductor and the "performers work together in a democratic fashion to achieve a shared vision") invites us to see *Firefly* within the codes of a particular western tradition (2008, 192). The problem is that this aspect of the show's format, which is vitally important, has been largely obscured in the first ten minutes. No show can possibly offer all of its format potential in the teaser to its pilot, but in this instance there is a real imbalance toward one area.

An equally important omission is Whedon's stated desire to offer a small sense of the utopian via the emergence of a new culture derived from "America and China . . . the two greatest superpowers on the planet." This culture, which would be achieved "once we went out forward and created new planets" will also result in "everybody who is American speak[ing] Chinese" (195). In addition to everyone speaking Chinese, there was also to be "Chinese writing everywhere. And it's just sort of been incorporated into American culture" (Havens 2003, 135). With the exception of two moments of Chinese expression (Mal's "Ta ma duh" and Kaylee's "Shr ah"), we see no evidence of this "incorporation" in "Serenity." Not until we move into Inara's shuttle do we *see* anything Chinese at all, and even that visual reference is simply a Chinese character on her black lacquer box. In many ways, this is no more an expression of the incorporation of a culture than a Chinese character on a T-shirt, such as the character Oz wore in "Wild at Heart" (*Buffy* 4.6). We do find more effort to visualize this aspect of the format later in the episode, but, as with the western, it has been significantly sidelined in the opening section (which, if it had been a normal-length show, would have accounted for nearly a third of the episode).

The Format of "The Train Job"

"The Train Job," written over a weekend after Fox had declined "Serenity," had the exact same mission: it had to present the format of the show. It may be that DeCandido correctly asserts that the introduction of Simon and River and the representation of Niska were not effective in this "world creation." However, the teaser is incredibly effective at setting up the three most important visual codes: the science fiction (which "Serenity" achieved brilliantly), the western (at which "Serenity" was less successful), and the "Chinese" (which "Serenity" did almost not at all).

The episode opens in a bar. The initial shot is a moment of typical Whedonesque brilliance. A steadicam moves through the bar at knee height. Our first encounter with this new world is, quite literally, childlike. We experience the bar from a position of smallness and unknowing, open to the possibility with which the movement provides us. From this place of partial views, we witness the jumbled, hectic setup of the bar. And immediately we see a hybrid world of many influences, different cultural heritages, people, and objects. We emerge from behind a chair leg and see a belly dancer dressed in red and patrons standing and sitting in muted colors, drinking alcohol, playing cards; a waitress or two move by with white-painted faces and kimono-style dresses; lanterns and birdcages hang from the rafters. This place is undeniably a saloon bar. The setting of the saloon establishes an aspect of the format that can be returned to, thus providing for interepisodic points of confluence and rhythm. Most notably, perhaps, "Shindig" (1.4) will open in a bar and include a fight. The explicit description of the bar as a "saloon" in the preoutline to Espenson's script for the episode makes it an unmistakably western locale.[2] As such, it launches us straight into a canvas of mixed styles and genres: we are in a place and of a time that is not our own and, therefore, likely to be science fiction; we are in a saloon and therefore gesturing toward a western; we are surrounded by cultural debris, the historical bric-a-brac of various cultures with a preponderance of Chinese and American. In seconds, the opening of "The Train Job" has provided us with the formal and visual template for the format.

As the camera moves us in its childlike discovery, we approach a table. The belly dancer puts something in the hand of the person sitting there, and the camera rises to show the person given the paper and two others. Wearing a russet-brown coat, the man nearest us (Mal) faces away. The other two (Zoe and Jayne) wear earthy greens and hints of brown and red. Their attire, in the hybrid saloon, signals the western motif in a way that ties the characters to this specific bar at this specific time, but also draws the show into the histories it was always hoping to. A game of some kind is being played, and drink is being drunk. Off-screen a drunken voice demands silence for a toast. We shift to a medium long shot (beautifully set up through the space next to some beaded curtains, thereby getting the sense of depth so crucial to all of Whedon's

2. I am indebted to Jane Espenson for letting me see the draft scripts for this episode.

shows); we see more of the saloon—the lanterns, the Chinese-looking women, the red colors—and we hear a brief history of the civil war and the victory of the Alliance over the Independents. The scene is economical: it tells the history and locates Mal in that history without us having to see the battle, it offers the chance for the first use of the word *Browncoats*, and, in between, it allows us to hear Mal order a drink in Chinese quite casually, as though Chinese has, indeed, just been incorporated into the more general culture.

Mal being called a "Browncoat" means that the costume (and color scheme) is absolutely related to his martial career but is not dominated by it. In fact, the costume has already been invested with the western before the military aspect is foregrounded. As such, the color palette is open to much more nuance and subtlety because it is not as dramatically overdetermined as it is in "Serenity." The improvisational aspect to Mal mentioned above in terms of camera shots is also an aspect of his character. In "Serenity" we see Mal fail in battle. We also see the show's capacity with humor when he shoots down an aircraft and looks triumphant only to realize it is crashing directly into where he is standing. In "The Train Job," Mal tells an Alliance supporter to say to his face the insult the supporter had mumbled. Apart from us seeing the sympathizer wearing a costume of dirty grays (a color relationship kept up throughout the format), we also see Mal's improvised, tricksy tactics. By having the Alliance-aligned man face him, Mal ensures that the man has not seen Zoe arrive, and she is able to punch him to the ground.

The ensuing fight sees Mal thrown through a window. This moment of pure western is radically recast as a sci-fi and western hybrid by virtue of the window being virtual and flicking back into pretend presence soon after. A similar ploy is used in "Shindig" when the billiard balls in the saloon flicker off. The importance of this visual in terms of format creation is that the science fiction and the western do not sit side by side (as they arguably did in the pilot "Serenity"); instead, they become integral to each other: being thrown through the window signals both sci-fi and western. At that moment, the second pilot brilliantly establishes the format. As the fight moves outside and Zoe, Jayne, and Mal are trapped against the edge of the sandy cliff (western), the ship *Serenity* appears from below and rescues them (sci-fi). Again, the scene is both/and, thereby further cementing in the brief teaser the essential facts of the format's visualization.

It is not just visually, however, that "The Train Job" is successful in the sci-fi, western, and Chinese aspects of the format. Musically, the episode (and therefore the franchise) opens with "vibrant dance music, featuring instruments such as sitar, strummed mandolin-like instruments, varied drums and bells, and folk-sounding flutes" (Neal 2008, 196), thereby fusing West-ern-style folk and Eastern-style dance in a sci-fi context.

Conclusion

Firefly is a great television show. However, its ability to succeed in the ways desired by Fox was always going to be compromised by a range of related but distinct problems. First among these issues, perhaps, was the primary desire that it emulate the success of *The X-Files*, in terms of both ratings and atten-dant merchandising. Whedon's classics on the WB and UPN had nothing like the audience figures of *The X-Files*, and, though superficially similar, Whedon's shows demanded more of their viewers in regards to long-term commitment and complexity of storytelling. It was not clear that Whedon's style of tele-vision writing (long form, story arced, supernatural or science fiction) would fit with a channel that had largely favored, even in its quality output, mainly anthology-style dramas (*The X-Files*) or domestic realism (*Party of Five*).

Additionally, the particular genres that Whedon was choosing to hybrid-ize had not been especially successful on network television in a long time in their own terms: a generic commingling of two relatively unpopular types of show into this new offering with its long-form story arc (the unexplored story of River) was not an obvious ratings winner, even if the simple presence of Whedon provided critical and cultural capital.

The format, then, was a typical piece of bravura creativity from Whedon, but one that was far from guaranteed to bring a large audience. The different focus in each of the two pilots indicates that beyond the generic question, issues of style, story, color, music, and so on had not yet been fully deter-mined, which also will have affected the capacity of viewers to fully engage. Without a fully formed and easily marketable format, the opportunities for franchising are limited, or reduced.

And what of Fox? The initial hire of Whedon was a forward-thinking one. It signaled, apparently, a desire to produce intelligent, complex, subtle shows. However, this creative-commercial desire soon gave way to two other commercial imperatives that seem to have overridden any sense of the ben-efits to be derived from a longer-term involvement with Whedon. The first was a short-termism that is insufficiently ready to allow a show to develop an audience over time. Without being an immediate big hit (that is, ranking high in ratings), *Firefly* was fighting a losing battle, and that battle was short indeed. Sadly for Whedon, he joined Fox at a moment of uncertain output, which can be seen, just for illustration's sake, in light of the slot of Monday night at 9:00 p.m. In the 2002–3 broadcast season, Fox aired a mere two episodes of a drama called *Girls Club* (2002) before axing it, five episodes of the reality show *Mr. Personality* (2003), and six episodes of the Monika Lewinsky–fronted reality offering *Married by America* (2003). Its fortunes were saved by the incredibly successful *Joe Millionaire* (2003), which became the number-two show in its time slot.

In addition to a general malaise, and of particular disappointment for production team and fans alike, one of the most galling aspects of *Firefly*'s cancellation is that its inability to attract large audiences immediately was owing to its launch in the middle of the Major League Baseball postseason. Erratic scheduling was compounded by a complete disregard for the intended broadcast sequence, which meant that any effort to produce a meaningful arc was made impossible.

It is too easy to simply criticize Fox for the failure of *Firefly*, but it is equally unhelpful to assert that it is the "fault" of the show. An intersecting nexus of histories, industrial contexts, financial imperatives, aesthetic choices, and business and sponsorship practices all contributed to the show's early demise. However, a vibrant post-Fox existence as a film, comic books, DVDs, and syndicated television reruns indicates that its strengths were always greater than its presumed weaknesses.

"Wheel Never Stops Turning"

Space and Time in Firefly *and* Serenity

ALYSON R. BUCKMAN

Joss Whedon's *Firefly* (2002) begins with Sergeant Malcolm Reynolds (played by Nathan Fillion) running through a battlefield, dodging bombs and bullets, until he reaches the small cave in which his platoon is quartered ("Serenity" 1.1).[1] The beginning of the film *Serenity* (2005), which continues the saga of *Firefly*, revolves around action as well: from a voice-over discussing the emigration of humans from a depleted Earth, to the escape of River and Simon Tam from a government facility, to the exterior shot of Malcolm Reynolds's ship, *Serenity*, entering the atmosphere of a planet, to the captain himself walking through the interior of *Serenity* (in a beautiful, long tracking shot), motion is emphasized. These active beginnings—indicative of the series and the film—express a central aspect of both texts: movement. Jes Battis notes the "perpetual motion" at the heart of *Firefly* (2008, para. 5). Spatially, temporally, narratively, cinematographically, and generically, movement of one sort or another is a near constant, which reflects the creativity of Whedon's approach and suggests new ways of thinking about both the interaction of space and time and these texts. We move from the advanced, twenty-sixth-century technology of the core planets to the nineteenth-century conditions of the rim,[2] from war story to science fiction to road movie to western, advancing

---

1. In this chapter, I follow the DVD order of episodes, which corresponds to Whedon's planned episode structure. Tim Minear was involved in this series as executive producer. My thanks to Charlotte Stevens, Tamy Burnett, Susan Fanetti, and Samira Nadkarni for their commentary on drafts of this chapter.

2. As Charlotte Stevens (2010) notes, this movement is encapsulated within the first few moments of the voice-over and accompanying images at the beginning of the film *Serenity*: the camera cuts from an image of terraforming to the futuristic and bright chrome buildings

the characterization of both crew and ship as we go; with the cancellation of *Firefly* and the fandom-inspired genesis of the film *Serenity*, we also move from the televisual to the cinematic form. This multilayered motion is presented through a camera that itself is rarely stationary. Such activity is reflective not only of the space in which the object moves but also of the time that such movement takes. It additionally illustrates shifts in characterization—or lack thereof—and whether characters are metaphorically stuck or in motion: that is, whether they are able to move onward from their pasts and to grow.[3] The relationship of the texts to history, including their ideological worldview, is important within this discussion of movement as well. In a nutshell, movement is at the heart of this multilayered and dynamic *Firefly* and *Serenity* 'verse, and it contributes to the richness of the text and characters.

According to Mikhail Bakhtin, genre is an intrinsic part of how both literal movement and figurative movement function. Bakhtin theorizes that genre influences the relationship between time and space within a text and produces certain types of characters. Additionally, it results in a particular ideological worldview. These coalescent elements create a "chronotope," which, literally translated, means "time space" (1982, 84). For instance, in "the adventure novel of ordeal," or classical Greek romance, the hero does not change as he engages with his quests.[4] He is tested and overcomes obstacles, but "nothing changes: the world remains as it was . . . feelings do not change, people do not even age" (91). Conversely, in the "adventure novel of everyday life," transformation is essential. These characters are free to act in surprising and nontraditional ways, and their biographies extend beyond the confines of the story, resulting in untapped potential, as Caryl Emerson argues (1986, 34–35). At the heart of the picaresque novel (a descendant of the adventure novel) exists a rogue or servant on the road, a character reminiscent of Captain Malcolm Reynolds (Mal). In the picaresque, as in *Firefly* and *Serenity*, moments in the protagonists' lives become one with their "actual spatial course or road—that is, with [their] wanderings" (Bakhtin 1982, 120). As the

---

and lush greenery of the core planets (the "beacon of civilization") to the desertlike conditions of the "savage outer planets" (one of which is depicted in the spreading shadow of an Alliance cruiser). The voice-over, we learn, is provided by a teacher giving a lesson.

3. See Ganser, Pühringer, and Rheindorf for more on the simultaneously literal and metaphoric journey within the chronotope of the road, one that bears similarities to space travel (2006, 5–6).

4. I purposely use the masculine gender here, as these Greek heroes were male.

previous point suggests, setting is highly relevant; Gary Saul Morson notes, "The social world defines and shapes from within the possibility of action, the succession of thoughts, and the world of choices" (1986, 14). Time and place are meaningful in a way that they are not in the epic, Bakhtin argues: "Time, as it were, *thickens* and takes on flesh, becomes artistically visible; likewise, space becomes charged and responsive to the movements of time, plot and history" (1982, 84; emphasis added). The chronotope, then, generates not only the events of the text but also its symbolism (Best 1994, 292–93). The symbols used are intimately connected to both the genre used and its tropes.

But what happens when an author (or an auteur) utilizes multiple genres and media that contradict each other in regard to narrative action, ones in which the narrative tropes are both progressive and regressive? Robert Stam writes that "concrete spatiotemporal structures," or chronotopes,[5] place limits on the possibilities of narration and characterization and thus influence the structure of the fictional world (2000, 204–5); however, this notion of chronotopes is reliant upon a fixed generic structure and medium. Whedon's mixing of genres[6] challenges the static connection between chronotope and genre and creates a text in which the constant movement of the form is in league with the restlessness of the content. Additionally, analysis of both the televisual and the cinematic forms of this story enables an understanding of how the chronotope may work differently in the two forms.

Firefly and *Serenity* combine a variety of tropes, predominantly from the western, science fiction, and road-trip genres, although heist, mystery, war, and horror tropes are used as well. In his discussion of chronotopes, Stam resists the consideration of genre as a delimited and stable category, since issues of taxonomy and essentialism frequently arise and obscure the intertextuality often found within particular instances of genre. "Any text," he writes, "that has slept with another text . . . has necessarily slept with all the texts the other text has slept with" (201–2). Thus, the road movie and the western often

---

5. Chronotopes were first theorized by Mikhail Bakhtin, who discussed solely the novel (1982, 84). As Janice Best (1994), Paula J. Massood (2005), and Robert Stam (2000) have shown, chronotopic analysis is also useful to other media. Stam finds film especially suited to chronotopic analysis in its construction of both timing and space through such respective elements as editing and mise-en-scène (2005, 27).

6. Whedon's use of multiple genres is one of the stamps of his work as an auteur; his earlier series, *Buffy the Vampire Slayer* and *Angel*, freely mix elements of teen romance, horror, comedy, film noir, and fantasy. Sharon Sutherland and Sarah Swan (2008) argue that *Firefly* and *Serenity* fit within the dystopic tradition as well.

use the same elements: the protagonist who cannot settle down, constantly keeps moving, and, along the way, encounters strangers and adventures. However, while Stam's points about intertextuality and the slipperiness of generic categories are valid, it remains useful to understand the basic boundaries of these genres in order to understand how the fiction works.

For instance, examining the narrative in regard to the contours of each of the aforementioned genres of *Firefly* and *Serenity* enables one to see the element of motion essential to the texts. The construction of the western looks backward to the nineteenth century in its manufacture and ideology; these texts are often guided by a conservative nostalgia for the sureties of Manifest Destiny, essentialized gender and race roles, and an allegedly simpler life. However, the narrative momentum of the text may either be the protection of resources that have been claimed, thus constructing a narrative of static resistance to change, or be the restlessness of the cowboy looking to move farther west, unable to settle down and always needing to strike out for the next frontier (yet written after the heyday of the cowboy and the closing of the frontier). By and large, the western contains within it a great deal of action: cattle drives, raids by "Injuns," and battles among landowners, criminals, and the law all make for a genre marked by movement.

Several important westerns are about internal movement within characters as well, such as *Stagecoach* (1939), *Red River* (1948), *High Noon* (1952), *Shane* (1953), *The Searchers* (1956), and *The Man Who Shot Liberty Valance* (1962). The American Civil War often impacts characterization within westerns, and this Civil War impact is true for *Firefly* and *Serenity* as well. Although such a topic requires a more thorough discussion elsewhere, for my purposes, suffice it to say that the Civil War is reimagined within the *Firefly/Serenity* universe ('verse) as the War for Unification between the Independents (a.k.a. Browncoats) and the Alliance; Whedon required an analogous historical moment to shore up his western-style fiction. Putting Mal on the losing side of the war[7] enabled Whedon to create a character full of bitterness at the victor, one whose anger at the Alliance remains unresolved and one who feels the need to, in the words of Huck in Mark Twain's *Huckleberry Finn*, "light out for the Territory" in the face of defeat ([1885] 2011, 372).

---

7. Whedon argues that Confederate elements in costuming and ideological positioning are used in *Firefly* and *Serenity* to position Mal on the losing side and not to suggest some latent racism or support of slavery within Mal (*"Serenity": The Official Visual Companion* 2005, 8). "Serenity" (1.1), "The Train Job" (1.2), and "Jaynestown" (1.7) make clear Mal's denunciation of slavery.

I do not have room to discuss all the western elements of *Firefly*, which seems more western than *Serenity* in terms of plot and setting, whereas *Serenity* is more connected to science fiction and the dystopic tradition within it.[8] However, the movement within *Firefly* is evasive, connecting it to aspects of the western. Mal is originally attracted to the ship *Serenity* as it represents the promise of a tenuous and small measure of freedom (a conservative, static approach), but he forces himself into increased motion by sheltering Simon and River Tam even as he attempts to maintain his former way of life. Such lighting out for the frontier—to "just get a little further" than the long arm of the Alliance ("Out of Gas" 1.8)—is one overlapping element among the western, science fiction space opera, and the chronotope of the road.[9]

Science fiction regularly looks to a future beyond the present of the author in addition to concentrating on forward movement; this practice is illustrated within both *Firefly* and *Serenity*. Barbara Maio argues that the western and science fiction share the motif of the "exploration of new territories" (2008, 204). Certainly, both regularly include immigrants or explorers (or both) who are seeking a new way of life elsewhere. Lorna Jowett adds "moving the boundaries of 'civilization' forward," a critique of capitalism, and a belief in Manifest Destiny through improving people to the similarities in western and science fiction narrative concerns (2008, 103–4). Generally speaking, science fiction is about moving forward in a linear narrative of progress and colonization (Battis 2008, para. 2). However, Jowett posits that *Firefly* offers a "guilt-free colonization scenario," since the planets colonized seem free of indigenous life; instead, the colonization occurs upon the Alliance's own subjects, as in the case of River (2008, 103). Battis writes that *Firefly* "is entirely a show about human expansion and exploration, human chaos and interaction in the farthest reaches of space" (2008, para. 3). He connects *Firefly* to the science fiction concern of what he calls "how you get there [to where you are going]," stressing the human interaction within and ethics of space travel and technology use (para. 36). We thus can see this connection between movement within *Firefly* and two of its principal genres.

Whedon has stated, "I wanted to create a show that took the past and the future and put them together by making them feel like the present" ("Here's

8. See Brian Thiessen on this issue as well (2006, 1).

9. Such overlap is evident in Gene Roddenberry's widely known pitch for *Star Trek* as "*Wagon Train* to the stars," referring to a well-known western television serial that aired from 1957 to 1965.

How" 2003). He accomplishes this aim in part by mixing these genres as well and utilizing other generic elements, as mentioned above. Different geographic portions of the 'verse also are split between these generic elements. The 'verse is divided into core and rim planets in an analogue of the wheel of fortune (or *rota fortunae*): the landscapes and people of the rim planets are akin to those of the western (for example, common elements are dirt roads, nineteenth-century clothing, travel by horses, and difficult, stressful lives in which resources are always an issue), whereas those of the core planets are futuristic (skyscrapers, good health care, plentiful resources, and high technological and educational levels abound).[10] The characters move repeatedly between these genres in a technologically advanced version of the stagecoach (Fred Erisman [2006] also calls the series "*Stagecoach* in Space").

The 'verse as a wheel is one element of Whedon's emphasis on movement. Mal tells a criminal middleman, "The wheel never stops turning, Badger"; Badger's response is, "That only matters to the people on the rim" ("Serenity"). There is a visual analogue to this dialogue, one that, according to Whedon and Fillion (2003), is meant to stress the line and the action therein. From behind and over Mal's shoulder (facing Badger), the camera circles around behind Badger to a zoom in for a close-up on Mal as he moves away from Badger. The camera then cuts to a close-up of Badger and zooms out.[11] The motion of the camera provides a sense of the dynamic motion of the phrasing; the phrasing itself indicates the less stable lower socioeconomic and political status of the rim planets. Whereas the core or hub represents stasis, comfort, and lack of mobility, those on the rim must continually move, shift, and adapt. Those on the rim are also the ones who fight for independence from the Alliance core. Thus, we can see how interrelated time, space, movement, and ideology are within these two texts. This interrelationship is furthered by the additional use of the trope of the road and its associated chronotope.

10. Maio argues that some of the "futuristic" design elements of the core planets originate from the period of the 1950s to 1970s (2008, 202). The code switching is not as fixed as I perhaps seem to suggest here; as Maio notes, Whedon often switches seamlessly between western and science fiction codes and back again within the same scene (203).

11. This pair of shots is only one example of cinematography on the move. For instance, tracking shots, which are habitually used in road movies (Ganser, Pühringer, and Rheindorf 2006, 4), are regularly used in *Firefly* and *Serenity* as well. Characters and camera often are in motion; in addition to regularly used handheld cameras and zooms, editing also creates a sense of movement.

Although there are no literal roads in space, *Serenity*'s pilot, Wash, must chart their course between planets. Often, he is forced to chart longer journeys in the hope of staying off the track of the Alliance. As a result of the crew's mobility between planets and their need at the beginning of *Firefly* to pick up passengers, the chronotopes of the road and of encounter are also at work within the series. Lily Alexander argues that the chronotope of the road is one of the first cultural chronotopes; whereas this road was revitalized through 1960s culture, by the end of the decade this road became a dead end, and the outsiders so vital to the chronotope of the road were relegated to the discourse of crime and punishment; finally, the road was replaced by the chronotope of space travel in the 1970 and '80s (2007, 30–31).[12] According to John Brinkerhoff Jackson, the road functions as a "zone of influence and control" (1994, viii); it is central to order, commerce, and warfare, as well as providing connection to the strange and foreign. It is thus a potential site of vulnerability as well (1994, 6).

Associated with the chronotope of the road is the chronotope of encounter, which represents flux and diversity: "The spatial and temporal paths of the most varied people—representatives of all social classes, estates, religions, nationalities, ages—intersect at one spatial and temporal point" (Bakhtin 1982, 243). Hence, mobility within socioeconomic strata defines the chronotope of encounter; this is another similarity with *Firefly*. Taking on passengers to make enough money to fuel their ship, the main crew of Captain Mal, second in command Zoe, pilot Wash, mechanic Kaylee, and mercenary Jayne are joined by Shepherd Book, a member of a religious order; Dr. Simon Tam; Tam's sister, River; and Dobson. A Companion, Inara, rents a shuttle in order to continue her career as a sort of geisha; her vocation is both legal and respectable in the twenty-sixth century. Whereas the main crew is marked by their low status, the passengers and Inara represent wider strata: Book is looking to "walk [the world] awhile," the once-prosperous Simon and River have chosen a life as fugitives from Alliance experimentation, and Dobson turns out to be an Alliance mole on the trail of the Tams.[13] This diversity within the group creates a good portion of the tension that arises as the crew tries to identify the mole. Mal's distaste for the upper class is also illustrated when he

12. Unlike Alexander, Ganser, Pühringer, and Rheindorf see the post-1960s road movie as a critique of American ideologies of home and patriotism in relation to Vietnam and increased American mobility (2006, 2).

13. The spectrum of characters creates a clear homage by Whedon to *Stagecoach* (for more on this, see Erisman 2006).

immediately dislikes and distrusts Simon owing to his clear upper-class status. Mal's misperception provides one of the first moments of possible character growth for him when he realizes that his biases have endangered his crew. The chance encounter with the Tams and Book also provide Mal's character with the opportunity to be more hero than scoundrel: it elevates him ("Serenity"). Over the course of the narrative, many of these characters will evolve, resulting in internal growth for Mal, River, and Simon; the beginnings of growth are evident in Jayne. These gains, however, are not necessarily permanent, and the impermanence is evidenced by Mal's more ambiguous and tortured character at the beginning of the film *Serenity*.

In addition to the social heterogeneity present within the chronotope of the road, this chronotope provides as well what Ganser, Pühringer, and Rheindorf term a "'snowballing' effect . . . with actions gaining momentum as the protagonists drive across a space that is anything but empty" (2006, 3). Other than the Reavers[14] and the Alliance, the 'verse includes Mr. Universe (a hacker extraordinaire who lives on his own moon), multiple trade stations and settlements, and other adventurers. Mal observes it is "gettin' awful crowded in my sky" ("Serenity"). Even when the ship is parked at the "corner of No and Where," as Mal remarks in "Out of Gas," another ship manages to come across them. In keeping with the "snowballing effect," the film *Serenity* follows the classical narrative formula of rising action, climax, and denouement as well: the crew's plans to finish a deal and leave River and Simon on Beaumonde are interrupted by River's initially inexplicable transformation into a "blitzkrieg of kung fu" (Burnett 2010). After learning Miranda is a key to unlocking the secrets of both River's brain and the Alliance and fleeing the Alliance Operative sent to capture River, the crew first travels there and then to Mr. Universe to broadcast the truth about Alliance "meddl[ing]," as River calls it. While the rest of the crew attempts to stave off

14. As several people have argued (see, for example, Rabb and Richardson 2008), the Reavers are the bogeymen of the 'verse and function similarly to the "Injuns" of classic westerns in *Firefly*, threatening the safe passage of *Serenity* within the system. Within the film *Serenity*, the origin story of the Reavers focuses on Alliance experimentation with an airborne drug (the Pax) on the planet Miranda. Vented throughout the environment, it was meant to remove aggression but instead resulted in two polar effects: extreme apathy or, in a minority of the population, intense aggression. *Serenity* creates an ironic commentary upon the construction of Native Americans within westerns and nineteenth-century society: in the Alliance's attempt to bring civilization to the 'verse and "make people better" (*Serenity*), they reap savagery and death.

the Reavers, Mal must fight the Operative to achieve his goal. These actions depend upon escalating action.

Even as the pace escalates, though, the ship is simultaneously still. Rather than moving through physical space in a small vehicle, these characters live in a spaceship, one that functions very much as a domestic space and, hence, also imbues the show with aspects of the domestic drama. The ship as home enables a sense of community and domesticity even as it provides a mobility that simultaneously conjures exile and migration. Although the latter might imply what Tim Cresswell (2004) calls "placelessness," the ship *Serenity* in fact becomes a tenth character ("*Serenity*: The Tenth Character" 2003) and is place-full.[15] Interior settings are as important to the action of the series as the development of characters, and they function symbolically as well: when the ship is defaced and then crippled badly in *Serenity*, nearly every member of the crew is challenged or traumatized, and its pilot is killed. The ship, the crew, and their mission must be rebuilt at the end of the film. Character, place, and time are conjoined, and, although I am able to discuss only a few examples, the function of time and space within *Firefly* is an especially rich area of inquiry that deserves further exploration.

The first example of important character development is tied to a thick chronotope I have discussed elsewhere: the war scene in Serenity Valley and the depiction of Malcolm Reynolds in the original pilot (see Buckman 2008). This chronotope is thick because of the way in which place and time cohere in these opening moments, which achieve a great deal; for instance, they set forth the terms of this 'verse, including the intertextuality and generic interplay that will be central to the narrative: war, science fiction, and western tropes all appear. The opening scenes also establish Mal as protagonist through point of view (POV) shots, shot length, dialogue, and narrative time; Serenity Valley is also recorded as a site of trauma. Within the Serenity Valley sequence, two chronotopic moments are essential to the narrative that follows: Mal kissing his cross pendant and Mal discovering that the ships he hoped were Browncoat "angels" are, instead, Alliance.

The shot of Mal kissing his cross lasts only a second, and, only a few minutes later, the camera focuses on Mal watching the Alliance ships descend—firing

15. See also Maio (2008, 209) for more on the construction of the spaceship *Serenity* as place. Additionally, there are multiple points at which *Serenity* is treated as a living entity. For instance, in "Heart of Gold" (1.13), Kaylee says that she will "ask *Serenity*" about some parts to refit a water system.

upon and killing fellow soldier Bendis in the process, contrary to Mal's earlier assurances to Bendis of their heavenly protection. Viewing Mal's expression of faith followed quickly by bitter defeat before his eyes in Serenity Valley is necessary to later understanding both his seeming contempt for faith and its expressions and the ways in which he is metaphorically stuck in Serenity Valley. The mise-en-scène is also essential, with Mal's face framed half in shadow, with low key lighting, no ambient sound (music replaces it), the slow-motion death of Bendis, and the slow dolly in to a close-up, full-frontal shot of Mal's shocked face. Whedon uses slow-motion photography literally to slow time, suggesting Mal is ensnared within Serenity Valley like an insect in amber. Whedon then cuts from this shot to Mal upside down "six years later," which suggests the continued upheaval of Mal's world (Buckman 2008, 42). Although important events occurred within those six years, as the audience sees in "Out of Gas," the lack of observable growth therein suggests that six years later is negligible for someone still stuck in the past.[16]

The need to move on from one's past or risk getting stuck there in a *Waiting for Godot*–like crisis is a point made by Cynthea Masson in her essay on *Angel*'s "The Girl in Question," and it is a point that reverberates throughout Whedon's work (2008b).[17] Mal continues to be burdened by his anger over God's (and Browncoat leaders') seeming desertion of him and the fight for independence at Serenity Valley, so much so that the ship, which consciously represents freedom to Mal ("Out of Gas"), works as a symbol of his stagnancy: "There's no place I can be since I've found Serenity," sings Sonny Rhodes in the series theme song. "Serenity," a word that represents a state of peace and equilibrium, instead is a sign of the battle never fully left behind: Mal carries it around with him through the sky (see also Pateman 2008, 212).

Badger remarks on Mal's entrapment in his past in the "Serenity" pilot, arguing that he is not a captain but "still a sergeant. Still a soldier. Man of honor in a den of thieves." In "The Train Job" (1.2), the audience learns Mal always visits "an Alliance-friendly bar . . . come U[nification] Day." Surrounded by Alliance-friendly barflies on the edge of a precipice, he remarks to Zoe, "This is why we lost [the war]. Superior numbers." Zoe dryly notes,

16. Battis implicitly suggests that we start with character change when he writes that Mal experiences defeat, "loses his faith and begins his slow, painful transition into the acerbic and bitter captain that we will meet later" (2008, para. 4).

17. Masson's essay (revised) is included in this volume.

"Thanks for the re-enactment, Sir." He is stuck, repeating time and place incessantly; whether he is conscious of his own lack of motion is debatable, even though he is reminded of it repeatedly, as in "Bushwhacked" (1.3), when an Alliance officer comments on the name of Mal's ship. Such inability to work through the past is one more aspect of generic characterization for the western hero and the war veteran, both of whom carry the past with them. Mal's costuming, of course, serves as a reminder of his past every day, since he wears the long brown duster of the appropriately nicknamed Browncoats.

As John Cawelti argues, the western hero is additionally alienated from the community as a result of his violent past (1999, 82); even within the group Mal has formed on the ship *Serenity*, only Zoe fought beside him (Wash, Jayne, River, and Simon did not fight, and Inara supported unification). In "War Stories" (1.10) we find that this violent past separates Mal and Zoe from other crew members when they treat apples as possible bombs. Their shared past creates tension between Mal and Wash, since Wash suspects Zoe is firmer in her loyalties to Mal than to her husband. Mal is alienated even more from the larger 'verse, as we see when he tries to find someone to whom he can sell his illicit cargo and must settle for Patience, who once shot him. In writing about the western elements of *Firefly*, Mary Alice Money notes, "The hero remains, ultimately, locked away, maintaining his status as loner even while we watch his memories unfold [in "Out of Gas"]" (2008, 123). For his own health and the well-being of his relationships with others, Mal must move internally as well as externally. For instance, in "The Train Job," Mal knowingly risks his crew and forfeits money when he returns stolen medicine rather than delivering it to Niska, the cruel, elderly crime boss from whom he received the contract for the burglary. The sheriff is impressed by Mal's decision: "A man learns all the details of a situation like ours . . . well, then, he has a choice." "I don't believe he does," Mal responds.

However, by the time of the film *Serenity*, Mal has developed his bitterness and alienation to the point that he leaves behind a villager seeking refuge from Reavers: "In the time of war, we would never have left a man behind," Zoe asserts. Cynically, Mal responds, "Maybe that's why we lost." He argues that he left this man behind to protect his own crew; the "mule" would not have taken the weight of an additional person, and he could not dump the money they had stolen because of their "powerful need to eat." His ethics of personal responsibility have changed between "The Train Job" and *Serenity*; he has sunk further into the morass of Serenity Valley.

One might argue that River is stuck as well, plagued as she is by uncertain and slow recovery as well as nightmares. These latter provide thick moments in which space and time intertwine within a dreamscape. The pain and terror River feels within the dreamscape presented in "The Train Job," for instance, are communicated visually and aurally through expressionistic sound, including a rhythmic noise that suggests a heartbeat. The cinematography of the nightmare scene is important: the bright lights, blurry quality of the picture, and use of spotlight drown out the details of the Alliance laboratory even as space and time are exceptionally important. The lights join with extreme close-ups of her head, hands, and puncture sites; off-center framing; lack of clarity; and slow motion to form a moment out of time and space that is simply nightmarish and never-ending. Even once she awakens, she continues to suffer emotional and physical trauma as a result of these experiments. Once onboard *Serenity*, River must be coaxed into the surgical bay because it reminds her of the trauma endured at the hands of the Alliance. This trauma is the first evidence—other than callous attitude and retro-fascist costumes—that the Alliance is suspect as a system.

As a result of its narrative placement within the series, the nightmare scene of the Alliance's manipulation of River becomes analogous to Niska's torture of those individuals who fail him and thus becomes a critique of the system in place, combining space, time, and ideology. The film *Serenity* will carry this critique further, by extending the plotline of involuntary experimentation on humans from River out to the Reavers. The origin story of the latter provided in *Serenity* differs importantly from the one offered by the crew in the series. In *Serenity*, the events on Miranda function as a parallel for River's abuse at Alliance hands, including her education and indoctrination. In the opening scene of the film, River's teacher is explaining the conflict between the Alliance and the Independents as one resulting from the misguided ignorance of the Independents. The scenery of this central planet is peaceful and lush, the classroom outdoors, and the teacher mild-mannered and soft-spoken. Time progresses at a normal, relaxed pace. Asking why the Independents would reject the Alliance, the teacher approaches River, who has offered that "we meddle. . . . We're in their homes and in their heads, and we haven't the right. We're meddlesome." The teacher responds, "River, we're not telling people what to think. We're just trying to show them how." She then stabs at River's forehead with River's stylus, and the time and space of the scene shift abruptly around River; the scene cuts on action from the stylus to a needle stabbed into River's head by one of the doctors in the lab. "She's dreaming." "Got that? Off the charts." "Scary monsters." The editing creates a direct link between education, experimentation on humans, and imperialism.[18] The teacher becomes the doctor's "scary monsters" just as, later, a Reaver will attack River during her memory of this moment.

The use of past images within a dreamscape that includes both past and present Rivers also suggests River's inability to move beyond this past in that all these elements are intertwined. However, coming to understand her history and its relation to the experiences of others enables her progress. It is River who finds the recording cylinder detailing the history of experimentation on planet Miranda's population, and the mise-en-scène suggests that the female scientist recording the information speaks directly to River through an eye-line match. River even mouths the holographic scientist's words simultaneously, seeming to know what the scientist will say. After Wash turns off the tape and River vomits, she states that she is "alright. I'm alright." Her repetition, her tone, and the surprised look on her face suggest that this new knowledge has allowed her to integrate the fragments of her self as she recognizes her own abuse by the Alliance as analogous to the abuse of the population of Miranda, which, although it occurred twelve years previously, seems to function as if in the present through the hologram. The fear of the Reavers evident in the holographic woman's words is very much a fear for the present crew as well. Hidden for those twelve years in a conscious manipulation of history and knowledge, Miranda remains static until the crew of *Serenity* discovers her secret. The dissolution of that secret enables River's forward movement within a place in which the action functions symbolically parallel to River's own past.

Now that River has control of this information, she has power over it; she is no longer controlled by the Alliance, and her crew does not need to fear her as an unknown danger. Knowledge, community, and moving onward have given her the ability to *not* be a Reaver.[19] This story is what the Alliance wanted to keep from River and the rest of the 'verse: by gaining access to

18. For more on *Serenity* and geopolitics and dystopia, see Bussolini 2008; Lackey 2004; Sutherland and Swan 2008; and Wilcox 2008.

19. As K. Dale Koontz (2008) has illustrated, the names Whedon chooses for his characters often carry symbolic weight. This understanding—plus the facts that "River" and "Reaver" sound so much alike and that they are both products of government experimentation that resulted in, respectively, a purposeful and an accidental increase in violence and aggression—suggests their function as analogues. See also Wilcox (2005, chap. 3) on the power of naming and J. Douglas Rabb and J. Michael Richardson (2008, 136) on the double signification of "Miranda" in *Serenity*.

knowledge, she becomes a threat to their control over both her body and the rest of the 'verse. Once the crew distributes that knowledge, however, she seems to cease being a threat. Place, time, and movement coalesce through Miranda, River, and Mal's pasts and the physical site and sight of this trauma in the present; this chronotope engages with the tropes of both science fiction and western genres of *Serenity*, leading to the trope of the last stand. Although the Reavers are more analogous to Native Americans in *Firefly*, the construction of a clear origin story for them in the film *Serenity* contradicts this function: they are not just "savages" patrolling the borders of space and attacking "innocent" travelers.[20] However, Whedon (2007) has discussed the scene in which the Reavers follow the ship *Serenity* disguised as a Reaver ship into an attack at Mr. Universe's moon as "the Indians ride over the hill and surprise the cavalry." Although the information that leads Mal and crew to Mr. Universe is rooted more fully in the science fiction trope of experimentation gone wrong, the intertextuality among western, science fiction, and road-trip generic elements assuredly leads to this moment.

What we see in these examples of River and Mal is the interaction of place with time, character, genre, and ideology. Each of these moments focuses on the individual and his or her loss of a sense of control over the world, a theme important to the borderland location of the western as well as a signal of the 'verse's postmodern construction and production; science fiction often relies upon motifs of control and autonomy as well, and road-trip movies often focus upon seizing control over one's life or resisting control over one's life by another. When both Mal and River gain the knowledge of Miranda in the film *Serenity*, it enables their action, their bursting forth from unproductive stasis. Mal feels free to embrace the alleged "bad guy" within, while River embraces her own agency; both commit to the last stand, a stand indeterminate in terms of its lasting effect. Like many protagonists of these other genres, they are willing to die to protect their ideals. This attitude is similar to Angel's stance in "Epiphany" (*Angel* 2.16): "If nothing we do matters, then all that matters is what we do." River and Mal have not dismantled the

---

20. See, for instance, Rabb and Richardson 2008 on the construction of the Reavers. They argue that *Serenity* illustrates the Eurocentric fabrication of the racial Other in the shift in origin stories presented between the series and the film. There is no "savage" per se, just our construction of the racial Other as savage. Agnes B. Curry argues, conversely, that Whedon reinscribes the trope of Native American as savage even as his expressed, verbalized intent was to deconstruct it (2008, para. 42).

Alliance, although they have certainly given the citizens a great deal to think about, and they may or may not have gained River's freedom. Taking action in itself has enabled internal progress, however.

The penultimate moments of Joss Whedon's *Serenity* are typical of Hollywood cinema: Captain Malcolm Reynolds and River Tam sit on the bridge of *Serenity*, and the former gives an aptly romantic speech about how love keeps a spaceship flying. Enemies currently vanquished and casualties tallied, Mal and River fly off into the metaphorical sunset of the western with their remaining crew, living to fight another day. While River muses that the "storm's getting worse" as they fly away from Mr. Universe's base, Mal replies, "We'll pass through it soon enough," potentially suggesting their happy ending and a neatly wrapped bit of closure; they then break through the clouds and fly toward the sun. A chronotopic analysis would suggest that this ending would be appropriate in that it does reflect the usual generic Hollywood ending; narratively, it also works since Mal and River seem to have resolved—at least in some measure—their internment within the past, found equilibrium, and more firmly established a community of equals.

Rather than a happy ending, however, it may be merely a momentary respite for Mal's "little albatross" and company. The last few moments of the film circle back to the beginning in homage to Wash and perhaps to suggest mere reprieve rather than full resolution. At the beginning of the film, after the initial credits, there is a long tracking shot, an exterior view of *Serenity* entering a planet's atmosphere. A piece of the ship tears off, at which point Mal exclaims, "What was that?!" In the closing moments of the film, a piece of the ship comes off and flies in front of the camera, effectively cutting the screen to black. In dialogue over the cut to black, Mal again asks, "What was that?!" This repetition suggests a more circular route than simple linear progress to the ending, and perhaps continues the movement of the narrative, breaking the potentially static ending.[21] The finale to *Firefly* (though not planned as such), "Objects in Space" (1.14), also emphasizes mobility at its end: the camera cuts from Zoe sewing up the wounded doctor to Mal and Inara to Kaylee and River playing jacks. We end with the current threat to the ship, Jubal Early, floating alone through space, having been defeated and

---

21. In 2010, Fanetti and Burnett also noted to me the complication of the narrative line through this reiteration of the beginning.

ejected from *Serenity*.[22] The endings of the series and the film remain fluid and true to their narrative momentum.

The chronotope of *Firefly* and *Serenity* is one that stresses movement within characters, time, setting, cinematography, and even the form. Set several hundred years in the future, *Firefly* and *Serenity* rely upon genres firmly rooted in the nineteenth and twentieth centuries. The western emphasizes the individual in conflict with both order and chaos, as represented respectively by the forces of civilization and "barbarism," and generally deals with a nation torn apart in the aftermath of the Civil War. The science fiction aspect provides models for dystopia and the depiction of scientific inquiry and rejection of control through science. Both genres contain elements of romanticism and a revised Manifest Destiny. The movement that is central to the series and the film is paralleled in these genres and is complicated through their focus, respectively, on the past and future. Even when the western moves forward, it is rooted within the past, whereas science fiction strives to move forward. This tension within the action is replicated in two characters who must reconcile with their pasts and move forward into their futures. Mal and his crew are trapped physically, temporally, and generically between the border and the core planets and between past and future, endlessly moving. The ending of *Serenity* suggests a possible resolution to this restlessness and an ability to move forward through the storm and attain at least a measure of freedom from Mal's and River's pasts. Considering the perpetual movement of Whedon's universe, perhaps River is right when she says to Kaylee in "Objects in Space" (1.14), "No power in the 'verse can stop [them]."

22. Nadkarni queries whether the last scene with Mal and Jubal is a sign of Mal taking back Serenity (both the spaceship and valley); he steps outside of it, defeats the threat, and protects his crew.

Metaphoric Unity and Ending

Sending and Receiving Firefly's *Last "Message"*

ELIZABETH L. RAMBO

"The Message" was the last episode of *Firefly* to be written and filmed, which partly explains why it is one of three unaired episodes: the series had been canceled before it could be broadcast. The unaired episodes are arranged in their originally intended viewing order on the *Firefly* DVD set: 1.11 "Trash," 1.12 "The Message," and 1.13 "Heart of Gold."[1] Cowriter and director Tim Minear calls "The Message" "kind of a spare parts episode in some ways" (Bernstein et al. 2007, 139), meaning that he and cowriter Joss Whedon had odds and ends of story and production ideas that they were able to use, giving the impression that the episode was thrown together without any coherent plan. However, if we consider the unaired *Firefly* episode "The Message" as the unintended conclusion to the series, we find that multiple messages are delivered textually, intratextually, and extratextually with the circumstances of its production. The result is that Whedon and Minear's "spare parts" coalesce to reiterate several themes or "messages" of the *Firefly* series as a whole, including alienated human nature, communication, family, and death, making it a fitting farewell to the show itself.

Alienated Humanity

In *Firefly*, Whedon deliberately posits a universe in which humans are the only intelligent creatures, implying, therefore, that we must take care of one

---

1. The DVD set presents the intended pilot episodes, "Serenity—Parts One and Two," as a single two-hour episode. This pilot was originally broadcast last, after the series had been officially canceled. The third unaired episode, "Heart of Gold," was originally filmed as Episode 12, but appears on the DVDs as Episode 13.

another because we are all we have; as the original line from W. H. Auden's (1969) poem has it, "We must love one another or die."[2] "The Message" teaser sequence satirizes the fear of the alien (the Other) as it opens in a "Space Bazaar" on a station, with dialogue presented almost as background noise or introduction, a carnival sideshow barker shouting, "We are not alone!" and going on to insist he will show proof of alien life. His claim is immediately undercut by Simon and Kaylee in the advertised exhibit, revealing that the supposed alien is an upside-down fetal calf. This scene presents us with one of the foundational elements of the series: the usual science fiction trope is the discovery that we humans "are not alone" in the universe because sentient beings from other planets find us, or vice versa. When Wash and Zoe view the fake alien, Wash spoofs this cliché, addressing the preserved calf with a line straight out of a B movie: "Do not fear me. Ours is a peaceful race, and we must live in harmony." The cliché exemplifies a typical Whedonesque rhetorical strategy of using sarcasm or satire to state or imply a truth: humans are alone, we are not "a peaceful race," and therefore it is imperative that we find ways to "live in harmony." Similarly, in the pilot, "Serenity," Wash, a character who frequently supplies humorous yet pointed commentary, is introduced playing with toy dinosaurs for whom he provides dialogue that at first seems cooperative until the carnivorous T-rex turns on the vegetarian stegosaurus, whom Wash imagines lamenting, "Curse your sudden but inevitable betrayal!" ("Serenity"). As hilarious as this scene may be—a spaceship pilot playing with toy dinosaurs—it epitomizes many scenarios of betrayal to come in *Firefly*, including the one in "The Message."

The teaser gives us several other vignettes of estrangement, alienation, or displacement, listed here to illustrate how this theme of alienation is packed into a relatively short introductory scene:

- Simon tries awkwardly to compliment Kaylee but insults her instead, leading Zoe to observe that he is not very good at talking to people in general, not just to girls.
- As Mal and Inara stroll through the bazaar, Mal catches a child pickpocket. On one hand, the moment demonstrates Mal's street smarts;

2. According to some accounts, Auden later wanted to change the line to a more accurate "We must love one another and die," which certainly also describes the Whedonverses (Mendelson 2000, 478).

on the other hand, a world in which children must pick pockets is not a just world.

- Mal and Inara in an intratextual moment argue over fencing "the Lassiter," alluding to the infamous weapon the crew stole in the previous episode "Trash" and demonstrating their unresolved conflicts from that episode. Though it is evident that Mal and Inara care for one another, they are unable to express these feelings effectively, leading to an unfortunate exchange in "Trash" in which Mal calls Inara a "whore" and she calls him a "petty thief." Their cooperation to outwit "Saffron" (a.k.a. Yolanda, Bridget, Our Mrs. Reynolds) does not eliminate the tension.

- Postmaster Amnon greets Mal, noting that "an old friend's face is a balm in this age," implying that friends are rare in the Alliance worlds.

- River remains out of place, alienated, among her comrades. Her awkward approach to what seems to be a common edible fair treat, the "ice planet," leads Jayne to comment that her mental talents do not compensate for her apparent lack of ordinary life skills.

- Jayne tries to hold back for himself the change from a purchase of ammunition. According to actor Alan Tudyk in the DVD commentary (Tudyk and Staite 2003), this bit of business was improvised by Adam Baldwin, and it not only fits the character, who has been shown consistently on the lookout for himself first, but also fits the alienation theme.

- Jayne's reception of a knitted cap from his mother, which Kaylee terms bemusedly "the sweetest hat ever," displaces his shipmates' view of him. Suddenly, the man whose deepest emotional commitment seems to be to a gun he has named "Vera" ("Our Mrs. Reynolds" 1.6) has a family whom he has been supporting—the message with the hat also mentions a father and someone named "Matty," possibly a sibling, who suffers "with the Damplung." The cap, yellow and orange with a pompom and earflaps, looks like something a five-year-old Norwegian might wear sledding, but Jayne wears it with pleasure and dignity throughout the episode, completely unaware or uncaring that anyone might find it "faintly ridiculous" (Bernstein et al. 2007, 141).

The causes of our alienation from one another are many; however, one common thread in several of these vignettes is communication—or the lack thereof—appropriate in an episode titled "The Message."

Communication

"The Message," not surprisingly, offers several examples of communication and miscommunication connecting or dividing the characters. In the teaser, Jayne has received one message, from his family, a message that both connects him to them and divides him from the *Serenity* crew—or at least divides the crew from their preconceptions of Jayne.

The episode's central message is delivered by the apparently deceased Tracey, recorded on a portable drive of some kind, and intended for Mal and Zoe, whom he says are the only ones he trusts to get him where he needs to go—"home" to his family. He says the "real world" has been a greater struggle for him than the war was, and concludes, "When you can't run anymore, you crawl, and when you can't do that, well—yeah, you know the rest . . . ," continuing the "old saying" introduced in the "Battle of Du Khang" flashback. Parts of this message are repeated in the middle and at the end of the episode, each time giving viewers a different perspective on the speaker Tracey and on the characters who listen to his message.

Communication fails in several ways after the crew discovers that Tracey is very much alive and that his "death" is part of his plan to smuggle contraband implanted organs. Tracey's paranoia leads him to act without full information and take Kaylee hostage when he thinks the captain has betrayed him to the Alliance agents pursuing him. In the scene that follows, Tracey tries various rhetorical angles to place the blame for his predicament on Mal and the crew, as he holds a gun to Kaylee's head and warns Mal, "Don't make me—," to which Mal responds, "Far as I can see, no one's made you do anything. You brought this on yourself." Tracey then argues that the *Serenity* crew members are equally criminals, that they have also left "a trail of bodies." Mal replies, "Weren't bodies of people helping me out." He is a hard man, but he has his code. Indeed, in previous episodes, we have seen that although he, Zoe, Jayne, and even River have killed a number of people, almost all of these people were actively attempting or seriously threatening to kill our heroes at the time.[3]

Now Tracey shifts his rhetorical attack, claiming he chose Mal and Zoe to ship him home because he remembered them as "saps," easy marks, who

---

3. Mal's representative line would be his response to Simon when they first meet: "You don't know me, son. So let me explain this to you once: if I ever kill you, you'll be awake, you'll be facing me, and you'll be armed" ("Serenity").

believed in glory and honor. "What are you now, Mal? What are we now?" he asks, a question that resonates throughout *Firefly*. Tracey's question implies that both he and Mal are unprincipled rogues, out for whatever they can get. Certainly, it is the persona Mal likes to wear, but in fact Mal represents what David Magill calls "ethical manhood," which upholds "individual freedom combined with ethical action" (2008, 83). Whatever doubts Mal and his crew may have about their other choices, their dedication to one another is unwavering.

The arrival of the corrupt Alliance agents is signaled by silence and Tracey's last verbal appeal to Mal's sympathy: "That call means you murdered me." Throughout this conversation, however, the unity of the *Serenity* crew is shown through unspoken communication: Mal glances at Jayne, who cocks his rifle, distracting Tracey. Tracey releases Kaylee to point his pistol at Jayne. Mal then shoots Tracey, this time fatally. All this action takes less time to watch than to read, and it ends with Mal's reply to Tracey: "No, son . . . I just carried the bullet a while." We do not need to be reminded of his words at the battle of Du Khang: "Everybody dies, Tracey. Someone's carrying a bullet for you right now, doesn't even know it."

If Tracey had been willing or able to communicate with his former comrades whom he claimed to trust ("You two are the only people I trust to get me where I'm going," according to his recorded message), he might have benefited. Tracey had assumed they would use him, as he tried to use them as marks, as he had evidently been using everyone he met. He is another example of the type of *Serenity*verse villains described by Linda Jencson (2008), villains who operate according to "[n]egative reciprocity . . . in which each party tries . . . to get the advantage of the other party," such as Saffron of "Our Mrs. Reynolds" and "Trash," who insists that "everybody plays each other; that's all anybody does" ("Our Mrs. Reynolds"). Tracey's similar reliance on negative reciprocity probably explains why he "never could get [his] life working right . . . not once after the war." Tracey had recorded in his original message, the memorial to his fake death, "It's the real world I couldn't survive." Now Tracey's inability to trust and communicate truth in that real world has indeed killed him.

Tracey's apologies are now accepted by Mal and Zoe and Kaylee, despite the fact that he has just tried to kill them all. Viewers, too, are probably convinced that in facing his real death, Tracey is sincere, if hapless, and now deserves the sympathy the crew gave him when he was only playing dead. They will fulfill "that stupid message" now for the sake of the "old saying" first partially introduced in the first act:

MAL: You know the old saying . . .

TRACEY: When you can't run, you crawl . . . and when you can't crawl,
you—when you can't do that . . .

ZOE: You find someone to carry you.

This message can connect hapless humans alienated from one another in a
brutal world. Yet Tracey still dies.

Family and Jayne's Hat

Several Whedon scholars have explored interpretations of the *Serenity* crew as a
metaphorical "family" (see, for example, Wilcox and Cochran 2008a; Koontz
2008), whereas members of the cast and crew, such as Nathan Fillion (2007,
52) and Joss Whedon (Bernstein et al. 2007, 13), have used the same term to
describe their experience of working on *Firefly*. In the "Battle of Du Khang"
flashback, we get another perspective on the foundation of the *Serenity* crew as
"family." Zoe and Mal function as a parental couple here,[4] and Jane Espenson
(2004b, 1), writer for *Firefly*, *Buffy*, *Angel*, and *Dollhouse*, notes the extratextual connection of these characters with real-life counterparts: "The Joss-as-
Mal, co–executive producer Marti Noxon-as-Zoe parallel struck all of us in
those days." In this scene, Zoe is the one who gives the tough love, advising
the clueless Tracey that if he does not take care to be more aware of his surroundings, she is "just gonna watch" him get killed. Mal, meanwhile, takes
over for the shell-shocked lieutenant and carries Tracey to safety.

Helping his family and possibly returning to them seem to be Tracey's
deepest motivations. Although his recorded message may have been a ploy, it
appears Tracey did intend the profits from his organ smuggling to go to his
family, and his last request is "You'll do it? Get me home?" Here Mal appears
as the authoritative father figure, while Zoe, in a rare demonstration of maternal gentleness, brushes Tracey's hair away from his forehead.

One of the more notable signifiers of "family" throughout "The Message"
is the "cunning" knitted hat Jayne receives from his mother in the opening
teaser. Burns argues that in the context of "The Message," the hat may appear
to be "just a hat, doing hat things," but it also "signifies an entire wealth of
background to this universe, where mothers still knit hats for their grown

4. Koontz describes Mal as the father figure, Inara as the maternal stand-in, and Zoe as
the "big sister" (2008, 73).

sons, where sons unconditionally love the hats their mothers send them" (2007, 22). This hat is too cute for an outlaw, but Jayne puts it on immediately and is seen wearing it in nearly every scene. Extratextually, *Firefly* fandom has come to associate Jayne's hat with devoted family ties and with fearlessness in the face of opposition, such as the corporate interests that doomed *Firefly*, just as Jayne accepts Wash's comment "Man walks down the street in that hat, people know he's not afraid of anything" without a trace of irony. "Jayne's cunning hat" may be more iconic for *Firefly* fans (also known as Browncoats) than any other item associated with the *Serenity*verse. Consider, for example, the Big Damn Knitters Livejournal community, which produced so many of the caps that they actually caused a yarn shortage in 2005 (*Browncoats* 2009). The parting insult from the corrupt Alliance agent Womack, "That hat makes you look like an idiot," makes no impression at all on Jayne. He only removes the cap as a gesture of respect at Tracey's funeral, in the final scene of "The Message," a scene that brings many of the episode's thematic "spare parts" together as a metaphorical representation of the death of *Firefly*.

Death and Birth, Sorrow and Laughter

The central themes of "The Message" are introduced at the end of the teaser with the opening of a large crate that the postmaster has been holding for Mal and Zoe, one in which they discover a coffin holding the apparent corpse of their old battle comrade Tracey (as yet unnamed).[5] The coffin introduces two linked themes of this episode: death and birth. As mentioned previously, "The Message" was the last episode to be written, and several actors, writer-director Tim Minear, and writer Joss Whedon have all noted that while they were filming "The Message," the crew was informed that *Firefly* had been canceled. The irony is overwhelming. The specific interconnections of these circumstances must be explored, for, as Matthew Pateman writes, "*Firefly* is steeped in death. . . . [T]he fact of death continues to dominate the affective and narrative drive of the story. . . . In other words, death is not simply

---

5. Jonathan M. Woodward, the actor who plays Tracey, also appeared in *Buffy* Season 7 as vampire psychologist Holden Webster and in *Angel* Season 5 as Knox, a Wolfram & Hart tech specialist secretly devoted to the ancient god-king Illyria. Like Tracey, each of these characters initially seems somewhat sympathetic, but ultimately betrays even those individuals he seems to like or love and dies. Woodward is one of four actors who has done the "hat trick" of appearing in these three Whedon series; the other three are Carlos Jacott, Jeff Ricketts, and Andy Umberger.

something that, on an episode-by-episode basis provides a narrative direction or plot fulcrum . . . ; rather, death offers a tonal and thematic center to the show, anchoring it into a deep moral seriousness, even at those moments of great comedy, romance, and action" (2008, 212–14). Pateman's essay does not mention "The Message" but could have easily done so. The scene in which Mal and Zoe open the crate and the coffin inside it parallels the scene from the (intended) first episode, the two-hour "Serenity," in which the crew opens a mysterious blue box containing the cryogenically suspended River Tam. The two scenes occur at different points in the respective episodes, but the similarity adds intratextual weight to "The Message" as a bookend to that opening episode (along with other parallel scenes to be discussed). Each box-opening scene occurs at the end of an "act"—"Serenity" act three, "The Message" teaser—and concludes with expressions (spoken and unspoken) of baffled bemusement. In "Serenity," Mal's response to the naked sleeping girl is a nonplussed "Huh." In "The Message," everyone gazes in astonishment at the body, and only Jayne is able to find words: "What'd you all order a dead guy for?" Similarly, each sleeper awakes screaming and struggling—for, of course, Tracey is only in an artificially induced death-like coma. River awakens near the beginning of the next act, and Tracey's "resurrection" comes several scenes later; nevertheless, both indicate that a state that appeared or was supposed to be peaceful was instead rather disturbing in some way. River, after regaining some kind of coherence, tells her brother, "Simon . . . they talk to me, they want me to . . . to talk . . . ," as if she has carried dreams or memories of her torture by the Alliance with her;[6] similarly, Tracey tells Mal and Simon his drug-induced coma was supposed to be dreamless, "but I . . . [d]reamt of my family"—assuming he is telling the truth at this point.

The two scenes differ significantly, though: The box-opening scene in "Serenity," *Firefly*'s intended pilot episode, is metaphorically associated with birth, as River appears "curled in a fetal position, which visually presents her as a child" (Buckman 2008, 42). In contrast, in the last-written, last-to-be-filmed episode, "The Message," the "corpsified" Tracey, shipped in a coffin, is inevitably associated with death. Jewel Staite comments that a sense the show was doomed—metaphorically marked for death—pervaded the set at times as the cast compulsively watched *Firefly*'s disappointing ratings: "It was just excruciating. So I was relieved that we finally had an answer" (Bernstein et al. 2007, 146). The metaphorical message of "The Message" has to do with

6. River's torture is made more explicit in the *Serenity* film.

how to deal with the departure of a beloved project—the *Firefly* series and the people involved with it.

The metaphorical death/birth parallels continue as the first act of "The Message" opens with a flashback to "The Battle of Du Khang, Seven Years Earlier," in which we are introduced to the body in the coffin as Mal and Zoe's Browncoat army buddy Tracey. This scene is parallel to the flashback to the "Battle of Serenity Valley" in the "Serenity" pilot teaser, which reveals the death of Mal's faith and the birth of Mal as we know him (Pateman 2008, 212–13). The "Battle of Du Khang" past version of Mal, however, is more like Jayne—boisterous and fearlessly optimistic—even as he warns, "Everyone dies, Tracey. Someone's carrying a bullet for you right now, doesn't even know it." (Writer-director Tim Minear says this line is his favorite [Bernstein et al. 2007, 139].) Contrasting their attitudes to life and war, Tracey feels the war is pointless and does not want to "die on this rock," but Mal prefers to go down fighting, wherever he may be. Mal must carry the wounded Tracey to safety (we presume), saying cryptically, "You know the old saying . . ." Expectations are set up that we *will* know this "old saying" by the end of the episode.

The extratextual connection of the very real impending doom of the *Firefly* series and the episode's metaphorical representation of death is particularly notable in the early scene in which the *Serenity* crew stands around Tracey's coffin, listening to his recorded message about "falling in with untrustworthy folk" and his desire to be returned to family and people he can trust. The camera pans to each one so we see that nearly all the crew members are touched by these words. Wash's immediate offer to redirect the ship to Tracey's family home on St. Albans confirms that they are all willing to fulfill the last request of a young man who might easily have been one of them, if things had gone differently. The metatext of this somber scene, however, is that it is remembered by Alan Tudyk ("Wash") (Tudyk and Staite 2003), Jewel Staite ("Kaylee") (2004), film editor and associate producer Lisa Lassek (Bernstein et al. 2007, 143), and Joss Whedon as one of "the best thing[s] that ever happened" (Bernstein et al. 2007, 6) because of a prank by Nathan Fillion ("Mal"), as described by Jewel Staite: "Nathan decided it would be hilarious to sort of follow the camera around as it moved from one of our faces to the other in the circle. . . . One minute he was beside Alan, the next beside Ron [Glass], and the next leaning on Gina [Torres]'s shoulder, and at the end when the camera pans down to Tracey, he's cuddling him in the casket. Again, we were all kind of tired and delirious, so this was probably a lot funnier to us than to anyone else, but we were literally crying with laughter . . ." (2004, 226). The interconnection of the somber canon scene with the joke version of the scene remembered with such pleasure highlights both the unity of the *Serenity* crew and the unity of the cast of actors, who knew their show was struggling and very likely to be canceled, though the official word had not yet been given. Jewel Staite, like several other members of the cast and production crew, notes that they had all become friends both on and off the set (Bernstein et al. 2007, 146).

In scenes that follow, we are shown each member of the crew dealing with the prospect of death in idiosyncratic ways. In Kaylee's brightly lit and colorful bunk, she listens to Tracey's recorded message again. Simon comes looking for her but turns away, as if realizing that he cannot compete with this eloquent dead boy created by Kaylee's compassionate imagination. Book prays over the coffin, while Jayne throws himself into physical activity, confessing, "Me, I see a stiff—one I didn't have to kill myself—I just get, you know, the urge to do stuff. Work out, run around, get some trim if there's a willin' woman around. . . . My kind of life don't last, Preacher," stating "a familiar philosophy that endorses physical/sensual pleasures and situates humanity as vulnerable in its embodiment" (Jowett 2008, 109). Yet Koontz points to this scene as one indication of Jayne as a character "having a certain degree of religious faith," when Jayne also asks the shepherd if he will "read over [him]" when his time comes (2008, 71). River scandalizes both Jayne and Book as she lies down on the coffin, saying, "I'm very comfortable." In light of later developments and considering her psychic abilities, we might wonder whether she is speaking for herself or for the "corpse."

The scene in which Mal and Zoe tell Inara "war stories"[7] about Tracey as they eat, drink, and laugh together also carries extratextual significance: sharing food and memories of the dead are typical elements of a wake or memorial service, reenacted here in miniature. In terms of the "death" of *Firefly*, cowriter and producer Joss Whedon notes that the day before he had had to come on set and tell the cast and crew that *Firefly* had been canceled and then proceed to shoot "the scene of Zoe and Mal laughing their asses off, talking about their friend who was dead, and in a way, there couldn't have been a more appropriate scene and they couldn't have been better in it, because we all had a friend who was dead. But the joy we got from it was so worth laughing about" (Bernstein et al. 2007, 138). Whedon highlights the synchronicity between the narrative lines of "The Message" and the circumstances of its production.

7. Telling "War Stories" is an allusion to an earlier episode with that title (1.10).

The juxtaposition of sorrow and laughter is also reflected in Jewel Staite's recollection that Whedon informed the cast and crew of *Firefly*'s cancellation during the scene in which the revived Tracey holds Kaylee hostage: "We still had another four days left to go and we had to buck up and just get over it, keep shooting. . . . But I don't remember the shooting of that episode being particularly sad. I remember us goofing off like crazy. We knew that they weren't going to fire us, because we were already [canceled]" (146). Staite's comment again emphasizes the extratextual connection between the circumstances of the episode and the death of the series. The death of the fictional Tracey and the death of *Firefly* the series became intertwined.

In the final scene of "The Message," we see the crew deliver Tracey's coffin, now serving its true purpose, to his home on the snowy planet, and Kaylee delivers the recording device to his family as Tracey's original message plays in voice-over for a third time, now more poignant for having ironically become truth. Whedon comments that because everyone now knew this episode was the last one, "the funeral scene was incredibly funereal" (138).[8] Snow falls everywhere, a visual metaphor for burial and death. Jayne removes his hat in a gesture of respect.[9] Viewing Jayne's hat as a symbol for family connections, here the respectful removal of his hat connects Jayne with Tracey's family. Kaylee takes Simon's hand, reconciling their rift in the episode's opening scenes. The last shot is on Mal, looking obliquely at the camera as if silently echoing Tracey's final voice-over, "Yeah, you know the rest."

This funeral scene is the second in two consecutive episodes—"Heart of Gold" also includes a touching funeral. In "Out of Gas" (1.8), Mal insists that "everyone dies alone," and the episode Joss Whedon chose as the final statement of the series, "Objects in Space" (1.14), also implies a lonely conclusion, with bounty hunter Jubal Early's last words as he drifts away into empty space, "Well, here I am." Yet in "The Message" and "Heart of Gold," the individuals who die pass away surrounded by comrades, and their passing is marked by one of the most communal of human rituals, a funeral. In the DVD commentary for "The Message," Alan Tudyk recalls that the funeral "was actually the last shot for *Firefly*," barring one or two "pickups" (Tudyk and Staite

8. According to *IMDb.com* ("Joss Whedon" 2012) and several *Firefly* fandom sources (Marsh 2012), Whedon himself makes an uncredited cameo appearance in the funeral scene, as if to acknowledge the metaphorical funeral of *Firefly*.

9. Koontz notes this incident as another indicator of Jayne's familiarity with, at least, and possible respect for religious faith (2008, 71).

2003).[10] The funeral scene has no dialogue, other than selected voice-overs from Tracey's "message," giving *Firefly* music composer Greg Edmonson an opportunity to make his own statement: "I didn't write that music for the Tracey character, I wrote it to say goodbye to the *Firefly* characters, who [*sic*] I desperately loved and didn't want to say goodbye to. . . . The music was maybe too emotional for what the Tracey character deserved, but I didn't really write it for him" (Bernstein et al. 2007, 157). The music in this scene provides one more link between "The Message" as unintended final episode, the death of *Firefly,* and the birth of the series in the pilot: Edmonson originally wrote the basic theme, which Jennifer Goltz (2004, 210) calls "Sad Violin," for the "Serenity" pilot, where it plays over Mal's desolation at the battle of Serenity Valley and in the scene where Simon (and the audience) is led to believe the already beloved Kaylee is dead. Perhaps purely on the facts, Tracey is, as cowriter Whedon says, "a guy we don't trust and don't like and haven't known before this episode" (Bernstein et al. 2007, 138), yet by the end of "The Message," he has made a place for himself in the family of the *Serenity* crew, a family united, according to Koontz, by the belief that they are their brothers' keepers (2008, 80).

Conclusion

"The Message" is rarely mentioned as a particularly significant or memorable *Firefly* episode. It was the last of three episodes never aired because the series was canceled, and, therefore, Whedon chose "Objects in Space" as the series' broadcast finale[11] as his last medium "to dramatize [*Firefly*'s] themes about the contingency and meaninglessness inherent in existing things—and about the only possible source of value, in our free choices" (Zynda 2005, 85). However, as the actual final episode to be written and filmed, "The Message" turns out to encompass several key "messages" of *Firefly,* including human alienation in a universe without "aliens," communication and miscommunication, family, and—most of all—death. Coincidentally, or synchronicitously, during filming of "The Message," Whedon had to notify the cast and crew that Fox had can-

10. Pickups are minor scenes or shots recorded after the conclusion of principal photography, often not requiring the main actors.

11. "Objects in Space" was followed by the intended series pilot, "Serenity," perhaps in response to fan appeals.

celed *Firefly*, and the circumstantial context may have influenced this episode more than any other. What began as a "spare parts" script by Tim Minear (Bernstein et al. 2007, 139) involving the death of an otherwise minor guest character became a metaphor for the death of the show and an opportunity for the unusually cohesive cast to bond one last time, both on- and off-screen.

Part Four

Dollhouse

Dollhouse

An Introduction

DAVID LAVERY

At a Paley Center "Inside Media" evening devoted to Joss Whedon's "brilliant but canceled" fourth television series, *Dollhouse* (Fox, 2009–10), the show's creator—tongue, characteristically, firmly planted in cheek—wonders out loud about the origins of his diegetic surrogate Topher Brink, the scientist who programs the Actives (or Dolls): "That Topher—what's wrong with him? He just creates these character people and then he just puppets them around, and he thinks it's OK to do that. Who's he based on? What monster?" (*"Dollhouse": Cast and Creators* 2010). Neither Whedon nor his cast and crew knew then that *Dollhouse* would, to pretty much everyone's surprise, be renewed a month later, but in the series finale, the jury was still out on the driven-nearly-mad-by-guilt, neural-apocalypse-causing Topher, as the following exchange makes apparent:

> PAUL BALLARD: The point is Topher thinks he can flip it. Create a pulse to restore all the wiped minds.
> ZONE: Yeah? He also thinks he's a little teapot short and stout.
> ADELLE DEWITT: Topher Brink is a genius! And you will keep a civil tongue in this house or we'll put your tongue in a stew. ("Epitaph Two: Return" 2.13)

Shakespeare, John Keats once insisted in an 1819 letter, "led a life of allegory: his works are the comments on it" (2011, 226). Whether we understand Joss Whedon—who would in 2012 turn to adaptation of the bard's *Much Ado about Nothing* as a relaxation project after wrapping the third-highest-grossing film of all-time—as an allegorical monster or genius,[1] *Dollhouse* is not likely to make or break his reputation.

With an origin myth that includes a sit-down at lunch with career-in-the-doldrums Eliza Dushku (*Buffy*'s bad girl Slayer Faith), desperate for a project, *Dollhouse* was never pure Whedon from the outset. The idea he came up with (according to some versions, during a visit to the men's room) was a science fictioner set in a (literally) underground Los Angeles company, a division of the ultrasinister Rossum Corporation, offering for hire for very large fees "secret agents," Dolls, both male and female, able to take on almost any role or task after being reprogrammed by futuristic neurological technology. Originally intended to be a network-friendly, relatively free from seriality, episodic series, *Dollhouse* was to give us Dushku (Echo) performing a different Active each week, thereby showcasing her acting talents.

From the beginning, however, *Dollhouse* was a troubled show. Its "rough takeoff—the scrapped pilot, the uncertain early episodes, the Friday death slot"—singled out by Scott Tobias in the *Onion A.V. Club* (2010) was a disconcerting development but basically déjà vu all over again: had not *Firefly* faced the very same obstacles? More significantly, complaints, troubling in regard to a show from "Joss Whedon: Feminist,"[2] were heard from the beginning about the show's questionable messages: were not the Dolls, as critics understandably asked, being sold into sexual slavery in some episodes? Many found fault as well with Dushku's acting, and some of the stand-alone stories were weak, to say the least. But the remainder of the ensemble cast was uniformly excellent, especially Olivia Williams as Adelle DeWitt, the head of the Los Angeles Dollhouse; Harry Lennix as Boyd Langston, Echo's "Handler" (and eventually much more); Enver Gjokaj and Dichen Lachman as prominent Dolls Victor and Sierra; and Fran Kranz as Topher.

Being a Whedon show, *Dollhouse* became, of course, much more than merely episodic. Echo faced her weekly challenges—as, to name only a few, a crisis negotiator ("Ghost" 1.1), backup singer and bodyguard ("Stage Fright" 1.3), burglar ("Gray Hour" 1.4), blind cult member ("True Believer" 1.5), a dead woman ("Haunted" 1.10), an FBI agent ("Vows" 2.1), a mom

1. See "The Genius of Joss Whedon" (Lavery 2002a), my afterword to Rhonda V. Wilcox and my collection *Fighting the Forces* (2002, 251–56).
2. The title of James Longworth's interview with Whedon (Lavery and Burkhead 2011, 42–63).

("Instinct" 2.2), a college student ("Belle Chose" 2.3). But in multiepisode story arcs, we also followed investigation of the Dollhouse's improbable existence by rogue FBI agent Paul Ballard (Tahmoh Penikett); met the mysterious psychopath Alpha (Alan Tudyk) ("Omega" 1.12; "A Love Supreme" 2.8); learned about the backstories of Echo/Carolyn, Victor, and Sierra ("Needs" 1.8; "Belonging" 2.4; "Stop-Loss" 2.9); tracked the crusade of Senator Daniel Perrin (Alexis Denisof) to expose the Dollhouse ("The Public Eye" 2.5; "The Left Hand" 2.6); ascended to the mysterious and frightening "Attic," a netherworld for failed Dolls and Rossum Corporation enemies ("The Attic" 2.10); and visited other Dollhouses and discovered Rossum's insidious schemes and ambitions ("Echoes" 1.7; "Getting Closer" 2.11; "The Hollow Men" 2.12).

By his own admission (in the Paley Center discussion and elsewhere), Whedon had put two women in charge, *Angel* veterans Sarah Fain and Mere Smith, in order to help deflect criticism, and, when they left the series after Season 1, replaced them with another pair of female showrunners: Michele Fazekas and Tara Butters (creators of the canceled CW show *Reaper* [2007–9]). Whedon's own credited involvement, however, was minimal.

One of the greatest, most innovative writers-directors in the history of the medium, Whedon would write *and* direct only two episodes—"Ghost" and "Vows" (2.1), the initial outings of both seasons—and write the very meta "Man on the Street" (1.6), perhaps the best aired episode of Season 1. And he would supply the story for and direct the unaired, available for the first time on DVD, "Epitaph One." International distribution of *Dollhouse* had required thirteen episodes, but Whedon and company had contracted for only twelve. So on the fly they gave us—for lagniappe—a dark tale set in an apocalyptic future, a nightmare world in which the Dollhouse's wiping technology has gone global, basically zombifying the human race. Shot on a Fox-placating shoestring budget, it stands as a splendid example of television's astonishing ability to do more with less, to transform necessity into genius. "Epitaph Two: Return" (2.13), the series' satisfying finale, would, of course, return to *Dollhouse*'s future tense.

What was *Dollhouse*? As unsatisfying and perplexing as it sometimes was, even to ardent Whedon proponents like the present author, it is hard to disagree with Scott Tobias's assessment (in an *Onion A.V. Club* recap of the finale) that, in retrospect, even the much-despised Fox "deserves credit for producing a show this ambitious and allowing it to air all but one episode for two seasons, despite deadly ratings." Unlike another canceled Whedon series, *Dollhouse* had its chance: "This wasn't a *Firefly* situation, where Whedon needed a movie to tie up loose ends. This was a complete series, and we should be grateful for what we got." Watching it again, beginning to end, over a few days' time, I found it substantially more satisfying than I had when parsed out over a couple dozen Fridays. I am going to tuck it away—perhaps in "my drawer of inappropriate starches"—and watch it again one day soon.

Reflections in the Pool

Echo, Narcissus, and the Male Gaze in Dollhouse

K. DALE KOONTZ

In 2009 Joss Whedon returned to network television with *Dollhouse*, a series advertised as a mainstream action-adventure show. This billing was typical Whedon misdirection. Rather than centering squarely on the "eye candy" presented by lithe actors with extremely short hemlines, *Dollhouse* had at the center of its subversive heart some complex questions of memory and selfhood to present for examination. Indeed, the very code name of the central character of the *Dollhouse* corps, "Echo," raises intriguing questions of autonomy and identity. It cannot be a coincidence that the character at the heart of the *Dollhouse* ensemble shares her name with a nymph who loses her ability to speak as punishment for challenging the prevailing power structure. Names are never a coincidence to Whedon; in fact, he has said that he can get blocked in writing a character until he knows the name of that character ("Interview with Joss Whedon" 2005). Knowing of that statement, it is useful to examine the origin of the name "Echo," which has quite a long history.

Echo's name is derived from the classic myth of Echo and Narcissus, and it is appropriate that a recent television series and a thousands-year-old myth can successfully illuminate one another. As cultural anthropologist Claude Lévi-Strauss observed, myths have no author in the traditional sense (Bloch 2009). Therefore, every subsequent society may expand and manipulate myths in any manner that is deemed useful. This very fluidity lends myths their staying power and is the primary reason myths continue to be retold in any number of artistic forms.

Though Whedon incorporates twists and turns into the traditional tale, *Dollhouse* remains rooted in the classical myth in three important ways and therefore provides an excellent means of examining the ways in which such a myth can be successfully altered to provide relevance for a new audience.

First is the structure Whedon uses. Much of *Dollhouse*, particularly the first season, can be traced to the classical myth of Echo and Narcissus as detailed in Ovid's *Metamorphoses*. In addition to the name "Echo" having its origin in this myth, the identities and roles of several other *Dollhouse* characters are rooted there as well. Second is the importance of gazing to the narrative. Specifically, Whedon's *Dollhouse* provides a springboard into Laura Mulvey's theory of the cinematic male gaze and its subsequent revisions. Third is the use of reflections and the ways in which perceived images can trick the viewer into accepting a false image as true. This theme is present from the first line spoken in *Dollhouse*: "Nothing is what it appears to be."[1] In this chapter, I weave together the intertextual threads of classical mythology, feminist critical theory, and popular culture by examining Whedon's *Dollhouse* with an eye toward discussing these three commonalities.

It is reasonable to begin this examination with a synopsis of Ovid's story, which is contained in his *Metamorphoses*. Briefly, Echo is a nymph who is both clever and lovely. She is also loyal to her friends, some of whom are involved in a dalliance with the philandering king of the gods, Jupiter. Echo loves her friends, so she decides to provide cover for them, detaining Jupiter's suspicious wife, Juno, with endless chatter so Jupiter can slip away undiscovered. When the furious Juno discovers Echo's role in concealing her husband's actions, she retaliates in a cruelly fitting fashion by removing Echo's ability to initiate conversation. The lively, laughing girl can now only repeat the last few words she has heard another say.[2]

A shell of her former self, Echo drifts aimlessly, waiting for someone to speak so she can talk back in the only way left to her. One day in her lonely wanderings, she glimpses a beautiful youth and instantly falls deeply in love with him. Unfortunately, Narcissus, the object of her desire, is both conceited and proud and has eyes only for his own perfection. Ignored by her beloved and unable to give voice to her desires, she fades away into nothingness,

---

1. This line comes from "Ghost," which was the first episode of *Dollhouse* to be broadcast on television and is not to be confused with "Echo," which was the pilot episode produced to pitch the show to Fox. Though "Echo" is included in the DVD set for Season 1 of the show, it was never aired as part of the broadcast run of *Dollhouse*.

2. Despite the assistance rendered to him by Echo, Jupiter declines to interfere in this turn of events, leaving the poor nymph to get along as best she can. Jupiter and Juno have what could most charitably be termed a complicated relationship that is not made easier by their uncomfortably close blood ties. Then again, gods get to do all sorts of things that are considered out-of-bounds for mere mortals.

leaving behind only the ghost of her voice. Narcissus succumbs to a similarly sad fate, dying of heartbreak when he cannot be with his own beloved, who was in this case his own perfect reflection (Ovid 1995, 91–97).

This nutshell version provides all that is necessary to begin the discussion, for within it are found the three main points of this chapter. First, I scrutinize the essential characters and structure of both the original myth and the retelling of it in *Dollhouse*. Next, I explore the crucial action of gazing in both versions of the myth. Finally, I examine the unreliable nature of reflections as mere distorted images. That the myth is contained in Ovid's *Metamorphoses* is in itself illuminating, considering that the common definition of a "metamorphosis" as found in the *Encyclopædia Britannica* is a "striking change of form or structure in an individual after hatching or birth." This transition is usually thought of in terms of physical change, such as a caterpillar transforming into a butterfly. Though Ovid's tales all concern metamorphosis, the changes do not necessarily concern biological states of being. Instead, as Larry Brown (2008) has stated, "Ovid is more interested in metamorphosis as a universal principle which explains the nature of the world: Troy falls, Rome rises. Nothing is permanent." Ovid's Echo transforms from one state to another over the course of the narrative, moving from a physical being to an incorporeal one, as well as undergoing a vast change in personality. Whedon's Echo does much the same, undergoing a weekly metamorphosis as she takes on a new persona for her assignment—one she is told will be "wiped" upon completion of the mission. It is important to note that neither Ovid's Echo nor Whedon's Echo chooses her "forms," and the transformations are not dictated by biology. Rather, both women have their metamorphoses thrust upon them. In the case of Ovid's Echo, the transformation is the result of crossing a powerful woman who has the ability and inclination to curse her supernaturally. In the case of Whedon's Echo, technology and the whims of wealthy clients dictate whether she will be an enthusiastic lover or a dedicated midwife, a hard-as-nails hostage negotiator or a blind believer.

The character of Echo is far from being the only character found in both versions of the Echo myth. Therefore, it is well worth the effort to examine the links in the dramatis personae that exist between Whedon's twenty-first-century tale and Ovid's original. As discussed, Ovid's version involves the following characters: *Jupiter*, chief god and Class A philanderer; *Juno*, queen of the gods and mightily jealous; *Echo*, who is punished harshly by Juno but is not entirely blameless in the events of her own story; and *Narcissus*, who is so focused on his own desires that his name is now the basis of a documented personality disorder. In Whedon's *Dollhouse*, Jupiter becomes the multinational Rossum Corporation, Juno becomes Adelle DeWitt, Echo becomes post-Caroline Echo, and Narcissus becomes Alpha.

At the heart of both the *Dollhouse* ensemble and the Ovid tale is Echo. In the classical myth, Echo is the chatterbox nymph who angers Juno by concealing Jupiter's dalliances and is punished by having her voice stripped from her. Like the classical Echo, when Whedon's Caroline becomes Echo, she is denied her voice—her autonomy, in this case—and is left only with the ability to act out the script written for her by others. Just as the traditional Echo can no longer speak first, but can be only a weak, partial response, Whedon's Echo loses her individuality, becoming a faint reverberation of a "real" person. Regardless of her own feelings and desires, Echo is there to be whomever and whatever the client wants: professional art thief, backup singer, sexy coed, beloved wife, or any of hundreds of other personalities kept on a shelf until ordered by a client.

Whedon's penchant for carefully naming his characters is clearly evident here. His Echo begins life as "Caroline," a name that is a feminized form of "Charles" (M. Campbell 2010a) meaning "man" (M. Campbell 2010b). In this way, Caroline is literally a type of Everyman (or Everywoman, in this case). In *Dollhouse* viewers see that anyone can have autonomy taken away and be made into a Doll. As events with Senator Daniel Perrin show in Season 2, even wealth and power are not absolute shields against this outcome. Anyone and everyone has the potential to become a Doll. An alternative meaning for the name "Caroline" is "free man" (K. Johnson 2008). This definition gives the name another level of significance, for Caroline will spend much of *Dollhouse* fighting to regain her lost freedom and to bring freedom to those individuals enslaved by Rossum. Through her actions, the classical myth is given a clever twist, as Whedon's "Echo" (Caroline's code name) later provides a voice for the mute and powerless.

Aside from her code name, Caroline has additional links to the classical Echo. The original Echo (there is an oxymoron for you!) is a nymph, a spirit of the woods and mountains. Whedon's Caroline begins as a well-intentioned "tree hugger" who wants to expose the plight of animals that are being used for apparently nefarious purposes by the all-powerful Rossum Corporation. I will discuss Echo's nemesis in more detail later. Another of the twists in Whedon's retelling of the myth is that the original Echo is punished for attempting to conceal the truth of Jupiter's dalliances, whereas Whedon's Echo is punished for attempting to reveal the truth about Rossum's activities. In both cases, Echo will pay for her actions by forfeiting her ability to "talk back."

Moreover, following Juno's curse, the classical Echo wanders aimlessly over the fields and woods, basically doing nothing. Whedon's Echo is shown to spend her "downtime" between engagements in a sort of null state. Viewers are told that Dolls are "innocent as children" while in the Dollhouse, spending their days in innocuous pastimes such as painting and gentle yoga, with no activities that might lead to troubling self-awareness.[3] The Dolls lack any real purpose until "activated" for an engagement, at which time Echo is programmed and costumed to be whatever the client has paid handsomely for the Doll to be.

Although Echo's name immediately conjures up the "Echo and Narcissus" myth, the names of the Dolls—Echo, Victor, Sierra, Whiskey, November, Alpha—are derived from the 1957 version of the NATO phonetic alphabet. This alphabet "where letters are substituted by spoken words from an approved list, was . . . developed to help prevent confusion between similar sounding letters/words, and to clarify communications that may be garbled during transmission" (Peña 2006). In a similar fashion, in Whedon's *Dollhouse*, the renamed Dolls are simply ciphers on a list, devoid of any individual, fixed meaning. These human ciphers take on meaning only when a Doll is activated, at which time the Doll stands in for a person of the client's choice.[4]

Echo is the central character in both Ovid's myth and Whedon's *Dollhouse*, and in both, her relationship to other characters is the driving force propelling the narrative forward. For instance, consider Juno. In Ovid's version of the myth, Juno is queen of the gods, married to the all-powerful, yet never faithful, Jupiter. She is the one who punishes Echo for trespassing into the bounds of her dysfunctional relationship with Jupiter. Whedon's Juno is Adelle DeWitt, who is described in the original casting notice for *Dollhouse* as

3. Dolls also go to sleep at night in pods arranged around a central core. The end result looks disturbingly like petals on some twisted type of flower. Seeing them, I am always reminded of my mother's admonishment that I put up my toys before going to bed, and I shiver at that image involving people.

4. Interestingly, the *O* in the phonetic alphabet is represented by "Oscar," not "Omega." The first season episode title "Omega" is likely a reference to the Christian concept of Alpha and Omega. These letters are the first and last letters of the classical Greek alphabet and are used in the Christian faith to refer to God as being eternal, as literally being both the beginning and the end. In *Dollhouse*, this meaning is skewed, as Alpha strives to turn Echo into his version of perfection, for Alpha's "Omega" is meant to be the culmination of the imprinting process.

"cold as an Alp" (SL@SpoilerTV 2008). Just as Juno is married to Jupiter but is not generally treated as an equal to him, Adelle is figuratively married to the Rossum Corporation, the shadowy force powering the Dollhouse. Adelle may be Rossum's symbolic bride, but it is no marriage of equals. Adelle is clearly shown to be intimidated by and subservient to Rossum for most of the series. Similar to Juno's level of knowledge regarding Jupiter's actions, Adelle is usually kept on a "need to know" basis, and that "need to know" is determined by Rossum. Following Caroline's disastrous run-in with Rossum, it is Adelle who takes away Caroline's voice. However, there is a key difference here: the classical Echo is summarily punished by Juno, whereas Whedon's Caroline is given a choice by Adelle. It may be only a "handmaid's tale" sort of choice, one full of sharp edges and nasty consequences, but it is a choice nonetheless. Dolls are people who have agreed under extreme duress to give Rossum five years of service, but this arrangement is far from a simple enlistment contract. Once a person agrees to become a Doll, that person's memory and personality are totally wiped, resulting in a "clean slate" ("Ghost" 1.1). Viewers are told that the person retains no memory whatsoever of his or her prior life. At the end of the five-year term, the original personality is reinstalled and, theoretically, the person resumes ordinary life. Therefore, when Caroline becomes a Doll, she permits Adelle to take away her voice. Like the classical Echo, she is now merely a reflection. The classical Echo is a reflection of sound, whereas Whedon's Echo is a reflection of whatever her primarily male clientele desire her to be. In both cases, Echo's body remains, but her voice is vanquished.

Just as Jupiter thought nothing of slaking his sensual appetites with any lesser being who caught his ever-roving eye, Rossum executives are shown treating the Dolls as disposable objects. As an example, Rossum executive Matthew Harding dismisses Adelle's venture into being a Dollhouse client named "Miss Lonelyhearts" by saying, "Everyone likes to take a little something home from the office once in a while" ("Belonging" 2.4). A wiped human being is not seen to be much different from a box of paper clips, although one is clearly more fun to play with. Whedon has thus cast the multinational Rossum Corporation in the role of the all-powerful god in Ovid's myth. The "Rossum Corporation" is a nod to the play *R.U.R.* written by Czech playwright Karel Čapek in 1920, a debt that is specifically acknowledged in "Getting Closer" (2.11). The title *R.U.R.* is an abbreviation of the name of the corporation at the heart of the play: Rossum's Universal Robots (Čapek and Čapek 1973). Whereas the term *robot* is associated today with clanking mechanical men, Čapek had other ideas, ones that are much more relevant to Whedon's Dollhouse. Rather than being constructed from metal,

Čapek's robots "are more accurately the product of what we would now call genetic engineering" and are the result of chemical manipulation (Jerz 2002). This description sounds eerily similar to the atmosphere of the Dollhouse, which is bristling with bleeding-edge technology.

Like the mind-wiped Dolls, Čapek's robots are supposed to be harmless. They are considered to be "mechanically perfect" but also soulless, God having been supplanted by modern technology (Kussi 1990, 41). The head of robotic psychology and education notes that there is a flaw, though. Despite having no emotions, "occasionally they go crazy somehow. . . . All of a sudden one of them goes and breaks whatever it has in its hand, stops working, gnashes its teeth—and we have to send it to the stamping-mill" (Čapek and Čapek 1973, 50). This "stamping-mill" that breaks down defective robots into their component parts to be used as raw material for new robots bears an uncanny similarity to the Dollhouse's infamous "Attic" where broken Dolls are sent to fulfill other, even darker, purposes than being programmed playthings for the ultrarich.[5] In both cases, signs of self-awareness are not to be tolerated in either robots or Dolls. Though Rossum is far more hands-on than Jupiter is in Ovid's version of the tale, both are determined to keep the status quo firmly in place rather than indulging uppity underlings who have newfangled ideas about the prevailing power structure.

There is one final character to address in the myth—Narcissus, whose quest for perfection results in the death of both Echo and himself. Stripped of her ability to initiate communication, Echo wanders the hills, silent and alone. When she spies Narcissus, she falls instantly in love. Nothing positive will result from Echo's passion, which is woefully one-sided. Narcissus scorns not only Echo, but all who lack the good fortune to be him. In answer to the prayers of a rejected would-be lover, the gods curse Narcissus to suffer the pains he has so thoughtlessly caused others. Therefore, when an exhausted Narcissus rests before a shimmering pool, he falls in mad love with his own perfect reflection. As Ovid states, he is not only the seeker, but also the one who is sought; "he is the arsonist—and is the scorched" (Ovid 1995, 94). Even though vain Narcissus realizes that the lovely image in the still pool is his own, it does nothing to quench his desire. Rather, he wishes to be torn in two so he can admire his perfect inamorato. In Riley's prose translation of the myth, Narcissus articulates his desire in this fashion: "I burn with the love of

---

5. For a more detailed discussion of Čapek's *R.U.R.* and its links to Whedon's *Dollhouse*, see Koontz 2010.

myself, and both raise the flames and endure them. What shall I do? . . . Oh! would that I could depart from my own body! a new wish, *indeed*, in a lover . . ." (Ovid 1893, para. 105). Narcissus burns with the desire for a perfect reflection of himself. Whedon's Narcissus is Alpha, who has an equally strong obsession with what he sees as his own perfection. Alpha sees himself as, quite literally, the "alpha male," the top of the evolutionary heap. Viewers see in the episode "Omega" (1.12) that Alpha had an instantaneous crush on Caroline/Echo, which is the inverse of Echo's passion for Narcissus in the classical version. At this point in the *Dollhouse* narrative, a Doll named Whiskey is shown to be the most requested and popular of the Dolls, but Alpha will brook no challengers to his Echo. Alpha's solution is to deeply slash Whiskey's face, a violent technique he had employed before he entered the Dollhouse and one he will employ again. The Dollhouse staff attempts to "fix" Alpha, but the treatment goes terribly wrong and the obviously disturbed Alpha is instead imprinted with multiple personalities. Living up to Ovid's description of Narcissus as being both "the arsonist and the scorched," the damaged (or "scorched") Alpha goes on a killing spree, disfiguring and slaughtering a large number of Dolls and staff. Ovid's Echo dies as collateral damage of Narcissus's vanity, whereas Alpha actively kills to escape the confines of the Dollhouse. Just as the original Narcissus's needs could be met only by Narcissus himself, so too can Alpha's needs be met only by Alpha. In the final analysis, neither Narcissus nor Alpha has room for any other, including Echo.

Like Narcissus, Alpha sees nothing wrong with who and how he is. Rather, his plan is to give Caroline/Echo the same treatment he received and imprint her with all the personalities that have ever been forcibly jammed into her head in response to the calculating will of a profit-driven corporation. To Alpha, this transformation will make her as highly evolved as he is, and Echo will thereby become his mirror image, to be, in Ovid's words, "that which I desire to stand apart from my own self" (1995, 96). Unable and unwilling to connect with others, Alpha is determined to possess Echo and make her what he wants her to be. In this desire, he is the same as any other client of the Dollhouse whose attitude toward the Dolls is one of "I bought it; this is what I want it to do." Humanity is therefore denied, and the Dolls are viewed very much like Čapek's robots. However, just because one has godlike power does not mean that one's schemes will unfold as planned.

Unable to split his love apart from himself, Narcissus tries again and again to clasp his beloved to him, unable to connect with others even after realizing that the image in the water is his own. Just as his watery reflection is shattered whenever Narcissus reaches out to possess himself, Alpha's personalities are broken fragments, unable to be resolved into a productive whole. Neither Narcissus nor Alpha can form meaningful connections with others. In Whedon's work, lacking the capacity to form significant relationships with others is portrayed as a deep and often fatal flaw. Unable to force his will on Echo, Alpha flees. Regardless of his purported devotion to Caroline/Echo, when trapped, Alpha deliberately drops the computer wedge containing the original Caroline to buy himself time to escape. Notably, the wedge falls toward certain destruction, only to be rescued by Paul Ballard in a cyberpunk version of saving the girl by saving the hardware that *contains* the girl. In Whedon's work, those individuals who can connect are shown to have an advantage over the ones who cannot.[6] Therefore, the first season concludes with Paul Ballard (who *can* connect) insisting that Mellie/November be freed from the remainder of her contract with the Dollhouse, while Alpha (who *cannot* connect) runs like a rabbit, perhaps returning to his underground existence to grow a new batch of medicinal carrots. Viewers discover the answer to the question "what happened to Alpha?" in Season 2, but other questions we might have about his character progression are left unanswered.

The second commonality between Ovid's myth and Whedon's *Dollhouse* is the act of gazing. Echo gazes upon Narcissus while Narcissus gazes into a pool. Both are transfixed by what they see, and both are utterly unable to see anything beyond these surface perceptions. Likewise, Whedon's *Dollhouse* is also preoccupied with the concept of gazing, and *Dollhouse* provides an excellent gateway into the feminist theory of the male gaze as it relates to film. The cinematic theory of the "male gaze" was first put forth by Laura Mulvey and has been subsequently expanded upon by other theorists. A fully detailed synopsis of the development of the theory of the male gaze would be too lengthy for this chapter; however, the fundamentals can be briefly summarized.[7] Whe-

6. Consider Buffy, whose many connections provide her with resources and strength the far more classically trained Slayer Kendra lacks. Buffy adapts and survives, whereas Kendra dies at the hands of Drusilla. Another example is found in Whedon's show *Angel*, which has as a major theme throughout its five-year run Angel's struggle to find a meaningful way to live in the human world. He finds his path lit by friendship and connection. In contrast, when characters isolate themselves from others, those characters often begin a slide down into a moral darkness that will require great effort and the rekindling of the fires of friendship and connection to reverse. As an example, consider Wesley's slide into darkness beginning in Season 3 of *Angel*.

7. Owing to length considerations, I do not even scratch the surface of the Freudian and Lacanian underpinnings of Mulvey's work. Readers whose interest in the development of the theory goes beyond the brief summary contained in this chapter would do well to seek out

don has often spoken of his admiration for the work of film scholar Jeanine Basinger and her influence on his own film studies while he was a student at Wesleyan University. Basinger's book on women as both stars and audience members provides a solid entryway into the discussion of Mulvey's cinematic theory. Basinger explains that Mulvey posits "that women have been made into passive objects for male viewing pleasure by male moviemakers" and "that women on the screen [are] there to fulfill male fantasies and desires, and to both relieve and express male anxieties" (1995, 208). Because movies are primarily made by men, spectators (both male and female) view the resulting images with a "male gaze." Women on-screen are often reduced merely to the status of simple objects rather than being portrayed in far more nuanced representations as autonomous, fully realized human beings.

Mulvey's theory has been expanded since it was initially proposed in 1975.[8] Basinger examines these refinements and encapsulates the work of influential scholars E. Ann Kaplan and Mary Ann Doane. Kaplan claims that a woman's real significance on-screen is quashed and replaced by meanings that continue the needs of the entrenched patriarchal structure. Doane claims that women are forced into two unacceptable options: to view images either as a female viewer who shares the male point of view (seeing women primarily as objects) or as a "transvestite" who identifies with the male hero. Either way, Doane theorizes that women are encouraged to view images of women as objects (208). Often, this on-screen objectification is blazingly obvious, as watching just about any episode of *Baywatch* (1989–99) can attest. Instances of the male gaze being used to reduce a woman to disjointed body parts can be found in lingering shots of a woman's legs, breasts, or backside in numerous examples from television, film, anime, and advertising. Contemporary scholars, notably Teresa de Lauretis, find some light in the gloom of these thoughts. De Lauretis theorizes a more complicated, dualistic view. Female viewers are still forced to identify with the passive woman in the film (for she

---

Mulvey's original essay "Visual Pleasure and Narrative Cinema" (1975) along with the work of theorists such as E. Ann Kaplan (*Women and Film: Both Sides of the Camera*), Mary Ann Doane (*The Desire to Desire: The Woman's Film of the 1940s*), and Teresa de Lauretis (*Technologies of Gender: Essays on Theory, Film & Fiction*).

8. In fact, the "male gaze" theory became so rampant at one point that it was actually parodied by Rhonda V. Wilcox (2002a) in a bitingly funny essay reviewing a mock text, "Visual Pleasure and Nasal Elevation," in which the nose, rather than the eye, is posited as the center of the viewing experience.

is often the *only* woman in the film), but these same viewers are "also identifying with the active elements of the movie, that is to say, with the male characters and subjects" (209). This binary view is presented as a step forward, but clearly there is still a long way to go for women to gain actual parity with men in the arena of nuanced depiction of gender in films and television.[9]

Throughout his career, Whedon has created and presented a number of strong female characters who are most definitely more than mere eye candy. An unrepentant feminist, Whedon has remarked that he was stunned by the "very casual, almost insidious misogyny" that pervades so much mainstream entertainment ("The Ladies' Man" 2005). Yet Whedon's Echo is often presented as a designer sex toy for the ultrarich to rent. This depiction seems to be a great leap backward, but such a conclusion does not reflect the case. Though these three threads—the prevalence of gazing in Ovid's myth, the contemporary theory of the male gaze, and Whedon's self-professed feminism—initially appear too disparate to be woven together coherently, as Adelle DeWitt tells Echo at the very beginning of *Dollhouse*, "Nothing is what it appears to be." Viewers must look more deeply into what is presented in *Dollhouse* to discern these connections.[10]

9. As an aside, there is another theory that dovetails nicely with the idea of the male gaze. The Bechdel Test for women in movies (so named for Alison Bechdel's 1985 comic *Dykes to Watch Out For*) consists of three simple questions to gauge the presence of women in a movie. That is all it measures—just the *presence* of women. It does not claim to measure whether a particular movie is "feminist" or whether a particular movie is "good." The questions are so simple one would think all movies could easily pass the test: Are there at least two women in the movie who have names? Do these women talk to each other? Do they talk to each other about something besides a man? Simple, perhaps, but the list of movies that fail the Bechdel Test is truly shocking. A few examples include *Watchmen* (2009), *Slumdog Millionaire* (2008), *Pulp Fiction* (1994), *The Princess Bride* (1987), *Ghostbusters* (1984), all of the *Lord of the Rings* (2001, 2002, 2003) films, *Shrek* (2001), and even Whedon's own film *The Avengers* (2012). Then again, the Roger Corman bayou-dames-on-the-lam picture *Swamp Diamonds* (1956) does meet the Bechdel criteria, so grains of salt must be taken. At any rate, *Dollhouse* passes the Bechdel Test with flying colors. See http://bechdeltest.com/.

10. Television scholars and critics continue to dive into the pool of *Dollhouse* to explore the deeper meanings of the show. In 2010, the Whedon Studies Association devoted a double issue of *Slayage* to the show (http://slayageonline.com/Numbers/slayage30_31.htm), and Eve Bennett's award-winning exploration of corporate power and the manipulation of fantasy in Dollhouse is included in the spring 2011 issue of *Slayage* (http://slayageonline.com/essays/slayage33/Bennett.pdf).

The series begins with grainy surveillance footage of Adelle DeWitt and Caroline Farrell having tea.[11] The coarse visual quality quickly disappears, as viewers are taken inside the room where it is revealed that Adelle is offering Caroline a five-year contract to be transformed into a Doll. Whedon's use of the gaze begins with this first scene—the audience sees the scene, not just through the eye of the camera, but also filtered through the additional layer of distance provided by the surveillance camera. In other words, we are watching a film within a film. Viewers are given another clue that appearances and perception within this world cannot be trusted to be true or even accurate from the first line of *Dollhouse*: "Nothing is what it appears to be." What the audience is given are merely reflections (and often twisted ones, at that) of events. Such distortion means that viewers will have to be very attentive to discern what is true and what is false. This distortion also extends to portrayals of characters positioned as good/bad and Madonna/whore. To see only one side of the coin is to be deceived.

Whedon seems aware that his initial portrayal of Echo goes against the grain of his openly feminist persona. Consider that the second scene of this first episode shows Echo racing a powerful motorcycle recklessly through traffic, trying to beat her client to an expensive restaurant, where the client is throwing himself a birthday party ("Ghost"). Wearing a beaded micro-mini-dress short enough to qualify as a shirt, she is next shown dancing provocatively with the client. The scene causes Whedon to exclaim in the episode's commentary, "Through the motorcycle to the skimpy dress, I was like, 'What have I become?'" (Whedon and Dushku 2009). Though on the surface Whedon appears to be reinforcing the core concept of the male gaze by presenting passive, objectified women in *Dollhouse* (even Adelle's authority is shown to be tightly leashed by the powerful men who make up Rossum), viewers are rewarded when they go beneath the slick surface. Whedon has not in fact surrendered his feminist mantle, despite the outward appearance of using Echo as mere titillation for his viewers. Indeed, this scene establishes several important points that Whedon returns to throughout the series. Rossum does not view Echo as a person as that term is usually considered. By becoming a Doll, she has been stripped of all autonomy. Her personality, her memories, even

11. Names are always worth paying attention to in Whedon's work, and *Dollhouse* is no exception. Even the seldom-used surnames of characters are laden with meaning. Adelle certainly is quick-witted, and Caroline is in her current mess because she behaved outside the bounds of established society—in a *feral* manner, if you will.

her name—all of these components have been scooped out of her skull and stashed on a hard drive on a shelf in a lab. Yet Echo is not a cipher. She retains flashes of memory, and she will not fade into thin air, as did Ovid's Echo. However, her fire of self-awareness burns only on the inside, while her outward appearance and demeanor remain a representation of total compliance.

Echo's clients may gaze upon her, but they never see an actual "her." Instead, they see what they have ordered, just as Ovid's Narcissus sees only what he wants to see when he gazes into the pool. Narcissus manufactures his beloved's identity; in *Dollhouse*, identity is uploaded into Echo by an outside source. In this way, Whedon asks a valuable question: are humans fungible goods? He asks this question in the commentary for "Man on the Street" (1.6) when he muses, "How are we socialized in such a way that all we see of each other is external?" (Whedon 2009). Echo and the other Dolls are initially presented as empty shells that have no meaning until a specific set of requested skills and traits are loaded into them, at which time the buyer projects the context and meaning onto the market-ready Doll.

Echo's clients are not the only ones shown to do so. Paul Ballard, the FBI agent who begins the series on a quest to expose the Dollhouse and find Caroline, is positioned as the chivalrous hero of the piece. He has been obsessively pursuing his goal to the point of dismissing crucial information as merely collateral. Nietzsche famously stated that "he who fights with monsters should look to it that he himself does not become a monster. And when you gaze long into an abyss the abyss also gazes into you" ([1886] 1990, 102). Ballard's obsession with discovering the truth of the Dollhouse is his abyss, and he has gazed into it far too long. The Dollhouse has unlimited resources that have been brought to bear on Ballard—he has been gazed into. As a result, Ballard will align himself with the monsters he has been fighting, and the result will lead to death and destruction, in part because reflections contain distorted knowledge. Just as Echo's clients see her only as their expensive, designed-to-order fantasy rather than a real person, Ballard first sees Echo as a static photographed image rather than a living being. Further, in "Man on the Street," he and Echo have their first in-depth interaction after he glimpses her reflection in a window. Again, he is drawn to the *image* of Caroline/Echo, rather than seeing her as an actual person, and his confusion over the image versus the reality will cause him to repeatedly underestimate the schemes and resources of the Dollhouse.

The confusion caused by reflected images being taken for the "real thing" leads to the third commonality *Dollhouse* shares with the classic myth of Echo and Narcissus: the inherent unreliability of reflections. Echo gazes upon

Narcissus and thereby condemns herself to fade away into nothingness as she fruitlessly attempts to gain the attention of a man who is the ultimate epitome of "girl, he's just not that into you." Echo is completely unable to see that Narcissus has no interest in her. Indeed, Narcissus is enchanted with his reflection in a pool and confuses perception and reality to the point of death. In the classic telling of the myth, Narcissus's doom is foretold by a seer who cryptically tells his mother that Narcissus will reach old age only "if he never recognizes himself" (Ovid 1893, para. 101). Narcissus's utter inability to distinguish reality from perception leads to his downfall and death.[12]

The folly of confusing perception with reality is a driving theme of *Dollhouse*. Whedon (2009) acknowledges that he is deliberately manipulating multiple points of view, saying in the commentary for "Man on the Street" that "this [show] is about perception and so the heavy use of reflections without being didactic is absolutely thematic." This "heavy use of reflections" is seen in *Dollhouse*'s repeated use of eyes and vision as a critical part of the overall narrative. An example is found in the first episode of the show in which Echo is programmed to be a hard-as-nails hostage negotiator who wears glasses because this persona is nearsighted ("Ghost"). The nature of vision being inherently deceptive is developed further in "True Believer" (1.5), when the vision centers in Echo's brain are rerouted to allow her eyes to be used as high-tech cameras so events in a secretive cult can be monitored. Echo's imprint is blind and is further programmed to believe that she has come to the cult compound as the result of a "vision." Another example comes from "Epitaph One" (1.13), the final, unaired episode of the first season. This episode concludes with three characters leaving the Dollhouse, which has been the scene of tremendous carnage. As the three emerge into the remains of Adelle DeWitt's once-plush office, their attention is seized by a wall of photographs. Gazing at the photos, viewers are able to identify several of the Dolls. One of the photos is the black-and-white photo of Caroline first seen by viewers at the end of the first episode as Alpha drops it into an envelope to send to Paul Ballard. Held by Caroline, who has been uploaded into the body of a prepubescent girl, viewers are brought full circle. Caroline is not in "her" body as she gazes at an image of herself, yet the body she is in retains all the memories of being Caroline. Over this scene, the haunting song "Remains" (written by

---

12. This confusion between the Self and the reflected self (or "not self") as it relates to the condition of narcissism has been remarked upon before, notably by Christopher Lasch (quoted in Lavery 2010, 14–15).

Maurissa Tancharoen and Jed Whedon) is heard, and two lyrics from the song stand out: "Shine light on me / Your image reflected is all you'll ever see" (2009). The image is all that remains of the woman who had been Caroline: although her memories are contained in the mind of the young girl holding her picture, the Caroline of the photograph no longer truly exists, having been forever altered by her experiences while in the Dollhouse, along with the relationships she developed and the secrets she uncovered while there. This Caroline can move forward, but the slate is most certainly not blank.

Reflections are used throughout *Dollhouse* as a means not only of indicating that what the viewer sees is not to be taken at full face value but also of looking backward ("reflecting") on past events to imbue those events with meaning. Whereas this technique of reflecting on the past to find meaning in those past events is often utilized in "real life," in *Dollhouse* it proves to be problematic. Danish philosopher Søren Kierkegaard once claimed, "Life is lived forward but understood backward" (quoted in Watkin 2004). In the Dollhouse, as well as at the edge of Narcissus's pool, this statement, like so many others, loses its inherent meaning. As Caroline holds the picture of herself, viewers must acknowledge that her meaning is not derived from a linear structure, but must be cobbled together from multiple points of view. By doing so, Caroline is able to move forward, unlike the classical Echo and Narcissus, who are both so invested in what they think they see that they are completely unable to move beyond that broken perception.

Whedon's *Dollhouse* is rooted in Ovid's myth, and his Echo has clear echoes of the classical Echo. One final point remains to be made about these connections. Central to the myth of Echo and Narcissus is the image of the pool: Narcissus stares into the pool, oblivious to his surroundings, while Echo flutters at the edge of the pool, yearning for her beloved to speak so she can at least say a word or two back to him. In the opening credits for the first season, Whedon's Echo is shown sitting gracefully at the bottom of a swimming pool, in quiet contrast to the chaos of multiple engagements swirling above her. There may be no better image with which to close this discussion. The image of a calm woman at rest underwater is unsettling, yet it makes perfect sense. After all, an "echo" is reflected sound, and sound travels faster underwater, although it is also distorted by the water. Whedon's Echo has a long way to travel to find her way back to Caroline, and both of them will be distorted and transformed by the journey. The final destination is not the country Caroline expected to find, for this Echo is not a simple reflection of someone else. Through her recollected experiences, Echo is her own new creation. In the first episode, Caroline belligerently challenges Adelle about the latter's use of the "clean slate" metaphor, claiming that there is no such thing, for "you always see what was on it before" ("Ghost"). She was only partially correct. Far from being a pale copy, Echo has not revealed what had previously been written on the "Caroline slate." Instead, she has completely overwritten that material, rendering herself far more palimpsest than slate. In a similar fashion, Whedon has not contented himself with simply retelling a myth. Rather, he has given viewers an entirely new lens through which to gaze at an epic story of identity, memory, and perception.

"There Is No Me; I'm Just a Container"

Law and the Loss of Personhood in Dollhouse

SHARON SUTHERLAND AND SARAH SWAN

Each of Joss Whedon's four television shows has explored, in some manner, what it means to be human.[1] *Buffy the Vampire Slayer* presented a world in which personhood is part of having a soul: beings with souls fall under the protection of the Slayer, while those beings lacking souls can be killed without compunction.[2] *Angel*, with its eponymous vampire-with-a-soul protagonist, took this examination further and delved into the potential of the formerly soulless to regain the rights of personhood through redemptive acts. In *Firefly*, Whedon's conception of the human became even more complex: the evil monsters facing the protagonists in this series were Reavers: human-made monsters.[3] Not surprisingly, then, Whedon's most recent television series, *Dollhouse*, also asks what it is to be human. Yet unlike the first three series, *Dollhouse* does not examine this question from the emotional distance of a world of demons and mystical creatures, nor from the remove of a space empire in the distant future; *Dollhouse* grounds its examination in a Los Angeles that seems in almost every way like the present one and directly tackles some of the most pressing and concerning human rights issues of the twenty-first century: slavery, human trafficking, and sexual exploitation. Whenever the Dollhouse setting or the complexity of the technology allow the viewers to separate themselves from a seemingly distant science fiction future, passing

---

1. This chapter's title comes from a statement made by Echo in "Omega" (1.12).

2. As the scholarship on this subject shows, the issue of the soul in the Whedonverses is complicated. See, for example, McLaren 2005. See also Erickson, this volume.

3. For a discussion of this issue, see Rabb and Richardson 2008.

comments root us to the present.[4] In *Dollhouse*, Whedon engages with this subject matter in complex and disturbing ways.

Slavery and human trafficking are unthinkable to most people in North America, yet somehow they continue to exist throughout the world, including in developed countries. Human trafficking is the fastest-growing criminal activity in the world today (Das 2007). Globally, estimates suggest that 27 million people are slaves (Kristof and WuDunn 2009, 9). Within the United States, the Department of Justice estimates that 14,500–17,500 people are brought into the country each year to work as slaves, while more than 200,000 American children are at high risk for trafficking into the sex industry annually (Wisconsin Office of Justice Assistance 2012). Relevant to the feminist Whedon, 80 percent of all slaves are estimated to be female, and 75 percent of all slaves are forced into commercial sexual exploitation (Kristof and WuDunn 2009, 10).

There can be no doubt that the subject matter of *Dollhouse*—sexual slavery and rape—is deeply disturbing. *Dollhouse* attempts to engage the viewer in these unsettling topics through a variety of devices, but most important through the oft-repeated argument that the Dolls volunteered for service. Characters like Topher Brink and Adelle DeWitt who clearly accept, to some degree, the fiction of volunteerism and eventual benefit to the Dolls help viewers to enter into the world of the Dollhouse. Once inside, *Dollhouse* asks difficult questions regarding the possibility of consenting to the removal of one's personhood.

Dollhouse also presents the complex ways that slavery and sexual exploitation interact with personhood and with society. Through its depiction of the rise and fall of a high-end sci-fi brothel, *Dollhouse* offers a nuanced and challenging presentation of many issues surrounding personhood, sex work, and exploitation; demonstrates how law can be used as a technology of exploitation; and forces us to consider the ways in which exploitation, and in particular the exploitation of women, ultimately threatens the humanity of everyone.

Contract, Consent, and Personhood

Given the central fiction that the Dolls are all willing participants in their five years of servitude, it is only natural that *Dollhouse* begins with a contract

---

4. For example, when Caroline/Echo is grappling with the confusion of having thirty-eight personalities through the magic of the Dollhouse's technology, Echo reminds us that we are in the immediate present "now that we have a black president" ("Omega"). Similarly, the entire episode "Man on the Street" operates as an anchor to the present as we see a cross-section of citizens that are clearly from our own world (1.6).

negotiation. In the opening scene, Adelle, the head of the Los Angeles branch of the Dollhouse, discusses the future with Caroline Farrell, a young activist detained after her attempt at blowing up a laboratory went horrifically awry.[5] The two are seated at a table, in a typical corporate boardroom or office, and Adelle describes the terms of the deal: Caroline will enter into a five-year term of service, and in return, the Dollhouse will ensure that she exits the contract a wealthy woman, free of legal and psychological consequences for the damage she has inflicted ("Ghost" 1.1).

In this scene, the Dollhouse uses law as a technology of manipulation and exploitation, designed to bring Caroline under its power.[6] As the "victim" of Caroline's laboratory invasion, the Dollhouse controls the legal consequences to her: they can make the consequences disappear or make them as dire as possible. Here, rather than an exogenous circumstance, the law is portrayed as a weapon in the arsenal of the Dollhouse. The Dollhouse uses its power, and Caroline's desire to escape legal, emotional, and moral responsibility for what has occurred, to motivate her to enter into the transaction. Caroline recognizes the kind of manipulation that is at play when she objects to Adelle's choice of the word *volunteering* to describe her level of agreement.[7] Caroline points out that the term is disingenuous, since the circumstances as presented have left her with no meaningful choice. Adelle, however, remains insistent that this exchange is fair, and she later reminds Caroline of her version of the agreement:

ADELLE: You wanted to forget . . . I eased your suffering.
ECHO: Is that what you think you are doing here? Taking away basic human rights? Free will? My right to choose, feel, remember?
ADELLE: All relinquished by you, to our care and discretion.
ECHO: Tell me why I would.

5. It is perhaps more accurate to say "In the opening scene as aired on Fox": Whedon originally intended an episode called "Echo" (included on the DVD) to open the series.

6. As Franke notes, technology, beyond its connotations of scientific advancement and new devices, also means "a manner of accomplishing a task," a way of bringing about a desired reality (1997, 693). See Bussolini in this volume.

7. Differing scholarly opinions on *Dollhouse* reflect the complexity of the question of Caroline's consent. Wilcox writes that "Caroline is under extreme pressure (in the pilot 'Ghost,' she says, 'I don't have a choice, do I?'), but she does, of her own will, choose to sign the contract" (2010, para. 4), whereas Perdigao asserts that "both Caroline and Priya are forced into service" (2010, para. 16).

> ADELLE: I can't. I would be breaking a promise I made to you. All I
> can say is that you couldn't live with the consequences of your own
> actions. And you no longer have to. ("Needs" 1.8)

In addition to setting up the threat of criminal sanctions as a powerful motivator to influence Caroline's actions, Adelle also uses the act of contracting to manipulate Caroline. Typically, parties use formal contracts because they want their agreement to be legally enforceable in a court of law. In this case, though, that protection is not the purpose of the contract. Even if it were possible to enforce a contract for illegal services (which at least some of the assignments appear to be), the Dollhouse would never try to enforce a contract with an Active in court, for, as Boyd says, "we'd spend our lives in jail if anyone ever found this place" ("Ghost").

The Rossum Corporation's reliance on contractual forms, then, has a different motivation. The contract provides a distance from the ugliness of the realities underlying the transaction. Rather than the lurid connections to slavery, prostitution, and human trafficking that appear when one person is asked to surrender her body for the use and purposes of another, the contract gives the exchange the flavor of a staid, legitimate business transaction. Further, it gives the illusion that the parties are coming to the contract as equals, each negotiating a position and each receiving something in exchange for the promises made and obligations assumed. Adelle warns Caroline at the beginning of the episode that "nothing is as it appears to be," and the contract is no exception: it hides the reality of what is being transferred.

The contract also serves another purpose: it creates a moral obligation in the minds of the soon-to-be-Actives. For instance, when in "Omega" Caroline's original personality is activated in the body of Wendy, and Echo invites Caroline back to her own body, Caroline at first resists, on the basis that she has committed herself to an agreement and cannot renege. Echo, though, recognizes that such a bargain is unconscionable and cannot be morally binding. She tells Caroline that she cannot "sign a contract to be a slave" ("Omega"). FBI agent Paul Ballard echoes this same belief when he states, "I don't even care that these people signed themselves over to you. There is no provision for consensual slavery. It is wrong. You know it's wrong" ("Briar Rose" 1.11).

To Echo and Paul, one simply cannot alienate one's personhood, contract or no contract. As Echo declares, "I have 38 brains. Not one of them thinks you can sign a contract to be a slave" ("Omega"). They see the legal form as incapable of legitimizing such a transaction. Yet just as the contract operates to hide the ugliness of the true transaction, and to give it a veneer of legality, Adelle, in particular, both humanizes and rationalizes the argument that persons should be entitled to make any choice affecting their own body and mind, including volunteering for slavery. While Adelle's own role is problematic (as discussed below), her sales pitch for the Dollhouse to clients, "recruits," and skeptics like Ballard provides a smooth and well-thought-out counterpoint, requiring the audience to engage intellectually with the arguments for prostitution and deeper questions of how far consent to commercial sexual activities can go.[8] Adelle is the face of sincere rationalization, an intelligent woman who believes wholeheartedly in the liberal values of personal choice and freedom to contract, and she finds the Dollhouse a morally acceptable concept within that worldview.

Volunteer Slavery

The paradox and tension inherent in "volunteering" to become a slave are primary themes throughout *Dollhouse*. In the Whedon-written episode "Man on the Street" (1.6), a television news reporter interviews various people about the "urban legend" of the Dollhouse. One interviewee says, "Oh, it's happening. If there's one thing people will always need, it's slaves. . . . There's only one reason someone would volunteer to be a slave: if they is one already. Volunteers! You must be out of your f***in' mind." Although Topher and Adelle insist that the Actives are volunteers, as the stories behind the Dollhouse's recruiting activities are flushed out, the voluntariness of all the Actives is called into question. As noted, Caroline is pressured into her contract under threat of legal penalties. So too is Sam Jennings, the former grad student who attempted to steal a drug from the Rossum Corporation in "Echoes" (1.7). For other Actives, psychological traumas lead them to the Dollhouse, or, rather, lead the Dollhouse to them. Madeline/November was approached following the sudden death of her young daughter, an event that left her "unable to function," and Anthony/Victor was similarly scarred due to post-traumatic stress disorder caused by military service. Most troubling of all, Priya/Sierra was mistakenly believed to be psychologically damaged, though it is later revealed that she had been drugged in order to have her forced into service as a Doll. Each Active, then, arrives at the Dollhouse for reasons that render their consent problematic: we do not see any psychologically healthy Actives making reasoned and freely considered decisions to join

8. For a comparison of prostitution in *Dollhouse* and *Firefly*, see Szabo 2011.

the Dollhouse. Indeed, we learn that the Dollhouse initially experimented on prisoners ("Omega"), a choice that resonates with a long history of abusive medical experimentation premised on beliefs that denied the full rights of personhood to persons of color and criminals (for example, the Tuskegee syphilis trials, Nazi experiments in concentration camps, and the Holmesburg scandal). And, of course, this experimentation resonates with recent debates regarding the lifting of restrictions on experimentation on prisoners (Obasogie 2010, 53), again reminding the viewer that the Dollhouse is a small remove from the present.

Once an Active has "volunteered," there are many features of the Dollhouse-Active relationship that link it to slavery. Most important, the Dolls cannot quit: there is no option for them to exit the contract through an exercise of free will.[9] During the five-year term, the Active must do whatever it is programmed to do. The Active is possessed, mind, body, and soul. She is made to perform acts that would be unthinkable to her usual self and is allowed no choice regarding them. Further, she is forever changed by the experience: the imprinting process requires a modification of the architecture of the brain of an Active, architecture that is never removed. Any technology that affects Active Dolls will also affect former Dolls, a lesson Madeline learns when the remote wipe in "The Public Eye" (2.5) affects her, even though she has been released from her contract (Calvert 2010, para. 9). The former Actives are also subject to continued surveillance and monitoring.

The two Actives whose contracts we see terminate, Madeline and Anthony, both end up back in the Dollhouse.[10] Madeline believes that she is free, only to be taken back to the Dollhouse when she attempts to expose the organization, and she ends up back in the chair.[11] Anthony undergoes a similar fate. Within twenty-four hours of his release, another unit of the Rossum Corporation kidnaps him and enfolds him into a military collective that threatens to remove his personality forever. When Paul Ballard rhetorically asks in "Getting Closer," "No one ever really leaves here, do they?" the answer is obvious (2.11).

9. "Any legitimate contract must still leave all parties involved with some rights, including the option to default on the contract" (Kreider 2011, 67).

10. Many Actives are released during "Getting Closer" (2.11), but we do not see what happens to them.

11. The technology used to insert different personalities in the brain is activated in "the chair."

The Dollhouse, like any slavery regime, adheres to the idea that "ownership gives an absolute right of disposal of and authority over the owned" (Gwaltney 1999, 37). Although the form of ownership in *Dollhouse* is notionally more akin to a form of lease, there are many instances when the Dollhouse acts as though it has inviolate rights of ownership over the Actives. For instance, Matthew Harding's order that Priya must be imprinted and sent permanently to Nolan indicates he believes he has an unlimited property right over her. Rather than believing in the principle that each individual has an intrinsic right to control over her body, the Dollhouse operates on the belief that that right can be transferred. Once it has been, the Dolls become mere objects rather than subjects. This feature is perhaps the most important element of slavery: to be a slave is to be an object rather than a subject. In this sense, slavery directly attacks personhood, since "to be a person certainly means not to be merely a thing or object" (33). In the Dollhouse, the Dolls are revenue streams and guinea pigs for new technologies rather than persons. In particular, the several references to Dolls as pets reinforce their subhuman status ("Needs").

Sexual Slavery and Prostitution

Volunteering to be a slave has special implications when the sexual nature of the slavery in *Dollhouse* is considered. Prostitution has been described as "volunteer slavery" or "a choice made by people who have no choice" (Farley 2006, 110). The issue of the voluntariness of sex work and prostitution remains a complex one, and *Dollhouse* offers no easy answers. One point of view sees prostitutes as sex slaves, another as entrepreneurs. In reality, though, "there are some in each category and many other women who inhabit a gray zone between freedom and slavery" (Kristof and WuDunn 2009, 10). The Dolls, with their multiplicity of circumstances and motivations for joining the Dollhouse, reflect reality in this regard. There are no simple explanations for how each individual ends up at the Dollhouse. The one commonality, as Boyd suggests when Sierra returns after killing Nolan, is that they are all, in some sense, broken ("Belonging" 2.4).

Regardless of how they got there, part of the Dolls' contract clearly involves the provision of sex work. We see them on numerous sexual engagements, some ostensibly "romantic" and some explicitly involving domination and submission. The connection between prostitution, personhood, and disassociation is poignantly represented on the series. Many real-life first-person accounts of prostitution and sex work describe psychological dissociation or distancing from the event.[12] The same type of distancing between the "self" and sexual performances is evident in the Dolls: their self is completely separate from the sex acts they perform while imprinted. Echo describes it well when she says to Topher, "You gut them [Dolls] and use their bodies as playthings!" ("Needs"). There is something quite distressing involved in watching a self-aware Echo attempt to console Paul when he expresses disgust at his role as her pimp. She tells him that the client is not so bad and that when she performs the acts, she will retreat behind another imprint ("A Love Supreme" 2.8).

Whether sex work is inherently damaging to the personhood of the individuals who perform it is an open question. Some sex-work positive views are voiced during the series, although some, at least, are from the client's perspective. Dr. Saunders, for instance, points out that having a desire that you have to keep secret can be debilitating. She notes that they provide Dolls for many same-sex engagements, despite the purported increase in gay rights. An interviewee in "Man on the Street" suggests he would like to be such a client, when he admits that he would enjoy a consequence-free sexual encounter with another man. A version of Echo (imprinted as an FBI agent) expresses a worker-side view that sex work need not be damaging, when she asks Paul, "Is this about the sex? I know for you the act of love is the most intimate and precious thing two people can share. But it's just bodies. It's useful. And Clark is pretty damn fun. Man's got a work ethic" ("Vows" 2.1). It should be noted, though, that FBI agent Echo had been performing sex work with Echo's body for a long time by this point in the series, so this detached view of sex could itself be the result of that experience.

Rape

For those individuals in the Dollhouse, as the line between person and nonperson becomes obscured, the line between rape and consensual sex becomes similarly blurry. Of course, rape is not a monolithic phenomenon: "all rapes are not alike." Different degrees and kinds of force, coercion, and manipulation are part of rape (Baker 2008, 186). *Dollhouse* presents a range of sexual

---

12. For instance, "I've learned not to be there when they touch me. When they touch my breasts, I tell myself they're not really touching me" (J. Edelstein 2008, 356).

encounters and many different forms of rape as it challenges its viewers to judge where the line between consent and rape occurs.

Interestingly, Adelle is often the voice of judgment regarding whether someone has crossed a moral line with the Dolls, particularly in regards to rape. In Adelle's view, removing a person's consciousness and then allowing others to engage in sexual activities with her body is not rape. Others, including the Supreme Court of Canada, take a different view. In a recent case, *R v. J. A.*, 2011 SCC 28, the Court was asked to decide whether consent to engage in erotic asphyxiation extends to sexual activities performed on one's body once unconscious. Simply put, the issue was "whether a person can perform sexual acts on an unconscious person if the person consented to those acts in advance of being rendered unconscious." The Court held that consent and unconsciousness were incompatible: consent requires "a conscious, operating mind, capable of granting, revoking or withholding consent to each and every sexual act." In other words, at least according to the Canadian interpretation of consent, each sexual engagement that Dolls are sent on is a form of rape.

Although Adelle believes that sex with the imprinted Dolls is not rape, she does view the Dolls as rapeable. In the innocent, infantile, unprinted Doll state, the Dolls are not aware of their sexuality, or, perhaps more specifically, are not thought to have sexuality. Adelle believes that in this state, sex with the Dolls is inevitably rape. She is particularly horrified when it is discovered that Sierra has been sexually assaulted in this state. When Adelle learns that Sierra's handler, Hearn, is the perpetrator, she sentences him to death for his crime. She sends him to his death at the hands of another woman, an ending that she says "did not lack for poetry" ("Man on the Street").

Nolan is also punished with death for raping Sierra/Priya. Nolan's rape of Sierra/Priya is more complex: he has arranged to have Priya placed in the Dollhouse against her will; he then purchased her body for sex in an imprinted state—a state that is normally considered by Adelle to be consenting. However, Priya's lack of consent in entering into the Dollhouse changes things for Adelle. She views what he has done as abhorrent, labeling him "a raping scumbag one tick shy of a murderer" for having Priya put in the Dollhouse under false pretenses ("Belonging"). In this case, Adelle sees clearly that Nolan has committed a fraud on the Dollhouse to bypass Priya's consent. Adelle's anger underscores the fact that her definition of consent to Dollhood differs from the version of other characters: she clearly draws the line at fraud, but continues to support the notion of consent under duress where others, such as Madeline and Anthony, are concerned.

The Clients

Adelle's view on what constitutes rape of the Dolls is particularly interesting when one considers that she herself is a client of the Dollhouse. Indeed, the very term *client*, the preferred nomenclature in the Dollhouse, is another form of obfuscation, in that it connotes a commercial transaction rather than a sexual one. As one character suggests while trying to come up with the appropriate label, a term like *the John* may be more appropriate ("Man on the Street"). The role of these clients or Johns in perpetuating prostitution and trafficking is becoming a larger part of the dialogue surrounding the sex trade, and in *Dollhouse*, we are offered a glimpse into the role clients play in forced prostitution. Throughout the series, we become intimately familiar with many of these clients, particularly the ones purchasing Echo. Unlike the Dolls, these men[13] are aware of what is happening, and they know exactly what they are buying: they understand that the Dolls are programmed to be whomever the clients want them to be. Many are repeat buyers, and they blithely accept the programming as equivalent to genuine consent. Their willingness to purchase these women (and, less often, men) is an important part of the reason the Dollhouse can exist.

Adelle hides her role as a client from the others at the Dollhouse. She disguises herself as the elderly Ms. Lonelyhearts to have sexual experiences with Victor, programmed as the debonair Roger. Adelle uses Victor for the purposes of her own pleasure, raising an issue that is further complicated when one considers that she insists on multiple engagements with him, despite Dr. Saunders's warnings that using the same imprint on the same Active multiple times is dangerous and could cause permanent harm. Although Adelle is quick to point the moral finger at Hearn for his abuse of Sierra, she does not appear to consider how closely aligned her actions are with his. Both she and Hearn are using someone else's body to take what they want, with no regard for the well-being of the other. Indeed, the Rossum Corporation's Matthew Harding suggests that Adelle and Nolan have committed similar wrongs when he chides her with the question, "You wouldn't let anyone take advantage of your charges, would you, Ms. Lonelyhearts?" ("Belonging"). Although Adelle would like to believe that her actions are not similar to Nolan's and Hearn's, Harding's admonishment rings true. When Adelle tries to draw a moral line against certain proposed actions by insisting, "We're not slave-merchants,"

---

13. The clients of the Dollhouse are shown to be predominantly male.

Harding again speaks the truth when he points out that, actually, they are ("Belonging").

Others in the Dollhouse have complicated relationships with the Dolls as well. Boyd pursues a relationship with Dr. Saunders, even though she is a Doll. Of course, once Boyd's identity as the founder of Rossum is revealed, this relationship takes on more sinister connotations, but even earlier, his connection with a Doll is problematic. Ballard, despite his mission to expose and close the Dollhouse, also becomes a client: he uses Echo in an FBI-like sting operation. Together, Boyd and Ballard represent a movement from men who should be enforcing law into clients of the Dollhouse. Their subversion (in Boyd's case, a misleading one) describes the morally gray approach of ends justifying means, as Ballard, in particular, crosses lines that were previously clear to him.

Personhood, Exploitation, and the End of Humanity

On *Dollhouse*, the technology that facilitates the prostitution, human trafficking, and rape of the Dolls eventually leads to a near apocalypse. A character in the unaired future history episode "Epitaph One" asks, "A brothel? You mean to tell me that the tech that punk-kicked the ass of mankind was originally designed to create more believable hookers?" Whereas the group in "Epitaph One" seems shocked that there could be a connection between creating "more believable hookers" and bringing about the end of the world, many scholars have demonstrated a profound connection between the status of women and the general health of a society (Kristof and WuDunn 2009, xix). Societies in which women are oppressed, and where forced prostitution and human trafficking are rampant, tend to be the most unhealthy societies, plagued with poverty, violence, and despair (xix). While critics and activists argue that participating in the enslavement of others metaphorically diminishes the humanity of all involved, in *Dollhouse* we see the loss of humanity on a literal level in the two "Epitaph" episodes. As Echo comments in "Ghost," "Actions have consequences," and the development of technologies that remove the personhood of an individual will clearly have broader repercussions.

Underlying the events that almost bring about an apocalypse is a layer of misogyny that is perhaps one of the most disturbing aspects of the world of the Dollhouse. Throughout, a pervasive misogyny permits the objectification of women—in particular, the commodification of bodies and the disavowal of the Dolls' personhood. The scene in which a middle-aged FBI agent watches the college-age Caroline on video illustrates this attitude. The agent refers to

Caroline as "a piece of tail" and tells Paul that because she is a Doll, Caroline is one of two things: "A: effectively dead, and B: a whore. A mindless whore, just your type" ("Man on the Street").

The misogyny that permits the dehumanization of women and the commodification of their bodies for men's pleasure is supported by "tech" that almost brings about the apocalypse. This "tech" can be read as a highly effective stand-in for the more mundane manipulation and intimidation of women into the sex trade in real life. The words of the professor in "Man on the Street" offer a chilling portent: "Forget morality. Imagine it's true, all right. Imagine this technology being used. Now imagine it being used on you. Everything you believe, gone. Everyone you love, strangers. Maybe enemies. Every part of you that makes you more than a walking cluster of neurons dissolved at someone else's whim. If that technology exists—it'll be used. It'll be abused. It'll be global. And we will be over. As a species. We will cease to matter. I don't know, maybe we should" ("Man on the Street"). Neuroscience is constantly advancing, and one day something like the tech in *Dollhouse* may not be merely a science fiction device (Muntersbjorn 2010). In the meantime, however, a different kind of technology is already being used, is being abused, and is global. When women are forced into prostitution and persons are enslaved, equally frightening forms of coercion are used to remove their dignity and humanity. The personhood of individuals in forced sex situations is stripped away through mental, emotional, and often physical coercion. Body and mind become separate, and the body is commodified. The mind or will becomes irrelevant, erased either through physical and mental abuse or through the "technology" of drugs. Once only bodies are of value, the jump from temporarily renting out Dolls to permanently selling the bodies of Dolls to the rich as "anatomy upgrades" (as suggested in "Haunted" [1.10] and seen in "Epitaph Two" [2.13]) is not large.

Despite the attempts of pimps to dehumanize the prostituted, stories of resilience and triumph appear. Caroline's story in some ways parallels the experiences of the small number of women who successfully escape from brothels and sex work: she proves that she is more than a trophy or a slave; she is a person, despite what happens to her and despite what uses her body may have been subjected to. Initially valued only for her body and the fruit of that body—her unique spinal fluid—Caroline comes to be much more than a body, even appearing embodied in more than one human form in "Epitaph Two." In some sense, this double embodiment shows that Caroline has transcended her body rather than having been defined by it. She is able to create a "posthuman subjectivity," to, as Alpha says, "ascend" (Hawk 2010a, para. 1).

Despite the attempt to objectify her, Echo undergoes subjectivization, "the process of becoming a subject . . . characterized by one's relation to power structures and by one's struggle to narrate the process" (para. 4). Ironically, Echo takes a power structure that is meant to oppress her and from it forms a personhood more resilient than the one she had before. The violence inflicted on her, both metaphorically in the form of the obviously unpleasant imprinting process and literally in the form of the many violent altercations with clients and others, had the potential to destroy not just her body but also her personhood. In destroying the familiar forms, however, Echo is able to reconstruct a new self, for "in the story of forgetting and remembering pain is the story of constructing (or sustaining) one's identity" (Perdigao 2010, para. 17).

Conclusion

In *Dollhouse*, Whedon offers a brutal depiction of the complexities of prostitution, human trafficking, and rape, examining through these most egregious violations of personhood what it means to be human and retain one's self. The slippery divisions between voluntary action, consent, and enslavement are depicted through the stories of the Actives and the clients, creating a nuanced and complex vision of the gray zone between consent and force. Perhaps *Dollhouse*'s most scathing comment is the subtle indictment of the viewers themselves as somehow complicit in the evil of slavery (Wilcox 2010): like the many citizens interviewed in "Man on the Street" who all know that the Dollhouse exists yet do nothing, the vast majority of North Americans are aware of the problems of forced prostitution, human trafficking, and the continuing commodification and objectification of people yet also do nothing. *Dollhouse* can certainly be read as a call to action to stop the growing harm of the contemporary slave trade. As Whedon reminds us, individuals can make a difference. Just as the Scoobies of *Buffy the Vampire Slayer*, the staff at Angel Investigations, and the very human crew of *Firefly* all make a difference in their battles against evil and injustice, Caroline/Echo and her colleagues in the battle against Rossum Corporation have an impact. Although they do not completely win the battle for human dignity and respect of personhood, the near-apocalyptic world of "Epitaph Two" contains traces of hope that all is not lost, and suggests that resistance is meaningful and important and may one day be successful.

Part Five

Beyond
the Box

Joining the Evil League of Evil

The Rhetoric of Posthuman Negotiation
in Dr. Horrible's Sing-Along Blog

VICTORIA WILLIS

Written by Maurissa Tancharoen, Jed Whedon, Joss Whedon, and Zack Whedon, *Dr. Horrible's Sing-Along Blog* garnered so many hits when Act 1 was released on July 15, 2008, that the online server crashed. After the acquisition of more bandwidth, and the attempted resolution of viewing problems for international viewers who wanted to participate in the Internet serial release, Acts 2 and 3 were released on July 17 and 19, respectively. With little advertisement other than word of mouth, the forty-two-minute *Dr. Horrible's Sing-Along Blog* won the 2009 Hugo Award for "Best Dramatic Presentation, Short Form," the 2009 People's Choice Award for "Best Internet Phenomenon," seven of the 2009 Streamy Awards for Web TV, and the 2009 Primetime Creative Arts Emmy for "Outstanding Special Class—Short-Format Live-Action Entertainment Programs." Additionally, *Time* listed *Dr. Horrible* as number 4 in its Top 10 TV Series of 2008 and number 15 in its Best Inventions of 2008, accolades that perhaps best represent the hybridity of the text.

In *Critical Studies in Television*'s *CSTOnline*, Stacey Abbott, David Lavery, and Rhonda Wilcox each discuss the multilayered hybridity of *Dr. Horrible*'s format. Abbott briefly outlines the shifts among the blog space, narrative world, and cinematic flourishings throughout the Web film and concludes, "In typical Whedon form *Dr. Horrible* is a curious hybrid" (2009b, para. 2). Lavery discusses the rising popularity of "transmedia storytelling" and claims that after *Dr. Horrible*, "the status will no longer be quo, for Whedon or for television" (2009, para. 7). In addition, Wilcox considers the conjunctions between the Web film's intertextuality and metatextuality and claims, "We don't just break the fourth wall in *Dr. Horrible*; as Zack Whedon says in 'Commentary! The Musical,' it feels 'like we're breaking the ninth wall.'

The complexity of the text gives us more and more to think about" (2009a, para. 10).

The complex hybridization of *Dr. Horrible* is the reason it appears on both *Time*'s Best TV Series of 2008 (a slot Lavery called "perplexing" since, after all, *Dr. Horrible* never actually aired on television [2009, para. 3]) and *Time*'s Best Inventions of 2008. The attempt to categorize *Dr. Horrible*'s genre and format is difficult at best and tends to focus on the narrative mode of "musical" and the cinematic format of "short film" more than anything else. However, for viewers who watched the initial release on the Internet, and then subsequently on DVD, this attempt at categorization is clearly not sufficient. The medium may indeed be the message, as Marshall McLuhan claimed, since something is certainly lost in the displacement from computer screen to TV screen (1995, 148). And that something, I contend, is us, the posthuman viewers, who watch as posthumans and whose watching makes us posthuman. The posthuman, according to N. Katherine Hayles, "does not require the subject to be a literal cyborg" (1999, 4). Rather, posthumanism is marked by the fluidity of boundaries between bodily self and environment, where the posthuman subject is constructed through interactions and feedback loops between not only the mind and the body to form the self, but also the self and the environment (2).

It is our posthuman negotiation and identification that are missing when we watch *Dr. Horrible's Sing-Along Blog* on the TV screen rather than the computer screen, because blogs are a format designed for computers, not television. When we watch and engage with blogs, we negotiate our posthumanness, our artificial extensions and engagements with the world around us, and we struggle with our posthuman identities even as we engage, posthumanly, in the world around us. When we watch *Dr. Horrible* on the computer screen, our posthuman identification is more actively engaged than when we watch it on the TV screen. *Dr. Horrible* serves both as an allegory of our struggles with posthuman identification through its narrative and as a re-creation of our experiences with posthuman negotiation through the format of the text. When we watch on the computer screen, where we normally view blogs, the narrative follows and demonstrates the circular negotiations that we engage in while encouraging us to engage in those negotiations, creating a feedback loop characteristic of the posthuman. To analyze how this circular (but not tautological) feedback loop is constructed in the text and in and with the viewer, we must trace the narrative and its multilayered loops from the beginning. By tracing the feedback loop(s) of the posthuman in *Dr. Horrible*, we can see and be what it means to be posthuman.

Superheroes and supervillains tend to be "super" on the merits of their superpowers. In superpower mythos, a hero or villain obtains or possesses powers through various tropes of artificiality or natural ability. The Massive Multi-player Online Role Playing Game *City of Heroes* provides a good but problematic breakdown of these tropes in its character builder (where players can choose the traits, powers, and appearance of their gaming character), offering players hero powers from the following origin categories: mutant, science, technology, natural, and magic (Harper 2010, para. 5). Kareem Harper summarizes these origins in a *City of Heroes* review:

> What Cryptic Studios did was take around 200 superheroes from comic history and narrow down their abilities into these five categories. Mutants are born with their powers, which usually awaken around puberty; science origin characters gained their powers through some weird scientific mishap or deliberate self-experimentation; for fans of the Punisher or Iron Man, technology origin characters use self-created gadgets to do the dirty crime fighting work; and natural origin characters, not unlike Batman, are ordinary guys that fine tuned their body to "above average" levels. Lastly, heroes with magical origins obtained their powers through a magical source, an artifact or maybe some arcane ritual. (para. 5)

Although these origin categories are a good starting point for analysis, they do present some problems. Superman, for example, is an alien, and I am not sure that "mutant" offers an accurate description of his powers. Batman still seems almost evenly divided between natural and technological (perhaps because his use of gadgetry tends to be emphasized in the films). Still, these origin categories indicate two major differences in superhero or supervillain powers: there are powers that are possessed, and there are powers that are acquired. And these powers are inside or outside the superhuman body. Captain Hammer possesses superstrength. Dr. Horrible invents and acquires the freeze ray. Either origin of power points toward the same result: both the hero and the villain are, or become, something other than human. They become superhuman. They are both hybrids of humanness and otherness that are more than human, that are beyond human. They are, in fact, posthuman. Superpowers, whether inside or outside the body, exert influence on the world that extends the subject's agency further than ordinary, everyday abilities could. Hayles argues, "The post-human subject is an amalgam, a collection of heterogeneous components, a material-informational entity whose boundaries undergo continuous construction and reconstruction" (1999, 3). The line of difference between the body and the tools used by the body to effect change in the surrounding world does not just become blurred; it evaporates. The acquired and possessed superpowers extend Horrible's and Hammer's abilities to participate in and interact both with the world around them and also with each other.

The posthumanity of Horrible and Hammer is more important than their villainy or heroism. As supervillain and superhero, Horrible and Hammer have more commonalities than differences. As Krueger suggests, "Perhaps this is the difference between a hero and a villain: A villain will seek to defeat a hero for the villain's sake; a hero will seek to defeat a villain for the villain's sake. It's a fight to save the enemy at the same time that it is a fight to defeat him" (2006, 1). Krueger's distinction is significant because he points out that a hero seeks to defeat a villain to save the villain from himself or herself. A superhero attempts to save the supervillain by defeating him or her, which is an attempt to stop the supervillain's immediate plans and also the supervillain's life of crime. The superhero wants the supervillain to reconsider a life of villainy and turn toward a life of heroism and goodness. Krueger's distinction makes little differentiation possible between Horrible and Hammer. Neither one attempts to save the other. Horrible's decision to kill Hammer is prompted by the epiphany that he can rid himself of an obnoxious romantic rival while at the same time fulfilling Bad Horse's assassination requirement to join the Evil League of Evil. Horrible's motives are entirely self-serving; even though he talks about changing the world, he simultaneously insults and mocks the people of that world, calling them "sheep," "lemmings," and "cavemen." Hammer, meanwhile, constantly pummels Horrible, bullying him more than attempting to defeat him. He never tries to save Horrible or convince him to renounce his life of crime and villainy. When Hammer picks up the damaged death ray and focuses it on Horrible, he says, "I don't have time for your warnings. You give my regards to St. Peter. Or whoever has his job, but in Hell," a malicious, muddled statement that indicates Hammer's intent to kill Horrible, not for the good of society but because Horrible has simply become too much of an annoyance to Hammer's own success. The hero, for Krueger, attempts to save the villain for the villain's sake; he or she attempts to save the villain's inherent goodness and humanity. But these men have no interest in each other's humanities; they are concerned only with each other's posthumanities. Horrible tells Hammer that his disguise is failing, referring not to Hammer's costume or persona, but his disguise as a hero ("Slipping").[1] Hammer is no more a hero than Horrible is; Hammer, like Horrible, is merely another posthuman.

1. All songs cited in this chapter are dated 2008.

Horrible and Hammer both appear to be more intent on their conflict with each other than with saving people or changing the world, regardless of what they say. At the same time, they agree more with each other than with anyone else, especially Penny. Both Horrible and Hammer sing that "a man's gotta do what a man's gotta do," a song that ends with Horrible's frustrated, and particularly appropriate, cry of "Balls!" ("A Man's Gotta Do"). Not only is this song one of only two during which Horrible sings with other characters (the other is "My Eyes," Billy's duet with Penny, where he claims that evil is ascending, while she claims the same for harmony), but this song is also literally a turning point for Horrible. He begins the song as Billy, talking to Penny in an alley. "She talked to me!" he rejoices, as Penny walks away. "Why did she talk to me NOW? Maybe I should . . . ," he trails off, and hesitates, looking between Penny and the courier van he is about to rob. Making his decision, based on the idea that "a man's gotta do what a man's gotta do," Billy proceeds with the robbery, ducking behind a stairwell and reemerging in his Dr. Horrible lab coat, gloves, and goggles. Horrible's decision to continue with his robbery is motivated by the same premise that Hammer uses to save lives, and it is this crux that will ultimately result in Penny's death.

After all, who is Penny? Arguably the least developed character (Buckman 2010, para. 17), Penny has no superpowers to speak of. Yet she is possibly the most heroic character in the story. She devotes herself to helping the homeless. She believes in human nature, human kindness, and hope. On her date with Hammer, after she has taken him to the homeless shelter, she sings that goodness is inherent in each individual and that it is a trait worth protecting ("My Eyes"). Her optimism and faith in humanity are even more poignant when she sings, "Dreams are easy to achieve, / if hope is all I'm hoping to be" ("Penny's Song"). For Penny, hope makes positive change possible and achievable. She seeks to be *the* element that helps people change lives for the better. Penny's faith in hopefulness and the intrinsic goodness of human nature seems to define her; she tries to *be* hope, and hope realizes dreams. Her volunteer work and outreach attempts emphasize her self-appointed role. She sings, "With hope you can do your part / to turn a life around," on her date with Hammer while she demonstrates the importance of helping the homeless to recruit him to her cause ("My Eyes"). She could have just as easily sung, "With *me* you can do your part to turn a life around" as she shows him the benefits the homeless reap from the shelter's (and her) generosity.

Oddly enough, Penny also uses the most ineffective rhetoric of anyone in the story. When she attempts to collect signatures for the Caring Hands Homeless Shelter, she sings to passersby that they do not need to read her petition, implying they do not need to care about her cause, and they do not ("Caring Hands"). Her appeals fail utterly as the passersby on the street hardly look at her. No one is interested in signing her petition or listening to her plea. It is Hammer who manages to convince the mayor to donate the building to the shelter—not Penny. And Hammer is credited with becoming a crusader for the impoverished and homeless; Penny herself even credits him when she sings to him, "We can open by Monday, thanks to you." "Thanks to me!" Hammer replies ("So They Say"). Hammer credits Penny only with making him aware of the homeless "thing."

Penny, who has no superpowers, also appears to have no power whatsoever. Her accomplishments are small in comparison to Hammer's or Horrible's; she helps people only on individual levels. When it comes to changing the fate of the world, or even the fate of a building, Penny does not have the power to enact change. As Alyson Buckman argues, "Penny's function is that of love interest for Horrible and Hammer; additionally, her optimism provides a foil for both Horrible's violent cynicism and Hammer's narcissism" (para. 17). Hope, it seems, is not enough after all; it certainly is not enough to create effective rhetoric or give Penny the power to act. To have the power to speak and act, the speaker must be posthuman.

Hammer, who is posthuman through his superpowers, is able to get far more people to participate than Penny does. Before beginning his speech at the building dedication ceremony, the Mayor introduces Hammer and says, "Justice has a name. And the name that it has, other than justice, is Captain Hammer. Ladies and Gentlemen, your hero!" The mayor, with his lack of rhetorical finesse, equates Hammer to justice and emphasizes that Hammer is the audience's hero. Hammer is not "our" hero, but "your" hero, a distinction that underscores how Hammer's heroism is constructed by his audience. Additionally, Hammer, during his speech, tells his audience that they are heroes, too. He not only sings, "Everyone's a hero in their own way," a statement he continually undermines by following with phrases such as, "you and you and mostly me and you," but he also encourages his audience to sing along ("Everyone's a Hero"). He shouts "Everybody!" and they become his chorus, responding with a claim to be heroes just as he is. Heroism is branded and labeled repeatedly, and its meaning is created in the call-and-response session of the song. Heroism is nothing but a name, a label, that is constantly reinforced in a feedback loop of language. However, Hammer's voice and his influence both become negated with Penny's death. After Penny's death, Horrible sings, "So you think justice has a voice?"; he asks us to consider whether everyone has a choice ("Everything You Ever"). Horrible, with his successful entrance into the Evil League of Evil, negates Hammer's speech and undermines his rhetoric by claiming that justice, Captain Hammer, has no voice. He disrupts the feedback loop of heroism branding in the exchanges between Hammer and the audience. Heroism, then, is less critical than the construction created in the feedback loop; the making is more important than the made. Posthuman subjectivity gives Hammer the agency to speak (and sing) and Horrible the agency to enact change.

During Hammer's speech, Penny becomes almost invisible, and she does not participate in the rhetorical constructions or feedback loops enacted by either Hammer or Horrible. While Hammer addresses his audience, Penny attempts to slip away unnoticed, away from Hammer's posthuman feedback loops, and his audience pays no attention to her. She is so invisible that Horrible, when he attempts to brace himself to shoot Hammer with his death ray, has not even realized she is still in the room. When the death ray explodes, Hammer runs out of the room shouting and crying without realizing Penny lies wounded and dying. At first, Horrible also fails to realize that she has been wounded, and only after glancing around the room does he see the girl of his dreams pierced by shrapnel. After her death, she receives some attention in the media frenzy of flashbulbs, although most of that attention is focused on Horrible as the reporters ask, "Dr. Horrible! Why'd you kill her?" Afterward, her death is headline news, but she is not. "The Country Mourns What's-Her-Name" and "Heroes [*sic*] Girlfriend Murdered" are splashed across the newspapers, while Horrible is lauded as the "Worst Villain Ever." Penny's death is far more significant than her life. The news media focus on Penny's death only in relation to Hammer and Horrible and neglect to mention Penny's attempts to help the homeless. If Penny is a hero, then she is an unsung hero (and to be unsung in a musical is to be horribly neglected indeed). Her death, rather than saving Horrible and turning him to a life of goodness and hope, gains him entry into the Evil League of Evil. Without superpowers, Penny cannot enter the posthuman world of Horrible and Hammer; in fact, she can hardly enter society at all. She does not appear to have a job, and we know her only through her involvement with the homeless shelter and her relationships with Hammer and Horrible. If Hammer and Horrible are not just posthuman, but posthumanism, then Penny is more than just humane—she is humanism itself. And *Dr. Horrible*, through its multilayered narrative, begins to reveal itself as an allegory of the positional struggles between posthumanism and humanism.

Humanism, for Corliss Lamont, focuses on helping others and making others happy. Lamont states, "For Humanism the central concern is always the happiness of people in this existence . . . a happiness worthwhile as an end in itself" (1997, 33). One of the only things we know about Penny is that she tries to make others happy; she tries to help others for the sake of helping. Her volunteerism, without reference to paid work, makes her efforts magnanimous and brings her happiness. As Lamont puts it, "Each of us will find a deeper and more sustained happiness in working for a noble purpose" (118). Penny's optimism and faith are part of humanism's belief in the affirmation of life and finding happiness and beauty in sheer existence (248). Penny, who went from being disconnected and alone to believing in the innate goodness of humanity and contributing to the betterment of others ("Penny's Song"), develops her morality through human association—another humanist principle (97). She rejects divine will, or fate, when she tells Billy, "Everything happens." Billy responds, "Don't say for a reason." "No," Penny replies, "I'm just saying that everything happens." Even Penny's death is humanistic, as it allows Horrible to achieve his goal and join the Evil League of Evil.

Penny's death, however, is not just humanistic; it also indicates that Horrible's struggle to join the league has been less a struggle between good and evil and more a struggle between his humanism and his posthumanism. Her death is the death of humanism and the beginning of posthuman identification. And this negotiation is what Horrible has wrestled with all along. Horrible, as the only character to appear in both villain garb and street garb, is not a hero in this story but a subject negotiating his own posthumanism. Horrible's negotiation is similar to the viewer's negotiation watching Dr. Horrible on a computer screen: even as we watch, we use technology to extend our consciousness, our thinking and feeling, and we are able to empathize with Horrible's posthuman negotiation as we engage in our own. When Billy is confronted with the choice to run after Penny during his heist or continue with his crime, he is confronted with the choice of following humanism or his attempts to become posthuman by the technological powers he acquires through villainy. He attempts to use his villainy to enter posthumanism through his use of technological devices to commit his crimes, but his villainy is not what allows him to become posthuman and sit at the Evil League of Evil table in his red lab coat and goggles. It is Penny's, and humanism's, death. The death of human-centered-ness, of humanism, also allows us, the viewers, to extend our consciousness using technology and decenter ourselves into posthumanity. To become posthuman, we must negotiate the end of human-centered-ness and the end of humanism.

And, in a sense, Horrible and Hammer kill Penny together. After all, Horrible and Hammer are simply two sides of the same coin: Horrible is posthuman through his acquisition of powers through technology, and Hammer is posthuman through his possession of powers through superstrength. In the final standoff between Horrible and Hammer, leading up to Penny's death, Horrible and Hammer become mirror images of one another. The statue of Captain Hammer that was to be unveiled at the dedication ceremony is not a statue, but Dr. Horrible, who, when unveiled, freezes Hammer. Hidden beneath the veil, standing exactly opposite of Hammer at the podium, Horrible disguises himself as the statue of Hammer while Hammer sings. The veil slips from Horrible as he laughs and fires his freeze ray, effectively turning Hammer into a statue himself. Shortly after Horrible has been unveiled and has frozen Hammer, he accuses Hammer, and Hammer's disguise, of "slipping," a noteworthy choice of phrasing since the veil has just slipped away from Horrible. Hammer remains a statue while Horrible sings, "Society is slipping, / everything's slipping away": the categorical distinctions and boundaries constructed and used by and in society are slipping even as the distinctions between Hammer and Horrible are slipping ("Slipping"). While Hammer is frozen into a statue, Horrible proclaims that "heroes are over with," and braces himself to kill Hammer with his newly designed death ray ("Slipping"). Hoping that Penny does not see, he gets ready to pull the trigger. The freeze ray fails, the effect from the blast wears off, and Hammer recovers. He punches Horrible and damages the Ray, which explodes in a stunning misfire that inadvertently kills Penny (although no one else is physically injured, barring Hammer, who feels pain for what is apparently the first time). Horrible's creation and introduction of the death ray and Hammer's punch damaging the ray and his misuse of the damaged weapon combine to result in Penny's death. Together, natural powers possessed and artificial powers acquired form the weapon that causes humanism's demise.

Horrible is the only character who plays two parts, one who is "natural" and one who is "artificial": Billy, the quiet, dorky "laundromat buddy," and Dr. Horrible, who has "a Ph.D. in Horrible-ness." As Billy, he wears jeans and hoodies and navigates the everyday world in the guise of a natural, ordinary guy. As Dr. Horrible, he wears a white lab coat, gloves, and goggles and schemes the downfall of society and heroes. Horrible blogs and invents freeze rays; Billy does laundry and eats frozen yogurt with Penny. In Horrible's laundry fantasy, Billy uses the freeze ray to stop time and sing to Penny, a moment just as fantasy driven as the time they dance together in the Laundromat. When Billy sings "Brand New Day" and dons his Horrible costume, he proclaims, "Penny will see the evil me" and seems to imply that his Horrible persona is his "real," natural persona and that Billy is a mask, a disguise he must wear to pass in the world ("Brand New Day"). Billy wears disguises too: he wears a mustache and apron to pretend to work in the homeless shelter (although he never pours the soup into the bowls), and he pretends to be a shrub to spy on Penny and Hammer's date. Horrible, however, is his reality, and his lab coat, goggles, and gloves, along with his technological devices, are who he believes he really is. Billy is a posthuman extension of his arsenal of artificial tools that he uses to "be an achiever, like Bad Horse."

However, this distinction between the "real" persona and disguise is muddled because the last character we see is not Horrible, but Billy. To further complicate matters, we last see Billy after Horrible has donned his Evil League of Evil attire: the red lab coat, black gloves, and goggles no longer worn on his head, but lowered over his eyes. Even after Horrible's final transformation into full-on Dr. Horrible (emphasized by his sung statement that Dr. Horrible has arrived), we return to Billy, in front of his computer screen, dressed in black and appearing in front of Horrible's blog as Billy for the first time, in the last scene ("Everything You Ever"). The transformation into Dr. Horrible as a member of the Evil League of Evil is not, then, complete, and the scene implies that it was Billy, all along, who was using Dr. Horrible as an extension of himself, as an artificial mask or disguise.

The conflict between natural and artificial, human and extension, is further complicated by the "naturalness" of the other characters. Hammer is never out of costume, and he proclaims, "I don't go to the gym, I'm just naturally like this," stating that his superhuman strength is an inherent quality, but also implying that his costume (and perhaps even his cheesy personality) is an essentialized part of who he is. Moist, Horrible's friend and presumably a member of the Henchmen's Union, appears to be naturally moist. He always wears jeans and T-shirts while sweating copiously and dampening things around him, regardless of whether he wants to or not. Bad Horse is actually a horse, but one who communicates through the Bad Horse Chorus. The Pink Pummeler, Purple Pimp, and members of the Evil League of Evil are seen only in costume. And Penny, who has no superpowers, is naturally ordinary, along with the Mayor, the newscasters, the homeless, and the groupies. In fact, the only costume changes we see, other than Horrible's, are by the groupies, when they cease being fans of Hammer and don Horrible T-shirts and goggles. Their costume change implies that they are "naturally" groupies and that fandom itself is an inherent (and defining) characteristic, rather than their likes or dislikes. Horrible, in contrast to these "natural" characters, negotiates boundaries between "natural" and "real" personhood and "artificial" masks and technologies.

When Penny lies on the floor, gasping and dying, she looks at Horrible and sees Billy. She says, "Billy? Is that you? Are you all right? It's okay. It's okay. Captain Hammer will save us." Penny's recognition of Horrible as Billy merges his two identities for the first time. Her reassurances, followed by her inclusion of "us," highlights Billy's humanism while combined with Horrible's posthumanist garb. Horrible, it seems, is more than posthuman; he is a hybrid of posthumanism and humanism. Penny's faith that Captain Hammer will save them separates them both from the "pure," "natural," posthumanism of Hammer, while simultaneously elevating that posthumanism, cloaked under the guise of superheroism. The multilayered hybridities are, indeed, complex. Posthumanism is already hybrid, a humanness that is constructed by a person's place, function, affect, and operation in systems, cultures, environments, and, yes, humanity. Horrible, like many of us, is an artificially extended posthuman, using technology to extend his effect on and existence in society. But every artificial extension is made possible by the natural capacity that humans have for extension, malleability, and change. Our innate posthuman qualities, such as neural plasticity, enable our artificial posthuman qualities, such as computers, smartphones, and blogs—our technologies that affect how we live in our world (Clark 2003, 5–6), which are, incidentally, not terribly dissimilar in function from the Bad Horse Chorus. Just as Bad Horse extends himself, through his chorus, to communicate both with Horrible and with the viewing audience, we, too, use tools, such as phones and computers, to extend our communicating consciousness out into the world. Our boundaries of consciousness, like Bad Horse's through his chorus, are blurred. With all these complexities, combinations, and hybridities, it is not surprising that, as Horrible says, "society is slipping, everything's slipping away," because our society is frequently like the one in *Dr. Horrible*, with categories and definitions, such as "hero and villain" or "good and evil," that do not quite seem to suffice. It is also not surprising that we look around, and want to run away, and say that it is, indeed, horrible.

With posthumanism, the death of humanism is not simply inevitable; it is a horrible necessity. This comic book world without heroes begins to make sense because we are all villains, all murderers, all committers of dastardly deeds from a humanistic point of view. Humanism is, after all, a beautiful ideology, one that declares that humans are the center of the universe, that humans are good and capable and wonderful, that humanity deserves hope and faith and will always come out on top. Our posthumanism—extending further even as we extend ourselves by using smartphones, computers, satellites, blogs, cybertexts, pacemakers, and robotics—kills the human-centered-ness essential to humanism each time we reach out and become more connected, more decentered, and more superhuman ourselves. The further we extend, the more we decenter our own humanness—paradoxically enough, by using the very traits that make up our humanity. We are, as Andy Clark claims, "creatures whose minds are special precisely because they are tailor-made for multiple mergers and coalitions" (7). It is this very human, and humanistic, trait that compels us to be more than human. And humanism, like Penny, dies a humanistic death. As Lamont states, "Humanism . . . submits that we can find plenty of scope and meaning in our lives through freely enjoying the rich and varied potentialities of this luxuriant earth; through preserving, extending, and adding to the values of civilization; through contributing to the progress of and happiness of humankind during billions and billions of years; or through helping to evolve a new species surpassing Homo sapiens" (1997, 117). Penny's death opens the door to the evolution of humans, of humanism, into the realm of the posthuman. By dying, she enables Horrible's move into the Evil League of Evil and into becoming a fully posthuman subject. And the death of humanism, much like the death of Penny, does, and should, bring tears to our eyes.

At the end of the story, in the final scene, Horrible sits at his blog as Billy for the first time, finishing his song with "and I won't feel a thing" ("Everything You Ever"). Billy's appearance at Horrible's blog is the realization of his own posthumanity: Billy is Dr. Horrible by extension, through his blog, his Horrible attire, his freeze ray, death ray, transmatter ray, and technological devices. His subject negotiation, his "victory," is indeed complete. Billy's engagement and effect on the world happen not through his ordinary "Billy-ness" but through the enhancements that make him Dr. Horrible. Dressed in black, his face contorted, Billy clearly does feel—he feels grief, remorse, regret, and heartbreak. Through Horrible's blog, Billy engages with his audience, and with us, extending his mind and emotions through the blog itself. Posthumanism implies a humanism beyond feeling and after emotion, a mechanized people in a mechanized world, attempting to divorce itself from the caring and optimism of humanism. But this view, of course, is incorrect. Even in the ability to mourn the passing of humanism, posthumanism's feeling shines through. Billy's posthumanism is, in a sense, what finally makes him human by allowing him to embrace both his Horrible-ness and his Billy-ness. There will always be a little something of humanism left, the seed from which posthumanism evolved, even if it seems like just a memory. There will always be a bit of humanism in posthumanism—another hybridization, implicit in the very joining of *post* and *human*. After all, it is our very humanity that allows us to be beyond humanity, to be, as Clark puts it, *"natural-born* cyborgs" (3).

It is this circular hybridity that confounds us, and compels us, as viewers at our computers in ways that do not quite match our experience viewing *Dr. Horrible's Sing-Along Blog* on DVD. As we watch the Web film on a computer screen, we begin to engage in the video blog, interacting with our screens, and our protagonist, more closely than we do when we watch a television screen. As with Henry Jenkins's description of participatory culture, where consumers and viewers interact to create new media dynamics (2006, loc. 187), we are asked to participate as blog viewers and media consumers, both with the actors and with the media format. With the greater physical proximity of the computer, the blog directly addresses us as viewers: instead of being asked to watch a narrative unfold, we are asked to listen to Horrible's journal, his Web log. We immediately become extended and folded into the story even as we later become more distanced by the cinematography. But we are always pulled back to the blog. We are asked to engage directly with the experience of the narrative, an experience that is normally considered humanistic, while engaging with that narrative posthumanly, through a computer and a blog frame. The narrative itself engages in transmedia storytelling and "unfolds across multiple media platforms with each new text making a distinctive and valuable contribution to the whole" (loc. 1979). Each shift within the narrative among blog, song, and film serves to hybridize these various media platforms within the narrative, while the Internet release, DVD release, Wiki, and comic serve to expand and hybridize the narrative in different mediums (*Horrible Wiki* 2008). The hybridity of *Dr. Horrible* echoes our own hybridity as humans becoming and being posthuman. Like Horrible, we must negotiate our hybridity even as we resist it, much as we resist the ending of the narrative itself. When we watch *Dr. Horrible's Sing-Along Blog* at our computers, it is our own confrontations with humanism and posthumanism that place us in a position to "sing along," as posthuman villains complicit in the deaths of our humanisms, which we think want to be saved, even though there are no heroes to save them. It is, in many ways, a pretty horrible position to be in; at the same time, we really cannot help it. Posthumanism, particularly in our technologically entrenched society, is an inevitable turn. It, like everything, happens.

Buffy's Season 8, Image and Text

Superhero Self-Fashioning

MARNI STANLEY

The extension of *Buffy the Vampire Slayer* into an eighth season in a new medium (comics) allows Joss Whedon and his writing team to explore the promise of the Potentials, who were introduced at the end of the televised series. In television's Season 7, they were seen as unequivocally a force for good and as an unlocking and recognition of the potential heroism of young women. The Potentials replace the model of the single Slayer—the Chosen *One*—with the idea of the chosen many who might coexist and collaborate for the greater good. But as Season 8 develops, the lives of the new army of Slayers are made more complicated as the utopian fantasy becomes the lived reality for the characters. The new young group of Slayers does not have the careful training and monitoring that the Watchers provided previous Slayers; thus, they are killed at a rather alarming rate. They do not all accept being chosen, and some—such as Genevieve and Simone—choose to use their powers for their own ends and even kill other Slayers. Buffy both is and is not a member of this tribe. As the Chosen One, and as the leader, she is isolated by experience, rank, and knowledge (including of the unknowable—such as elements of the future, or even death and the afterlife). For the second time in her young life, Buffy has to deal with a massive change foisted upon her by powers beyond her control. In high school she discovered she was the Slayer of her generation, the Chosen One; now she finds herself the leader of eighteen hundred Slayers, responsible, suddenly, for the care, training, and governance of an army. Her most profound dilemma is caused by her difficulty in making authentic choices, a difficulty that stems from her inability to feel at home in her new role. Instead of risking herself and a few informed and consenting friends, she now puts at risk hundreds of young women she does not know and who are undertrained and unknowledgeable. Both the script and the art of the Season 8 comics delineate Buffy's struggle to stay connected in a world where meanings are constantly breaking down and where she is forced into making choices on a scale she cannot control. The narrative arc of Season 8 celebrates Buffy's struggle with absurdity and authentic action as she makes both good and bad choices, finally reaffirming her commitment to her role as Slayer and finding a deeper understanding of her own authentic choices, even at the expense of apparently abandoning, at least temporarily, the army of Slayers.

Whedon's interest in existential issues has been well established by critics, most notably J. Michael Richardson and J. Douglas Rabb in *The Existential Joss Whedon*; the main themes of Season 8 continue those philosophical preoccupations. One of the key concerns of Buffy in this comic book season is the question of whether the Slayers are a force for good. Issues of criminality among the Slayers (including Bank-Robber Buffy), violence, rogue Slayers, the endangering of peaceful people, bad public relations, and, most disturbingly, Buffy's acquisition of personal power she thinks comes from the deaths of hundreds of young Slayers all challenge Buffy's sense of the meaning of her work. Buffy begins with a deficit—she is chosen rather than given a choice. Even without having had choice at the beginning, Buffy can still make authentic choices through her commitment to her duties, but only if she finds them meaningful. Because she is under threat, she is pushed toward clarity. Jean-Paul Sartre, the preeminent philosopher of existentialism in the twentieth century, describes his experience in the French Resistance in World War II: "Because we were hunted down, every one of our gestures had the solemn weight of commitment. . . . Exile, captivity, and especially death (which we usually shrank from facing at all in happier times) became for us the habitual objects of our concern. . . . [T]he choice that each of us made of his life and his being was an authentic choice because it was made face to face with death, because it could always have been expressed in these terms: 'Rather death than . . .'" (1947, 499). Buffy confronts death often enough that her attention is constantly called back to the question of her authentic self. Over the course of the season, Buffy battles—along with vamps, demons, and villains—the classic existential obstacles of anguish and absurdity. Because the established meanings she has tried to hold onto are fragile or challenged by new paradigms, she fears, if not the onset of meaninglessness, then, at the very least, loss of control over the meaning of her work to others.

An existential lens is a useful frame through which to look at heroes such as Buffy because it is a philosophy that focuses on actions and the ongoing necessity of acting as a means of forging an authentic self. Sartre defines existentialism as a "doctrine that makes human life possible and also affirms that every truth and every action imply an environment and a human subjectivity" ([1946] 2007, 18). Existentialism denies us the ability to fall back on the excuses created by belief in predeterminers such as human nature. Instead, it argues that each person is the sum of his or her actions and decisions: a person does not remain a hero because she was one once; she must make new heroic choices. As Sartre states, "What we mean to say is that a man is nothing but a series of enterprises, and that he is the sum, organization and aggregate of the relations that constitute such enterprises" (38). Buffy's much-changed and rapidly changing situation in Season 8 presents her with many decisions, and each time she is faced with a choice that she must then act upon. For each decision, there are two possibilities—one of acting in bad faith and the other of taking authentic action. To act in bad faith is to be self-deceiving and deny there is a choice or provide false justification, as we will see Buffy do with Xander. As Sartre argues, "If we define man's situation as one of free choice, in which he has no recourse to excuses or outside aid, then any man who fabricates some deterministic theory, is operating in bad faith" (47).

The opposite of an action in bad faith is an authentic action that requires the person to acknowledge both freedom of choice and one's duty to all of humanity to take responsibility. Authentic actions require an understanding of the state of being in anguish. Sartre explains, "Existentialists like to say that man is in anguish. This is what they mean: a man who commits himself, and who realizes that he is not only the individual that he chooses to be, but also a legislator choosing at the same time what humanity as a whole should be, cannot help but be aware of his own full and profound responsibility" (25). Such a commitment is an authentic choice in the sense that Sartre uses the phrase in the passage on the French Resistance quoted above.

The final existential concept that is crucial to Buffy's situation is meaning making. Sartre declares, "Life has no meaning *a priori*. Life itself is nothing until it is lived, it is we who give it meaning, and value is nothing more than the meaning we give it" (51). Furthermore, he argues, "if I regard a certain course of action as good, it is I who will choose to say that it is good, rather than bad" (26). To sum up, then, everything that is a decision is also a responsibility, and our actions are free (though subject to constraints), not predetermined, which allows us to fashion ourselves and make meaning but also creates feelings of anguish and abandonment. Buffy's world has entered a state of extreme flux (there is no going back for someone whose entire hometown is now a giant blast crater), and she has lost or is in the process of losing many familiar things. The choices she must now make are more meaningful, but also more anguishing.

Buffy enters a new phase of her life and work in Season 8, but so too does her story as the *Buffy* canon shifts to a new medium. Comics shift our attention away from actors' performances (although in this case, we may still try to "hear" the script as if read by the original players) and onto text and art. There are some added benefits: freed from the financial constraints of filming, the creative team for the comics can flit to Italy, Japan, Tibet, or New York of the future and have giant sets (such as a Scottish castle) and unlimited helicopter-shot perspectives. The look of Season 8 is characterized by conventional comic techniques such as the use of predominantly straight-line grids to contain the panels (each individual framed drawing) and clear time sequences, design elements that do not draw attention to themselves. Similarly, the art, led by George Jeanty as the main penciller, works to distinguish characters clearly and avoids confusing effects. While Buffy may be struggling to find meaning, the writing team, which includes Whedon, has gone for well-structured storytelling with a lot of familiar humor. The non-attention-grabbing visual aesthetics, combined with familiar stylistic devices in the script, such as the distinctive speech styles of the different characters, keep our attention on what is happening to Buffy and the Scoobies rather than on the change of medium. The creative team of artists and writers has worked to create familiarity in spite of the medium change; Buffy may be suffering from alienation, but that condition is not a desirable one in fans.

Alienation, Sartre has argued, comes from the sense of being an "other" even to oneself (1992, 382); references to Buffy's alienation begin in the first frame of the first issue of Season 8. "The Long Way Home," the first episode (told over four issues of the comic), begins with the title on a black page over a single panel showing a shot of the earth from outer space with the sun rising on the horizon. Superimposed over the art is this narration: "The thing about changing the world . . . once you do it, the world's all different." In the penultimate scene of this issue, Buffy will return, in her narration, to the subject of changing the world. Variations on this same phrase also appear twice in the final comic of Season 8, helping to frame the argument and sustain the focus on making choices and their consequences. But here at the beginning of this season, we turn the page to find a double-page splash with Buffy large in the foreground, armed with a gun, flanked by three Slayers. She appears to be flying, though at a second glance we see that they are all tethered to a helicopter. This early simulation of flight foreshadows the actual flying she will do later in the season. We also see from this spread that she is the narrator who uttered the words on the previous page; it is *her* world that is all different. As she says, "Everybody calls me 'ma'am' these days." Over the next nine pages of this sequence, we cut between things that look very familiar to her fans (derelict churches, graveyards, big ugly demons getting stomped by Buffy) and things that look very unfamiliar (Buffy's new back-up Slayers, Xander running a command center with a large staff of computer operators and psychics, and Buffy handling modern automatic weapons). Buffy has also lost her anonymity. The four-star general tracking her calls her a "charismatic, uncompromising, and completely destructive" leader of an army. Whereas before she could always step back into the trappings of normalcy, now there are no more time-outs. Already struggling to be content in the role of Slayer, now Buffy has to find peace with being the leader of the Slayers.

Buffy's final two scenes in this issue use contrasts of scale to create a visual frame that emphasizes the scope of her problem in coming to terms with her new role. In the first of the two scenes, Buffy visits giant Dawn. Their unhappy confrontation takes place over a wonderfully executed two-page spread where Dawn, unable to move about in the confining space, is drawn in a single pose that spans all four of the vertical panels, while Buffy, unconfined, appears in a different position in each panel as she moves from bottom left corner in the first panel to top right corner in the final panel, where she stands with her hand on the door, ready to exit. As we turn the page, we find her moving outside, giant Dawn's frowning face partially framed in the door behind her. As Buffy emerges from the room, she notes, "We haven't really gotten along since . . . since we changed the world." The warm pink light of the sunset contrasts with her sad and worried expression. We see a long shot of the castle, partially in ruins and isolated on a high hill, as she begins a list of things she misses, beginning with "home," "mom," and "the gang." The final panel of the sequence shows Buffy silhouetted against the now dark-pink sky as she finishes a thought from the previous panel: "Suck it up Summers; you're a big girl now." Visually, she is not a big girl in this panel: she is a small silhouetted figure against a sky of heavy clouds and a landscape of mountains and forests. The panel opposite, at the bottom of the first page of the scene, shows her even more miniaturized, barely a figure at all, a mere stroke of the pen on the highest battlement of the castle.

This first issue beautifully sets up the narrative arc of the season. Buffy begins the season feeling isolated and not at home in her world. Things are out of control; her sister is a giant (and Willow is not around to fix that magical problem), and she has to command the five hundred Slayer-soldiers accompanying her as well as thirteen hundred others. Buffy instructs herself to get on with it, but she faces a long journey of challenge and discovery to make this new role authentically hers. As her isolation and her scale in the landscape remind us, the task before her is large and ultimately hers alone.

Buffy's altered status is reinforced as a problem that must be resolved as the season continues. "The Long Way Home," Part 4 (8.4), comes to an end with Buffy back in a bunker in Sunnydale, rescuing Willow from a military installation that is using Warren and Amy to get to the Slayers. At the end, Buffy argues with the general about his motives, and he tells her that, whether she knows it or not, "you're not human" and further that "you're at war with the human race," completely reversing her heroic self-image. Immediately after he makes this statement, we see Buffy, on the final page of the issue, isolated on a largely black ground. The page is composed of five equally sized horizontal panels. Buffy's face—first perplexed, then sad, then angry—is centered in each of the first four panels. The strong horizontal compression in the panels combined with the vertical alignment of the four images of her head and the eerie blue light behind her makes Buffy look otherworldly, perhaps the "not human" the general has just called her. In addition, this strong compression also reiterates the limits or constraints within which the self has nevertheless to take authentic action. Replying to the general's charge that she is at war, she utters an "oh" in the top panel, where she appears confused, and "kay" in the fourth panel, where confusion looks to have been replaced by intensely focused anger. Through this reply, Buffy acknowledges her acceptance of the general's interpellation of her and, in doing so, surrenders her heroic and positive self-image. The fifth and final panel contains her monogram, executed in three shades of red, literally putting her seal on the argument and signing off on her acceptance of this new self-concept.

As well as not feeling at home in this new role that has changed her world, Buffy also feels isolated by a series of betrayals that further her disconnection from old friends and allies and make her unsure of connections she thought were stable and enduring. In "No Future for You" (8.6–9), Buffy discovers that Giles has been working with Faith on an assignment in England. After Buffy first gets pulled across space into a fight with Faith and then pulled back again by Willow, she phones Giles to accuse him of working behind her back and endangering her. He refuses to explain what his plan has been, so she hands the phone to Willow. When Xander tries to explain Giles's actions by saying that "maybe the boss just needs some alone time," Buffy replies, "What other kind is there?" (8.9). In this compressed horizontal panel, Buffy is alone on a black and blue ground that echoes the look of the sequence of panels with the general from the end of "The Long Way Home," Part 4. This panel is one-fifth of the page, as were the panels of the earlier sequence, and Buffy's head is in approximately the same position, though turned in profile and looking sad rather than angry. Her hair is wet; she looks bedraggled.

Her rhetorical question hangs in the air, unanswerable, as we cut back, at the top of the facing page, to England and the fight between Faith and Genevieve. At the bottom of that page, in a horizontal panel roughly the size of the one Buffy occupies opposite it, Genevieve throws a pair of garden shears. Although we know they are aimed at Faith, their placement and trajectory, coupled with the lack of contextual background in the panel, make them appear to be aimed at Buffy's head, emphasizing the appearance of vulnerability. Unbeknownst to Buffy, Giles commits to "playing social worker to the Slayers" with Faith at the end of the episode. This decision creates a backstory for why he leaves his estate to Faith (8.40), an act that Buffy will interpret as another form of betrayal and evidence of her own failure. Although "No Future for You" is largely about Faith, it is a crucial piece of Buffy's struggle with the changing nature of her key relationships of many years' standing. Giles was her mentor, teacher, and guide, but now he wants, as he puts it, to play "Steed" to Faith's "Peel," moving from Watcher to Avenger.[1] For Buffy, he becomes another lost father; she is bewildered by, not comprehending of, his choices.

In the events of "Time of Your Life" (8.16–19), Buffy feels undermined by another betrayal that propels her into a New York of the future where there is, once again, only one Slayer, Fray, and where Willow appears to be a dark witch. Eventually, Buffy is compelled, by circumstances she cannot control, to slay this Willow just at the moment she is rescued back into her own time by good Willow. She does not feel that she understood these events or that she had any choice other than to kill Willow. In subsequent episodes, she is haunted by this act until in "Retreat," Part 3 (8.28), Willow tells Buffy that she is not the same Willow that Buffy kills in the future. Willow implies that by her actions, Buffy may even prevent that dark Willow from rematerializing. But even if the outcome is positive, Buffy has spent a great deal of time worrying about her actions and feeling alienated from Willow. She struggles to make meaning out of these events but cannot do so without help. Furthermore, Willow's attitude makes light of what, for Buffy, has been a very distressing experience.

1. John Steed and Emma Peel were the most noteworthy characters in the British spy series *The Avengers* (1961–69).

Finally, and most damning for Buffy in terms of the choices she makes, she feels betrayed by both Dawn and Xander as they fall in love. In "Retreat," Part 3, as the time for battle draws near, a number of characters, including Buffy, are preoccupied with the choices they must make in their lives. Buffy and Faith discuss being Slayers—Faith wants to let it go; Buffy wants to continue: "I need to feel that connected." But she also wants changes because she does not "want to stand . . . *over* people anymore." Dawn and Xander discuss the possibility of having a life not consumed by work, and Willow discusses, with her ex-boyfriend Oz, her fears that she will never have a family, while Oz urges her to give her magic to the earth and let it "slide away," as he has done with his wolf. This issue is also the one in which Buffy confesses to Willow that she, Buffy, will eventually kill Willow, but Willow is so preoccupied playing with Oz's baby that she cannot give Buffy the cathartic moment Buffy needs. In the midst of this emotional turmoil, Buffy goes to tell Xander she has made peace with Willow and finds him passionately kissing Dawn. She reacts with a shocked expression that is repeated in two nearly identical panels below their kiss, literally a double take. The exact repetition of her face (only the speech bubble changes between the two panels), eyes wide, mouth open in shock, creates a binocular effect, emphasizing her fixed stare. The frame and focus marks on these two panels remind us that Andrew is filming Buffy's shocked response; the filming is another kind of betrayal because Andrew is taking a private moment public and out of her control. Andrew has never been a part of her trusted inner circle, but Dawn and Xander are. Their kiss destabilizes her sense of who she is in relation to the people around her.

A few issues later, in "Turbulence," Buffy herself makes a play for Xander, and when he does not respond, she teases him that he is a "disgusting paedophile" or "cradle robber" (8.31). Xander tells her to mind her own business and begins to walk off. The page ends with Buffy isolated on a black ground, her head and shoulders outlined in red, gazing upward and crying, "What about me?" The black ink of the ground bleeds off the edges of the page and up under the panel above, flooding the scene with her anguish. Her ploy works, and Xander stops to continue the conversation. He tells her off for making her move only now that he is interested in Dawn. When Buffy denies it, he reminds her that even if she is telling the truth, "once you saw us together you should know the decent thing to do would be to keep it to yourself!" He calls her on her selfishness and reminds her that she is betraying Dawn by her actions. When she starts to cry, he does not abandon her but gives her a hug. Still, when he walks off at the end of the scene with his arm around Dawn, she mutters (indicated by the reduced size of the lettering in her speech bubble) about their "diving right in to the P.D.A. there." It is hard for Buffy to act in good faith in regard to Dawn and Xander because their relationship changes things she felt were certainties in her life. Even though she acknowledges that she has behaved badly, she cannot resist continuing to act in bad faith by mocking them, thereby isolating herself even further from her closest associates.

This episode has one more disturbing revelation for Buffy on the subject of alienation. "Turbulence" ends with Buffy and Willow flying off to deal with the wrathful Tibetan goddesses who have been unleashed. She tells Willow the news about Dawn and Xander in a series of three horizontal panels in the middle of the page. In reply to the news, Willow throws back her head and laughs, saying, "Gah! I thought they'd never figure that out," while Buffy looks at her astonished. The last panel of the page is pure black. We can feel Buffy's brain blinking as she tries to process what this statement means. Willow, who has been away from Dawn and Xander much more than Buffy, has observed the changes between them, whereas Buffy has not. The blackout panel gives Buffy a moment to catch up, to think about whether the lack of connection she has bemoaned on a number of occasions in Season 8 is not because of her own lack of attention to the people she purports to hold dear. This episode is full of "turbulence" for Buffy, who finds a number of her certainties disturbed. Her powers are fantastically altered, and revelations from Willow, Dawn, and Xander agitate her, putting her emotions in turmoil. She has, at least in part, been alienated by her own self-serving choices; she is not who she thought she was to friends and family precisely because she has not been playing the role of loving friend or sister.

The other existential challenge Buffy faces is the experience of absurdity, the inherent meaninglessness of the human condition. The meanings we project onto events are fragile and subject to breaking down and to challenges by other people offering contrary meanings. These issues are raised in "A Beautiful Sunset" (8.11). Buffy tells the Slayer Satsu (with whom she will have a brief affair [8.12] that she will later refer to as a "phase" [8.31]) that she knows Satsu is in love with her and warns her off: "People who love me tend to . . . oh, die . . . maybe go to a hell dimension, or burn up, or they start letting vamps suck on 'em and they leave, they all leave, even my friends, sooner or later everybody realizes there's something wrong . . . something wrong with me, or *around* me, or . . ." This speech takes place over two panels. The first clause is said over a close-up of Buffy with her scythe held close, cutting across her face in the composition. It is an image of Slayer Buffy, powerful and in control. The remainder of the speech takes place over a tight close-up of Buffy's face, brows furrowed in anxiety, with a mud-spattered Satsu in the background, also looking worried. The final image in this sequence, which immediately precedes the attack by the mysterious figure known as Twilight, shows Buffy turned away, her head buried in her hands, tears pouring down her face. The image bleeds (has no border) at the bottom of the page. It is one of the few panels in the whole season that has no background at all—only white space. In the context of such strong colored grounds (the rest of the sequence is full of the rich hues late in a sunset), the white has the effect of floating the weeping Buffy in a space without time or place. As she cries, she says, "Wow. Did not mean to end up there." (In the comics, Buffy omits the first-person pronoun regularly; it is a habit of her speech that perhaps expresses an underlying sense of alienation from the self.) Visually, she has ended up nowhere—floating on blankness, overwhelmed by accumulated sorrows, and unable to make any meaning other than the observation that perhaps she deserves to be alone—perhaps she is a curse on the people she loves.

When Twilight arrives to fight her and challenge her perspective, he offers other meanings. He contradicts her view of the new Slayers. He argues there are too many of them, and, because the world cannot contain them all, they will be made to suffer. He asks her to consider whether they have changed the world or helped her and then departs, leaving her with newly planted doubts. This doubt is reinforced by his address to his associates (a mix of US military and assorted demons) upon his return to his base. He tells the assembly, "The trick is to strip her of her greatest armor . . . her moral certainty" (8.11). Whedon, who wrote this episode, ends the scene with a double tease. As Twilight begins to lift his mask, he says, "and if there's one thing I've learned about the Slayer . . ." We turn the page, expecting him to be revealed, only to find him scratching his neck before pulling the mask back down. We do not hear him finish his thought, either; instead, the scene ends with his asking, "Where was I?" Through this double tease, Whedon reminds us of the readers' role as meaning makers, as interpreters and knowledge gatherers. He sets up the expectation that we will learn two important things when we turn the page; then he thwarts us. As Paul Atkinson, drawing on the work of Benoit Peeters, argues in his article "The Graphic Novel as Metafiction," in the comic book, "there is a sense in which the past, present and future coexist. . . . [T]here is an opportunity . . . for the viewer to preview the whole page, and, as such, no image, except for those at the turn of the page, [is] . . . unexpected" (2010, 112). Here Whedon beautifully plays with that attribute of the comic to give us an unexpected outcome that torments us because it substitutes nondisclosure for revelation; he deliberately disappoints our desire to know.

The final scene of "A Beautiful Sunset" again relates to the subject of making meaning and the question of whether it is possible to be a leader and still feel "connected." Is it part of being a leader to be, at least in part, alienated from the people you lead and from yourself, especially if it is not a role you chose for yourself? An injured and much-bandaged Buffy stands with Xander on the castle battlements. Expressing the doubts planted by Twilight, she asks Xander if the Slayer army is doing any good. After describing its energy and potential, Xander offers that the Slayer army is much more than the sum of its parts. As he struggles to find a word to express his thoughts, Buffy offers him one with which she has been struggling: "connection." She then asks, "Why can't I feel it?" Xander replies, "Maybe the leader, the girl who brings it all together, is the one that has to give that up." We cut from the close-up of Buffy and Xander to a horizontal panel of the Slayers practicing their fighting skills and then back to a tight close-up of Buffy, again in a compressed horizontal panel. Her eyes are downcast, her face bandaged. She is poised against the muddy brown of the castle wall, the background erased of detail, as she speaks the line "Yay me." Again, her monogram on a black ground fills the bottom horizontal panel of the page, emphasizing her isolation and singularity; there are many Slayers, but there is only one Buffy the Vampire Slayer. She accepts his interpretation of events, but with resignation; it is not a wished-for outcome.

The themes of alienation and authenticity discussed in this chapter are beautifully delineated in Issue 5 of Season 8, "The Chain." This episode, written by Joss Whedon, functions as a parable on the subject of being true to one's authentic self in spite of the constraints imposed by those things over which one has no control."The Chain" begins with a beautiful Jo Chen cover that explicitly echoes the cover of the first comic in the season. A woman who appears to be Buffy stands, gaze downcast, in a pose and attitude very close to the one she wore on the Chen cover of Issue 1 and wearing the same red "Buffy the Vampire Slayer" tank top. Now the top is tattered and torn, and her right arm is raised, not to hold her scythe, as in the cover of Issue 1, but apparently to rip off her own masklike face. The episode deals with an unnamed young woman who is one of the two Slayers chosen to be Buffy's doubles (whom Buffy mentions in the opening scene of the first episode of the season). We never learn exactly who made the decision to provide Buffy with decoys; she simply says, "The guys figured I was a target, set up two other Slayers to be me. One's underground. Literally" (8.1). "The Chain" opens with a horned demon uttering the name "Buffy Summers"; when we turn the page, we are confronted with a large panel of the demon holding her aloft and declaring her dead (8.5). The bottom two panels are narrated by the woman who reassures us she is not the real Buffy. Our initial response is relief; we do not yet relate to this impostor. We cut away first to a young jock asking, "Who the hell are you?" This panel appears twice in the comic, first to interrupt her death and move to the backstory of faux Buffy and then, at the end of the backstory, to restart the sequence of her death. The first time the panel appears it is the top horizontal panel of the third page, and the second time it is the bottom horizontal panel of the fourth-from-last page. His question "Who the hell are you?" clearly bears repeating for emphasis. The meaning we make of ourselves, in existential terms, *is* who we are. Even when a situation is not our choice, our understanding of it can be a choice. After his first appearance, we cut to faux Buffy underground accompanied by a little fairy who urges her to flee. Instead, faux Buffy tells her to take a message to the surface while she thinks, "Here's how it works. You don't get a choice."

Her situation speaks to the issue of whether the Slayers are truly equal. As she thinks about her training and transformation, she remembers a day when Giles came to give a speech to the Slayers and how he told them they were a chain, connected and equal. However, when she gets her assignment, she cannot help questioning that notion of equality. Why is she a decoy for someone else? As she is sent underground, she asks these questions: "Did I get the hardest, darkest path to walk 'cause I'm strong, I'm good, I can handle the heavier burden? Or am I weak and expendable. The one that won't be missed" (8.5). She answers her own questions with, "There is no truth. There's just what you believe." (She makes this statement in a panel where she is covered by a slimy slug monster and surrounded by little Tinker Bell–like fairies). Here is the existentialist answer to the absurdity of life. There is no greater meaning; there is only the meaning we make. This unknown young woman chooses not to be self-serving but to fashion herself as heroic and to trust that doing so is her authentic action. Her death is inevitable, so her only choice is the manner of her death. She consciously chooses to act according to her ideal self, to, as she says, "face the darkness like a woman." It does not matter, she thinks as she lies dying, whether anyone knows who she is, because she knows, and she has been true to that envisioned self. She has found, as Kierkegaard said in 1835, "a truth which is true for me . . . the idea for which I can live or die" (2001, 15). She has answered for herself what she calls the real questions: "Can I fight? Did I help? Did I do for my sisters? My comrades, children, slimy slug-clan . . . there is a chain between each and every one of us. . . . You either feel its tug or you ignore it." She explicitly does not need us to know who she is because her last thought is "You don't even know who

I am. But I do." She has chosen not to ignore the tug of connection and to serve the cause, even on to death, without ego or complaint. She feels her heroism herself, not because it is celebrated by others.

It is not a coincidence that Whedon appears in an advertisement for the cause of gender equity in this particular episode. The ad appears in the middle of the young woman's speech to the creatures of the underworld about commitment and connection and how nobody wins if they do not overcome their differences and stand together. The ad is for one of Whedon's favorite causes, "Equality Now: taking action for the human rights of women and girls everywhere." In the ad, he stands in a garden wearing a T-shirt with the organization's logo. By placing himself, literally, in the middle of this conversation, Whedon identifies one way that he sees himself as part of the chain and invites his fans to contemplate their own roles.[2] His presence in this episode, which deals with the responsibility we each have to make meaning of our lives, is a reminder that there are always choices to be made, regardless of the constraints we face.

Buffy is constrained by the fact that she did not choose to be the Slayer and, even now that she has the backing of the new Slayers, is forced into another unchosen role as the leader; thus, their existence has increased, not removed, the burdens upon her. She will always be alienated to some extent because, while she is alive and in that role, no one can take that burden from her. Buffy faces a number of challenges and tests in Season 8, and she sometimes makes choices that are self-serving and in bad faith. As the season begins to draw to a close and more changes, most notably a complete change in her powers, again befall her, we see her start to make her choices more measuredly and with a greater sense of connectedness. As we have seen, she does back off from tormenting Xander and Dawn, not graciously, but she understands she must because continuing to harass them only furthers the disconnection she feels. More important, as the leader of her troops, she orders them to pick up all the wounded they can after the massive battle in Tibet. At first she orders her people just to collect their own injured, but then she changes her mind and issues the order: "Protect everything that bleeds, okay?" (8.30). Faced with the giant wrathful goddesses who are mowing down everything in their path indiscriminately, she opts to see the common humanity of the enemy rather than their oppositional role.

2. The ad appears in the original single issue only.

In "Twilight," Part 4 (8.35), Buffy is faced with her greatest choice, the one that challenges the whole meaning of connection, of the chain. In "Twilight," Part 3 (8.34), Buffy has sex—cosmic, earth-shattering, universe-generating sex—with Angel, as Giles pontificates about how they are both reaching a higher metaphysical plane and altering the balance of the universe. (It is difficult to resist an inappropriate joke on the big bang theory at this point.) Their mating, both at the height of their powers, means, Giles argues, that "we humans won't matter at all" (8.34). At the end of this issue, Buffy and Angel are catapulted into a magical realm of Edenic beauty. At the start of "Twilight," Part 4, Buffy is convinced that this paradise-like landscape must be a trap. No threat manifests itself, but back on Earth their actions have created "a dimensional rift—It's raining demons!" (8.34). Although Angel says this place, also known as Twilight, is "a higher plane" and a "place of pleasure" and even "Paradise" (8.35), Buffy, in contrast, views it as a false temptation, a test, or a distraction from her true role. She argues that "it's not a higher plane! It's a Daffy Duck cartoon!" (8.35) as she walks out the door of a realistically drawn room into a blank white space. (The Daffy Duck cartoon most playful about the fluidity of the environment, which the animator keeps changing around Daffy, is Chuck Jones's brilliant 1953 short "Duck Amuck.") As Buffy and Angel argue in a blank space, Buffy says she wants to see her friends; as she draws her hand down for emphasis, the world becomes visible, and she can peel back the white space like tearing paper. Similarly, Angel can close it back up just by pulling the edges together. Buffy opens a window into the world and sees the great battle raging there. Angel does not want her distracted, so he draws the window closed and tries to convince her that the outcome is beyond their control and the world must end sometime. Buffy argues that it does not have to be today. While Xander calls Buffy to help, Angel tries one last time to get her to stay, arguing, "If you stay here, we can evolve" (8.35). But Buffy replies, "F#*% evolution," and climbs back into the world, Angel right behind her. They cross into a double-page splash of the two of them battling in the center of a vortex of demons. Three inserts across the bottom of the spread focus on Xander, Giles, and Dawn as each looks up and sees the fight and calls out the single word *Buffy*. They have been calling her to action; she has answered the call. So, apparently, has Spike, who appears as the final image of this episode (8.35).

Adding Spike back into the mix allows Buffy to revisit the meaning of all her key relationships over the course of Season 8 (Riley appears in "Retreat" [8.26–30]). The last episode, written by Joss Whedon, is "Last Gleaming"

(8.36–40). Spike brings with him a crucial piece of information about the "Seed of Wonder" (8.36), which is the totem Giles had referred to earlier (8.34). The destruction of the seed is the only thing that "can stop the earth from being destroyed" (8.37). Spike offers Buffy an explanation: "So what do you say, luv . . . fancy a bit of exposition?" (8.37). But at the crucial moment, when he is about to reveal how to save the world, Buffy distracts herself (and us) by filling her head (and the rest of the page) with an imagined passionate kiss with Spike. We know it is taking up too much space in her head because the panel bleeds under the surrounding panels, expanding in her consciousness. It is an active fantasy: her hand is under his shirt, pushing it up and cupping his left pectoral muscle. Because Buffy had been talking about Angel just prior to this fantasy, Spike thinks her distraction results from thoughts of Angel, but only four panels later Buffy is picturing herself in bed with Spike, clearly midcoitus. Buffy is also remembering what is unique about Spike; as she puts it, "You were the guy I told the things I wasn't supposed to tell. . . . You're my dark place, Spike" (8.37). By revisiting what he meant to her, Buffy can better understand both his draw for her and the strong triangulation among herself, Angel, and Spike.

Although everyone else fails to recognize Angel in his masked role as Twilight, Spike takes one look at a bit of digital video of Twilight flying and declares, "Ooh, that'd be Angel then" (8.36). When Angel complains to Buffy about Spike's reappearance, she retorts, "Would you have preferred he showed up a few hours ago?" (8.36), which would have been when she and Angel were having sex. When, in the battle over the Seed of Wonder, Angel tries to kill Spike by flying him into the sunshine, Buffy rescues Spike and chides them both: "I liked it better when you were kissing" (8.39). Buffy is acknowledging that the three of them are caught up in some not quite consummated ménage that she needs to understand (make meaning of) either to move on from them or to choose between them.

This last episode also richly complicates the issues of betrayal that have been so much the season's subject. Willow revisits Aluwyn (her goddess lover who first appeared in the Willow one-shot comic in Season 8). Aluwyn tells Willow that she needs to protect the Seed of Wonder to protect magic in the world; this command sets Willow in conflict with Buffy, who seeks to destroy it. Meanwhile, Buffy finds herself in a fight, seemingly to the death, with Angel, her former and now present lover. Perhaps the formation of Twilight (the place) was, Buffy says, "cosmic vengeance. That I had coming" (8.39). This thought is one choice of meaning for her. Giles knows that only the Slayer's scythe can break the Seed of Wonder, so he fetches it from Faith, who is using it in a battle with demons. This retrieval leaves Faith looking as though she feels betrayed, but before Giles can swing the weapon at the seed, Angel kills Giles, a terrible betrayal of the trust Buffy once had in Angel. Buffy then takes up the scythe, smashing it through the seed and causing Willow (in the sky fighting monsters) to plummet to the earth, deprived of all her powers and crying, "We lost!" (8.39), in her lover Kennedy's arms. Willow feels betrayed by Buffy's choice to end magic, a choice that simultaneously ends Willow's ability to access the realm that Aluwyn inhabits.

The accumulating betrayals are a major source of the turbulence of Buffy's life, and they literally unbalance and threaten her. In the fifth and final part of "Last Gleaming," the conclusion of Season 8, Buffy acknowledges the "ripples of hurt" (8.40) now moving through her world. Willow feels betrayed by Buffy; Buffy feels betrayed by Angel and even by Giles, who left his estate to Faith. When Spike tells her she did great and no one else can know how hard her choices were, she bursts into tears and, fleeing him, falls through a window. Clumsiness is not her thing; earlier in this issue, we see someone trip her while she is carrying a big tray of coffee (yes, she is back in food service), and she flips and catches it on her foot. Now even her body is betraying her. Willow decides she loves the now unreachable Aluwyn more than Kennedy and breaks up with Kennedy. Even the little fairy who loved faux Buffy in "The Chain" (8.5) reappears on the penultimate page as among the people whom Buffy's actions have hurt. Simone (the murderous rogue Slayer) now also reappears with a picture of Buffy on her assassination list. This issue begins with the phrase "The trouble with changing the world is . . ." (8.40). The phrase is not completed at its first iteration, but the second time, near the comic's end, Buffy finishes the thought, "The trouble with changing the world is . . . you don't." At most, "you move it up a little." This negative view contradicts the opening line of Season 8 in which she had argued that you can change the world, although she was not then sure she was keen on the changes. Now she seems to have reached the conclusion that what she thought were substantive changes were largely cosmetic: the big issues of life and death, love and trust, remain unchanged.

One of Buffy's greatest challenges this season has been the leadership of the many Slayers she had helped to create. Now many are dead, and many more have been "put through the meat grinder," as Faith expresses it (8.40). Although they still have their powers, no new Slayers will be created now that the Seed of Wonder is destroyed. Buffy has abandoned her leadership of them, and they are angry; the ones in San Francisco (where she now lives) feel justified in harassing and attacking her. When three former members of the

Slayer army attack her, Buffy defends herself enough to render them impotent and then confronts them: "I'm Buffy the Vampire Slayer and you're a bunch of whiny thugs. You come after me again . . . you so much as look at me funny . . . then I will fight you" (8.40). Buffy knows it is just the beginning of the reprisals. As Buffy contemplates the consequences of all the hurt around her, she is shown on a white ground, bright-red blood running down the side of her face as she turns her head toward a victim's cry from somewhere outside the frame. As she locates the source of the cry, she thinks about failing to change the world, but on the final page we see first the victim, a young woman, with the menacing silhouette of a vampire closing in, and then a close-up of the vampire with Buffy silhouetted on a rooftop behind him. The next panel is a close-up of her eyes and bloody cheek, focusing on her eyes as she thinks, "You hope." The final panel, taking up most of the bottom half of the page and bleeding under and spilling over the panels above it, shows Buffy, stripped back to basics, armed only with a stake, leaping into battle on the thought "Let's go to work." She uses the plural even though she is leaping alone into the fight. This image echoes, in both pose and color palette, Buffy's entrance into Season 8 in the first spread of the first comic. There she leaped through the sky backed by three Slayers, including Satsu, two helicopters, and a lot of high-tech weaponry. In her final leap, the technology is gone and she has only a simple wooden stake, normal street clothes, and her little golden cross around her neck, with the moon as her sole witness. Although we know the Slayer army remains and Season 9 will have to deal with them, Buffy remains true to herself by reaffirming her identity and her obligations.

Buffy's last line also directly quotes Angel's last line of the television series *Angel*. In "Not Fade Away" (5.22), Angel, in the final seconds of the series, uses the line to rally Illyria, Gunn, and Spike for the showdown with the demons unleashed by the team's destruction of the Circle of the Black Thorn. For Angel, the plural is literal; he still has backup, and although the scale of the demon army is unprecedented, it is business as usual. Buffy's use of the exact same phrase, in the context of her isolation, serves only to emphasize that she has lost both her original Scoobies and her Slayer army.

This first comic book season of *Buffy* has successfully forwarded both the main characters and their stories. Although fans may miss the actors and the action of the show, if they can adjust to the new medium, they will find that the writers and artists of Season 8 have kept the plot developing, creating much potential and momentum for Season 9. The final cover of Season 8 by Jo Chen echoes the covers of Numbers 1 and 5. Again we see Buffy alone in her red shirt, and, as in the first cover, she is holding the Slayer's scythe.

Now it is angled down in front of her, the blade clearly broken. Her clothes are tattered, her face is scratched, her eyes are downcast, and her brow is furrowed. She is much altered from the first cover. She has faced the challenge of changes she cannot control, and she has struggled to make choices she can live with and to understand that if she knows the meaning she wants to make of her life, then she can affirm that meaning by making authentic decisions. By rejecting the self-indulgent pleasures of a paradise that would have literally cost the earth, she reaffirms her commitment to her role as Buffy the Vampire Slayer. But she has paid a high price. Constrained by so many forces beyond her control, she has hurt and been hurt by almost everyone she has loved. Her affirmation of her role and of hope and her leap back into work suggest she has resolved her existential dilemma insofar as she is still confident that she has found something worth fighting for. But never has she been so alone in her pursuit of the meaning of her life.

Watchers in the Woods

Meta-Horror, Genre Hybridity, and Reality TV Critique
in The Cabin in the Woods

KRISTOPHER KARL WOOFTER

The Cabin in the Woods (2012, produced 2010) is perhaps the most deeply cynical work to come from the pen of Joss Whedon. And, taken with Whedon's most recent television project, *Dollhouse* (2009–10), the film marks a dark turn in Whedon's collaborative output that suggests the writer-director-producer to be engaged in a critical struggle with the genres and media formats that have provided outlets for his most influential ventures in popular entertainment.[1] Cowritten and directed by longtime Whedon collaborator Drew Goddard (and featuring allusions to Goddard's own work on both *Lost* [2004–10] and *Cloverfield* [2008]), *The Cabin in the Woods* (hereafter *Cabin*) wants to be an evisceration of a horror genre in crisis in the first decade of the twenty-first century. Indeed, Whedon and Goddard have both acknowledged their film's gestures toward "critiquing" (O'Heir 2012; Fernandez 2012) what they see as an especially brutal and vulgar turn in horror to so-called torture porn[2] (Whedon, Goddard, and Bernstein 2012, 9) in films like *Saw* (2004)

---

1. In an interview for *"The Cabin in the Woods": The Official Visual Companion*, Whedon has remarked: "To talk about yourself as an artist while promoting a horror film is like begging people not to see it" (Whedon, Goddard, and Bernstein 2012, 172).

2. A contested term in horror film scholarship, *torture porn* was first coined in 2006 by *New York Magazine* critic David Edelstein in an article inspired by films such as *The Passion of the Christ* (2004), *Wolf Creek* (2005), and *Hostel* (2006), and addresses what Edelstein perceived as a shift in twenty-first-century horror toward violent imagery that both exceeds the needs and logic of narrative and sutures audiences into an identification with a sadistic point of view. Adam Lowenstein (2011) offers an alternative to this reductive framing of what he terms *spectacle horror*. Derived from Tom Gunning's ([1986] 2006) discussion of a "cinema

and *Hostel* (2005). The film received many positive reviews to this effect, with critics such as Christopher Orr of the *Atlantic* labeling the film a successful "deconstruction" (2012) of the horror genre, NPR's Ian Buckwalter praising the film for its "many intellectual pleasures" (2012), and Roger Ebert suggesting that "the film itself [is] an act of criticism" (2012). Although I find this critical response framing *Cabin* as a paradigm shifter for horror to be misguided, I do not wish to dwell here on the film's successes or failures as meta-horror. Instead, I suggest that Whedon and Goddard's script has at its center concerns that render *Cabin* rather more interesting as a hybrid product of a number of coalescing scholarly and popular discourses around horror-genre "exhaustion," Frankfurt School–derived notions of media manipulation in service of what Theodor Adorno and Anson Rabinbach dubbed the "Culture Industry" ([1963] 1975), and the supposedly demoralizing effects on passive audiences willing to "submit" themselves to the everyday-horror spectacle of reality TV.

Aping and mocking reality TV programs such as *Big Brother* (1999–present) and *Survivor* (2000–present) and video games such as *Resident Evil* (many incarnations, 1996–present), *Cabin* revolves around the production of an elaborate survival horror event. Two acerbic showrunners, Hadley and Sitterson, preside over the machinery of horror in an underground control room described in the film's screenplay as "a wonderland of screens, switches and dials" (Whedon and Goddard 2012, 54). This clinical space of clean lines and curves resembles a cross between NASA headquarters and the military command center of *Buffy the Vampire Slayer*'s (1997–2003) fourth-season Initiative, another space for the production and containment of monsters. Hadley and Sitterson's monster-event production facility exists solely to harness a group of victims for an elaborate ritual sacrifice to "placate the Ancient Ones" (*The Cabin in the Woods* 2012),[3] a host of angry Lovecraftian gods who (apparently akin to a bunch of bored viewers of *The Real Housewives* [various cities, 2006–present]) demand a bloody sacrifice equal to, or better than, they saw last season. This annual ritual, for reasons unclear in the film's diegesis but quite clear in the film's meta-horror/reality TV discourse, must

---

of attractions" (quoted in Lowenstein 2011, 44), spectacle horror "address[es] the audience directly" (46) and viscerally, courting their expectations and emotions rather than encouraging their "identification" (44).

3. Where possible, I cite the screenplay published in *"The Cabin in the Woods": The Official Visual Companion* (Whedon and Goddard 2012). I cite the film here because this line, spoken by the ritual's "director" (played by Sigourney Weaver), does not appear in the published screenplay.

be staged as a high-tech horror spectacle, with a group of unwitting young people maneuvered into their roles as sacrificial victims based upon what Goddard claims to be the horror genre's "five very clear [character] archetypes" (the "scholar," the "jock," the "fool," the "whore," and the "virgin") (Whedon, Goddard, and Bernstein 2012, 16). Once these roles have been "cast," it is Hadley and Sitterson's responsibility to manipulate the players into making the (poor) choices that will render it necessary for them to be punished in proper order, according to long-standing ritual (in the diegesis) or horror convention (in the film's meta-discourse).

The film closes on the spectacular image of a giant god-fist thrusting out of the ground, as though to hit the reset button on the whole operation—and the world—in what Goddard identifies as a "Lovecraftian apocalypse" (2012, 6). This message in *Cabin* is clear: the horror genre—caught in its own vacuum of prepackaged, ritualized formula—must self-destruct before it can be "reborn." *Cabin*'s take on the genre thus fits squarely within a problematic critical and popular discourse that frames discussions of horror genre hybridity in eschatological terms of repetition, decline, self-destruction, and renewal. Whedon and Goddard are not alone (currently or historically) in pushing this essentializing evolutionary framework of an exhausted genre looking to find new footing through the courting of extremes. Scholarly work on horror has constructed similar monolithic critical binaries that, for example, have been responsible for the highly problematic framing of 1940s horror as a decade that fell victim to formula and excess after horror's so-called classical period, typically represented by the 1930s Universal monster films. Genre scholar Steffen Hantke has recently written how millennial and twenty-first-century horror scholarship has adopted its own "rhetoric of crisis" (2007, 2010). Hantke even goes as far as suggesting that horror scholars themselves must do the work of genre rejuvenation because he sees the worlds of academia and film production as "operat[ing] in almost perfect isolation from" each other (2007, 200). Though Whedon and Goddard would most certainly disagree with this point, their approach in *Cabin* participates in the scholarly rhetoric of crisis that Hantke identifies. On the film's overall goals, Whedon has remarked, "You look at something as ugly, stupid and morally bankrupt as the remake of *Texas Chainsaw* [*Massacre*, by Marcus Nispel in 2003] and you go, 'Not only do we keep performing this ritual, but it's clearly degenerating.' So why do we keep doing it? Why do we keep returning to it? I'm as fascinated and appalled by it as I am delighted, and so welcome to both" (Whedon, Goddard, and Bernstein 2012, 10). In other words, *Cabin* is intended as "both" celebration and evisceration of formula, "both" ritual and subversion of the power of ritual, which in this framework must also include a sort of loss or forgetting of the "original" purpose of the ritual. Although it is difficult to argue with Whedon's claim that the typical horror remake is creatively bankrupt (and barely interesting even as a form of nostalgia), it is a problem to equate the recent spate of Hollywood horror remakes with a "degenerati[on]" into *formula*, since the self-conscious deployment of convention as formula is the very essence of the horror genre, not to mention a major draw for its fans.

The problem with such a framing of horror (or any genre) as Whedon describes here, and as *Cabin* enacts through its thematic parallels between genre decline and apocalyptic excess, is threefold. First, it derives from the persistent elitist perspective in journalism and popular culture that sees horror as a crude, degraded genre appealing only to the most primitive desires and emotions and always in danger of going off the rails. Second, it belies the horror genre's *inherent* reflexivity and consequently upholds outdated theoretical constructs of horror viewership as passive consumption of prepackaged genre commodities. And third, it follows retroactively assigned narratives of genres as "progressing" through clearly marked evolutionary stages of development that tend to skirt notions of variation and hybridity. Referencing Thomas Schatz's (1996) work, Rick Worland highlights the kind of evolutionary "taxonomy" functioning here, characterized by "experimental, classical, refinement, and baroque phases" (2007, 18). According to this schema, generic codes and conventions form from a sort of primordial stew of styles and themes, then "stabiliz[e]" through repetition. Further experimentation with now established conventions moves the genre into a baroque phase marked "by increasing stylistic adornment and self-consciousness." In this final phase, conventions are "reject[ed] or ridicul[ed] . . . as inadequate, obvious, and outdated" (19). To speak of a baroque phase is thus to note a state of genre exhaustion and crisis, where mimicry has supplanted originality, and genre objects become products of empty ritual, doomed to be repeated through formula, parodies, mash-ups, and endless sequels. Such a baroque aesthetic characterizes meta-horror films like the *Scream* series (1996, 1997, 2000, 2011) and *Cabin*, all of which make straightforward use of as many conventions as they ridicule (because they know that horror fans love the genre's function *as* ritual).

As Worland notes (2007, 20), at least one problem with an evolutionary framing of genre is that it cannot account for hybridity; it overlooks difference, those films that constitute ruptures in the critical narrative (itself something of a formula) or have not been tagged by scholars as indicating a key "shift" into a new "phase." The evolutionary model also denies what Rick Altman emphasizes as the "ongoing *process*" ([1999] 2010, 54; emphasis in the original) of genre formation, a complex interplay of a number of important factors, including genre scholarship, fan practices, production conditions, specific historical and cultural contexts, and artistic vision. Important to Altman's conceptualization of genre is that hybridity is not merely the mark of renewed experimentation in the wake of the stagnation that marks the end of a cycle of films, but is integral to the notion of genres as *continual* processes. Considered in terms of genre hybridity, *Cabin* is more interesting than its irreverent reenactment of horror's always-already reflexive play with convention would suggest it wants to be. Like its titular cabin, and the control room beneath it, the film sits on a fault line of convergent discourses around realism, representation, and genre fatigue.

Cabin diverges from other meta-horror films such as Brian DePalma's *Blow Out* (1981), Sam Raimi's *Evil Dead 2: Dead by Dawn* (1986), Wes Craven's *New Nightmare* (1994), and George A. Romero's *Diary of the Dead* (2007). Whereas these films work *within* generic conventions to highlight themselves as formal constructs of spectacular excess and affect, *Cabin* takes a superior stance to its subject matter (and often its audience). In an early scene in which the five sacrificial archetypal characters enter the "woods," the film announces that it will use horror's often confrontational posture (that is, its conventionalized attractions) to undercut the pleasure to be derived from what Noël Carroll calls horror's "drama of iterated disclosure" (1990, 35), or the gradual process of revealing the nature of what is monstrous in the film.[4] Goddard frames the scene from an extreme height; moments after the characters enter, a screeching bird careens into the "electrical grid" (Whedon and Goddard 2012, 63) separating the real world from the virtual reality space of the survival-gaming arena, revealing the "woods" to be a sham. For viewers of the film, after this cue it no longer matters what lurks in these virtual woods, but instead what sideways pleasures might be derived from contemplating from a god's- (or bird's-) eye view the manipulation of these characters into their prescribed roles. Thus begins a process by which *Cabin* continually attempts to dislocate both viewer identification *and* the pleasurable contemplation of attractions by constructing a rather chilly spectatorial position that can derive pleasure solely by looking *askance* at the proceedings.

---

4. Although Carroll's argument is limited in its sidelining of the affective power of spectacle horror, it is important for signaling the epistephilic drive of the conventional horror narrative as one of the genre's key sources of pleasure.

The film's resulting diminishment of affect for the sake of critical distance is something *Cabin*'s detractors have pointed out. *Village Voice* critic Mark Olsen notes that the film undermines any successful identification with the characters or proceedings because it "is first and foremost about itself, interested only in a fundamental adherence to rules of its own devising and fenced off from the world at large" (2012). And *New York Post* critic Kyle Smith, lumping the film among the many "rip-offs" of both *The Truman Show* (1998) and *Scream*, laments that "every time things get horrifying . . . , we cut back to the tech wizards who are orchestrating the whole experience. The 'scares' are therefore 'ironic' and, being safely cordoned off behind these 'quotation marks,' aren't scary" (2012). Whether the purpose of *Cabin* is to "scare" its viewers or to engage them in a game of genre critique (in horror, it is often both), the film's entrance into a discourse that would prompt Smith to note its similarity to films such as *The Truman Show* is of interest. Smith's allusion to Peter Weir's satirical film about a childlike man (played by Jim Carrey) who comes to realize that his entire life is filmed as a reality TV show, places *Cabin* within an emergent tendency in millennial and twenty-first-century Hollywood cinema to critique media (mis)representations of reality by gesturing to the aesthetics and questionable ethics of reality TV.

In aligning itself against reality TV, *Cabin* engages peripherally with horror's recent remediation of documentary tactics and realism. As in horror films such as *The Blair Witch Project* (1999), *Home Movie* (2007), and the *Paranormal Activity* series (2009, 2010, 2011, 2012), where recording technologies become invasive tools of self-surveillance, *Cabin* draws upon a contemporary discourse that considers visual representation as offering neither infallible access to nor insulation from the real. In *Cabin*, the "stoner" character, Marty, is the only character who can see beyond the survival horror-gaming simulacrum created by Hadley, Sitterson, and company. "*We are not who we are*" (Whedon and Goddard 2012, 94; emphasis in the original), he remarks while observing the altered behavior of his friends as they are manipulated into their roles by the showrunners. On numerous occasions, Marty hears the whispered directions coming from the control room and utters the words *puppeteers* and *puppets* (94, 105) to himself, as though gradually entering into consciousness of both "cabin" and "woods" as constructs orchestrated by an invisible hand. Marty is also the film's only observer of the genre conventions that dictate the proceedings, and in this role, he is meant as a stand-in for a viewer who is critical of tired horror formula: "Really?" he responds skeptically, when Curt, "the jock," is manipulated by piped-in gas to suggest the group "split up" to "cover more ground." Finally, Marty serves as a mouthpiece linking the film's meta-discourse on genre to its apocalyptic themes around media saturation. By the time he discovers a hidden surveillance camera in the film's eponymous cabin and exclaims, "Oh my god, I'm on a reality show. . . . My parents are gonna think I'm such a burnout" (108), Marty has already come to be seen as a savvy observer of popular culture and a mouthpiece for the film's nihilism. Before Marty and friends enter the "woods," Jules (who will later be manipulated into the role of "whore" by a combination of her hair dye and an artificial mist of pheromones) asks Marty if society is "crumbling." He responds: "Society is *binding*. It's filling in the cracks with concrete. No cracks to slip through. Everything is recorded, filed, blogged, chips in our kids so they don't get lost—society *needs* to crumble. We're all too chickenshit to let it" (56). Later in the film, Marty's actions will precipitate just such an end.

It is worth noting that Fran Kranz, the actor playing Marty, also plays Topher Brink, the character who initiates the techno-apocalypse in Whedon's *Dollhouse*. Brink is initially perhaps the worst of *Dollhouse*'s many morally bankrupt characters, designing a machine that facilitates the use and abuse of people as mere bodies, commodities to be used by (sacrificed to) elitist consumers. Brink, like Marty, will eventually sacrifice himself for the greater good by the series' end. As Marty, Kranz may be *Cabin*'s most "burned-out" character, but he is also its most tuned-in, his drug use having expanded his mind enough to counteract Hadley and Sitterson's manipulative, mind-altering strategies. Marty's increasing awareness of both "cabin" and "woods" as a mediated reality eventually leads him to discover the agents behind (or, better, *beneath*) the illusion when he leads "virgin" Dana down into an elevator shaft and sets off a chain of events that destroys both virtual and real worlds. Both Marty and Topher Brink become redemptive figures, showing an increasing awareness of the Baudrillardian sense of the world-as-mediated-illusion that dictates postmodernist and late-capitalist discourses. Fran Kranz's presence in *Cabin* alone is, then, something of a meaningful transtextual reference point for fans of Joss Whedon in that it suggests links between series and film. Whedon has acknowledged the similarities between *Dollhouse* and *Cabin* in words that echo this skeptical Topher Brink/Marty intertext, stating that "we are all controlled, we are all experimented upon, and we are all dying from it. And we are all completely unaware of it. We are taught not to be kind. We are taught not to be forward-thinking. We are taught not to be as much as we can be. We are taught to be insecure. We are taught to be subservient. We are taught to be aggressive. And we are taught to buy, buy, buy. . . . And these are things that are going on every day, all the time, in everybody's life. So the person [who is] experimented upon is me, it's everyone, and it's constant" (Whedon, Goddard, and Bernstein 2012, 19). Once again, there is in Whedon's comments the sense of exhaustion associated with the Frankfurt School critique of the Culture Industry as offering a grand "deception" (Adorno [1963] 1975, 16). *Cabin* presents such a deception through the narrative logic of a reality game show like *Survivor*, which constructs only an illusory sort of agency: participants negotiate virtual conflicts, and all apparent choices lead to predetermined solutions.

Further parallels between *Cabin* and Whedon's *Dollhouse* serve to illuminate Whedon and Goddard's apparent interest in the influence of reality TV on its audience's sense of (and paranoia regarding) the real as involving a relatively high degree of mediation and manipulation. *Thematically*, both works critique the ethics of visual and virtual technologies as they come into the dystopian service of exploitation and surveillance. The cold, clinical technicians and masterminds in the control rooms of both *Dollhouse* and *Cabin* exist to deploy a group of "dolls" or "puppets" based on types and stereotypes derived from genre characterizations like avatars in a game. These new "watchers" read like perversions of the protective, even fatherly, "Watchers" of Whedon's *Buffy the Vampire Slayer* in that they observe from a place of extreme disconnect. *Formally*, both *Dollhouse* and *Cabin* feature an associative narrative structure, where the aforementioned chilly creator types observe their made-to-order fantasy constructs out in the field, commenting on them from behind the scenes in dialogue that either telegraphs the narrative's major themes, offers humorous critical commentary on the proceedings, or both. *Reflexively*, there is here an implicit critique of the Hollywood Dream Factory, with a group of "actives"[5] and the "watchers" who control and manipulate them in the interest of dispensing illusions. The "watchers" in this case extend also to the viewers, whose cinematic gaze, or supposedly fickle televisual "glance,"[6] is constructed and rewarded by the hypercontrolled on-screen spectacle of events in both *Cabin* and *Dollhouse*.

5. In Whedon's *Dollhouse*, "Actives" are the employees of the Rossum Corporation who sign away their identities and hire out their bodies for the purpose of acting out pleasure scenarios for high-paying clients.

6. This hotly contested term, first conceptualized by John Ellis ([1982] 1992), describes televisual viewership as distracted and disrupted because of the primarily domestic space of television reception.

As I have mentioned, *Cabin*'s control-room "watchers" and technicians have a mandate to manufacture a traumatic event in the form of spectacular ritual sacrifice. The ostensibly ritual function of what Cynthia Freeland calls "ordinary horror" (2004, 244) on reality TV as being akin to, in Hadley's words, "throw[ing] a virgin into a volcano" (*The Cabin in the Woods* 2012) has been much criticized (including by Freeland herself) as essentializing the reality TV viewer into a dissolute, fulfillment-seeking receptacle. Some of *Cabin*'s critical stance on reality TV derives from the wider scholarly discourse that laments the loss of the utopian potential of digital media to work as a democratizing force in the way we represent our reality in the media (see, for example, Dovey 1996). Again, this critical framework meditates on the failure of new recording technologies to hand over the power of representing history from institutional forces and "official" grand narratives of history to a more localized individual with agency. To this effect, fake-found-footage horror films such as *Paranormal Activity 2* and Christopher Denham's *Home Movie* (2007) feature characters introducing pervasive recording technologies into their own homes as a way of signifying the simultaneous technophilia and technophobia endemic to a paranoid surveillance society. *Cabin* stems from this recent trend in horror, locating such surveillance tactics squarely in the realm of corporate interests that seek to create and serve empty rituals to a consuming public willing to accept the artificial lives of others ("as seen on [reality] TV!") as akin to their own.

In *Cabin*, Whedon and Goddard thus align themselves (perhaps consciously, perhaps unconsciously) with a critical discourse on reality TV that Craig Hight calls "the 'trash TV' position," where reality programming is seen to manifest "increasing trends toward blatant exploitation within commercial television and clear signs of a decline in the collective taste and intelligence of contemporary mass audiences" (2004, 244). Importantly for a film like *Cabin*, Hight argues that popular millennial films such as *The Truman Show* and *EdTV* (1999), and the lesser-known *Series 7: The Contenders* (2001), struggle with "how to critique television as a medium without directly attacking viewers who are likely to also form the audience for the film itself" (235). Similarly, Whedon and Goddard are interested in how the various types of spectacle on display in their film might be received, yet they often have difficulty deciding what kind of viewer is out there watching. Much of the film's humor derives from scenes that juxtapose the "spectacle horror" (Lowenstein 2011, 42) of the film's five sacrificial victims with scenes of the control-room types behaving how Whedon and Goddard seem to feel horror audiences behave: by ogling the victims' half-naked bodies, laughing and shouting at their suffering, betting on the futile choices they will make, or ignoring them altogether while they go for more beer and chips. Whedon has suggested that Hadley and Sitterson are meant as stand-ins for himself and Goddard (Whedon, Goddard, and Bernstein 2012, 13), but *Cabin*'s two showrunners also seem to represent the way Whedon and Goddard imagine viewers behave in cinemas or at home: by turns ogling and distracted, desirous and detached. The resulting inconsistencies in the film's address (both diegetic and in the space of reception) can tell us much about how the film enacts the current relationship among genre, fandom, industry, medium, and technology.

Like many horror films, *Cabin* generates some of its unease by reminding viewers of their own position as witnesses to a series of violent or gory spectacles that offer a mixture of pleasure and recoil. *Cabin*'s extreme self-awareness in the highlighting of its viewers' relationship to such horror "attractions" (Gunning [1986] 2006) occurs especially in numerous scenes in the control room where members of the production crew are, by turns, glued to or fickly distracted from key scenes of sex and violence splashed across their multiple monitors. Goddard directs one such scene to allow viewers a few moments to become absorbed as the Buckners, the "zombie redneck torture family" (Whedon and Goddard 2012, 91), crawl out of their graves. Suddenly and shockingly, Sitterson enters the frame, directly facing (and confronting) viewers as he addresses his colleagues. Sitterson's body literally takes over the frame, blocking viewer investment in the Buckners' rise and revealing the source of the image to be one of many displayed on the control-room monitors.

In a similar scene, Jules ("whore") and Curt ("jock") wander the woods in search of sex, and the film cuts away to show Hadley, Sitterson, and company staring in awed anticipation of the requisite "boobies" (99). In yet another, the production team parties with their backs to multiple monitors showing the brutal beating of Dana, the film's indomitable "virgin." The former scene with Jules and Curt takes its own brutal turn, showing a topless Jules, yanked off of Curt (by a bear trap attached to her spine) during foreplay and subsequently beheaded by a member of the Buckners. But the latter scene is perhaps the more disturbing for its implications of a horror viewership distracted both literally and morally from the on-screen violence they actively ignore—an especially troubling conceit considering the complex range of responses *Cabin*'s audience in the multiplexes and living rooms might have while witnessing such a wholesale dismissal of spectacular suffering-for-the-masses.

Perhaps most telling in *Cabin*'s fraught representations of horror viewers is that, outside of the control-room space in which the producers themselves view the events, there is no logical space of reception in the diegesis for the elaborately produced rituals in the film. The events occurring in the diegesis of the film are akin to a military experiment: they are not intended for a mass audience; no one is watching this at home. There are potentially three logical configurations of viewership in the film's diegesis: the showrunners of the ritual sacrifice, the gods who demand the sacrifice, and the sacrificial players themselves (who on occasion watch each other). The gods demand blood, but who demands the spectacle? None of the above answers is really satisfying, and the difficulty in locating just whom this reality game show is supposed to address reveals *Cabin*'s struggle to situate its own audience. Is it to address a jaded audience? An uncritical, distracted audience? Should the film address a horror audience critical of a "degraded" reality TV aesthetic or a reality TV audience aware of the degree to which that format is self-aware and manipulative in ways similar to horror? At an impasse as to how to represent their audience within the diegesis, Whedon and Goddard opt to answer: no one is watching, at least in earnest.

Whedon and Goddard's criticisms seem largely to cite recent horror entertainment as the perpetration of a manipulative fraud on the public, yet *Cabin* has trouble deciding whether to frame horror viewers as victims of this fraud, as its coconspirators, or as primed for its exposure. The film encourages viewers to speculate that their reality is informed by continual surveillance and media manipulation, yet its mashed-up critique of the horror genre and reality TV fits squarely with Adornian contentions regarding a "Culture Industry" that "deludes" its consumers "with false conflicts" and exchanges "consciousness" for "conformity" ([1963] 1975, 17). Su Holmes and Deborah Jermyn suggest that a similar tendency in recent scholarship to debate the degree to which reality TV dupes or manipulates its audiences stems from difficulties addressing reality TV's inherent reflexivity (2004, 12). That is, reality TV addresses viewers through self-consciously hypermediated representations of reality (often involving game scenarios, but also revealing narrative and construct as part of the pleasure of viewing), and it pushes a degree of hyperbole and excess that encourages viewers to consider the packaged nature of the product they are watching. Thus, reality TV is, like horror, girded by a sense of its viewers' expectations and critical savvy based upon convention. It courts their outrage, their sense of humor, their sympathies, their knowledge, and their desire to be shocked by both act and accident. To emphasize only the audience's consumption at best, and its corruption and manipulation at worst, is to see ideology operating at a level that completely overcomes agency and subjectivity.

Television and its viewership have become a convenient target for a threat-ened cinema, which responds by both thematizing and co-opting a TV aes-thetic. In keeping with this hybridizing, *Cabin* works most clearly as both a commentary on and an emulation of the way reality TV forms are seen to have "invaded" horror cinema. *Cabin*'s struggle to figure its viewership derives from Whedon and Goddard's need to be critical of a perceived empty excess in recent horror that they seem to suggest is parallel to the rhetorical excesses and ethical transgressions of reality TV. Accordingly, *Cabin* is constructed largely of scenarios featuring viewers caught somewhere between mockery and distraction, confronting a product that is largely exploitative and emptied of any real substance. There is a difference between critical self-reflection and cynicism regarding horror viewership, and *Cabin* seems to take the latter tack, supporting the view that intelligent viewers must approach the genre from a position of derision to avoid being duped.

Joss Whedon Throws His Mighty Shield

Marvel's The Avengers *as War Movie*

ENSLEY F. GUFFEY

*M*arvel's The Avengers (hereinafter *The Avengers*), written and directed by Joss Whedon, currently holds more all-time box-office records than any other film. Furthermore, *The Avengers* is ranked the number-one film of all time for domestic opening-weekend receipts, having grossed US$207,438,708 in three days (*Box Office Mojo* 2012). With worldwide earnings totaling more than $1.5 billion in theaters (*Box Office Mojo* 2012), as well as positive reviews from 86 percent of top critics, and 93 percent of all critics, *The Avengers* is a true blockbuster (*Rotten Tomatoes* 2012). The film features action, humor, explosions, and beautiful stars in sexy clothing. It is based upon an enduring comic book title, and on the surface is yet another Hollywood big-budget, highest-common-consumer-denominator release. As with most projects helmed by Joss Whedon, however, first appearances are very deceiving.

Beyond its global, mass-market success, *The Avengers* has allowed Whedon to combine many of the most profound influences in his creative life to create a work of art that transcends the superhero movie genre. Indeed, Whedon's film is a true generic hybrid. Elements of possession by external forces via Loki's spear, a Hulk so truly monstrous and frightening that for the first half of the movie the creature is not even named, and the physical otherness of the Chitauri and their toothy, eel-like "Leviathans" all bring elements of horror to the story (*The Art of "Marvel's The Avengers"* 2012, 226). The ubiquitous intelligence/counterintelligence organization and advanced technology of the Strategic Homeland Intervention, Enforcement, and Logistics Division (S.H.I.E.L.D.) add an enormous vein of high-tech spy thriller to the mix. The superhero genre is front and center, of course, with a group origin story that forces the characters involved to come together and use their powers to confront a threat that is both too large and too powerful for conventional (or even unconventional yet merely human) forces to handle. Furthermore, *The Avengers* brings along the problematic baggage of five years of previous films dealing with the individual stories of four of the central heroes and forty-plus years of comic book continuity and memory.

This brief sketch gives some idea of the difficulties facing the production of *The Avengers* and poses the question of how, exactly, Whedon managed to bring all of these elements and genres together into a mostly harmonious, effective, and—not least of all—successful film. Whedon himself was well aware of the difficulties he faced:

> It's the same problem I had with *Serenity* and swore I'd never have again. Tracking the information you have to get across in the movie is more difficult. . . . You have to know how much people need to know, because some audiences come in knowing everything, and you don't want to tell them too much, and some of them will come in knowing nothing (about the previous Marvel films) and you don't want to tell them too much. You want some things to be inferred. It's fun to see a movie that has texture beyond what you know. If you feel there's a life outside the frame, then you feel good about it. You don't necessarily have to lay everything out. Organizing was the most exhausting part of the film because it wasn't all there. (quoted in Dawson 2012)

Whedon's solution for dealing with this inescapably rich text grew from his own education and creative experience. Simply put, he solved these problems with genre.

According to Whedon, "from the start I wanted to make a war movie. I wanted to put these guys through more than what they would be put through in a normal superhero movie" (quoted in Dawson 2012). Specifically, Whedon gathered all the disparate elements of *The Avengers* within the generic form of the classic combat film as defined by his former film studies professor at Wesleyan University, Jeanine Basinger. In her book *The World War II Combat Film: Anatomy of a Genre* (2003), Basinger delineates the generic form of a combat film and traces its evolution, variants, and typologies from World War II to the twenty-first century. A devoted student of Basinger, Whedon has maintained a close relationship with her since his graduation from Wesleyan. In 2008, Nikki Stafford reported that Whedon "not only keeps in touch with [Basinger], but calls her on a regular basis, asks for her help and input and criticism, and will go spend weeks at her house hashing out ideas." It is therefore all but certain that Whedon would be thoroughly familiar with this important book by a woman he has called one of "two great teachers in my life" and that his application of the combat film genre to *The Avengers* would be heavily influenced by Basinger's work (Roth 2010).

Importantly, the foundations to interpret *The Avengers* as a combat film were already present in the film's source texts. Briefly, the film takes its basic story line from a combination of those stories presented in the first issues (1963–64) of *The Avengers* comic book and the thirteen issues of Marvel's alternate-universe reboot of the franchise, *The Ultimates* (2003–4). In Stan Lee and Jack Kirby's original *Avengers* comic story line, Loki, having been banished from Asgard by his half-brother, Thor, and adoptive father, Odin, seeks revenge by trying to set Thor at odds with the only force on Earth that might be capable of defeating the God of Thunder: the Incredible Hulk. Through a series of plot conveniences, Loki's scheme backfires and inadvertently causes Thor, the Hulk, Iron Man, the Wasp, and Ant-Man to unite as a team to defeat him (*Marvel Masterworks: "The Avengers"* 2011, 1–22).

In the first *Ultimates* series of thirteen issues, written by Mark Millar and penciled by Bryan Hitch, S.H.I.E.L.D. is an enormously powerful, technologically advanced, and American-controlled paramilitary intelligence organization run by General Nick Fury. By Issue 8, S.H.I.E.L.D. includes agents Natasha Romanoff (the Black Widow) and Clint Barton (Hawkeye), who are working with Tony Stark (Iron Man), Bruce Banner (the Hulk), Henry Pym (Ant- and Giant-Man), and Janet Pym (the Wasp) to create a team of superpowered individuals to act as a reaction force against criminal-minded superpowered people and other threats usually outside the scope of regular law-enforcement and military organizations. This story line culminates with the Ultimates fighting off an invasion by the shape-shifting alien race known as the Chitauri (*The Ultimates* 2010).

Whedon was familiar with both series, as demonstrated by his introduction for the collected *Ultimates* graphic novel (2004a). Indeed, Whedon would repeat and expand upon many of the ideas he touched on in his introduction in various interviews about *The Avengers* film. Of the 1963 *Avengers* comic iteration, he wrote that the last panel of the first issue was unforgettable, showing the characters "standing strong as an indelible statement of, 'Seriously, what are these guys doing together?' . . . It didn't work. It worked great. The Avengers lived on through endless incarnations, endless line-ups, and two coasts" (Whedon 2004a).[1] On the *Ultimates* reboot of the franchise, he wrote, "It doesn't work. It works (I think you know where I'm going with this) great. It works because Mark Millar deconstructs the idea of heroes just enough for you to be truly worried about their chances when the world IS in need of saving, and truly excited when they succeed" (2004a).

Much of this description already fulfills some of the key requirements Basinger identifies as necessary for a combat film. Such a film must have a group that is "a mixture of unrelated types, with various ethnic and socio-economic backgrounds. They may be from different military forces, and/or different countries. They are of different ages. Some have never fought in combat before, and others are experienced." This mixed group was already present in both comic book versions, and in both cases it is a strange mish-mash of people, personalities, and powers that on the surface seems unwork-able, if not ridiculous. Likewise, both groups have important objectives. As Basinger states, however, the group must undertake a *military* objective: "The objective may have been a secret, or it may have been planned in advance, or it may have grown out of necessity" (2003, 68). Although defeating Loki in *The Avengers* comic may not qualify as an objective of the type called for by the combat film genre, defending Earth from alien invasion in *The Ultimates* most definitely does.

Thus, two central elements of the combat film genre are already present, and Whedon was not slow to incorporate them as he approached *The Aveng-ers*: "If it's about the origin of a team that doesn't make sense together, and they really don't, then you have to use the *Dirty Dozen* [1967] model, which is an hour and 40 minutes of training and 20 minutes of Nazi-killing. So I laid out my ideas, the biggest one being, I think it's a war movie. That's the only way you can make these people feel like they might lose. . . . And I felt it even more strongly when I watched *Black Hawk Down* [2001]. I was like, O.K., that's the movie I want to make" (quoted in Itzkoff 2012). The combi-nation of Loki and the Chitauri, and the necessity of confining their planned invasion of Earth to Manhattan Island, creates a "hold the fort"–type military objective against an enemy force that has the capability of truly endangering the lives of the group members (Basinger 2003, 68).

1. In 1984, Marvel spun off a new comic series from *The Avengers*, based on the West Coast of the United States and called *The West Coast Avengers* (changed in 1989 to *Avengers West Coast*). The series ended in 1994.

The disparate nature of the group also provides for another key element Basinger cites: "Conflict breaks out within the group itself. It is resolved through the external conflict brought down upon them" (69). In both comic book iterations, tensions among the heroes are immediately present and often erupt into violent struggles between team members. Whedon reinterprets these types of conflicts as the inevitable friction arising when you get together a group of supreme individualists, some with egos seemingly larger than their powers, and try to make them function as a unified team.

In Whedon's *The Avengers,* the group-conflict element noted by Basinger occurs first as Iron Man and Thor fight over custody of Loki until, stalemated against each other, and somewhat shamed by Captain America, they get back to the job at hand. Second, and most effectively, Steve Rogers and Tony Stark are in the middle of an escalating argument with each other when the possessed Hawkeye leads a commando-style raid on the vessel in order to free Loki and disable the ship. Cap and Iron Man are forced to work together to save the ship, while the rest of the team engage in individual struggles that ultimately convince them of the necessity of teamwork in the face of a common foe. While these are the most violent examples of this generic element in action, the most important ongoing conflict for the overall narrative is that which takes place between Tony Stark and Steve Rogers.

These characters fulfill two of the most important roles in the combat film genre: the hero and the hero's adversary (Basinger 2003, 49). Both comic book iterations of the Avengers have in common the leader of the group, a figure whom even superheroes consider a hero: Captain America. As Millar and Hitch had done with the first issue of *The Ultimates,* Marvel Studios used Captain America's World War II origin and career as the direct prequel to *The Avengers* with *Captain America: The First Avenger* (2011).[2] The importance of this character to Whedon's interpretation of *The*

2. In fact, Whedon's first job for Marvel's film division was as a script doctor for *Captain America*. Although the extent of Whedon's work on that script is unknown, and goes uncredited (as is usual for script doctoring), in a 2010 interview with Ed Gross, Whedon states that "there were a couple of opportunities to find [Captain America's] voice a little . . . and make the connections so that you understood exactly why he wanted to be who he wanted to be. And progressing through the script to flesh it out a little bit." Furthermore, comparing his work on *Captain America* to previous script-doctoring work, Whedon notes, "It was fun in this case, because . . . they'll actually use the things I wrote, which is rare" (quoted in Gross 2010). This statement suggests that Whedon potentially had a great deal of input in developing Captain America's character for both *Captain America* and *The Avengers*.

Avengers cannot be underestimated. As he explained in an interview with *Business World Weekender*'s Angela Dawson: "Captain America was kind of my Ground Zero for this film. The idea of someone who had been in World War II, had seen people laying down their lives in the worst kinds of circumstances in a world where the idea of community and the idea of a man being part of something, as opposed to being isolated from or bigger than the whole, is a very different concept of manhood. The idea of the soldier, the person who is willing to lay down his life, is very different than the idea of the superhero" (2012). This view of Captain America, and indeed of the American soldier in World War II, is so fundamental that it is worthwhile to review the history behind it.

The character of Captain America was introduced in 1941 in *Captain America Comics*, Issue 1, by Jack Kirby and Joe Simon (Sanderson 1996, 100). During the comic's World War II production run, Captain America fought on the home front, facing down various foes, particularly agents of the Axis powers such as the Red Skull as well as other assorted baddies. The character became "one of the most popular heroes of the 'Golden Age of Comics' [ca. 1938–51]" (102). In many ways, the wartime Captain America is pure pop-culture propaganda: the little guy from Brooklyn who, with the help of advanced American science, overcomes tremendous obstacles to fight for his country in a war against capital-*E* Evil.

Resurrected in March 1964 by Stan Lee and Jack Kirby in *The Avengers*, Issue 4, Captain America became the leader and ethical center of the group, and despite various name and costume changes, sabbaticals, and even (temporarily) dying, Steve Rogers as Captain America continues in this role today. He also became a much more complex and introspective character, a man out of time, haunted by his past, particularly the loss of his World War II sidekick, Bucky Barnes (*Marvel Masterworks: "Captain America"* 2010, 80). As Cap came into his own as a solo character in the mid-1960s in Marvel's *Tales of Suspense* title, Lee and Kirby tweaked his past, using the comic to recount Captain America's service and adventures in the European theater of World War II, where he often came into conflict not merely with Nazi superagents, such as Red Skull, but also with the regular German military.[3] It was this later iteration of Captain America's military career that became the primary canon for all subsequent interpretations, including Joss Whedon's.

3. Cap's encounters even include a memorable meeting with Adolf Hitler himself in *Tales of Suspense* Issue 67. See *Marvel Masterworks: "Captain America"* 2010, 93–94.

Although Whedon has referred to Captain America/Steve Rogers as having "an in with the audience, in that this world is stranger to him, so he is an identification figure," the character also connects with both the audience and even Whedon himself extradiegetically by tapping into the popular interpretation and mythology of the American soldier in World War II (*Clevver Movies* 2012). During the last decades of the twentieth century, as the United States marked the fortieth and fiftieth anniversaries of World War II, a very triumphant and nationalistic narrative emerged as the dominant popular memory of the war. This mythologized memory narrative extended to the American combat soldier as well. Books such as Tom Brokaw's *Greatest Generation* (1998) and Stephen E. Ambrose's *Band of Brothers* (1992) (later made into a popular miniseries on HBO) and Steven Spielberg's film *Saving Private Ryan* (1998) cemented the popular image of the American citizen-soldier as a paragon of masculine and military virtue.

As summarized by John Bodnar, this view of the "average American soldier" in World War II defines him as "a good man able to wage deadly warfare without becoming corrupted by the violence. He is the opposite of the brutal figures of Germans and Japanese that appeared in most Hollywood productions about the war. In the hands of Brokaw, Ambrose, and Spielberg, he is not only able to fight the good fight but to come away from the experience a better man" (2010, 214). Further, American GIs were presented as "model men who are more loving than dangerous and are committed to family and nation more than to violence and power" (213). These words could easily be applied to the classic characterization of Captain America/Steve Rogers, and Stan Lee and Jack Kirby leaned heavily on this view of the war and the American GI in their 1960s stories of Captain America in World War II. Though presenting a grittier and more violent Cap in their *Ultimates* reboot, Millar and Hitch also hewed close to the core of this reading.

Whedon's *Avengers* repeatedly references this mythologized view of the Second World War, most obviously during a scene set in modern-day Germany in which Loki forces a crowd of people to kneel before him and promises to remove the burden of freedom from humanity as a whole. He is first opposed by an elderly man and then by Captain America himself; both men reference Adolf Hitler and Nazi Germany. Notably, although some seventy years of suspended animation in Arctic ice has prevented Cap from aging, the old man and Captain America are *contemporaries*. For both, memories of the Second World War and Nazi Germany are far more present than for anyone else in the crowd. In appearing in the nick of time to save the one person with the guts to stand up to Loki, no matter how hopeless such defiance may be,

Captain America embodies the American popular memory of World War II, wherein the United States, and the United States alone, saved the world from evil. The vaguely Jewish folk music melody backing the elderly man's stand also evokes the Holocaust, which Bodnar notes has been appropriated in the American memory narrative of the war and has become "a central part of [the American] victory narrative and celebration" (221). For American audiences steeped in this traditional, triumphal framing of World War II as America's "good war," the scene is profoundly effective.[4]

Moreover, this scene also evokes the traditional interpretation of the American fighting man as seen in combat films from 1943's *Bataan* to 2001's *Black Hawk Down*. The Captain America that Whedon brings to the screen is the ultimate good American soldier who fought in the ultimate good war, and although the audience may on some level realize that this representation is a myth, it is also treasured as something of an ideal. As Whedon himself puts it, "I'm basically Tony [Stark] and I wish I was Steve [Rogers]. I believe everything that Steve says, but at the end of the day, I'm more like Tony" (quoted in Itzkoff 2012). Steve Rogers/Captain America thus fulfills the role of the hero—and then some. As for Tony Stark/Iron Man, he is the perfect foil to Captain America and perfectly fulfills the role of the hero's adversary: "This man is the group cynic, an important stand-in for audience doubts, and for its unwillingness to face the hardships the war will bring. Such a character becomes an appropriate initiation figure into the change-of-attitude that will be required for the task at hand" (Basinger 2003, 49). The exchange between Steve Rogers and Tony Stark shortly before the helicarrier is attacked is telling in this regard:

> ROGERS: Big man in a suit of armor. Take that off and what are you?
> STARK: Genius, billionaire, playboy, philanthropist.
> ROGERS: I knew guys who had none of that and were worth ten of you. . . .
>   You're not the guy to make the sacrifice play, to lay down on a wire and let the other guy crawl over you. (*Marvel's The Avengers* 2012)

Here is where Stark begins, but by the end of the film, not only has he accepted Captain America's leadership, but he has also *become* the guy who will "make

---

4. For a differing view on this scene's effectiveness, see Nadkarni 2012. In the audio commentaries to the DVD release of the film, Whedon acknowledges that many see the scene as "ham-handed," but states that he "liked the idea of a guy in Germany . . . who had a sense of history to him" (Whedon 2012).

the sacrifice play" as he alters the trajectory of a nuclear missile to destroy the Chitauri mother ship, an action that is likely to lead to his own death. It is Stark and Rogers who carry the film's debate over why we fight, and circumstances force Stark to submerge his individualism, at least temporarily, for the good of the group and in order to achieve the objective, become a soldier, and successfully wage a war. The same story is played out by the Hulk, Thor, Hawkeye, and the Black Widow as each faces off against Loki and their own inner demons individually and unsuccessfully, until they are forced to function as part of a team.

Although a standard generic formulation, Stark's journey from cocky überindividualist with all of the answers and a healthy distrust for authority to a member of a group who lays down his life for the greater good is problematic. Despite finding hard evidence of Nick Fury's duplicity in weaponizing the power of the Cosmic Cube, and repeated assertions that he is neither a soldier nor willing to follow Fury's orders, in the end Stark does exactly that. His independence is undermined by the earnestness of Captain America, on the one hand, and Fury's cold-blooded manipulation of Agent Phil Coulson's death, on the other. The individual is subsumed for the good of the group, a situation that is usually anathema in an American culture that lionizes individualism above all but is oddly acceptable in wartime.

This partial surrendering of individual agency for the good of the whole is particularly important in a genre within which the group is usually read as representing the American melting pot. However, Basinger reminds us that "the representation is not a simple one. We are a mongrel nation—ragtail, unprepared, disorganized, quarrelsome among ourselves, and with separate special interests, raised, as we are, to believe in the individual, not the group. At the same time, we bring different skills and abilities together for the common good and from these separate needs and backgrounds we bring a feisty determination. No one leads us who is not strong, and our individualism is not set aside for any small cause. Once it is set aside, however, our group power is extreme" (2003, 46–47). A better description of the generic spirit behind Whedon's *The Avengers* may not be possible.

This extraordinarily Americentric interpretation of the world, and particularly of World War II, is not without its problems. As Samira Nadkarni has pointed out, *The Avengers* as a whole can be read as a piece of American propaganda in which the technocratic, post-9/11 America is melded with the mythologized spirit of sacrifice and unity of America in World War II to produce a triumphal narrative in which "the war for Earth has been won for us. And specifically, won for us by America" (2012). Whedon offers a slight critique of this framing with the well-placed mistrust in S.H.I.E.L.D. and Fury's motives held by Tony Stark, Bruce Banner, and even Steve Rogers, but overall he hews close to a triumphal American narrative.

In the past, Whedon has not hesitated to offer incisive critiques on this kind of nationalistic framing of America and American history.[5] Therefore, that he should present just such a narrative in *The Avengers* may well indicate a conscious choice on Whedon's part. The two films cited by Whedon as his major influences for *The Avengers*—*The Dirty Dozen* and *Black Hawk Down* (as noted above)—support this interpretation, as both films, while certainly variations within the American war film genre, present stories in which ultimately the assumed American national virtues of pluralism, training, and heroism prove victorious against seemingly overwhelming odds. Also, the story of the Avengers, whether told in comic books or on film, is quintessentially an American story of the same type, told from an American point of view. That Whedon should retain this structure seems evidence less of blind nationalism on his part than of a desire to maintain the heart of that narrative itself and to create a traditional generic piece. And for Whedon, this heart centers on S.H.I.E.L.D. agent Phil Coulson.

In the roll call of combat film generic elements, Agent Coulson plays a vital part, for it is essential that at least one member of the group die. Coulson's death not only helps to unify the team, but also serves as an example of heroic action. Coulson, after all, is not a superhero, but merely a well-trained human being. Nonetheless, he challenges Loki, a being of godlike power, in an attempt to save Thor. Coulson also harks back to a figure that emerged in some of the earliest combat films produced during World War II itself, a figure Basinger terms "the dead father figure . . . who originally rounds up the group of volunteers for an important mission" (2003, 48). Coulson, who has spent five films "rounding up" this team by this point, clearly fulfills this role. He is a man who truly believes in heroes. Coulson's final words to Loki, "You lack conviction," mark the core of the film. All the team members need to acquire conviction, to believe in something larger than themselves in order to overcome their personal struggles and form a coherent team. Coulson has always had it, and he recognizes its lack not just in Loki but in the Avengers themselves. Steve Rogers must find the means to live in the contemporary world and deal with his past. Tony Stark must overcome his innate selfishness

5. For example, see the *Angel* (1999–2004) episode "Why We Fight" (5.13), the series *Firefly* (2002–3), and the feature film *Serenity* (2005).

and egotism. Thor must find his place in relation to Earth and his vow to protect it. Bruce Banner must find a way to be at peace with "the other guy" and to accept that the Hulk is a part of him. Natasha Romanoff must deal with the "red in [her] ledger," and Clint Barton must prove that he is himself again (*Marvel's The Avengers* 2012). These problems are solved by the mission, the duty and necessity of risking everything to save Earth and the innocents on it (as represented by the inhabitants of New York City) from another world war and from enslavement by Loki and the Chitauri. The Avengers have the conviction that comes with serving a just cause (which again recalls the popular memory of America's role in World War II), and this conviction begins with Coulson's sudden death at Loki's hands. Basinger notes that this death "becomes a basic unit of the combat genre. The metaphoric meaning is obvious. In war, one will lose security, home, and comfort. A sacrifice will be made, and this initial loss in the storyline depicts this for the viewing audience in narrative terms" (2003, 49).

Ultimately, of course, a combat film must culminate in combat. The climax of the combat film is a battle, during which a character (or characters) demonstrates that he or she has changed and grown (Basinger 2003, 69). Whedon gives us this climax in spades with the battle of New York. The team gels at last, and each individual willingly places him- or herself under the command of Captain America in order to effectively fight the seemingly endless Chitauri horde. The fight is a classic hold-the-fort-style last stand, with Cap telling the team and the audience that "until we close that portal our priority is containment" and "Loki's gonna keep this fight focused on us and that's what we need. Without it [the Chitauri] could run wild" (*Marvel's The Avengers* 2012). The next twenty-five minutes of the film is constant combat, by the end of which every member of the Avengers is exhausted, battered, and bloody. Whedon crafted the battle carefully, as he told Adam Rogers: "It can't just be 'fight until we reach the 1:50 mark and then go home.' . . . You gotta think they might fail" (2012). This sense of endangerment is summed up in what is supposedly one of Whedon's favorite scenes in the film as Thor and Captain America—both with Christ-like wounds on their left sides, and both clearly showing signs of the strain and exhaustion of combat—face the fact that they might not survive the battle, yet (with a quip by Captain America) return to the fight nonetheless (Rogers 2012).

It is also worth noting that the Avengers and their allies do not kill anyone with a face. The humans shown being killed by S.H.I.E.L.D. agents or the Avengers are all masked, as is the case with the commando team led by the possessed Hawkeye against the helicarrier. Although plenty of Chitauri are destroyed, they are presented throughout as an anonymous enemy, the opposite of the protagonist group's distinct individuals (Basinger 2003, 55), not "people" at all, in other words, and (based upon their sudden collapse with the destruction of their mother ship) perhaps not even autonomously sentient.[6] This dehumanizing of the antagonists is not at all unusual in the war film genre. In *The Avengers*, it serves a double purpose: to distance the heroes from the act of killing people and to create maximum contrast and impact with Phil Coulson's death at Loki's hands. For all of the rhetoric about the realities of war throughout the script, the film very carefully exonerates the heroes from participation in the act of deadly violence that is central to war.

Further, like the presentation of the Japanese in the 1943 film *Bataan*, the Chitauri are both high-tech in terms of their military equipment and animalistic in their cruelty and barbarity (Basinger 2003, 55). The Chitauri, while willingly attacking the Avengers, are also directly targeting *unmasked* (that is, fully "real" and human) civilians, apparently rounding them up to be slaughtered en masse. Our heroes, of course, are seen risking their lives to save these innocents, who are stand-ins for all of humanity. The battle is thus framed in terms of the noblest and most venerable of causes: the heroes fight to protect the innocents of the entire world from evil.

This careful distancing of deadly violence from the heroes and the dehumanization of their opponents are a conscious use of genre on Whedon's part. The American combat film genre has proved to be remarkably flexible in terms of the messages it can convey, from the classic prowar propaganda of the films made during World War II itself to the devastating antiwar sentiments conveyed in films such as *Catch 22* (1970) or *Platoon* (1986) (see Basinger 2003, 109–98). With *The Avengers*, however, Whedon is quite deliberately crafting a very traditional "good guys versus bad guys" war film. He directly calls the audience's attention to that fact by having characters speak to it twice during the film. As he journeys to S.H.I.E.L.D.'s helicarrier with Steve Rogers, Agent Coulson reveals his lifelong hero worship of Captain America and the fact that he helped redesign Cap's uniform:

STEVE/CAP: The Uniform? Aren't the Stars and Stripes a little . . . old fashioned?

---

6. In his commentary to the DVD release of *The Avengers*, Whedon himself expresses a profound distaste for this bit of plot convenience. See Whedon 2012.

COULSON: Everything that's happening, the things that are about to come to light . . . people might just need a little old-fashioned.

And again, after Coulson's death, Nick Fury explains the Avengers Initiative to Cap:

FURY: Phil Coulson died still believing in that idea, in heroes. Well, it's an old-fashioned notion. (*Marvel's The Avengers* 2012)

Whedon is addressing the audience with these lines, telling us that *The Avengers* is not only a war film but a deliberately old-fashioned war film.[7]

We are not going to get any real moral ambiguity here or lingering meditations on the futility and ugliness of war; we are going to get heroes, flawed though they may be, who go through hell for all the right reasons and win through to save the day and make us proud. We are not getting *Platoon* (1986); we are getting *The Sands of Iwo Jima* (1949). This classic style of war film also complements the superhero genre, allowing Whedon to preserve a fundamental continuity with the comic book origins of the characters as people who violently fought evil but rarely took a life and, therefore, remained untouched by the violence they perpetrated.

Despite the problems inherent in the traditional combat film, Whedon's use of this framework for *The Avengers* has proved to be very successful. In his astute review of the film, Devin Faraci (2012) notes that *The Avengers* has touched on something in the culture that has largely been missing in other interpretations and reinterpretations of traditional superheroes: "That something, I believe, boils down to sincerity. *The Avengers* is a movie that wears its heart on its sleeve, that does not have much cynicism and contains zero ironic distancing. It's a movie that is not afraid to be big, to be silly and to embrace very traditional images of heroism. . . . [*The Avengers'*] heroism is uncomplicated. . . . This is old-fashioned good guys doing good things because they should. That's refreshing, and it's something we want to see in the world around us right now." Whedon has thus given us something fundamental with *The Avengers*. By being unafraid to make a comic book movie in

---

7. Indeed, in his audio commentary to the DVD release of the film, Whedon notes of Fury's "old-fashioned" line that "if there is a single line in the movie that explains what the idea behind the movie is, it's that" (Whedon 2012).

spite of an increasingly cynical mass media, a global economic recession, and America's involvement in two seemingly unending and very messy wars, and by calling upon the traditional American myth of the "good war"-style World War II combat film for the generic structure of that comic book movie, Joss Whedon has given us our heroes back and, with them, a little more hope than we had when we walked into the theater.

Part Six

Overarching
Topics

Stuffing a Rabbit in It

Character, Narrative, and Time in the Whedonverses

LORNA JOWETT

In *Twin Peaks* (1990–91), Laura Palmer is memorably described as being "filled with secrets" (1.2). In *Dollhouse*, on the other hand, a character initially sees Echo as "just an empty hat. Till you stuff a rabbit in it" ("The Target" 1.2). Any television character can be seen as an empty hat that becomes potentially full of secrets (or rabbits): the processes of creating, writing, directing, acting, shooting, or editing are all ways of stuffing that rabbit in it. The episodes mentioned in this necessarily brief examination "propel the possibilities of television drama," as Matthew Pateman says (2006, 109), because they demonstrate that the Whedonverse series are highly conscious of how television narrative and character work and how viewers read them. The Whedonverse series are not unique in using narrative and time to develop characters or even to interrogate identity. On the contrary, their consistent meditation upon the (de)construction of subjectivity over time is something that makes them typical of contemporary television and exemplary quality television drama.

As Catherine Johnson observes, VCR and DVD technology changes the way television is produced as well as the way it is consumed: "As television becomes less ephemeral, series with ongoing and complex narrative structures become more commercially viable" (2005, 117). Niche marketing also enables long-form narratives to succeed commercially. Character is thus increasingly important to television drama. Popular hits such as *Lost* (2004–10) successfully combine cult elements with mainstream television, some argue, by focusing on character (see Pearson 2009). The revival of *Doctor Who* (2005–present) develops its main characters within existing mythology but also in line with audience expectations of contemporary quality television.

The importance of characters in television drama generally is the first of two important premises underpinning this examination. Even in fantasy,

297

horror, and science fiction, where once the spectacle of the fantastic was fore-grounded, now, Catherine Johnson notes, genre television places "emphasis on the *reactions* of characters to the unknown over the representation of the fantastic itself. . . . [C]limactic cliff-hangers . . . end with a close-up of the face of a recurring character, rather than a dramatic special effect or action sequence" (2005, 80). Serious television drama started taking on aspects of soap opera narrative forty or fifty years ago, and soap elements are now common in any ensemble cast show. An ensemble cast allows for more stories because there are more characters and their interactions set up more narrative possibilities. Character interactions also afford narratives that resist closure, typically running alongside self-contained episodes or season story arcs. For these reasons, Rhonda Wilcox (2005) and others have championed *Buffy* as a serial narrative on a par with the novels of Dickens—and Dickens is a favorite of Joss Whedon.

The second premise intersects with the first. Television has a history of representing time, and conventions (narrative, visual, aural) for doing so have been firmly established. We are all familiar with flashback or backstory; we are accustomed to titles telling us where and when we are or to interpreting a montage of images designed to show time passing. In the fantastic, time can be represented and used in ways not possible for more "realistic" television drama. Strict conventions of realism preclude even flashbacks, and shows such as *The Wire* and *The Shield* (both 2002–8) generally avoid disruption of "real" time and naturalistic continuity. The fantastic, on the other hand, can include vampire characters who have lived for hundreds of years, or parallel time streams, and parallel characters inhabiting them. It opens up endless possibilities for rendering time and memory and exploring subjectivity.

The Whedonverse shows apply and adapt conventional television strategies for developing character, foregrounding subjectivity as fluid and constantly reconstructed. Time can function, for instance, to provide direction, dynamism: as Whedon comments, "People move on. You have to move forward all of the time" (quoted in Havens 2003, 114). Whether through point of view, narration, memory, or prophecy, perceptions of time and identity are always limited, contingent, and open to interpretation. Here the focus is on memory.

Memory Retrieval

All of the Whedonverse series use flashback to extend the temporal range of their narratives. *Buffy* often moves back in time and is not limited to the recent past, showing the 1970s ("Fool for Love" 5.7), the 1860s ("Becoming, Part

One" 2.21), or even prehistory ("Restless" 4.22). As Stacey Abbott notes of *Angel*, vampire protagonists mean that flashbacks become "an integral strand to the fabric of the series" (2009a, 21–22). Flashbacks are a form of memory retrieval, but they also provide novelty. Instead of the usual setting and cast of characters, an entirely new setting, in space and time, can be offered as well as entirely new characters, though generally a familiar character links present and past, introducing us to the past as part of his or her memory.

Flashbacks thus evoke additional pleasures, providing a display of period detail through sets and costumes. Period drama can efface history, presenting nostalgic, heritage spectacle, yet Helen Wheatley's *Gothic Television* suggests that period horror has the opposite effect, exposing a dark side to that heritage, functioning as feel-bad or antinostalgic period drama (2006, 49). Period setting in *Angel* often invokes this darkness, whether the McCarthyism and paranoia of the 1950s ("Are You Now, or Have You Ever Been?" 2.2) or the double dealing of war time ("Why We Fight" 5.13), and the darkness is often human, not demonic. Glen Creeber observes that older generations of television commentators familiar with the British tradition of social realism castigate recent television drama for "an explicit concern with the personal and private 'politics' of everyday life rather than concentrating on grand political issues and wider socio-economic debates" (2004, 116). However, Creeber goes on to suggest that a subjective rendering of history, society, and politics can be more realistic than an epic, moralizing tale, as *Angel* demonstrates. Similarly, *Firefly*'s focus on a small group of diverse characters casts a critical eye on colonization from the double vantage point of science fiction's defamiliarization and history's reevaluation of the past.

If period spectacle can liven up a familiar cast and setting, so can backstory. Roberta Pearson notes that it "augments character" and "introduces the novelty and divergence necessary in a long-running programme" (2009, 153). To achieve this result, flashbacks need neither last long nor provide concrete information, as *Buffy*'s "Dark Age" (2.8), an episode revealing some of Watcher Rupert Giles's backstory, demonstrates. The flashbacks here are brief impressionistic glimpses presented as dreams rather than memories, disturbing in form as well as content. Because we never clearly see or hear what is going on, the flashbacks are augmented by characters' explanations of them and by other evidence of Giles's history, such as the Mark of Eyghon tattoo or the personal testimony of Ethan Rayne, a fellow Eyghon worshipper from his past. Ethan becomes a recurring character from here on and is often used to illuminate Giles's less establishment traits, his alter ego, Ripper. As the episode title suggests, Giles, despite his stuffy demeanor (in the episode, the teens suggest that even "his diapers were tweed"), had a dark age, resisting responsibility, dropping out of college, and then experimenting with demon worship.

Giada Da Ros comments that the "fact of being character-driven instead of plot-driven is the basis of good fiction," going on to observe, "What makes a soap a soap is how much these personal elements are left showing, how much they shine through and how much they become themselves action" (2004, para. 26). The Whedonverses do not employ typical unending soap narrative, nor do they go to the extremes of a show like *Lost*, which is almost entirely predicated on character and flashback. Nevertheless, Carlton Cuse's remark that *Lost*'s "flashback stories are the emotional core of the series" (quoted in Pearson 2009, 143) is relevant to Whedon. Seconds-long flashbacks from "The Dark Age" add a new dimension to Giles's relationship with Buffy and the Scoobies by identifying similarities between them rather than differences. They also position Giles, like other Whedonverse characters, as someone who seeks to redeem his past mistakes but finds that his dark side puts the people he cares about in danger.

The use of personal history by Whedon and company to enhance narrative is most obvious in *Angel*. The first extended period flashbacks in *Buffy* concerned Angel's past, either as soulless Angelus or as reensouled Angel, and are an integral element in the spin-off. "Throughout the series," Abbott succinctly observes, "Angel has been represented as a man who is haunted by his past, which every once in a while emerges into the present to torment him" (2009a, 78). The unfolding of Angel's backstory knits together past and present, his history, and the story of other characters. This knitting together is nowhere more evident than in Season 3 of *Angel*, a season that Abbott describes as "a family melodrama built around the return of pregnant Darla, Angel's former vampire-lover, the birth of Angel and Darla's son, Connor . . . , and the breakdown of Angel's family [of friends] at Angel Investigations" (35). The whole arc operates with heightened intensity because "the fears and anxieties associated with childbirth and parenthood, the traditional subject of melodrama" are intertwined "with Holtz's centuries-old quest for vengeance" (36), offering a multilayered representation of time, memory, character, and narrative.

Eighteenth-century vampire hunter Daniel Holtz's story begins in the first episode of Season 3 ("Heartthrob") as Angel tells a story about Angelus and Darla being pursued by Holtz. Their shared history unfolds slowly across several episodes and not in chronological order—the flashback story of Holtz's family tragedy is not concluded until "Lullaby" (3.9). In the past, Holtz is visited by the demon Sahjhan, who makes him an offer. Holtz accepts, is frozen in time, and is revived centuries later to continue hunting Angelus; thus, mystical time travel allows him to appear in the present narrative as well as in flashbacks. Holtz's character is presented as anachronistic through costume (a present-day riding coat replaces his eighteenth-century cloak) and speech (formal and distinctively patterned).

When Angel and Holtz first meet in the present ("Quickening" 3.8), Holtz still thinks he is tracking Angelus. Before they meet again, flashbacks reveal that Angelus and Darla not only slaughtered Holtz's family but also turned his daughter into a vampire so that Holtz felt compelled to kill her. With dramatic irony, and what Pateman calls intratextual "involution," the second meeting (in "Lullaby") takes place in an alley where Darla has just given birth to Angel's son by staking herself. Involution, as Pateman describes it, is a formal strategy where "contact between two points (whether intra- or intertextual) . . . magnifies the connotative and interpretive power of both" (2006, 120). Here, knowing that Holtz holds Angelus responsible for the death of his family, we expect that Holtz will take revenge by killing Angel's son. The tension is heightened by visual manipulation of time. Holtz emerges from the burning building in slow motion, crossbow at the ready, but then normal speed resumes, only to have time slow in a different way as he takes in the sight of Angel with his son during a lengthy pause. A more conventional television drama might use this moment as a cliffhanger ending—teasing the audience with the knowledge that it will be another week before the situation is resolved—but, as so often with Whedonverse shows, our expectations are subverted. The episode ends with Holtz letting Angel go.

Fantasy is used to bring Holtz, a character from Angelus's past, into the present. Similarly, the childhood of Angel and Darla's son, Connor, is compressed via the device of interdimensional travel. When Connor is abducted by Holtz in "Sleep Tight" (3.16) and the two enter a portal into the hell-like dimension Quor-toth, Connor too becomes a time traveler. Thus, Angel's mourning for his abducted baby son lasts only three episodes, and then Connor returns in "The Price" (3.19), already a young man. The fantasy elements of the series allow for this telescoping of time, yet self-conscious reference is also made to the ways televisual form can manipulate or exaggerate the pace of events. Gunn comments, "He was wearing diapers a coupla weeks ago, now he's a teenager," and Cordelia replies, "Tell me we don't live in a soap opera" ("A New World" 3.20). High melodrama and fantasy likewise combine at the end of the season, which brings Holtz's long revenge to fruition. The aged Holtz agrees that Connor should leave him (his adopted father and kidnapper) and return to Angel. "Every time you look upon his face, every time he calls you father," he tells Angel, "you will be reminded of that which you took and can never give back" ("Benediction" 3.21). Here, Holtz predicts a future in which Angel's present is forever tainted by the past actions of Angelus, however hard Angel seeks redemption. Holtz's elaborate vengeance sets Connor against Angel, and the season finale leaves Angel chained at the bottom of the ocean. Time, it seems, has caught up with Angelus, even if he is now Angel—and the audience has to wait for the next season to see the story continue.

Angel's development is delineated here and in other major season arcs through remorse, redemption, loves, and losses. Any flashback providing backstory offers both contrast and similarity between past and present. The appearance in flashbacks of the human Liam, Angelus, and Angel demonstrates the distance between these versions of the character as well as the similarities. Despite Giles's uncharacteristic behavior in "The Dark Age"—"lost weekending" in his apartment, as Buffy describes it—his care for the young people he aids, teaches, and nurtures is reinforced, as is his mission to resist the seduction of dark powers. For vampires like Angel and Spike, change is supposedly impossible: changelessness is part of being a vampire. Yet Angel's story repeatedly proves that even biologically fixed vampires can change.

Memory as Story

As *Angel* demonstrates, backstory can provide more than just character history. Flashbacks in the Whedonverses are generally related to ongoing narratives. This point may sound obvious, yet it is not always the case in serial television. Pearson notes that *Lost*'s "flashbacks don't initiate independent plot lines, but directly connect to the established mythology" (2009, 154), whereas in *The Sopranos* (1999–2007) "flashbacks illuminate the character's interiority, but they don't necessarily advance the plot in terms of connecting directly to present-day development" (142). Whedonverse flashbacks tend to do all of it and often reflect on narrative too, foregrounding the process of remembering and (re)telling the past. For example, in *Buffy*'s "Fool for Love," Spike tells Buffy how he killed other Slayers in the past. Frequent mismatches between what he says and what we actually see signal the unreliability of his first-person narration.[1] Episodes such as this use flashback as a means of structuring the plot and of reflecting on the process of memory (remembering an event may not be the same as living it at the time or retelling it later). *Firefly*'s episode "The Message" (1.12) uses a straightforward flashback to set in motion a process

---

1. On the narrative technique of "Fool for Love," see Albright in this volume.

of memory retrieval that demonstrates how the past is interpreted in personal and subjective ways.

"The Message" begins with a war flashback that initiates a series of narratives and revisions of those narratives. Captain Mal and second in command Zoe's shared war history is an ongoing thread in *Firefly*. It unites them, as seen in the pilot or "Out of Gas" (1.8), but often appears to exclude others (see "War Stories" 1.10). This episode is different because Mal and Zoe's shared experiences are now set alongside another set of memories, war comrade Tracey's. Although all three remember the same events, different responses to them are explored as the episode unfolds, matched with a sense of how the events' meanings might change for an individual over time. The events themselves are retrieved for us through a short flashback to the "Battle of Du-Khang / Seven Years Earlier" that follows the opening credits. The flashback is fairly conventional, introduced by titles that situate it in time and space. It records interactions among the three characters, focusing on Tracey. It is the straight story yet to be embellished by different memories and different interpretations.

The episode teaser shows the crew on a space station collecting their mail, and most viewers remember this episode because ex-mercenary Jayne receives a hand-knitted hat from his mother. Mal and Zoe claim a rather different package: the body of Tracey. The accompanying audio message states that Tracey's life has not gone well since the war and requests that Mal and Zoe return his body to his parents for burial. His faith that they will do so derives from his memory of their shared experience, invoked by his words: "You two carried me through that war and now I need you to carry me just a little bit further, if you can." Tracey's later comment, "Never could get my life working right, not once after the war," and his slide into debt and crime (revealed as the episode unfolds) reflect aspects of war as trauma, its effects on combat veterans. The personal history of the three war veterans thus invokes a larger history. Moreover, in this series, the story of the war is told by the losers, not, as is more common, the winners. The film *Serenity* (2005) interrogates in more detail Alliance rewriting of history, a feature common to the dystopian form (see Baccolini 2003). Even in "The Message," it is made clear that the military record of the battle is distinct from personal experience of it.[2] The flashback focuses on the perspective of the characters. In it both Zoe and Mal

2. For a discussion of the parallels between "The Message" and the cancellation of the *Firefly* series, see Rambo in this volume.

save Tracey's life, and each passes on advice to him. We also see Mal order the remaining personnel to join up "with the 22nd" so they can survive, overturning existing orders that take no account of the changing situation on the ground. The commanding officer is catatonic and in no state to countermand Mal, yet Mal tells Tracey that he does not want to blot the lieutenant's record in case he "ever gets his mind back." In this way, the episode suggests that although the military has a "record" of the battle of Du-Khang, it is not necessarily an accurate one.

A military record might be factual and objective; Tracey's audio recording is personal, designed to inspire emotion. When the crew first hear it, Jayne takes his hat off as a sign of respect (and the sequence makes clear that the message, not the body, prompts this reaction). Later, as part of a montage showing the crew's response, we see mechanic Kaylee listen to it again in her quarters, a scene suggesting regret for a life cut short. In the kitchen of the ship, however, the memories of Tracey that Mal and Zoe share with associate and friend Inara inspire laughter, albeit coupled with reflection. Memory evokes emotion, and Tracey exploits this sentiment. His involvement in organ smuggling is later revealed, and we find he is using his history with Mal and Zoe and a faked death to secure safe passage from Alliance pursuers. That is, he is counting on exactly the kind of emotional kick delivered by the flashback and the reminiscing.

Tracey's position in the narrative thus shifts from dead, down-on-his-luck veteran to live, manipulative criminal. His opportunism is contrasted with Mal's notion of honor. The preceding episodes have emphasized how important the war is to Mal and Zoe, so trading on it as Tracey does strengthens the impact of his betrayal. David Magill, discussing masculinity in *Firefly* and *Serenity*, notes that when Tracey admits his actions, his "labeling of Mal's lessons as 'stories' demonstrates that he has not internalized them" (2008, 83). Tracey remembers Mal's "stories and his homilies, of glory and honor," and here memory and narrative seem to be about interpretation. He must believe that Mal and Zoe are "saps" who take these "stories . . . of glory and honor" seriously; otherwise his planned ruse would not work. Moreover, it is necessary for him to describe them cynically, so he can dismiss their shared memories and follow through with his betrayal.

For the audience, however, Mal and Zoe's memories of Tracey, delivered through the flashback and the stories they tell, reinforce our emotional response to these familiar characters. The flashback tells us who Zoe and Mal were; their responses to the present situation tell us who they are. Before he dies, Tracey asks the captain, "What are we now, Mal?" He may have changed;

Mal and Zoe have not. They have stuck to a code; he has not. They will stick by war comrades; he is prepared to betray and use them. Thus, when Tracey threatens Kaylee, Mal shoots him to protect the crew. His words to Tracey from the war flashback are repeated here at the episode's climax, bringing the narrative full circle: "Everybody dies, Tracey. Someone's carrying a bullet for you right now, doesn't even know it. The trick is, die of old age before it finds you." Mal shoots Tracey despite saving his life years ago and answers his protest with a reference to the apparent irony of these actions: "No, son. Murdered yourself. I just carried the bullet a while."

The final scene, showing the crew bringing Tracey's body home, is a further irony. They fulfill his "last request," and his message, designed to fool the saps who believe in honor, is (re)invested with emotion. Music sets the tone, but the only spoken words are the message repeated for the last time, more full of meaning and pathos than ever. The falling snow suggests that although mortals die, the seasons turn and time moves on. Memory retrieval here structures a complex narrative that debates the human condition.

Memory Loss

Robert J. Thompson identifies "memory" as a key element of quality television (1996, 14), meaning that television drama can build up a history of narrative events, remembered by the characters, by the show (continuity), and by the audience. (This narrative practice works in contrast to, for example, typical sitcom: a format that traditionally resets itself with each new episode.) This practice can happen to varying degrees. Thus, Pearson notes that in general "the requirement for a certain degree of stability and repetition shapes the narrative arc of the central characters of serial television dramas, denying them life-altering epiphanies that would threaten the series' format" (2009, 154), and observes that even a highly regarded serial drama such as *The Sopranos* sidesteps real development. Its "greatness," she suggests, "lies partly in its extensive exploration of a character who changes very little over the course of six seasons, who remains as complex at the end as he was at the beginning" (156). Some might disagree, but the point is really about how far television can build up real character development. Some development was present in *Buffy* because most of the core characters *were* teenagers but grew up, a version of real time borrowed from soap operas, designed as endlessly ongoing serial narratives. Moreover, given that the longest-running of the Whedonverse shows are partly or wholly about redemption, real change (in the form of "life-altering epiphanies") is essential. Change has no effect without memory, which these shows employ to a high degree. As writer Jane Espenson notes, "Story-telling that doesn't reset to status quo after every episode rewards faithful viewers" (2010b, 45). Such rewards are now an essential part of quality television, leading to the ongoing serial narratives that define many critically acclaimed dramas.

If flashback is a form of memory retrieval, memory loss enables something different. Incidents of memory loss tend to be bubble episodes, self-contained stories that do not necessarily affect ongoing characters or narratives. In this sense, as Abbott notes, they are "often sanctioned transgression designed to capitalize upon audience's taste for innovation" (2010a, 95). The obvious exception here is *Dollhouse*, where memory loss is integral: Dolls can be programmed and are permanently wiped of memory and personality, ready to receive whatever memory and personality fit their next engagement. The philosophy behind this representation of memory, demonstrated in cult science fiction films like *Blade Runner* (1982), also underpins memory-loss episodes from the Whedonverses that preceded and perhaps inspired *Dollhouse*. The reimagined *Battlestar Galactica* (2003–9) and its treatment of the Cylons are a wonderfully innovative development of *Blade Runner*'s replicants, and it is no surprise that *Battlestar* is referenced directly in *Dollhouse* (in "Meet Jane Doe" [2.7] Topher says that Bennett "went all Cylon" on him, for example). Put simply, these fictions debate this question: Are we who we are or who we remember we are? And if identity is the sum of our experiences (memories), what happens if we lose those memories?

Wilcox explains that *Buffy*'s "Tabula Rasa" (6.8) offers "predictors of future episodes, blueprints of events to come" (2005, 60); that is, losing memories of the past is tied to foreshadowing the future. The episode also suggests that an essential core to characters persists, despite memory loss. Although some comic misunderstandings ensue (Giles and Anya decide they are romantic rather than business partners; the two Brits, Giles and Spike, assume that they must be related), other character interactions suggest residual bonds and traits. Dawn and Buffy feel a connection, as do Willow and Tara; Buffy "chooses not only heroism but also leadership," as Wilcox notes (62). In shows so strongly invested in character, it is hardly surprising that relationships show through. In *Dollhouse*, Sierra and Victor's romantic bonding functions to humanize the Dolls before we meet their "originals," Priya and Tony, and to contrast Echo's rather different ability to remember.

In *Angel*'s "I Will Remember You" (1.8), Angel remembers what happened with Buffy when he was human for a day, even though nobody else does. Similarly, the other characters' memories of Connor are wiped in "Home" (4.22) to give Connor a chance at a normal life, though Angel retains his memories of his son. This arc reverses *Buffy* Season 5, when Dawn is inserted into the narrative, which is "retconned" to accommodate her. (*Retcon* derives from "retroactive continuity," when, as Espenson explains, "the only way to make it happen is after the fact" [quoted in Kaveney 2004c, 107].) Yet a later episode exposes Angel's choice and reveals that Connor's new life is potentially under threat.

Connor's distinctive relation to time is highlighted continually. When he unexpectedly returns fully grown from Quor-toth, his line "Hi, Dad" forms the closing line of "The Price" and the opening of the next episode ("A New World"), a manipulation of television temporality that adds impact. This line is then repeated as the closing line of "A New World" when Connor is reunited with Holtz, revealing his divided identity as Connor, Angel's son, and Stephen, Holtz's adopted son. When the memory-wiped Connor reappears in Season 5's "Origin" (5.18), his first line is, "Hey, Dad," as he walks past Angel to join his "new" father. The same line invites us to spot the difference each time.

It is revealed in "Origin" that warlock Cyvus Vail "built" Connor's new memories, apparently turning him into a different person. Other characters' memories have also been altered, effectively erasing Connor from their pasts. Illyria tells Wesley that reality has not been changed, suggesting that what we term reality is simply our subjective experience. "You are a summation of recollections," she says, and "each change is simply a point of experience," but he insists, "We're more than just memories." Connor is prophesied to kill demon Sahjhan, so when Sahjhan meets Connor, he says, "Ah, you're him," to which Connor replies, "Yeah, I'm me." Yet he is neither the warrior Sahjhan thinks he is nor the son Angel remembers. Instead, he is the summation of the recollections Vail has so skillfully "built." This situation seems to contradict the essential core of being demonstrated in *Buffy*'s "Tabula Rasa" by implying that new memories, real or counterfeited, make a new person—a concept exploited to the full in *Dollhouse*. By the end of "Origin," there are, in Illyria's words, "two sets of memories, those that happened and those that are fabricated," and for the characters, "it's hard to tell which is which." But, like Giles, Joyce, and most of the adult population of Sunnydale in *Buffy*'s "Band Candy" (3.6), in order to continue his normal life, Connor *chooses* to forget that he remembers what had been magically wiped away: "I gotta go back to my life now. . . . I need to take care of my parents," he tells Angel.

However, because Connor knows that Angel is his biological father, he returns for the final battle in the series finale to "take care of" his other parent. In contrast, Buffy sacrificed herself for Dawn in the finale of *Buffy* Season 5 on the strength of her false memories, choosing to believe those memories rather than a forgotten world, a history without Dawn (compare "Normal Again" 6.17). Thus, Pateman notes that even though all of the characters discover that their memories of Dawn "are false, they cannot erase them and *do not seem to want to*" (2006, 200; emphasis added). The Whedonverses emphasize free will in addition to fluid subjectivity, and these stories suggest that in choosing which memories to believe, characters choose who they are.[3]

Whedonverse series are sparing with slow motion, but the Connor arcs of *Angel* use it relatively often. In places, slow motion intensifies action and emotion—a prime example being the *Matrix*-style bullet-time sequence during the fight between Angel and Connor after Connor returns from Quor-toth ("A New World"). But the use of slow motion here also highlights the malleable nature of time itself, especially as it relates to memory and identity: "He was wearing diapers a coupla weeks ago, now he's a teenager." Other moments, as when Connor walks away from Angel to return to his new parents at the end of "Origin," suggest visually that Angel wants to slow time down, to delay the inevitable.

These episodes and arcs also draw attention, as Margaret L. Carter notes about parallel-universe stories, to the process of writing television (2003, 179). Such erasures highlight the carefully constructed diegetic world *as* a construction, written according to the conventions of television narrative. Abbott offers some insights into this self-reflexivity when she discusses voice-over in *Angel*'s "Spin the Bottle" (4.6): Lorne narrates this episode, as if to an audience in his club, Caritas, acknowledging advertisement breaks and speaking straight to the camera in midscene (2009a, 93). Similarly, although the introduction of Dawn in the fifth season's first episode may be as "seamless" as Pateman describes (2006, 200) because of the competence of Whedon and company, it also works because it is self-reflexive. The decision to have "Real Me" (5.2) shift to Dawn's narrative point of view, with voice-overs of her diary entries, was made early in the process of developing Dawn's character (Fury 2003). We are abruptly jerked out of the usual format of the show by the introduction of a new character we know does not fit; the jarring effect is heightened by this shift in narrative perspective. Yet allowing Dawn to speak directly to us introduces her more intimately, and her first full episode works to show how she *does* fit into the familiar diegetic world, presenting clearly well-worn interactions with regular characters who "have a history with her, even though we as an audience know that she never existed before," as writer

---

3. On the choices of memory and ethics, see Rabb and Richardson in this volume.

David Fury notes (2003). It is not until later in the episode that the narrative draws attention to the fact that Dawn has been suddenly inserted, when a madman tells her, "You don't belong." And it is some time later in the season that an explanation is offered: Dawn is a mystical form of energy, the Key, hidden in the form of Buffy's sister for protection.

An Empty Hat?

Having experimented with the many and varied ways that television characters are constructed by stuffing a rabbit into the empty hat, Whedon and company's *Dollhouse* initially seems to be a formal experiment to achieve drama *without* the relation of character to narrative. In the first season, very little insight is given into most of the nonwiped characters' histories. Perhaps this reticence was intended to hint, in a variation on *Blade Runner* and *Battlestar*, that nobody was "real" (as it turned out, some were not). *Dollhouse* builds memory loss into its basic premise, and the finale of Season 1 ("Epitaph One" 1.13) also gives us an alternate timeline, a flashforward, reworking previous Whedonverse uses of time.

"Epitaph One" is a kind of "Restless" (*Buffy*), a season finale that acts as a coda to the resolution of the season arc in the penultimate episode, a disruption of conventional television season structure. Moreover, this season finale does not follow in continuous chronology; instead, it leaps forward in time, and we are thrown into "a whole new world" (Jed Whedon and Tancharoen 2009)—it creates a memory gap. In this way, it both ruptures the world of the show and denies viewers their familiarity with that world. The familiar titles do not roll. The characters use strange terms, what writers Jed Whedon and Maurissa Tancharoen call "future lingo" (2009), familiar words given new meanings ("tech," "actuals," "birthmarks"). The episode does not even provide familiar characters in new roles with new histories (clues about how the memory gap might be filled), as other alternate timeline stories do. We are well into the episode before the first familiar face, Whiskey, appears, like a ghost in the ruins of the Dollhouse. Familiar characters are mostly restricted to flashbacks—ghosts in this new world—and we do not see Echo herself until a flashback in the last act. Even the familiar characters appearing in the present of the episode are not as we know them: Whiskey is not Dr. Saunders; the downloaded Caroline is not Echo.

Time, history, and memory are played with on several levels. The diegetic flashbacks that the protagonists see of the past are memories downloaded into a wiped mind. Whereas a few, the earliest, are flashbacks for us too, because they cover events that precede the present of the first season, most are flash-forwards, contained in a frame story that itself is a flashforward. The main story is filmed on video and the flashbacks on film, affording clear aesthetic distinctions between the two time streams. A flash of light segues from one to the other; again, style visualizes time and time shifting. For the characters, the scenario operates like a conventional not-too-distant future dystopia (more extreme than the rest of the series), where the protagonists seek to recover the history that brought them to this grim present. For the audience, it shows possible consequences of events we have followed for twelve episodes. The episode title reinforces that it is history—"Epitaph"—but it is unfinished history, as implied by "Epitaph One."

"Epitaph Two: Return" does indeed follow at the end of Season 2, in another strategic use of serial television time, but the cancellation of the show perhaps affects its presentation. It offers a more conventional postapocalyptic history that now slots into the present-day narrative, signposted at the end of the penultimate episode, which leaps "10 years later" for its last few minutes. This sequel might be a satisfying narrative continuity, but it is less experimental than "Epitaph One." Sergio Angelini and Miles Booy comment that "setting a concluding episode decades in the future was pioneered by" J. Michael Straczynski's *Babylon 5* (1993–98), noting that it was soon adopted by other shows. They observe that this strategy "allows for the creation of stories set between the penultimate and final parts and thus encourages fans to fill in the narrative blanks" (2010, 25). "Epitaph One," unaired on first broadcast in the United States, was designed to function as a series finale if the show was not renewed. And indeed it is the gap between the present and the future, the blank that Season 2 fills to an extent, that entices. On the DVD commentary, the writers mention parcels of information that could be picked up—or not—in future episodes (Jed Whedon and Tancharoen 2009). The wall of photographs that the protagonists find as they leave the building functions as a link between present and future, as well as a memorial for the show if it is canceled. But in hindsight, it too plays on *possibility*: the final shot is a photograph of Caroline, not Echo.

It is a demonstration of Whedon and company's skill in knitting together television narrative and character that they can invest even empty hats like the Dolls with emotional resonance for audiences, making us *want* to fill in the blanks. *Dollhouse* eventually does develop character through experience and memory, though it continues to draw attention to both the empty hat and the rabbit used to stuff it. "If people don't care when you [kill] off a great character, then you haven't done it right," says Whedon (quoted in Havens 2003,

44). The Whedonverse series bind narrative development to character development and narrative memories to audience memory so successfully that we always *do* care. *Doctor Who* showrunner Russell T. Davies acknowledges that he used *Buffy* as a template when reimagining the series (see Chapman 2006, 185), and it is evident in the way *Doctor Who* uses memory. Along with their formal innovation in television style and structure, the Whedonverse series' emphasis on character, time, and memory ensures that they will continue to influence television in the future.

Adventures in the Moral Imagination

Memory and Identity in Whedon's Narrative Ethics

J. DOUGLAS RABB

AND J. MICHAEL RICHARDSON

Our principal purpose is to show how what we call Joss Whedon's narrative ethics uses story rather than rules or principles to justify moral judgments or ethical choices. We see the technology of implanted memory used by the Rossum Corporation in Whedon's *Dollhouse* as, among other things, a metaphor for narrative applicable throughout Whedon's creations. Each implanted personality brings with it a life story, invoking Whedon's narrative ethics. Cognitive scientist George Lakoff, graduate supervisor of Whedon-verses writer-producer Jane Espenson, argues that the human brain thinks primarily in terms of cognitive metaphors (see Rabb and Richardson 2009). Relating narrative and cognitive metaphor, Lakoff goes on to explain, "Narratives and melodramas are not mere words and images; they can enter our brains and provide models that we not merely live by, but that define who we are" (2008, 231). There is a sense, then, in which we are all like the Actives created by the Rossum Corporation, constructed through *Dollhouse* and other narratives. As Harry Lennix, the actor who played Boyd, Echo's handler, puts it, "I think we're all in a Dollhouse" (quoted in Wilcox 2010, epigraph).

The big reveal in the antepenultimate *Dollhouse* episode "Getting Closer" is, of course, that Rossum is not the proper name of the corporation's head or founder, but is "just a name, from a play, actually" (2.11). When Caroline learns this bit of information, she is also told that, "although technically you're not robots, it seemed to fit." We think it is significant that Caroline is told this information *before* she has been turned into Echo. She is not yet an Active or a Doll, much less a robot. The term *Rossum* comes from Karel Čapek's 1921 play *R.U.R.*, which first introduced the word *robot*, from the

312

Czech *robota*, denoting serfdom. *R.U.R.* stands for *Rossum's Universal Robots* (2004; see Koontz 2010). We suggest that the statement—you're not robots, but the term seemed to fit—is not meant for Caroline alone. In this narrative, all of us are being addressed as dolls, or doll-like creations constructed by a series of narratives, including Whedon's *Dollhouse*, thus raising ethical questions concerning authenticity: are we alone scripting our own lives? The various narratives we read often contain, and sometimes even support, conflicting values. Any narrative ethics must give us some way of deciding among these conflicts. We show, through a study of Whedon's various narratives, how this way of deciding is possible.

We like to contrast narrative ethics with both a principlist ethics based on rules and a utilitarian or consequentialist ethics based on the evaluation or optimization of consequences. Principlist and utilitarian ethical theories are sometimes combined in a so-called supreme principle of morality such as, "Everyone ought to follow the optimific principles, because these are the only principles that everyone could rationally will to be universal laws" (Parfit 2011, 1:411). Optimific principles are ones that "would make things go best" (1:410). By appealing to or following such principles, we are said to be making objective rational moral decisions. On the other hand, a narrative ethics relies more on imagination and emotion than on this kind of deductive or calculative reason alone. Nonetheless, narratives can guide our actions and help us decide what kind of persons we really want to be. Whedon presents what we would call narrative arguments against both moral principlism and utilitarianism, the two most prominent ethical theories. Buffy herself is certainly not governed by rules, yet she survives in her very dangerous vocation, unlike Kendra, the rule-bound (principlist) Slayer. As Zoe-Jane Playdon observes, "Kendra is trained: Kendra is killed. Buffy is educated: Buffy survives" (2002, para. 15). Playdon explains the difference between training and education by noting that "the goal of education is 'transformation,'" whereas training involves the transmission of rules, principles, commands, or "a set of behaviors" (para. 12). As we will see, stories and narratives themselves can be educational and thus transformative. Buffy does not slavishly follow rules—she does not even have the *Slayer's Handbook*—and freely breaks rules when necessary. But when in the episode "Selfless" she is confronted with an especially difficult moral choice, she laments with considerable frustration that she cannot make her decision by simply appealing to rules or principles: "There's no mystical guidebook, no all-knowing council—human rules don't apply. . . . There's only me. I am the Law" (7.5). Whedon never says that making moral decisions without rules is easy.

As we said above, he also rejects a consequentialist (utilitarian) approach based on choosing the lesser of two evils. In the *Buffy* episode "Choices," Wesley and the Scooby Gang wrestle with the problem of whether to trade Willow's freedom for an item central to the rituals surrounding the Mayor's ascension (3.19). Wesley's priority, as a Watcher, is to prevent at all costs the Mayor's ascension and the opening of the Hellmouth. He argues that they must destroy "the key to the Mayor's ascension. Thousands of lives depend on our getting rid of it. Now I want to help Willow as much as the rest of you, but we will find another way." Wesley is clearly willing to sacrifice Willow's life in order to save thousands of others. He represents the rational, utilitarian, or consequentialist approach to decision making. Buffy agrees that rational choice would require the sacrifice of the one to save the many, but it is made clear that rational choice is not her main priority. During their argument with Wesley, Giles attempts to calm them down by saying, "All right! Let's deal with this rationally," whereupon Buffy retorts, "Why are you taking his side?" Wesley thinks that they should find another way to rescue Willow; the Scooby Gang believes they should find some way to stop the Mayor and save Sunnydale that does not involve risking, much less sacrificing, Willow. This passage, we contend, is a narrative argument rejecting, through example, a utilitarian or consequentialist approach to ethics. It is not the only instance in which the Whedonverses confront the moral issue of sacrificing the one to save the many. How they deal with it depends upon the circumstances at the time, depends on the story, as we would expect in a narrative ethics. For example, Buffy kills Angel in order to save the world from being destroyed by a vortex that only Angel's blood will stop from opening. In this case, the vortex had already started opening, and there was just no other way to stop it ("Becoming, Part Two" 2.22). Similarly, Giles finds it necessary to kill the character Ben who, through no fault of his own, is the vessel that the Hellgod Glory must use to manifest herself and destroy the world. Giles is not happy about being forced into the position of choosing the lesser of two evils. In this case, Buffy had refused to do so. But what is important here is Giles's comment on his having to take a human life: "I've sworn to protect this sorry world and sometimes that means saying and doing what other people can't. What they shouldn't have to" ("The Gift" 5.22). Giles's moral judgment here, that we should not have to kill innocent people, is a rational judgment, though it is not based on principles, consequentialist or otherwise. Still, it is obvious from the story, the context, that it is a true statement, an objective judgment. A nonethical example might make this idea clearer. For example, as every Whedon scholar knows, the artistic judgment "*Firefly* should not have been cancelled so quickly" is obviously true. Giles's point here, and the point of this particular story, is that we should not have to kill innocent people; that is not how the world ought to be.

If a narrative ethics does not appeal to principles, how are moral judgments justified? We saw above that cognitive scientist George Lakoff argues that "narratives . . . provide models that we not merely live by, but that define who we are." As we will see, cognitive science has provided compelling evidence that principlism and utilitarianism are outmoded given recent discoveries about how the brain functions. Whedon's narrative ethics, which we regard as a post-Christian love ethics, is not unlike the conclusion of *R.U.R.*, in which two robots have discovered the ability to love, as illustrated by their willingness to sacrifice themselves for each other.

Whedon seems to like narratives in which the correct moral choice involves self-sacrifice. In the dramatic ending to *Dollhouse*, Topher atop a high tower chooses to sacrifice himself to save the world in the process of returning humanity to its pre-Rossum state, reminiscent of Buffy's sacrificial leap off another tower at the end of *Buffy* Season 5. An overarching theme in the Whedonverses seems to be that the best way to find yourself is through self-sacrifice. For example, at the end of *Buffy* Season 6, Xander the humble carpenter is a Christ figure offering to sacrifice himself to save the world from the wrath of dark Willow, whom he still loves. Buffy herself is constantly engaged in self-sacrifice, from giving up a normal social life, not to mention her life itself in Seasons 1 and 5, through killing Angel in Season 2, to giving up what looks to be a new reality of an eternal paradise with Angel in Season 8 at the end of "Twilight," Part Four (2010, 8.35), in the graphic narrative continuation of the *Buffy* story. In this graphic narrative, Buffy and Angel seem to have acquired such control over their own lives that they can quite literally write their own story. The place reacts to them, as is indicated by the blank backgrounds in many of the panels, bringing to mind the "clean slates" in *Dollhouse* and the "Tabula Rasa" episode of *Buffy* (6.8). As Angel says, "It's the one thing the best philosophers had right. We build it ourselves. . . . Paradise is ours to write" ("Twilight," Part Four). But this place is not the paradise Buffy chooses to write. She is more than willing to choose to sacrifice even the happiness of paradise in order to rescue her friends. Buffy is still writing her *own* narrative and thus defining her authentic identity.

We learn from such narratives to set our own goals and write our own stories. Near the end of *Dollhouse*, Caroline/Echo commits herself to the original goal of Caroline, fighting the Rossum Corporation. Caroline was first brought before its executives because she was caught trying to bomb a

Rossum facility she believed was engaged in unethical animal experimentation. She has just learned that they experiment not only on animals but also on people. She is obviously not freely choosing to enter the Dollhouse and become an Active; her freedom is not restored until she rediscovers and adopts Caroline's original goal of doing something about the unethical activities of Rossum. By then, she can draw upon all the knowledge, talents, and personalities Rossum has imprinted on her. It is a lesson of truly Shakespearean proportions: with Caroline/Echo, Rossum has, Macbeth-like, instilled "bloody instructions, which, being taught, return to plague th'inventor" (1.7.9–10). The Dolls/Actives have had their original memories, personalities, and identities neurologically wiped and others superimposed. We say "superimposed" because, as Caroline/Echo observes when Adelle offers her "a clean slate," "You ever tried to clean an *actual* slate? You always see what was on it before" ("Ghost" 1.1). No matter how hard one tries, one cannot get slates, or neural networks, perfectly clean. Traces of what used to be there remain, like the *scriptio inferior*, the "underwriting," on a palimpsest. In Season 2, all these traces that have receded into the background, the whole sequence of memories, skills, and identities, become activated, sometimes within Echo's conscious control, sometimes not. As Sherry Ginn observes in her article on the scientific plausibility of neurological tampering, "Echo clearly shows awareness of . . . implanted personalities, as well as her original primary personality" (2010, para. 8). As she *chooses* to fight Rossum (Caroline's original goal), Echo gradually acquires the power to *deliberately* utilize the memories and skills that Rossum has forced upon her. Here is a unique case of what is called interpretive memory.

The main point is that memory itself is interpretive. How we remember the past and thus how the past influences us in the present can be determined by our future goals, our projects. We not only choose our goals, but thereby also choose our memories, *how* we remember the past. This point is Sartrean. We know that, at an early age, Whedon was deeply influenced by the existential philosopher Jean-Paul Sartre (Whedon 2003b). As Sartre argues, our memories themselves are actually interpretations of what we have experienced. Changing ourselves by changing our goals in life can also change these interpretations, change the way we remember the past, and thus change the way the past influences us, our feelings, our emotions, and our behavior. The memories are not just false memories, as some psychologists argue (Ginn 2010, para. 11). Phyllis Sutton Morris explains in *Sartre's Concept of a Person*, "Sartre is not saying that we are able to change the brute facts of the remembered past; his point, rather, is that there is an element of choice in our remembering. . . . We decide what our past means by acting in the present to achieve one kind of goal as opposed to some other kind of goal" (1976, 73). As Sartre himself puts it, "The meaning of the past is strictly dependent on my present project" ([1943] 1972, 640). Even though in a narrow sense the past may determine our present, it is also the case that the future (in terms of our sometimes newly chosen goals) reaches into that past to produce the present. It is our choice of goals that really decides who we are. As Morris puts it, "What links present action to memories of past events is, at least in part, an interpretive connection which can only be understood in terms of the individual's chosen future end" (1976, 73). The interpretation of these memories turns out to be stories that we tell ourselves and as such are personal stories that can be used as a narrative ethics with all its transformative power. As narrative ethicist J. T. Banks observes, "Narrative inevitably expresses and transforms who we are at every level of our being: the organic, the symbolic, the social, and the spiritual" (2002, 219).

The line connecting *Dollhouse* to *Buffy* and *Angel*, *Firefly*, and *Serenity* is clear. Using neurotechnology or magic to manipulate memory and mind is a recurrent theme in the Whedonverses. It is, for example, apparent in the story arcs of Riley, River, Spike, and Echo, as well as Buffy herself in "Normal Again" (*Buffy* 6.17). The question that arises for a narrative ethics is how much of the individual's original personality, character, and identity remain and to what extent it can be recovered or restored if the person chooses a new goal. In the case of *Buffy*'s Initiative operative Riley Finn, who chooses to fight against the Initiative and Adam, the monster soldier they created, it would seem that recovery is fairly straightforward: he needs to get weaned off the drugs the Initiative has been surreptitiously feeding him and to rip out its implanted controlling chip. It is rather more difficult with *Firefly*'s River Tam. As we see her in *Serenity*, River is, not unlike Echo in *Dollhouse*, a composite of the original bright young girl, an Alliance fighting machine, and a repository of knowledge and skills she gradually discovers she has—all of which she chooses to use in both rejecting the Alliance and joining and protecting her adopted family. Thus, she turns the skills the Alliance forced upon her back upon the Alliance itself. As Alyson Buckman observes, River "undercuts the authorship of her being" by the male voice, "rewriting herself into action" by becoming "River the Reaver Slayer in *Serenity*" (2008, 46–48). River, like Riley, chooses her own narrative and thus chooses who she really wants to be. By constructing their own stories, they are each rejecting the oppression imposed upon them by the Initiative and the Alliance, respectively.

The Spike story arc in *Buffy* and *Angel* is practically the paradigm of interpretive memory through choosing a new goal, the quest for his soul. There is some question about whether Spike set out deliberately to have his soul restored. Stacey Abbott argues in some detail that "the dialogue in the scene when Spike requests the restoration of his true self is deliberately written so that it can be interpreted either as the removal of the chip or the return of his soul." But Abbott does not accept this ambiguity, arguing that the final episodes of Season 6 "clearly suggest that Spike went to hell and back again to have the chip removed and be once again what he was: a vampire" (2005a, 333). However, Rhonda V. Wilcox argues, "Whether the reader believes Spike chose to undergo horrendous trials from a conscious or subconscious desire for a soul, certainly it is significant that he is given the soul as a result of his own agency (as opposed to Angelus, who had his soul forced upon him)" (2005, 37). Other commentators speak of Spike's setting out "in search of a soul" (Beagle 2004, 117), leaving "Sunnydale to win himself a conscience—a soul" (Holder 2004, 156), and laboring for the "retrieval of his soul" (G. Stevenson 2003, 88). This critical response certainly makes it sound like a conscious choice, and there is no indication in these commentaries of any ambiguity concerning Spike's choice. Because the major commentators we have cited cannot agree about the motivation of Spike's quest, we suggest that it is indeed ambiguous. We argue that Spike himself resolves this ambiguity by choosing the life of a hero. In choosing *this* goal, Spike selects his narrative—the story he tells himself (and others)—and thus remembers his quest as one for a soul. In the *Angel* episode "Destiny," for example, Spike declares, "I fought for my soul. Went through the demon trials. Almost did me in a dozen times over, but I kept fighting. 'Cause I knew it was the right thing to do. It's my destiny" (5.8). Through choosing his goal, then, choosing good over evil and love over hate, Spike determines (chooses) how he remembers his quest. Spike's story is certainly an excellent example of interpretive memory; it functions as a model of behavior, thus showing how narrative ethics can be used to change lives, create authentic identities, and help with difficult choices.

Interpretive memory also plays a significant role in *Dr. Horrible's Sing-Along Blog*. As Alyson Buckman observes, in *Dr. Horrible* storytelling "is referenced in a variety of ways, including the emphasized act divisions, coming as they do at the beginning of each installment. It is also referenced through the opening set-up of the blog format, which makes manifest both the story and the gaze" (2010, para. 8). In reminiscing about his Wonderflonium robbery, Dr. Horrible offers two interpretations of the event and hence of his story. In one, he refers to his "famously successful heist last week. I say successful in that I achieved my objective." In the other interpretation, he notes that it "was less successful in that I inadvertently introduced my arch-nemesis to the girl of my dreams. . . . She called him sweet. How is he sweet? Right, freeze ray. As of tonight I am *in* the Evil League of Evil, if all goes according to plan" (Act 2). Of course, all does not go according to plan. In the end, his freeze ray fizzles and his death ray gun explodes, killing Penny with some of the shrapnel, suggesting perhaps he had chosen the wrong goal, since, as Buckman notes, it was ironically achieved at the cost of Penny's life (para. 10). On the other hand, he was required to kill someone in order to qualify for entry into the Evil League of Evil, which illustrates just how incompatible his two objectives really are: love of one who does good (helping the homeless) or joining Bad Horse and the Evil League of Evil. Whether Dr. Horrible remembers the heist as "famously successful" or "less successful" depends upon his chosen goal.

Interpretive memory, and thus transformation through story, plays a recurring role in the Whedonverses. When we reread the Buffyverse in light of *Dr. Horrible*, we can more readily perceive interpretive memory in, for example, Spike's story arc, thus adding further confirmation to Wilcox's reading of Spike's quest, as well as our own reading. Spike, of course, chooses the role of the hero, chooses self-sacrifice over self-gratification, whereas Dr. Horrible does not so much choose evil as let the opportunity for choice and transformation slip away. Horrible himself realizes it, singing the plaintive words "so you think justice has a voice and we all have a choice," while carrying Penny's lifeless body (Act 3). At this point, he is beginning to realize that his past choices have resulted in the death of the woman he loves, and that he has cut himself off from the range of choices he once had. *Dr. Horrible's Sing-Along Blog* is thus a cautionary tale, a negative mode of narrative argument, of narrative ethics. The fact that we are watching a cautionary tale is emphasized in part by the external stance the blog format allows the viewer; as Buckman notes, "The gaze is not hidden in an attempt to make what we have been watching seem real (as is the case with most Hollywood-produced cinema) and authentic; instead, the gaze is made manifest and, thus, more readily deconstructed" (para. 16).

Dollhouse is likewise a cautionary tale. For example, at the end of "Epitaph One," we see Caroline, embodied in a prepubescent girl, looking out at the apocalypse and describing the results of the misused neurotechnology as "children playing with matches" (1.13). The memory implantation in *Dollhouse* can be read as metaphor on a number of levels. We have already indicated that on one level, these memories can serve as a metaphor for narrative. On the purely technological level, they symbolize the abuse of neurotechnology and a narrow calculative sense of reason. Throughout the Whedonverses, there is a concern about the dehumanizing effects of technology and the misuse of reason. For example, James B. South's early critical response argues that "there is present in *Buffy the Vampire Slayer* a real worry about the uses of technology and the ways in which it can dehumanize humans" (2001, 98).[1] In *Dollhouse*, the importance of invoking the Czechoslovakian play *R.U.R.* becomes clear when we realize that the name "Rossum" is an allusion to the Czech word *rozum*, meaning "reason." Its use in *Dollhouse* seems to substantiate our point that *Dollhouse* is in part another Whedon narrative argument against a *purely* rational theory of ethics.

Whedon never *totally* rejects reason; what he attacks is the misuse of reason. Moral choice is not found in the narrow binary option of good over evil, much less in rationalizing the choice of the lesser of two evils. Rather, authentic moral choice, freedom, consists in the ability to prevent evil from entering the world (see J. Richardson and Rabb 2007, 7). This kind of moral choice is metaphorically represented in the Buffyverse as attempts to close the Hellmouth or to prevent it from opening. The power to do so Whedon usually associates not so much with reason, but with passion, love, and self-sacrifice as well as with choosing appropriate goals. In *Dollhouse*, Echo, Victor, and Sierra, once they adopt the goal of fighting against Rossum—which, like the Initiative in *Buffy* and the Alliance in *Firefly* and *Serenity*, represents a misuse of reason—all seem to be able to choose, integrate, order, and utilize their implanted memories and skills. As William Faulkner says in *Requiem for a Nun*, "The past is never dead. It's not even past" (1966, 92). In *Dollhouse*, it seems interpretive memory can be used to cope with the victimization involved in technologically implanted identity.

Dollhouse can also be seen as a metaphor for our own lack of freedom in contemporary society. The *Dollhouse* episodes illustrate the *illusion* of freedom left to people manipulated (scripted) by others. When the neurally wiped Dolls vacantly ask if they may leave the imprinting lab, each is told, in a patronizing voice, "If you like." In the unaired *Dollhouse* episode "Epitaph One," true freedom is regained when the characters finally choose appropriate goals, thus becoming who they truly are. Similarly, in our own lives, we achieve true freedom, as opposed to vacant choice, only when we make decisions about appropriate goals and who we really want to be. We see it throughout Whedon's work: for instance, in *Serenity*, Mal announces that he "aim[s] to

1. On technology and magic in Whedon, see Bussolini in this volume.

misbehave" and decides to confront and expose the Alliance. Likewise, Angel begins to cope with his memories as Angelus only when the good demon Whistler shows him that Buffy needs help as the Slayer and he decides he wants to "become someone" ("Becoming, Part One," *Buffy* 2.21). Angel thus helps Buffy fight evil in Sunnydale, and eventually continues fighting evil by working to help the helpless when he moves to Los Angeles. Angel's project, incidentally, echoes Penny's helping the homeless, something Dr. Horrible might have chosen to do to win the girl of his dreams. After all, Spike started to reform in order to win Buffy, not really because it was the right thing to do. People who do the right things for the wrong reasons often end up doing them for the right reasons in the long run, both in the Whedonverses and, we suggest, in our own lives as well.

These and similar examples also illustrate one positive way in which stories work as arguments in narrative ethics. It is crucial to distinguish narrative argument from the more formal logical argument associated with traditional moral theory. As David B. Morris notes in "Narrative, Ethics, and Pain: Thinking *with* Stories," "In contrast to principle alone, narrative in its detailed, emotion-rich representation of experience can help us recognize implicit values and negotiate conflicts of moral action" (2002, 213). It is important to note that the title of Morris's paper is thinking *with* stories not just thinking *about* stories. This difference is what distinguishes narrative ethics from literary criticism, even though the ethicist draws upon methodologies developed by the literary critic. As John Rodden explains, "A rhetoric of narrative does still include a substantial rational component, but its concepts are less dry or mechanical or head-centered and instead more full-bodied and even impassioned. They are rational but also emotive and ethical" (2008, 151). In his defense of narrative in ethics, philosopher of cognitive science Mark Johnson argues, "There are many things wrong with our received view of moral reasoning as consisting primarily in discerning the appropriate universal moral principle that tells us the single 'right thing to do' in a given situation" (1993, 1). Johnson critiques what he calls the "Enlightenment folk theory of Faculty Psychology" that we have inherited from seventeenth- and eighteenth-century science and philosophy. The plausibility of any ethics based on principles presupposes this folk theory of faculty psychology, which assumes that "our mental acts can be broken down into separate and distinct forms of judgment" (207). According to the "Enlightenment folk theory of Faculty Psychology" and the correlative "Moral Law Folk Theory," in moral judgment the faculty of reason is used to rule our emotions, feelings, and desires, to keep such passions in line. Although (as cognitive science has shown) the theory operates for the most part unconsciously, Johnson observes, "this folk theory of Faculty Psychology is shared by virtually everyone in Western culture" (15). Johnson's work puts beyond dispute that "folk theories that are based on Enlightenment Faculty Psychology, its distinction among types of judgment, and its correlative distinction among realms of experience . . . are, for the most part, shown to be wrong by cognitive science" (208). We think that it is ironic that the supreme principle of morality that we cited at the beginning of this paper was first presented and defended in the 2002 Tanner Lectures presented at the University of California, Berkeley, the home of Lakoff's Institute for Cognitive Studies. Yet there is no mention of Lakoff or Johnson or cognitive science in these Tanner Lectures or in the two-volume 1,365-page tome that followed from them and purports to give the most complete rational foundation for objective moral judgments since Kant (Parfit 2011). In striking contrast to the received time-honored view that "man is a *rational* animal," Johnson, following Lakoff, begins his own study with the provocative claim: "My central thesis is that human beings are fundamentally *imaginative* moral animals" (1993, 1). That belief is the reason he claims that narrative and imagination are more important in moral decision making than appeals to calculative reason and rational moral principles. As Lakoff and Johnson have shown based on the findings of cognitive science, "Moral Law theories must be rejected" (189).

Some may be suspicious of narrative as ethical argument because they cannot see how to decide, how to choose between competing narratives. We conclude this discussion by showing how it is possible. The Whedonverses themselves contain a number of narratives that critically examine moral perspectives diametrically opposed to what we have called Whedon's post-Christian love ethics, an ethics embodied in stories in which compassion, cooperation, community, and self-sacrifice seem to save the day. We have called this a post-Christian love ethics simply to acknowledge Whedon's atheism. We are happy to follow others in calling it a feminist Christian love ethics (Playdon 2002). The opposite of this kind of communitarian love ethics would be a radical individualism governed by what some might call the virtue of selfishness. We see this ethics portrayed in the Whedonverses in Jayne's story arc in *Firefly/Serenity* and in the story of the unreformed Faith in *Buffy* and *Angel*. Here we will concentrate on the Jayne narrative, as we have discussed the fate of Faith in some detail elsewhere (J. Richardson and Rabb 2007, 26–62).

Jayne is certainly a radical individualist living by what some might call rational egoism, wanting whatever would be best, but best for himself. He is not unlike the "heroes" of Ayn Rand's two massive novels *The Fountainhead* and *Atlas Shrugged*. One of Rand's characters actually argues at some length that "the world is perishing from an orgy of self-sacrifice" ([1943] 1993, 684). Jayne certainly can make no sense of the notion of self-sacrifice.

In the *Firefly* episode "Jaynestown," Jayne's former partner in crime, Stitch, accuses Jayne of leaving him behind to be captured. Jayne replies, "You'd'a done the same" (1.7). To this comment, Stitch offers the following indignant rebuke: "Not ever! You protect the man you're with. You watch his back! Everybody knows that—'cept the 'hero of Canton.'" We can see the beginning of moral development in Jayne when a local throws himself in front of Jayne to shield him from Stitch's shotgun blast. The local is killed. Jayne finds this kind of self-sacrifice totally inexplicable, saying over and over, "Don't make no sense." Yet he also wonders, "Don't know why that eats at me so." He seems not yet to understand why rational self-interest ought not to be a guide to action. By the time he has sold River and her brother Simon to the Alliance, and is about to be ejected into the vacuum of space by a furious Mal, Jayne is beginning to recognize the folly of rational self-interest. At least he pleads with Mal not to tell River and Simon, who have by this time been rescued, what he has done. He is beginning to realize that what others think of him matters. This glimmer of a change of heart is enough to allow Mal to spare Jayne's life. Jayne is not portrayed as all bad.

Jayne can be seen as a parody of the ideal man as conceived by Rand. *The Fountainhead* and *Atlas Shrugged* are really narratives extolling Jayne-like selfishness. We can even make Jayne sound somewhat more respectable. After all, he was the hero of Canton and had a statue erected in his honor. Simon and River Tam were criminal fugitives in the eyes of the legitimate government, hence the price on their head. From Rand's perspective, Jayne cannot really be faulted for accepting this legitimate bounty. He is support-ing a government that has all the virtues of which Rand would approve. It is an alliance, or combination, of American laissez-faire capitalism and Chinese productive and bureaucratic efficiency. So, from the perspective of narrative ethics, how do we decide between the communitarianism of Whedon's narra-tives and the ethical egoism of an Ayn Rand or a Jayne Cobb?

Whedon's television narratives, true to his communitarian approach, are in fact written by a number of people. As Rhonda Wilcox notes, "One of the great themes of the show—the importance of community, trust, friendship—is found not only in the episodes but also their creation" (Wilcox 2005, 6). And she quotes Whedon as saying, "I have people with whom I trust my artistic *life*" (7). On the other hand, the lone author Ayn Rand takes a much more narrow principlist approach to writing. She even admits that "without an understanding and statement of the right philosophical principle, I cannot create the right story" (quoted in Peikoff 1996, 6). Her right philosophical principle is of course nothing but rational self-interest, ethical egoism (Rand [1968] 1993, vii). We should point out that mainstream moral philosophers like Derek Parfit, whom we cited above, maintain that "Rational Egoism is best regarded, not as a moral view, but as an external rival to morality" (2011, 1:166). This notion still leaves us with a question: "Why be moral?" But this question is best answered by narrative argument using your moral imaginations to decide just what kind of monster, if any, you are willing to become.

Ultimately, choosing among narratives is up to the reader. But this choice has important consequences. Narratives shape character. Stories wire brains, influencing memory and identity. The kind of narrative we accept will affect the kind of persons we become and the sorts of goals we are likely to choose and how we achieve them. As Tony Adams reminds us, "If stories remain riddled with ideas about how to live well . . . we must critically evaluate these stories. . . . But we must not approach stories with a prescription or typology for analysis. . . . Every situation is different and a preformed set of principles runs the risk of doing violence to a story and its author" (2008, 179). Whedon's portrayal of interpretive memory as story that can determine identity is a warning that his own narratives may be transformative and that ultimately his audience is responsible for interpreting his text and how it influences them. Essentially, Joss Whedon is an ethical atheist embedding his moral position within narratives. Because, as we have shown, these narratives are also arguments supporting self-sacrifice and a (post-)Christian communitarian love ethic, we conclude that, existentially, Joss Whedon is also an atheistic ethicist.

Technology and Magic

Joss Whedon's Explorations of the Mind

JEFFREY BUSSOLINI

Joss Whedon demonstrates an abiding fascination with the processes of the mind and their modification. Scientific (or magical) alteration of perception, knowledge, and mental state is foundational to the stories of *Firefly* and *Dollhouse* and is a fundamental component of several major plot arcs in *Buffy the Vampire Slayer*. At issue is not only a plot device or story model but also an ongoing imaginative reflection about qualities of mind and a deep artistic-ethical critique of the instrumentalization of subjects through unchecked use of technological manipulations. Writing of such problematic instrumentality in terms of the critical analysis of mind/body dualism that also animates the analysis here, science studies scholar Donna Haraway notes, "Self-sure . . . hierarchy . . . takes heart from the primary dualism that parses body one way and mind the other. That dualism should have withered long ago in the light of feminist and many other criticisms, but the fantastic mind/body binary has proved remarkably resilient" (2008, 71).[1]

Whedon uses technology and magic to pose significant ethical and epistemological questions about memory and manipulation, and in many respects, magic and technology function similarly for him. While Whedon has a sustained critical analysis of technology, we might also think of Arthur C. Clarke's famous Third Law: "Any sufficiently advanced technology is indistinguishable from magic" (1973, 21). Whedon's renderings remind us of the Greek root τέχνη (*technē*) that refers equally to "art, skill, method of making,"

---

1. Donna Haraway is perhaps a particularly appropriate theoretical guide for considering *Buffy the Vampire Slayer*: she called three cats who lived on her property Willow, Giles, and Spike (2008, 276–77).

to "craft, cunning, sleight, wiles, devices," and to "a way, manner, means whereby a thing is gained" (Liddell, Scott, and Jones [1940] 1996, 1785). In their definitions (as in Whedon's texts), modern technology, magic, and art significantly overlap, and each aspect of the etymology is important. It is precisely as an artistic meditation on technology and on other "means whereby a thing is gained" that Whedon's stories are so effective.[2]

The analysis in this essay hews especially closely to instances presented in Whedon's texts to evaluate some prominent considerations about mind and mental processes. Like Haraway, Whedon touches on persistent philosophical questions about thought, engages with science fiction and fantasy accounts of mental tweaking, and reflects critically on contemporary real-world situations that confront humanity (and related species). He repeatedly refers to the character of Gigolo Joe from Steven Spielberg's film *AI* (2001) as a touchstone for these questions. Joe is an android who has been programmed to mimic love and act as a male prostitute. Whedon wonders where the mimicry leaves off, where the "real" love begins, and how much it can be requited. The number and intensity of the questions presented along these lines in the Whedonverses make it impossible decisively to answer them in the scope of this essay, and indeed Martin Heidegger has pointed out that the identification and posing of questions are often more important than conclusively answering them (Heidegger 1977, 1984). However, the main aspects of Whedon's "theory of mind" are an immanent rather than split-level ontology of mind, an astute awareness of the unknowable consequences of tampering with mind, a strong interest in socialization, and a deep-seated ethical rejection of coercive measures.

Whedon's interest in socialization is shown in a Paley Media Center event about *Dollhouse*. He is posed a particularly apropos question regarding human experimentation on Adam in *Buffy*, River and the Reavers in *Firefly*, and the Dolls in *Dollhouse* (*"Dollhouse": Cast and Creators* 2010). Whedon says that he is "very obsessed with the robot mythos as a modern-day Frankenstein thing, which all goes back to what are we, who made us, why are we the way we are? And human experimentation, for me, is a lot about socialization, is a lot about what does society tell us we have to become and what is actually innate within us?"

---

2. The significant identity between art and technology in *technē* is Martin Heidegger's point of conceptual departure in "The Question Concerning Technology" (1977; etymology especially, 12–14).

Whedon is fascinated by socialization and social interaction—as anyone who has partaken in the "American high school" genre of film and television must be. In an interesting slip, Whedon describes Gigolo Joe as "this Doll (oops! Doll, person, robot) out there searching for love, but it's really about whether or not we can love them, and how we imprint on people, and what we need from people. I don't trust people and I don't like them" (*"Buffy the Vampire Slayer" Reunion* 2009). Several elements bear noting: individual self versus socialization, abiding fascination with science fiction as device for studying the human condition, lack of importance attached to ontological state (Doll, person, robot) next to deeper elements of personality and lived experience, the role of love in our social and individual selves, and misanthropy. Jane Espenson has noted that "Joss is never about the stuff, but about the stuff behind the stuff" (2004b, 1). By closely considering Whedon's texts, my analysis similarly seeks to situate this technico-psychological theme in these texts by drawing upon questions in literature and philosophy that serve to inform this theme.[3]

Several narratives in the Whedonverses are critical of the explicitly mechanist conception in which mind is entirely explainable and controllable through the physical matter of the brain. Whedon casts the science fiction dream of transferring or modifying consciousness as scientifically flawed and ethically abhorrent. His scenarios ask why such mechanistic modification would be pursued (or whose interests would be served) and what it would mean for the existence of those subjects altered. Though not a technophobe, Whedon nonetheless inquires about how science and technology are applied within problematic social and political structures.

Whedon's contention is not that technological interventions do not work, but rather that they work differently than intended according to hasty and haughty forms of knowledge that seek neatly to explain the world while disregarding the entropic effects of ignorance, uncertainty, and finitude. Whedon seems especially interested in side effects, unintended consequences, and persistence of personality despite extraordinary modification. Deeply fascinated by fundamental questions about mind, including how perception and memory operate, he presents disturbing scenarios in which the world threatens to be very different from the way that we ordinarily perceive or think of it.

3. The primary philosophical frame of reference is the conflict between the mechanistic dualism of Descartes and the immanent expressionism of Spinoza (also considered in different ways by Donna Haraway and Martin Heidegger); the major literary referent is Mary Shelley's *Frankenstein*.

Whedon's figurings of mind include several aspects. First, he returns repeatedly to the notion of the blank slate, the tabula rasa, but does not believe that it exists (which is consonant with his rejection of the mind/body binary): some form of one's nature reasserts itself, a phenomenon that repeatedly occurs in the Whedonverses. Second, he is intrigued by some of the problems that captivated René Descartes: the Evil Genius problem (we cannot be sure that the world is real, and we may be only a brain kept in a vat and fed sensations by an Evil Genius) and radical doubt (a first step in Descartes's overcoming of the vat problem, beginning by doubting everything that we hold to be evident or sure, leading to his famous dictum of *cogito ergo sum*), for instance ([1641] 1960, 80–82).[4] However, Whedon appears skeptical of Cartesian mechanism, rejecting simple causal explanations and technological interventions based on it. The notion that the mind can be purely and simply transferred from one body to another corresponds to Descartes's notion that it is a separate entity controlling the actions of the body. Whedon holds to a more complicated, or immanent, Spinozist account in which mind and body are but different expressions of the same "nature" underneath,[5] which explains why there is no "blank slate," and elements of former identity reemerge despite technical manipulation—as viewers see starkly illustrated in *Dollhouse*'s less-than-perfect mind transfer and the persistence of underlying identity in *Buffy* episodes such as "Tabula Rasa" (6.8).

Manipulations of the Mind in *Buffy*

Buffy has several story arcs that bear upon the modification of mind through technological or magical means. Season 4 in particular, with the introduction of the Initiative as a government project attempting to weaponize

4. Descartes rejected explanations of the mind and spirit in mechanistic terms and, to defend free will, held mind to be a different type of substance from physical matter. Nonetheless, Descartes's physical mechanism has overgrown this distinction and been applied to explaining the mind. The first, second, and sixth Meditations especially concern us here. I have slightly emended the translation based on the Latin *genium aliquem malignum* ("Evil Genius" versus "Evil Spirit").

5. As opposed to the dualist (actually tripartite) division of being that is set out by Descartes, Spinoza proposes a univocity of being in which all substance, including body, mind, and god, exists as part of the same single entity that he calls nature. Rather than seeing the mind as the motor force for will and the body, Spinoza is interested in the capacity and ingenuity of the body, claiming that "we do not yet know what a body can do." *The Ethics*, pts. 1–2, bear especially upon the body and the mind.

demons, deals with the use of technology to modify mind and behavior in demons, humans, and cyborgs. As such, the season most directly comments on high-technology Big Science and the military-industrial complex, and it contains instances of Whedon's emphases on immanent mind, unanticipated consequences, and the profoundly unethical status of coercive manipulation. Several *Buffy* episodes, especially "Normal Again" (6.17) and "Tabula Rasa," also take up magic-induced manipulations of mind and combine a problematization of self-evident perceptions of the world with the persistence of identity despite magic used to suppress it.

"Chips All Around," Part 1: Adam and Riley, Children of the Initiative

As the plot with the Initiative expands and the "Big Bad" of Season 4 is revealed to be Adam, we see that the intent of the secret organization is well beyond the simple "neutering" of demons for public safety (Maio 2004, 121; Wilcox 2005, 164). Rhonda Wilcox calls the Initiative a "demon-fighting experimental, governmental, scientific-military unit" and "government-run military-industrial-complex which represents, of course, the military-industrial complex" (2005, 53, 64). Cynthea Masson (2010a) analyzes the troubling fascist elements deeply embedded in the Initiative. Barbara Maio refers to it as "a paramilitary group conducting experiments on creatures they capture using modern technology and advanced arms" (2004, 117). Adam is the ultimate instantiation, "a Frankensteinian combination of human, demon, and machine bits": pieces (such as stabbing spikes) of several different types of demons together with human parts and technical systems including computers and a plutonium power source assembled for their tactical advantages (Wilcox 2005, 48).

Difficulty is caused for the Initiative when Adam becomes fully self-aware and begins trying to make sense of who he is. This arc echoes Whedon's invocation of Frankenstein and Gigolo Joe. Although Adam is not the same type of sympathetic character, we can "sympathize" with him in that he has been purpose-built and programmed with certain (violent, rational) ends in mind. As he becomes independent, he seeks to understand the goals for which he has been built. Made as a killer, from parts of other killers, he sees a young boy in the forest (a parallel to the scene in Mary Shelley's novel) and kills him, but not before seeking a dialogue with him ("Goodbye Iowa" 4.14).

Adam is genuinely curious, hoping that his interlocutor can help him understand his existential questions. Actor George Hertzberg does a particularly effective job of rendering both his naïveté and his malevolence. Adam is not necessarily evil, though his pairing of infant perplexity with murderous instincts and cold technical knowledge is deeply disconcerting. Maio notes that "Adam is a monster without emotions, and with extreme strength linked to a keen mind" (2004, 122). He is almost Socratic in his pursuit of knowledge and seems to be puzzled by the most basic (also the most abstract) issues of life and existence. Wilcox refers to the Initiative as "that bastion of scientific rationality" (2005, 32). Built as a soldier and as a scientific experiment, Adam, metonymically the Initiative, sees the world in those terms. Verbal questioning (Socratic dialogue) and vivisection (advocated by Descartes) are part and parcel of the same process for him, and indeed the boy's frank answer ("You're a monster") to his question seems to make perfectly reasonable his subsequent killing of the boy.

Though Adam's murder of the boy may be read as fulfillment of his demon personality, it equally represents a process of exploration through which he seeks to understand the world and his place in it. In a disconcerting expository monologue in "Goodbye Iowa," Adam ruminates about his identity: "I've been thinking about the world. I wanted to see it, learn it. I saw the inside of that boy and it was beautiful, but it didn't tell me about the world. It just made me feel. So now I want to learn about me. Why I feel. What I am. So I came home. I'm a kinematically redundant, biomechanical demonoid designed by Maggie Walsh. She called me Adam and I called her mother." Adam here speaks as a child, identifying home and mother as sources of answers to his most fundamental questions. Adam is frightening not necessarily because of his malevolence—in some ways he is not malevolent at all, merely curious—but because he is a being of such power and possible destruction who is without ethical awareness. Guided by a sterile scientific empiricism and demonic indifference toward life, killing for him is an aesthetic act or a source of information, albeit unsatisfying and inconclusive information. While the Initiative-planted chip prevents the vampire Spike from harming or killing humans, Spike's ethical orientation is intact. Adam is perfectly able to harm or kill humans or other creatures without restraint, but his ethical orientation has been strangely vitiated (likely the "design flaw" he speculates he has—he seems indifferent about killing, unlike the gleefully violent evil Spike and Angelus).

Seeking to discover more about himself, Adam places a diskette into a drive embedded in his chest. Riley challenges him, objecting to Adam's claim that Walsh is his mother. Adam produces another diskette labeled "Finn" and places it into his drive, exclaiming, "Oh! Mother made you too." As Riley angrily denies it, saying that he has a real mother, Adam continues, "A birth mother. Yes. But after you met Maggie, she was the one who shaped your basic operating system. She taught you how to think, how to feel. She fed you chemicals to make you stronger—your mind and body. She said that you and I were her favorite children. Her art. That makes us brothers. Family." In an unlikely place, here is one of the chosen families of the Buffyverse—at least by Adam's reckoning.

The soldiers are similarly confounded as they try to make sense of their "programming" while withdrawing from the powerful chemicals that Walsh administered to them (one of the several prominent drug addiction and withdrawal themes to be found in the Buffyverse). As all that he has known and trusted slips away (hence the episode title, "Goodbye Iowa"), Riley becomes confused and belligerent, as unsure as Adam of his place in the world. Adam is not denouncing or being aggressive with Riley in their interactions, but sympathizing with him by trying to help Riley understand more about his existence and, in the process, better understand his own.

Riley draws his gun and attempts to shoot Adam, who easily disarms him, stabs him, and defeats everyone in the room, including Buffy, killing Dr. Angelman in the process. Adam shows no anger or lasting hostility, but gratitude, saying, "Thank you. This has been very interesting," before he flees the Initiative. Adam's uncanny mixture of seeming goodwill, dialogue, and violence is the manifestation of the several different parts of his cobbled-together self. He is simultaneously a scientific subject who attempts to understand the world through rational means and a demon to whom murder comes naturally. Perhaps most important, he is, like Gigolo Joe in Whedon's explanation, the Dolls of *Dollhouse* or River from *Firefly*, a technologically modified cyborg subject who is trying to understand his existence and self.

Striving to comprehend his role, Adam looks to Riley and the other soldiers as his colleagues and siblings, a choice the soldiers abhor. They are all agents of the Initiative who have been at the center of its research process, the guinea pigs of an experiment gone awry. The reductio ad absurdum of this strange kinship network is Adam's attempt to realize his own interpretation of his "mother" Dr. Walsh's vision in "Primeval" (4.21). Walsh herself, Dr. Angelman, and Forrest are forged into biomechanical humanoids, and Adam activates Riley's chip to constrain and control him.

Riley's excision of his own chip in "Primeval" is instructive. To begin with, his chip has been placed not in his brain, contemporary seat of "mind," but in his chest, near his heart and intercostal thoracic nerves. This placement accords much more closely with Greek and other ancient reckonings of the spirit or θυμός (*thumos*) in the torso as the seat of thought and feeling (which is now approximated again in recent research on the importance of emotional, heart, or distributed intelligence).[6] Adam activates Riley's chip to control him and inform Riley about his plan without Riley's responding or resisting. Despite this element of technical control, Riley ultimately fights against his "programming" to take up a piece of broken glass and cut out his chip, demonstrating both that the control exercised by the chip is imperfect and that Riley's underlying identity is more important and persistent than his technological programming.

"Chips All Around," Part 2: Spike's Chip

Our first exposure to the inside of the Initiative—a "demon's-eye view," if you will—comes via Spike's capture by the organization ("The Initiative" 4.7). The narrative choice of letting the viewer experience the story through Spike's point of view makes following his unfolding experience, and the mental and ethical questions that arise, germane. Like Adam and Riley, Spike has been subject to technical manipulation of his mind. He easily escapes from the Initiative, but soon learns that he can no longer attack humans without the chip causing him intense neurological pain.[7] His attempt to bite Willow in her dorm room is thwarted by it, which raises pertinent questions for a consideration of mind and the chip. Not all of these issues can be decisively dealt with here, if at all, but they are indicative of vexing problems that are opened up by the narrative. Can it be said to be ethical for Spike to avoid biting or killing only because he is restrained by the chip? Concerning vampire vital organs: if vampires do not use their hearts (we know they do not beat) or their lungs (Angel cannot resuscitate Buffy in "Prophecy Girl" [1.12], although vampires can smoke cigarettes), what precisely is the continuing motor force of the brain in their existence? Is it merely the physical pain that acts as the deterrent? Despite these lingering questions, Spike's arc reveals that one of the major research goals of the Initiative is to use technology as a means to render demons "safe" to humans.

Over this and subsequent seasons, there is a good deal of ethical and existential debate within the Buffyverse about the significance of the chip. Spike

---

6. In Combo-Buffy's battle with Adam in "Primeval" (during which Buffy combines with Willow, Xander, and Giles), it is her (their) pulling out of Adam's heart reactor that ultimately defeats an enemy who had earlier seemed unstoppable.

7. How he is able to escape the Initiative without the pain of the chip is an open question, as he is clearly attacking several men; perhaps they are demons.

proclaims that he is still evil and that he would help in indirect ways to bring harm to the Slayer or humans. Although he initially refrains from violence against humans and helps the Scoobies only because of the chip and mercenary enticement (being paid), Spike's motivations become more complex. When he discovers that he can attack demons without the pain of the chip, he takes part in the combat and violence that he relishes, although this choice places him on ambiguous moral ground vis-à-vis other demons, who beat him for turning on his own kind. The chip is at best a partial modification of Spike's behavior—a blunt instrument, as it were—that causes as many ethical conundrums as it resolves.

With the chip, Spike charts a convoluted and zigzagging path between self-interested subject of behaviorist conditioning and closely trusted ally of the Scoobies—in certain situations, such as protecting Dawn, Spike is the only one accepted by Buffy, an indication that it is more than just the restraint of the chip that motivates her. Spike transitions from selfish to somewhat selfless as he realizes the faith that has been placed in him and thanks Buffy by saying, "I know that I'm a monster, but you treat me like a man, and that's . . ." ("The Gift" 5.22). Spike does not finish his sentence, yet the implication is clear. He says that he will protect Dawn "until the end of the world, even if that happens to be tonight." Neither Buffy's trust nor Spike's loyalty is accounted for by the chip and suggests development in his thinking and social relationships.

Notwithstanding his moral development, Spike is subject to severe regressions in conduct. The discovery that Spike can strike Buffy without the conditioning response of the chip after she is brought back from the dead in Season 6 is unsettling to both of them: not least because it strongly implies that Buffy "came back wrong"—perhaps even soulless herself.[8] The discovery also sets the stage for a frequently sadomasochistic sexual relationship that is troubling to many viewers. Although the end of Season 5 sees Buffy place an unprecedented level of trust in Spike and Spike claims to love her in Season 6, the relationship is selfish and debased from both sides. Buffy's friends are shocked to find out (though Giles takes the news with humor), and the originally consensual sadomasochistic relationship turns ugly and coercive when Spike attempts to rape Buffy in the bathroom of her house. At this point, the particular failings of the chip are in evidence. Spike cannot directly attack (ensouled) humans without suffering the pain the chip triggers, but he can still attack

8. For further considerations on a number of issues in this section, and indeed in the chapter overall, see McLaren 2005. See also Erickson, this volume.

them via indirect means, as the chip itself provides no blanket action against violence or evil intent. In line with Whedon's immanent account of mind, the technological attempts to modify Spike's behavior do not alter his underlying character, which continues to manifest. As a result, Spike decides that he must seek a more profound transformation of his mind and ethos (although the fact that he does so reveals, ironically, that he seems to have a moral motivation to do so). In addition, the fact that he requires a soul to "truly" change indicates the importance of the spirit or soul to underlying identity in the Buffyverse— as we see starkly illustrated in the character of Angel/Angelus. This tension is precisely the one explored by Scott McLaren (2005) in his article on the ontology of the soul in the Buffyverse.

"Normal Again" and "Tabula Rasa"

One of the most philosophically significant *Buffy* episodes is surely "Normal Again," and a close reading of it discloses significant aspects of Joss Whedon's theory of mind. Buffy, affected by the sting of a demon, hallucinates that she is in a mental institution, schizophrenic, being treated for severe delusions about a life as the Slayer. In moments of lucidity, she sees and converses with her parents (still together, her mother living) and the doctor, who urge her not to return to imaginary friends Xander and Willow and sister Dawn. Although the situation promises to be resolved with the administration of an antidote derived from the stinger of the same demon, with Buffy returning to normal consciousness among friends, there is a lingering doubt that the entire world of Sunnydale is a fantasy in the mind of an institutionalized young woman. Malaise is heightened in that we never see Buffy ingest the antidote, discarding the first batch and asking Willow for more shortly before the final scenes. Compare this complex uncertainty to the notorious snow-globe shot from the final episode of *St. Elsewhere* (1982–88), "Last One" (1988), which implies that the hospital and the entire series have been the imaginings of an autistic child gazing into the globe.

"Normal Again" disturbs us because it so artfully casts the "normal" world of Sunnydale as fantastic aberration. Indeed, the doctor's description of the delusion to Buffy—a Hellmouth where demonic activity is rife and the world is frequently threatened with destruction—makes Sunnydale sound like a six-year hallucination. Buffy is diagnosed by the doctor as egocentric for seeing herself as the center of overblown conflicts involving monsters. Writer Diego Gutierrez (2004) observes in the DVD commentary that the episode can be unsettling to viewers, and even to writers and crew, as Buffy is pathologized for doing precisely what they all do: "buy into this reality."

The message about mind is Janus-faced: that we must affirm our existence and experience and that they could be radically different than we perceive and narrate them. As Gutierrez points out, the episode not only shows different Sunnydales but also cuts uncomfortably across the Buffyverse and the "real world" of the viewers. At one of the points of greatest emotional intensity, Buffy decides that she must kill her imaginary friends in Sunnydale to be sane. She subdues Willow, Xander, and Dawn and sets the demon free against them, nearly allowing it to kill them.

As in the *St. Elsewhere* finale, the episode closes with a discomfiting image. The Buffy of the mental institution becomes fully nonresponsive, and the doctor says that he thinks they have lost her. He and Buffy's parents remain standing over her as she sits crumpled against the corner of her asylum room, right hand limply attached to the loose neck of her gown, staring into space (the "thousand yard stare" Dawn references earlier). Franco La Polla points out that "logically this last scene did not have to be shown, as Buffy's choice would have once and for all canceled out the illusion of the clinic. Whedon leaves us, precisely, with the suspicion that there is a grain of truth in this parallel world" (2007, 85). Given what we know of alternate universes from *Buffy*, it would seem that the price of Buffy's return to her reality in Sunnydale is the permanent catatonia of the Buffy in the institution. Although she makes a leap of faith that her existence in Sunnydale must be the "real" one, there is a troubling doubt that Buffy's life as perceived and remembered may be an elaborate deception.

Though more comedic than "Normal Again," the episode "Tabula Rasa" contains important reflections about mind as acted upon by magic. When Willow's memory spell goes awry and has a much wider effect than intended, the Scoobies have no recollection of their names or positions in the social group. As a result, Spike thinks that his name is Randy and he is Giles's son (both realize that they have English accents), Anya and Giles think that they are a soon-to-be-married couple, and Buffy chooses to be called "Joan." The assumed relations among the group provide grounds for a good deal of comical banter, such as assumed father-son tensions between Giles and Spike. However, the persistence of underlying identity is also strongly borne out, as "Joan" still recalls how to fight vampires and Willow realizes, "I think I'm kinda gay." The title of "Tabula Rasa" is hardly coincidental. Although ostensibly the episode is presented as the wiping clean of the slates of the respective characters' minds, the underlying message is in line with the leitmotif of the persistence and emergence of identity and self despite this supposed erasure.

Mental Manipulation in *Firefly*

Whereas *Buffy* contains prominent story arcs that concern modifications of mind, *Firefly* and *Serenity* are predicated upon extreme technologies of mental manipulation. A wince-inducing shot from early in *Serenity* shows River Tam's teacher jabbing a stylus directly into her forehead. The school falls away and is replaced by a laboratory where Alliance scientists are experimenting on her, the stylus replaced by a giant needle. While Captain Malcolm Reynolds is a main character, River is arguably the protagonist of *Firefly*, as her story constitutes the central mystery and cuts closer to the vital heart of the "'verse." Lorna Jowett expresses River's centrality in writing that "objectification of humans by the Alliance is demonstrated through River" (2008, 103).[9]

Like Adam, River has been subjected to intensive experimentation in order to create a superwarrior. After the crew discovers River on board *Serenity*, her brother, Simon, offers an explanation to a skeptical Mal and crew about who, or what, she is. He recounts that River was recruited at age fourteen by a government-sponsored academy that subjected her to experiments and modifications, as Simon learned in a coded letter he received from her months later, saying, "They're hurting us. Get me out" ("Serenity" 1.1). As the series progresses, River, Simon, and the crew learn more about River's personality and what was done to her. The film retells or reimagines some of this ground and significantly adds to River's backstory in disclosing the origin of the Reavers and her role as a weapon against them. As a result of the cruel experiments, her cyborg nature (technologically augmented like Adam or the Initiative soldiers, River's physical and mental capacities have been significantly extended), and her self-consciousness of being a weapon, River oscillates between extreme incapacitation that makes her reliant on others and extraordinary skill in reasoning and combat that enables her to single-handedly save the *Serenity* crew/family. Like Adam, Spike, or Riley, she is often unsure of her place or proper role.

The classic original formulation of the cyborg or cybernetic organism comes from speculations in the 1960s about the technological necessities of

---

9. Although Jowett convincingly argues that River is not a cyborg, I hold that she is for reasons explicated in this section.

space travel. More pertinent for us here is Donna Haraway's essay "A Cyborg Manifesto" in her *Simians, Cyborgs, and Women* (1991). Haraway's considerations are particularly apropos regarding River because, although she may not have visible technical components like Adam, she has clearly been technically modified. Dominique Lestel, drawing on Hannah Arendt, argues that the most relevant cyborgs of the future are not necessarily explicit machine-human hybrids like Frankenstein's monster, but humans who have been modified by means, for example, of genetic engineering and neurological intervention (2007, 214). Haraway places particular emphasis on communication technologies as modifications of our bodies and on the role of cyborgs in communication networks: in *Serenity*, River is the only one who is able to receive the message contained in the "Fruity Oaty Bar" advertisement scene in the Maidenhead Bar. An important resonance with Haraway (1997) is the critique of essence, purity, and originality, which is one of her main arguments in *Modest_Witness@Second_Millenium*. In that book, Haraway is troubled by blanket critiques of genetic engineering that rely on a bedrock notion of purity or naturalness. She sees those discourses as uncomfortably close to racist claims of purity and discreteness. The key to River's successful healthy transformation lies not in the removal of her technological modifications (which Simon seems first to envision), and thus the return to her natural state, but in inhabiting her modified cyborg nature.

Reavers

Though the Reavers are frequently mentioned or discussed in *Firefly* and figure centrally in the story line of the episode "Bushwacked" (1.3), they remain largely mysterious until the film *Serenity*. On the planet Miranda, the crew learns in a scientist's chilling final message that it was the Alliance itself that created the Reavers. Experiments to regulate mood with a chemical called G-Paxilon Hydrochlorate inadvertently produced the opposite effect in a small number of cases. None of us who has seen the film can easily forget this scene. There is a striking similarity between the fictional name "Pax" and the actually existing drug Paxil, which was also designed to promote calmness but results in extremely violent responses in some fraction of those individuals who take it (Bussolini 2008). A technological attempt at a quick fix—in this case, a docile and nonaggressive population (perhaps a dangerous goal to begin with)—backfires with unintended consequences that dwarf the scale of the original problem. Whedon is clearly fascinated by technology and existence, but he highlights the intractability of human limitation, error, and violence even and especially in light of utopian projections. The attempt to control the "group mind" through the Pax produces extreme violence, while the attempt to create River as a weapon against the Reavers produces a cyborg who comes to claim and inhabit her own nature along lines much different from what the Alliance had anticipated.

Mind in *Dollhouse*

Like *Firefly*, *Dollhouse* is centrally predicated upon technologies to modify the mind and offers a parallel message about technological hubris. The Dollhouses are enabled by neuroscientific research that has rendered possible the recording, downloading, wiping, and transplanting of individual consciousnesses (Ginn 2010; Connelly and Rees 2010). Topher Brink, the self-proclaimed genius who is responsible for the technological aspects of the Los Angeles Dollhouse, claims that this process is flawless, the wipes are "clean," and the personalities can be easily swapped among different bodies with no complications. In the Whedonverses, however, such a process could never be easy or flawless owing to unintended consequences and the persistence of mind (Calvert 2010, para. 7–9).[10] The once and future killer Alpha shows clearly that the process is neither fully understood nor flawless.

In the first scene of the series (as aired), in the episode "Ghost" (1.1), Adelle DeWitt and Caroline have a discussion that bears upon the theme of the tabula rasa, and Caroline gives voice to what could be Whedon's own views on the matter (Wilcox 2010, para. 5). Adelle speaks of the contract with the Dolls and says that the Dollhouse can offer "a clean slate" in return for their periods of service. Caroline responds by asking her, "You ever try to clean an actual slate? You can always see what was on it before." As much as technology can be used to wipe or modify the minds of characters (here the Dolls), there is something of underlying personality or "nature" that strives to reassert itself. The technophiles of the Dollhouse hold to the Cartesian mechanist notion that the mind is a separate substance that controls the body and can be swapped at will. Caroline expresses the immanent, nondualistic Spinozist version according to which mind and body are intricately intertwined and

10. Calvert (2010) considers the supposed "cleanness" of these wipes in terms of mind and embodiment in an analysis that cuts close to the Spinozist frame of this essay. From different perspectives, Julie Hawk (2010b), Ian G. Klein (2010), and Kate Rennebohm (2010) also explore these questions. See also Rabb and Richardson, this volume.

defy efforts purely and simply to separate them. The story line of *Dollhouse* is structured largely around two parallel and interrelated processes for Echo/Caroline: the recall of memories and feelings from her life as Caroline as well as the coming to awareness as a person of Echo in defiance of her assigned role as a "Doll" in a "natural state." Caroline can be compared to the cyborg River in that she, too, comes to inhabit and affirm her altered state rather than yearn for the essence of a "pure" premodification life. The characters of Sierra and Victor are powerful in this respect, as they manifest an ongoing drive for companionship with one another despite being "wiped" repeatedly (Ginn 2010, para. 7; Perdigao 2010, para. 10, 19).

Throughout the series, Echo becomes increasingly aware of herself as a Doll. She rejects the easy classification of herself and the other Dolls as somehow less than human or as partial people. She asserts that it is less ontological state (unaltered human versus Doll) that determines personhood than experience in living. She is another of Whedon's characters who both experience the persistence of underlying identities and strive to make sense of themselves and the world.

Conclusion

In the Whedonverses, there is a parallel among the Dolls, River, and Adam (and his kin Riley and Spike). All of them have been subject to extensive technological manipulation, but all are primarily concerned with fundamental questions about their identity and the meaning of existence. All of them are aware of a certain "script" or datum that is meant to determine their existence, yet they all either fight against or reinterpret this script in light of their own lived (and felt) experience. They hark back to the figure of Gigolo Joe whom Whedon mentioned in the Paley Center *Dollhouse* event, a "technical" being who nonetheless is determined by, and occupied by, the most fundamental questions of existence. As Whedon explains in part of his description of *Dollhouse* at the Paleyfest event, this questioning is about what is innate within us and why we are the way we are, and, crucially, whether we can love these characters and what it is that we "need from people" by doing so.

As part of his emphasis on the process of reflection about one's own existence, Whedon is critical of manipulations, technical or magical, that instrumentalize subjects rather than treat them as autonomous agents. Thus, the Scoobies, chiefly Tara as the intended target of the spell, feel betrayed by Willow and her memory magic in "Tabula Rasa." By the same token, Riley and the Initiative soldiers feel wronged by Professor Walsh because she subjected them to technical modification without their knowledge. Part of the particular deviousness of the demon in "Normal Again" lies in the fact that its venom disrupts Buffy's perception and thus her agency. As a consequence, Buffy leaves her friends vulnerable to the demon, ready to sacrifice them against their will to regain her sanity. In this respect of emphasizing autonomy and agency, Whedon agrees with Kant in the Second Formulation of the Categorical Imperative: "Act in such a way that you treat humanity, whether in your own person or in the person of any other, never merely as a means to an end, but always at the same time as an end" ([1785] 1993, 30). Donna Haraway explains how the type of calculative manipulation explored and decried by Whedon has thrived on the persistence of the "fantastic mind/body binary" (2008, 71).

In combination with the emphasis on lived experience and the attempt to understand oneself, Joss Whedon also maintains a complexly immanent view of mind and being. There is no tabula rasa, or clean slate, because mind and body are intricately interwoven rather than separate substances. It is for this reason that technological interventions to swap personalities and memory spells alike are doomed to unforeseen consequences and ultimate failure in the Whedonverses.

From Old Heresies to Future Paradigms

Joss Whedon on Body and Soul

GREGORY ERICKSON

God and Soul

In the unaired pilot episode of *Dollhouse*, Boyd Langton has a conversation with Topher Brink about the ethics of repeatedly wiping and programming their "Actives." Boyd proposes the idea that the Actives or "Dolls" are perhaps still "people" and questions the morality of "those things we program them to do." He refutes Topher's argument that the Actives' engagements actually provide them heightened life experiences, saying, "There's nothing real about it. They're programmed." Topher responds by listing Boyd's most embodied habits ("You eat eggs every morning but never at night"), including the ones imposed by popular culture ("Your stomach rumbles every time you drive by a big golden arch"), and concludes, "Everybody's programmed, Boyd" ("Echo" 1.0).

This exchange simultaneously rehearses ancient debates over body and soul, modern philosophical dialogues on essentialism and existentialism, and futuristic anxieties about the posthuman. From *Buffy* and *Angel* through *Firefly* and *Dollhouse*, Joss Whedon has dramatized the difficulty of understanding the tension between what we do and who we are, between action and being, and between our desire for and suspicion of the "real." What is the relationship between memory and reality? Creator and created? Flesh and spirit? These tensions—what Scott McLaren refers to as the tension "between the ontological and the existential" (2005, para. 2)—as Whedon repeatedly shows us, raise questions at the core of human self-definition. For theologian Charles Winquist, "we think we know what we mean when we say I and that this I is a person, which, in turn, gives a substantial meaning to the word 'person'" (1998, 225). This certainty, however, is shadowed by doubt, a doubt that Whedon demonstrates by challenging the defined boundaries of the human soul and, by extension, our changing definitions of ourselves. His dramas often focus on human figures who, in one way or another, lose their "soul" as they change from one status to another: human to vampire, human to Reaver, human to Active, human to god. The question of what is lost or gained in each case is directly related to our cultural associations about the human soul.

It remains a popular metaphor in our society to equate the lack of a soul with a defective moral conscience, and therefore, when we assume the existence of a soul, we assert the exceptionalism of our "humanity." To insist that any being (African slave, Islamic terrorist, Cylon) has no soul is to separate "it" from us. A soulless being's actions do not represent humanity or threaten our conceptions of who we are, and our actions toward them can be justified outside accepted morality codes. On *Buffy* and *Angel*, the soul is often connected to a conscience or a state of "goodness."[1] Although the equation of the soul with morality or the good is obviously problematic, Whedon's most interesting characters, from Spike to Illyria to Topher, both confirm and subvert traditional and essentialist notions of a soul. As J. Renée Cox, among others, points out, characters such as Whistler, Clem, and, most prominently, Spike are examples of "soulless" beings who still make moral choices (2008, 27–29). Although Whedon seems to imply that the human soul may be a necessary if imaginary construct, he also demonstrates its essential instability. By interlacing pagan and Christian ideas of the soul and the body with futuristic technodriven speculation, and by presenting narrative forms that challenge viewers' sense of identity, linearity, and coherence, Whedon offers a reenvisioning of the soul as a relational concept that is simultaneously physical, spiritual, and technological.

A soul, dictionaries tell us, is the "incorporeal essence of a person," a definition that follows ancient Christian and Greek thinkers. For Plato, the soul "sheds its wings and wanders until it lights on something solid, where it settles and takes on an earthly body" (1997, 524). A familiar Catholic catechism claims "the soul is a living being without a body, having reason and free will." In both cases, the soul serves as a separate moral command center for the body, yet is still defined in opposition to the body. The uncertainty at the core of the body-soul relationship has historically defined and divided various branches of religion, and the variety of answers to questions of body and soul dominated the development of the Christian church for the first five hundred years of its

---

1. Questions of the soul in Whedon's work, particularly *Buffy* and *Angel*, have received much attention. See, for example, Abbott 2003; Cox 2008; and McLaren 2005.

existence and are embedded in the subconsciousness of Western culture. More than fifteen hundred years ago, Augustine wrote, "God and the soul. That is what I desire to know, nothing more" (quoted in Schaff [1888] 2007, 539). In these few words, Augustine defines two concepts, God and the self, as central epistemological quests, the mystery of which continues to underwrite most of Western thought. The modern equivalent of Augustine's statement can be found in Gayatri Spivak's comment that "humankind's common desire is for a stable center, and for the assurance of mastery" (1976, xi). Yet the desire to know both god and soul, the familiar Whedonian quest for one's source and one's identity, participates in a paradox contained in claiming anything as certain, a paradox that often resides in our perception of our corporeal existence—the human body—and its connection to the soul.

Whedon retraces Augustine's quest by addressing analogous questions of the materiality, origin, and significance of the soul. The soul, in Whedon's vampire dramas, though it appears to be opposed to evil, does not come from a place of good and is often a commodity, a "thing" separated from its source and originating outside of its host body.[2] Angel receives his soul in the form of a gypsy curse, and when Spike is "ensouled" at the end of the sixth season of *Buffy*, it is through a process of bloody combat tests put to him by a demon. The soul, like other objects of supernatural power in *Buffy* and *Angel* (holy water, crosses), is separated from its theological origins and its grounding in good or evil. Yet the soul's "objectivity," its materiality, paradoxically calls it into question. When the soul is made immanent, it is just another material object, just another part of this world, devoid of mystery. How can a soul be a true soul if it can be stored in an urn or conjured and implanted by a gypsy curse, a demon, or a nascent Wiccan? Whedon's dramas reveal how the soul stands for the material evidence of individual identity but that it also represents the impossibility of defining an individual. This transcendent/immanent tension—at the root of a Jewish and Christian tradition that simultaneously desires a personal god *and* a god beyond all naming and imagination—is characteristic of religious constructions that continually restage this paradox. It is the transcendence of Moses's ineffable God versus the immanence of Aaron's Golden Calf, the transcendence of a ghostly spirit and the immanence of ectoplasm, and the transcendence of an omnipotent Creator and the immanence of a naked man bleeding on a cross. In each pairing, we desire and need both, however imaginary they may be.

2. For a detailed analysis of the soul in Whedon's Buffyverse, see McLaren 2005.

But whereas body/soul may seem like another immanent/transcendent binary, we now question the ontology of the body as well as the soul. Rapid advances in digital, genetic, biotechnological, and cybernetic science have initiated a new sense of uncertainty about our bodily presence, and these emerging new technologies have led to increased anxieties about the clear boundaries of the human body. Today's humans may have several online bodiless "avatars" through which they experience much of the world; the concept of gender is no longer fixed, either psychologically or physically; reproduction can occur without sexual activity; eyes, limbs, and organs are improved or replaced with increasing ease; and the ubiquity of portable global positioning systems and Google devices has partially replaced or augmented memory. Even the boundaries of the soul have been implicitly challenged through DNA research that demonstrates that our personal information is not just "stored" in brains but exists in a more living form in our genes; the idea of "I am who I am" easily becomes "Who am I?" We do not know what is on the other side of all this technology; like Buffy, we are afraid that we may "come back wrong" ("Dead Things" 6.13), not fully human anymore.

The Monstrosity of Echo

Although issues of artificial intelligence and cyborg and transhuman rights may seem in the distant future, it is today's popular art that will prepare us to react to these new moral challenges. Science fiction and fantasy genres have always tested the borders of possible thought, allowing both creator and perceivers to imagine social situations outside traditional constraints, accepted boundaries, and received ideas. Whedon destabilizes many of the common assumptions that accompany belief and skepticism. He engages with new technologies (artificial intelligence, mind control, cyborgs) and ancient fears (vampires, demons, werewolves) to present belief and nonbelief in a reimagined context—often pushing viewers to accept or sympathize with positions outside what they could have previously imagined. Whether we consider ourselves religious or not, following a Whedon drama often means we find ourselves drifting away from the essentialist foundation of our assumed humanism or the implied divinity in our sense of purpose. The questions inherent within the narrative of these texts go directly to updated twenty-first-century anxieties about the existence of God: Can only God create humans? Can only humans create humans? Can only humans create God? What does it mean to destroy one's creator? At what point are we no longer human, and at that point, what happens to our gods? Do machines have souls? Do we?

The soul, as Freud writes, was likely the first "double" of the body and was a "creation that belongs to a primitive phase in our mental development" ([1899] 2003, 143). But if the double was "originally an insurance against the extinction of the self" (142), then this "primitive phase" has returned in technologically driven theories of the future in which we find ourselves again fearing extinction and a loss of selfhood. Ray Kurzweil predicts, "Well before the twenty-first century is completed, people will port their entire mind file to the new thinking technology" (2000, 126). Just being able to imagine this possibility means that the idea of the double as an immortal soul is now a scientific concept as well as a religious one. *Dollhouse*, for example, depicts multiple forms of immortality: saving an imprint of oneself for after death, moving from one body to another, downloading an imprint into someone else. If the first double was the soul, will these new doubles have a soul?

This question, which may define the future of humankind, cannot be understood outside of our theological backgrounds, programming that is deep within our ideological DNA. The Christian concepts of the resurrection and eternal life of the soul that emerged in the first centuries after Christ were, of course, not new or unique. What was new was *bodily* resurrection, which is the reason Christians have historically emphasized the empty tomb and the body of Christ. This balance of presence and absence, body and soul, can be seen in the earliest Christian philosophers, orthodox and heretical. In the third century, Tertullian emphasized the immortality of the body as well as the soul. What is "raised" after death, he wrote, is "flesh, suffused with blood, built up with bones . . . undoubtedly human" (quoted in Pagels 1989, 4). On the other hand, for many Gnostics, the idea of a bodily resurrection was naïve. Their belief was that the entire material world, especially the human body, was base matter not deserving of resurrection or immortality. The only hope was to find a spark of divinity within one's soul and help it escape the material world. Within Christianity, these questions are echoed in early theological debates: Did God create Christ? Was Christ created at all, or is he eternal? If his body was not eternal or divine, then what was it? These theological positions still resonate today in questions of body and soul, both inside and outside religious contexts, and could be paraphrased in language appropriate for Topher or Angel.[3] As David Noble argues in *The Religion of*

---

3. For example, Topher's insistence that he is responsible for creating a new "whole person" ("Ghost" 1.1) is essentially a theological statement that will be implicitly debated throughout the series.

Technology, "Masked by a secular vocabulary and now largely unconscious, the old religious themes nevertheless continued subtly to inform Western projects and perceptions" (1999, 104). Although the theological roots of our modern ideology have been concealed over time (often by the very sciences it produced), this unstable core exists as a shadow, continuing to color our thinking and action, often in ways we do not perceive or understand.

In *Dollhouse*, Whedon uses the cyborg-like Actives to pose difficult questions that continue to acknowledge their theological nature. The cyborg, as a hybrid creature between human and machine, as simultaneously biological and technological, destabilizes categories on which Western logic depends. This figure resonates strongly within our imagination because it dissolves the distinction between born and made, a dialectic that lies at the core of artistic creation, personal identity, and Christianity.[4] The Actives of the Dollhouse force us to question the relationship of the body to identity and to think about how we define a human. A Doll, says DeWitt, is "our heart's desire made flesh" ("The Target" 1.2), obviously echoing New Testament language and inviting comparison between an Active and the man/god Jesus. One of the most significant questions within early Christianity considered the creation or noncreation of Jesus. The position that became orthodox claimed that he was not "created" but has always been ("Begotten not made," says the Nicene Creed). This formulation left unresolved the question of whether Christ was man or god (or if perhaps his body was man and his soul was god). His presence as somehow both man and god, or what Slavoj Žižek refers to as the "monstrosity of Christ" (2009, 40), acts as an ancient cyborg that calls categories into question, much as Echo does in *Dollhouse*. Each is clearly not human according to accepted definitions, yet each demands to be accepted as human. "What is she?" Topher asks in awe, a question that has no answer ("A Love Supreme" 2.8).

Trying to answer Topher's question moves us in the direction of postmodern theologies that read the body of Christ not as a truth that ensures doctrines of a church, but as a container of memories that generates alterities within the Christian tradition. Like Echo's body (and the body of a vampire), the body of Christ disrupts conventional category constructions. Christ was a new type of being, an alien intruder into a world with which he had no ontological connection; he changed the conception of history and challenged

4. The same question can also be found in Islam, where the debate is whether the Koran was created or has eternally existed.

categories of life and death. The bodies of vampires and Actives also challenge these categories. Alpha's gift of Paul's imprint to Echo in "Epitaph Two: Return" (2.13) raises the same ontological issues as the vampire's "undeath" or Christ's "being." Paul, who was already an imprint of his "true" self, has been killed, but his imprint is now inside Echo. Where does he exist? What is he? These new questions of "being," even as they restate the old, can no longer be settled by creed and dogma and church councils. Neither can these issues be resolved through current scientific and philosophical thought, which is limited by the questions we can imagine. We need new frameworks through which to imagine new questions.

Chip versus Soul: "Same Diff"?

Although one of the themes in *Buffy* is its privileging of the irrationality of magic and mysticism over the supposed rationality of science and technology, these polarities are blurred in the figure of Spike. In Season 4 of *Buffy*, after the Initiative installs a chip in his brain that prevents him from harming humans, Spike begins to express compassion, kindness, and love, all supposedly without the presence of a soul. The complex relationship between the spiritual and the technological is articulated by Dawn, who defends Spike by comparing him to the ensouled Angel: "Spike has a chip. Same diff" ("Crush" 5.14). What makes this line so important is that it conflates two ways—the theological and the technological—of understanding the human consciousness. These two paths have been traditionally held apart, but in the future we will no longer be able to separate them. In these few words, Dawn encapsulates the twenty-first-century theological issues that drive *Dollhouse*. Dawn, like a programmed Active, comes with a "lifetime" of memories that on some level are not "real," that are created outside of normal human processes. Dawn and viewers realize, implicitly, the randomness of the origin of the soul and of an essentialist "humanity." Dawn has been created through mystical means and Spike through both evil and digital, and Dawn understands what Spike represents. Not fully human, each attains a form of selfhood that must be recognized as somehow deserving of "human" rights.

For theologian Elaine Graham, "Definitive accounts of human nature may be better arrived at not through a description of essences, but via the delineation of boundaries" (2002, 11). These boundaries are created, threatened, and negotiated through narratives and stories. In *Firefly*, it is the Reavers who threaten to reveal the lack of an essential humanity. The most horrific double Whedon has yet created, Reavers mirror Freud's definition of the "uncanny" as a "species of the frightening that . . . had long been familiar" ([1899] 2003, 124). The bodies of the Reavers communicate several historical and religious narratives suggestive of both American Indian and space aliens.[5] As in narratives of Indians and aliens, whose otherness both served to define normative "humanness" and to articulate Western anxieties of the body, Reavers' bodies are recognizably human, yet their deviance is defined by bodily destruction, self-mutilation, rape, and cannibalism. Although Mal and his crew think of Reavers as evil, the show also suggests that Reavers were once like us. From this point of view, Jayne's comment on Reavers, that "them people ain't human," is more profound than he could ever know ("Bushwhacked" 1.3).

Reavers, as Mal explains, exist because "they got out to . . . that place of nothin' . . . and that's just what they became" ("Bushwhacked"). Although *nothing*, in this case, is coded as evil, a void for humans to resist, historically the concept of nothingness has been used to represent dark *and* light, the abyss *and* possibility. Although mainstream and popular religion tends to categorize nothingness as evil or as frightening, there has always been a mystical apophatic branch within Judaism and Christianity that embraced the idea of nothing as either a path to or a description of the divine. For thinkers from Plato to medieval mystics to postmodern theologians, because God cannot be something that "is," it is more accurate to refer to God as "nothing." Yet within most religious thought, nothing remains a dark and threatening concept, opposed to the positive attributes of real and present. The complex concept of nothing is deeply connected to the contradictory function of the soul. The soul gives us an assurance that we are not nothing, that we exist as humans, yet at the same time, our soul may very well be just nothing. All "creatures," orthodox Christians insisted, like the world itself, come into existence "out of nothing." The eternal uncreated God was safe from the fall into nothing; God, as he who *is*, was the only force against this sinful abyss. The fourth-century Arius committed his greatest heresy in claiming that Christ was indeed "created" by God "out of nothing," affirming that "once he was not." Arius's claim that Christ like man was also created, that he too came from nothing, forced thinkers to theorize the act of creation and the concept of nothing and nothingness. The ultimate decision to reject Jesus as a created being was directly related to the fear of nothing.

5. See Barbeito (2005) for an interesting discussion of the relationship of Indian and alien narratives and bodily anxieties. On the American Indian/Reaver connection, see Rabb and Richardson 2008.

According to this theology, because humans are by nature mortal, because they are "made out of what is not," they are therefore always on the edge of being drawn back into this originary abyss, or, in the terms of *Firefly*, we are all potential Reavers on the edge of nothing. The episode that most completely develops the idea of nothing and of the Reavers ("Bushwhacked") concludes as River and Simon cling to the hull of the ship to avoid detection by the Alliance.[6] Unlike Simon, who is terrified, River gazes in joyful awe into the black space. River, whose name of course resembles *Reaver*, and who, like them, is the result of irresponsible technology, has just like the Reavers reached a "place of nothing," but unlike them, she thrives. It is in her relationship to the idea of nothing that the character of River can be seen as suggesting a path that is not traditional faith or traditional humanism; it is neither the religion of Shepherd Book nor the atheism of Malcolm Reynolds, but rather a path that offers multiple directions. River transforms nothing and blackness into new possibilities. Only for River (a truly posthuman construct) can a negative also be something positive, an emptiness not to be feared. The posthumanity of River (like Echo's) allows her to redefine the nothing of the medieval mystic, to conflate theology and technology into a new way of understanding being.[7] By looking into nothing, River looks away from the defined self, away from the teleological straight path of history, and away from absolutes. Meaning is not in things, as both Mal and Book want to insist, but between them, in the interplay, the relationality, and the empty space.

Like River in *Firefly*, Echo offers alternatives to linear or fundamentalist constructions of meaning, and, like Whedon's earlier dramas, *Dollhouse* questions the connection between body and soul and assumptions of stable identity. The show presents a central character who, for much of the series, essentially does not exist. By the end of the series, we must accept a hero who was nonexistent in the beginning, a character that the show and the viewers have created out of the narrative itself. What makes *Dollhouse* most challenging is that it both affirms and questions traditional expectations of identity and the human soul. *Dollhouse* begins as an affirmation of Western traditional identity: we assume the self to be a bounded container separate from other similarly bounded containers and in possession of its own capacities and abilities that must be protected. In the opening episodes, Caroline has been

6. For a more complete reading of the concept of nothing in this episode of *Firefly*, see Erickson 2008.

7. On the character Dr. Horrible and posthumanism, see Willis in this volume.

robbed of her identity, and her "container," which was not protected properly, needs to have its own "capacities and abilities" returned so "she" can return to her separate "bounded" state as an unquestioned self. This quest for the essence that is Caroline appears to be the main thrust of the series. Yet by the end of Season 1, this premise and definition have been problematized; by the end of Season 2, they have been almost completely reformulated.

These subversive ideas gradually emerge during the first season through the repeated suggestion that we all resemble Dolls in one way or another; various "human" characters comment that they feel empty, programmed, or as if they are constantly remade to match another's wishes.[8] In the Season 1 broadcast finale, "Omega" (1.12), the tension arising from each of these themes is heightened and dramatized. Alpha, who had smashed his "original self," kidnaps Echo, all of her imprints, and a young woman (Wendy). In his own version of Topher's imprint chair, Alpha imprints Wendy with Echo's original personality, Caroline Farrell; he then initiates a "composite event" on Echo, creating a hybrid consciousness he calls Omega. "Nietzsche predicted our rise," Alpha says. "Something new. The Übermensch."

Alpha's language, as he prepares Echo to receive a dumping of all of her previous imprints, resonates with language of a gnostic secret knowledge of the divine spark that transcends the physical body: "And she will ascend. She will know." He dismisses the importance of the body, saying, "It's just a body. They're all pretty much the same." Alpha's plan is for Echo to kill Caroline/ Wendy; from the death of Caroline will rise Omega, a life from death that is simultaneously pagan, Christian, Nietzschean, and posthuman. Alpha intones, "The Gods require blood. New life from death. . . . The old Gods are back." As he switches on the imprinting process, crying, "Alpha meet Omega," music and lighting and a montage of Echo's past imprints build to a classic Franken-steinian moment. At the moment of the season's climax, Echo leaps out of the chair. She is a new creation and the other characters respond appropriately:

WENDY/CAROLINE: Oh, God.
ALPHA: Oh, gods.

8. For example, in early episodes, a client fabricates his whole background ("The Target" 1.2); a superstar singer complains, "I'm not a real person. I'm everybody's fantasy" ("Stage Fright" 1.3); and the happiness of the Actives is implicitly compared to the happi-ness of cult Christians: "True happiness," it is said of the cultists, "requires some measure of self-awareness" ("True Believer" 1.5).

This moment of creation is indeed a religious one, and the tension between expressions of mono- and polytheism comments on the relationship of the technology to the characters' perceptions of soul, body, and identity. Monotheism is linked to a belief in a stable single identity, so Wendy/Caroline calls out for God. At the same time, Alpha celebrates his creation of another superior being like himself with the plural, "Oh, gods." Neither mono- nor polytheistic, Echo simply says: "I get it." She does not argue with Alpha's statement "We're not just humans anymore," answering him, "We're not anybody; because we're everybody."

The episode introduces a new, more ambiguous relationship of self to imprint and body, and the language of the characters reflects this ambiguity. As "Caroline" (in Wendy's body) looks at "herself" (Echo), she cannot find the spatial language to express her desire: "I want my brain back," she says, then "I want back in my brain." Echo is equally challenged to express her ontology: "There is no me. I'm just a container," and then, "I'm Echo. . . . She's [Echo's] nobody. I'm just the porch light waiting for you [Caroline]." The difficulty is in determining the ontology of identity: Cellular? Digital? Memory? Spirit? In this scene, all are open to manipulation. The theo-techno-onto-relationship of essential self, digital implant, and physical body becomes a postmodern, posthuman trinity. Echo embodies these three previously incompatible understandings. It is up to us to accept or reject this logic, both here and throughout this episode.

In the same episode, Dr. Saunders, who along with Boyd has represented the moral "humanist" voice throughout the season, is revealed to be an Active, code-named Whiskey, who was imprinted with "Dr. Saunders's" personality after Alpha killed the original doctor. The most moving moment in this episode occurs when Dr. Saunders/Whiskey confronts Topher after she confirms her fears that she is indeed an Active. "Aren't you curious to see who you really are?" asks Topher, a question that contradicts his usual nonessentialist denials of any sort of core or soul. "I know who I am," she replies, leaving us wondering what she means. This episode continues to give us these unreadable moments. When the following exchange takes place between Paul and Topher, we do not know how to interpret it:

PAUL: I still don't believe you can wipe away a person's soul.
TOPHER: (*incredulously*) Their what?
PAUL: Who they are at their core. I don't think that goes away.
TOPHER: You'd be wrong about that.

Which character are we supposed to agree with? Does Topher mean that he can wipe away a soul or that he does not believe in the soul? Is Paul indeed *wrong*? Does *Dollhouse* seem to come down on one side or the other in this debate?

This episode challenges us to make a decision and then forces us to question it. As viewers, we are culturally conditioned to feel that it is "right" for Caroline to return to her body, yet we celebrate the power Echo now has. "I kick ass," Caroline-in-Wendy's body says admiringly of her former body, which feels like an emotional turning point. Finally we have a hero to root for, finally a vehicle for Whedon's dramatic language. We *want* lines such as "I'm done laying back in the chair. I'm ready to rinse and spit." Yet the lasting impression of this episode is not heroism but the tortured moral ambiguity of Topher and the existential anguish of Whiskey. When Echo whispers "Caroline" at the end of the episode (and, many thought, the end of the series), we do not know who it is or what we should want for her.

Although "Omega" seemed to be written as a final judgment on the ethics of what the Dollhouse does, Season 2 establishes Echo as far more than a "porch light" and, in fact, as something much closer to what Alpha envisions. Beginning with "Omega" and continuing through Season 2, *Dollhouse* helps us think about whether there is an instinctive drive toward disembodied transcendence deeply embedded in the human consciousness. Such an instinct has been expressed scientifically by thinkers such as Hans Moravec (1990), who proposes that human identity is essentially an information pattern rather than an embodied essence. Like Topher and Alpha, Moravec is a "postbiological" thinker who believes in a future world where corporeal embodiment will become optional and where we will be able to, and will probably want to, leave our bodies behind. On the other hand, many cognitive philosophers believe that the human body largely determines the nature of the human mind, arguing that only machines connecting to the world through a body could achieve a true artificial intelligence. Either position will require deeply resisted shifts in our definition of body and soul.

Part of the problem is our failing to recognize technological innovation as a fundamental aspect of human existence. This cognitive step is what *Dollhouse* can help us imagine. We must gradually let go of the idea that the body is "for" Caroline and realize that the "tech" has produced a new being. In the series finale, both Echo and Alpha are said to have "evolved," a word that suggests both a biological process and teleological improvement. Are Echo and Alpha, as evil Alpha says in "Omega," now higher beings? In the future, will the newly wiped single personalities be envious of their powers and try to overthrow them or accept them as a higher species or even gods? Echo and Topher, like Buffy and Willow, have indeed "changed the world," but is it a happy ending? Is it an ending at all?

Posthuman Narrative: Not What You Want, but What You Need

Our body, as is increasingly understood, is integral to how we understand and relate to the world. If we start to see the body not as a guarantee of a stable existence, but rather as a space through which to ask questions—much the same way we have learned to comprehend the mind—then the whole way we process knowledge changes. And as Mark Taylor proposes, if it is "possible to argue that not only the unconscious but the body is structured like a language," then we increasingly come to see that the body is not a closed system, but a "nonsystematic play of differences that is riddled with gaps" (1993, 220–21). Our language system, whether we claim to be believers or not, contains in it assumptions about God, body, soul, and morality. "Morality," as Topher says, "is programming too" ("Ghost"), and the history of our programming in the West is steeped in Christian narratives. We are, as humans, created by stories that we continue to tell ourselves. In a posthuman, post-Christian world, then, the way we tell our stories will necessarily change. If popular art is what will give us tools to move outside of this model, then new forms of narrative create new possible moral paradigms.

Firefly, *Dollhouse*, and the final seasons of *Buffy* all present structures of narrative that model unstable systems that refuse to conform to a linear and coherent identity. The final two seasons of *Buffy* were constantly disruptive to audience's expectations and desires, upsetting the progress of story line and character while drawing attention to these disruptions, forcing viewers to reconsider the consistency of the show's narrative. Seasons 6 and 7 created tension between viewers' desire for coherence and an unsettling awareness of its fragility. Season 6, in particular, linked disruption of a complex narrative to a questioning of bodily integrity. For example, when the Buffy-bot is torn into pieces, it symbolically links the role of the body with the role of fragmented narrative, serving as a metaphor for the disjointed Season 6 and encapsulating questions about how Buffy will react to her own death. If our certainty resides in the faith that we know who we are, and that we know the limits of our own skin, then from the pieces of the Buffy-bot to scenes of rupture, flaying, rape, and torture, Season 6 investigates this sense of certainty through challenges to the idea of bodily integrity (see Erickson and Lemberg 2009; Wilcox 2009b, 95–98).

Like the final seasons of *Buffy*, *Dollhouse* links formalist challenges of narrative to questions of identity by subverting assumptions about the continuity of self, knowledge, and narrative. The narrative of the show stretches and challenges its own boundaries. It seems to change direction; characters behave in ways that do not seem consistent, and elements such as the unaired pilot ("Echo") and "Epitaph One" suggest various directions, almost creating parallel worlds. Depending on whether they had seen "Epitaph One," viewers were literally watching a different second season. Much of the early critical work on *Dollhouse* has focused on the relationship of a fragmented narrative and the fragmented selves that make up each Active. Lisa Perdigao describes *Dollhouse* as an "unorthodox television series that seems disordered, like the multiple personality disordered Alpha and Echo" (2010, para. 11). For Julie Hawk, "Echo's subjectivization process . . . is wrapped up in narrative considerations. . . . [T]he subject is the story and the story is the subject" (2010a, para. 2). In other words, the radical "constructedness" of Echo's posthuman psyche "resembles the constructedness of narrative" (para. 6). The show resists efforts at totalization and definitive interpretations; it leaves, as Topher says of his wiping process, "unpredictable remainders" ("The Target"). Like its central premise, *Dollhouse* challenges ideas of an essential core, a coherent object, or a single linear narrative. Even Adelle, Paul, Boyd, and Topher, like the Dolls that they manipulate, shift in ways we cannot understand. On a second viewing of the series, do we really believe that Boyd was always a cofounder of Rossum or that DeWitt was acting throughout most of Season 2 to bring the Dollhouse down? Perhaps or perhaps not. Again, the decision is ours. There is no single truth. Art, like the Actives, imitates life.

The function of art, as a wiped and innocent Echo is told in "Gray Hour" (1.4), is to show us "who we are." Perdigao points to how the description of the Picassoesque painting in "Gray Hour" is a "reflection of our world and our fragmentation in the narrative medium of television . . . illustrating how the broken Dolls of *Dollhouse* and the broken narrative of the series can be put together to make meaning" (para. 4). But although the point of Picasso's cubist paintings may be the perceiver's reconstruction, art can also demonstrate the impossibility of a coherent whole. A Picasso painting is still framed, contained as a single unit, separate from its surroundings. But the frames around *Dollhouse* (an unaired pilot, "Epitaph One," and "Epitaph Two: Return") do not really belong; they violate all the rules of traditional narrative and commercial television. The art of *Dollhouse* forces us to consider whether Echo ultimately learns to cohere as a single subject or if she accepts an essential fragmentation. The plot of *Dollhouse* blocks closure. Like Echo, we must hold on to multiplicities.

Conclusion: Playing with Matches

In "Man on the Street" (1.6), a professor says of the Dollhouse, "If that technology exists . . . then we will be over. As a species we will cease to matter." What *Dollhouse* ultimately asks is whether that scenario is necessarily "wrong." Like Echo, like Buffy, like River, and like the early Christians, both heretical and orthodox, future generations will again need to rethink the relationship of the human body and soul. They may discover that their most sacred of beliefs no longer work, but that in this realization exists a new path. Whether it is Buffy, who destroys the ancient apostolic succession that created her, or River and Echo, who learn to embrace what others see as unnatural hybrid identities, Whedon's dramas suggest the need to create voids to allow new meanings. Echo, as Hawk writes, "follows a trajectory that results in changing the system, changing the narrative. Not satisfied with humanism, especially since she isn't strictly speaking, a human anymore, Echo effectively hacks into the narrative that she was told was a read-only file" (para. 20). Maybe what is necessary is to kill our idea of the soul, to create a lack in order to rebuild. Playing with matches can indeed "burn the house down" ("Epitaph Two" 2.13), but fire also initiates new growth. Žižek makes the point that today's art no longer generates sublime objects, but instead works to create a "(Sacred) Place" of emptiness (2000, 31). Here is the role of the "art" that Echo creates at the end of "Gray Hour" when she begins to draw a face in the fogged-over mirror and then wipes it away to reveal her own reflection. More Marcel Duchamp than Picasso, Echo's drawing not only is unfinished, but also disappears as she wipes it away, leaving a reflection of her literally vacant self. If her drawing is meant as a representation of the self, then she creates a void by wiping away both creation and creator. Her new creation will no longer be able to be reflected or framed; instead, "Echo" will become a relational network of bodies and souls, unable to be contained. This new conception of creation, art, and identity is what Echo—and Joss Whedon—offers: art that is neither transcendent nor immanent but helps us imagine something different, something other. Whedon the atheist ultimately gives us not a rejection of all religion but a vision that acknowledges the death of god and the soul and finds in this death new emergent ideas and possibilities.

"Hot Chicks with Superpowers"

The Contested Feminism of Joss Whedon

LAUREN SCHULTZ

Joss Whedon is often proclaimed a feminist auteur, thanks largely to *Buffy the Vampire Slayer*, a series he created to defy expectations of females in fantasy and horror films. In interviews, he explains he was tired of seeing the blonde who "was cute, had sex, was bouncy and frivolous, [and] always got her ass killed. I just felt really bad for her. I thought, I want to see the movie where she walks into a dark alley, a monster attacks her, and she just wails [*sic*] on him" (Longworth 2002, 209). Although he envisioned a kick-butt heroine, Whedon wanted to emphasize the character's physical and emotional strength instead of her sexuality. The heroine he created was still young and nubile, but Buffy Summers learns to control her own physical capabilities, a control that empowers her to shape her own identity. Consequently, many consider Buffy an important feminist role model and icon, despite problematic aspects of the character and show. Referenced more than Whedon's other series, *Buffy* established his reputation as a feminist auteur and heightened expectations for his future work.

His feminism was repeatedly challenged in the fall of 2009 when Whedon launched his controversial show *Dollhouse*. The series is set in a high-tech house of prostitution, where a group of scientists scan and remove individuals' personalities, replacing them with newly constructed personalities and thus creating human "Dolls." Dollhouse administrators then rent these Dolls to wealthy clients with elaborate fantasies—a plot that relocates prostitution, human trafficking, and rape culture to the realm of science fiction and fantasy. Whedon had already established himself capable of examining sophisticated ethical concepts in SFF with *Buffy*, *Angel*, *Firefly*, and *Serenity*, but *Dollhouse* advertisements and plots were so provocative that viewers had difficulty accepting the show as feminist. Despite their physical prowess, Whedon's

Dolls do not have the control over their bodies that Buffy exercises over hers. As playthings of wealthy individuals, the Dolls are constantly objectified by clients' whims, the camera, and the viewer's gaze.

Although certain criticisms of the show are warranted, the provocative elements of *Dollhouse* must be judged in accordance with both the series' narrative, which works against the objectification of the characters, and Whedon's body of work. This juxtaposition allows us to understand *Dollhouse* as part of his ongoing feminist project—a dialogue about gender politics, sexuality, and control of the body. Although in *Dollhouse* Whedon approaches these subjects very differently than in *Buffy* and *Firefly*, he uses similar visual cues and complex narrative techniques throughout all his series to examine the process of emotional and sexual awakening, and ultimately his most controversial show is no less feminist than the shows that preceded it. Though *Dollhouse*'s graphic images and controversial plot have caused many to question his ideology, Whedon is a dedicated feminist auteur whose belief in gender equality consistently and productively informs even his works that feminists find most problematic.

Dollhouse was not the first of Whedon's works to draw concerned feminist criticism; the many scholarly debates over portrayals of gender, sexuality, and the physical body in *Buffy*, *Angel*, *Firefly*, and *Serenity* provide an important framework for interpreting *Dollhouse*. In his other series, Whedon links discourse regarding power with controversial depictions of the female body; by revisiting these themes, he interrogates social concepts of gender using multiple perspectives, techniques, and genres. Whedon insists that despite challenges working in the industry, "I still love television because, like with *Dollhouse*, we get to examine the question that we're interested in over and over from all these different angles" ("Defining Moments" 2010). This philosophy is, in fact, an important aspect of his work that makes him a true auteur: a consistent exploration of similar subjects. The thematic relationship between his various series invites multiple readings, fueling productive conversations about feminine sexuality and power—therefore, his position as a feminist must be understood as a complex stance.

Although not all of Whedon's works are explicitly feminist, the ways each series addresses the subjects of gender, sexuality, and the physical body provide insight into the other texts. Some scholars laud *Buffy* for its feminist ethos, arguing that the show "undoes the helpless female stereotypes," thus providing "a positive role model for young women, one which feminism should celebrate" (Vint 2002, para. 3). But even those scholars who praise *Buffy* acknowledge that despite the significant number of physically and intellectually empowered female characters, they are all "hot chicks with superpowers," as the Slayer Faith observes in the episode "End of Days" (7.21). Accordingly, the show has been critiqued for the homogenous appearance of its heroines. Both of the Slayers featured most prominently in the series (Buffy and Faith) are Caucasian, as are many of the young Slayers who participate in the final battle; the predominance of Caucasians in the series has led scholars to discuss the series' lack of racial diversity (Ono 2000; Edwards 2002; Payne-Mulliken and Renegar 2009).[1] Because all the Slayers are young and pretty and often wear suggestively cut clothing, others have scrutinized Buffy's low necklines and short skirts (Fudge 1999) and examined the show's narrow representations of motherhood and aging (St. Louis and Riggs 2010; Battis 2005; Williams 2002). Furthermore, much has been written about *Buffy*'s depictions of sexuality and gender roles, not only in the contexts of normative and deviant heterosexual relationships (see Symonds 2004; Jowett 2005; McCracken 2007; Price 2010; Burr 2003; Call 2007), but also within lesbian relationships (Beirne 2004; Cochran 2008). Willow and Tara were the only long-term lesbian partners portrayed on television in the early 2000s (Wilts 2009, 44); as a result, both fans and scholars debated the implications when Tara's homicide and Willow's murderous reaction forced the groundbreaking characters into the Dead/Evil Lesbian Cliché (Wilts 2009; Tabron 2004). Critics have also analyzed gender and sexuality in *Angel, Firefly, Serenity*, and *Dr. Horrible's Sing-Along Blog* (see Davidson 2004; Marano 2007; Aberdein 2008; Beadling 2008; Comeford 2009; Sutherland and Swan 2010). However, despite the aspects of these shows that feminists find problematic, the complexity of these series and the larger statement that they form regarding Whedon's complex stance on women's rights encourages dialogue about feminist issues and social problems, which is also true of the debate surrounding *Dollhouse*.

Rape culture, human trafficking, and male prostitution are uncomfortable topics that mainstream media often hesitate to portray or discuss; consequently, negative buzz surrounded *Dollhouse* even before its premiere because Whedon sought to tackle these subjects. His reputation ripened the subject for debate: as one viewer posted online, "Whedon is always the guy who gets called out" for including misogynist elements in his shows because the media have labeled him a feminist ([H]ypatia 2009), a characterization he

---

1. Although throughout the first six seasons of the series Slayers Kendra, Nikki Wood, the First Slayer, and the nameless Chinese Slayer are not Caucasian, they are marginalized in various ways, and we see all but the First Slayer killed off quickly.

has welcomed. Whedon affirmed his commitment to feminism in his 2006 Equality Now speech, declaring that misogyny "is life out of balance—and that imbalance is sucking something out of the soul of every man and woman who's confronted with it" (Whedon 2006). Yet advertisements for *Dollhouse* were explicitly sexual, objectifying Eliza Dushku through close-ups slowly panning her scantily clad body. Critics questioned whether a series depicting such callous objectification and abuse of women (and men) could be the product of a feminist's imagination. Soon after the show premiered, some viewers even began accusing Whedon of misogyny, bluntly articulating their thoughts in online forums.

Whether he expected such severe accusations or not, Whedon anticipated backlash to his new show. He "designed [*Buffy*] to be a feminist show—not a polemic, but a very straight-on feminist show" (Whedon 2002), and as Jason Middleton (2007) argues, the way *Buffy* is shot and edited generally works against fetishizing the female characters. In contrast, Whedon intended *Dollhouse* to approach feminist subjects from a different perspective than his first series. He told *TV Guide*'s Matt Mitovich that "I think a lot of people who watch *Dollhouse* are going to be challenged . . . because it's a very touchy show. It's going to deal with some ugly issues, but yes, I am absolutely a feminist" (2009). With this comment, Whedon assured fans that his belief in gender equality continued to guide his work.

Because Dushku was presented so provocatively, however, commentators continued to criticize *Dollhouse*. "Fox has a new and improved dream girl for the Friday-night fantasies of teenage boys, and she arrives tonight wearing a hey-look-me-over, super-short dress—the perfect model of female allure and submission," writes David Zurawik (2009) of the *Baltimore Sun*, describing Echo as "a 21st century version of geisha girl-meets-Charlie's Angels, with an unmistakable subtext of the heroine as prostitute always eager to please." With this description, Zurawik highlights the issue that many viewers had with the show: from the opening sequence of the first episode ("Ghost" 1.1), Dushku's body is prominently displayed and objectified in an overtly sexual manner. After a flashy motorcycle race, Dushku's character, Echo, and her partner cut loose on the dance floor, and as a low-angle shot tracks forward, viewers' eyes are drawn to Dushku dancing in the center of the frame. Medium close-ups present her torso and well-toned legs in a slinky dress that barely covers her buttocks. Whedon may not have had control over the *Dollhouse* advertising campaign, but he did control the camera work and costuming on the show. Yet both Whedon and Dushku confess to being uncomfortable with the scene. During the commentary, Whedon describes her costume as "the skimpy dress," admitting that as he was filming, "I was like, 'what have I become?'" The actress then laughs, "Why is the camera down there?" and Whedon responds, "I'm not going to lie—I put it down there," without offering any explanation (Whedon and Dushku 2009). The camera angles and costumes of this particular scene, as well as the way Whedon and his series star banter about the objectification of Dushku's body, offer little to counter Zurawik's criticism of *Dollhouse*. Although Whedon assured viewers that he is "absolutely a feminist" during his *TV Guide* interview, he does not defend his artistic choices during the commentary for "Ghost."

Other critics made observations similar to Zurawik's, particularly during the first weeks of the show's broadcast when the focus was on explaining the premise of the Dollhouse. The plot eventually shifts its focus, from the Dolls' engagements to the treacherous bureaucratic struggles within the organization and the Dolls' growing awareness of their former lives. The first episodes, however, develop the Dollhouse concept and establish that "Actives" are supposed to be perfectly blank slates—which made it difficult for many viewers to identify with the characters. One viewer posted that "*Buffy* allowed the whole 'power fantasy' thing to happen for women, the same way a comic book like *Superman* or *Batman* or *Ironman* can for men. I can watch *Buffy* and see a variety of those power fantasies, from the geeky girl who gets to date the band member, to the girl who gets to kick ass and take names while looking awesome and dealing in quips. Who am I supposed to identify with in *Dollhouse*? This is why the show doesn't work for me at all" (Anna 2009). As this viewer and others observed, without character development to humanize the Actives, the audience will likely see them as empty shells instead of human beings. Interpretations of the text as antifeminist are understandable in this context; it is reasonable to question whether Whedon is a feminist if he presents the victims of prostitution as disposable objects.

Critics faulted Whedon not only for sexually objectifying the Actives but also for *Dollhouse*'s graphic and violent images. The *Washington Post*'s Tom Shales (2009) argues that "the producers and director get carried away in the second episode, the camera languishing over shots of naked, nubile bodies scarred by slices and other gruesome wounds." Shales's description targets one of the more explicit group-shower scenes found throughout the series. Although most of these scenes are not violent in nature, this particular scene from "The Target" (1.2) depicts the bloody aftermath of a killing spree in the Dollhouse. Even when the scenes are benign, they could be considered gratuitous sexual content, and *Dollhouse*'s combination of violent and sexual images upset many. Some viewers may overlook the graphic imagery and consider how *Dollhouse*'s complicated narrative examines complex social issues, but others may be unable to get beyond the images. As one viewer notes, "This is the problem with literary theory: Someone shows you 44 minutes of rape and you start talking about the deeper commentary on patriarchal values entrenched in mass media culture, and somehow overlook the fact that millions of people are sitting in their living rooms watching 44 minutes of rape" (Lewis 2009). Because viewers could watch *Dollhouse* in much the same way some would watch soft-core pornography, the show's visual style must be interrogated, and both fans and scholars should acknowledge the potentially damaging nature of its explicit images. As Rhonda V. Wilcox states in her article "Echoes of Complicity," Whedon asks viewers to evaluate whether they are "*examining* exploitation or *participating* in it" (2010, para. 4), which is in fact the task of literary theory and academic scholarship—to consider the positive and negative aspects as well as positive and negative implications of a complex work such as *Dollhouse*. In doing so, scholars and fans continue the dialogue regarding mass media and societal values that the work is attempting to initiate, but viewers must also acknowledge that most often, they are both examining and participating in exploitation, given the graphic nature of *Dollhouse* and similar works.

In considering both the positive and the negative aspects of the show, we must examine how Whedon's use of sexually graphic and violent images emphasizes the level of dehumanization occurring within the Dollhouse and works to prevent viewers from becoming comfortable with the exploitation of the Actives. Dolls, after all, live in a comfortable spa-like facility; the group showers seem much more pleasant and benign than communal prison showers because of the luxurious setting. After a few episodes, viewers could become desensitized to the rape regularly portrayed on the show. Although the narrative does not explicitly comment upon the dehumanization of the Dolls at every turn, jarring images such as the violent flashbacks remind viewers that though they are pampered, Actives are still brain-wiped prostitutes who are regularly exploited and placed in dangerous situations.

The narrative complexities of *Dollhouse* provide an important counterpoint to the show's graphic images, and those viewers who defended *Dollhouse* against dismissive reviewers and angry bloggers cited Whedon's narrative techniques to argue that the show upholds feminist ideals. One poster observes, "The surface elements are not feminist, not progressive, and very-reaffirming of kyriarchal values. But just like the construction of the Dollhouse itself, the surface doesn't tell the story" ([W]hatsername 2009). Rather, viewers must look below the surface to understand the feminist potential of a show existing both in spite of and because of its sexualized presentation of the female body. As noted, the initial premise of *Dollhouse* is not complex, yet multiple inter-connected story lines, narrative twists, and moral ambiguities complicate and further Whedon's feminist agenda. Whedon states that when writing *Buffy*, he frequently used narrative juxtaposition to engage both viewers' intellect and their emotions in complicated ways (Whedon 2002). But Whedon's first series also declares its feminist agenda outright, whereas *Dollhouse* does not explicitly express a particular set of values; instead, the series relies heavily on intercut images and contrasting narrative elements to raise questions regard-ing gender and exploitation.[2]

The episode "Belle Chose" (2.3) illustrates particularly well how Whedon uses narrative juxtaposition in *Dollhouse*. Cynthea Masson (2010c) argues that characters perform the act of interpretation in several contexts throughout the episode, modeling how to decode the intricate text of *Dollhouse*; thus, the epi-sode becomes a meta-commentary and guide. Viewers must read the subtext, paying careful attention to how various threads of the narrative are woven together, to grasp the underlying moral commentary. Throughout the series, the Dollhouse is presented as a safe haven for the Actives and its local adminis-trators (Adelle DeWitt, Boyd Langdon, Topher Brink, and later Paul Ballard) as caring, protective, and sympathetic. But in "Belle Chose," the actions of DeWitt and the others are closely juxtaposed with the deeds of disturbed serial killer Terry Karrens. As Karrens mirrors the Dollhouse administrators and employees, the audience is reminded that DeWitt, Brink, Langdon, and Ballard are involved in the exploitation of human beings—which complicates the viewer's sympathies a great deal.

Throughout "Belle Chose," the Dollhouse's exploitative nature is rein-forced through the comparison of DeWitt and her subordinates with Kar-rens as well as through scenes juxtaposing two different sets of living "dolls." While Dollhouse Actives are literally reprogrammed to fulfill their clients' fantasies, Karrens drugs his victims until paralyzed and then arranges them into a tableau. In a large garage, he re-creates a summer afternoon game of croquet with his sisters, mother, and Aunt Sheila, using women he kidnapped. Initial close-up shots show Karrens's hands, carefully adjusting shoelaces and

---

2. Although beyond the scope of this essay, both scholars such as Wilcox (2010) and fans such as Sady (2009) have also noted that, throughout *Dollhouse*, Whedon directly invites viewers to question and scrutinize his role as creator and his own complicity in exploitative elements of television and media, particularly through the character of Topher Brink.

the collars of women's polo shirts; under the fluorescent lighting, it looks as though it might be a store employee, adjusting mannequins' clothing in a window display. Subsequent close-ups show him smoothing sweaters over torsos and rearranging hair and then reveal the women's frozen expressions and panicked eyes—the faces of living human beings. The camera captures a bead of sweat trickling down one woman's forehead, emphasizing the horror of Karrens's actions.

This scene, which shows Karrens playing with his victims as though they were dolls, is juxtaposed with a scene in which Dollhouse employee Paul Ballard takes Active Echo to be outfitted for an "engagement." As Echo is led away to try on clothing, the man from the wardrobe department tells Ballard, "Changing their insides is nothing. Zip, zip. But the outsides—that's art." This comment is played for laughs, but it highlights the incredible importance Dollhouse administrators place on the appearance and functionality of the Actives' bodies, something that often takes precedence over their well-being as individuals. Although the dialogue in this scene is humorous, the previous scene with Karrens and his victims does not allow an uncomplicated moment of comedy. Although Actives are routinely given new wardrobes for their engagements, after seeing Karrens play dress up with his victims, viewers should find it much more unsettling to watch Echo being led away to change costumes. The juxtaposition of these two scenes emphasizes that both Karrens's victims and the Actives' bodies are being appropriated without their consent.[3] Throughout the episode, many intercut scenes and narrative juxtapositions reinforce the comparison between the Dollhouse administrators and the more overtly sinister serial killer; these narrative techniques help reveal the feminist perspective of Whedon and his creative team.

Other episodes similarly rely on narrative juxtaposition to create a feminist subtext and explicate the unstated perspective(s) of the show's creators and writers. In "Belonging" (2.4), intercut images of the Active Sierra at different stages of her life emphasize how the Dollhouse has manipulated and exploited her. We meet Priya, a woman still in possession of her own personality and free will, before she becomes Sierra. Priya angrily rejects the romantic advances of Dr. Nolan Kennard, a scene that fades abruptly into a shot of them blissfully kissing. The stark contrast between her reaction to Kennard in the two scenes shows something significant has taken place to change her opinion

---

3. On the vexed issue of consent and the Dollhouse contract, see Sutherland and Swan in this volume.

of him; the episode then reveals she has been turned into a Doll version of herself so Kennard can have a sexual relationship with her. This arrangement essentially amounts to serial rape, and by juxtaposing images of Priya at different stages of the story, the writers reiterate the vile nature of her kidnapping and exploitation. In some scenes, the Doll Priya is reserved and sweet, happily accepting Kennard's previously unwanted affections. Interwoven with these scenes are others that show her with ratty hair, dark bags under her wild eyes, her face streaked with tears as she insists men with guns are poisoning her. These disturbing images of Priya help build to the narrative climax: just before she has her revenge on Kennard, scenes of a smiling and happy Priya are closely intercut with scenes of a crazed, violent Priya struggling against orderlies who force her into a straitjacket. These images show such an extreme contrast and are pieced together with such a rhythm that the tension builds to a breaking point before Priya/Sierra kills Kennard.

Following this climax, shots of Priya/Sierra covered in Kennard's blood recall the graphic images from the show's second episode—the same images of a bloodied Echo sitting in the showers that prompted criticism from the *Washington Post*'s Tom Shales. But such violent images make it nearly impossible to ignore the depravity of the Dollhouse's activities, despite the sympathetic nature of many of the organization's employees. Graphic scenes of violent sex and sexualized violence make it impossible to believe, as DeWitt and Topher initially tell themselves, that the Dollhouse protects its Actives. Episodes such as "Belonging" and "Belle Chose" leave viewers extremely uncomfortable and permit little doubt that Whedon and his team abhor all forms of exploitation. Juxtaposition, then, is crucial to expressing Whedon's unequivocal condemnation of rape, human trafficking, and prostitution.

To fully understand the feminist potential of *Dollhouse*, though, we must consider not only Whedon's visual presentation and narrative techniques but also the thematic concerns of the show in conjunction with the prominent themes of his previous series and films. As noted, many of Whedon's works feature "hot chicks with superpowers." With these characters, he explores issues related to feminine sexuality and control of the female body, and in *Dollhouse*, he revisits his thematic concerns with the body as a site of struggle for social, political, and emotional power.

One particular feminist narrative Whedon revisits and develops throughout his work is what I call the "awakening narrative." This story line most often involves a young teenage girl's emotional and sexual awakening, which in the Whedonverses tends to coincide with her discovery, exploration, and acceptance of her physical strength, other powers and abilities, or both.

Whedon depicts this metamorphosis most prominently with several *Buffy* and *Firefly* characters, all of whom first appear during early or midadolescence. In a variation on this narrative, *Dollhouse* becomes distinctly focused on the "awakening" of the Actives midway through the first season. Not only does this story line thematically mirror the social, emotional, and sexual awakenings of other characters in the Whedonverses, but it also builds upon these story lines. Although Willow, Cordelia, and many others provide interesting and important variations on Whedon's awakening narrative, Buffy's and River's story lines provide especially striking comparisons to the *Dollhouse* Actives because Whedon uses similar imagery to highlight the growing personal awareness of these particular characters. Studying such closely matched imagery and narrative arcs helps us understand Whedon's continuing preoccupation with the same feminist themes, although these themes may not be obvious upon first viewing *Dollhouse*.

Buffy's awakening narrative portrays both her sexual development and her struggle to decide how her role as the Slayer will shape her identity overall. The series therefore depicts her "awakening" to both her desires and her extraordinary strength, and at times these are pitted against each other, illustrating how young women must juggle different roles, responsibilities, and types of power. Particular sequences that present Buffy waking from her dreams emphasize her burgeoning sexuality. As scholars such as Wilcox (2005), Melanie Wilson (2009), and Sara Swain (2010) have noted, the first image of our heroine in the entire series presents Buffy lying in bed, rolling back and forth as she experiences monstrous nightmares. Close-ups emphasize her smooth skin and full lips; lying between the pure white sheets and under a white comforter, she is the picture of sweetness and purity ("Welcome to the Hellmouth" 1.1). By presenting her as asleep, childlike, and vulnerable, Whedon introduces Buffy to his audience as sexually innocent. The moment she suddenly shakes herself awake, looking disoriented, can then be read as foreshadowing the sexual and emotional awakening that begins as she accepts her role as the Slayer and develops a relationship with the vampire Angel. Whedon states that this narrative arc was intended to portray typical adolescent sexual experiences, and even the supernatural consequence of their sexual encounter—the loss of Angel's soul—was meant to mimic the rejection that a normal teenager might experience after having sex (Whedon 2002). The show continues to trace her sexual awakening and development, and as Swain (2010) notes, the postcoital rejection and long-term abuse that Buffy suffers at the hands of Angelus significantly shape and hinder her romantic and sexual relationships from that point forward.

Whedon emphasizes the complexity of Buffy's development by repeatedly showing the heroine awakening from a literal sleep, visually calling attention to her growing sexual and emotional awareness. Several scholars argue that Buffy's dream sequence in the episode "Surprise" (2.13), which opens with Buffy once again stirring from sleep, is the moment of her sexual awakening (Wilcox 2005; M. Wilson 2009; Swain 2010). But although this dream certainly indicates that she is considering whether to consummate her relationship with Angel, this moment is one of many sexual awakenings that the heroine experiences throughout the show's seven television seasons. During the sequence, Buffy awakens and gets out of bed to get a drink, but when she opens the door to the bathroom, she finds herself in the local nightclub; it becomes obvious that she has "woken up" only within her own dream. After watching the vampire Drusilla kill Angel, she awakens, actually coming out of her dream at this point and jolting upright in alarm. Buffy's multiple "awakenings" in this sequence indicate that although she will engage sexually and emotionally with Angel on a level that she previously has not, there remains potential for her to discover new depths to her desires in the future, which she then does during her sexual trysts with Spike in Season 6.[4] In other words, Buffy experiences not one moment or phase of sexual awakening, but rather a series of awakenings, and with each step she takes, she becomes a more confident and empowered young woman. More realistic than a single rite of passage or initiation to the adult world, Buffy's series of awakenings provide a credible model of a young woman's maturation process, and the imagery used throughout the series reemphasizes the idea that self-awareness is a process or journey with many significant moments.

Whedon reworks this imagery with the character River, who remains peripheral for much of the short-lived series *Firefly* but eventually emerges as an important feminist role model and pivotal character in *Serenity*, a film featuring the same characters. Both of these texts are vital to understanding River's awakening narrative, which bridges what Whedon explores in *Buffy* and *Dollhouse*. Significantly, whereas Buffy becomes physically powerful at the onset of her sexual maturation process and is therefore able to defend herself against sexual assault, River's story is about a young girl who has not been

---

4. Buffy's sexual evolution continues in the Season 8 comics, where she experiences another awakening after beginning a lesbian relationship. Readers interested in the portrayal of Buffy's sexuality in Season 8 may note Carlen Lavigne's presentation "Buffy the Lesbian Separatist" (2009) and Frohard-Dourlent (2010).

able to prevent the violation of her body. Consequently, her journey is just as much about self-discovery as about reclamation and recuperation of her body and her identity.

Mirroring many scenes from *Buffy*, "Objects in Space" (*Firefly* 1.14) opens with River waking up in her bunk, foreshadowing the episode's awakening narrative. Lying under an off-white blanket and white sheets, River has skin and lips that are equally pale; similar to Buffy's frequent placement on white sheets and in a white wardrobe in dream sequences, these details suggest that River is pure—but somewhat unnaturally so. This visual characterization matches her overall depiction as a sixteen-year-old who acts more like a girl of five or six; the abuse of the Alliance doctors and scientists likely caused her to regress to a safer role. A close-up shows her lying completely still; suddenly, her eyes flash open and her lips part slightly. In terms of what has literally happened, the psychic River has been awakened by the thoughts of bounty hunter Jubal Early, which she can hear from some distance away. Besides depicting River regaining consciousness, this scene can be read as a moment of sexual awakening and the following scenes as a metaphor for River's exploration of her own body. Although *Serenity* is always referred to as "she," in this episode the ship is specifically equated with River, and after the shot of her in bed, she ambles through the ship and engages with *Serenity* in a very sensual way. Wide-eyed, she strokes the ship's walls and the mess-hall doorway as she crosses the threshold. She looks around with both fascination and bewilderment, as though she has not seen the ship before and does not understand what she is experiencing. This scene suggests she has retreated within a childlike persona for so long that she finds her sexuality quite baffling.

The thoughts and feelings of the other crew members, which River is able to psychically experience, reinforce this interpretation of the scene. Simon and Kaylee flirting, a sweetly romantic exchange, affirms the sensual nature of River's experiences. She encounters Jayne and Shepherd Book, discussing whether Book is allowed to have sex; upon hearing their vulgar thoughts, she retreats in shock and fright. She passes Zoe and Wash making out in the cockpit and psychically shares their experiences—in surround sound. As Wash runs his hands over his wife's body, shown in several close-up shots, River gasps. Swaying back and forth, she clutches and strokes her own arm. The moment is accompanied by a nondiegetic soundtrack of ocean waves, which emphasizes the way unfamiliar sexual feelings are washing over River. She backs away and then witnesses a conversation between Mal and Inara fraught with romantic and sexual tension. These interactions highlight River's own tension and confusion, reinforcing the idea first suggested by the image of her roused from sleep—that she is experiencing a sexual awakening.

Throughout "Objects in Space" and the film *Serenity*, River gains confidence in her own strength and takes possession of her own physical and psychic powers, becoming a heroine in her own right. Once timid, River single-handedly mows down a mob of Reavers when her brother and shipmates are injured. Though never depicted as fully comfortable with her sensuality, she becomes much more comfortable with herself overall and among the crew. Like Buffy, she is portrayed as both having a specific moment of awakening and continuing to mature and evolve.

On *Dollhouse*, the characters are not teenagers, so the Dolls' awakening is not the initial sexual awakening of early adolescence. Instead of a process of discovery, the Dolls experience a process of reclamation. Throughout the narrative arc, they take steps to regain control of their physical bodies and rediscover their identities, which are portrayed as being closely tied to their sexuality, and the story line continually depicts the female body as a site of conflict—others are vying for control both over and within these people. This struggle for power becomes particularly interesting when their original genetic makeup and the "Active architecture" that scientist Topher Brink has installed begin to war with each other for control over the body and identity of each Active. The Dolls must fight to reverse the brain-wiping process in order to "awaken" their true selves, a process that each of them experiences differently.

Through an oft-repeated sequence, Whedon emphasizes the thematic focus on the Dolls' reawakenings. Each time the Actives are wiped of a personality imprint, they stir from their unconscious state and ask, "Did I fall asleep?" Although they do not suspect him, it is while they "sleep" that scientist Topher Brink removes their memories, personality, and power. Therefore, almost every *Dollhouse* episode includes a sequence of one or more Actives waking up in the chair used to imprint them with new personalities. Despite the fact that they are supposedly asleep, the Actives' eyes remain wide open while they are being imprinted, so these sequences visually contrast the scenes of Buffy's and River's eyes flashing open. As the procedure ends, the Actives are breathless and gasping from the intense neurological exchange that takes place during the brain wipe, but they immediately become calm and trusting of the people around them. According to Dollhouse protocol, whenever an Active asks, "Did I fall asleep?" a nearby scientist or handler is to respond, "For a little while." This scripted exchange provides the Actives with false reassurance that they are now "awake," but they do not truly awaken until they begin to sense aspects of their original personalities and memories from their former lives, aspects deeply buried in their brains.

This awakening journey takes place over the course of the entire two seasons but becomes much more intense during the second season. The Actives have more frequent flashbacks to their original selves and become more conscious of personalities imprinted (supposedly only temporarily) in their brains. As these two types of memories emerge, the characters begin to understand what has been done to them. With this knowledge, they become less trusting and vulnerable; information they collect about the Dollhouse and its technologies often serves as either a catalyst or a milestone in the Actives' awakening. This process empowers them to break away from the control of Dollhouse administrators, reshape their identities based on both their previous selves and their experiences as Dolls, and establish new lives altogether.

Though Echo and the other Actives become fully aware of the theft of their identities and their subsequent exploitation in the episodes preceding the second-season finale, Whedon drives home the "awakening" narrative in "Epitaph Two" (2.13). The episode is set in the future when a large portion of the population has had their personalities "remote-wiped" and has not been imprinted with alternate personas. Topher, aware of the widespread damage that his technology has done, designs a way to restore the personalities of all the "Dumb Shows," and DeWitt and another character guide a group of these helpless individuals out of the Dollhouse so they are exposed to the pulse meant to restore their original identities. With blank expressions on their faces, the Dumb Shows gaze at the destruction around them; then Topher sets off the pulse, but viewers do not see the moment when it hits the group. Instead, the image of the blast cuts straight to a shot of DeWitt and her companion standing and surveying bodies that are peacefully laid out on the street, as though they have fallen asleep curled up next to each other. As they stir, they look up at DeWitt and around at the destroyed street, some of them showing more distress than others. But as they stand, the soundtrack helps create a hopeful atmosphere. Brink has essentially hit the reset button, returning these individuals' personalities and offering them a chance to rebuild their lives. Instead of in the Dollhouse labs underground, this moment takes place outside in the sunlight, symbolizing group empowerment that mirrors the sharing of Slayer power in the seventh-season finale of *Buffy*. Although no one asks DeWitt, "Did I fall asleep?" this climactic moment fulfills the promise of every artificial awakening that the Actives experienced within the Dollhouse: these once-powerless individuals now have the chance to (re)create themselves.

Ultimately, Whedon's awakening narratives explore what it means for a person—female or male—to establish an identity within the context of existing power structures that seek to control weaker members of society. Whereas Buffy's and River's narratives provide productive feminist role models for young women during adolescence, through the narratives of the Dollhouse Actives, Whedon expands this discourse on sexual awakening to include other possibilities. *Dollhouse* explores the stories of women at different stages of life, as well as both men and women who must rediscover or reclaim their sexual and emotional identities after some form of trauma.

Whedon's ongoing interest in portraying the liberation of both women and men indicates he is dedicated to feminist ideals and invested in developing a broader humanist ideology. The analysis of his various shows and these awakening narratives in particular illustrates that Whedon's belief in gender equality consistently informs even those works of his that feminists find most problematic, and the complexity of his narrative techniques spurs productive—albeit uncomfortable—conversations. In a retrospective of *Dollhouse*, Whedon states that he hopes "people can take feminists' ideals away from [the show]. The idea was very simply this woman doesn't exist. She literally doesn't exist and she builds herself from scratch. To me, that is the most powerful act that a person can do" ("Defining Moments" 2010). With *Dollhouse*, Whedon clearly intended to fuel a debate that would move his continuing commentary on sexuality, power, and the female body to a new arena. The awakening narratives in each of Whedon's series are tied to the others, a connection that creates a powerful overarching commentary on these subjects. Whether or not viewers agree that *Dollhouse* tackles feminist issues in an appropriate and effective manner, an analysis of these several series confirms that Whedon is indeed a feminist auteur.

Whedon Studies

A Living History, 1999–2013

TANYA R. COCHRAN

It was a spring evening in 2000.[1] After a long day of grad school, I plopped down on the sofa next to my apartment mate, Carla, who was already engrossed in her favorite guilty pleasure: Joss Whedon's *Buffy the Vampire Slayer* (1997–2003). Demons and vampires flashed across the television screen. Suddenly, slaying ensued. I snapped my head toward Carla. With a reproachful gasp, I cried, "*What* are you watching?" Carla sighed deeply, without peeling an eye away from the action, "Isn't Angel the most beautiful man you've even seen?!" Maybe. *But it's just not right*, I thought, *young girls fraternizing with vampires!* I felt a bit sanctimonious.

Carla summarized the plot: Angel used to be Angelus, an infamously cruel vampire, until he fed on the wrong woman, a gypsy whose family then cursed Angelus with a soul. Now Angel had spent a few hundred years trying to redeem himself, his soul a constant reminder of how cruelly he had tortured people in the past. But because he and Buffy had fallen in love and then consummated their love, Angel had experienced a moment of pure pleasure—the one occurrence, according to the terms of the curse, that would cause him to become the soulless Angelus once again. Now Buffy was heartbroken. Her first sexual encounter had resulted in the loss of her lover's soul and the re-creation of a vicious vampire; rightly, she was devastated.

---

1. An earlier, less-developed version of this essay appears in "Toward a Rhetoric of Scholar-Fandom" (2009), the doctoral dissertation I completed at Georgia State University in Atlanta under the direction of Lynée Lewis Gaillet, Mary Hocks, and Baotong Gu.

All I could muster was, "What kind of show is this?!" But when Carla lost interest because Angel (and David Boreanaz) left the narrative for a while, I kept peeking through splayed fingers and listening with wide-open ears.[2]

Soon I found myself in an uneasy position, inhabiting the liminal space between enthusiast and scholar. As my master's degree in rhetoric and composition at the University of Tennessee–Chattanooga unfolded, my pleasure for what at first seemed no more than a silly teen series increased; as my skills in rhetorical analysis sharpened, so my interest in studying contemporary media—especially television and fandom—intensified. In fact, my academic interest in these topics had begun just before I stumbled onto *Buffy*. As a scholar-fan,[3] I had initially become intrigued by Chris Carter's *The X-Files* (1993–2002), and it was the anthology *"Deny All Knowledge": Reading "The X-Files"* (2006) coedited by David Lavery, Angela Hague, and Marla Cartwright and including a chapter by Rhonda V. Wilcox (coauthored with J. P. Williams) that fortuitously led me, with the encouragement of my adviser, Eileen Meagher, to attend only my second professional and very first popular culture conference, the fall 1999 meeting of the Popular and American Culture Associations in the South in Roanoke, Virginia. That gathering altered the course of my graduate research as well as my career and introduced me, though only from a distance at that time, to Lavery and Wilcox, who were quickly to become the architects (some say "parents") of *Buffy* Studies. Soon I joined the growing number of intellectuals interested in Whedon's emerging body of work. More than a decade and a half later, it seems appropriate to review and record this community's living history.[4]

Though philosophers and scholars often wrestle with the accuracy of textbook histories, few would debate the importance of attempting to capture the moments and events that contribute to the development of an idea, an event, a community, a nation. In academia, documenting the emergence of a field or discipline, and specialties within a field, serves many purposes, one of which

2. My "Discovering *Buffy*" story represents only one of many. A collection of such narratives appears on the *Slayage* website at http://slayageonline.com/discoveringbuffy/index .htm.

3. This hyphenated term, its synonym *academic-fan* (or *aca-fan*, a term coined by Henry Jenkins), and the reverse of both (*fan-scholar* and *fan-academic*) were first explored in detail by Matt Hills in *Fan Cultures* (2002). These expressions refer to a liminal hybrid identity, one that has been a novel topic of scholarly inquiry in the past decade.

4. I am not the first to record portions of this history. Begin with Lavery 2004, Wilcox 2006, and Hornick 2012a for additional historical accounts of *Buffy* and Whedon Studies.

is self-reflection. Whereas some researchers posit that the body of scholarship focused on the works of Joss Whedon constitutes a subfield of television studies, itself a subfield of media or communications studies, others reject such a thesis.[5] A few in academia have also questioned the intensity of passion devoted by fellow scholars to such an endeavor.[6] Despite these debates, Whedon Studies has experienced significant growth since the first scholarly essays on *Buffy* were published in 1999. Defined at that time by only a few articles in several journals and a handful of conference presentations, today Whedon Studies represents a substantial body of academic literature (see bibliographies by Macnaughtan [2011] and Hornick [2012b]); *Slayage*, a blind peer-reviewed electronic journal celebrating in 2014 its thirteenth anniversary; *Watcher Junior*, a nearly decade-old blind peer-reviewed undergraduate journal; and the Whedon Studies Association (WSA), a US nonprofit organization with an international membership, initiated in 2008 and established in 2009 and now cosponsoring with the *Slayage* journal biennial conferences that began in the summer of 2004. Because of this progress, herein I chronicle some major milestones and note several significant figures who have made this specialized interdisciplinary area of study a reality. Because that reality involves me, I also narrate my own relationship with and role in the community of scholars, colleagues, and friends.

5. There are several scholars worth exploring on this topic; however, begin with Bradney 2006 for an overview.

6. In the 2003 essay "Feeling for Buffy: The Girl Next Door," Levine and Schneider stated their concern that current scholarship on *Buffy* lacked rigor because it bore the marks of fannishness. At that nascent moment in the history of Whedon Studies, they argued that little or no necessary self-reflection had been done, insisting that although *Buffy* deserved "a degree of scholarly attention," it was merely "a well-made and fairly unremarkable instance of popular culture" (2003, 301). Time has demonstrated otherwise. While the scholar-fan's identity and productions remain a valid topic of investigation, evidence suggests that *Buffy* is remarkable. That evidence includes a steady stream of academic as well as popular papers presented, essays written, and books published; many high school and college professors who continue to use *Buffy* to teach film, feminist theory, and philosophy (among other topics), or who simply teach *Buffy* and other Whedon texts (see, for example, Kreider and Winchell 2010); and new generations of young people around the globe who develop an appreciation for *Buffy* by way of syndication, DVD, or Internet streaming services. Levine, Schneider, and others who share their perspective about scholar-fans in general mistakenly assume that an academic's fannish passion produces *only* scholarly impotence when it can produce—and actually *has* produced—scholarly fecundity. Although my purpose is not to provide an elaborate response to these charges, such charges *are* present in the community's history, not unlike the histories of many fields and subfields that once were not but now are integrated into and respected by academia. Such challenges aid in any discipline's development because they obligate a new area of study to define itself.

In the early 1990s, budding script doctor and writer Joss Whedon penned the screenplay for the motion picture *Buffy the Vampire Slayer* (1992). After being submitted to the production company, the script was out of Whedon's hands, and the author had little to do with the final product, a film about which he later openly shared his disappointment. Whedon has repeatedly cited the casting of the film and the misinterpretation of the script as reasons for his dissatisfaction. He realized that, unfortunately, the chance to tell his story of the teen heroine in the way he had envisioned had likely passed; second chances are rare in Hollywood. It was with surprised joy, then, that Whedon was approached by Twentieth Century Fox several years later with an opportunity to bring Buffy and her cohorts to the small screen. On March 10, 1997, *Buffy the Vampire Slayer* premiered on the WB Television Network. Though quickly drawing the attention of its target teen audience, within a season and a half the series had captured a more diverse audience. In January 1998, *Mediaweek* reported that on the Tuesday *Buffy* aired alongside the series premiere of *Dawson's Creek* (1998–2003), "The night delivered record numbers in every under-50 demographic" ("WB Slays Records on Tuesday"). Among those viewers were many delighted entertainment critics as well as quite a few intrigued academics representing a variety of disciplines—from literature and linguistics to law and library science.[7]

In the summer of 1999, just two years after the series' premiere, some of the first academic publications analyzing *Buffy* appeared in the *Journal of Popular Film and Television*, essays by scholars Rhonda Wilcox and A. Susan Owen. In "'There Will Never Be a "Very Special" *Buffy*': *Buffy* and the Monsters of Teen Life," Wilcox (1999) notes the marked differences between the series and its contemporaries, programs such as *7th Heaven* (1996–2007), *Party of Five* (1994–2000), and *The Wonder Years* (1988–93). Specifically, she argues that the "very special episode"—on teen suicide, alcoholism, or the perils of encroaching adulthood—is a literal way of addressing the issues of teenage life, one that can seem melodramatic, didactic, and belittling to young adult viewers. In contrast and on at least two levels, *Buffy* deals with the same issues in a symbolic manner. On one level, fantastic monsters represent real-world problems. For example, when on Buffy's seventeenth birthday she

---

7. In "Mapping the Whedonverses," Hornick "introduce[s] the uninitiated to some of the best scholarship and resources available" in Whedon Studies (2012a, 458). Consequently, I attempt to avoid unnecessary repetition. See her piece for a detailed account of and some recommendations for such scholarly reading.

and Angel have sex for the first time, Buffy wakens to a stranger—a heartless, cruel, and soulless Angelus. Angel's transformation into Angelus produced a profound effect on many female fans who attested to the story line's reflection of their own realities.

On an even more sophisticated level, *Buffy* addresses the challenges of real life through language: "Buffy confronts the vampires of adulthood not only with weapons, but with words of her own," language that "starkly contrasts with that of the adults" (23, 16). As Wilcox observes, Buffy and her friends are not distinguished from adults simply by the words they choose. Whereas the adult characters may select more erudite vocabulary or generally know more about the world than their young charges, the teenagers "know different things," especially popular culture things: "When Buffy says in the ["I Robot, You Jane" (1.8)] episode, 'My spider sense is tingling,' she has to apologize to Giles: 'Pop culture reference—sorry.' When she complains in 'The Pack' [1.6] that Giles is refusing for once to consider a supernatural explanation, she says, 'I can't believe that you of all people would Scully me,' assuming knowledge of *The X-Files* television character famous for stretching rational explanations to cover unusual events" (22). Beyond references to popular culture, Wilcox notes that the teens rearrange word order for emphasis; turn verbs into nouns, adverbs into adjectives, and adjective into nouns; or make "metaphorical or metonymic substitutions" (22). These linguistic choices are deliberate on the part of Whedon and his team of writers, who have Willow remark, "The Slayer always says a pun or witty play on words, and I think it throws off the vampires" ("Anne" 3.1)—vampires, observes Wilcox, who are often linguistically associated with the adults in the series.

I detail Wilcox's argument for several reasons. Foremost, her essay was one of the first academic essays on *Buffy* to be published as well as the first one I read as an emerging scholar. After viewing only a few episodes of *Buffy* through splayed fingers and with wide-open ears, I desired more than the primary text; I required secondary sources—and not only fan sites or *Entertainment Weekly* reviews. So I went to the university library. I distinctly remember feeling surprised and then giddy the day I used the phrase "Buffy the Vampire Slayer" for what I thought would be a futile keyword search of the Modern Language Association Bibliography.[8] Because I had read her chapter in *"Deny*

---

8. Again, my story is not unique. While offering feedback on this chapter, one of my coeditor-friends, Cynthea Masson, noted in the margin, "This moment at which you enter the phrase into the MLA [database] is pivotal—this is exactly what happened to me. There comes

All Knowledge," I promptly recognized Wilcox's name in the very short list of results. With haste, I then filled out the paper-based interlibrary loan form and impatiently waited for an employee at a distant institution to locate the journal, make a photocopy of the essay, and send that copy to my university library where I could claim it. Once I had it in hand, I read voraciously and found my own experience echoed in the pages of the argument: I, too, was drawn to *Buffy* by its deeply affective metaphors and its clever and innovative dialogue. In fact, the language struck me (at that time in my midtwenties) on a more personal level than any after-school television special ever had or could have. Like Wilcox, I recognized the teens' language as part of their heroism and, by extension, part of my own everyday heroism.

In the same issue of the *Journal of Popular Film and Television*, A. Susan Owen, in *"Buffy the Vampire Slayer*: Vampires, Postmodernity, and Postfeminism,"* reads the show through the intersections of the elements listed in her subtitle, particularly noting both how the "television narrative appropriates body rhetorics and narrative agency from traditionally masculinist metanarratives in the horror and mystery genres" and how the characters navigate feminist politics and a postmodern world all while living in an idyllic—at least on the surface—contemporary American suburb (1999, 24). In addition to essays by Wilcox and Owen, that same summer linguist Michael Adams published the first of a two-part article in *Verbatim: The Language Quarterly* titled "Slayer Slang (Part 1)" (1999a) in which he explores *Buffy*'s impact on American English.[9] Also, at the University of North Texas, Ashley Lorrain Smith devoted a portion of her master's thesis, "Girl Power: Feminism, Girlculture, and the Popular Media" (1999), to the series, its genre, and its young female audience, and Dawn M. Heinecken addressed *Buffy* in a portion of her doctoral dissertation, "The Women Warriors of Television: A Feminist Cultural Analysis of the New Female Body in Popular Media" (1999). Before these academic publications were available, professors and students who were interested in *Buffy* had to rely solely on popular sources such as newspapers, magazines, and websites—such as the ever-helpful and thoughtful *WHEDONesque*—for discussions about the program. As a result, especially the articles written by Adams, Owen, and Wilcox became the scholarly bedrock

---

a moment in every potential Whedon scholar's life where the words 'Buffy the Vampire Slayer' are typed into a search engine—and thereafter, life changes."

9. In the fall, Michael Adams (1999b) published the second half on his *Verbatim* article, the work that led to his book-length study also titled *Slayer Slang* (2003).

for those of us beginning to study *Buffy*, foundational pieces that continue to be cited today.[10]

During 2000, *Buffy* was the subject of a half-dozen new academic essays and began to be a popular topic for conference presentations. Also that year, the first dissertation devoted entirely to the television series—*"Buffy the Vampire Slayer:* The Insurgence of Television as a Performance Text"—was completed by Michele Byers at the University of Toronto.[11] Just prior to this time, Lavery and Wilcox, longtime members of and acquaintances through the Popular and American Culture Associations in the South, began soliciting and receiving proposals for an anthology that would eventually be called *Fighting the Forces: What's at Stake in "Buffy the Vampire Slayer"* (see figure 1). They were, however, not the only ones thinking of preparing such a collection.

Published in 2001 by Tauris Parke was editor Roz Kaveney's *Reading the Vampire Slayer: An Unofficial Critical Companion to "Buffy" and "Angel"* (an updated version was published in 2004). I include the collection in this history yet distinguish it from *Fighting the Forces* according to traditional definitions of academic research.[12] This distinction is not to suggest the collection was unimportant to Whedon Studies; quite the opposite. It, too, became foundational work. As Wilcox has rhetorically queried, "Why ignore any source of knowledge or understanding?" (2006, 42).[13]

10. Also published in 1999 in the trade magazine *American Libraries* was GraceAnne DeCandido's "Bibliographic Good vs. Evil in *Buffy the Vampire Slayer*," an essay that explores how Buffy's Watcher, the librarian Giles, was influencing the public perspective of real librarians.

11. According to Macnaughtan, the earliest known academic piece that considered Whedon's work was the 1995 master's thesis "A Feminist Named Buffy? Women in Horror Films of the 1990s" by Alta E. Dethlefsen (2011, 263). As the date of the thesis suggests, Dethlefsen considered the film rather than the television series.

12. For example, *Reading the Vampire Slayer* is published by a popular press and aimed at a mainstream—albeit intelligent—audience (2004a). (I must note that the same press, though a different imprint, published *Investigating "Firefly" and "Serenity": Science Fiction on the Frontier* [2008b], the scholarly collection I coedited with Rhonda Wilcox.) A text such as Kaveney's might be considered *quasi* academic, a hybrid text, as it appeals in both content and style to fans as well as scholars. Also, the chapters in Kaveney's collection are written not by career scholars but by a mix of scholars, graduate students, and freelance journalists. Citations to scholarly works are in some cases fewer than would be expected in a purely academic collection, though citations to scholarly and popular works are included. Certainly, this anthology poses a challenge to categorization. Notably, it continues to be regularly cited by academics.

13. Wilcox's "In 'the Demon Section of the Card Catalogue': *Buffy* Studies and Television Studies" (2006) was published in *Critical Studies in Television* and reprinted by permission in *Slayage* the same year.

CFP: Buffy the Vampire Slayer (collection; 4/21/00)

Fighting the Forces: Essays on the Meaning of Buffy the Vampire Slayer

Rhonda Wilcox and David Lavery solicit your ideas, abstracts, or completed essays for an in-development book on *Buffy the Vampire Slayer*. The series is the intersection of many contending forces—gender, generation, culture, and more. Buffy's complex and ambivalent heroism is central to a series which is itself complex both thematically and structurally. From its language to its narrative arcs, from single characters to social cohorts, from pop culture allusions to foreshadowings of Columbine, Buffy constitutes a text worthy of study and appreciation. Possible topics range from allusions and ancillary texts to vampires, women in production, and Xander. Please see our website at <http://www.mtsu.edu/~dlavery/buffybook.html or contact us by email>:

Rhonda Wilcox
Humanities
Gordon College
Barnesville, GA 30204
<rhonda_w@falcon.gdn.peachnet.edu>

David Lavery
English Dept.
P.O. Box 70
Middle Tennessee State University
Murfreesboro, TN 37132
<dlavery@frank.mtsu.edu>

1. The original call for essays posted by Wilcox and Lavery on March 17, 2000, to the University of Pennsylvania's archive.

Quickly after *Reading the Vampire Slayer* appeared, *Fighting the Forces* (Wilcox and Lavery 2002) became the first academic collection devoted to the analysis of *Buffy*. The editing process, though, had begun in the late fall of 1999, when Lavery and Wilcox released their call for papers. The two quickly found themselves overwhelmed with submissions. In fact, the coeditors ultimately pored over 144 abstracts, knowing they could accept only 20 or so of the ones submitted. It was out of this difficult decision-making process that Lavery developed the idea for an online journal. In their letter to scholars whom they could not include in their anthology, Lavery and Wilcox announced the journal and solicited submissions (see figure 2). Shortly, a similar call would be posted to UPenn's announcement archive. As the coeditors explain, they learned that "two other collections of essays [one of them *Reading the Vampire Slayer*] on *Buffy* were also in the works. It seemed obvious that there was a not-soon-to-be-exhausted international critical and scholarly interest" ("Site History" 2012). As a result, in January 2001, even before *Fighting the Forces* had been published, *Slayage: The Online International Journal of "Buffy" Studies* made its debut on the World Wide Web.[14] From the journal's inception, Lavery and Wilcox, supported by an international editorial board,[15] have acted as coeditors of the blind refereed journal and maintain that *Slayage* "will continue to be published at least four times a year as long as interest warrants" ("Site History" 2012). To date, academic interest in the works of Joss Whedon has not significantly waned: *Slayage* published more than thirty issues and more than 150 essays in its first eleven years. Yet scholarship on Whedon's various texts is more widely distributed; publication venues—both academic and popular—are plentiful. As a result, Lavery and Wilcox, with the editorial board's support, made a decision in early 2012 to reduce the frequency of issues. Currently, the journal is published biannually rather than quarterly.

Because a handful of collections, *Slayage*, and several other journal issues devoted to *Buffy* all were published within months of one another, a sudden surplus of scholarly work became available. Consequently, it was necessary

14. As Wilcox notes, the idea for the journal began with David Lavery, who was inspired by *Whoosh!*, online birthplace of the International Association of *Xena* Studies; the actual "title *Slayage* was suggested by video artist / art writer Richard Gess" (2006, para. 6).

15. Editorial board members include or have included the following: Stacey Abbott, Michael Adams, Gerry Bloustien, Viv Burr, Tanya R. Cochran, Lynne Edwards, Greg Erickson, Lorna Jowett, Roz Kaveney, Donald Keller, Tanya Krzywinska, Matthew Pateman, Patricia J. Pender, Elizabeth L. Rambo, Jana Reiss, James B. South, and Sue Turnbull. The current associate editor is Deborah Wilson Overstreet.

19 May 2000

Rhonda Wilcox and I have now finished examining over one hundred and twenty proposals for FIGHTING THE FORCES: ESSAYS ON THE MEANING OF BUFFY THE VAMPIRE SLAYER[*] and have selected the finalists for the book. We are sorry to inform you that your proposal was not one of them.

We both want to thank you for your interest in our project. The overwhelming response to the call for papers for FIGHTING THE FORCES has, however, inspired a spin-off.

We are contemplating starting an electronic [Buffy] journal, similar to WHOOSH, the online XENA journal. It will be called SLAYAGE and will be edited by Rhonda and me. The journal will be refereed by an editorial board now in development. Each submission will be read by at least two critics, and, if found worthy, published on the web. The website for SLAYAGE can be found here: <http://www.mtsu.edu/~dlavery/slayage.html>.[**]

Please feel free to resubmit your finished essays to SLAYAGE.

Unless we hear an objection from you, we will keep your name on a mailing list and inform you of further developments as we find a publisher for FIGHTING THE FORCES.

David Lavery and Rhonda Wilcox

* Note that the final title of the collection is *Fighting the Forces: What's at Stake in Buffy the Vampire Slayer* (2002).
** Today, the site is located at <http://slayageonline.com>.

2. This letter is shared with permission by the authors and marks the first mention of *Slayage* as an academic journal.

to begin a bibliography as a time-saving device for researchers desiring to become or remain informed. In the December 2002 issue of *Slayage* (2, no. 3), Derik A. Badman published the "Academic *Buffy* Bibliography," the first list of approximately 160 entries that he was simultaneously hosting on a Web page (no longer available). In the introduction to the *Slayage* version, Badman admits that he "was not able to limit the scope of this project with any clear cut boundaries" (para. 2). Consequently, the entries are based on his own understanding of what constitutes "academic." Internet content especially posed a challenge, because there was simply too much of it to sift through and judge. For a brief time, David Lavery attempted to build upon Badman's work and keep an updated bibliography on the *Slayage* website; he even began to maintain two versions—one strictly alphabetical, the other divided into the discipline, method, or approach each source represented—from aesthetics to textual criticism, from criminal justice to political science. The task, however, was all-consuming as more and more scholarship appeared across many disciplines. In 2005, Alysa Hornick (2012a) volunteered to assume responsibility for the bibliography. Today, still in her hands, *Whedonology: An Academic Whedon Studies Bibliography* (2012b) is an "always-evolving," extremely valuable document to Whedon Studies. Proving the usefulness of such texts, in 2011 Don Macnaughtan published *The Buffyverse Catalog: A Complete Guide to "Buffy the Vampire Slayer" and "Angel" in Print, Film, Television, Comics, Games, and Other Media, 1992–2010*, a selectively annotated text that includes both academic and important popular sources.[16]

Interest in keeping track of and publishing essays on Whedon's texts has never been limited to seasoned scholars. Thus, in July 2005, coeditors Lynne Edwards and Katy Stevens, in association with *Slayage*, launched *Watcher Junior: The Undergraduate Journal of "Buffy" Studies*, a blind refereed publication.[17] The electronic journal, now subtitled *The Undergraduate Journal of Whedon Studies*, currently boasts six volumes and eight issues comprising twenty-six essays. After several years at the helm, Edwards and Stevens passed editorial duties and site maintenance over to David Kociemba and Kristen

16. Badman, Hornick, and Macnaughtan have master's degrees in library and information science.

17. Editorial board members include or have included the following: Jes Battis, Tanya R. Cochran, James Francis Jr., Hélène Frohard-Dourlent, Candra Gill, Jacob Held, Alysa Hornick, Jodie A. Kreider, Lori C. Patton, Caroline Ruddell, Cynthia Ryan, Lauren Schultz, Arwen Spicer, Jennifer Stokes, Meghan K. Winchell, and Kristopher Karl Woofter.

Romanelli, respectively. Additionally, Kociemba and Romanelli regularly engage with readers on the journal's blog.

The same interest that has kept *Slayage* and *Watcher Junior* viable remains alive and well among academic conference participants. The number of conference presentations on *Buffy* and *Angel* (1999–2004), *Buffy*'s spin-off, sharply increased at the beginning of the new century, jumping from fewer than ten in 2000 to close to one hundred in 2002.[18] The dramatic increase in such presentations was largely owing to one conference. In October 2002, the University of East Anglia in the United Kingdom became the first academic institution to host a conference devoted to Whedon's *Buffy*. Titled "Blood, Text, and Fears: Reading around *Buffy the Vampire Slayer*," the event was organized by Catherine Fuller, Scott MacKenzie, Carol O'Sullivan, and Claire Thomson and was a collaborative effort among several university departments: the School of Language, Linguistics, and Translation Studies; the School of English and American Studies; and the British Centre for Literary Translation. In a university press release, Thomson comments on the interest the call for proposals attracted: "We were astonished to be inundated with submissions from scholars of all ages and degrees of distinction, from all over the world" (quoted in "Blood, Text, and Fears" 2002). Actually, this bringing together of intellectuals from a multitude of disciplines and institutions was one of the organizers' goals, a goal they easily met. Approximately 160 people were in attendance, 60 of them presenters from Australia, Canada, Italy, New Zealand, the United Kingdom, and the United States.[19] According to MacKenzie, other goals for the conference included exploring the cultural significance of *Buffy* and *Angel*, particularly through disciplinary lenses—philosophy, literary theory, gender studies, musicology—and dismantling the distinction between "'high-brow' and 'popular' culture": "Why shouldn't well-made television tell us just as much about ourselves and our world as canonical literature?" (quoted in "Blood, Text, and Fears" 2002). To most media scholars, the answer to MacKenzie's question is obvious: television does just that.[20]

18. It is difficult to accurately record conference presentations, as programs are not always accessible. The numbers I report here are estimates based on the careful work of Macnaughtan (2011) and Hornick (2012b).

19. *Salon.com*'s Stephanie Zacharek (2002), a conferee and presenter, reports that the two-day program could accommodate only half of the approximately 120 proposals submitted to the conference organizers.

20. See Turnbull 2004 and Wilcox 2006 regarding the reciprocal relationship between *Buffy* and television studies.

As was the case with conference presentations, a dramatic increase in academic essays occurred at the beginning of the new century. Between 2000 and 2001, scholarly journal articles rose from fewer than five to nearly thirty. This excess was mostly the result of *Slayage*; it published more than twenty essays in 2001. Nevertheless, significant cross-pollination occurred in academia in regard to *Buffy* and, more and more often, *Angel*. In addition to *Slayage*, essays appeared in *Educational Studies*, *European Legacy*, *Intensities: The Journal of Cult Media*, *Journal of American and Comparative Cultures*, *Journal of Popular Culture*, *Popular Culture Review*, and *Television Quarterly*. Even though in its first decade *Slayage* published approximately two dozen essays a year, journal articles continued to proliferate, peaking at nearly forty in 2005, two years after *Buffy* ended its seventh and last season on television. Of course, some of these fertile years occurred because periodicals such as *Refractory: A Journal of Entertainment Media* and the *European Journal of Cultural Studies* devoted special issues in 2003 and 2005, respectively, to Whedon's works.[21] Again, these refereed essays addressed disparate topics from a wide range of disciplinary perspectives and thus appeared in a variety of publication venues—both print and online.

Also worth noting are the many popular sources that were being produced at this time, mainstream works that meaningfully influenced scholarship on Whedon. Though not an exhaustive list, these works included three volumes of *The Watcher's Guide* published by imprints of Simon and Schuster in 1998, 2000, and 2004. Respectively, the guides were coauthored by Christopher Golden and Nancy Holder; Holder, Jeff Mariotte, and Maryelizabeth Hart; and Paul Ruditis. Also published in 2002 was Nikki Stafford's *Bite Me! An Unofficial Guide to the World of "Buffy the Vampire Slayer,"* a volume updated and rereleased in 2007. Importantly, Holder and Stafford would later play key roles in the academic conferences on Whedon's texts organized by Lavery and Wilcox and sponsored by *Slayage*.

During the same decade (2001–11), nearly twenty single-authored books that analyze, in particular, *Buffy* and *Angel* were published,[22] as well as more than fifteen edited collections that examine not only *Buffy* and *Angel* but also

21. Currently, *Refractory*'s special issue on *Buffy the Vampire Slayer* resides at http://blogs.arts.unimelb.edu.au/refractory/category/browse-past-volumes/volume-2/.

22. Notably, not all of these books were written in English. For example, significant works were published in Italian and German, respectively: Barbara Maio's *Buffy the Vampire Slayer* (Aracne, 2004) and Marcus Recht's *Der Sympathische Vampir: Visualisierungen von Männlichkeiten in der TV-Serie "Buffy"* (2011).

Firefly (2002), *Serenity* (2005), *Dr. Horrible's Sing-Along Blog* (2008), and *Dollhouse* (2009–10). Well over a hundred doctoral dissertations and master's theses—in Danish, English, French, German, Icelandic, Italian, Norwegian, Portuguese, and Spanish—were penned and approved (Macnaughtan 2011, 262–67). Also, nearly forty chapters were included in anthologies devoted to broad media-related topics rather than specifically to *Buffy* and its televisual siblings. Since 2011, of course, even more work has appeared, and much is forthcoming, including at least two important anthologies that consider race and (dis)ability in Whedon's texts, topics that have been underexplored. The first, tentatively titled "Beyond Light and Dark: Race, Ethnicity, Power, and Privilege in Joss Whedon's Works," is being edited by Mary Ellen Iatropoulos and Lowery A. Woodall III, the latter, tentatively titled "Blood, Body, and Soul: Health, (Dis)Ability, and Medicine in Joss Whedon's TV Worlds," by Tamy Burnett and AmiJo Comeford. Though difficult to track, around the globe and in sites from classrooms to conferences, it appears that roughly seventy-five to a hundred papers on Whedon's various narrative worlds (or Whedonverses) are delivered each year, some the result of Whedon-centric conferences like "Blood, Text, and Fears" and some the result of focused subject areas such as "The Works of Joss Whedon," an area of the Southwest Texas Popular and American Culture Association chaired by Alyson R. Buckman (California State University–Sacramento) and Tamy Burnett (University of Nebraska–Lincoln). *Slayage* itself began to sponsor such gatherings in 2004.

Once the online journal was established and it was clear to Lavery and Wilcox that interest was not only healthy but also thriving, the seemingly obvious next step was to organize a conference. Two other conferences and three symposia had already occurred: as mentioned above, the University of East Anglia's "Blood, Text, and Fears" (October 19–20, 2002), organized by Fuller, MacKenzie, O'Sullivan, and Thomson; as well as the University of Melbourne's "The Buffyverse: A Symposium" (November 21, 2002), organized by Angela Ndalianis; the University of South Australia–Adelaide's "Staking a Claim: Exploring the Global Reach of *Buffy*" (July 22, 2003), organized by Geraldine Bloustien; the University of Melbourne's "Spectacle, Rhythm, and Eschatology" (July 24, 2003), organized, again, by Ndalianis; and, in London, Open University's "Greeks and Romans in the Buffyverse: Classical Threads in Fantasy and Science Fiction on Contemporary Television" (January 7–8, 2004).[23]

---

23. Though not entirely devoted to Whedon's work, a group of *Buffy*-centric papers was also presented in July 2003 at "Sonic Synergies, Creative Cultures" at the University of South

All five of these events, though, had been in locations outside of the United States, the birthplace of Whedon's many narratives. As a result, Lavery and Wilcox planned the first *Slayage* conference on *Buffy the Vampire Slayer* to be hosted in Nashville, Tennessee, by Middle Tennessee State University, the institution with which Lavery was and still is affiliated.

Many scholars, fans, fan-scholars, and scholar-fans anticipated the conference that ran from Thursday, May 27, 2004, to Monday, May 31. Approximately four hundred people were present, making it a very well-attended, topically varied, and disciplinarily diverse event.[24] Delivered during that Memorial Day weekend were four keynote addresses, by TV critic David Bianculli (*Fresh Air with Terry Gross*), popular author Nancy Holder, philosophy professor James B. South (*"Buffy the Vampire Slayer" and Philosophy: Fear and Trembling in Sunnydale* [2003]), and media scholar Sue Turnbull; six featured presentations, by Michael Adams, Gerry Bloustien, David Lavery, John Pungente, Jana Reiss (*What Would Buffy Do? The Vampire Slayer as Spiritual Guide* [2004]), and Rhonda Wilcox; and nearly two hundred papers, mine included.

A sense of seriousness infused the panels—serious thought, analysis, critique. Yet, certainly, festiveness also permeated the halls of the Nashville Renaissance Hotel. Serious fun: an ideal blend. At the Thursday-evening opening reception, I remember seeing a lone conferee in Spike cosplay[25] as well as both fan and scholar attendees excitedly engaged in conversation. During the Friday-night banquet, Mr. Pointy Awards (named for Buffy's favorite wooden stake) were announced for best article-length and book-length scholarship published that year as well as best conference paper delivered at *Slayage*,[26] Buffy-centric books were distributed as door prizes, and there was singing, a

---

Australia–Adelaide. Importantly, one of the keynote addresses concerned *Buffy* Studies and was delivered by David Lavery. The presentation was later published in *Slayage* (Lavery 2004).

24. I am greatly indebted to my longtime friend Wendy Campbell for making me aware of the first *Slayage* conference and attending it with me.

25. *Cosplay*, an amalgamation of *costume* and *play*, refers to a type of performance art or costumed role playing common among science fiction, fantasy, and anime fans.

26. That year, the book-length award was given to Michael Adams for *Slayer Slang*, the article-length award to Jes Battis for "'She's Not All Grown Yet': Willow as Hybrid/Hero in *Buffy the Vampire Slayer*," and the conference paper award to Sue Turnbull for "'Not Just Another *Buffy* Paper': Towards an Aesthetics of Television." The tradition of recognizing the best published scholarship in Whedon Studies has continued every year since then. A full listing of award nominees and recipients can currently be found on the *Slayage* website. In 2010, under the auspices of the Whedon Studies Association, the article and book awards became juried. The conference paper award continues to be voted on site by all conferees.

group rendition of the entire "Once More, with Feeling" (6.7) *Buffy* episode. Everything seemed to take place on a grand scale, as if this gathering would be the only one of its kind. Indeed, it was grand enough to garner the attention of both local and international news agencies and publications, among them the *Toronto Star*, the Associated Press, London's *Times Higher Education Supplement*, and CNN's *Headline News*.

At the closing ceremony, Lavery and Wilcox asked an important question of the audience members: was there enough interest to continue holding conferences? The overwhelming response from the international assembly was affirmative. Planning began for a second biennial conference.

In the meantime, Viv Burr organized "Bring Your Own Subtext: Social Life, Human Experience, and the Works of Joss Whedon." The two-day event was held at the University of Huddersfield (United Kingdom), June 29–July 1, 2005. Invited speakers were Tanya Krzywinska and Zoe-Jane Playdon. Also, "Beyond *Buffy*? 'Teens' on TV: Audience, Industry, Identity" was held June 2006 at Oxford Brookes University (United Kingdom).

The "*Slayage* Conference on the Whedonverses," a new moniker to represent Whedon's growing number of texts, was held May 26–28, 2006, at Gordon College (now Gordon State College) in Barnesville, Georgia, institutional home to Rhonda Wilcox. Keynote speakers included film studies scholar Stacey Abbott (noted for her multiple works on *Angel*), Michael Adams, Nancy Holder, and Roz Kaveney. Featured presentations were delivered by Gerry Bloustien, Lynne Edwards, Lorna Jowett (*Sex and the Slayer: A Gender Studies Primer for the "Buffy" Fan* [2005]), and David Lavery.

A year later, in 2007, Sabrina Boyle organized "It's the End of the World . . . Again: Why *Buffy* Still Matters: A *Buffy the Vampire Slayer* Mini-Conference," a one-day event that convened at the University of North Carolina–Greensboro on March 16 and featured Rhonda Wilcox as keynote speaker. Also, "*Buffy* Hereafter: From the Whedonverse to the Whedonesque: An Interdisciplinary Conference on the Work of Joss Whedon and Its Aftereffects" was held in Istanbul, Turkey, October 17–19. Tuna Erdem was the convener of this academic gathering.

In 2008, the third *Slayage* conference was hosted June 5–8 by local arrangements chair Kevin Durand at Henderson State University in Arkadelphia, Arkansas. Keynote presentations were delivered by Wesleyan University's Jeanine Basinger, one of Joss Whedon's film professors; culture and media studies scholar Matthew Pateman (*The Aesthetics of Culture in "Buffy the Vampire Slayer"* [2006]); literature professor Elizabeth L. Rambo (coeditor, *Buffy Goes Dark* [2009]); and Nikki Stafford. Featured speakers included Stacey

Abbott, David Lavery, J. Michael Richardson and J. Douglas Rabb (coauthors, *The Existential Joss Whedon: Evil and Human Freedom in "Buffy the Vampire Slayer," "Angel," "Firefly," and "Serenity"* [2006]), and Rhonda Wilcox.

A year later, "Buffy Tueuse de Vampires" convened at Cité Internationale Universitaire de Paris on June 26, 2009.

In 2010, the fourth *Slayage* conference was hosted by local arrangements chairs Tamara Wilson and James Wilson at Flagler College in St. Augustine, Florida. Over June 3–6, keynote speakers included Janet K. Halfyard (coeditor, *Music, Sound, and Silence in "Buffy the Vampire Slayer"* [2010]), Lorna Jowett, and K. Dale Koontz (*Faith and Choice in the Works of Joss Whedon* [2008]). Featured presentations were given by me (Tanya Cochran), David Lavery, Cynthea Masson, and Rhonda Wilcox.

Though not academic and not conferences, two major events related to Whedon Studies occurred between the fourth and fifth *Slayage* meetings. On her Quality Television blog *Nik at Nite*, Nikki Stafford introduced in January 2011 a yearlong "*Buffy* Rewatch." A team of writers—from fans to scholars—contributed thoughtful, accessible commentary on each episode of all seven seasons of the television series. For some readers, it was the first time they had watched *Buffy*. Many willfully gave in to the pleasure of the text and the talk. On March 4, 2011, writer and editor Robert Moore launched "Spotlight: Joss Whedon" for *PopMatters*, a culture magazine published online. Over the course of the next month and a half, a large team of writer-commentators, including many academics as in the case of the "*Buffy* Rewatch," participated in critiquing for a mainstream audience every major Whedon text. The spotlight was so popular that Titan Books approached *PopMatters* about collecting and printing the essays, aiming for a release date several months prior to the opening weekend of Whedon's *The Avengers* (2012). With the quick and astute work of Mary Alice Money as editor, *Joss Whedon: The Complete Companion* appeared as planned in the spring of 2012—with new content to boot.

The fifth biennial *Slayage* conference was hosted July 12–15, 2012, by local arrangements chairs Hélène Frohard-Dourlent, Sharon Sutherland, and Sarah Swan at the University of British Columbia–Vancouver, marking the first time a *Slayage* conference was held outside of the continental United States. Keynote speakers included women's and gender studies professor Tamy Burnett (coeditor, *The Literary "Angel": Essays on Influences and Traditions Reflected in the Joss Whedon Series* [2010]), media and cultural studies scholar Jonathan Gray (*Show Sold Separately: Promos, Spoilers, and Other Media Paratexts* [2010]), and medievalist Cynthea Masson (noted for numerous published academic essays representing every major Whedon text and coeditor of this volume). Featured presentations were delivered by Alyson Buckman, Hélène Frohard-Dourlent, Nancy Holder, and Ananya Mukherjea.

Before the next *Slayage* conference, "Joss in June: A Conference on the Works of Joss Whedon" was scheduled for June 29, 2013. The one-day event convened at the LeGrand Conference Center on the campus of Cleveland Community College in Shelby, North Carolina. Hosts Dale Guffey[27] and Ensley F. Guffey intentionally encouraged participants to focus on Whedon's comics, as little scholarly work has been done in the area. In addition to audience members, they welcomed approximately forty presenters, and Rhonda Wilcox delivered the keynote address on Whedon's film of Shakespeare's *Much Ado about Nothing*.

In February 2013, members of the Whedon Studies Association voted to hold the sixth biennial conference, an event marking the tenth anniversary of the gathering, at California State University–Sacramento, institutional home of local arrangements chairs Alyson Buckman and Susan Fanetti. In honor of the anniversary, special events and guest speakers were planned.

Though the number of participants fell after the inaugural *Slayage* conference, a decline to be expected, attendance at subsequent meetings has remained stable and enthusiasm has not diminished. However, having no central organization for support—especially financial and administrative—the third conference in Arkansas included an open discussion among attendees and conveners Lavery and Wilcox concerning the feasibility of subsequent meetings. The possibility of not gathering in 2010 disappointed many; some proposed action. By the conclusion of the conference, several future locations had been discussed—including British Columbia and Quebec as well as California, Florida, and Nebraska—and fellow scholars had stepped forward to offer financial and administrative support to ensure that the conference continued. In a surprising turn, Lavery and Wilcox discovered that a benefactor, Tom Connelly, wished to give a substantial monetary gift. With the promise of such a considerable donation, *Slayage* and Whedon scholars were about to take a new and important path in their unfolding history.

Hearing of a potential patron for future conferences, I, a regular *Slayage* conference attendee and member of the community, began to think and casually discuss with a colleague and friend, Meghan Winchell, the need for a formal organization. In August 2008, I scribbled down a list of possible names for the conceptual association, a list with which I planned to approach

27. Dale publishes under the name K. Dale Koontz.

Lavery and Wilcox. By this time, both were close friends of mine, and Rhonda and I had together recently completed the edited collection *Investigating "Firefly" and "Serenity": Science Fiction on the Frontier* ([2008]).[28] Before I could contact either, though, Rhonda e-mailed me with the news that she and David had been mulling over a similar idea: seeking nonprofit status for *Slayage* in order to responsibly accept monetary gifts. In September 2008, Rhonda requested that I join her and David as a founding board member of the Whedon Studies Association, the name that seemed most appropriate to us. I agreed, yet everything was very informal; after all, we had just appointed ourselves executive officers of a yet-to-be-created organization. In essence, the decisions we were making simply represented a grassroots movement in the direction of something more formal but still intangible.

In the following two months, however, the intangible quickly became tangible as Rhonda pursued legal status. Registered in the state of Georgia, the Whedon Studies Association became an educational nonprofit entity on October 16, 2008. Two and a half months afterward, on December 30, our inaugural board meeting occurred by means of conference call from Rhonda's home in Decatur, Georgia (because I visit my immediate family and home state every Christmas, I was physically present for a holiday British-style tea at Rhonda's beforehand [as was colleague and friend Mary Alice Money], and David joined us via phone from his home in Murfreesboro, Tennessee). It was a thoroughly joyous occasion—for many reasons.

As secretary-treasurer of the new association, I began soliciting names of charter associates in February 2009 when the announcement about the WSA was made public on the *Slayage* website (see figure 3). When this volume went to press, the organization had close to three hundred associates, a number more or less equal to the longer-established William Faulkner Society. In the fall of 2009, Rhonda, David, and I as board members and executive officers voted (with the approval of the editorial board) to change *Slayage*'s subtitle to *The Journal of the Whedon Studies Association*, a more accurate reflection of the journal's content and now affiliation. During this time, with Rhonda's assistance, I also began the task of completing the extensive paperwork necessary for the association to secure its 501(c)(3) or tax-deductible designation under the US federal income tax Internal Revenue Code, a status it was

---

28. I appreciate Rhonda collaborating with a novice coeditor. What I learned during our editorial and publishing process, I have passed on to students and peer scholars—a practice of sharing knowledge consistently observed among Whedon and his creative partners.

The Whedon Studies Association

[1] The Dickens Society, the Wordsworth-Coleridge Association, the Flannery O'Connor Society—for generations, scholars have been banding together to support each other in the study of admired works of important creators. We are using the first 2009 issue of this journal to announce the official formation of the Whedon Studies Association, a non-profit organization devoted to the study of the works of Joss Whedon and his associates.

[2] The word "official" is purposefully chosen. In an informal sense, there has been an "association" of Whedon scholars since October of 2002, when University of East Anglia at Norwich professors Carol O'Sullivan, Claire Thomson, Catherine Fuller, and Scott MacKenzie hosted over 200 scholars for the first international conference on Joss Whedon, focusing on his first and most famous television show, *Buffy the Vampire Slayer*. Since then, scholars have gathered at places as far-flung as Adelaide, Australia (convener Geraldine Bloustien), Istanbul, Turkey (convener Tuna Erdem), and Nashville, Tennessee (convener David Lavery and coconvener Rhonda Wilcox). The latter was the location of the first of the biennial *Slayage* conferences, the regular meetings of which have supported the extensive growth of Whedon scholarship. Whedon scholarship now includes the publication of a journal (once specifically on [*Buffy the Vampire Slayer*], but now open to submission on any Whedon-associated work); multiple scholarly books in any given year; articles published in a variety of scholarly venues; annual awards for the best work in the field; dissertations and theses by Ph.D.'s, M.A.'s, and honors undergraduates; a comprehensive bibliography of books, articles, and conference papers in the field (maintained by Alysa Hornick), and more. It seems only appropriate that this very active scholarship should be supported by an official association, and during the course of 2008, Tanya Cochran, David Lavery, and Rhonda Wilcox took the steps to legally establish the Whedon Studies Association.

[3] It is our hope that this organization will further the study of the work of Whedon and his associates long after the current generation of scholars is active. As a peer-reviewed journal, the *Slayage* journal—now officially the Whedon Studies Association journal—is a complex and challenging

3. The official announcement of the Whedon Studies Association written by its president, Rhonda V. Wilcox.

enterprise; David Lavery, who originally conceived it, and Rhonda Wilcox, the other founding editor, hope to see it continue after their eventual retirement. It should also be noted that the establishment of this non-profit organization will facilitate the literal "association," the gathering, of Whedon scholars. While the WSA still plans to arrange conferences in connection with sponsoring universities, the establishment of the WSA as a legal entity will give greater independence of decision-making, particularly in terms of choice of location (e.g., the WSA hopes to return the next conference to a hotel setting).

[4] We invite all Whedon scholars, whether writers or readers, to join the organization. Please send your name and email address to the WSA's secretary/treasurer Tanya Cochran at wsamembers@gmail.com. (Please send in your name even if you have been previously associated with the *Slayage* conference or other related scholarly endeavors.) Those who enroll in the WSA will receive first notice of new issues of the journal; information about upcoming conferences; shared calls for papers for upcoming books; announcements of association meetings; and more. In terms of the organization's finances (and, as Buffy discovered in season seven, there are indeed costs for simply existing), the WSA proposes to operate in a fashion somewhat similar to NPR (the U.S.'s National Public Radio). For anyone who can provide monetary assistance, $25.00 is the suggested contribution for those who are employed full-time; $10.00 is the suggested contribution for those employed less than full-time (presumably most students). However, we invite all devotees of Whedon scholarship to join the association, with or without financial contribution. We propose to call those who join in the first year "charter associates." We hope for hundreds of WSA scholars to gather face to face at the next *Slayage* / WSA conference in 2010.

---Rhonda V. Wilcox

granted on April 12, 2010. During that same spring, the WSA Facebook page, at the initiative of Shelley S. Rees, went live.[29] A virtual space for informal conversations and networking, it currently has close to four hundred participants who are quite active.

In the spring of 2012, as I and my coeditors were preparing the manuscript of this book, the WSA had its first open election. The organization's vice president simultaneously acts as president-elect, a provision that ensures the WSA maintains continuity. However, because David Lavery wished not to assume the presidency, I was encouraged to run for the position, something I eventually did. As Rhonda and David stepped back from officer duties, it became my responsibility and goal to pass on as much institutional memory as possible so that the association flourishes in the future. The year 2012 marked, then, not only the fifth biennial conference but also the beginning of a democratic transfer of leadership. From this point forward, WSA officers will be elected by their peers, the associates of the organization, and serve two-year terms. I am pleased and honored to be coming to a resting point in this living history as president of the WSA and to be serving alongside the other elected officers: vice president Stacey Abbott, secretary Kristopher Karl Woofter, and treasurer Cynthia A. Burkhead. In 2014, at the sixth biennial conference, I will be even more pleased and honored to hold with Rhonda the title of past president, knowing that Whedon Studies and the WSA will continue to prosper in the hands of our very capable scholar-friends.

I was attracted to *Buffy*, to Whedon, to his other narratives for many reasons. But I was especially drawn in by the abiding theme of chosen family. Chosen family is exactly what I have found, what I have made for myself. Not just in the stories, but also in this community, among those individuals who, like me, continue to explore and enjoy the intellectually complex and rewarding works of Joseph Hill "Joss" Whedon. In many ways, Whedon himself will determine whether scholarship on his various texts has a relatively short or long life. Two major film works were released in 2012, *The Cabin in the Woods* and *Marvel's The Avengers*; a film adaptation and television series premiered in 2013, Shakespeare's *Much Ado about Nothing* and *Marvel's Agents of S.H.I.E.L.D.*; and a *Dr. Horrible* sequel is supposedly on the horizon. With these and other texts, a long, healthy life seems likely.

---

29. In addition to Shelley, three Whedon Studies associates have from its debut maintained the Facebook page: Alyson Buckman, Hélène Frohard-Dourlent, and Ian Klein.

References

Contributors

Index

References

Abbott, Stacey. 2003. "Walking the Fine Line between Angel and Angelus." *Slayage: The Online International Journal of "Buffy" Studies* 3, no. 1. http://slayage online.com/Numbers/slayage9.htm.

————. 2005a. "From Madman in the Basement to Self-Sacrificing Champion: The Multiple Faces of Spike." *European Journal of Cultural Studies* 8, no. 3: 329–44.

————. 2005b. "Kicking Ass and Singing 'Mandy': A Vampire in LA." In *Reading "Angel": The TV Spin-off with a Soul*, edited by Stacey Abbott, 1–13. London: I. B. Tauris.

————. 2006. "'Cavemen vs. Astronauts—Weapons to Be Determined': Angel, Spike, and the Buddy Genre." Paper presented at SCW2: The *Slayage* Conference on the Whedonverses, Gordon College, Barnesville, GA, May 26–28.

————. 2009a. *Angel*. Detroit: Wayne State Univ. Press.

————. 2009b. "Dr. Horrible's Sing-Along Blog: A Cult TV Event without the TV." *CSTOnline*, Jan. http://www.criticalstudiesintelevision.com/index.php?siid =8871.

————, ed. 2010a. *The Cult TV Book*. London: I. B. Tauris.

————. 2010b. "Innovative TV." In *The Cult TV Book*, edited by Stacey Abbott, 91–99. London. I. B. Tauris.

Aberdein, Andrew. 2008. "The Companions and Socrates: Is Inara a Hetaera?" In *Investigating "Firefly" and "Serenity": Science Fiction on the Frontier*, edited by Rhonda V. Wilcox and Tanya R. Cochran, 63–75. New York: I. B. Tauris.

Achebe, Chinua. 1989. *Hopes and Impediments: Selected Essays*. New York: Doubleday.

Adams, Michael. 1999a. "Slayer Slang (Part 1)." *Verbatim: The Language Quarterly* 24, no. 3: 1–4.

————. 1999b. "Slayer Slang (Part 2)." *Verbatim: The Language Quarterly* 24, no. 4: 1–7.

————. 2003. *Slayer Slang: A "Buffy the Vampire Slayer" Lexicon*. Oxford: Oxford Univ. Press.

————, ed. 2006. "Beyond Slayer Slang: Pragmatics, Discourse, and Style in *Buffy the Vampire Slayer*." Special issue, *Slayage: The Online International Journal of "Buffy" Studies* 5, no. 4. http://slayageonline.com/Numbers/slayage20.htm.

Adams, Tony E. 2008. "A Review of Narrative Ethics." *Qualitative Inquiry*, no. 14: 175–94.

Adorno, Theodor W., and Anson G. Rabinbach. (1963) 1975. "Culture Industry Reconsidered." *New German Critique*, no. 6: 12–19.

"Afterlife." 2001. *Buffy the Vampire Slayer*. Season 6. Episode 3. Written by Jane Espenson. Directed by David Solomon. Los Angeles: Twentieth Century Fox Home Entertainment, 2003. DVD.

A.I. 2001. Written by Steven Spielberg and Stanley Kubrick. Directed by Steven Spielberg. Los Angeles: Dream Works.

Alexander, Lily. 2007. "Storytelling in Time and Space: Studies in the Chronotope and Narrative Logic on Screen." *Journal of Narrative Theory* 37, no. 1: 27–64.

Altman, Rick. (1999) 2010. *Film/Genre*. London: BFI.

"Amends." 1998. *Buffy the Vampire Slayer*. Season 3. Episode 10. Written and directed by Joss Whedon. Los Angeles: Twentieth Century Fox Home Entertainment, 2010. DVD.

"Angel." 1997. *Buffy the Vampire Slayer*. Season 1. Episode 6. Written by David Greenwalt. Directed by Scott Brazil. Los Angeles: Twentieth Century Fox Home Entertainment, 2010. DVD.

Angel. 1999–2004. Los Angeles: Twentieth Century Fox Home Entertainment. DVD.

"Angel: The Final Season." 2005. *Angel*. Season 5. Disc 6 (featurette). Los Angeles: Twentieth Century Fox Home Entertainment, 2006. DVD.

Angelini, Sergio, and Miles Booy. 2010. "Members Only: Cult TV from Margins to Mainstream." In *The Cult TV Book*, edited by Stacey Abbott, 19–27. London. I. B. Tauris.

Anna. 2009. "The Problem with *Dollhouse* Is Not That I Don't Understand Subtlety." *The Angry Black Woman* (online forum). Apr. 29, 2:39 p.m. http://theangryblackwoman.com/2009/04/28/the-problem-with-dollhouse-is-not-that-i-dont-understand-subtlety/.

"Anne." 1998. *Buffy the Vampire Slayer*. Season 3. Episode 1. Written and directed by Joss Whedon. Los Angeles: Twentieth Century Fox Home Entertainment, 2001. DVD.

"Are You Now or Have You Ever Been?" 2000. *Angel*. Season 2. Episode 2. Written by Tim Minear. Directed by David Semel. Los Angeles: Twentieth Century Fox Home Entertainment, 2003. DVD.

Armson, Rosalind. 2011. *Growing Wings on the Way: Systems Thinking for Messy Situations*. Devon: Triarchy Press.

Arnzen, Michael. 2008. "Weirdness Isolation and Sunnydale Syndrome." *Popular Uncanny* (blog), Aug. 9. http://www.gorelets.com/uncanny/theory/weirdness-isolation-and-sunnydale-syndrome/.

The Art of "Marvel's The Avengers." 2012. Written by Jason Surrell. Book design by Jeff Powell. New York: Marvel Worldwide.

Ashworth, Peter D. 2000. *Psychology and "Human Nature."* New York: Routledge.

Atkinson, Paul. 2010. "The Graphic Novel as Metafiction." *Studies in Comics* 1, no. 1: 107–25.

"The Attic." 2009. *Dollhouse.* Season 2. Episode 10. Written by Maurissa Tancharoen and Jed Whedon. Directed by John Cassaday. Los Angeles: Twentieth Century Fox Home Entertainment, 2010. DVD.

Auden, W. H. 1969. "September 1, 1939." In *Modern British Poetry,* edited by Louis Untermeyer, 461–62. New York: Harcourt, Brace, and World.

Baccolini, Raffaella. 2003. "'A Useful Knowledge of the Present Is Rooted in the Past': Memory and Historical Reconciliation in Ursula K. Guin's *The Telling.*" In *Dark Horizons: Science Fiction and the Dystopian Imagination,* edited by Raffaella Baccolini and Tom Moylan, 113–34. London: Routledge.

Bacon-Smith, Camille. 2003. "The Color of the Dark." *Slayage: The Online International Journal of "Buffy" Studies* 2, no. 4. http://slayageonline.com/Numbers /slayage8.htm.

"Bad Girls." 1999. *Buffy the Vampire Slayer.* Season 3. Episode 14. Written by Douglas Petrie. Directed by Michael Lange. Los Angeles: Twentieth Century Fox Home Entertainment, 2006. DVD.

Badman, Derik A. 2002. "Academic *Buffy* Bibliography." *Slayage: The Online International Journal of "Buffy" Studies* 2, no. 3. http://slayageonline.com/Numbers /slayage7.htm.

Baker, Katharine. 2008. "Once a Rapist? Motivational Evidence and the Relevancy of Rape Law." In *Women and the Law,* edited by Libby Adler, Lisa Crooms, Judith Greenberg, Martha Minow, and Dorothy Roberts, 186–99. 4th ed. New York: Foundation Press.

Bakhtin, Mikhail. (1941) 1993. *Rabelais and His World.* Translated by Hélène Iswolsky. Bloomington: Indiana Univ. Press.

———. 1982. *The Dialogic Imagination: Four Essays.* Edited by Michael Holquist. Austin: Univ. of Texas Press.

Baldwin, Kristen, and Bruce Frets. 1997. "The Week." *Entertainment Weekly,* Mar. 14, 68.

Bales, Kevin. 2000. *Disposable People: New Slavery in the Global Economy.* Berkeley: Univ. of California Press.

"Band Candy." 1998. *Buffy the Vampire Slayer.* Season 3. Episode 6. Written by Jane Espenson. Directed by Michael Lange. Los Angeles: Twentieth Century Fox Home Entertainment, 2010. DVD.

Banks, J. T. 2002. "The Story Inside." In *Stories Matter: The Role of Narrative in Medical Ethics,* edited by R. Charon and M. Montello, 218–26. New York: Routledge.

Barbeito, Patricia Felisa. 2005. "'He's Making Me Feel Things in My Body That I Don't Feel': The Body as Battleground in Accounts of Alien Abduction." *Journal of American Culture* 28, no. 2: 201–15.

"Bargaining, Part One." 2001. *Buffy the Vampire Slayer.* Season 6. Episode 1. Written by Marti Noxon. Directed by David Grossman. Los Angeles: Twentieth Century Fox Home Entertainment, 2010. DVD.

"Bargaining, Part Two." 2001. *Buffy the Vampire Slayer.* Season 6. Episode 2. Written by David Fury. Directed by David Grossman. Los Angeles: Twentieth Century Fox Home Entertainment, 2010. DVD.

Basinger, Jeanine. 1995. *A Woman's View: How Hollywood Spoke to Women, 1930–1960.* Middletown, CT: Wesleyan Univ. Press.

———. 2003. *The World War II Combat Film: Anatomy of a Genre.* Rev. ed. Middletown, CT: Wesleyan Univ. Press.

———. 2008. "Joss Whedon, Film Major: A+ All the Way." Keynote address presented at SCW3: The *Slayage* Conference on the Whedonverses, Henderson State Univ., Arkadelphia, AR, June 5–8.

Battis, Jes. 2003. "'She's Not All Grown Yet': Willow as Hybrid/Hero in *Buffy the Vampire Slayer.*" *Slayage: The Online International Journal of "Buffy" Studies* 2, no. 4. http://slayageonline.com/Numbers/slayage8.htm.

———. 2005. *Blood Relations: Chosen Families in "Buffy the Vampire Slayer" and "Angel."* Jefferson, NC: McFarland.

———. 2008. "Captain Tightpants: *Firefly* and the Science Fiction Canon." In special issue on *Firefly* and *Serenity,* edited by Rhonda V. Wilcox and Tanya R. Cochran. *Slayage: The Online International Journal of "Buffy" Studies* 7, no. 1. http://slayageonline.com/Numbers/slayage25.htm.

Beadling, Laura L. 2008. "The Threat of the 'Good Wife': Feminism, Postfeminism, and Third-Wave Feminism in *Firefly.*" In *Investigating "Firefly" and "Serenity": Science Fiction on the Frontier,* edited by Rhonda V. Wilcox and Tanya R. Cochran, 53–62. New York: I. B. Tauris.

Beagle, Peter S. 2004. "The Good Vampire: Angel and Spike." In *Five Seasons of "Angel": Science Fiction and Fantasy Writers Discuss Their Favorite Vampire,* edited by Glenn Yeffeth, 115–24. Dallas: BenBella Books.

"A Beautiful Sunset." 2008. *Buffy the Vampire Slayer.* Season 8. Issue 11. Written by Joss Whedon. Pencils by George Jeanty. Milwaukie, OR: Dark Horse Comics.

"Beauty and the Beasts." 1998. *Buffy the Vampire Slayer.* Season 3. Episode 4. Written by Marti Noxon. Directed by James Whitmore Jr. Los Angeles: Twentieth Century Fox Home Entertainment, 2010. DVD.

Beckett, Samuel. 1954. *Waiting for Godot.* New York: Grove Press.

"Becoming, Part One." 1998. *Buffy the Vampire Slayer.* Season 2. Episode 21. Written and directed by Joss Whedon. Los Angeles: Twentieth Century Fox Home Entertainment, 2010. DVD.

"Becoming, Part Two." 1998. *Buffy the Vampire Slayer.* Season 2. Episode 22. Written and directed by Joss Whedon. Los Angeles: Twentieth Century Fox Home Entertainment, 2010. DVD.

Beeden, Alexandra, and Joost de Bruin. 2010. "*The Office*: Articulations of National Identity in Television Format Adaptation." *Television and New Media* 11, no. 1: 3–19.

Beirne, Rebecca. 2004. "Queering the Slayer-Text: Reading Possibilities in *Buffy the Vampire Slayer.*" *Refractory: A Journal of Entertainment Media*, no. 5. http://refractory.unimelb.edu.au/2004/02/03/queering-the-slayer-text-reading-possibilities-in-buffy-the-vampire-slayer-rebecca-beirne/.

"Belle Chose." 2009. *Dollhouse*. Season 2. Episode 3. Written by Joss Whedon and Tim Minear. Directed by David Solomon. Los Angeles: Twentieth Century Fox Home Entertainment, 2010. DVD.

"Belonging." 2009. *Dollhouse*. Season 2. Episode 4. Written by Joss Whedon, Maurissa Tancharoen, and Jed Whedon. Directed by Jonathan Frakes. Los Angeles: Twentieth Century Fox Home Entertainment, 2009. DVD.

"Benediction." 2002. *Angel*. Season 3. Episode 21. Written and directed by Tim Minear. Los Angeles: Twentieth Century Fox Home Entertainment, 2005. DVD.

Berger, Peter L., and Thomas Luckmann. 1966. *The Social Construction of Reality: A Treatise in the Sociology of Knowledge*. Garden City, NY: Anchor Books.

Bernstein, Abbie, Bryan Cairns, Karl Derrick, and Tara DiLullo. 2007. *Firefly: The Official Companion*. Vol. 2. London: Titan Books.

Best, Janice. 1994. "The Chronotope and the Generation of Meaning in Novels and Paintings." *Criticism* 36, no. 2: 291–317. http://findarticles.com/p/articles/mi_m2220/is_n2_v36/ai_15435238.

"Bewitched, Bothered, and Bewildered." 1998. *Buffy the Vampire Slayer*. Season 2. Episode 16. Written by Marti Noxon. Directed by James A. Contner. Los Angeles: Twentieth Century Fox Home Entertainment, 2010. DVD.

"Birthday." 2002. *Angel*. Season 3. Episode 11. Written by Mere Smith. Directed by Michael Grossman. Los Angeles: Twentieth Century Fox Home Entertainment, 2006. DVD.

The Blair Witch Project. 1999. Directed by Daniel Myrick and Eduardo Sanchez. Santa Monica, CA: Artisan Entertainment. DVD.

Blanchot, Maurice. (1955) 1981. *The Gaze of Orpheus, and Other Literary Essays*. Translated by Lydia Davis. Barrytown, NY: Station Hill Press.

Blank, Jonah. 2000. *Arrow of the Blue-Skinned God*. New York: Grove Press.

Blitgen, M. John Carol. 1967. "*No Exit*: The Sartrean Idea of Hell." *Renascence: Essays on Value in Literature*, no. 19: 59–63.

Bloch, Maurice. 2009. "Claude Lévi-Strauss Obituary." *Guardian*, Nov. 3. http://www.guardian.co.uk/science/2009/nov/03/claude-levi-strauss-obituary.

"Blood, Text, and Fears." 2002. Univ. of East Anglia, Oct. 15. http://www.uea.ac.uk/mac/comm/media/press/2002/oct/Blood,+text+and+fears.

"Blood Ties." 2001. *Buffy the Vampire Slayer*. Season 5. Episode 13. Written by Steven S. DeKnight. Directed by Michael Gershman. Los Angeles: Twentieth Century Fox Home Entertainment, 2003. DVD.

"Blue." 2002. Written by Joss Whedon and Angie Hart. Song heard in "Conversations with Dead People." *Buffy the Vampire Slayer.*

Bodnar, John E. 2010. *The "Good War" in American Memory.* Baltimore: Johns Hopkins Univ. Press.

"The Body." 2001. *Buffy the Vampire Slayer.* Season 5. Episode 16. Written and directed by Joss Whedon. Los Angeles: Twentieth Century Fox Home Entertainment, 2002. DVD.

Bowman, Laurel. 2002. "Buffy the Vampire Slayer: The Greek Hero Revisited." Univ. of Victoria. http://web.uvic.ca/~lbowman/buffy/buffythehero.html.

Box Office Mojo. 2012. "*Marvel's The Avengers.*" http://boxofficemojo.com/movies /?id=avengers11.htm.

Bradney, Anthony. 2006. "The Politics and Ethics of Researching the Buffyverse." *Slayage: The Online International Journal of "Buffy" Studies* 5, no. 3. http:// slayageonline.com/Numbers/slayage19.htm.

"Brand New Day." 2008. Music written by Jed Whedon and Joss Whedon. Lyrics written by Joss Whedon. Song in *Dr. Horrible's Sing-Along Blog.*

"Briar Rose." 2009. *Dollhouse.* Season 1. Episode 11. Written by Jane Espenson. Directed by Dwight Little. Los Angeles: Twentieth Century Fox Home Entertainment, 2009. DVD.

Brinkley, Douglas. 2006. *The Great Deluge: Hurricane Katrina, New Orleans, and the Mississippi Gulf Coast.* New York: HarperCollins.

Brooks, Peter. 1992. *Reading for the Plot: Design and Intention in Narrative.* Cambridge, MA: Harvard Univ. Press.

Brown, Larry A. 2008. "Ovid's Metamorphoses." *Larry A. Brown* (personal website). http://larryavisbrown.homestead.com/files/xeno.ovid1.htm.

Browncoats. 2009. "Big Damn Knitters." *Wikia.* http://browncoats.wikia.com/wiki /Big_Damn_Knitters.

Brown-Jeffy, Shelly, and Steve Kroll-Smith. 2009. "Recovering Inequality: Democracy, the Market Economy, and the 1906 San Francisco Earthquake and Fire." In *The Political Economy of Hazards and Disasters*, edited by Eric C. Jones and Arthur D. Murphy, 83–103. New York: Altamira Press.

Buchanan, Ginjer, 2004. "Who Killed *Firefly*?" In *Finding Serenity: Anti-heroes, Lost Shepherds, and Space Hookers in Joss Whedon's "Firefly,"* edited by Jane Espenson (with Glenn Yeffeth), 47–54. Dallas: BenBella Books.

Buckman, Alyson. 2008. "'Much Madness Is Divinest Sense': *Firefly*'s 'Big Damn Heroes' and Little Witches." In *Investigating "Firefly" and "Serenity": Science Fiction on the Frontier*, edited by Rhonda V. Wilcox and Tanya R. Cochran, 41–49. New York: I. B. Tauris.

———. 2010. "'Go Ahead! Run Away! Say It Was Horrible': *Dr. Horrible's Sing-Along Blog* as Resistant Text." *Slayage: The Journal of the Whedon Studies Association* 8, no. 1. http://slayageonline.com/Numbers/slayage29.htm.

Buckwalter, Ian. 2012. "*Cabin in the Woods*: A Dead-Serious Genre Exorcism." NPR.org, Apr. 12. http://www.npr.org/2012/04/12/150299147/cabin-in-the-woods-a-dead-serious-genre-exorcism.

Buffy the Vampire Slayer. 1992. Written by Joss Whedon. Directed by Fran Rubel Kuzui. Twentieth Century Fox.

Buffy the Vampire Slayer. 1997–2003. Los Angeles: Twentieth Century Fox Home Entertainment. DVD.

"Buffy the Vampire Slayer" Reunion: Cast and Creators at Paleyfest. 2009. Los Angeles: Paley Center for Media. DVD.

Burnett, Tamy. 2010. Personal correspondence to Alyson Buckman. Nov. 14.

Burns, Maggie. 2007. "Mars Needs Women: How a Dress, a Cake, and a Goofy Hat Will Save Science Fiction." In *Serenity Found: More Unauthorized Essays on Joss Whedon's "Firefly" Universe*, edited by Jane Espenson (with Leah Wilson), 15–25. Dallas: BenBella Books.

Burr, Vivien. 2003. "Ambiguity and Sexuality in the Buffyverse: A Sartrean Analysis." *Sexualities* 6, nos. 3–4: 343–60.

"Bush Stunned by Conditions in New Orleans." 2005. *New Orleans Times-Picayune*, Sept. 3, A1. http://www.nola.com/katrina/pages/090305/a1.pdf.

"Bushwhacked." 2002. *Firefly*. Season 1. Episode 3. Written and directed by Tim Minear. Los Angeles: Twentieth Century Fox Home Entertainment, 2010. DVD.

Bussolini, Jeffrey. 2005. "Los Alamos Is the Hellmouth." *Slayage: The Online International Journal of "Buffy" Studies* 5, no. 2. http://slayageonline.com/Numbers/slayage18.htm.

———. 2008. "A Geopolitical Interpretation of *Serenity*." In *Investigating "Firefly" and "Serenity": Science Fiction on the Frontier*, edited by Rhonda V. Wilcox and Tanya R. Cochran, 139–52. New York: I. B. Tauris.

Button, Gregory V. 1999. "The Negation of Disaster: The Media Response to Oil Spills in Great Britain." In *The Angry Earth: Disaster in Anthropological Perspective*, edited by Susanna M. Hoffman and Anthony Oliver-Smith, 113–32. New York: Routledge.

Byers, Michele. 2000. "*Buffy the Vampire Slayer*: The Insurgence of Television as a Performance Text." PhD diss., Univ. of Toronto.

The Cabin in the Woods. 2012. Written by Joss Whedon and Drew Goddard. Directed by Drew Goddard. Vancouver: Lionsgate.

[C]actusflower. 2004. "5-20: 'The Girl in Question' 2004.05.05." *Television without Pity* (online forum). May 6, 12:25 a.m. http://forums.televisionwithoutpity.com/index.php?showtopic=3116537&st=210.

Call, Lewis. 2007. "'Sounds Like Kinky Business to Me': Subtextual and Textual Representations of Erotic Power in the Buffyverse." *Slayage: The Online International Journal of "Buffy" Studies* 6, no. 4. http://slayageonline.com/Numbers/slayage24.htm.

Callander, Michelle. 2001. "Bram Stoker's Buffy: Traditional Gothic and Contemporary Culture." *Slayage: The Online International Journal of "Buffy" Studies* 1, no. 3. http://slayageonline.com/Numbers/slayage3.htm.

Calvert, Bronwen. 2010. "Mind, Body, Imprint: Cyberpunk Echoes in the Dollhouse." In "Fantasy Is Not Their Purpose: Joss Whedon's *Dollhouse*," edited by Cynthea Masson and Rhonda V. Wilcox. Special issue, *Slayage: The Journal of the Whedon Studies Association* 8, nos. 2–3. http://slayageonline.com/Numbers/slayage30_31.htm.

Campbell, Joseph. 2004. *Pathways to Bliss: Mythology and Personal Transformation.* Edited by David Kudler. Novato, CA: New World Library.

Campbell, Mike. 2010a. "Caroline." *Behind the Name.* http://www.behindthename.com/name/caroline.

———. 2010b. "Charles." *Behind the Name.* http://www.behindthename.com/name/charles.

Čapek, Karel. 2004. *R.U.R. (Rossum's Universal Robots).* Translated by Claudia Novack. New York: Penguin Group. Kobo edition.

Čapek, Karel, and Josef Čapek. 1973. *R.U.R.* Translated by Paul Selver. Edited by Harry Shefter. New York: Pocket Books.

Carroll, Noël. 1990. *The Philosophy of Horror; or, Paradoxes of the Heart.* New York: Routledge.

Carter, Margaret L. 2003. "A World without Shrimp." In *Seven Seasons of "Buffy,"* edited by Glenn Yeffeth, 176–87. Dallas: BenBella Books.

Catanzey. 2004. "5-20: 'The Girl in Question' 2004.05.05." *Television without Pity* (online forum). May 5, 10:09 p.m. http://forums.televisionwithoutpity.com/index.php?showtopic=3116537&st=120.

Cate, Hollis L. 1972. "The Final Line of Sartre's *No Exit*." *Notes on Contemporary Literature* 2, no. 5: 9–10.

Cawelti, John. 1999. *The Six-Gun Mystique Sequel.* Bowling Green, OH: Bowling Green State Univ. Popular Press.

"The Chain." 2007. *Buffy the Vampire Slayer.* Season 8. Issue 5. Written by Joss Whedon. Pencils by Paul Lee. Milwaukie, OR: Dark Horse Comics.

Chapman, James. 2006. *Inside the TARDIS.* London: I. B. Tauris.

Chester-Wallis, Raymond. 2009. "A Legal Perspective on Consent and Sexual Acts in *Dollhouse*." Unpublished paper.

"Choices." 1999. *Buffy the Vampire Slayer.* Season 3. Episode 19. Written by David Fury. Directed by James A. Contner. Los Angeles: Twentieth Century Fox Home Entertainment, 2003. DVD.

"Chosen." 2003. *Buffy the Vampire Slayer.* Season 7. Episode 22. Written and directed by Joss Whedon. Los Angeles: Twentieth Century Fox Home Entertainment, 2006. DVD.

"City Of." 1999. *Angel.* Season 1. Episode 1. Written by David Greenwalt and Joss Whedon. Directed by Joss Whedon. Los Angeles: Twentieth Century Fox Home Entertainment, 2001. DVD.

Clark, Andy. 2003. *Natural-Born Cyborgs: Minds, Technologies, and the Future of Human Intelligence*. New York: Oxford Univ. Press.

Clarke, Arthur J. 1973. *Profiles of the Future: An Enquiry into the Limits of the Possible*. New York: Harper and Row.

Clevver Movies. 2012. "Joss Whedon Talks *The Avengers* and Captain America's Role." By Tatiana Carrier. *DailyMotion.com*, Mar. 15. http://www.dailymotion .com/video/xpgedp_joss-whedon-talks-the-avengers-inspiration-captain-america -s-role_shortfilms.

Clover, Carol J. 1992. *Men, Women, and Chain Saws: Gender in the Modern Horror Film*. Princeton, NJ: Princeton Univ. Press.

CNN. 2010. "Humanitarian Crisis in Haiti Escalates; Haitian Adoptions in Limbo; Chaos as Food Aid Arrives; Doctors Asked to Evacuate Hospital Due to Security Concerns; Dead Dumped in Mass Graves." *Anderson Cooper 360 Degrees*. Transcript for Jan. 15, 2010. http://transcripts.cnn.com/TRANSCRIPTS/1001 /15/acd.01.html.

Cochran, Tanya R. 2008. "Complicating the Open Closet: The Visual Rhetoric of *Buffy the Vampire Slayer*'s Sapphic Lovers." In *Televising Queer Women*, edited by Rebecca Beirne, 49–63. New York: Palgrave.

Comeford, AmiJo. 2009. "Cordelia Chase as Failed Feminist Gesture." In *"Buffy" Meets the Academy: Essays on the Episodes and Scripts as Texts*, edited by Kevin K. Durand, 150–60. Jefferson, NC: McFarland.

Connelly, Tom, and Shelley Rees. 2010. "Alienation and the Dialectics of History in Joss Whedon's *Dollhouse*." In "Fantasy Is Not Their Purpose: Joss Whedon's *Dollhouse*," edited by Cynthea Masson and Rhonda V. Wilcox. Special issue, *Slayage: The Journal of the Whedon Studies Association* 8, nos. 2–3. http://slayage online.com/Numbers/slayage30_31.htm.

"Consequences." 1999. *Buffy the Vampire Slayer*. Season 3. Episode 15. Written by Marti Noxon. Directed by Michael Gershman. Los Angeles: Twentieth Century Fox Home Entertainment, 2002. DVD.

Contat, Michel, and Michel Rybalka. 1974. *The Writings of Jean-Paul Sartre*. Vol. 1, *A Biographical Life*. Translated by Richard C. McCleary. Evanston: Northwestern Univ. Press.

"Conversations with Dead People." 2002. *Buffy the Vampire Slayer*. Season 7. Episode 7. Written by Jane Espenson and Drew Goddard (uncredited: Marti Noxon and Joss Whedon). Directed by Nick Marck. Los Angeles: Twentieth Century Fox Home Entertainment, 2005. DVD.

"Conviction." 2003. *Angel*. Season 5. Episode 1. Written and directed by Joss Whedon. Los Angeles: Twentieth Century Fox Home Entertainment, 2005. DVD.

Cox, J. Renée. 2008. "Got Myself a Soul? The Puzzling Treatment of the Soul in *Buffy*." In *The Truth of "Buffy": Essays on Fiction Illuminating Reality*, edited by Emily Dial-Driver, Sally Emmons-Featherston, Jim Ford, and Carolyn Anne Taylor, 24–37. Jefferson, NC: McFarland.

Creeber, Glen. 2004. *Serial Television: Big Drama on the Small Screen*. London: BFI.

Cresswell, Tim. 2004. *Place: A Short Introduction*. Malden, MA: Wiley-Blackwell.

"Crush." 2001. *Buffy the Vampire Slayer*. Season 5. Episode 14. Written by David Fury. Directed by Dan Attias. Los Angeles: Twentieth Century Fox Home Entertainment, 2005. DVD.

Curry, Agnes B. 2008. "We Don't Say 'Indian': On the Paradoxical Construction of the Reavers." In special issue on *Firefly* and *Serenity*, edited by Rhonda V. Wilcox and Tanya R. Cochran. *Slayage: The Online International Journal of "Buffy" Studies* 7, no. 1. http://slayageonline.com/Numbers/slayage25.htm.

"The Dark Age." 1997. *Buffy the Vampire Slayer*. Season 1. Episode 8. Written by Dean Batali and Rob Des Hotel. Directed by Bruce Seth Green. Los Angeles: Twentieth Century Fox Home Entertainment, 2007. DVD.

Da Ros, Giada. 2004. "When, Where, and How Much Is Buffy a Soap Opera?" *Slayage: The Online International Journal of "Buffy" Studies* 4, nos. 1–2. http://slayageonline.com/Numbers/slayage13_14.htm.

Das, P. Mohan. 2007. "Health—Human Trafficking: Human Trafficking Fastest Growing Organised Crime." UNODC United Nations Office on Drugs and Crime. http://www.unodc.org/india/en/uni_colombo_ht_20.html.

Davidson, Joy. 2004. "Whores and Goddesses." In *Finding Serenity: Anti-heroes, Lost Shepherds, and Space Hookers in Joss Whedon's "Firefly,"* edited by Jane Espenson (with Glenn Yeffeth), 113–30. Dallas: BenBella Books.

Dawson, Angela. 2012. "Whedon Corrals Marvel Superheroes in *The Avengers*." *Business World Online Weekender*, May 10. http://www.bworldonline.com/weekender/content.php?id=51507.

"Dead Things." 2002. *Buffy the Vampire Slayer*. Season 6. Episode 13. Written by Steven S. DeKnight. Directed by James A. Contner. Los Angeles: Twentieth Century Fox Home Entertainment, 2005. DVD.

DeCandido, GraceAnne A. 1999. "Bibliographic Good vs. Evil in *Buffy the Vampire Slayer*." *American Libraries* 30, no. 8: 44–47.

DeCandido, Keith R. A. 2004. "'The Train Job' Didn't Do the Job." In *Finding Serenity: Anti-heroes, Lost Shepherds, and Space Hookers in Joss Whedon's "Firefly,"* edited by Jane Espenson (with Glenn Yeffeth), 55–62. Dallas: BenBella Books.

"Defining Moments: A Retrospective with Joss Whedon." 2010. *Dollhouse*. Season 2. Disc 4 (featurette). Los Angeles: Twentieth Century Fox Home Entertainment. DVD.

Dempsey, John. 1997. "Femme Leads Earn Piece of the Action." *Variety*, July 14, 25.

Derrida, Jacques. 1993. *Aporias: Dying—Awaiting (One Another at) the "Limits of Truth."* Translated by Thomas Dutoit. Stanford, CA: Stanford Univ. Press.

Descartes, René. (1641) 1960. *The Meditations on First Philosophy*. In *Discourse on Method and Meditations*. Translated by Laurence J. Lafleur. Indianapolis: Liberal Arts Press. Latin original at http://la.wikisource.org/wiki/Liber:Meditationes _de_prima_philosophia.

"Destiny." 2003. *Angel*. Season 5. Episode 8. Written by David Fury and Stephen S. DeKnight. Directed by Skip Schoolnik. Los Angeles: Twentieth Century Fox Home Entertainment, 2006. DVD.

Dethlefsen, Atla E. 1995. "A Feminist Named Buffy? Women in Horror Films of the 1990s." Master's thesis, Univ. of South Carolina.

Diehl, Laura. 2004. "Why Drusilla's More Interesting than Buffy." *Slayage: The Online International Journal of "Buffy" Studies* 4, nos. 1–2. http://slayage online.com/Numbers/slayage13_14.htm.

"Dirty Girls." 2003. *Buffy the Vampire Slayer*. Season 7. Episode 18. Written by Drew Goddard. Directed by Michael Gershman. Los Angeles: Twentieth Century Fox Home Entertainment, 2004. DVD.

"Dollhouse": Cast and Creators Live at the Paleyfest. 2010. Los Angeles: Paley Center for Media. DVD.

Donne, John. (1633) 1941a. "Song." In *The Complete Poetry and Selected Prose of John Donne and the Complete Poetry of William Blake*, 3–4. New York: Modern Library.

———. (1633) 1941b. "The Sunne Rising." In *The Complete Poetry and Selected Prose of John Donne and the Complete Poetry of William Blake*, 6. New York: Modern Library.

"Doppelgangland." 1999. *Buffy the Vampire Slayer*. Season 3. Episode 16. Written and directed by Joss Whedon. Los Angeles: Twentieth Century Fox Home Entertainment, 2010. DVD.

"Doublemeat Palace." 2002. *Buffy the Vampire Slayer*. Season 6. Episode 12. Written by Jane Espenson. Directed by Nick Marck. Los Angeles: Twentieth Century Fox Home Entertainment, 2004. DVD.

Doug. 2004. "Oh the Horror!!" *All Things Philosophical on "Buffy the Vampire Slayer" and "Angel": The Series* (online forum). May 6, 06:22:49. http://www.atpobtvs.com/existentialscoobies/archives/may04_p01.html.

Dovey, Jon. 1996. "The Revelation of Unguessed Worlds." In *Fractal Dreams: New Media in Social Context*, edited by Jon Dovey, 109–34. London: Lawrence and Wishart.

Dowd, Maureen. 2005. "United States of Shame." *New York Times*, Sept. 3. http://www.nytimes.com/2005/09/03/opinion/03dowd.html.

Dr. Horrible's Sing-Along Blog. 2008. Written by Maurissa Tancharoen, Jed Whedon, Joss Whedon, and Zack Whedon. Directed by Joss Whedon. Mutant Enemy, 2008. DVD.

Durand, Kevin K., ed. 2009. *"Buffy" Meets the Academy: Essays on the Episodes and Scripts as Texts*. Jefferson, NC: McFarland.

Early, Frances. 2003. "The Female Just Warrior Reimagined: From Boudicca to Buffy." In *Athena's Daughters: Television's New Women Warriors*, edited by Frances Early and Kathleen Kennedy, 55–65. Syracuse, NY: Syracuse Univ. Press.

"Earshot." 1999. *Buffy the Vampire Slayer*. Season 3. Episode 18. Written by Jane Espenson. Directed by Regis B. Kimble. Los Angeles: Twentieth Century Fox Home Entertainment, 2002. DVD.

Ebert, Roger. 2012. *"The Cabin in the Woods." Chicago Sun Times*, Apr. 11. http://rogerebert.suntimes.com/apps/pbcs.dll/article?AID=/20120411/REVIEWS/120419993.

"Echo." 2009. *Dollhouse*. Unaired pilot. Written and directed by Joss Whedon. Los Angeles: Twentieth Century Fox Home Entertainment, 2009. DVD.

"Echoes." 2009. *Dollhouse*. Season 1. Episode 7. Written by Elizabeth Craft and Sarah Fain. Directed by James Contner. Los Angeles: Twentieth Century Fox Home Entertainment, 2009. DVD.

Edelstein, David. 2006. "Now Playing at Your Local Multiplex: Torture Porn." *New York* 39, no. 4: 64.

Edelstein, Judy. 2008. "In the Massage Parlour." In *Women and the Law*, edited by Libby Adler, Lisa Crooms, Judith Greenberg, Martha Minow, and Dorothy Roberts, 355–60. 4th ed. New York: Foundation Press.

Edwards, Lynne. 2002. "Slaying in Black and White: Kendra as Tragic Mulatta in *Buffy*." In *Fighting the Forces: What's at Stake in "Buffy the Vampire Slayer,"* edited by Rhonda V. Wilcox and David Lavery, 85–97. Lanham, MD: Rowman and Littlefield.

Edwards, Lynne, Elizabeth Rambo, and James South, eds. 2009. *Buffy Goes Dark: Essays on the Final Two Seasons of "Buffy the Vampire Slayer" on Television*. Jefferson, NC: McFarland.

Ellis, John. (1982) 1992. *Visible Fictions: Cinema, Television, Video*. New York: Routledge.

Elsaesser, Thomas. 1987. "Tales of Sound and Fury: Observations on the Family Melodrama." In *Home Is Where the Heart Is: Studies in Melodrama and the Woman's Film*, edited by Christine Gledhill, 43–69. London: BFI.

Emerson, Caryl. 1986. "The Outer Word and Inner Speech: Bakhtin, Vygotsky, and the Internalization of Language." In *Bakhtin: Essays and Dialogues on His Work*, edited by Gary Saul Morson, 21–40. Chicago: Univ. Chicago Press.

"Empty Places." 2003. *Buffy the Vampire Slayer*. Season 7. Episode 19. Written by Drew Z. Greenberg. Directed by James A. Contner. Los Angeles: Twentieth Century Fox Home Entertainment, 2006. DVD.

"End of Days." 2003. *Buffy the Vampire Slayer*. Season 7. Episode 21. Written by Douglas Petrie and Jane Espenson. Directed by Marita Grabiak. Los Angeles: Twentieth Century Fox Home Entertainment, 2006. DVD.

"Enemies." 1999. *Buffy the Vampire Slayer*. Season 3. Episode 17. Written by Douglas Petrie. Directed by David Grossman. Los Angeles: Twentieth Century Fox Home Entertainment, 2002. DVD.

"Entropy." 2002. *Buffy the Vampire Slayer*. Season 6. Episode 18. Written by Drew Z. Greenberg. Directed by James A. Contner. Los Angeles: Twentieth Century Fox Home Entertainment, 2004. DVD.

"Epiphany." 2001. *Angel*. Season 2. Episode 16. Written by Tim Minear. Directed by Thomas J. Wright. Los Angeles: Twentieth Century Fox Home Entertainment, 2006. DVD.

"Epitaph One." 2009. *Dollhouse*. Season 1. Episode 13. Written by Joss Whedon, Maurissa Tancharoen, Jed Whedon, Tracy Bellomo, and Andrew Chambliss. Directed by David Solomon. Los Angeles: Twentieth Century Fox Home Entertainment, 2009. DVD.

"Epitaph Two: Return." 2010. *Dollhouse*. Season 2. Episode 13. Written by Maurissa Tancharoen, Jed Whedon, and Andrew Chambliss. Directed by David Solomon. Los Angeles: Twentieth Century Fox Home Entertainment, 2010. DVD.

Erickson, Gregory. 2008. "Humanity in a 'Place of Nothin'": Morality, Religion, Atheism, and Possibility in *Firefly*." In *Investigating "Firefly" and "Serenity": Science Fiction on the Frontier*, edited by Rhonda V. Wilcox and Tanya R. Cochran, 167–82. New York: I. B. Tauris.

Erickson, Gregory, and Jennifer Lemberg. 2009. "Bodies and Narrative in Crisis: Figures of Rupture and Chaos in Seasons Six and Seven." In *Buffy Goes Dark: Essays on the Final Two Seasons of "Buffy the Vampire Slayer" on Television*, edited by Lynne Edwards, Elizabeth Rambo, and James South, 114–29. Jefferson, NC: McFarland.

Erisman, Fred. 2006. "*Stagecoach* in Space: The Legacy of *Firefly*." *Extrapolation* 47, no. 2: 249–58.

Espenson, Jane. 2002. Unpublished drafts for "Shindig."

———, ed. (with Glenn Yeffeth). 2004a. *Finding Serenity: Anti-heroes, Lost Shepherds, and Space Hookers in Joss Whedon's "Firefly."* Dallas: BenBella Books.

———. 2004b. Introduction to *Finding Serenity: Anti-heroes, Lost Shepherds, and Space Hookers in Joss Whedon's "Firefly,"* edited by Jane Espenson (with Glenn Yeffeth), 1–3. Dallas: BenBella Books.

———, ed. (with Leah Wilson). 2007. *Serenity Found: More Unauthorized Essays on Joss Whedon's "Firefly" Universe*. Dallas: BenBella Books.

———, ed. (with Leah Wilson). 2010a. *Inside Joss' "Dollhouse": From Alpha to Rossum*. Dallas: BenBella Books.

———. 2010b. "Playing Hard to 'Get': How to Write Cult TV." In *The Cult TV Book*, edited by Stacey Abbott, 45–53. London. I. B. Tauris.

Esslin, Martin. (1961) 2004. *The Theatre of the Absurd*. 3rd ed. New York: Vintage Books.

Everett, Todd. 1997. "Buffy the Vampire Slayer." *Variety*, Mar. 16, 1.

"Everyone's a Hero." 2008. Music and lyrics written by Joss Whedon. Song in *Dr. Horrible's Sing-Along Blog*.

"Everything You Ever." 2008. Music and lyrics written by Joss Whedon. Bridge written by Jed Whedon. Song in *Dr. Horrible's Sing-Along Blog*.

"Faith, Hope, and Trick." 1998. *Buffy the Vampire Slayer*. Season 3. Episode 3. Written by David Greenwalt. Directed by James A. Contner. Los Angeles: Twentieth Century Fox Home Entertainment, 2002. DVD.

"Family." 2000. *Buffy the Vampire Slayer.* Season 5. Episode 6. Written and directed by Joss Whedon. Los Angeles: Twentieth Century Fox Home Entertainment, 2010. DVD.

Fanetti, Susan. 2010. Personal correspondence to Alyson Buckman. Nov. 7.

Faraci, Devin. 2012. "*The Avengers* Defeated Irony and Cynicism." *The Devin's Advocate* (blog). *Badass Digest*, May 20. http://badassdigest.com/2012/05/20/the-avengers-defeated-irony-and-cynicism/.

Farley, Melissa. 2006. "Prostitution, Trafficking, and Cultural Amnesia: What We Must *Not Know* in Order to Keep the Business of Sexual Exploitation Running Smoothly." *Yale Journal of Law and Feminism*, no. 18: 109–44.

Faulkner, William. 1966. *Requiem for a Nun*. New York: Random House.

"Fear Itself." 1999. *Buffy the Vampire Slayer.* Season 4. Episode 4. Written by David Fury. Directed by Tucker Gates. Los Angeles: Twentieth Century Fox Home Entertainment, 2010. DVD.

Fernandez, Maria Elena. 2012. "*The Cabin in the Woods* Spoilers: Drew Goddard Speaks Freely." Interview with Drew Goddard. *Daily Beast*, Apr. 16. http://www.thedailybeast.com/articles/2012/04/16/the-cabin-in-the-woods-spoilers-drew-goddard-speaks-freely.html.

Ferrante, Anthony C. 2001. "Future at Stake." *Fangoria*, no. 199: 50–53, 82.

Fillion, Nathan. 2007. "I, Malcolm." In *Serenity Found: More Unauthorized Essays on Joss Whedon's "Firefly" Universe*, edited by Jane Espenson (with Leah Wilson), 49–53. Dallas: BenBella Books.

Firefly. 2002. Los Angeles: Twentieth Century Fox Home Entertainment. DVD.

Foer, Franklin. 1997. "Highlights from the Week in Criticism." *Slate.com*, Dec. 25. http://www.slate.com/articles/news_and_politics/summary_judgment/1997/12/_2.single.html.

"Fool for Love." 2000. *Buffy the Vampire Slayer.* Season 5. Episode 7. Written by Doug Petrie. Directed by Nick Marck. Los Angeles: Twentieth Century Fox Home Entertainment, 2007. DVD.

Franke, Katherine. 1997. "What's Wrong with Sexual Harassment?" *Stanford Law Review* 49, no. 4: 691–772.

Freeland, Cynthia A. 2004. "Ordinary Horror on Reality TV." In *Narrative across Media: The Languages of Storytelling*, edited by Marie-Laure Ryan, 244–66. Lincoln: Univ. of Nebraska Press.

Freud, Sigmund. (1899) 2003. *The Uncanny*. Translated by David McLintock. New York: Penguin.

———. 1959. "The Uncanny." In *Collected Papers*, 4:368–407. New York: Basic Books.

Frohard-Dourlent, Hélène. 2010. "Les-Faux Representations: How *Buffy* Season Eight Navigates the Politics of Female Heteroflexibility." In *Sexual Rhetoric in the Works of Joss Whedon*, edited by Erin B. Waggoner, 31–47. Jefferson, NC: McFarland.

Fudge, Rachel. 1999. "The Buffy Effect; or, A Tale of Cleavage and Marketing." *Bitch Magazine*, no. 10. http://bitchmagazine.org/article/buffy-effect.

Fury, David. 2003. "Real Me." *Buffy the Vampire Slayer*. Season 5. Episode 2. Disc 1 (commentary). Los Angeles: Twentieth Century Fox Home Entertainment, 2007. DVD.

Ganser, Alexandra, Julia Pühringer, and Markus Rheindorf. 2006. "Bakhtin's Chronotope on the Road: Space, Time, and Place in Road Movies since the 1970s." *Linguistics and Literature* 4, no. 1: 1–17. http://facta.junis.ni.ac.rs/lal/lal2006/lal2006-01.pdf.

Genette, Gérard. 1980. *Narrative Discourse: An Essay in Method*. Translated by Jane E. Lewin. Ithaca, NY: Cornell Univ. Press.

"Get It Done." 2003. *Buffy the Vampire Slayer*. Season 7. Episode 15. Written and directed by Doug Petrie. Los Angeles: Twentieth Century Fox Home Entertainment, 2010. DVD.

"Getting Closer." 2010. *Dollhouse*. Season 2. Episode 11. Written and directed by Tim Minear. Los Angeles: Twentieth Century Fox Home Entertainment, 2010. DVD.

"Ghost." 2009. *Dollhouse*. Season 1. Episode 1. Written and directed by Joss Whedon. Los Angeles: Twentieth Century Fox Home Entertainment, 2009. DVD.

"The Gift." 2000. *Buffy the Vampire Slayer*. Season 5. Episode 22. Written and directed by Joss Whedon. Los Angeles: Twentieth Century Fox Home Entertainment, 2010. DVD.

"Gingerbread." 1999. *Buffy the Vampire Slayer*. Season 3. Episode 11. Written by Thania St. John and Jane Espenson. Directed by James Whitmore Jr. Los Angeles: Twentieth Century Fox Home Entertainment, 2010. DVD.

Ginn, Sherry. 2010. "Memory, Mind, and Mayhem: Neurological Tampering and Manipulation in *Dollhouse*." In "Fantasy Is Not Their Purpose: Joss Whedon's *Dollhouse*," edited by Cynthea Masson and Rhonda V. Wilcox. Special issue, *Slayage: The Journal of the Whedon Studies Association* 8, nos. 2–3. http://slayageonline.com/Numbers/slayage30_31.htm.

"The Girl in Question." 2004. *Angel*. Season 5. Episode 20. Written by Steven S. DeKnight and Drew Goddard. Directed by David Greenwalt. Los Angeles: Twentieth Century Fox Home Entertainment, 2006. DVD.

Gliatto, Tom. 1997. "Buffy the Vampire Slayer." *People*, Mar. 31, 17. http://www.people.com/people/archive/article/0,,20121679,00.html.

Goddard, Drew. 2012. Foreword to *"The Cabin in the Woods": The Official Visual Companion*, by Joss Whedon, Drew Goddard, and Abbie Bernstein, 6. London: Titan Books.

Goffman, Erving. 1963. *Stigma: Notes on the Management of Spoiled Identity*. New York: Simon and Schuster.

Goltz, Jennifer. 2004. "Listening to Firefly." In *Finding Serenity: Anti-heroes, Lost Shepherds, and Space Hookers in Joss Whedon's "Firefly,"* edited by Jane Espenson (with Glenn Yeffeth), 209–15. Dallas: BenBella Books.

"Goodbye Iowa." 1999. *Buffy the Vampire Slayer.* Season 4. Episode 14. Written by Marti Noxon. Directed by David Solomon. Los Angeles: Twentieth Century Fox Home Entertainment, 2006. DVD.

Gordon, Lois. 2003. "*No Exit* and *Waiting for Godot*: Performances in Contrast." In *Captive Audience: Prison and Captivity in Contemporary Theater*, edited by Thomas Richard Fahy and Kimball King, 166–88. New York: Routledge.

"Graduation Day, Part One." 1999. *Buffy the Vampire Slayer.* Season 3. Episode 21. Written and directed by Joss Whedon. Los Angeles: Twentieth Century Fox Home Entertainment, 2010. DVD.

"Graduation Day, Part Two." 1999. *Buffy the Vampire Slayer.* Season 3. Episode 22. Written and directed by Joss Whedon. Los Angeles: Twentieth Century Fox Home Entertainment, 2010. DVD.

Graeber, David. 1998. "Rebel without a God: Buffy the Vampire Slayer Is Gleefully Anti-authoritarian—and Popular." *In These Times*, Dec. 27, 30.

Graham, Elaine. 2002. *Representations of the Post/Human: Monsters, Aliens, and Others in Popular Culture.* New Brunswick, NJ: Rutgers Univ. Press.

Grant, Peter S., and Chris Wood. 2004. *Blockbusters and Trade Wars: Popular Culture in a Globalized World.* Vancouver: Douglas and McIntyre.

Graves, Robert. 1992. *The Greek Myths: Complete Edition.* London: Penguin.

"Gray Hour." 2009. *Dollhouse.* Season 1. Episode 4. Written by Sarah Fain and Elizabeth Craft. Directed by Rod Hardy. Los Angeles: Twentieth Century Fox Home Entertainment, 2009. DVD.

"The Greek Myths." 2008. *In Our Time.* BBC Radio 3, Mar. 13.

Greenblatt, Stephen. 2004. *Will in the World: How Shakespeare Became Shakespeare.* New York: W. W. Norton.

Gross, Ed. 2010. "Joss Whedon Discusses His Contributions to the First Avenger: Captain America." *Earth's Mightiest Fansites: Captain America*, Aug. 17. http://www.earthsmightiest.com/fansites/captainamerica/news/?a=7535.

Gunning, Tom. (1986) 2006. "The Cinema of Attraction[s]: Early Film, Its Spectator, and the Avant-Garde." In *The Cinema of Attractions: Reloaded*, edited by Wanda Strauven, 381–88. Amsterdam: Amsterdam Univ. Press.

Gutierrez, Diego. 2004. "Normal Again." *Buffy the Vampire Slayer.* Season 6. Episode 17. Disc 5 (commentary). Los Angeles: Twentieth Century Fox Home Entertainment, 2006. DVD.

Gwaltney, Marilyn. 1999. "Androids as a Device for Reflection on Personhood." In *Retrofitting Blade Runner: Issues in Ridley Scott's "Blade Runner" and Philip K. Dick's "Do Androids Dream of Electric Sheep?,"* edited by Judith Kerman, 32–40. Athens, OH: Bowling Green State Univ. Popular Press.

Halfyard, Janet K. 2010. "Love, Death, Curses, and Reverses (in E minor): Music, Gender, and Identity in *Buffy the Vampire Slayer* and *Angel*." In *Music, Sound, and Silence in "Buffy the Vampire Slayer,"* edited by Paul Attinello, Janet K. Halfyard, and Vanessa Knights, 15–31. Burlington, VT: Ashgate.

"Halloween." 1997. *Buffy the Vampire Slayer*. Season 2. Episode 6. Written by Carl Ellsworth. Directed by Bruce Seth Green. Los Angeles: Twentieth Century Fox Home Entertainment, 2002. DVD.

Hamlet. 1996. Written by William Shakespeare and adapted by Kenneth Branagh. Directed by Kenneth Branagh. Los Angeles: Castle Rock Entertainment.

Hantke, Steffen. 2007. "Academic Film Criticism, the Rhetoric of Crisis, and the Current State of American Horror Cinema: Thoughts on Canonicity and Academic Anxiety." *College Literature* 34, no. 4: 191–202.

———. 2010. "They Don't Make 'Em Like They Used To: On the Rhetoric of Crisis and the Current State of American Horror Cinema." In *American Horror Film: The Genre at the Turn of the Millennium*, edited by Steffen Hantke, 7–32. Jackson: Univ. Press of Mississippi.

Haraway, Donna. 1991. *Simians, Cyborgs, and Women: The Reinvention of Nature*. New York: Routledge.

———. 1997. *Modest_Witness@Second_Millennium.FemaleMan_Meets_OncoMouse: Feminism and Technoscience*. New York: Routledge.

———. 2008. *When Species Meet*. Minneapolis: Univ. of Minnesota Press.

Harbin, Leigh. 2005. "'You Know You Wanna Dance': Buffy the Vampire Slayer as Contemporary Gothic Heroine." *Studies in the Humanities* 33, no. 1: 22–38.

Haring, Lee. 2004. "Framing in Oral Narrative." *Marvels and Tales* 18, no. 2: 229–45.

Harper, Kareem. 2010. "City of Heroes (Cryptic Studios/NCsoft)." Review of *City of Heroes* by Cryptic Studios. *Optimgamerz*. http://www.optimgamerz.com/review/city-of-heroes/.

Harris, Marvin. 1989. *Our Kind: Who We Are, Where We Came from, Where We Are Going*. New York: HarperCollins.

"The Harvest." 1997. *Buffy the Vampire Slayer*. Season 1. Episode 2. Written by Joss Whedon. Directed by John T. Kretschmer. Los Angeles: Twentieth Century Fox Home Entertainment, 2010. DVD.

Haskins, Rob. 2010. "Variations on Themes for Geeks and Heroes: Leitmotif, Style, and the Musico-dramatic Moment." In *Music, Sound, and Silence in "Buffy the Vampire Slayer,"* edited by Paul Attinello, Janet K. Halfyard, and Vanessa Knights, 45–60. Burlington, VT: Ashgate.

"Haunted." 2009. *Dollhouse*. Season 1. Episode 10. Written by Jane Espenson, Maurissa Tancharoen, and Jed Whedon. Directed by Elodie Keene. Los Angeles: Twentieth Century Fox Home Entertainment, 2009. DVD.

Havens, Candace. 2003. *Joss Whedon: The Genius Behind "Buffy."* Dallas: BenBella Books.

Hawk, Julie L. 2010a. "Hacking the Read-Only File: Collaborative Narrative as Ontological Construction in *Dollhouse*." In "Fantasy Is Not Their Purpose: Joss Whedon's *Dollhouse*," edited by Cynthea Masson and Rhonda V. Wilcox. Special issue, *Slayage: The Journal of the Whedon Studies Association* 8, nos. 2–3. http://slayageonline.com/Numbers/slayage30_31.htm.

———. 2010b. "More than the Sum of Our Imprints." In *Inside Joss' "Dollhouse": From Alpha to Rossum*, edited by Jane Espenson (with Leah Wilson), 247–57. Dallas: BenBella Books.

Hayles, N. Katherine. 1999. *How We Became Posthuman: Virtual Bodies in Cybernetics, Literature, and Informatics*. Chicago: Univ. of Chicago Press.

"Heart of Gold." 2002. *Firefly*. Season 1. Episode 13. Written by Brett Matthews. Directed by Thomas J. Wright. Los Angeles: Twentieth Century Fox Home Entertainment, 2003. DVD.

"Heartthrob." 2001. *Angel*. Season 3. Episode 1. Written and directed by David Greenwalt. Los Angeles: Twentieth Century Fox Home Entertainment, 2006. DVD.

Heidegger, Martin. 1977. "The Question Concerning Technology." In *The Question Concerning Technology, and Other Essays*, edited and translated by William Lovitt, 3–35. New York: Harper and Row.

———. 1984. *Early Greek Thinking*. Edited and translated by David Farrell Krell. New York: Harper and Row.

Heinecken, Dawn M. 1999. "The Women Warriors of Television: A Feminist Cultural Analysis of the New Female Body in Popular Media." PhD diss., Bowling Green State Univ.

"Helpless." 1999. *Buffy the Vampire Slayer*. Season 3. Episode 12. Written by David Fury. Directed by James A. Contner. Los Angeles: Twentieth Century Fox Home Entertainment, 2010. DVD.

Hendershot, Cyndy. 1998. *The Animal Within: Masculinity and the Gothic*. Ann Arbor: Univ. of Michigan Press.

"Here's How It Was: The Making of *Firefly*." 2003. *Firefly*. Season 1. Disk 4 (featurette). Los Angeles: Twentieth Century Fox Home Entertainment, 2003. DVD.

"Hero." 1999. *Angel*. Season 1. Episode 9. Written by Howard Gordon and Tim Minear. Directed by David Semel. Los Angeles: Twentieth Century Fox Home Entertainment, 2003. DVD.

Hight, Craig. 2004. "'It Isn't Always Shakespeare, but It's Genuine': Cinema's Commentary on Documentary Hybrids." In *Understanding Reality Television*, edited by Su Holmes and Deborah Jermyn, 233–51. New York: Routledge.

Hills, Matt. 2002. *Fan Cultures*. New York: Routledge.

"Him." 2002. *Buffy the Vampire Slayer*. Season 7. Episode 6. Written by Drew Z. Greenberg. Directed by Michael Gershman. Los Angeles: Twentieth Century Fox Home Entertainment, 2006. DVD.

Holder, Nancy. 2004. "Death Becomes Him: Blondie Bear 5.0." In *Five Seasons of "Angel": Science Fiction and Fantasy Writers Discuss Their Favorite Vampire*, edited by Glenn Yeffeth, 153–66. Dallas: BenBella Books.

Holder, Nancy, with Jeff Mariotte and Maryelizabeth Hart. 2000. *The Watcher's Guide*. Vol. 2. New York: Pocket Books.

"A Hole in the World." 2004. Season 5. Episode 15. Written and directed by Joss Whedon. Los Angeles: Twentieth Century Fox Home Entertainment, 2005. DVD.

"The Hollow Men." 2010. *Dollhouse*. Season 2. Episode 12. Written by Michelle Fazekas, Tara Butters, and Tracy Bellomo. Directed by Terrence O'Hara. Los Angeles: Twentieth Century Fox Home Entertainment, 2010. DVD.

Holmes, Su, and Deborah Jermyn. 2004. "Introduction: Understanding Reality TV." In *Understanding Reality Television*, edited by Su Holmes and Deborah Jermyn, 1–32. London and New York: Routledge.

"Home." 2003. *Angel*. Season 4. Episode 22. Written and directed by Tim Minear. Los Angeles: Twentieth Century Fox Home Entertainment, 2006. DVD.

Home Movie. 2007. Directed by Christopher Denham. New York: IFC Films. DVD.

Hornick, Alysa. 2012a. "Mapping the Whedonverses: Whedon Studies, 1999 and Beyond." In *Joss Whedon: The Complete Companion: the TV Series, the Movies, the Comic Books, and More*, edited by Mary Alice Money, 457–64. London: Titan Books.

———, ed. 2012b. *Whedonology: An Academic Whedon Studies Bibliography*. http://www.alysa316.com/Whedonology/.

Horrible Wiki. 2008. *Wikia*. http://drhorrible.wikia.com/wiki/Horrible_Wiki.

Howard, Megan. 1997. "Slayer-Speak." *Entertainment Weekly*, Oct. 31, 84.

Huffer, Lynne. 1998. *Maternal Pasts, Feminist Futures: Nostalgia, Ethics, and the Question of Difference*. Stanford, CA: Stanford Univ. Press.

Hurley, Kelly. 2007. "Abject and Grotesque." In *The Routledge Companion to Gothic*, edited by Catherine Spooner and Emma McEvoy, 137–46. New York: Routledge.

"Hush." 1999. *Buffy the Vampire Slayer*. Season 4. Episode 10. Written and directed by Joss Whedon. Los Angeles: Twentieth Century Fox Home Entertainment, 2006. DVD.

"Hush." 2003. *Buffy the Vampire Slayer*. Season 4. Disc 3 (featurette). Los Angeles: Twentieth Century Fox Home Entertainment, 2003. DVD.

[H]ypatia. 2009. "The Problem with *Dollhouse* Is Not That I Don't Understand Subtlety." *The Angry Black Woman* (online forum). May 1, 2:34 p.m. http://theangryblackwoman.com/2009/04/28/the-problem-with-dollhouse-is-not-that-i-dont-understand-subtlety/.

Iatropoulos, Mary Ellen, and Lowery A. Woodall III, eds. Forthcoming. "Beyond Light and Dark: Race, Ethnicity, Power, and Privilege in Joss Whedon's Works." Jefferson, NC: McFarland.

IGN FilmForce. 2003. "An Interview with Joss Whedon: The *Buffy the Vampire Slayer* Creator Discusses His Career." *IGN,* June 23. http://www.ign.com /articles/2003/06/23/an-interview-with-joss-whedon?page=10.

"The I in Team." 2000. *Buffy the Vampire Slayer.* Season 4. Episode 13. Written by David Fury. Directed by James A. Contner. Los Angeles: Twentieth Century Fox Home Entertainment, 2006. DVD.

"The Initiative." 1999. *Buffy the Vampire Slayer.* Season 4. Episode 7. Written by Doug Petrie. Directed by James A. Contner. Los Angeles: Twentieth Century Fox Home Entertainment, 2006. DVD.

"Innocence." 1998. *Buffy the Vampire Slayer.* Season 2. Episode 14. Written and directed by Joss Whedon. Los Angeles: Twentieth Century Fox Home Entertainment, 2006. DVD.

"Intervention." 2001. *Buffy the Vampire Slayer.* Season 5. Episode 18. Written by Jane Espenson. Directed by Michael Gershman. Los Angeles: Twentieth Century Fox Home Entertainment, 2010. DVD.

"Interview with Joss Whedon about *Serenity.*" 2005. *Science Fiction and Fantasy World.* http://www.sffworld.com/mul/130p0.html.

"I Only Have Eyes for You." 1998. *Buffy the Vampire Slayer.* Season 2, Episode 19. Written by Marti Noxon. Directed by James Whitmore Jr. Los Angeles: Twentieth Century Fox Home Entertainment, 2002. DVD.

"I Robot, You Jane." 1997. *Buffy the Vampire Slayer.* Season 1. Episode 8. Written by Ashley Gable and Thomas A. Swyden. Directed by Stephen Posey. Los Angeles: Twentieth Century Fox Home Entertainment, 2010. DVD.

Itzkoff, Dave. 2012. "Joss Whedon on Assembling *The Avengers.*" *New York Times,* Apr. 11. http://artsbeat.blogs.nytimes.com/2012/04/11/joss-whedon -assembles-the-avengers-for-the-biggest-film-of-his-career/.

"I Will Remember You." 1999. *Angel.* Season 1. Episode 8. Written by David Greenwalt and Jeannine Renshaw. Directed by David Grossman. Los Angeles: Twentieth Century Fox Home Entertainment, 2005. DVD.

Jackson, John Brinkerhoff. 1994. *A Sense of Time, a Sense of Place.* New Haven, CT: Yale Univ. Press.

"Jaynestown." 2002. *Firefly.* Season 1. Episode 7. Written by Ben Edlund. Directed by Marita Grabiak. Los Angeles: Twentieth Century Fox Home Entertainment, 2003. DVD.

Jencson, Linda. 2001. "Disastrous Rites: Liminality and Communitas in a Flood Crisis." *Anthropology and Humanism,* no. 26: 46–58.

———. 2008. "'Aiming to Misbehave': Role Modeling Political-Economic Conditions and Political Action in the *Serenity*verse." *Slayage: The Online International Journal of "Buffy" Studies* 7, no. 1. http://slayageonline.com/Numbers/slayage 25.htm.

———. 2010a. "Elite Panic Can Slow Aid in Disaster." *Charlotte (NC) Observer,* Jan. 20. http://www.charlotteobservor.com/viewpoint/v-print/story/1191107.html.

———. 2010b. "Watching Haiti Die: News Coverage of the January 2010 Haitian Earthquake." Paper presented at the annual meeting of the Popular Culture Association in the South, Savannah, GA, Oct. 7–10.

Jenkins, Henry. 2006. *Convergence Culture: Where Old and New Media Collide*. New York: New York Univ. Press. Kindle edition.

Jerz, Dennis G. 2002. "R.U.R. (Rossum's Universal Robots)." *Dennis G. Jerz* (blog). http://jerz.setonhill.edu/resources/RUR/index.html.

Johnson, Catherine. 2005. *Telefantasy*. London: BFI.

Johnson, Kevin. 2008. "German Language/Etymology." *AllExperts*. http://en.all experts.com/q/German-Language-1585/2008/6/etymology-1.htm.

Johnson, Mark. 1993. *Moral Imagination: Implications of Cognitive Science for Ethics*. Chicago: Univ. of Chicago Press.

"Joss Whedon." 2012. *IMDb.com*. http://www.imdb.com/name/nm0923736/#Actor.

Joss Whedon's Dollhouse. 2009–10. Los Angeles: Twentieth Century Fox Home Entertainment. DVD.

Jowett, Lorna. 2005. *Sex and the Slayer: A Gender Studies Primer for the "Buffy" Fan*. Middletown, CT: Wesleyan Univ. Press.

———. 2008. "Back to the Future: Retrofuturism, Cyberpunk, and Humanity in *Firefly* and *Serenity*." In *Investigating "Firefly" and "Serenity": Science Fiction on the Frontier*, edited by Rhonda V. Wilcox and Tanya R. Cochran, 101–13. New York: I. B. Tauris.

"Judgement." 2000. *Angel*. Season 2. Episode 1. Story by Joss Whedon and David Greenwalt. Teleplay by David Greenwalt. Directed by Michael Lange. Los Angeles: Twentieth Century Fox Home Entertainment, 2002. DVD.

"Just Rewards." 2003. *Angel*. Season 5. Episode 2. Written by David Fury and Ben Edlund. Directed by James A. Contner. Los Angeles: Twentieth Century Fox Home Entertainment, 2006. DVD.

Kalbear. 2004. "5-20: 'The Girl in Question' 2004.05.05." *Television without Pity* (online forum). May 6, 1:23 a.m. http://forums.televisionwithoutpity.com/index.php?showtopic=3116537&st=240.

Kant, Immanuel. (1785) 1993. *Grounding for the Metaphysics of Morals*. Translated by James W. Ellington. Indianapolis: Hackett.

Kaveney, Roz, ed. 2004a. *Reading the Vampire Slayer: The New, Updated, and Unofficial Guide to "Buffy" and "Angel."* London: I. B. Tauris.

———. 2004b. "'She Saved the World. A Lot.': An Introduction to the Themes and Structures of *Buffy* and *Angel*." In *Reading the Vampire Slayer: The New, Updated, and Unofficial Guide to "Buffy" and "Angel,"* edited by Roz Kaveney, 1–82. London: I. B. Tauris.

———. 2004c. "Writing the Vampire Slayer: Interviews with Jane Espenson and Steven S. DeKnight." In *Reading the Vampire Slayer: The New, Updated, and Unofficial Guide to "Buffy" and "Angel,"* edited by Roz Kaveney, 100–131. London: I. B. Tauris.

———. 2005. "A Sense of the Ending: Schrodinger's *Angel*." In *Reading "Angel": The TV Spin-off with a Soul*, edited by Stacey Abbott, 57–72. London: I. B. Tauris.

Keats, John. 2011. *Letters of John Keats to His Family and Friends*. Edited by Sidney Colvin. Cambridge: Cambridge Univ. Press.

Kermode, Frank. 1967. *The Sense of an Ending: Studies in the Theory of Fiction*. New York: Oxford Univ. Press.

Kierkegaard, Søren. 2001. "Journals and Notebooks." In *The Kierkegaard Reader*, edited by Jane Chamberlain and Jonathan Rée, 13–26. Oxford: Wiley, Blackwell.

Kimmel, Daniel M. 2004. *The Fourth Network: How Fox Broke the Rules and Reinvented Television*. Chicago: Ivan R. Dee.

King, Neal. 2003. "Brownskirts: Fascism, Christianity, and the Eternal Demon." In *"Buffy the Vampire Slayer" and Philosophy: Fear and Trembling in Sunnydale*, edited by James B. South, 197–211. Chicago: Open Court.

Kirkland, Ewan. 2005. "The Caucasian Persuasion in *Buffy the Vampire Slayer*." *Slayage: The Online International Journal of "Buffy" Studies* 5, no. 1. http://slayage online.com/Numbers/slayage17.htm.

Klein, Ian G. 2010. "'I Like My Scars': Claire Saunders and the Narrative of Flesh." In *Inside Joss' "Dollhouse": From Alpha to Rossum*, edited by Jane Espenson (with Leah Wilson), 117–31. Dallas: BenBella Books.

Kociemba, David. 2009. "Understanding the Espensode." In *Buffy Goes Dark: Essays on the Final Two Seasons of "Buffy the Vampire Slayer" on Television*, edited by Lynne Edwards, Elizabeth Rambo, and James South, 23–39. Jefferson, NC: McFarland.

———. 2010. "From Beneath You, It Foreshadows: Why the First Season Matters." Paper presented at SCW4: The *Slayage* Conference on the Whedonverses, Flagler College, St. Augustine, FL, June 3–6.

Koontz, K. Dale. 2008. *Faith and Choice in the Works of Joss Whedon*. Jefferson, NC: McFarland.

———. 2010. "Czech Mate: Whedon, Čapek, and the Foundations of *Dollhouse*." In "Fantasy Is Not Their Purpose: Joss Whedon's *Dollhouse*," edited by Cynthea Masson and Rhonda V. Wilcox. Special issue, *Slayage: The Journal of the Whedon Studies Association* 8, nos. 2–3. http://slayageonline.com/Numbers /slayage30_31.htm.

Kreider, Jodie A., and Meghan K. Winchell, eds. 2010. *"Buffy" in the Classroom: Essays on Teaching with the Vampire Slayer*. Jefferson, NC: McFarland.

Kreider, S. Evan. 2011. "*Dollhouse* and Consensual Slavery." In *The Philosophy of Joss Whedon*, edited by Dean A. Kowalski and S. Evan Kreider, 55–68. Lexington: Univ. Press of Kentucky.

Kristof, Nicholas, and Sheryl WuDunn. 2009. *Half the Sky: Turning Oppression into Opportunity for Women Worldwide*. New York: Alfred A. Knopf.

Kromer, Kelly. 2006. "Silence as Symptom: A Psychoanalytic Reading of 'Hush.'" *Slayage: The Online International Journal of "Buffy" Studies* 5, no. 3. http://slayageonline.com/Numbers/slayage19.htm.

Krueger, Jim. 2006. Introduction to Vol. 1 of *Justice*, by Jim Krueger and Alex Ross. New York: DC Comics.

Kunzelman, Michael. 2011. "Michael Lohman, Former New Orleans Cop, to Be Sentenced for Cover-up of Police Shootings during Katrina." *Huffington Post*, Nov. 2. http://www.huffingtonpost.com/2011/11/02/excop-to-be-sentenced-for_n_1071072.html.

Kuppers, Petra. 2004. "Quality Science Fiction: *Babylon Five*'s Metatextual Universe." In *Cult Television*, edited by Sara Gwenllian-Jones and Roberta Pearson, 45–59. Minneapolis: Univ. of Minnesota Press.

Kurzweil, Ray. 2000. *The Age of Spiritual Machines: When Computers Exceed Human Intelligence*. New York: Penguin.

Kussi, Peter, ed. 1990. *Toward the Radical Center: A Karel Čapek Reader*. North Haven, CT: Catbird Press.

Lackey, Mercedes. 2004. "*Serenity* and Bobby McGee: Freedom and the Illusion of Freedom in Joss Whedon's *Firefly*." In *Finding Serenity: Anti-heroes, Lost Shepherds, and Space Hookers in Joss Whedon's "Firefly,"* edited by Jane Espenson (with Glenn Yeffeth), 63–73. Dallas: BenBella Books.

"The Ladies' Man." 2005. *Age*, Sept. 25. http://www.theage.com.au/articles/2005/09/22/1126982178268.html.

Lakoff, George. 2008. *The Political Mind: Why You Can't Understand 21st-Century Politics with an 18th-Century Brain*. New York: Viking Penguin.

Lamont, Corliss. 1997. *The Philosophy of Humanism*. 8th ed. Washington, DC: Humanist Press. PDF file. http://www.corliss-lamont.org/philos8.htm.

La Polla, Franco. 2007. "L'appocalisse come Weltschmerz: Le radici culturali di *Buffy*." In *"Buffy the Vampire Slayer": Legittimare la Caciatrice*, edited by Barbara Maio, 79–96. Rome: Bulzoni Editore.

"Last Gleaming." 2010. *Buffy the Vampire Slayer*. Season 8. Issue 36–40. Written by Joss Whedon. Pencils by George Jeanty. Milwaukie, OR: Dark Horse Comics.

"The Last One." 1988. *St. Elsewhere*. Written by Bruce Paltrow and Mark Tinker. Directed by Mark Tinker. Los Angeles: NBC Television Drama.

Lavery, David. 2002a. "Afterword: The Genius of Joss Whedon." In *Fighting the Forces: What's at Stake in "Buffy the Vampire Slayer,"* edited by Rhonda V. Wilcox and David Lavery, 251–56. Lanham, MD: Rowman and Littlefield.

———. 2002b. "'A Religion in Narrative': Joss Whedon and Television Creativity." *Slayage: The Online International Journal of "Buffy" Studies* 2, no. 3. http://slayageonline.com/Numbers/slayage7.htm.

———. 2003. "Apocalyptic Apocalypses: The Narrative Eschatology of *Buffy the Vampire Slayer*." *Slayage: The Online International Journal of "Buffy" Studies* 3, no. 1. http://slayageonline.com/Numbers/slayage9.htm.

———. 2004. "'I Wrote My Thesis on You!': *Buffy* Studies as an Academic Cult." *Slayage: The Online International Journal of "Buffy" Studies* 4, nos. 1–2. http://slayageonline.com/Numbers/slayage13_14.htm.

———. 2009. "'The Status Is Not Quo': Television's *Horrible* Future." *CSTOnline*, Jan. http://www.criticalstudiesintelevision.com/index.php?siid=8872.

———. 2010. "Due Back on the Planet Earth: Toward a Definition of Spaciness." In *The Collected Works of David Lavery. David Lavery* (personal website). http://davidlavery.net/Collected_Works/Essays/Due_Back.pdf.

———. 2012. "The School of Whedon." *David Lavery* (personal website). http://david.lavery.net/Joss/School%5Fof%5FWhedon/.

Lavery, David, and Cynthia Burkhead, eds. 2011. *Joss Whedon: Conversations.* Jackson: Univ. Press of Mississippi.

Lavigne, Carlen. 2009. "Buffy the Lesbian Separatist: Cinnamon, Sex, and Gender in *Buffy the Vampire Slayer*—Season 8." Paper presented at Queen City Comics Conference, Regina, SK, Canada, May 2.

"Lessons." 2002. *Buffy the Vampire Slayer.* Season 7. Episode 1. Written by Joss Whedon. Directed by David Solomon. Los Angeles: Twentieth Century Fox Home Entertainment, 2003. DVD.

Lestel, Dominique. 2007. *Les amis de mes amis.* Paris: Seuil.

Levine, Elana. 2007. "*Buffy* and the 'New Girl Order': Defining Feminism and Femininity." In *Undead TV: Essays on "Buffy the Vampire Slayer,"* edited by Elana Levine and Lisa Parks, 168–89. Durham, NC: Duke Univ. Press.

Levine, Michael P., and Steven Jay Schneider. 2003. "Feeling for Buffy: The Girl Next Door." In *"Buffy the Vampire Slayer" and Philosophy: Fear and Trembling in Sunnydale*, edited by James B. South, 294–308. Chicago: Open Court.

Lewis, Joseph. 2009. "The Problem with *Dollhouse* Is Not That I Don't Understand Subtlety." *The Angry Black Woman* (online forum). Apr. 28, 9:40 p.m. http://theangryblackwoman.com/2009/04/28/the-problem-with-dollhouse-is-not-that-i-dont-understand-subtlety/.

Liddell, H. G., R. Scott, and H. S. Jones. (1940) 1996. *A Lexicon of Ancient Greek.* Oxford: Oxford Univ. Press.

"Lies My Parents Told Me." 2003. *Buffy the Vampire Slayer.* Season 7. Episode 17. Written by David Fury and Drew Goddard. Directed by David Fury. Los Angeles: Twentieth Century Fox Home Entertainment, 2004. DVD.

"Life Serial." 2001. *Buffy the Vampire Slayer.* Season 6. Episode 5. Written by David Fury and Jane Espenson. Directed by Nick Marck. Los Angeles: Twentieth Century Fox Home Entertainment, 2010. DVD.

"Listening to Fear." 2000. *Buffy the Vampire Slayer.* Season 5. Episode 9. Written by Jane Espenson. Directed by David Solomon. Los Angeles: Twentieth Century Fox Home Entertainment, 2006. DVD.

London, Jack. (1903) 2003. *The Call of the Wild.* New York: Aladdin Classics.

"The Long Way Home." 2007. *Buffy the Vampire Slayer*. Season 8. Issue 1–4. Written by Joss Whedon. Pencils by George Jeanty. Milwaukie, OR: Dark Horse Comics.

Longworth, James L., Jr. 2002. *TV Creators: Conversations with America's Top Producers of Television Drama*. Syracuse, NY: Syracuse Univ. Press.

"Lovers Walk." 1998. *Buffy the Vampire Slayer*. Season 3. Episode 8. Written by Dan Vebber. Directed by David Semel. Los Angeles: Twentieth Century Fox Home Entertainment, 2004. DVD.

"A Love Supreme." 2009. *Dollhouse*. Season 2. Episode 8. Written by Jenny DeArmitt. Directed by David Straiton. Los Angeles: Twentieth Century Fox Home Entertainment, 2010. DVD.

Lowenstein, Adam. 2011. "Spectacle Horror and Hostel: Why 'Torture Porn' Does Not Exist." *Critical Quarterly* 53, no. 1: 42–60.

"Lullaby." 2001. *Angel*. Season 3. Episode 9. Written and directed by Tim Minear. Los Angeles: Twentieth Century Fox Home Entertainment, 2005. DVD.

Lury, Karen. 2005. *Interpreting Television*. London: Hodder Arnold.

[L]uxgladius. 2004. "5-20: 'The Girl in Question' 2004.05.05." *Television without Pity* (online forum). May 6, 1:12 a.m. http://forums.televisionwithoutpity.com /index.php?showtopic=3116537&st=225.

Macnaughtan, Don. 2011. *The Buffyverse Catalog: A Complete Guide to "Buffy the Vampire Slayer" and "Angel" in Print, Film, Television, Comics, Games, and Other Media, 1992–2010*. Jefferson, NC: McFarland.

Magill, David. 2008. "'I Aim to Misbehave': Masculinities in the 'Verse." In *Investigating "Firefly" and "Serenity": Science Fiction on the Frontier*, edited by Rhonda V. Wilcox and Tanya R. Cochran, 76–86. New York: I. B. Tauris.

Maio, Barbara. 2004. *Buffy the Vampire Slayer*. Rome: Aracne.

———. 2008. "Between Past and Future: Hybrid Design Style in *Firefly* and *Serenity*." In *Investigating "Firefly" and "Serenity": Science Fiction on the Frontier*, edited by Rhonda V. Wilcox and Tanya R. Cochran, 201–11. New York: I. B. Tauris.

"Man on the Street." 2009. *Dollhouse*. Season 1. Episode 6. Written by Joss Whedon. Directed by David Straiton. Los Angeles: Twentieth Century Fox Home Entertainment, 2009. DVD.

"A Man's Gotta Do." 2008. Music and lyrics written by Jed Whedon. Song in *Dr. Horrible's Sing-Along Blog*.

Marano, Michael. 2007. "River Tam and the Weaponized Women of the Whedonverse." In *Serenity Found: More Unauthorized Essays on Joss Whedon's "Firefly" Universe*, edited by Jane Espenson (with Leah Wilson), 37–48. Dallas: BenBella Books.

Marck, Nick, Jane Espenson, Drew Goddard, Danny Strong, and Tom Lenk. 2004. "Conversations with Dead People." *Buffy the Vampire Slayer*. Season 7. Episode 7. Disc 2 (commentary). Los Angeles: Twentieth Century Fox Home Entertainment, 2006. DVD.

Marsh, Erica. 2012. "'The Message': *Firefly* Episode." In *The Encyclopedia of Buffy Studies*, edited by David Lavery and Rhonda V. Wilcox. http://slayageonline.com/EBS/firefly/episodes/themessage.htm.

Marvel Masterworks: "The Avengers." 2011. Vol. 1. Written by Stan Lee. Pencils by Jack Kirby. New York: Marvel Worldwide.

Marvel Masterworks: "Captain America." 2010. Vol. 1. Written by Stan Lee. Pencils by Jack Kirby. New York: Marvel Worldwide.

Marvel's The Avengers. 2012. Written and directed by Joss Whedon. Manhattan Beach, CA: Marvel Studios.

Masson, Cynthea. 2008a. "'But She Was Naked! And All Articulate!': The Rhetoric of Seduction in *Firefly*." In *Investigating "Firefly" and "Serenity": Science Fiction on the Frontier*, edited by Rhonda V. Wilcox and Tanya R. Cochran, 19–30. New York: I. B. Tauris.

———. 2008b. "What the Hell? *Angel*'s 'The Girl in Question.'" Paper presented at SCW3: The *Slayage* Conference on the Whedonverses, Henderson State Univ., Arkadelphia, AK, June 5–8.

———. 2010a. "'Evil's Spreading Sir, and It's Not Just over There!': Nazism in *Buffy* and *Angel*." In *Monsters in the Mirror: Representations of Nazism in Post-war Popular Culture*, edited by Sara Buttsworth and Maartje Abbenhuis. Westport, CT: Praeger.

———. 2010b. "'It's a Play on Perspective': A Reading of Whedon's Illyria through Sartre's *Nausea*." In *The Literary "Angel": Essays on Influences and Traditions Reflected in the Joss Whedon Series*, edited by AmiJo Comeford and Tamy Burnett, 159–72. Jefferson, NC: McFarland.

———. 2010c. "Who Painted the Lion? A Gloss on *Dollhouse*'s 'Belle Chose.'" In "Fantasy Is Not Their Purpose: Joss Whedon's *Dollhouse*," edited by Cynthea Masson and Rhonda V. Wilcox. Special issue, *Slayage: The Journal of the Whedon Studies Association* 8, nos. 2–3. http://slayageonline.com/Numbers/slayage30_31.htm.

Masson, Cynthea, and Rhonda V. Wilcox, eds. 2010. "Fantasy Is Not Their Purpose: Joss Whedon's *Dollhouse*." Special issue, *Slayage: The Journal of the Whedon Studies Association* 8, nos. 2–3. http://slayageonline.com/Numbers/slayage30_31.htm.

Massood, Paula J. 2005. "*Boyz N the Hood* Chronotopes: Spike Lee, Richard Price, and the Changing Authorship of *Clockers*." In *Literature and Film: A Guide to the Theory and Practice of Film Adaptation*, edited by Robert Stam and Alessandra Raengo, 191–207. Oxford: Blackwell.

McCracken, Allison. 2007. "At Stake: Angel's Body, Fantasy Masculinity, and Queer Desire in Teen Television." In *Undead TV: Essays on "Buffy the Vampire Slayer,"* edited by Elana Levine and Lisa Parks, 116–44. Durham, NC: Duke Univ. Press.

McLaren, Scott. 2005. "The Evolution of Joss Whedon's Vampire Mythology and the Ontology of the Soul." *Slayage: The Online International Journal of "Buffy" Studies* 5, no. 2. http://slayageonline.com/Numbers/slayage18.htm.

McLuhan, Marshall. 1995. *Essential McLuhan*. Edited by Eric McLuhan and Frank Zingrone. New York: Basic Books.

McNeilly, Kevin, Christine Sylka, and Susan R. Fisher. 2001. "Kiss the Librarian, but Close the Hellmouth: 'It's Like a Whole Big Sucking Thing.'" *Slayage: The Online International Journal of "Buffy" Studies* 1, no. 2. http://slayageonline .com/Numbers/slayage2.htm.

"Meet Jane Doe." 2009. *Joss Whedon's Dollhouse*. Season 2. Episode 7. Written by Maurissa Tancharoen, Jed Whedon, and Andrew Chambliss. Directed by Dwight Little. Los Angeles: Twentieth Century Fox Home Entertainment, 2010. DVD.

Mendelson, Edward. 2000. *Later Auden*. New York: Farrar, Straus, and Giroux.

"The Message." 2002. *Firefly*. Season 1. Episode 12. Written by Joss Whedon and Tim Minear. Directed by Tim Minear. Los Angeles: Twentieth Century Fox Home Entertainment, 2007. DVD.

"Metamorphosis." 2010. In *Encyclopædia Britannica Online*. http://www.britannica .com/EBchecked/topic/377827/metamorphosis.

Middleton, Jason. 2007. "Buffy as *Femme Fatale*: The Cult Heroine and the Male Spectator." In *Undead TV: Essays on "Buffy the Vampire Slayer,"* edited by Elana Levine and Lisa Parks, 145–67. Durham, NC: Duke Univ. Press.

Mikosz, Philip, and Dana C. Och. 2002. "Previously on *Buffy the Vampire Slayer*." *Slayage: The Online International Journal of "Buffy" Studies* 2, no. 1. http:// slayageonline.com/Numbers/slayage5.htm.

Miles, Lawrence, Lars Pearson, and Christa Dickson. 2003. *Dusted: The Unauthorized Guide to "Buffy the Vampire Slayer."* New Orleans: Mad Norwegian Press.

Miller, Jessica Prata. 2003. "'The I in Team': Buffy and Feminist Ethics." In *"Buffy the Vampire Slayer" and Philosophy: Fear and Trembling in Sunnydale*, edited by James B. South, 35–48. Chicago: Carus.

Millman, Joyce. 1997. "The Year in Television, 1997." *Salon.com*, Dec. 12. http:// www.salon.com/ent/tv/1997/12/24best2.html.

MindPieces. 2004. "Comments on 3833: Herc Gives 'The Girl in Question' 4.5 Stars." *Whedonesque* (online forum). May 6, 07:14. http://whedonesque.com /comments/3833.

Mitovich, Matt. 2009. "Video: Whedon Answers Your Questions about Sarah Michelle, Feminism, His Ultimate Project, and More." *TVGuide.com*. Video, 8:09. Posted Feb. 26. http://www.tvguide.com/News/VIDEO-Whedon-Gellar -1003385.aspx.

Mittell, Jason. 2006. "Narrative Complexity in Contemporary American Television." *Velvet Light Trap*, no. 58: 29–40.

Money, Mary Alice. 2002. "The Undemonization of Supporting Characters in *Buffy*." In *Fighting the Forces: What's at Stake in "Buffy the Vampire Slayer,"* edited by Rhonda V. Wilcox and David Lavery, 98–107. Lanham, MD: Rowman and Littlefield.

———. 2008. "*Firefly*'s 'Out of Gas': Genre Echoes and the Hero's Journey." In *Investigating "Firefly" and "Serenity": Science Fiction on the Frontier*, edited by Rhonda V. Wilcox and Tanya R. Cochran, 114–24. New York: I. B. Tauris.

Moravec, Hans. 1990. *Mind Children: The Future of Robot and Human Intelligence.* Cambridge, MA: Harvard Univ. Press.

Morris, David B. 2002. "Narrative, Ethics, and Pain: Thinking *with* Stories." In *Stories Matter: The Role of Narrative in Medical Ethics*, edited by R. Charon and M. Montello, 196–218. New York: Routledge.

Morris, Phyllis Sutton. 1976. *Sartre's Concept of a Person: An Analytic Approach.* Amherst: Univ. of Massachusetts Press.

Morson, Gary Saul. 1986. "Who Speaks for Bakhtin?" In *Bakhtin: Essays and Dialogues on His Work*, edited by Gary Saul Morson, 1–19. Chicago: Univ. of Chicago Press.

Much Ado about Nothing. 1993. Written by William Shakespeare and adapted by Kenneth Branagh. Directed by Kenneth Branagh. Los Angeles: Samuel Goldwyn.

Much Ado about Nothing. 2013. Written by William Shakespeare and adapted by Joss Whedon. Directed by Joss Whedon. Santa Monica: Bellwether Pictures.

"*Much Ado about Nothing* Press Release." 2011. *Much Ado the Movie.* http://much adothemovie.com/documents/MuchAdoPressRelease.pdf.

Mukherjea, Ananya. 2008. "'When You Kiss Me, I Want to Die': Gothic Relationships and Identity on *Buffy the Vampire Slayer.*" *Slayage: The Online International Journal of "Buffy" Studies* 7, no. 2. http://slayageonline.com/Numbers /slayage26.htm.

Mulvey, Laura. (1975) 2000. "Visual Pleasure and Narrative Cinema." In *Film and Theory: An Anthology*, edited by Robert Stam and Toby Miller, 483–94. Oxford: Blackwell.

———. 1975. "Visual Pleasure and Narrative Cinema." Reprint of the original articles published in the autumn 1975 issue of *Screen*. *Scribd.* http://www.scribd .com/doc/7758866/laura-mulvey-visual-pleasure-and-narrative-cinema.

Muntersbjorn, Madeline. 2010. "Disgust, Difference, and Displacement in the *Dollhouse.*" In "Fantasy Is Not Their Purpose: Joss Whedon's *Dollhouse*," edited by Cynthea Masson and Rhonda V. Wilcox. Special issue, *Slayage: The Journal of the Whedon Studies Association* 8, nos. 2–3. http://slayageonline.com/Numbers /slayage30_31.htm.

"My Eyes." 2008. Music written by Jed Whedon. Lyrics written by Maurissa Tancharoen, Joss Whedon, and Jed Whedon. Song in *Dr. Horrible's Sing-Along Blog.*

Nadkarni, Samira. 2010. Personal correspondence to Alyson Buckman. June 13.

———. 2012. "Months after the Fact, Sami Rambles on about *Avengers.*" *Sami AndNemanjaGoToTheMovies* (blog), Oct. http://samiandnemanjagotothemovies .tumblr.com/post/32974005326/months-after-the-fact-sami-rambles-on-about -avengers.

Neal, Christopher. 2008. "Marching Out of Step: Music and Otherness in the *Firefly/Serenity* Saga." In *Investigating "Firefly" and "Serenity": Science Fiction on the Frontier*, edited by Rhonda V. Wilcox and Tanya R. Cochran, 191–201. New York: I. B. Tauris.

"Needs." 2009. *Dollhouse.* Season 1. Episode 8. Written by Tracy Bellomo. Directed by Felix Alcala. Los Angeles: Twentieth Century Fox Home Entertainment, 2009. DVD.

Nelson, Robin. 2007. *State of Play: Contemporary "High End" TV Drama.* Manchester: Manchester Univ. Press.

"Never Kill a Boy on the First Date." 1997. *Buffy the Vampire Slayer.* Season 1. Episode 5. Written by Rob Des Hotel and Dean Batali. Directed by David Semel. Los Angeles: Twentieth Century Fox Home Entertainment, 2010. DVD.

Newcomb, Horace, and Robert S. Alley. 1983. *The Producer's Medium: Conversations with Creators of American TV.* New York: Oxford Univ. Press.

"New Moon Rising." 2000. *Buffy the Vampire Slayer.* Season 4. Episode. 19. Written by Marti Noxon. Directed by James A. Contner. Los Angeles: Twentieth Century Fox Home Entertainment, 2006. DVD.

"A New World." 2002. *Angel.* Season 3. Episode 20. Written by Jeffrey Bell. Directed by Tim Minear. Los Angeles: Twentieth Century Fox Home Entertainment, 2005. DVD.

Nietzsche, Friedrich. (1886) 1990. *Beyond Good and Evil.* Translated by R. J. Hollingdale. London: Penguin.

"Nightmares." 1997. *Buffy the Vampire Slayer.* Season 1. Episode 10. Written by David Greenwalt. Directed by Bruce Seth Green. Los Angeles: Twentieth Century Fox Home Entertainment, 2010. DVD.

Noble, David. 1999. *The Religion of Technology: The Divinity of Man and the Spirit of Invention.* New York: Penguin.

"No Future for You." 2007. *Buffy the Vampire Slayer.* Season 8. Issue 6–9. Written by Brian K. Vaughn. Pencils by George Jeanty. Milwaukie, OR: Dark Horse Comics.

"Normal Again." 2002. *Buffy the Vampire Slayer.* Season 6. Episode 17. Written by Diego Gutierrez. Directed by Rick Rosenthal. Los Angeles: Twentieth Century Fox Home Entertainment, 2007. DVD.

"Not Fade Away." 2004. *Angel.* Season 5. Episode 22. Written by Jeffrey Bell and Joss Whedon. Directed by Jeffrey Bell. Los Angeles: Twentieth Century Fox Home Entertainment, 2006. DVD.

Nowell-Smith, Geoffrey. 1987. "Minnelli and Melodrama." In *Home Is Where the Heart Is: Studies in Melodrama and the Woman's Film*, edited by Christine Gledhill, 70–79. London: BFI.

Obasogie, Osagie K. 2010. "Prisoners as Human Subjects: A Closer Look at the Institute of Medicine's Recommendations to Loosen Current Restrictions on Using Prisoners in Scientific Research." *Stanford Journal of Civil Rights and Civil Liberties* 7, no. 1: 41–82.

"Objects in Space." 2002. *Firefly*. Season 1. Episode 14. Written and directed by Joss Whedon. Los Angeles: Twentieth Century Fox Home Entertainment, 2003. DVD.

O'Connor, John J. 1997. "Just the Girl Next Door, but Neighborhood Vampires Beware." *New York Times*, Mar. 31, C11. http://www.nytimes.com/1997/03/31 /arts/just-the-girl-next-door-but-neighborhood-vampires-beware.html.

O'Heir, Andrew. 2012. "Joss Whedon on His Two Big Movies." Interview with Joss Whedon. *Salon.com*, Apr. 13. http://www.salon.com/2012/04/13/interview _joss_whedon_on_his_two_big_movies/.

Oliver-Smith, Anthony. 1999. "The Brotherhood of Pain: Theoretical and Applied Perspectives on Post-disaster Solidarity." In *The Angry Earth: Disaster in Anthropological Perspective*, edited by Anthony Oliver-Smith and Susanna M. Hoffman, 156–72. New York: Routledge.

Olsen, Mark. 2012. "*Cabin in the Woods* Can't See the Forest for the Trees." *Village Voice*, Apr. 11. http://www.villagevoice.com/2012-04-11/film/cabin-in-the -woods-can-t-see-the-forest-for-the-trees/full/.

"Omega." 2009. *Dollhouse*. Season 1. Episode 12. Written and directed by Tim Minear. Los Angeles: Twentieth Century Fox Home Entertainment, 2009. DVD.

"Once More, with Feeling." 2001. *Buffy the Vampire Slayer*. Season 6. Episode 7. Written and directed by Joss Whedon. Los Angeles: Twentieth Century Fox Home Entertainment, 2003. DVD.

Ono, Kent A. 2000. "To Be a Vampire on *Buffy the Vampire Slayer*: Race and ('Other') Socially Marginalizing Positions on Horror TV." In *Fantasy Girls: Gender in the New Universe of Science Fiction and Fantasy Television*, edited by Elyce Rae Helford, 163–86. Lanham, MD: Rowman and Littlefield.

"Origin." 2004. *Angel*. Season 5. Episode 18. Written by Drew Goddard. Directed by Terrence O'Hara. Los Angeles: Twentieth Century Fox Home Entertainment, 2005. DVD.

"Orpheus." 2003. *Angel*. Season 4. Episode 15. Written by Mere Smith. Directed by Terrence O'Hara. Los Angeles: Twentieth Century Fox Home Entertainment, 2004. DVD.

Orr, Christopher. 2012. "*The Cabin in the Woods* Disembowels the Slasher Film." *Atlantic*, Apr. 13. http://www.theatlantic.com/entertainment/category/film /page/11.

[O]stentatious. 2004. "5-20: 'The Girl in Question' 2004.05.05." *Television without Pity* (online forum). May 6, 8:02 a.m. http://forums.televisionwithoutpity.com /index.php?showtopic=3116537&st=285.

"Our Mrs. Reynolds." 2002. *Firefly*. Season 1. Episode 6. Written by Joss Whedon. Directed by Vondie Curtis Hall. Los Angeles: Twentieth Century Fox Home Entertainment, 2003. DVD.

"Out of Gas." 2002. *Firefly*. Season 1. Episode 8. Written by Tim Minear. Directed by David Solomon. Los Angeles: Twentieth Century Fox Home Entertainment, 2007. DVD.

"Out of Mind, Out of Sight." 1997. *Buffy the Vampire Slayer*. Season 1. Episode 11. Written by Ashley Gable and Thomas A. Swyden. Directed by Reza Badiyi. Los Angeles: Twentieth Century Fox Home Entertainment, 2010. DVD.

Overbey, Karen Eileen, and Lahney Preston-Matto. 2002. "Staking in Tongues: Speech Act as Weapon in *Buffy*." In *Fighting the Forces: What's at Stake in "Buffy the Vampire Slayer,"* edited by Rhonda V. Wilcox and David Lavery, 73–84. Lanham, MD: Rowman and Littlefield.

Ovid. 1893. *The Metamorphoses*. Translated by Henry T. Riley. *Project Gutenberg*, 2007. http://www.gutenberg.org/files/21765/21765-h/files/Met_I-III.html#bookIII.

———. 1995. *The Metamorphoses*. Translated by Allen Mandelbaum. San Diego: Harcourt.

Owen, A. Susan. 1999. "*Buffy the Vampire Slayer*: Vampires, Postmodernity, and Postfeminism." *Journal of Popular Film and Television* 27, no. 2: 24–31.

"The Pack." 1997. *Buffy the Vampire Slayer*. Season 1. Episode 6. Written by Matt Kliene and Joe Reinkemeyer. Directed by Bruce Seth Green. Los Angeles: Twentieth Century Fox Home Entertainment, 2010. DVD.

Pagels, Elaine. 1989. *The Gnostic Gospels*. New York: Vintage.

"Pangs." 1999. *Buffy the Vampire Slayer*. Season 4. Episode 8. Written by Jane Espenson. Directed by Michael Lange. Los Angeles: Twentieth Century Fox Home Entertainment, 2004. DVD.

Paranormal Activity 2. 2010. Directed by Tod Williams. Hollywood: Paramount Home Entertainment. Blu-Ray.

Parfit, Derek. 2011. *On What Matters*. 2 vols. Oxford: Oxford Univ. Press.

"Passion." 1998. *Buffy the Vampire Slayer*. Season 2. Episode 17. Written by Ty King. Directed by Michael E. Gershman. Los Angeles: Twentieth Century Fox Home Entertainment, 2010. DVD.

Pateman, Matthew. 2006. *The Aesthetics of Culture in "Buffy the Vampire Slayer."* Jefferson, NC: McFarland.

———. 2008. "Deathly Serious: Mortality, Morality, and the Mise-en-scène in *Firefly* and *Serenity*." In *Investigating "Firefly" and "Serenity": Science Fiction on the Frontier*, edited by Rhonda V. Wilcox and Tanya R. Cochran, 212–23. New York: I. B. Tauris.

Payne-Mulliken, Susan, and Valerie Renegar. 2009. "The Rhetorical Construction of Sisterhood in the Final Season." In *"Buffy" Meets the Academy: Essays on the Episodes and Scripts as Texts*, edited by Kevin K. Durand, 57–77. Jefferson, NC: McFarland.

"Peace Out" 2003. *Angel*. Season 4. Episode 21. Written by David Fury. Directed by Jefferson Kibbee. Los Angeles: Twentieth Century Fox Home Entertainment, 2006. DVD.

Pearson, Roberta. 2009. "Chain of Events: Regimes of Evaluation and *Lost*'s Construction of the Televisual Character." In *Reading "Lost,"* edited by Roberta Pearson, 139–58. London: I. B. Tauris.

Peikoff, Leonard. 1996. The 1991 introduction to *Atlas Shrugged*, by Ayn Rand, 1–8. New York: Signet.

Peña, Fabio. 2006. "Signal Flags and Phonetic Alphabet." *NavSource Naval History*. http://www.navsource.org/archives/sfpa.htm.

"Penny's Song." 2008. Music written by Jed Whedon. Lyrics written by Maurissa Tancharoen and Jed Whedon. Song in *Dr. Horrible's Sing-Along Blog*.

Perdigao, Lisa. 2010. "'This One's Broken': Rebuilding Whedonbots and Reprogramming the Whedonverse." In "Fantasy Is Not Their Purpose: Joss Whedon's *Dollhouse*," edited by Cynthea Masson and Rhonda V. Wilcox. Special issue, *Slayage: The Journal of the Whedon Studies Association* 8, nos. 2–3. http://slayage online.com/Numbers/slayage30_31.htm.

The Pez. 2004. "5-20: 'The Girl in Question' 2004.05.05." *Television without Pity* (online forum). May 5, 9:18 p.m. http://forums.televisionwithoutpity.com /index.php?showtopic=3116537&st=45.

"Phases." 1998. *Buffy the Vampire Slayer*. Season 2. Episode 15. Written by Rob Des Hotel and Dean Batali. Directed by Bruce Seth Green. Los Angeles: Twentieth Century Fox Home Entertainment, 2010. DVD.

[P]iranesi. 2004. "5-20: 'The Girl in Question' 2004.05.05." *Television without Pity* (online forum). May 6, 2:48 a.m. http://forums.televisionwithoutpity.com /index.php?showtopic=3116537&st=255.

Plato. 1997. *Phaedrus*. Translated by Alexander Nehamas and Paul Woodruff. In *Plato: Complete Works*, edited by John Cooper. Indianapolis: Hackett.

Playdon, Zoe-Jane. 2002. "'The Outsiders' Society': Religious Imagery in *Buffy the Vampire Slayer*." *Slayage: The Online International Journal of "Buffy" Studies* 2, no. 1. http://slayageonline.com/Numbers/slayage5.htm.

"Power Play." 2004. *Angel*. Season 5. Episode 21. Written by David Fury. Directed by James A. Contner. Los Angeles: Twentieth Century Fox Home Entertainment, 2006. DVD.

Powley, Edward H. 2009. "Reclaiming Resilience and Safety: Resilience Activation in the Critical Period of Crisis." *Human Relations* 62, no. 9: 1289–1326.

"The Price." 2002. *Angel*. Season 3. Episode 19. Written by David Fury. Directed by Marita Grabiak. Los Angeles: Twentieth Century Fox Home Entertainment, 2005. DVD.

Price, Jessica. 2010. "The Role of Masculinity and Femininity in *Buffy the Vampire Slayer*." In *Sexual Rhetoric in the Works of Joss Whedon*, edited by Erin B. Waggoner, 215–25. Jefferson, NC: McFarland.

"Primeval." 2000. *Buffy the Vampire Slayer*. Season 4. Episode 21. Written by David Fury. Directed by James A Contner. Los Angeles: Twentieth Century Fox Home Entertainment, 2006. DVD.

"Production Pilot." 1997. *Buffy the Vampire Slayer*. Season 1. Episode 0. Written and directed by Joss Whedon. http://www.buffyworld.com.

"Prophecy Girl." 1997. *Buffy the Vampire Slayer*. Season 1. Episode 12. Written and directed by Joss Whedon. Los Angeles: Twentieth Century Fox Home Entertainment, 2010. DVD.

"The Public Eye." 2009. *Dollhouse*. Season 2. Episode 5. Written by Andrew Chambliss. Directed by David Solomon. Los Angeles: Twentieth Century Fox Home Entertainment, 2010. DVD.

Punamaki, Raija-Leena. 2010. "Posttraumatic Growth in a Middle Eastern Context: Expression and Determinants of PTG among Palestinians." In *Posttraumatic Growth and Culturally Competent Practice: Lessons from Around the Globe*, edited by Tzipi Weiss and Roni Berger, 31–48. Hoboken, NJ: Wiley.

"Puppet Show." 1997. *Buffy the Vampire Slayer*. Season 1. Episode 9. Written by Dean Batali and Rob Des Hotel. Directed by Ellen S. Pressman. Los Angeles: Twentieth Century Fox Home Entertainment, 2010. DVD.

Quarantelli, E. L. 1985. "Realities and Mythologies in Disaster Films." *Communications: The European Journal of Communication*, no. 11: 31–44. http://www.degruyter.com/view/j/comm.1985.11.issue-1/comm.1985.11.1.31/comm.1985.11.1.31.xml.

———. 1987. "Disaster Studies: An Analysis of the Social Historical Factors Affecting the Development of Research in the Area." *International Journal of Mass Emergencies and Disasters* 5, no. 3: 285–310.

Queenan, Joe. 1997. "High Stakes." *TV Guide*, May 17–23.

"The Quickening." 2001. *Angel*. Season 3. Episode 8. Written by Jeffrey Bell. Directed by Skip Schoolnik. Los Angeles: Twentieth Century Fox Home Entertainment, 2005. DVD.

Rabb, J. Douglas, and J. Michael Richardson. 2008. "Reavers and Redskins: Creating the Frontier Savage." In *Investigating "Firefly" and "Serenity": Science Fiction on the Frontier*, edited by Rhonda V. Wilcox and Tanya R. Cochran, 127–38. New York: I. B. Tauris.

———. 2009. "Myth, Metaphor, Morality, and Monsters: The Espenson Factor and Cognitive Science in Joss Whedon's Narrative Love Ethic." *Slayage: The Online International Journal of "Buffy" Studies* 7, no. 4. http://slayageonline.com/Numbers/slayage28.htm.

Rambo, Elizabeth. 2009. "*Buffy* 1.5: Never Kill a Boy on a First Date." *The Painful Nowning Process* (blog), Nov. 22. http://elrambo.wordpress.com/2009/11/22/buffy-1-5-never-kill-a-boy-on-the-first-date/.

Rand, Ayn. (1943) 1993. *The Fountainhead*. New York: Signet.

———. (1957) 1996. *Atlas Shrugged*. New York: Signet.

———. (1968) 1993. Introduction to the twenty-fifth Anniversary Edition of *The Fountainhead*, v–xi. New York: Signet.

Recht, Marcus. 2011. *Der Sympathische Vampir: Visualisierungen von Männlichkeiten in der TV-Serie "Buffy."* Frankfurt am Main: Campus Verlag.

"Redefinition." 2001. *Angel*. Season 2. Episode 11. Written by Mere Smith. Directed by Michael Grossman. Los Angeles: Twentieth Century Fox Home Entertainment, 2006. DVD.

"Remains." 2009. Written by Maurissa Tancharoen and Jed Whedon. Song heard in "Epitaph One." *Dollhouse*.

Rennebohm, Kate. 2010. "'The Mind Doesn't Matter, It's the Body We Want': Identity and the Body in *Dollhouse*." In *Inside Joss' "Dollhouse": From Alpha to Rossum*, edited by Jane Espenson (with Leah Wilson), 5–19. Dallas: BenBella Books.

"Reptile Boy." 1997. *Buffy the Vampire Slayer*. Season 2. Episode 5. Written and directed by David Greenwalt. Los Angeles: Twentieth Century Fox Home Entertainment, 2010. DVD.

"Restless." 2000. *Buffy the Vampire Slayer*. Season 4. Episode 22. Written and directed by Joss Whedon. Los Angeles: Twentieth Century Fox Home Entertainment, 2010. DVD.

"Retreat." 2009. *Buffy the Vampire Slayer*. Season 8. Issue 16–19. Written by Jane Espenson. Pencils by George Jeanty. Milwaukie, OR: Dark Horse Comics.

"Revelations." 1998. *Buffy the Vampire Slayer*. Season 3. Episode 7. Written by Douglas Petrie. Directed by James A. Contner. Los Angeles: Twentieth Century Fox Home Entertainment, 2002. DVD.

Rice, Lynette. 2001. "Slayer It Ain't So." *EW.com*, Mar. 23. http://www.ew.com/ew/article/0,,280397,00.html.

Richardson, David. 2004. "*Angel* Hits 100." *TV Zone*, no. 173: 32–35.

Richardson, J. Michael, and J. Douglas Rabb. 2007. *The Existential Joss Whedon: Evil and Human Freedom in "Buffy the Vampire Slayer," "Angel," "Firefly," and "Serenity."* Jefferson, NC: McFarland.

Rilke, Rainer Maria. 1996. *Werke: Kommentierte Ausgabe in vier Banden*. Vol. 2. Frankfurt am Main: Insel.

Rob. 2004. "Re: Reaction to 5-20 'The Girl in Question.'" *All Things Philosophical on "Buffy the Vampire Slayer" and "Angel": The Series* (online forum). May 6, 07:22:41. http://www.atpobtvs.com/existentialscoobies/archives/may04_p01.html.

Robinson, Tasha. 2001. "Joss Whedon—Web Exclusive." *Onion A.V. Club*, Sept. 5. http://www.avclub.com/articles/joss-whedon-web-exclusive,13729/.

Rodden, John. 2008. "How Do Stories Convince Us? Notes toward a Rhetoric of Narrative." *College Literature* 35, no. 1: 148–73.

Rogers, Adam. 2012. "With *The Avengers*, Joss Whedon Masters the Marvel Universe." *Wired.com Underwire*, Apr. 30. http://www.wired.com/underwire/2012/04/ff_whedon/all/1.

Rosenberg, Howard. 1997. "So, Like, She Hates Vampires, Y'Know?" *LA Times*, Mar. 10. http://articles.latimes.com/1997-03-10/entertainment/ca-36747_1_vampires-buffy-wb.

Roth, Michael. 2010. "Why We Teach." *The Blog* (blog). *Huffington Post*, Dec. 3. http://www.huffingtonpost.com/michael-roth/why-we-teach_b_791871.html.

Rotten Tomatoes. 2012. *"Marvel's The Avengers."* http://www.rottentomatoes.com/m/marvels_the_avengers/.

Sady. 2009. *"Dollhouse,* Joss Whedon, and the Strange and Difficult Path of Feminist Dudes: Some Thoughts." *Tiger Beatdown* (blog), Apr. 20, 10:55 a.m. http://tigerbeatdown.blogspot.com/2009/04/dollhouse-joss-whedon-and-strange-and.html.

Sanderson, Peter. 1996. *Marvel Universe.* New York: Harry N. Abrams.

Sartre, Jean-Paul. (1943) 1972. *Being and Nothingness: A Phenomenological Essay on Ontology.* Translated by Hazel E. Barnes. New York: Washington Square Press.

———. (1946) 2007. *Existentialism Is a Humanism.* Translated by Carol Macomber. New Haven, CT: Yale Univ. Press.

———. (1947) 1989. *"No Exit," and Three Other Plays.* New York: Vintage International.

———. 1947. "Republic of Silence." In *Republic of Silence,* edited by A. J. Liebling, 498–500. New York: Harcourt, Brace.

———. 1976. *Sartre on Theater.* Translated by Frank Jellinek. New York: Pantheon Books.

———. 1992. *Notebooks for an Ethics.* Translated by David Pellauer. Chicago: Univ. of Chicago Press.

Schaff, Philip, ed. (1888) 2007. *Nicene and Post-Nicene Fathers.* Vol. 7. New York: Cosimo.

Schechet, Nita. 2005. *Narrative Fissures: Reading and Rhetoric.* Madison, NJ: Fairleigh Dickinson Univ. Press.

"School Hard." 1997. *Buffy the Vampire Slayer.* Season 2. Episode 3. Story by Joss Whedon and David Greenwalt. Teleplay by David Greenwalt. Directed by John Kretchmer. Los Angeles: Twentieth Century Fox Home Entertainment, 2001. DVD.

"Seeing Red." 2002. *Buffy the Vampire Slayer.* Season 6. Episode 19. Written by Steven S. DeKnight. Directed by Michael Gershman. Los Angeles: Twentieth Century Fox Home Entertainment, 2010. DVD.

"Selfless." 2002. *Buffy the Vampire Slayer.* Season 7. Episode 5. Written by Drew Goddard. Directed by David Solomon. Los Angeles: Twentieth Century Fox Home Entertainment, 2004. DVD.

"Serenity." 2002. *Firefly.* Season 1. Episode 1. Written and directed by Joss Whedon. Los Angeles: Twentieth Century Fox Home Entertainment, 2003. DVD.

Serenity. 2005. Written and directed by Joss Whedon. Los Angeles: Universal Studios. DVD.

"Serenity": The Official Visual Companion. 2005. London: Titan.

"*Serenity*: The Tenth Character." 2003. *Firefly*. Season 1. Disk 4 (featurette). Los Angeles: Twentieth Century Fox Home Entertainment, 2003. DVD.

[S]ervo. 2004. "5-20: 'The Girl in Question' 2004.05.05." *Television without Pity* (online forum). May 5, 9:07 p.m. http://forums.televisionwithoutpity.com/index .php?showtopic=3116537&st=0.

Shakespeare, William. 1984. *Macbeth*. Edited by Kenneth Muir. Arden Shakespeare. London: Methuen.

————. 2002. *Much Ado about Nothing*. In *The Complete Pelican Shakespeare*, edited by Stephen Orgel and A. R. Braunmuller, 371–400. New York: Penguin.

Shales, Tom. 2009. "*Dollhouse*: On Fox, a Strange New Toy." *Washington Post*, Feb. 13. http://www.washingtonpost.com/wp-dyn/content/article/2009/02/12 /AR2009021203994.html.

"Shindig." 2002. *Firefly*. Season 1. Episode 4. Written by Jane Espenson. Directed by Vern Gillum. Los Angeles: Twentieth Century Fox Home Entertainment, 2003. DVD.

Siegel, Carol. 2005. *Goth's Dark Empire*. Bloomington: Indiana Univ. Press.

"Site History." 2012. *Slayage: The Journal of the Whedon Studies Association*. http:// slayageonline.com/pages/Slayage/site_history.htm.

SL@SpoilerTV. 2008. "*Dollhouse*: Casting News." *SpoilerTV*. http://www.spoilertv .com/2008/03/dollhouse-casting-news.html.

"Sleeper." 2002. *Buffy the Vampire Slayer*. Season 7. Episode 8. Written by David Fury and Jane Espenson. Directed by Alan J. Levi. Los Angeles: Twentieth Century Fox Home Entertainment, 2006. DVD.

"Sleep Tight." 2002. *Angel*. Season 3. Episode 16. Written by David Greenwalt. Directed by Terrence O'Hara. Los Angeles: Twentieth Century Fox Home Entertainment, 2005. DVD.

"Slipping." 2008. Music and lyrics written by Joss Whedon. Song in *Dr. Horrible's Sing-Along Blog*.

Smith, Ashley Lorrain. 1999. "Girl Power: Feminism, Girlculture, and the Popular Media." Master's thesis, Univ. of North Texas.

Smith, Kyle. 2012. "Just *Woods* Schlock." *New York Post*, online edition, Apr. 12. http://nypost.newspaperdirect.com/epaper/viewer.aspx.

SNeaker. 2004. "5-20: 'The Girl in Question' 2004.05.05." *Television without Pity* (online forum). May 5, 9:05 p.m. http://forums.televisionwithoutpity.com /index.php?showtopic=3116537&st=0.

Solnit, Rebecca. 2009. *A Paradise Built in Hell: The Extraordinary Communities That Arise in Disaster*. New York: Viking.

"Something Blue." 1999. *Buffy the Vampire Slayer*. Season 1. Episode 1. Written by Tracey Forbes. Directed by Nick Marck. Los Angeles: Twentieth Century Fox Home Entertainment, 2010. DVD.

"So They Say." 2008. Music written by Jed Whedon and Joss Whedon. Lyrics written by Joss Whedon. Song in *Dr. Horrible's Sing-Along Blog*.

"Soul Purpose." 2004. *Angel*. Season 5. Episode 10. Written by Brent Fletcher. Directed by David Boreanaz. Los Angeles: Twentieth Century Fox Home Entertainment, 2005. DVD.

South, James B. 2001. "'All Torment, Trouble, Wonder, and Amazement Inhabits Here': The Vicissitudes of Technology in *Buffy the Vampire Slayer*." *Journal of American and Comparative Cultures* 24, nos. 1–2: 93–102.

Spinoza, Baruch. 1955. *The Ethics*. Translated by R. H. M. Elwes. New York: Dover. Latin original at http://users.telenet.be/rwmeijer/spinoza/works.htm?lang=E.

"Spin the Bottle." 2002. *Angel*. Season 4. Episode 6. Written and directed by Joss Whedon. Los Angeles: Twentieth Century Fox Home Entertainment, 2005. DVD.

"Spiral." 2001. *Buffy the Vampire Slayer*. Season 5. Episode 20. Written by Steven S. DeKnight. Directed by James Contner. Los Angeles: Twentieth Century Fox Home Entertainment, 2006. DVD.

Spivak, Gayatri Chakravorty. 1976. Preface to *Of Grammatology*, by Jacques Derrida, ix–lxxxvii. Baltimore: Johns Hopkins Univ. Press.

St. Louis, Renee, and Miriam Riggs. 2010. "'And Yet': The Limits of *Buffy*'s Feminism." *Slayage: The Journal of the Whedon Studies Association* 8, no. 1. http://slayageonline.com/Numbers/slayage29.htm.

Stafford, Nikki. 2007. *Bite Me! The Unofficial Guide to "Buffy the Vampire Slayer": The Chosen Edition*. Toronto: ECW Press.

———. 2008. "Slayage Conference: Jeanine Basinger." *Nik at Nite* (blog), June 12. http://nikkistafford.blogspot.com/2008/06/slayage-conference-jeanine-basinger.html.

———. 2011. Personal conversation with Matthew Pateman.

"Stage Fright." 2009. *Dollhouse*. Season 1. Episode 3. Written by Maurissa Tancharoen and Jed Whedon. Directed by David Solomon. Los Angeles: Twentieth Century Fox Home Entertainment, 2009. DVD.

Staite, Jewel. 2004. "Kaylee Speaks: Jewel Staite on *Firefly*." In *Finding Serenity: Anti-heroes, Lost Shepherds, and Space Hookers in Joss Whedon's "Firefly,"* edited by Jane Espenson (with Glenn Yeffeth), 217–27. Dallas: BenBella Books.

Stam, Robert. 2000. *Film Theory: An Introduction*. Oxford: Blackwell.

———. 2005. "Introduction: The Theory and Practice of Adaptation." In *Literature and Film: A Guide to the Theory and Practice of Film Adaptation*, edited by Robert Stam and Alessandra Raengo, 1–52. Oxford: Blackwell.

[S]teffie. 2004. "5-20: 'The Girl in Question' 2004.05.05." *Television without Pity* (online forum). May 5, 9:30 p.m. http://forums.televisionwithoutpity.com/index.php?showtopic=3116537&st=60.

Stevens, Charlotte. 2010. Personal correspondence to Alyson Buckman. Nov. 20.

Stevenson, Gregory. 2003. *Televised Morality: The Case of "Buffy the Vampire Slayer."* Lanham, MD: Hampton Books.

Stevenson, Robert Louis. (1886) 1991. *The Strange Case of Dr. Jekyll and Mr. Hyde.* Mineola, NY: Dover.

"Stop-Loss." 2009. *Dollhouse.* Season 2. Episode 9. Written by Andrew Chambliss. Directed by Felix Alcalá. Los Angeles: Twentieth Century Fox Home Entertainment, 2010. DVD.

"Storyteller." 2003. *Buffy the Vampire Slayer.* Season 7. Episode 16. Written by Jane Espenson. Directed by Marita Grabiak. Los Angeles: Twentieth Century Fox Home Entertainment, 2004. DVD.

"Superstar." 2000. *Buffy the Vampire Slayer.* Season 4. Episode 17 Written by Jane Espenson. Directed by David Grossman. Los Angeles: Twentieth Century Fox Home Entertainment, 2010. DVD.

"Surprise." 1998. *Buffy the Vampire Slayer.* Season 2. Episode 13. Written by Joss Whedon and Marti Noxon. Directed by Michael Lange. Los Angeles: Twentieth Century Fox Home Entertainment, 2002. DVD.

Sutherland, Sharon, and Sarah Swan. 2008. "'The Alliance Isn't Some Evil Empire': Dystopia in Joss Whedon's *Firefly/Serenity.*" In *Investigating "Firefly" and "Serenity": Science Fiction on the Frontier,* edited by Rhonda V. Wilcox and Tanya R. Cochran, 89–100. New York: I. B. Tauris.

———. 2010. "Lilah Morgan: Whedon's Legal Femme Fatale." In *The Literary "Angel": Essays on Influences and Traditions Reflected in the Joss Whedon Series,* edited by AmiJo Comeford and Tamy Burnett, 54–65. Jefferson, NC: McFarland.

Swain, Sara. 2010. "Losing It: The Construction of Virginity in *Buffy the Vampire Slayer.*" In *Sexual Rhetoric in the Works of Joss Whedon,* edited by Erin B. Waggoner, 173–84. Jefferson, NC: McFarland.

Symonds, Gwyn. 2004. "'Solving Problems with Sharp Objects': Female Empowerment, Sex, and Violence in *Buffy the Vampire Slayer.*" *Slayage: The Online International Journal of "Buffy" Studies* 3, nos. 3–4. http://slayageonline.com/Numbers/slayage11_12.htm.

Szabo, Tait. 2011. "Companions, Dolls, and Whores: Joss Whedon on Sex and Prostitution." In *The Philosophy of Joss Whedon,* edited by Dean A. Kowalski and S. Evan Kreider, 103–16. Lexington: Univ. Press of Kentucky.

Tabron, Judith. 2004. "Girl on Girl Politics: Willow, Tara, and New Approaches to Media Fandom." *Slayage: The Online International Journal of "Buffy" Studies* 4, nos. 1–2. http://slayageonline.com/Numbers/slayage13_14.htm.

"Tabula Rasa." 2001. *Buffy the Vampire Slayer.* Season 6. Episode 8. Written by Rebecca Rand Kirshner. Directed by David Grossman. Los Angeles: Twentieth Century Fox Home Entertainment, 2007. DVD.

Tagg, Philip. 1989. "An Anthropology of Stereotypes in TV Music?" *Philip Tagg* (personal website). http://tagg.org/articles/xpdfs/tvanthro.pdf.

"The Target." 2009. *Dollhouse.* Season 1. Episode 2. Written and directed by Steven S. DeKnight. Los Angeles: Twentieth Century Fox Home Entertainment, 2009. DVD.

Taylor, Mark C. 1993. *Nots*. Chicago: Univ. of Chicago Press.

———, ed. 1998. *Critical Terms for Religious Studies*. Chicago: Univ. of Chicago Press.

"Teacher's Pet." 1997. *Buffy the Vampire Slayer*. Season 1. Episode 4. Written by David Greenwalt. Directed by Bruce Seth Green. Los Angeles: Twentieth Century Fox Home Entertainment, 2010. DVD.

"Ted." 1997. *Buffy the Vampire Slayer*. Season 2. Episode 11. Written by David Greenwalt and Joss Whedon. Directed by Bruce Seth Green. Los Angeles: Twentieth Century Fox Home Entertainment, 2002. DVD.

Tedeschi, R. G., and L. G. Calhoun. 1996. "The Post-traumatic Growth Inventory: Measuring the Positive Legacy of Trauma." *Journal of Traumatic Stress* 9, no. 1: 445–71.

"That Vision Thing." 2001. *Angel*. Season 3. Episode 2. Written and directed by Jeffrey Bell. Los Angeles: Twentieth Century Fox Home Entertainment, 2003. DVD.

Thiessen, Brian. 2006. "'No More Running': *Firefly*, the Western, and the Genre of *Serenity*." Paper presented at SCW2: The *Slayage* Conference on the Whedonverses, Gordon College, Barnesville, GA, May 26–28. http://www.slayage online.com/SCW_Archive/Thiessen.pdf.

Thompson, Robert J. 1996. *Television's Second Golden Age*. Syracuse, NY: Syracuse Univ. Press.

Thompson, Terry. 2001. "Melville's *Moby-Dick*." *Explicator* 59, no. 3: 130–32.

Tierney, Kathleen J., et al. 2006. "Metaphors Matter: Disaster Myths, Media Frames, and Their Consequences in Hurricane Katrina." *Annals of the American Academy of Political and Social Science*, no. 604: 57–79.

"Time of Your Life." 2008. *Buffy the Vampire Slayer*. Season 8. Issue 16–19. Written by Joss Whedon. Pencils by George Jeanty. Milwaukie, OR: Dark Horse Comics.

Tobias, Scott. 2010. "Epitaph Two: The Return." *Onion A.V. Club*, Jan. 29. http:// www.avclub.com/articles/epitaph-two-return.37694/.

"To Shanshu in L.A." 2000. *Angel*. Season 1. Episode 22. Written and directed by David Greenwalt. Los Angeles: Twentieth Century Fox Home Entertainment, 2006. DVD.

"Touched." 2003. *Buffy the Vampire Slayer*. Season 7. Episode 20. Written by Rebecca Rand Kirshner. Directed by David Solomon. Los Angeles: Twentieth Century Fox Home Entertainment, 2006. DVD.

Tracy, Kathleen. 1998. *The Girl's Got Bite: The Unofficial Guide to Buffy's World*. Los Angeles: Renaissance.

"The Train Job." 2002. *Firefly*. Season 1. Episode 2. Written by Joss Whedon and Tim Minear. Directed by Joss Whedon. Los Angeles: Twentieth Century Fox Home Entertainment, 2003. DVD.

Transformers. 2007. Written by Roberto Orci, Alex Kurtzman, and John Rogers. Directed by Michael Bay. Los Angeles: Paramount Pictures.

"Trash." 2002. *Firefly*. Season 1. Episode 11. Written by Ben Edlund and Jose Malina. Directed by Vern Gillum. Los Angeles: Twentieth Century Fox Home Entertainment, 2003. DVD.

"The Trial." 2000. *Angel*. Season 2. Episode 9. Written by David Greenwalt. Directed by Bruce Seth Green. Los Angeles: Twentieth Century Fox Home Entertainment, 2002. DVD.

"True Believer." 2009. *Dollhouse*. Season 1. Episode 5. Written by Tim Minear. Directed by Allan Kroeker. Los Angeles: Twentieth Century Fox Home Entertainment, 2009. DVD.

The Truman Show. 1998. Directed by Peter Weir. Hollywood, CA: Paramount Home Entertainment. DVD.

Tudyk, Alan, and Jewel Staite. 2003. "The Message." *Firefly*. Season 1. Episode 12. Disc 4 (commentary). Los Angeles: Twentieth Century Fox Home Entertainment, 2007. DVD.

"Turbulence." 2010. *Buffy the Vampire Slayer*. Season 8. Issue 31. Written by Joss Whedon. Pencils by George Jeanty. Milwaukie, OR: Dark Horse Comics.

Turnbull, Sue. 2004. "'Not Just Another *Buffy* Paper': Towards an Aesthetics of Television." *Slayage: The Online International Journal of "Buffy" Studies* 4, nos. 1–2. http://slayageonline.com/Numbers/slayage13_14.htm.

Turner, Graeme. 2005. "Genre, Format, and 'Live' Television." In *The Television Genre Book*, edited by Glen Creeber, 6–7. London: British Film Institute.

Twain, Mark. (1885) 2011. *Adventures of Huckleberry Finn*. New York: Scholastic.

"Twilight." 2010. *Buffy the Vampire Slayer*. Season 8. Issues 32–35. Written by Brad Meltzer. Pencils by George Jeanty. Milwaukie, OR: Dark Horse Comics.

Twin Peaks. Season 1. Episode 2. 1990. Written by Mark Frost and David Lynch. Directed by David Lynch. Los Angeles: Universal Pictures. 2001. DVD.

"Two to Go." 2002. *Buffy the Vampire Slayer*. Season 6. Episode 21. Written by Douglas Petrie. Directed by Bill Norton. Los Angeles: Twentieth Century Fox Home Entertainment, 2010. DVD.

"The Ultimates": The Ultimate Collection. 2010. Written by Mark Millar. Penciled by Bryan Hitch. New York: Marvel Worldwide.

Vint, Sherryl. 2002. "'Killing Us Softly?': A Feminist Search for the 'Real' Buffy." *Slayage: The Online International Journal of "Buffy" Studies* 2, no. 1. http://slayageonline.com/Numbers/slayage5.htm.

"Vows." 2009. *Dollhouse*. Season 2. Episode 1. Written and directed by Joss Whedon. Los Angeles: Twentieth Century Fox Home Entertainment, 2010. DVD.

"Waiting in the Wings." 2002. *Angel*. Season 3. Episode 13. Written and directed by Joss Whedon. Los Angeles: Twentieth Century Fox Home Entertainment, 2003. DVD.

"War Stories." 2002. *Firefly*. Season 1. Episode 10. Written by Cheryl Cain. Directed by Jim Contner. Los Angeles: Twentieth Century Fox Home Entertainment, 2007. DVD.

Watkin, Julia. 2004. "Quotations from Kierkegaard." *Kierkegaard Quotations and Questions.* http://www.utas.edu.au/docs/humsoc/kierkegaard/resources/Kierk quotes.html.

Watkins, Jeff. 2012. "Joss Whedon, Man of My Heart." *Atlanta Shakespeare Tavern.* http://www.shakespearetavern.com/index.php?/shiny.

"WB Slays Records on Tuesday." 1998. *Mediaweek,* Jan. 26. LexisNexis Academic.

"The Weight of the World." 2001. *Buffy the Vampire Slayer.* Season 5. Episode 21. Written by Doug Petrie. Directed by David Solomon. Los Angeles: Twentieth Century Fox Home Entertainment, 2002. DVD.

Weiss, Tzipi, and Roni Berger. 2010. *Posttraumatic Growth and Culturally Competent Practice: Lessons from Around the Globe.* Hoboken: Wiley.

"Welcome to the Hellmouth." 1997. *Buffy the Vampire Slayer.* Season 1. Episode 1. Written by Joss Whedon. Directed by Charles Martin Smith. Los Angeles: Twentieth Century Fox Home Entertainment, 2010. DVD.

Westerfield, Scott. 2003. "A Slayer Comes to Town." In *Seven Seasons of "Buffy,"* edited by Glenn Yeffeth, 30–40. Dallas: BenBella Books.

[W]hatsername. 2009. "The Problem with *Dollhouse* Is Not That I Don't Understand Subtlety." *The Angry Black Woman* (online forum). Apr. 28, 6:57 p.m. http://theangryblackwoman.com/2009/04/28/the-problem-with-dollhouse-is-not-that-i-dont-understand-subtlety/.

"What's My Line? Part One." 1997. *Buffy the Vampire Slayer.* Season 2. Episode 9. Written by Howard Gordon and Marti Noxon. Directed by David Solomon. Los Angeles: Twentieth Century Fox Home Entertainment, 2010. DVD.

"What's My Line? Part Two." 1997. *Buffy the Vampire Slayer.* Season 2. Episode 10. Written by Marti Noxon. Directed by David Semel. Los Angeles: Twentieth Century Fox Home Entertainment, 2010. DVD.

Wheatley, Helen. 2006. *Gothic Television.* Manchester: Manchester Univ. Press.

Whedon, Jed, and Maurissa Tancharoen. 2009. "Epitaph One." *Dollhouse.* Season 1. Episode 13. Disc 4 (commentary). Los Angeles: Twentieth Century Fox Home Entertainment, 2009. DVD.

Whedon, Joss. 2002. "Innocence." *Buffy the Vampire Slayer.* Season 2. Episode 14. Disc 4 (commentary). Los Angeles: Twentieth Century Fox Home Entertainment, 2002. DVD.

———. 2003a. "Interview with Michael Patrick Sullivan." *Undergroundonline.com.* http://www.whedon.info/Joss-Whedon-UnderGroundOnline-com.html.

———. 2003b. "Objects in Space." *Firefly.* Season 1. Episode 10. Disc 4 (commentary). Los Angeles: Twentieth Century Fox Home Entertainment, 2003. DVD.

———. 2003c. "Waiting in the Wings." *Angel.* Season 3. Episode 13. Disc 4 (commentary). Los Angeles: Twentieth Century Fox Home Entertainment, 2003. DVD.

———. 2004a. Introduction to *"The Ultimates": The Ultimate Collection.* New York: Marvel Worldwide.

———. 2004b. "Spin the Bottle." *Angel*. Season 4. Episode 6. Disc 2 (commentary). Los Angeles: Twentieth Century Fox Home Entertainment, 2004. DVD.

———. 2005a. "A Hole in the World." *Angel*. Season 5. Episode 15. Disc 4 (commentary). Los Angeles: Twentieth Century Fox Home Entertainment, 2005. DVD.

———. 2005b. "Joss on Music: Pre-production Memo." In *"Serenity": The Official Visual Companion*, 30–34. London: Titan Books.

———. 2006. "Joss Whedon Equality Now Award Acceptance Speech." *YouTube.com*. http://www.youtube.com/watch?v=QoEZQfTaaEA&feature=related.

———. 2007. "Feature Commentary with Writer/Director Joss Whedon." *Serenity: Collector's Edition*. Los Angeles: Universal Studios. DVD.

———. 2009. "Man on the Street." *Dollhouse*. Season 1. Episode 6. Disc 2 (commentary). Los Angeles: Twentieth Century Fox Home Entertainment, 2009. DVD.

———. 2012. "Audio Commentary with Director Joss Whedon." *Marvel's The Avengers*. Manhattan Beach, CA: Marvel Studios, 2012. Blu-Ray.

Whedon, Joss, and Eliza Dushku. 2009. "Ghost." *Dollhouse*. Season 1. Episode 1. Disc 1 (commentary). Los Angeles: Twentieth Century Fox Home Entertainment, 2009. DVD.

Whedon, Joss, and Nathan Fillion. 2003. "Serenity." *Firefly*. Season 1. Episode 1. Disc 1 (commentary). Los Angeles: Twentieth Century Fox Home Entertainment, 2003. DVD.

Whedon, Joss, and Drew Goddard. 2012. *The Cabin in the Woods*. Screenplay. In *"The Cabin in the Woods": The Official Visual Companion*, by Joss Whedon, Drew Goddard, and Abbie Bernstein, 44–151. London: Titan Books.

Whedon, Joss, Drew Goddard, and Abbie Bernstein. 2012. "Into the Woods: Joss Whedon and Drew Goddard on the Making of the Film." In *"The Cabin in the Woods": The Official Visual Companion*, by Joss Whedon, Drew Goddard, and Abbie Bernstein, 8–43. London: Titan Books.

Whitaker, Thomas R. 1999. *Mirrors of Our Playing: Paradigms and Presences in Modern Drama*. Ann Arbor: Univ. of Michigan Press.

White, Hayden. 1985. *Tropics of Discourse: Essays in Cultural Criticism*. Baltimore: Johns Hopkins Univ. Press.

"Who Are You?" 2000. *Buffy the Vampire Slayer*. Season 4. Episode 16. Written and directed by Joss Whedon. Los Angeles: Twentieth Century Fox Home Entertainment, 2010. DVD.

"Why We Fight." 2004. *Angel*. Season 5. Episode 13. Written by Drew Goddard and Steven S. DeKnight. Directed by Terrence O'Hara. Los Angeles: Twentieth Century Fox Home Entertainment, 2005. DVD.

Wilcox, Rhonda V. 1999. "'There Will Never Be a "Very Special" *Buffy*': *Buffy* and the Monsters of Teen Life." *Journal of Popular Film and Television* 27, no. 2: 16–23.

———. 2002a. "Visual Pleasure and Nasal Elevation: A Television Teleology, by Taryn P. Cursive-Waters." Reprint of the 2002 original chapter published in *Teleparody:*

Predicting/Preventing the TV Discourse of Tomorrow, edited by Angela Hague and David Lavery, 15–19. London: Wallflower Press. *David Lavery* (personal website). http://davidlavery.net/Teleparody/Wilcox.pdf.

———. 2002b. "'Who Died and Made Her the Boss?': Patterns of Mortality in *Buffy*." In *Fighting the Forces: What's at Stake in "Buffy the Vampire Slayer,"* edited by Rhonda V. Wilcox and David Lavery, 3–17. Lanham, MD: Rowman and Littlefield.

———. 2005. *Why "Buffy" Matters: The Art of "Buffy the Vampire Slayer."* New York: I. B. Tauris.

———. 2006. "In 'The Demon Section of the Card Catalogue': *Buffy* Studies and Television Studies." *Critical Studies in Television* 1, no. 1: 37–48.

———. 2008. "'I Do Not Hold to That': Joss Whedon and Original Sin." In *Investigating "Firefly" and "Serenity": Science Fiction on the Frontier*, edited by Rhonda V. Wilcox and Tanya R. Cochran, 155–66. New York: I. B. Tauris.

———. 2009a. "'Breaking the Ninth Wall' with *Dr. Horrible's Sing-Along Blog*: Internet Creation." *CSTOnline*, Jan. http://www.criticalstudiesintelevision.com /index.php?siid=8962.

———. 2009b. "'Set on This Earth Like a Bubble': Word as Flesh in the Dark Seasons of *Buffy*." In *Buffy Goes Dark: Essays on the Final Two Seasons of "Buffy the Vampire Slayer" on Television*, edited by Lynne Edwards, Elizabeth Rambo, and James South, 95–113. Jefferson, NC: McFarland.

———. 2010. "Echoes of Complicity: Reflexivity and Identity in Joss Whedon's *Dollhouse*." In "Fantasy Is Not Their Purpose: Joss Whedon's *Dollhouse*," edited by Cynthea Masson and Rhonda V. Wilcox. Special issue, *Slayage: The Journal of the Whedon Studies Association* 8, nos. 2–3. http://slayageonline.com/Numbers /slayage30_31.htm.

Wilcox, Rhonda V., and Tanya R. Cochran. 2008a. "'Good Myth': Joss Whedon's Further Worlds." Introduction to *Investigating "Firefly" and "Serenity": Science Fiction on the Frontier*, edited by Rhonda V. Wilcox and Tanya R. Cochran, 1–11. New York: I. B. Tauris.

———, eds. 2008b. *Investigating "Firefly" and "Serenity": Science Fiction on the Frontier*. New York: I. B. Tauris.

Wilcox, Rhonda V., and David Lavery, eds. 2002. *Fighting the Forces: What's at Stake in "Buffy the Vampire Slayer."* Lanham, MD: Rowman and Littlefield.

"Wild at Heart." *Buffy the Vampire Slayer*. 1999. Season 4. Episode 6. Written by Marti Noxon. Directed by David Grossman. Los Angeles: Twentieth Century Fox Home Entertainment, 2010. DVD.

Williams, J. P. 2002. "Choosing Your Own Mother: Mother-Daughter Conflicts in *Buffy*." In *Fighting the Forces: What's at Stake in "Buffy the Vampire Slayer,"* edited by Rhonda V. Wilcox and David Lavery, 61–72. Lanham, MD: Rowman and Littlefield.

"Willow: Goddesses and Monsters." 2009. *Buffy the Vampire Slayer*. Season 8. Willow one-shot. Written by Joss Whedon. Pencils by George Jeanty. Milwaukie, OR: Dark Horse Comics.

Wilson, Melanie. 2009. "Buffy's Dream in 'Surprise.'" In *"Buffy" Meets the Academy: Essays on the Episodes and Scripts as Texts*, edited by Kevin K. Durand, 125–30. Jefferson, NC: McFarland.

Wilson, Steve. 2001. "Laugh, Spawn of Hell, Laugh." In *Reading the Vampire Slayer: An Unofficial Critical Companion to "Buffy" and "Angel,"* edited by Roz Kaveney, 78–97. New York: Tauris Park Paperbacks.

Wilts, Alissa. 2009. "Evil, Skanky, and Kinda Gay: Lesbian Images and Issues." In *Buffy Goes Dark: Essays on the Final Two Seasons of "Buffy the Vampire Slayer" on Television*, edited by Lynne Edwards, Elizabeth Rambo, and James South, 41–56. Jefferson, NC: McFarland.

Winquist, Charles. 1998. "Person." In *Critical Terms for Religious Studies*, edited by Mark C. Taylor, 225–38. Chicago: Univ. of Chicago Press.

Wisconsin Office of Justice Assistance. 2012. *Wisconsin Human Trafficking Protocol and Resource Manual*. http://www.wcadv.org/wisconsin-human-trafficking -protocol-and-resource-manual.

"The Wish." 1998. *Buffy the Vampire Slayer*. Season 3. Episode 9. Written by Marti Noxon. Directed by David Greenwalt. Los Angeles: Twentieth Century Fox Home Entertainment, 2010. DVD.

"The Witch." 1997. *Buffy the Vampire Slayer*. Season 1. Episode 3. Written by Dana Reston. Directed by Stephen Cragg. Los Angeles: Twentieth Century Fox Home Entertainment, 2010. DVD.

Worland, Rick. 2007. *The Horror Film: An Introduction*. London: Blackwell.

Wright, John C. 2004. "Just Shove Him in the Engine; or, The Role of Chivalry in Joss Whedon's *Firefly*." In *Finding Serenity: Anti-heroes, Lost Shepherds, and Space Hookers in Joss Whedon's "Firefly,"* edited by Jane Espenson (with Glenn Yeffeth), 155–68. Dallas: BenBella Books.

Wynne-Davies, Marion, ed. 2001. *"Much Ado about Nothing" and "The Taming of the Shrew."* Houndsmill, UK: Palgrave.

"The Yoko Factor." 2000. *Buffy the Vampire Slayer*. Season 4. Episode 20. Written by Doug Petrie. Directed by David Grossman. Los Angeles: Twentieth Century Fox Home Entertainment, 2010. DVD.

Yun Hui Tsu, Timothy. 2008. "Making Virtues of Disaster: 'Beautiful Tales' from the Kobe Flood of 1938." *Asian Studies Review*, no. 32: 197–214.

Zacharek, Stephanie. 2002. "Deconstructing *Buffy*." *Salon.com*, Nov. 9. http:// www.salon.com/2002/11/09/buffy_conference/.

ZachsMind. 2004. "Comments on 3833: Herc Gives 'The Girl in Question' 4.5 Stars." *Whedonesque* (online forum). May 6, 21:31. http://whedonesque.com /comments/3833.

"The Zeppo." 1999. *Buffy the Vampire Slayer.* Season 3. Episode 13. Written by Dan Vebber. Directed by James Whitmore Jr. Los Angeles: Twentieth Century Fox Home Entertainment, 2002. DVD.

Žižek, Slavoj. 2000. *The Fragile Absolute.* London: Verso.

————. 2009. *The Monstrosity of Christ: Paradox or Dialectic?* London: MIT Press.

Zurawik, David. 2009. "Welcome to the *Dollhouse.*" *Baltimore Sun,* Feb. 13. http://articles.baltimoresun.com/2009-02-13/news/0902120062_1_dollhouse-eliza-dushku-buffy.

Zynda, Lyle. 2005. "We're All Just Floating in Space." In *Finding Serenity: Anti-heroes, Lost Shepherds, and Space Hookers in Joss Whedon's "Firefly,"* edited by Jane Espenson (with Glenn Yeffeth), 85–95. Dallas: BenBella Books.

Contributors

STACEY ABBOTT is a Reader in Film and Television Studies at Roehampton University. She is the author of *Celluloid Vampires* (2007) and *Angel* (2009), the editor of *Reading "Angel": The TV Spin-off with a Soul* (2005) and *The Cult TV Book* (2010), and the author or coeditor of many other works. With Lorna Jowett, she is the coauthor of *TV Horror: Investigating the Dark Side of the Small Screen* (2013). She is Series Editor of the I. B. Tauris Investigating Cult TV series. She is a member of the editorial board of *Slayage: The Journal of the Whedon Studies Association*.

RICHARD S. ALBRIGHT is an Associate Professor of English at Harrisburg Area Community College in Pennsylvania, where he teaches composition and literature. After majoring in English literature at Lehigh University, he pursued a career as a systems analyst before deciding that his dream of an academic career was not to be denied. He eventually returned to Lehigh a generation after his previous sojourn there, earning his PhD in 2002. Besides his work on *Buffy*, he has published *Writing the Past, Writing the Future: Time and Narrative in Gothic and Sensation Fiction* (2009) and journal articles on nineteenth-century British literature.

ALYSON R. BUCKMAN is a Professor in the Humanities and Religious Studies Department at California State University, Sacramento, where she teaches courses in film, popular culture, American Studies, and multiculturalism. Her publications include work on Alice Walker, Octavia Butler, Marge Piercy, *The Gilmore Girls*, *Firefly*, and *Dr. Horrible's Sing-Along Blog*. She is actively involved with the Southwest/Texas Popular Culture/American Culture Association as well as the Whedon Studies Association.

JEFFREY BUSSOLINI is Associate Professor at the City University of New York and Codirector of the Avenue B Multi-Studies Center. He has published on *Buffy the Vampire Slayer*, *Firefly*, and *Serenity*. He also researches human/animal interactions (especially feline/human) and the ethnography of national security institutions. He has been a visiting scholar at Macquarie University (Centre for Research on Social Inclusion, Centre for Integrative Study of Animal Behaviour) and the University of New South Wales (School of the Humanities).

TANYA R. COCHRAN, PhD, is Associate Professor of English at Union College in Lincoln, Nebraska. Her interests include fandom and gender studies as well as the intersection of faith and learning. An editorial board member for *Slayage: The Journal of the Whedon Studies Association* and its undergraduate partner, *Watcher Junior*, she is also the president of the Whedon Studies Association (2012–14) and one of its cofounders. Her publications include *Investigating "Firefly" and "Serenity": Science Fiction on the Frontier* (2008), coedited with Rhonda V. Wilcox; essays in multiple anthologies; and articles for journals such as *Transformative Works and Cultures.*

GREGORY ERICKSON is an Associate Professor at the Gallatin School of New York University where he teaches courses on religion, literature, music, and popular culture. He is the author of *The Absence of God in Modernist Literature* (2007) and the coauthor of *Religion and Popular Culture: Rescripting the Sacred* (2008).

ENSLEY F. GUFFEY'S publications include "'We Just Declared War': Buffy as General" in *Watcher Junior: The Undergraduate Journal of Whedon Studies.* A May 2012 summa cum laude BA in history (University of North Carolina at Greensboro), he is a graduate student at East Tennessee State University.

JANET K. HALFYARD is a musicologist and Director of Undergraduate Studies at Birmingham Conservatoire, UK. Her publications include *Danny Elfman's "Batman": A Film Score Guide* (2004), the edited collection of essays *Music, Sound, and Silence in "Buffy the Vampire Slayer"* (2009), and the edited collection *Music and Fantasy Cinema* (2012) as part of the Equinox Genre, Music, and Sound series. She has published many other articles on film and television music.

LINDA J. JENCSON teaches anthropology at Appalachian State University. She is the author of several essays on Whedon, including "'My Rifle's as Bright as My Sweetheart's Eyes': Joss Whedon's *Firefly* and the Songs of the Clancy Brothers" in *Buffy, Ballads, and Bad Guys Who Sing: Music in the Worlds of Joss Whedon* (2011).

LORNA JOWETT is a Reader in Television Studies at the University of Northampton, UK. She is the author of *Sex and the Slayer: A Gender Studies Primer for the "Buffy" Fan* (2005) and coauthor with Stacey Abbott of *TV Horror: Investigating the Darker Side of the Small Screen* (2013). She has published many articles on television, film, and popular culture, and is on the editorial board of *Slayage: The Journal of the Whedon Studies Association.*

DAVID KOCIEMBA is the President of the Affiliated Faculty of Emerson College union. Focusing on the work of Todd Haynes, spoilers, *Glee*, Joss Whedon, and Jane Espenson, he has written for the journals *In Medias Res, Slayage,* and *Transformative*

Works and Cultures, along with the anthologies *Buffy Goes Dark* (2009), *Finding "Battlestar Galactica"* (2008), *Supernatural Youth* (2011), *"Buffy" in the Classroom* (2010), and *Buffy and Angel Conquer the Internet* (2009). Kociemba is the editor of *Watcher Junior*, a peer-reviewed journal of undergraduate scholarship on Joss Whedon.

K. DALE KOONTZ, JD, is an Instructor at Cleveland Community College in western North Carolina, where she teaches courses in communication and film. She is the author of *Faith and Choice in the Works of Joss Whedon* (2008), which explores themes of redemption and consequences in Whedon's work. She was a keynote speaker at the fourth biennial *Slayage* Conference on the Whedonverses (2010) at Flagler College.

DAVID LAVERY, PhD, is Professor of English at Middle Tennessee State University (1993–present). He is the author, coauthor, editor, or coeditor of more than twenty books, including *Joss Whedon: Conversations* (2011) and *Joss Whedon, a Creative Portrait: From "Buffy the Vampire Slayer" to "The Avengers"* (2013), and has published books on the space age, *Lost*, *Twin Peaks*, *The X-Files*, *The Sopranos*, *Buffy the Vampire Slayer*, teleparody, *Seinfeld*, *Deadwood*, *My So-Called Life*, *Gilmore Girls*, *Heroes*, *Battlestar Galactica*, cult TV, and *Supernatural*. A founding coeditor of the journals *Slayage*, *Critical Studies in Television*, and *Series/Season/Show* and cofounder of the Whedon Studies Association, he has lectured around the world on the subject of television.

CYNTHEA MASSON works in the English Department at Vancouver Island University. Her PhD in English (McMaster University) focused on medieval literature and the rhetoric of mysticism. Though she has published in the field of Medieval Studies, the majority of her academic work and publications since 2005 has been in the area of Whedon Studies. Her combined familiarity with medieval literature and the Whedonverses led to a paper on Chaucer's *Wife of Bath* as portrayed in *Dollhouse* ("Who Painted the Lion? A Gloss on *Dollhouse*'s 'Belle Chose'" in the 2010 *Slayage* double issue that she edited with Rhonda V. Wilcox, "Fantasy Is Not Their Purpose: Joss Whedon's *Dollhouse*"). Her fiction includes *The Elijah Tree* (2009), a novel that combines theories of medieval mysticism with contemporary issues of faith and sexuality. She is currently working on her second novel, *The Alchemists' Council*.

ANANYA MUKHERJEA is an Associate Professor of Sociology at the City University of New York College of Staten Island and in public health at the CUNY Graduate Center. She is the editor of *Understanding Emerging Epidemics: Social and Political Approaches* (2010) and has published on popular culture studies in the journals

Slayage and *Studies in Popular Culture* and in collections on the *Twilight* phenomenon and on HBO's *True Blood* series. She received the 2008 Mr. Pointy Award (for best article) from the Whedon Studies Association, of which she is a charter associate. She is on the board of the Foucault Society.

MATTHEW PATEMAN is Professor of Contemporary Popular Aesthetics at Sheffield Hallam University, South Yorkshire. He is the author of *The Aesthetics of Culture in "Buffy the Vampire Slayer"* (2006). His research takes him from Buffy to Bowie, Orwell to Whedon, postmodernism to St. Paul. His published work on literature, philosophy, and television seeks to historicize the aesthetic. He is currently working on a book about Joss Whedon.

J. DOUGLAS RABB is Professor Emeritus, Philosophy, at Lakehead University in Thunder Bay, Ontario, Canada. He is coauthor, with J. Michael Richardson, of *The Existential Joss Whedon* (2007) and a number of papers on the Whedonverses. Their work has appeared in *Slayage* and in *Investigating "Firefly" and "Serenity"* (2008). As an executive founding member of the Centre for Health Care Ethics, his principal research interests are in cross-cultural values and worldviews. He is coauthor, with Ojibwa philosopher Dennis H. McPherson, of *Indian from the Inside: Native American Philosophy and Cultural Renewal* (2011) and a number of articles, including most recently "Indigeneity in Canada: Spirituality, the Sacred, and Survival," in *Aboriginal History: A Reader* (2012).

ELIZABETH L. RAMBO is Associate Professor of English at Campbell University, specializing in medieval literature. A charter member of the Whedon Studies Association and a member of the editorial board of *Slayage: The Journal of the Whedon Studies Association*, she coedited *Buffy Goes Dark: Essays on the Final Two Seasons of "Buffy the Vampire Slayer" on Television* (2009) with Lynne Y. Edwards and James B. South, published several essays on *Buffy* and *Angel*, and contributed to Nikki Stafford's "Great Buffy Rewatch" on the *Nik at Nite* blog (2011). Her medieval scholarship includes Celtic Studies, Arthurian legends, and medievalism in popular culture.

J. MICHAEL RICHARDSON, Professor of English at Lakehead University in Thunder Bay, Ontario, is coauthor, with J. Douglas Rabb, of *The Existential Joss Whedon* (2007) and a number of papers on the Whedonverses. Their work has appeared in *Slayage* and in *Investigating "Firefly" and "Serenity"* (2008). He has also coauthored, with Kim Fedderson, a number of articles on Shakespeare and popular culture, which have appeared in *College Literature*, *Apocalyptic Shakespeare* (2009), and *Macbeth: New Critical Essays* (2008). He has also published on Edmund Spenser, most notably *Astrological Symbolism in Spenser's "The Shepheardes Calender"* (1989).

LAUREN SCHULTZ has an MA in literature from American University in Washington, DC, and has previously taught at Rockville Community College in Rockville, Maryland, and Mercy College in Dobbs Ferry, New York. She currently works as a professional grant writer in the New York City area. Her previous publications include "Concepts of Identity When *Nancy Drew* Meets *Buffy*," in *"Buffy" Meets the Academy* (2009).

MARNI STANLEY (PhD, Oxford) works at Vancouver Island University, where she teaches English and Women's Studies. Her academic work and publication areas include Victorian literature, film, television, graphic narratives, and comics.

SHARON SUTHERLAND is Assistant Professor at the University of British Columbia Faculty of Law at Allard Hall, where she teaches mediation, a judicial externship program, and ethics. Her research interests include child protection mediation, improvisational theater, and law and popular culture. Her publications include chapters in *Reading "Angel"* (2005), *The Literary "Angel"* (2010), and *Investigating "Firefly" and "Serenity"* (2008).

SARAH SWAN is a JSD candidate at Columbia University. Her research interests include law and culture, private law, and feminist legal theory. She has published essays in *Reading "Angel"* (2005), *The Literary "Angel"* (2010), and *Investigating "Firefly" and "Serenity"* (2008).

RHONDA V. WILCOX, PhD, is Professor of English at Gordon State College, cofounder and past president (2008–12) of the Whedon Studies Association, and past president of the Popular Culture Association in the South. She is editor of *Studies in Popular Culture* and coeditor and cofounder of *Slayage: The Journal of the Whedon Studies Association*. She is the author of *Why "Buffy" Matters: The Art of "Buffy the Vampire Slayer"* (2005) and coeditor, with David Lavery, of *Fighting the Forces: What's at Stake in "Buffy the Vampire Slayer"* (2002); with Tanya R. Cochran, of *Investigating "Firefly" and "Serenity": Science Fiction on the Frontier* (2008); and, with Sue Turnbull, of *Investigating "Veronica Mars"* (2011).

VICTORIA WILLIS is a Research Analyst at Georgia State University in the Office of Institutional Research with a PhD in English. Her research focuses on rhetoric and popular culture. Her "Be-in-tween the Spa[ ]ces: The Location of Women and Subversion in Jazz" won the William M. Jones Best Graduate Student Paper award for the *Journal of American Culture*.

KRISTOPHER KARL WOOFTER is a PhD candidate in Film and Moving Image Studies at Concordia University and teaches courses on horror and the Gothic at Dawson College in Montreal. He is codirector of Montreal's Miskatonic Institute of Horror Studies and has served for six years as cochair for the Horror Area of the Popular Culture / American Culture Association. He has published on *Buffy the Vampire Slayer* and has a forthcoming (2013) coauthored essay on the intersection of the Gothic and documentary in the journal *Textus*. His current research involves the merging of horror film, documentary, mockumentary, pseudodocumentary, and reality TV.

Index